Tracing your Ancestors in the National Archives

Tracing your Ancestors in the National Archives

7th edition

Amanda Bevan

the national archives

Seventh edition first published in 2006 by
The National Archives
Kew, Richmond
Surrey, TW9 4DU, UK

www.nationalarchives.gov.uk

The National Archives was formed when the Public Record Office
and Historical Manuscripts Commission combined in April 2003.

First published in 1981 by HMSO (0 11440 114 4)
Second edition 1982 (0 11440 180 2)
Third edition 1984 (0 11440 186 1)
Fourth edition 1990 (0 11440 222 1)
Fifth edition published in 1999 by PRO (1 873162 61 8)
Sixth edition 2002 (1 903365 34 1)

ISBN 1 903365 89 9
      978 1 903365 89 2

Cover: main image by Pier Photography
Portraits from the National Archives except:
front left and second from right (courtesy of Robert Pols)
front second from left (Time & Life/Getty Images)

Designed by Ken Wilson | point 918
Typeset by Gem Graphics, Trenance, Cornwall
Cover designed by Briony Chappell
Printed in the UK by CPI Bath Press

Contents

Foreword to the Seventh Edition of Tracing Your Ancestors in The National Archives

Since joining the National Archives as Chief Executive last October, I have become even more aware that many of our users – onsite and online – visit our reading rooms and website primarily because they have a hunger to know more about the history of their ancestors. They are drawn to the National Archives not only by the wealth of source material that we hold here but also by the expertise and friendliness of our staff, both at Kew and the Family Records Centre, who are committed to making the records available to the widest possible audiences. In order to do this successfully, complex information about the records has to be presented in a clear, straightforward manner that stimulates but never patronises the reader. I am delighted to see that all these virtues are exemplified in this seventh edition of *Tracing Your Ancestors*.

Important changes have taken place since the publication of the sixth edition four years ago. The Public Record Office and the Historical Manuscripts came together to form the National Archives in April 2003. This means that, as well as consulting original sources that are held by The National Archives, family historians can also obtain information from us about relevant material kept in other places – for example, manor court records, family papers and estate archives. Building on the success of this merger, we are keen to work with other organisations in offering seamless services to family historians whenever this is practicable.

The other striking change is the rapid development of online services aimed at the family historian – hence the new subtitle of this edition, 'the website and beyond'. We have provided for the first time, either through our own website or in partnership with other organisations, online access to a huge amount of material, including census returns and wills, without which the family historian cannot hope to make serious progress. I am committed to making the digitisation of even more family history sources over the next few years a top priority for the National Archives. At the same time, there eventually comes a point when all the obvious online sources have been exhausted, and this guide will also help determined family historians to carry out their own detective work among the original records.

The continuing success of the television series *Who Do You Think You Are?*, which can attract audiences of about five million people, convinces me and my colleagues that the so called 'family history bubble' is not about to burst in the near future. On the contrary, the galloping pace of technological change and rising user expectations make it quite likely that before too long there will be a steady stream of requests for this seventh edition to be updated. Meanwhile I should like to congratulate Amanda Bevan for compiling this massively erudite and very readable volume, which is clearly destined to become an indispensable reference work for all those who are keen to find out more about their British ancestors.

Natalie Ceeney
Chief Executive
The National Archives

March 2006

Acknowledgements

This is the seventh edition of *Tracing Your Ancestors* – under a slightly different title this time, to reflect both the joining of the Public Record Office and the Historical Manuscripts Commission into one National Archives in 2003 and the transformation of research brought about by the internet. *Tracing Your Ancestors in the Public Record Office* was first published in 1981, a slim tome edited by my colleagues Jane Cox and Tim Padfield. It was our first foray into the world of family history publishing, and was hugely successful. Responsibility for its upkeep passed to me in 1990. Since then, it has grown in size with every new edition. This is a proper reflection of the enormous range of interest developed by family historians. In the old days, when 'Cox and Padfield' was first published, there was still some doubt in official minds about genealogy as a serious endeavour. There is none now. Family history is true democratic history, and family historians are often outstanding researchers.

As usual, I have relied on my excellent and knowledgeable colleagues. In particular, I would like to thank Dave Annal, Vanessa Carr, Alan Bowgen, Paul Carter, James Cronan, Bruno Derrick, Karen Grannum, Guy Grannum, Abi Husainy, Liz Hore, Ann Morton, Lee Oliver, Bruno Pappalardo, Mark Pearsall, William Spencer, and Chris Watts for subject and record advice; Emma Allen, Hazel Bagworth-Mann, Jone Garmendia, Sue Hurley, Frieda Midgley, Gemma Richardson and Colin Williams for advice on the website applications; Natalie Ceeney for taking time to write the Foreword; Roger Nixon for his advice on making the book more useable; and Catherine Bradley, Sheila Knight, Sian Morris, Judy Spours and Ken Wilson for producing it. Chapters 48 and 49, though revised, are still based largely on the work of Ruth Paley and Helen Watts respectively. Any errors or infelicities throughout the book are my responsibility.

I would particularly like to thank my father William Bevan (ex-Merchant Navy and RAF) for helping me make sense of the Merchant Navy – and for all the support and encouragement he and my dear late mother Sonia Bevan have given me over the years. My greatest thanks as ever are owed to Tom, Anna, Edmund and Miles Brass, whose family life has suffered again. They are still not interested in the subject, but have nobly kept me going with tea and sympathy.

Amanda Bevan

March 2006

1 Getting the best results: the website and beyond

1.1   Why do you need this book?

Online sources for family history are now so popular that many people expect researching their family history to be exclusively an internet activity. You can certainly get a fair way towards creating a family tree like this – but why restrict yourself when you may be able to discover so much more? Family history websites contain only a minute proportion of what is available to the dedicated searcher. For example, several million individual documents from the National Archives can be seen on our own website, but these represent about 0.01 per cent of the records used by family historians in our reading rooms at Kew.

Moving away from the standard sources of the census and the birth, marriage and death records (which apply to most people) takes you into areas of the records relating to subsets of people – for example, those who joined the Army or went to sea, or who resorted to the law courts for justice. Here survival rates of documents can be patchy, the organisation of the records can be complicated and things don't always mean what they appear to say – but the rewards can be great, if you know where to look.

This book is your guide. It gives detailed advice and background information about nearly 1,500 series of major interest to family historians, so that you can identify likely sources to investigate. The standard sources are covered in three chapters; another 58 give advice on accessing the kind of records that don't apply to everyone, but might apply to some of the people you are researching. It's a traditional compendium of archivists' knowledge, inherited and accumulated over the last 500 or so years. But this edition also gives access to a wholly new set of skills accumulated by staff at the National Archives over the last ten years in using the online versions of the data. You are (or will be) the expert on your family history: we know how to look for the evidence that you need. This new skill set combined with older knowledge is what makes the difference between a successful search and an illusory one. A successful search looks in the right place in the right way: you may not find what you want (not everything survives) but you won't miss it by error. Sometimes a negative answer is the best you can get – but it is far better than missing what was there all the time simply because you were looking in the wrong way.

1.2 About the National Archives

The National Archives (of England, Wales and the United Kingdom) was formed in April 2003 by bringing together the Public Record Office and the Historical Manuscripts Commission. We hold the shared public archive created by the central government of the United Kingdom in its various historic forms over the past thousand years. We have inherited this from a large number of medieval and later government archives (kept in such places as the Tower of London, Westminster Abbey and the State Paper Office). Our holdings are primarily the archives of

• overarching national institutions, such as the armed services or the Foreign Office;
• the internal government of England and Wales;
• the records of the law courts of England and Wales.

These government archives run unbroken from Domesday Book in 1086. The respective National Archives of Scotland and Ireland, the National Archives of Northern Ireland and the National Library of Wales hold most of their purely national archives of their time as part of the United Kingdom, and of their time as independent states. However, much centrally generated or stored material about all these countries (especially Wales) is held in the National Archives at Kew. We are also one of the world's major international archives, with vast holdings on the former British colonies and on foreign relations over eight centuries, and one of the greatest map archives of the world.

From the Historical Manuscripts Commission, the National Archives inherited the responsibility to advise the private owners and custodians of other archives and record offices, and to help them make their holdings available according to their own priorities. We maintain the National Register of Archives on site and online, and also the union online catalogue called Access to Archives (or A2A). This is a growing collection of online catalogues from hundreds of private and public archives across England. So, even for access to other archives, the National Archives is a good place to start.

All this may sound rather daunting, but I hope you will be pleasantly surprised on visiting the National Archives or using our website. We do try to make things as easy and friendly as we can, and you will find enquiry staff in the various reading rooms to help you towards the best sources. As using historical records does require patience, understanding, lateral thinking and some dedication, it's a good thing that family historians make excellent researchers: perhaps your personal commitment stokes up curiosity and determination.

1.3 About the National Archives' website

The National Archives website is at **www.nationalarchives.gov.uk**. You can search here for catalogue descriptions of records held in the National Archives and also of documents held in local and private archives across England and, to some extent, Wales. On the website you can find catalogues of records, copies of records, databases and advisory material, and you can also access many services. The website has online exhibitions like 'Moving Here' (about immigration) and educational resources such as our online tutorials in palaeography and Latin. Our website also acts as a portal to the linked census websites, where online access to the 1841–1901 censuses is available for a small fee. There are also several smaller databases, such as the National Register of Archives, the Hospital Records Database, the Trafalgar Ancestors Database, the Manorial Documents Register and the Library Catalogue. These can all be found by clicking on the relevant part of the red bar at the top of the webpage to open up drop-down menus.

We also have a new site search facility that searches across the content of the website itself and the major databases hosted on it: you can access this directly from our home page. (Other databases will be added gradually, so check on the website to see what is currently included.) This is important because using it can take you right away from the National Archives. The website hosts three separate databases of roughly equal size (each getting on for ten million records).

- The *catalogue* of nearly 15,000 separate series of public records kept in the National Archives (and a very few kept elsewhere: see 1.10 for details).
- *Documents Online*, which provides indexes and digital images of the contents of some of the most popular family history series (and individual documents from several other series) in the National Archives.
- *Access to Archives*, or A2A, which contains local and private archives across England. (Wales has its own equivalent to A2A at **www.archivesnetwork wales.info**.) These archives are also served on our website by the *National Register of Archives* (which brings together information on archives of

particular people, families, businesses and organisations in public and private hands across England *and* Wales) and the *Archon Directory* of contact details for these and other places.

Our new site search therefore gives you the opportunity, for the first time, to search across the majority of historic documents kept in England (but relating potentially to the whole world).

Put in your search term and your hits will come back divided into subject categories. Once you click on each hit, you will be taken into the source from which it came. For example, you may find that four hits relating to Ebenezer Wouldbegood take you far afield: the first to his will in Documents Online; the second to a chancery lawsuit in the National Archives catalogue; the third to his estate papers in the Barsetshire Record Office noted in the National Register of Archives; and the fourth to details of his correspondence as secretary of the West of England Pig Breeders Association, now held by the University of Barset, and listed in A2A. You can then go direct to the holders of these records for further information on how to access them or how to get copies (the Archon directory holds the contact details). This will save an enormous amount of time in locating relevant sources – and may open up whole areas of research that you had not dreamt of.

As you go from our site search into a variety of databases, you need to be aware of how best to use each one. Although this book concentrates on the public records kept in the National Archives, and accessed mostly through using the catalogue and Documents Online as separate databases, it does include details on these other resources at 1.12–1.14. Other parts of the book make reference to local or private archives: you can explore these suggestions further using the tools on our website. Local and private archives do have their own foibles and problems, and you may need to consult specialist guides and indexes to use them effectively. (Examples are local probate courts and parish registers, whose records are not searchable online through A2A.)

1.4 Understanding our catalogue

The National Archives' catalogue contains descriptions of unique documents, each with a unique reference: they usually look like wo 12/135 or ADM 188/59 – up to four letters followed by two sets of numbers. (Other archives have their own patterns of references: 8ANC7/67–87 or MS5036/5088, for example.) Some of our references are based on ancient descriptive systems and so look very odd – E 134/22Geo2/Mich5 or E 317/Leics/13, for example.

Take a proper note of document references so that you can find them again, cite them as evidence if you want to publish your research and point other people towards them. Much of our advice service is taken up with helping people to find the right document reference for the information they want: please write references down, with a note of what they are. These references are used to order documents out of the storage areas, or to request copies. You also need to note where you found the information in the document. This is usually a page or folio number (a folio is a leaf in a book, numbered on the front but not the back – the back of folio 235 is called 235v).

The National Archives holds about 375 separate collections of records from government departments, the armed services and the courts, occupying about 178 kilometres of shelving. Each of these collections has its own department code of up to four letters. Each department code contains a number of series of records (arranged by subject or type of record): some have over a thousand series, others only one. In all, the 375 department codes contain about 15,000 series, each numbered from 1 within their code – so we have ADM 1, WO 1, C 1 and so on. The 15,000 series contain millions of documents, described at 'piece' or 'item' level (an item is part of a piece, like a page in a book). (Most are only described at piece level, leaving much still to be discovered.)

The most common department codes used by family historians are

ADM	Admiralty Royal Navy and Royal Marines
AIR	Air Ministry and the Royal Air Force
ASSI	Clerks of Assize
BT	Board of Trade, and Registry of Shipping and Seamen
C	Chancery
CHES	Palatinate of Chester (basically the county of Chester)
CO	Colonial Office
CP	Court of Common Pleas
CRIM	Central Criminal Court
CUST	Customs and Excise
DL	Duchy of Lancaster (basically the possessions of the Duke of Lancaster, that is, the monarch)
DURH	Palatinate of Durham (basically the county of Durham)
E	Exchequer
FO	Foreign Office
HO	Home Office
IR	Inland Revenue
J	Supreme Court of Judicature
KB	Court of Kings Bench
MEPO	Metropolitan Police
PC	Privy Council
PCOM	Prisons Commission
PIN	Ministry of Pensions
PL	Palatinate of Lancaster (basically the county of Lancashire)
PMG	Paymaster General

PROB	Prerogative Court of Canterbury
RAIL	Railways
REQ	Court of Requests
RG	Registrar General – General Register Office
SP	State Papers
STAC	Court of Star Chamber
T	Treasury
TS	Treasury Solicitor
WO	War Office – the Army

(To find out more about the history of these departments, go to our online catalogue, type the code letters into the 'Go to' box and then click on the 'Full details' tab.) For a full list of series used in this book, see the Series Index.

This book is full of references to documents each uniquely identified in this system. If you find one that looks interesting and is expressed, for example, as CUST 20/154–159, this is a reference to several pieces – to volumes 154, 155, 156, 157, 158 and 159 in the series CUST 20. To find out which of these you actually want, go to the online catalogue, type CUST 20/154 into the 'Go to reference' box and then choose 'Browse from here'.

If we take the catalogue of the National Archives to be a full listing of the contents of all these 15,000 series, then it is rather a shapeless beast, covering a wide variety of formats: parchment volumes, index cards, printed books, typescript and manuscript index volumes, paper lists and online databases. However, most people mean the online catalogue, which does indeed give details of all series, although it does not contain full listings of all series.

The online catalogue of public records describes these records at up to seven different levels – although only the three shown in italics below *have* to be used: you need to be aware of this because it has an impact on searching and browsing.

Department	*WO = War Office*	*C = Chancery*
Division	Records of the Armed Forces from commands, headquarters, regiments and corps	Records of the Chancery as central secretariat
Series	*WO 95: War Office: First World War and Army of Occupation War Diaries*	*C 143: Chancery: Inquisitions Ad Quod Damnum, Henry III to Richard III*
Sub-series	Part iii Gallipoli, Dardanelles	
Sub-sub-series	Royal Naval Division	
Piece	*WO 95/4290: Royal Naval Division*	*C 143/318: Inquisitions taken as a result of applications to the Crown for licences to alienate land*

Item	WO 95/4290	
[can't order these – order as piece]	Assistant director medical services [this item has no separate number: it is in a box with three other war diaries]	C 143/318/24: Ralph de Middelneye, knight, and Elizabeth his wife to settle the manor and hundred of Poorstock (Dorset) ... on themselves and the heirs of their bodies, with remainder to Maurice, younger son of Thomas de Berkelee of Berkeley, the elder, knight ...

The National Archives, like other ancient archives, has an enormous amount of 'legacy data' about its holdings. We are only the current generation of people looking after government records: many of our catalogues are modern forms of work carried out in the sixteenth century or even earlier by our predecessors (one of whom was known as the Clerk of Hell, after the stinking cellar where that part of the archive was kept). I think the oldest one still in use as the main means of access to a particular collection dates from about 1558. Much of this data survives in a variety of formats in what we call 'supplementary finding aids'.

There is also a problem of material that is in the online catalogue but effectively uncatalogued. In the National Archives we have hundreds of series of records where the only catalogue description is 'correspondence' and a date range – 1802–1805 or 1832 January – not an adequate description for the 300 or so letters sent or received in that time period. Most of these are from the eighteenth and nineteenth centuries – the time of the growth of Empire, of the industrial revolution, of huge changes taking place in our society and in the world – and yet most of these papers are almost inaccessible. We cannot blame our nineteenth-century colleagues, who were busy opening up medieval and early modern records using the advent of cheap printing to make published versions of these records freely available through municipal libraries across the land. But we are now beginning to exploit the opportunity of the internet equivalent of 'cheap printing' to open up these wonderful treasure houses of information to the world.

Throughout this book, you will see examples of fascinating information opened up by correspondence cataloguing projects across a variety of subjects (particularly criminals requesting pardons; the setting up of the new poor law system; the history of the Caribbean; and internees in Britain and abroad during the First World War). I think that future historians will look back at this period as one of great discovery. This is not a static catalogue: so much is being added that you may find it worth having another look at areas you have already researched.

1.5 Searching our catalogue

When I suggest here looking at or searching a particular series of records, I mean you to use the catalogue search of the National Archives' own catalogue at **www.nationalarchives.gov.uk/catalogue**, not the site search (which searches other archives as well). (For browsing, see 1.7.)

Searching by keyword in the catalogue is easy and can be very fruitful: many people will not need to go any further. To search the catalogue, you need to have a search term. This is any word (you can substitute an * if you want to search solely by year and series or department code). The best search terms are those which are most likely to crop up in catalogue entries. Place-names are good, as are surnames or occupations. Surnames that come from place-names or occupations can cause problems: searching for Birmingham or Butcher brings up far too many entries. (The search is currently limited to 3,000 results.) Forenames can be a problem, as our catalogue enters them as they were written in the original paper finding aid, abbreviations and all: see 1.6 for advice.

SEARCH TIPS

The system is set to search for exactly what you type in. For example, if you put in James Maltby you will get only those hits where James appears immediately before Maltby. There are ways round this:

- use AND: James AND Maltby will find Maltby, James;
- use NOT, NEAR, OR;
- use brackets in complicated searches, for example, Inn AND (Southwark OR Lambeth OR St Olave);
- use a ? in place of each single letter that you are not sure of. Sm?th will find Smith and Smyth; Br?nn?ysund finds both Brönnöysund and Bronnoysund;
- use an asterisk to pick up variant spellings. Rob*n* will find Robins, Robbins, Robyns, Robbyns and Robinson;
- don't use apostrophes; if you want to find O'Connor, type it as O Connor;
- to search by date only in a given series, put an * as the search term, enter a range of years and restrict the search to that series. This can be an excellent way to get around large series that are not listed in detail.

Or the search term can be restricted to a range of years or a range of departments. If you know you are looking for Army records about Aldershot and that Army records are mostly in the wo code (standing for War Office), try restricting the search to wo to avoid getting swamped with records from the education departments, the census or the Ordnance Survey about Aldershot.

A search on the National Archives catalogue may give you thousands of hits or only a few – but not what you want. Unfortunately, this is because the data behind the search is still patchy. It's the same old data, created by archivists over the last 500 years to widely differing standards. Some of it is poor; some of it is fine for using on paper; some of it is excellent informative material but is expressed in ways which make it difficult to find on a search. It doesn't mean we don't have what you want.

Many catalogue entries

- put names back to front – Smith, John not John Smith;
- use the spellings of surnames as given in the documents – Rigmaiden, Rigmaden, Rigmarden, Rigmayden, Rygmayden, Rygmadyn, Rygmayn – even when it is clear that they refer to the same person;
- only indicate the range of surnames – Baa–Badc;
- use abbreviations – D.A.D.P.S.;
- use only the date to describe similar documents in a series, leaving the description field empty;
- give very brief descriptions because they rely on an index, or a publication or a website to provide the real data;
- simply provide only the information needed by the government department or court that created them.

A common problem is putting in too many search terms. *Malta AND Naval AND hospital* will not pull up all references to the Naval hospital at Malta. If, for example, a whole series is described as Naval Hospital Records, then the entry for a piece relating to the hospital in Malta will just read Malta, and this search will not pick it up. The search does not marry up words from series titles (Naval Hospital) with words in the description of individual pieces (Malta). You may need to investigate the 'advanced search' options or simply restrict your search terms to relevant series (which you can identify from this book): our site search (1.3) is an easy alternative.

1.6 Searching our catalogue: common subject terms, and abbreviations

Subjects may need a bit of lateral thinking. Most catalogue entries will not use the kind of subject terms that many people try to search on. There is no point putting in 'family history' unless you want to get back a research guide telling you what sources exist for family history. If you are not sure what search terms to use, find the advice in this book indicating a particular series for that subject, type that reference into the 'Go to' box and have a look at sample entries.

We have analysed the subject search terms most frequently used, and find for the following subjects people frequently missed what they wanted by not using a helpful term.

Best term	Alternate terms in catalogue	Don't use these terms
First World War	Great War, 1914–1918, 1914–1919, 1914–1920	1st World War, World War One, WW1, WW 1, WWI, WW I, FWW
Second World War	1939–1945	2nd World War, World War Two, WW2, WW 2, WWII, WW II, SWW, Great Patriotic War
Will	Probate, Personal estate, Testament	

We did try altering our search engine to look for all forename abbreviations, but doing this messed up too many other aspects of the search. You may need to search separately for these variations.

FORENAME ABBREVIATIONS USED IN THE CATALOGUE

Alexander, Alex, Alexr
Alfred, Alf
Anthony, Antony, Anth, Antho
Benjamin, Ben, Benjn, Benj
Charles, Chas
Daniel, Dan, Danl
Edmund, Edmond, Edm, Edmd
Edward, Edw, Edwd
Elizabeth, Elizth, Eliz
Francis, Fras
Frederick, Fred, Fredk
George, Geo
Henry, Hy, Hen, Harry
Humphrey, Humfrey
James, Jas
Jeffrey, Jeff, Jeffy
John, Jno
Joseph, Jos
Joshua, Josh
Michael, Mich
Matthew, Mattw
Nicholas, Nicolas, Nic, Nich
Philip, Phillip, Phil
Richard, Ric
Robert, Robt
Samuel, Sam, Saml
Stanley, Stan
Thomas, Thos, Th, Tho
Victoria, Vic, Vict

Counties are another area where the catalogue is full of variants.

ENGLISH COUNTY ABBREVIATIONS USED IN THE CATALOGUE

Bedfordshire, Beds, Bedf, Bedford
Berkshire, Berks
Buckinghamshire, Bucks, Buckingham
Cambridgeshire, Cambs, Camb, Cambridge
Cheshire, Ches, Chesh, Chester
Cornwall, Corn, Cornw
Cumberland, Cumb
Derbyshire, Derb, Derbs, Derbys, Derby
Devon, Devonshire
Dorset, Dorsetshire, Dors
Durham, Durh, County Durham
Gloucestershire, Glos, Gloucs, Gloucester
Hampshire, Hants, Southampton
Herefordshire, Heref, Hereford
Hertfordshire, Herts, Hertford
Huntingdonshire, Hunts
Lancashire, Lancs, Lanc, Lancaster
Leicestershire, Leics, Leic, Leicester
Lincolnshire, Lincs, Linc, Lincoln
Middlesex, Midd, Middx
Monmouthshire, Monm, Monmouth

Norfolk, Norf
Northamptonshire, Northants
Northumberland, Northumb
Nottinghamshire, Notts, Nottingham
Oxfordshire, Oxon, Ox, Oxford
Shropshire, Salop
Somerset, Somersetshire, Som
Staffordshire, Staffs, Staff, Stafford
Suffolk, Suff
Surrey, Surr
Sussex, Suss
Warwickshire, Warw, Warwick
Westmorland, Westmorcld, Westmorcland
Wiltshire, Wilts
Worcestershire, Worcs, Worc, Worcester
Yorkshire, Yorks, Ebor, York
West Riding, W.R., WR, W. R, W R
East Riding, E.R., ER, E. R, E R
North Riding, N.R., NR, N. R, N R

WELSH COUNTY ABBREVIATIONS USED IN THE CATALOGUE
Anglesey, Anglesea, Ang
Breconshire, Brec, Brecknockshire, Brecon, Brecknock
Caernarvonshire, Caern
Cardiganshire, Card
Carmarthenshire, Carm
Denbighshire, Denb
Flintshire, Flint
Glamorganshire, Glam
Merionethshire, Merion
Montgomeryshire, Mont
Pembrokeshire, Pemb
Radnorshire, Rad

Searching for medieval and early modern records can be hampered by the huge number of variant spellings. Archival practice was to give the spelling of names and places as was used in the document, which is fine for browsing a paper version but not good for searching. You may need to build up your own collection of variant spellings. The published versions of earlier records include variant forms in their indexes.

1.7 Browsing our catalogue

If your searches are unsuccessful, try browsing a suggested series instead. Browsing allows you to look up all the catalogue descriptions as in a paper list. At the National Archives in Kew, you can use the paper catalogue, as this can sometimes be easier; elsewhere, you can do it on screen. From the Catalogue homepage, type the series code (e.g., HO 47) into the 'Go to reference' box. This will take you to a description of that series (always useful to read – and it may give you details of any supplementary finding aids or published versions that exist). Then click on the 'Browse from here' box. This will take you to a list of series in which HO 47 is followed by HO 48, HO 49 and so on. Many people get lost at this point: clicking on the underlined text will just take you round in a circle. The trick here is to go instead for the folder symbol or series code on the left. Clicking on this will take you into the next level down – the descriptions of each document.

You can also choose between two different views to display a list, by reference or by hierarchy. Hierarchy is a good choice for large series, as it sorts references into sub-series. For example, ADM 1 has 31,080 pieces. Sort it by hierarchy, and these are reduced to about nine sub-series arranged by date, each with further sub-sub-series arranged by subject. This makes navigating a long list much easier. Displaying by reference usually means in numerical order.

1.8 What to search and what to browse?

One of the main problems with using the catalogue effectively is that it depends on knowing what to search and what to browse. I recommend always starting with a search, because you never know what may crop up unexpectedly. If you are looking for a specific person or surname or place, try a search on that first: you may be lucky.

As only a small proportion of our catalogue is fully searchable, you will need to learn how to browse as well. This book helps you by indicating the relevant series for particular subjects and categorising these series by how best to access them. As you look through the book, you will see references like WO 97 or HO 45 with symbols after them. Below are the **symbols** and their meaning; they are also reproduced on the very last page of the book for ease of consultation.

[1]	Searchable online by surname
[2]	Searchable online by forename AND surname (James AND Maltby)
[3]	Searchable online by initial AND surname (J AND Maltby)
[4]	Searchable online by county
[5]	Searchable online by place
[6]	Searchable online by subject or by name of regiment, unit or ship
[7]	Brief description in catalogue (sometimes just a date range, or ranges of names or numbers): no searchable data on individuals. May need to browse the catalogue (or search by * and date), or use the paper catalogue and then read the most likely record. For how to browse the catalogue, see 1.7
[8]	Brief description in catalogue: no searchable data on individuals. The document itself contains an index

P	Best searched in paper catalogue at the National Archives: detailed descriptions are not in online catalogue
S	Best searched in published work: detailed descriptions are not in online catalogue
F	Best searched in or with a supplementary finding aid at the National Archives: detailed descriptions are not in online catalogue
V	Use variants spellings or wildcards
W	Searchable on another website (often free at the National Archives)

1.9 Traditional searches: going beyond the website

The 5,500 page *PRO Guide* gives an overview of the history and content of the records in our care. Its last update was in 1998, so it is out of date for modern records. However, very many series are no longer being added to, so for older records this problem is not significant. The *Guide* occupies several loose-leaf volumes and is divided into three parts. Part 1 contains the history of government. Part 2 contains series or class descriptions in alphabetical order of department code. Part 3 is the index to the other two parts. It can still be a very useful aid, particularly when you want to check on or compare several series quickly. You may find that some areas of the records still rely on the *Guide* as published in 1963–1968, based on the one published in 1923, based on the one published in 1896. These can all still be useful for overviews of earlier records, and are especially useful if you are trying to track down a reference to a document from a publication of that period. The current system of assigning each document a letter code, a series number and a piece number only dates from the 1920s, and was not really adopted by historians until the 1960s or 1970s, so there are plenty of obsolete references in existence in their footnotes. If you come across one, ask for advice or use one of the older *Guides* to puzzle it out. Several printed copies of the 1998 *Guide* are available at the National Archives and at the Family Records Centre. You may be able to find a microfiche edition locally. Remember to check on the catalogue as well for new accessions and the most up-to-date information.

Also at the National Archives are the paper catalogue (from which the online catalogue was created) and large numbers of volumes of printed, typescript and manuscript lists and indexes, plus many card indexes. Modern forms of supplementary finding aids also exist: we have many indexes on CD-Rom, created by family history societies and private researchers, accessed from all the public terminals. We even have two immense series of ancient finding aids, treated as records, which can still be of great value: IND 1 for contemporary 'indexes' created by the original keepers or creators of the records and OBS 1 for similar material, which has been superseded. These are best explored in a publication (ask at the enquiry desks), the List and Index Society's *Catalogue of Index Volumes and Obsolete Lists and Indexes*. You will find several references to volumes from IND 1 throughout this book. Most have to be ordered up as documents in the usual way, but some are on the open shelves in the Map Room at Kew.

1.10   Ordering documents to be produced or copied

The catalogue provides both a description and links into a document ordering system, where you can request the original to be produced at the archives or copies to be made. (The system differs slightly on site and off site.) You can also order copies at **www.nationalarchives.gov.uk/shop** or on site. You can order documents to be ready for when you arrive. It normally only takes twenty to thirty minutes for documents to be fetched once ordered, but some documents are kept off site and take three days. Most of these are relatively unpopular series: any mentioned in this book are indicated.

You must have a valid reference to order documents or copies – and this means one that our ordering system accepts. You can only order records at piece or item level (see the table in 1.4). Some documents are described at item level but ordered at piece level, which causes a lot of confusion. Pieces and items have got rather muddled. If you imagine that an item is a page in a book, or one document among many rolled in a bundle, and the piece is the book or the bundle, you can see why some items cannot be ordered by themselves, and why you have to order the parent piece instead. But other items can be ordered. (I always assumed there was some logic behind this, but now I rather doubt it – all depends on how documents were catalogued or stored or boxed or re-boxed in the past.)

The basic point is that if you want to order a document and find you cannot, it is probably because it is an unorderable item. The simple solution is to knock off the last numbers and try again – but keep a note of the lopped off numbers to help you find your place when the larger book or bundle appears. For example, if you want to order c 13/282/45 but the catalogue will not let you, try instead to order c 13/282 and look for number 45 in the large bundle. If you want to order copies, make sure that you include instructions that you only want number 45.

If you have an obsolete reference from a published book to something clearly held by us, or real problems in ordering, get in touch and we will sort out the modern reference for you.

A few series included in our own catalogue are not actually kept by the National Archives (this is indicated in the catalogue). The ones you are most likely to come across are POST, kept by the British Postal Museum and Archive, and ADM 354, kept by the National Maritime Museum.

1.11 Documents Online

Documents Online allows you online access to our collection of (currently) over seven million digital images of public records, including excellent family history sources. It's obviously very convenient to be able to download an image straight away, but for me the real benefit is the indexing – seven million digital images means seven million index entries. When you consider that most of these have come from only five series of records, and that we have nearly 15,000 series, you can see that there is still much to discover about the actual contents of the records.

Searching the index is free, and it currently costs £3.50 to download an image. (Documents Online can now be used free of charge at the National Archives and the Family Records Centre. Printing facilities are available in most of the reading rooms, but you cannot email images or save them to disk.)

The main family history topics covered so far are:

WILLS
More than one million wills proved in the Prerogative Court of Canterbury from 1384 to 1858, as well as original wills of famous people such as William Shakespeare, Jane Austen, Sir Francis Drake, Samuel Pepys and Christopher Wren. (See 10.3 for advice and context: series are PROB 11 and PROB 1.)

ROYAL NAVAL SEAMEN
Service details for more than 500,000 seamen who were in the Royal Navy at 1873 or who joined between 1873 and 1923. (See 28.4.3 for advice and context: series is ADM 188.)

FIRST WORLD WAR CAMPAIGN MEDALS
Almost all of the men and women who saw active service overseas were awarded a campaign medal, making this the most complete listing of all men and women, officers and soldiers who served in the British Army or Royal Flying Corps during the First World War. (See 26.1.1 for advice and context: series is WO 372.)

SECOND WORLD WAR MERCHANT SEAMEN'S MEDALS
This contains a record of medals claimed and issued to more than 100,000 merchant seamen from 1946 to 2002. Each entry gives details of the seaman's name, discharge book number and the medals, ribbons and clasps issued to him. Some entries also list date and place of birth. (See 35.15 for advice and context: series is BT 395.)

1.12 The National Register of Archives

The National Register of Archives (NRA) is the central point for information about the nature and location of manuscripts relating to

British history. It is maintained by the Historical Manuscripts Commission, which joined with the Public Record Office to form the National Archives in 2003. The Register is a collection of over 44,000 unpublished lists and catalogues of records and manuscripts held elsewhere: it does not hold any of the actual records and manuscripts. The catalogues can be consulted at the National Archives (and each one can be seen at the place where the records and manuscripts are kept).

The National Register contains information about historical records created by some 46,000 individuals, 9,000 families, 29,000 businesses and 75,000 organisations. So much material obviously needed indexing, and indexing brought together entries for the same people, places or organisations that were actually kept in many different locations. The index to the National Register of Archives has therefore grown into a major research tool in itself. The entry for Winston Churchill, for example (carefully identified as 'Churchill, Sir Winston Leonard Spencer (1874–1965) Knight Statesman and Historian'), notes 95 separate collections of his papers. In 1995 the indexes of the NRA were made available online, and are now at **www.nationalarchives.gov.uk/nra**. As more and more catalogues and lists have been made available online the indexes have provided links to these – some of which are in A2A and others in our own catalogue. However, most of the hard-copy lists in the NRA are not available online.

There are five online indexes to the NRA: the business index, the organisations index, the personal index, the families and estates index and the diaries and papers index. You can search the indexes in the following ways:

- Simple Search, designed so that you can search more than one index simultaneously, although it is not possible to search all five at once;
- Advanced Search, which allows more refined searches of each index;
- the site search on our homepage, which allows for some subject searching of the indexes.

Entries found under the different indexes to the NRA vary to some extent but all share certain common elements; once you understand these you will easily be able to interpret the results of most of your searches. Many individual index entries have numerous sub-entries referring to different groups of records, but each will follow the pattern outlined below. A typical index entry will include the following details:

- the name of the individual, family, business or organisation that created the records, and information such as a personal epithet (such as pig breeder, soldier);
- a short summary of the records themselves, usually including the covering dates of the collection;
- the location of the records, usually a name of a record repository;

- a reference number of the records and for some entries a link to an online catalogue;
- an NRA number if a hard-copy catalogue of a particular collection has been sent in;
- references to published sources, copies of which will normally be available in the search room and in good reference libraries.

Each results page has a general explanation of the information given.

If you are accessing the website from in or near the National Archives, you may want to come and look at the hard-copy catalogues of records held elsewhere but sent in to the National Register of Archives. These are now in the Research Enquiries Room. These can be an excellent source to browse for context once you have found a relevant hit. If the mythical Mr Wouldbegood (of 1.3) had turned out in A2A to be in correspondence with Lord Emsworth about pigs, a search in the National Register of Archives might turn up the Emsworth estate papers in the Blandings Castle Muniment Room. These may not be easy to get at, but the NRA reference points to a paper catalogue at the National Archives to inspect for peripheral mentions of the fraud in the Pig Breeders' accounts, the direct cause of the chancery suit.

1.13 Access to archives held elsewhere: A2A

Access to Archives, or A2A, allows you to search and browse for information in detailed catalogues of archives in England outside the National Archives, dating from the 900s to the present day. These are archives cared for in over 340 local record offices and libraries, universities, museums and national and specialist institutions across England, where they are made available to the public. Some of the major catalogues are from the Oriental and India Office Collections at the British Library, the Canterbury Cathedral Archives, private collections at the National Army Museum, the Bodleian Library and so on – a really astounding roll call of institutions small and large that guard our documentary heritage.

Using A2A, you can search for relevant documents across all these catalogues quickly and easily. Once you have references to documents, you can contact the holder of the documents (*not* the National Archives) to arrange to see them or to obtain copies. The database is updated regularly, so revisit often for newly included catalogues.

You can use our site search to find material in A2A (see 1.3) or you can use its own search engine at **www.nationalarchives.gov.uk/a2a**. Although this is a powerful search engine, a simple general search using one word (such as a surname) is the best start. There may be only a few hits for the name and a more specific search could well exclude some of them. There may be too many hits, but at least you will get an idea of the quantity and can then start to make your search more specific. If you start with a more complex search term and get no results, you may not know which of your search terms to change. Try some of the following suggestions:

SEARCH DATES

There are two options to search using dates that produce two different outcomes.

Specific year If you search for a specific year your search will retrieve individual catalogue entries concerning that year or covering a range of dates including that year.

Search between range of years This search will find hits in catalogues where the date range of the entire catalogue overlaps, includes or is included in the date range you are searching. This can seem confusing. For example, Joseph Jones' will is dated 1869, but the catalogue it is in dates from 1086–1972; so a search for his will between the dates 1600 and 1650 would still find this catalogue entry because the overall dates of the catalogue overlap those specified, although the catalogue entry found is outside the date range.

Remember also that not every catalogue entry is dated. The date, particularly of older records, may not be known.

DATES OF CATALOGUES

This allows you to restrict your search to catalogues that have been added to A2A since the last time you searched so that you can repeat searches without going over the same results.

NEAR AND ADJ

If you want to search for a combination of words in a single file description the best way is to use **NEAR**. NEAR by itself searches for words next to each other, but NEAR2, NEAR3 and NEAR4 search for words 2, 3 or 4 words away from each other. For example, the search for the will of Joseph Jones mentioned above was 'will NEAR8 Hereford', a search that looks for the words will and Hereford within 8 words of each other, in any order. You can vary the number of words simply by changing the number.

ADJ works in the same way as NEAR, but searches for the words in the order that you type them. This is useful to search for phrases with the word 'and' or 'or' in them, for example, 'bricks and mortar'. If you use this phrase as a search term, the actual search you are running is for the word 'bricks' and the word 'mortar' within the same catalogue, and 67 catalogues are found. If you use the term 'bricks ADJ1 mortar', which looks for the two words within one word of each other, only 11 catalogues are found.

1.14 Directory of Archives: Archon

The Archon directory includes contact details for record office and other archives in the United Kingdom (and also for institutions elsewhere in the world) that have substantial collections of manuscripts noted in the National Register of Archives. You can either search it directly at **www.nationalarchives.gov.uk/archon** or via the site search. You will also find direct links to Archon from hits on A2A or the NRA. A typical entry would give contact details; correspondence address; telephone and fax numbers; email address; website; an online map; access information, opening hours, etc; and a list of the paper catalogues sent to the NRA and available at the National Archives.

1.15 The Library of the National Archives

Our Library is a specialist history reference library that has been in existence for over 150 years. It has not been open to the public for very long and it is still a rather underused resource. Its catalogue can be seen at **www.nationalarchives.gov/library**. The Library is also responsible for free access on site to the many of the subscription-only websites that are so useful: *The Times*, the *Dictionary of National Biography* and the *Parliamentary Papers* are the ones I use regularly, but there are many others to explore.

The Library has excellent sets of periodicals and journals for all kinds of history. Its holdings of local record society publications are a tremendous resource and you may even find that the information you are looking for has been printed. It also holds a very large collection of books relating to the myriad of subjects covered by the records in the National Archives. There are long runs of annual publications, such as the *Army List*, *Crockford's Clerical Directory*, the *India List*, the *Court and City Register*, the *Imperial Calendar*, the *Annual Register of World Events* (from 1758 to date), *Burke's Landed Gentry* and collections of local and professional directories. However, there is a very good online source for local directories from 1750 to 1919 at **www.historicaldirectories.org**.

1.16 Getting the best results: the website and beyond: bibliography

M S GIUSEPPI, *A Guide to the Manuscripts preserved in the Public Record Office* (London, 1923)

C J KITCHING, 'The National Register of Archives: adapting to meet researchers' needs in the twenty-first century' in *Recusant History*, vol. 25, no. 2 (2000)

List and Index Society, *Catalogue of Index Volumes (IND 1) and Obsolete Lists and Indexes (OBS 1)* (List and Index Society, vol. 232, 1988)

Public Record Office, *Guide to the Contents of the Public Record Office* (London, 1963, 1968)

Public Record Office, *Guide to the Contents of the Public Record Office* (Public Record Office, 1998 edition)

S R SCARGILL BIRD, *A Guide to the Principal Classes of Documents preserved in the Public Record Office* (London, 1896)

2 The National Archives and the Family Records Centre

2.1 Family history research: starting out

The best place to begin family history research is not on the web, nor in an archive or records office, but at home, gathering as many facts, memories and memorabilia as you can from members of your family. You may be surprised at how much you can accumulate. Putting it together will bring out all kinds of queries when you realise that there are unexplained gaps. Answering those queries may lead to more questions, and so on until you find that you need to start looking outside the family for information. You will find that you probably have to revisit family memories as you find out more.

A record office is not the place to start research because neither local nor central government has ever had much interest in recording family history. We sometimes get questions from people who expect to find a government file on their family kept over the centuries. This was not the case. Records were kept only when people came into contact with government at some point – when their birth, marriage or death was registered; when they completed a census return; when they entered one of the armed services; when they committed a crime; when they were supposed to pay taxes; or when they had recourse to a court of law. Because government had no interest in tracking individuals, there are no official indexes to records giving all the references to, say, John Smith of Little Puddington.

You really do need to have a list of answerable questions, and as much information as you can, before you go to the trouble and expense of visiting a record office. To help you work out what questions you can expect to get answers to, try your local library for *recent* books on how to research family history: there are many good ones available.

Some books are particularly interesting. Mark Herber's *Ancestral Trails* is an unsurpassed overview of both local and national records that can be used by family historians. A lawyer himself, the author has a real gift for clearly explaining the legal framework behind so many of the most valuable records. Peter Christian's *The Genealogist's Internet* (now in its third edition) is an invaluable guide to making good use of the huge number of online resources. David Hey's *Journeys in Family History* sets the social and historical context against what you can find in the records. David Hey has also produced *Family Names and Family History*, which shows how very many surnames and families remain local to their place of origin. Some surnames can even be traced back to individual farmsteads. Apparently, 1,000 surnames covered 60 per cent of the population. But there were very many more – 30,000 rare ones were used by only 10 per cent of the population. Working on these lines, you may also wish to investigate *The British 19th Century Surname Atlas* CD-Rom (see **www.archersoftware. co.uk**). This can be a very useful source indeed for finding variant spellings of surnames, as well as their local distribution, and it is easy to use and not expensive. You should make sure that you are not duplicating research someone else has already done. Try the listing of surnames that have been registered by researchers with the Guild of One Name Studies (**www.one-name.org**).

At some point you may discover the Society of Genealogists in central London (**www.sog.org.uk**: address in 62). They have an incomparable library of published and unpublished source material, including transcripts of many parish registers: for an overview, see Churchill, 'Off the Shelf' (details in the bibliography at the end of this chapter). You can pay an annual fee to join the Society, or you can pay a small daily or hourly charge to use the library. Try to contact your local family history society, which could be extremely helpful in providing guidance if you run into problems. A list of family history societies and like bodies appears in the *Family History News and Digest*, the journal of the Federation of Family History Societies (**www.ffhs.org.uk**: address in 62). They also publish an excellent series of brief and inexpensive guides to records. You may also discover locally run courses in family history techniques and sources.

If London is out of reach, look for one of the worldwide Family History Centres run by the Church of Jesus Christ of Latter-day Saints. Through them, you can access on microfilm vast runs of records vital to the pursuit of family history. You can view these films at their local centres for a small fee. Most need to be ordered from their headquarters in Utah and take about a month to arrive. To find out the nearest centre, look at **www. familysearch.org**. Their main UK centre is the Hyde Park Family History Centre (addresses in 62).

Once you know what questions you want to ask in an archive or record office, and where you can reasonably expect to get them answered, you need to find out how to get there. You could invest in Gibson and Peskett's inexpensive pamphlet, *Record Offices and How to Find Them* (a typically practical and helpful FFHS guide, which includes maps). Another way is to check the directory of archives and record offices online at **www.archon.nationalarchives.gov.uk**.

2.2 Using the internet

You may be annoyed to find that this book assumes that you have access to the internet. This is because so much is now available there that to ignore it would be to cut yourself off from some wonderful sources of information and advice. It is really astounding how much has become available and how quickly on official, commercial and amateur sites. (When I say amateur I mean that these sites are a labour of love, created by people with real knowledge and interest and a desire to share it.) In only a few years, the internet has become one of the most valuable tools for family history. Some sites offer free databases, which include their own search engine. Other sites charge fees or a subscription rate, or charge fees for downloading images of documents. (If you don't have access at home, try your local library or an internet café.) Many libraries provide library-card holders with free access to subscription databases for specialised resources such as newspapers, biographies, encyclopedias and periodicals. Many of these are also free onsite at the National Archives and Family Records Centre.

A good place to start is with the family history gateway site, **www. familyrecords.gov.uk**. This leads you on to the official websites for the various United Kingdom national archives you will need to use for family history research. Another UK-based site of great interest is **www.genuki. org.uk**, which covers every county in the UK and has much information on family history societies. A site that you will use time and again is **www.familysearch.org**, which gives free access to millions of index entries. Two excellent US-based sites are **www.cyndislist.com**, with over 65,000 links to other sites, and **www.rootsweb.com**, with over 19,000 mailing lists. A really good overview of what sites exist (and there are thousands of them) is given in Peter Christian's *The Genealogist's Internet*. To keep up to date, check out his regular 'Internet Section' in *Ancestors*, the National Archives' own family history magazine.

A word of warning: much of the information online comes from secondary sources. This means that the original (which may be damaged or illegible) has been read and copied out, perhaps several times, before reaching you in a list or index. It may not be accurate and should not be taken as proof. You must evaluate the information yourself: think about its source, how it fits with what you know and how it fits with what is likely. Try to check original sources whenever you can. Many archives and record offices are able to send you copies of the original documents for only a small charge, and you can often use the internet to order by email.

2.3 Visiting the National Archives

The National Archives is based on the banks of the River Thames at Kew, near Richmond, just south-west of London. It occupies a very large building with several reading rooms and advice points. The staff are there to advise you on how best to carry out your research, so please feel free to approach the enquiry desks if you have a question or aren't sure how to proceed.

You do not need to make an appointment to use the National Archives. Our reading rooms are currently open Monday to Saturday until 5 p.m., with late night opening on Tuesday and Thursday until 7 p.m. They open at 9 a.m., except on Tuesdays (10 a.m.) and Saturdays (9.30 a.m.). Documents cannot be ordered or read until 9.30 a.m. We are closed on Sundays, public holidays and during stocktaking (normally a few days at the beginning of December). There is a restaurant on site, where you can also eat your own food, as well as a bookshop, an internet café and a museum.

You will need to get a reader's ticket at the National Archives. This is issued at Reception when you arrive on production of some positive means of identification. We ask for a passport, banker's card or driving licence. Foreign nationals should bring a passport or some other form of national identification document. Children of 14 and over can be issued with a reader's ticket if they come with (and are vouched for by) their parents or other adult. If they come by themselves, they must bring a letter of recommendation from their school, on headed notepaper and signed by the head teacher.

Our first responsibility is to preserve the records for this and future generations – they are unique and in many cases ancient or fragile. Large bags, coats and mobile phones are not allowed in the research areas at the National Archives. Lockable hangers are provided for coats, and there are free lockers for other belongings. Pens and coloured pencils are not allowed in the reading rooms. Graphite pencils and laptop computers are allowed: power points and locking points are available. The shop has supplies of paper, tracing paper and pencils and magnifying sheets. If you want to trace anything, ask for an acetate sheet to put over the document first. To help preserve the documents, please make use of the foam wedges and covered weights supplied – instructions for their use are on display.

Many of our most popular documents are seen as copies (microfilm, microfiche or digitised image) that you can access yourself. Less frequently used documents are seen in the original, and you need to put in an order to get these fetched for you. You can order three original documents at a time; as soon as they arrive you can order another three, and so on throughout the day. They take about twenty minutes to arrive. If you want to order documents to be ready before you get to the National Archives, you can ring us up or email the order from our website.

Copies of documents can be bought in many formats: you can scan them yourself using our scanners or print them from microfilm or microfiche. You can now also bring your own camera to photograph documents. You will need to register your camera with us the first time you do this, and to abide by the rules relating to photography. You cannot use flash, a phone camera, a camcorder or a tripod. We do provide camera stands. We also run a copying service that you can access via our website, or by letter, email or phone.

Readers with disabilities should know that there is a lift to all floors, and that the facilities are wheelchair friendly. We have aids to help readers with impaired vision, but those with severe impairment are advised to come with a sighted friend. Equally, if you have mobility or lifting difficulties it may be a good idea to come with a friend. Many of the documents are heavy and unwieldy – and are often very dirty. The National Archives is housed in a very large building, and there can be distances to cover between different sources of information. If you contact us in advance, we can provide wheelchair assistance for the 100 metres plus from the car park and you can borrow a wheelchair for use within the building itself. There are disabled parking bays at the rear of the building, available on a first-come, first-served basis. You can find more details on our website at **www.nationalarchives.gov.uk/visit/disabled.htm**.

Our contact details are:

Post	The National Archives, Kew, Richmond, Surrey TW9 4DU
Telephone	+44 20 8876 3444 for international calls, 020 8876 3444 for UK calls
Email	Please use our contact form at **www.nationalarchives.gov.uk/contact/form**
Fax	020 8878 8905
Minicom	020 8392 9198

If you are walking to the National Archives, our pedestrian entrance is off Ruskin Avenue (the nearest station, Kew Gardens, is about 10 minutes' walk: the route is signposted). The entry for cars is off the south circular road (Mortlake Road): follow the signs to the Kew Retail Park. We have a good-size car park, but on busy days it does fill up.

2.4 Visiting the Family Records Centre

The Family Records Centre is run jointly by the National Archives and the General Register Office of England and Wales. It opened in 1997 on the closure of the Census Rooms at the Public Record Office's former site in Chancery Lane, and of the General Register Office public search room at

St Catherine's House. Some books and people still use the old names. Here you can see

- censuses (in surrogate form) from 1841–1901. Access to the census online before 1901 is free here;
- the major archive of wills before 1858;
- Nonconformist records of births, marriages and deaths before 1837;
- Fleet marriage registers before 1754;
- indexes to civil registers of birth, marriage and death, 1837 to date;
- indexes to adoption records, 1927 to date.

The other main family history sources held outside the National Archives and the Family Records Centre are

- parish registers of births, marriages and deaths before 1837: held locally, usually in county record offices;
- wills proved in local church courts before 1858: usually in county record offices;
- wills after 1858, held at the Principal Registry of the Family Division's Probate Searchroom (sometimes still referred to as being at Somerset House).

The Family Records Centre is in Islington, London (just across the road from the London Metropolitan Archives, in case you want to plan a double trip) and is open from 10 a.m. on Tuesdays, 9.30 a.m. on Saturdays and 9 a.m. every other weekday. It closes at 7 p.m. on Tuesday and Thursday, and 5 p.m. on the other days. The Family Records Centre is closed on Sundays and public holidays. No reader's ticket is needed. Pens can be used, and there are power points for laptops in the census and wills search room. There are many computers for accessing family history sources online, and an expert staff to turn to for advice. There is a shop and an eating area in the building, and several places nearby sell meals and sandwiches. There are lockers that take a £1 coin, returned after use. If you want to take copies, there are self-service reader-printers.

There is ramp access for wheelchairs and a lift to both floors. There are three parking spaces reserved for disabled readers, which you have to book in advance by ringing 020 7533 6436. There are some motorised microfilm readers with zoom facilities for disabled readers, and magnifiers are available for printed sources or copies. If you have severely impaired vision, try to come with a sighted friend. A friend may also be of help if you have limited mobility: once in the building, there is still a considerable amount of walking backwards and forwards during the course of a visit.

Contact details are:

Post   Family Records Centre, 1 Myddelton Street, London EC1R 1UW
Minicom   020 8392 9198
Website   **www.familyrecords.gov.uk/frc**

Census, will and general enquiries: 020 8392 5300, fax 020 8487 9214, email frc@nationalarchives.gov.uk

Certificate, adoption or overseas enquiries: 0845 603 7788, fax 020 8392 5307, email certificate.services@ons.gsi.gov.uk. Postal enquiries for certificates should be sent to the General Register Office, Smedley Hydro, Trafalgar Road, Southport, Merseyside PR8 2HH. You can also order certificates online at **www.gro.gov.uk**.

The Family Records Centre is very busy and popular, even now that so much is available online, as many people find the staff guidance and access to websites a real help. It has an extensive range of leaflets giving you up-to-date guidance on how to use the records and find aids there.

2.5 Children and archives

Thousands of children every year come on school trips to the education rooms at the National Archives and go away enthused and excited. Others come on our family days and behind the scenes tours. But reading rooms in archives are not really suitable for young children: they are quiet or silent areas where records can be consulted without fear of damage.

At the National Archives, any children must stay with you at all times, in case of emergency. If they cause a disturbance to other readers, you will have to take them out of the reading rooms. Children are rarely as interested in your research as you might wish and get bored quickly. Spinning round on chairs attracts disapproving glances from other readers. A child can't even colour in quietly, as only graphite pencils are allowed at the National Archives. If you need to bribe your way to a day at the National Archives or Family Records Centre, note that the shops at both sites sell a range of 'historic' gifts, which may appeal to children or to the person looking after them for you!

From the age of 14 school pupils can get their own ticket for the National Archives if an adult with a reader's ticket accompanies them and vouches for them.

2.6 Paying for research

The ideal for all family research is to do it yourself, as only you can judge what unexpected information in a source ties in with what you already know about your family. However, personal visits to archives or record offices are not always possible. You then have several options for research at the National Archives:

- you can ask someone to come for you – a friend or a family member;
- if you know the exact document reference, you can order copies on the website or by post. We can do a small amount of identification within a box or volume;

- you can pay someone to do the work for you.
  With this last option you have two choices (you can find out more about both on our website or by contacting us):
- a professional independent researcher, who has the knowledge and experience of someone who undertakes work in a variety of archives and registries, not just in the National Archives. Ideally, they should be able to advise on how to overcome problems in your research into your family tree;
- our own paid service provides a search in a specific range of records for a piece of specific information, but not the wider commitment of a good independent researcher.

We have several lists of independent researchers on our website, and we supply a printed list in response to a phone call or written request. Please indicate what area of research interests you, as independent researchers specialise in different subjects. The arrangement between you and the independent researcher will be of a purely private nature. The Association of Genealogists and Researchers in Archives (see 62) can also put you in touch with a researcher accredited to the Association. You may find helpful the article by Adolph, 'How to hire a genealogist – getting the best use out of professional researchers'.

2.7 The Friends of the National Archives

Some researchers find themselves so hooked on using archives that they want to do something to help make them more widely available. The Friends of the National Archives is a group of volunteers who take part in large cataloguing projects, such as indexing soldiers' discharge papers or death duty registers, much to our gratitude. They also receive a newsletter, access to events and discount in the bookshop. For more details or to volunteer, please look at **www.nationalarchives.gov.uk/ friends** or write to the Friends of the National Archives (address in 62).

2.8 Publications, indexes and pedigrees

You may arrive at the National Archives with a specific query or with a planned programme of research. When you have an odd half-hour while waiting for a document, it may be worth taking a side-step to look elsewhere to see if any extra information can be picked up quickly.

There are four easy places to check for information in print or online about a particular person. The first is the *Dictionary of National Biography*, which is in the Library in hard copy and free online at the National Archives. This contains brief biographies of many thousands of people who were considered to be of some national significance. The second is the *British Biographical Archive*. This is a compilation of over 300 other English language biographical dictionaries published between 1601 and 1929, put together on microfiche in a single alphabetical order of surname. It is on open access in the Microfilm Reading Room. It has a printed index called the *British Biographical Index*, available in our Library, which is a useful source in its own right as it provides a summary of the entries and acts as an index to the fiches. The fourth is a CD-Rom, available in the Library, called the *Biography Database 1680–1830*. The current issue contains over 100 directories (national, town and trade); over 1,500 book subscription lists; apprenticeship lists from the Stationers' Company 1701–1800; birth, marriage, death and bankruptcy notices from the *Gentleman's Magazine from 1731–1750*; and much more. It contains roughly 900,000 records and is searchable by name, title, office, occupation and address. It is updated regularly to include more sources.

Indexes to records are available not only at the National Archives. Other record offices and libraries obviously have their own indexes, and very many people index records for their own purposes, which they are prepared to search for a fee. There may be an index somewhere that will save you days of work or suggest new lines of enquiry. To find out, look at Gibson and Hampson, *Specialist Indexes for Family Historians*, which should be available at every enquiry desk.

Another source worth checking as you garner more names for your family tree is the large number of pedigrees that have ended up in the public records, usually in support of some legal claim. You can search our catalogue using 'pedigree' as the search term. This will bring up many pedigree cattle, but possibly also an entry for your family. Most of the pedigrees are listed or indexed only by the 'principal person' – the pivotal person in the legal proof of entitlement to whatever was being claimed. An early work by Wrottesley, *Pedigrees from the Plea Rolls, 1200–1500*, may be worth looking at.

2.9 New skills and knowledge: language, writing, dates and money

As you move back in time from the twentieth century, you need to acquire new skills and knowledge to understand the documents properly. You will come across odd forms of writing, different methods of dating, archaic measurements, incomprehensible legal phrases and, of course, Latin (in general use for many legal records until 1733). This is all on top of the fact that in very many documents (particularly registers where a few clerks were entering similar information year in, year out) there are all kinds of abbreviations, which meant something at the time but which now might as well be in double Dutch.

LANGUAGE AND WRITING

Reading the writing can often be a skill in itself: classes are a good way to learn this skill of palaeography, or you could try our course at **www.**

nationalarchives.gov.uk/palaeography. Excellent self-help books are also available, such as Marshall's *Palaeography for Family and Local Historians*. However, the problem is that handwriting changes enormously over time – many letter forms are completely different in different centuries. Most courses concentrate on the earlier material. Having done them, I can read most sixteenth-century hands quite fluently, but I do find nineteenth-century clerk's copperplate a real trial. For books to help with understanding the writing, and the Latin, see 2.10 or try our Latin course at **www.nationalarchives.gov.uk/latin/beginners**.

The multi-volume *Oxford English Dictionary* is very helpful when you are satisfied that you have read a word correctly but you still have no idea what it means. This can be accessed online free at the National Archives. It is especially helpful as it gives dated examples of usage. For legal phrases and procedures, there are several legal dictionaries at the National Archives. For understanding old weights and measurements, try Chapman, *How Heavy, How Much and How Long? Weights, Money and Other Measures Used by Our Ancestors*.

DATES

You need to learn a few old ideas about dating practices and then refer to a crib to help you date documents correctly. Munby's *Dates and Time* is a fascinating account of the subject, but you may still need access to Cheney and Jones's classic *Handbook of Dates*. For much of the documented past, people in England dated years not by the calendar year (e.g., 1780) but by the regnal year (how long the monarch had been on the throne). A new regnal year began on the anniversary of the monarch's accession to the throne. Thus, 1 Elizabeth I ran from the death of Mary on 17 November 1558 to 16 November 1559; 2 Elizabeth I ran from 17 November 1559 to 16 November 1560; and so on, until 45 Elizabeth I stopped at her death on 24 March 1603 and the new year of 1 James I began.

Another problem with years is that although New Year's Day was celebrated on 1 January, the actual year number did not change until 25 March. This was the Annunciation or Lady Day, nine months to the day before Christmas. This practice did not change officially until 1752, but for some decades beforehand dates from January to 24 March were expressed as being in two years – as 1641/2, for example. You will find that most dates given in National Archives lists and publications are amended to the modern form of the year.

The third issue to look out for is Old Style and New Style – the difference between English dates and European dates from 1582. Pope Gregory XIII reformed the calendar in 1582 by cutting out ten days to return to the solar year. Other countries followed this lead at different times: broadly speaking, Catholic states adopted the New Style in the sixteenth century, Protestant states in the eighteenth century and Orthodox states in the twentieth century. People corresponding between countries would date their letters with both dates – for example, 12/22 December 1635. All kinds of oddities crop up. In 1688 William of Orange left Holland on 11 November and arrived in England on 5 November. In the United Kingdom the change took place in 1752, when Wednesday 2 September was followed immediately by Thursday 14 September. This was ignored by the accounting and hiring records, so that the old accounting day of Lady Day (25 March) slipped to 5 April ('old Lady Day'), still the start of the financial year in Britain.

In early modern documents you often find that instead of using the day and month, saint's days and religious feasts are used, so that you could find the phrases 'Tuesday after the Annunciation' or 'in the eve of St Martin'. To translate these, you need to know the date of the feast day and the calendar for that particular year. You can find both in the lists and tables in Cheney and Jones's *Handbook of Dates* (available at all the enquiry desks).

The legal system had its own calendar, based around the old agricultural and religious cycles. The legal year began with the Michaelmas term (starting on 6 October) followed by the Hilary, Easter and Trinity terms. Between the terms were the vacations. In the Lent vacation (Hilary to Easter) and the Summer vacation (Trinity to Michaelmas), the judges from the central courts travelled round the country on the assize circuits. Details of the legal terms for each year are given in the latest edition of the *Handbook of Dates*.

MONEY

Before decimalisation in 1971, our money was expressed in ancient units, as follows:

£1 in units of 12 and 20
£1 = 20 shillings or 240 pennies (not a coin)
1 shilling = 12d (pennies)
1 guinea = £1 1s

£1 in quarters and eighths
10s = a rose noble or a royal coin (medieval and Early Modern)
5s = 1 Crown
2s 6d = half a Crown

£1 in thirds (medieval and Early Modern)
13s 4d = 1 mark (not a coin)
6s 8d = half a mark (a noble or angel coin)

Some of these were actual coins. Larger sums of money such as marks were not actual coins, but were terms used in speech and in accounts.

2.10 The National Archives and the Family Records Centre: an introductory bibliography

Many of the books cited in the bibliography at the end of each chapter are available in our reference library. Some are for sale in the shops at the National Archives and at the Family Records Centre. Our bookshop also runs a mail order service: for more information, check the website (see 2.53). Most of the books recommended are in the Guildhall Library (a public library with an excellent genealogical collection), the library of the Society of Genealogists and in good reference libraries. You could try inter-library loan through your local lending library, which is usually available for a very small fee. Our library does not lend on inter-library loan.

If you want to explore the historical background, try the Royal Historical Society's online bibliography of books and articles at **www.rhs.ac.uk/bibl**. Another interesting site is British History Online at **www.british-history.ac.uk/**. This is a digital library containing some of the core printed primary and secondary sources for medieval and modern history.

British Biographical Archive (London, 1984 continuing)

P CARTER and K THOMPSON, *Sources for Local Historians* (Chichester, 2005)
P CHRISTIAN, *The Genealogist's Internet* (National Archives, 2005, 3rd edn)
Dictionary of National Biography (Oxford, 2004 and **www.oxforddnb.com**)
M HERBER, *Ancestral Trails: The Complete Guide to British Genealogy and Family History* (2nd edn, Society of Genealogists, 2004)
D HEY, *Family Names and Family History* (London, 2000)
D HEY, *Journeys in Family History* (National Archives, 2004)
R POLS, *Family Photographs 1860–1945* (National Archives, 2002)
G WROTTESLEY, *Pedigrees from the Plea Rolls, 1200–1500* (London, c. 1906)

Practical help

A ADOLPH, 'How to hire a genealogist – getting the best use out of professional researchers', *Ancestors* 42 (2006)
C R CHAPMAN, *How Heavy, How Much and How Long? Weights, Money and Other Measures Used by Our Ancestors* (Lochin Publishing, 1996)
C R CHENEY and M JONES, *Handbook of Dates for Students of English History* (London, 2000)
E CHURCHILL, 'Off the Shelf' [Society of Genealogists], *Ancestors* 38 (2005)
J S W GIBSON, *Unpublished Personal Name Indexes* (FFHS, 1987)
J S W GIBSON and P PESKETT, *Record Offices and How to Find Them* (FFHS, 2002)
J S W GIBSON and E HAMPSON, *Specialist Indexes for Family Historians* (FFHS, 2001)
H MARSHALL, *Palaeography for Family and Local Historians* (2004)
L H MUNBY, *Dates and Time: A Handbook for Local Historians* (1997)
L H MUNBY, *How Much Is That Worth?* (British Association for Local History, 1996)
Ancestors, The National Archives

General guides to the National Archives and the Family Records Centre

S COLWELL, *New to Kew?* (National Archives, 2006)
S COLWELL, *The Family Records Centre: a User's Guide* (National Archives, 2002)

3 Censuses of England, Wales, Isle of Man and the Channel Islands, 1801–1901

3.1 Census returns

From 1801 onwards, information about the population of England, Wales, the Isle of Man and Channel Islands has been collected every ten years by means of a census. The census returns taken together form the most important and useful modern source for genealogical, local, demographic and other studies in the care of the National Archives. Until very recently, they were difficult and time-consuming to access because of their sheer size, despite the work of devoted cataloguers and indexers over the years. However, the internet has made possible their publication in a searchable way that really has transformed their role in family history. The census returns are the nearest we can come to a ten-yearly snapshot of a family's development, and they can record children whose existence might otherwise have gone undetected, or travels to another part of the country that we might not have suspected. As the information given to the census enumerator is treated as confidential for 100 years, the 1911 census will not be open to the public until 2012.

Censuses started in 1801, but until 1841 were simply headcounts and did not name individuals. The returns from 1841 onwards should in theory give information about all people in England, Wales, the Isle of Man and the Channel Islands on a specific night in the census years. The census recorded everyone present at each specific address overnight on the chosen enumeration date (always a Sunday, and from 1851 in the spring), so an entire family unit, plus collateral relatives, lodgers, employees, servants and friends may be included. From 1851, the relationship of everyone to the head of the household is given. Not everyone was at home, of course, and not everyone had a home. There are many institutional entries for barracks, schools, ships and even prisons and asylums (not all of which give names).

There are some pitfalls in using the censuses. One is errors in transcription in the indexes. There are many, and you may need to do some lateral thinking to get round them. Once you get to the right entry, interpreting the evidence is not always as straightforward as it might appear. A good general rule is that the younger the person described the more accurate the information on age and place of birth. One thing you do need to be aware of is that the people themselves supplied the information in the census. There is no guarantee as to its accuracy. We know, for example, that far more people described themselves as naturalised citizens than ever took out naturalisation papers. Apparently it also happens regularly that the number of women describing themselves as between 30 and 40 is always significantly less than the number of the same women who had described themselves as 20 to 30 ten years before, even allowing for any deaths. Family relations could be entered in ways quite other than the truth – and unless the enumerator who helped with and collated the census forms happened to know the actual circumstances, who would know any differently?

3.2 Where to read the census returns

The census returns can be read anywhere that has an internet connection! The censuses for 1851 to 1901 (and imminently to be joined by 1841) are now all fully searchable and viewable online on a variety of websites: some are subscription based, others pay as you go. At the National Archives or Family Records Centre you can get free access to most of these services, but you will need to pay our standard charges for prints from them.

1841	**www.britishorigins.com** [not complete at the time of writing]	HO 107
1851	**www.ancestry.co.uk**	HO 107
1861	**www.ancestry.co.uk**	
	www.1837online.com	RG 9
1871	**www.ancestry.co.uk**	
	www.britishorigins.com [not yet complete]	RG 10
1881	**www.ancestry.co.uk**	RG 11
1891	**www.ancestry.co.uk**	RG 12
1901	**www.ancestry.co.uk**	
	www.1901censusonline.com	RG 13

They all offer slightly different search facilities; see Christian, *The Genea-logist's Internet* for an analysis of and advice on using these (and many other) sites.

If you want to look at the census returns on microfiche or microfilm, you can still do this at the Family Records Centre for 1841–1901, and at the National Archives for the 1901 census only. Many local archives and libraries have bought the films or fiches for their own locality (for library holdings see **www.familia.org.uk**. This method of access is particularly useful if you are undertaking a local study, or want to set people in their local context. Another way to do this is to use the unindexed scans of census pages available from **www.stepping-stones.co.uk**, which offers CDs of the 1841–1871 censuses, and the opportunity to view the 1851 census online. Another source for buying CDs of the censuses (split into counties) is **www.britishdataarchive.com**.

At Kingston-upon-Thames, there is a project to put all Victorian data from census, birth, marriage and death registers, burial and other sources into a single searchable database (to search this go to **http://localhistory. kingston.ac.uk/db_forms/LocalHistoryForm.asp**).

3.3 Contents of the 1841–1901 censuses

Information in the census varies slightly over time. The greatest difference is between 1841 and the rest.

1841 June 6	Pencil. Gives full name, age, sex and occupation. For those under 15, ages were given exactly (if known). For people over 15, ages were rounded **down** to the nearest five years. (For example, someone of 64 would appear as 60, another of 29 as 25.) Some information relating to the place of birth was also given, but was restricted to whether or not a person was born in the county of residence (Y for Yes, N for No) and, if not, whether in Scotland (S), Ireland (I) or foreign parts (F). Indicates which individuals lived in a particular house, and the individual households within that house, but does not give relationships between members of the same household.
1851 March 30	Ink. Groups people by household. Gives full address, name, age last birthday, marital status, relationship to the head of the household, sex, occupation, parish and county of birth, and various medical disabilities.
1861 April 7	As 1851
1871 April 2	As 1851
1881 April 3	As 1851
1891 April 5	Ink. Gives full address, name, age last birthday, marital status, relationship to the head of the household, sex, occupation, parish and county of birth, and various medical disabilities, employment status and (for Wales) language spoken.
1901 March 31	As 1891

Within each census, the records are arranged by place, grouped in the registration districts used for the registration of births, marriages and deaths. Maps of these registration districts can be found in RG 18 ⑥, and can be seen at the National Archives and at the Family Records Centre. However, they are not detailed: if you have a street name from a census and want to find it on a map, you would be better off getting in touch with the local record office or local studies library for that town. The National Archives does not hold a set of detailed town maps for 1841 to 1901 (but see 51.4 for detailed maps and property surveys from 1910 to 1913).

3.4 Contents of the 1801–1831 censuses

The censuses of 10 March 1801, 27 May 1811, 28 May 1821 and 29 May 1831 were confined to the compilation of numerical totals (by parish) of the following: houses habited and uninhabited; families; men and women; occupations (in broad categories); and various statistics of baptisms, marriages and burials. A partial enumeration of age was taken in 1821 and a more extensive investigation into occupations took place in 1831. People's names were not recorded in the official returns for these years.

Most of the information in these records was published in Parliamentary Papers: an incomplete set can be seen at the National Archives. The original documents were destroyed in 1904, with the exception of the clergymen's returns of numbers of baptisms, marriages and burials by parish, 1821–1830, which survive in HO 71 ☐.

However, in the course of carrying out the censuses, some local enumerators did compile unofficial listings of named individuals. Those that survive in local record offices are listed by Gibson and Medlycott in *Local Census Listings 1522–1930* or in Chapman's *Pre-1841 Censuses and Population Listings*.

3.5 Census returns: other places

For Scottish and Irish censuses, see 13 and 14. Colonial census returns, if they survived, will be kept in the appropriate national archives. However, the National Archives does hold a few colonial censuses. The best known of these are the censuses of convicts (and some free settlers) in New South Wales and Tasmania, 1788–1859 (HO 10: see 47.12 for further details). In addition, the National Archives has a census of 1811 from Surinam, detailing slaves and free black and white inhabitants (CO 278/15–25); a 1715 census of the white population of Barbados (CO 28/16); a census of the colony of Sierra Leone on 30 June 1831 (CO 267/111); and a census of Heligoland (which was British between 1807 and 1890) in 1881 (CO 122/37).

3.6 Censuses of England, Wales, Isle of Man and the Channel Islands, 1801–1901: bibliography

A ARMSTRONG, *Farmworkers of England and Wales: a social and economic history 1770–1980* (Iowa, 1988)

M E BRIANT ROSIER, *Index to Census Registration Districts* (FFHS, 1995)

C CHAPMAN, *Pre-1841 Census and Population Listings* (Dursley, 1994)

S COLWELL, *The Family Records Centre: a User's Guide* (National Archives, 2002)

J S W GIBSON and E HAMPSON, *Marriage, Census and Other Indexes for Family Historians* (FFHS, 7th edn, 1998)

J S W GIBSON and M MEDLYCOTT, *Local Census Listings, 1522–1930, holdings in the British Isles* (FFHS, 1994)

D HEY, *How our ancestors lived: a history of life a hundred years ago* (National Archives, 2002)

D HEY, 'Sons of Toil' [agricultural labourers], *Ancestors* 23 (2004)

E HIGGS, *Life, Death and Statistics: civil registration, censuses and the work of the General Register Office, 1836–1952* (Hatfield, 2004)

E HIGGS, *Making sense of the census revisited: census records for England and Wales, 1801–1901 – a handbook for historical researchers* (London, 2005)

S LUMAS, *Making Use of the Census* (National Archives, 2002)

M MEDLYCOTT, 'Some Georgian Censuses': The Militia Lists and 'Defence Lists', *Genealogists' Magazine*, vol. XXIII, pp. 55–59

D MILLS and C PEARCE, *People and Places in the Victorian Census: A Review and Bibliography, 1841–1911* (Historical Geography Research Group, 1989)

M NISSEL, *People count: A history of the General Register Office* (London, 1987)

K SCHURER and T ARKELL, eds, *Surveying the People* (Oxford, 1992)

P M TILLOT, 'The Analysis of the Census Returns', *Local Historian*, vol. VIII (1968–69)

4 Civil registration of births, marriages and deaths from 1 July 1837

4.1 Registration and reality

Birth, marriage and death certificates or records are one of the main entry routes into family history. After 1 July 1837, certificates of birth, marriage and death were issued by the state at the time of registration. Before then, they were usually only issued by churches when required as proof. If you are lucky, you may have records of these vital events in the collective life of a family already among your family papers – notes in a Bible or a birthday book, or bundles of certificates. If so, you have a head start in your research. The major registers of certificates are not held by the National Archives – to many people's surprise – but by the General Register Office. This chapter will give an overview of what records exist for after 1837, and the next chapter on what you can use before 1837.

Before using certificates as proof of anything, it's probably a good idea to think about how and why people supply the personal information they do. The records concerned with recording the existence of an individual are both easy and complex. They can be easy to find or hard to find, easy to understand or hard to understand. Sometimes they hide more than they reveal, other times they seem to reveal a truth that then turns out after years of research not to be true. To the people originally concerned, these records had a different significance than they do to us now. They came with all kinds of baggage – proof of respectability, religious faith (and by inference loyalty) and legal claim to anything from entitlement for poor relief to inheritance of property.

Although not actually intended as such, in a way they represent the church and state view of how life should be conducted, which was forced upon the teeming variety of actual existence. People were required to comply – but they also tried to put the best face on things from their own perspective. We do it ourselves – giving our occupation in a way that sounds impressive, for example. And in many ways the system was not foolproof. The fact of a registration many miles away did not actually prevent a bigamous marriage. In a place where your business was not known, it was quite easy for people to hide the actual facts of their lives while giving every appearance of conforming to the expectations of society. This was obviously not so easy in a rural parish, or in an earlier society where church courts kept a close eye on morality, or in a street where everyone knew their neighbours' business.

4.2 The central civil register

For people whose families have moved around, the index to the central register of the General Register Office of England and Wales (GRO) is the best place to start. However, if you know that your family stayed in one locality, you may find it more convenient to use the local register office for that area (see 4.3).

The Family Records Centre in central London holds the thousands of huge index volumes to the central register of births, deaths and marriages registered in England and Wales since civil (non-religious) registration began on 1 July 1837. The indexes are arranged by date of registration, and then alphabetically. There are four sets for each year, covering each quarter and labelled with the last month in each quarter – March, June, September and December. From 1983, the indexes cover the whole year. The indexes to the Adopted Children Register from 1927 are also here.

The Family Records Centre holds indexes to the main collection of records of birth, death and marriage of English and Welsh people at sea, abroad or in the armed services (see 7 and 8). Registers and indexes of Scots and Irish births, marriages and deaths (at home, overseas and in the services) are kept by the General Register Offices of Scotland, Ireland and Northern Ireland: see 13 and 14.

The actual central registers of birth, marriage and death are not kept at the Family Records Centre but at the GRO's head office at Southport. From the Family Records Centre, applications to buy a certified copy of the central register entry (identified from the indexes) are sent to Southport, and the certificate is then either posted to you or returned to the Family Records Centre for collection. However, you don't have to go to the Family Records Centre to access the central register. If you have enough information, you can order a certificate online at **www.gro.gov.uk**, even without knowing the index entry: a certificate costs more this way but the saving of time may make it worthwhile.

The General Register Office has started a major programme to digitise its registers and create a new index to them. This will not be available for some years, but in the meantime you can search the existing indexes online at **www.1837online.com** on a subscription basis; this will take you to images of the index. An alternative is to search the FreeBMD Project's incomplete but rapidly growing database of index entries at **http:// freebmd.rootsweb.com**. This offers slightly different search facilities: see Christian, *The Genealogist's Internet* for an analysis of and advice on using these (and many other) sites. Increasingly, many family historians and societies are publishing indexes and transcripts on the web: see Raymond, *Births, Marriages and Deaths on the Web* for a guide. If you don't have access to the internet, several of the larger record offices and libraries have copies of the indexes to the central register on microfiche: a list of where they are held can be supplied by the Family Records Centre.

If you are able to identify the certificate you want, you can order a copy direct from Southport by post, phone or online at **www.gro.gov.uk**. If you can give the year, volume and page reference, the cost is less. The address of the GRO at Southport is given in 62.

This is not really the place for detailed advice on researching certificates. The Family Records Centre produces its own guidance in a booklet called *General Register Office: Tracing Records of Births, Marriages and Deaths*. There is also the specialist publication by Colwell, *The Family Records Centre: A User's Guide*, and a pocket guide on *Using Birth, Marriage and Death Records* by Annal. In addition, the subject is covered in all the general genealogical guides and in several specific ones. There is also much advice available online: for a good overview, try **www. familyrecords.gov**.

4.3 Local civil registers

Registration of birth, marriage and death took place locally (as it still does). The local registrars sent in returns every quarter to the Registrar General for copying into the central register, but they also kept their own local registers. As a result there are two series of registers, equally valid. The local registers have their own indexes – the index entries from the index to the national register will not work. The local indexes are more accurate than the central index, which was created from copies of copies – errors have naturally crept in. (The interesting book by Foster discusses errors in the marriage register indexes.) And obviously the local office may be the best place to go if the family is known to have stayed put.

Local civil registers are normally still kept by the local register offices or by the District Registry. These offices are usually prepared to help family historians, but this is not their main business, so don't ask too much of them. You will still have to buy copy certificates, but you should be able to access the indexes. The level of access varies from office to office.

To find the local register office, try the telephone directory or the library. If you can access the internet, look at **www.genuki.org.uk**, which has a list county by county with contact details and information about whether you can make an appointment to search the indexes and about how to order a copy.

If you are interested in finding out more about registration procedures, try Lewis's 1888 *Synoptical Index of Regulations*, available in the Library at the National Archives. Files of correspondence about individual cases are in RG 48 at the National Archives.

4.4 No entry in the indexes?

Failure to find a birth, marriage or death entry in the indexes may be for any of the following reasons:

- Before 1875 there was no penalty for non-registration and there may be omissions in the birth and death registers. A study by Hughes comparing Liverpool baptismal records with registered births has shown a shortfall of almost 33 per cent as late as 1874. You may need to look at parish and non-parochial registers until 1875;
- Before 1927 there was no formal adoption procedure and there is no record of the birth of the adopted child under the name by which he or she was known;
- There may have been a clerical error when the entry in the local registrar's register was transferred to the central register. The local registers are more accurate;
- Surnames could be spelled differently, especially if the informants were illiterate. The official completing the certificate would use his preferred version of Gardener, Gardiner, Gardner or Gairdner, for example – and the next time that family registered an event it might have been a different official with a different preference;
- Some people were known by a forename that was not the first forename on their birth certificate. Euphrosyne Stella may well have chosen to be known as Stella;
- The child may not have been named by the date of registration. Entries under the sex of the infant are given at the end of each surname section;
- In the nineteenth century at least 10 per cent of marriages took place after the birth of the first child;
- Many couples concealed the fact that they were not married by simply adopting the same name: on a birth certificate it would look as though they were married. This would only work in a town large enough to guarantee anonymity, or in a new locality;
- A birth or marriage may have been registered by the Army: see 8.8 and 24.1;
- Registers of births on Lundy Island, in the Bristol Channel, were treated as foreign registers and are in the National Archives, in RG 32–RG 35, indexed by the general indexes in RG 43. Some records from the Channel Islands were treated the same way;
- Did the event happen somewhere outside England and Wales? Try the

registers of births, marriages and deaths at sea or overseas for people normally resident in England and Wales, or the armed forces registers (see 7 and 8);

- People normally resident in Scotland, Ireland and Northern Ireland will be found in the registers kept there (including registers of births, marriages and deaths at sea or overseas) (see 13 and 14).

It may be worth checking the Registrar General's correspondence on births, marriages and deaths from 1874 at the National Archives (RG 48). These papers include files on individual cases of difficulty, but some are closed for 50 or 75 years.

The General Register Offices will not issue copy certificates in cases where the original entry has been marked as invalid – a bigamous marriage, for example, which was uncovered and the entry annotated with details of conviction of the bigamist. However, they should at least tell you that this is the case, even if you cannot get a certified copy. (See Park's article on bigamy and Bevan's article on divorce for information on this difficult topic.)

4.5 Adoptions

Before 1927 there was no system of legal adoption and it is usually extremely difficult to trace private arrangements. Some charities, such as Barnardos, arranged adoptions and may conduct searches for a fee. Certificates of any adoption in England and Wales since 1 January 1927 may be obtained from the Family Records Centre. They show the date of the adoption, the name of the child adopted and the full name and address of the adoptive parents. The Family Records Centre has booklets available at the downstairs enquiry desk on *Access to Birth Records*, *The Adoption Contact Register* and *Information for Adopted People and their Relatives*. You can also look at **www.gro.gov.uk** for advice. For information on foundlings, see 6.2.

4.6 Civil registration of births, marriages and deaths from 1 July 1837: bibliography

D ANNAL, *Using Birth, Marriage and Death Records* (Public Record Office, 2000)

A BEVAN, 'Divorce 1858 onwards', *Ancestors* 10 (2002)

S COLWELL, *The Family Records Centre: A User's Guide* (Public Record Office, 2002)

M W FOSTER, A *'Comedy of Errors' or the Marriage Records of England and Wales 1837–1899* (New Zealand, 1999) (The review of this by A Camp in *Family Tree Magazine*, vol. 15 no 5 gives a useful summary of the problems with marriage indexes.)

General Register Office, *Abstract of Arrangements respecting Registration of Births, Marriages and Deaths in the UK and other Countries of the British Commonwealth of Nations, and in the Irish Republic* (London, 1952)

General Register Office, *General Register Office: Tracing Records of Births, Marriages and Deaths* (ONS, 1997)

E HIGGS, *Life, Death and Statistics: civil registration, censuses and the work of the General Register Office, 1836–1952* (Hatfield, 2004)

D HUGHES, 'Liverpool infant mortality rates *c.* 1865–1874: A city much maligned?' in *Lancashire Local Historian*, no 6, 1991, pp. 32–43

J LEWIS, *Synoptical Index of the Regulations for the duties of Superintendent Registrars, Registrars of Births and Deaths, and Registrars of Marriages, and incidentally also of the Statutes relating to the Registration of Births, Marriages and Deaths in England And Wales* (London, 1888)

M NISSEL, *People Count, A History of the General Register Office* (London, 1987)

P PARK, 'Double dealing: matrimony and bigamy', *Ancestors* 24 (2004)

S A RAYMOND, *Births, Marriages and Deaths on the Web* (2 vols, Federation of Family Historians, 2005)

5 Religious registration of births, marriages and deaths before 1 July 1837

5.1 Parish registers and online indexes

Before 1 July 1837, no national records of birth, marriage or death were kept. An attempt had been made in 1538 to set up such a system when the new Church of England was required to keep parish registers of baptism, marriages and burials. (Very few in fact survive from 1538: the average starting date for surviving registers is 1611 for England and 1708 for Wales.) The information could be copied out in case of need by the cleric in charge, who would certify that it was a true copy. These earlier certificates of an entry in the register can therefore take many forms – some were simple letters, others entered onto a pre-printed form. For centuries, certificates of baptism had to be provided by people wishing to take up positions of trust in government (civil or armed servants of the state) to prove that they were members of the state Church of England. You may be able to find one of these copy certificates, but the usual course is to go to the church register or a transcript of it. These records are more difficult to find than the later civil registers, as they are scattered among local record offices, but they are usually open to inspection. If you want to buy a copy, it does not need to be certified and therefore costs less.

However, after 1538 religious diversity grew extensively, so that not everyone attended the parish church to be included in the parish register. The National Archives holds a collection of registers from outside the parish system, called non-parochial registers (sometimes called Nonconformist registers, but containing Anglican records as well): see 5.4.

The nearest thing there is to a union index to both parish and non-parochial registers is the *International Genealogical Index*, known as the *IGI*, freely accessible at **www.familysearch.org**. This is an index to births, baptisms and marriages worldwide: it does not include deaths (see 5.3 for a death index). The indexes to the British Isles cover the period from the beginning of parish registers to about 1885. (Religious registration was required in England and Wales from 1538, in Scotland from 1552 and in Ireland from 1634, but few of the earliest registers survive.) The indexes for England and Wales are mainly to Church of England parish registers and to nearly all the non-parochial registers at the National Archives.

Family Search does have a very good feature, which is rather hidden. If you find an entry for, say, an Anna Brass, click on the entry at the bottom of the screen marked Batch No. This will take you back to the search screen, with the box for Batch No completed. Click on Search again and it will pull up all the entries taken from the same source – so that Anna Brass is joined by Timothy Brass and surrounded by the names of people she probably knew.

There are some drawbacks to the *IGI*. Its coverage is not complete, as some registers have not been included. There is no guarantee that the registers that have been covered are included in full. In addition, useful information that may appear in the register, such as age or father's occupation, is not given in the *IGI*.

If you do find a likely ancestor in the *IGI*, you are strongly advised to check the source, or a transcript of it, yourself. Family Search gives the following advice, which can be followed in many parts of the world:

- In Family Search, go to the Family History Library Catalog. The catalog lists all of the Church of England records, both microfilmed originals and transcripts, in the collection of the Family History Library. Select the catalog, and search for church records by locality on county or parish levels. [You can then request a copy of the relevant microfilm to be sent to your nearest Family History Centre. A list of centres worldwide can be found on the homepage, together with a link to the Family History Library Catalog. Family History Centres are branch facilities, the main one being in Salt Lake City, and can provide access to most of the microfilms and microfiche in their huge collection.]   (Reproduced from **www.familysearch.org**)

Alternatives routes are the *Phillimore Atlas and Index of Parish Registers* or the *National Index of Parish Registers* to discover the location of the parish register or a copy of it. The Society of Genealogists has a vast collection of parish register transcripts. If the entry refers to a Nonconformist chapel, then it is most probably in our set of non-parochial records and can be seen on microfilm at the National Archives or the Family Records Centre (see 5.5). Some of the Nonconformist registers contain a lot more information than is included in the *IGI*.

An alternative to the *IGI* is being developed by the Federation of Family History Societies at **www.familyhistoryonline.net/**: it currently has over 20 million entries from parish registers and is well worth using.

5.2 Marriages before 1837 and online indexes

The Boyd Marriage Index has a 12-per cent coverage of English marriages between 1538 and 1837. It is also searchable at **www.britishorigins.com**, which has various other indexes of use as well. See Churchill for the background.

For London, try the Pallot Marriage and Baptism Indexes, covering the years *c*. 1780–1837. These index marriages and baptisms from all but two of the City of London parishes, and many more besides, and extracts from Nonconformist registers. You can access them on **www.ancestry. com** as a charged service. Some of the entries relate to registers that no longer survive, owing to bomb damage during the Second World War, and for anyone looking for a London marriage this is an indispensable source.

A Marriage Licence Allegation was a document sworn by one of the prospective parties, usually the groom, to the effect that there was no impediment to the marriage and as to where the marriage could take place. The National Archives has some marriage licences for the Chapel Royal, Whitehall, 1687–1754 and 1807 in RG 8/76–78, but in general this is not the place to look for these documents. See Gibson's *Bishops' Transcripts and Marriage Licences*. The website British Origins has two Marriage Licences Allegation indexes containing the names of over 670,000 people issued with marriage licences between 1694 to 1850, identifying couples (particularly Londoners) who intended to marry: these are searchable at **www.britishorigins.com**.

See 5.13 for advice on less formal marriages recorded in the Fleet marriage registers.

5.3 Deaths: the *National Burial Index*

The *IGI* does not include deaths – and deaths can be difficult to trace. The Federation of Family History Societies is tackling the problem by indexing burial registers in its *National Burial Index* (*NBI*), published on CD-Rom and now in its second edition. The information has been extracted from the burial registers kept by parishes, Nonconformists, Catholics and secular cemeteries. Where these details are available they include surname and forename, age, date of burial and county and parish or cemetery of burial.

So far the index contains over 13 million burial records, reflecting the enormous benefit of the voluntary work in its compilation by members of the Federation of Family History Societies.

However, at the moment the *NBI* is an incomplete tool. If you do not find the person you are looking for, see 8.6 for more suggestions.

5.4 Non-parochial registers in the National Archives

The National Archives does hold a major source for registered baptisms, marriages and burials in England and Wales – its very large collection of non-parochial religious registers. Some of the registers date from after 1837, but they can still be useful as a complement to the civil registers, as failure to use the civil registration system was not penalised until 1875. They are all seen on microfilm, at the Family Records Centre as well as at Kew.

The non-parochial registers are often referred to as 'Nonconformist registers'. However, in addition to several thousand Protestant Nonconformist registers, the collection also includes a number of Church of England registers from churches outside the usual parish structure, 77 Catholic registers, a few registers of foreign churches in England and some cemetery records.

Before 1837, the parish register was the only official place to register baptisms, marriages and burials. Thousands of people refused to comply with the Church of England rites and wished to be baptised and buried by their own church and to record these events in the registers of their own faith. However, from 1754 to 1837, marriages had to be performed by a beneficed Anglican clergyman in order to be acknowledged in law. Exceptions were made for Quakers and Jews because of the detailed way they recorded marriages. In order to ensure the legitimacy of their children and their ability to inherit, other Nonconformists had to marry in the Anglican church and have the event recorded in the parish register. Nonconformist registers between 1754 and 1837 therefore record details of births/baptisms and deaths/burials only. After 1837, they may include marriages as well.

When civil registration was set up in 1837, parliamentary commissioners collected most Nonconformist registers and some Anglican non-parochial registers. The registers were deposited in the new General Register Office, where they were used to issue birth certificates that had the status of a legal record (now RG 4–RG 6). Another collection was made in 1857 (some were placed in RG 8 and some in RG 4). On both occasions Catholic and Jewish congregations retained the registers of most of their churches and synagogues. Not all Nonconformist registers were surrendered to the General Register Office. Some remained with the congregations (or the minister or priest) and still do so; yet others are in county record offices, or with the archives of the colleges and societies of the various denominations. Look at the *National Index of Parish Registers* for guidance on their known whereabouts.

Both the 1837 and the 1857 collections were transferred to the National Archives in 1961 and became widely available for the first time. Other registers were later deposited at the National Archives in RG 8 for safe keeping. Many, but not all, of the births and baptisms in the authenticated registers in RG 4 (but not RG 8) have been included in the *International Genealogical Index.*

5.5 Using Nonconformist registers

At the National Archives and Family Records Centre you can access several thousand Nonconformist registers and certificates from England and Wales. The main churches represented in the National Archives' holdings are the Society of Friends or Quakers, the Presbyterians, the Independents or Congregationalists, the Baptists, the Wesleyan and other Methodists, the Moravians, the Countess of Huntingdon's Connexion, the Bible Christians and the Swedenborgians, as well as various foreign churches. The English Independent congregation of St Petersburg, Russia also deposited its registers of births, baptisms and burials, 1818–1840 (RG 4/4605).

With the exception of the Quaker registers (see 5.8), Nonconformist registers are in RG 4 ⑤⑥ and RG 8 ⑤⑥, largely depending on whether they were collected by the 1837 or the 1857 commission. Most of the registers are in RG 4 and have been indexed in the *IGI*; there are many fewer in RG 8, and these are not centrally indexed. However, they are exactly the same kind of registers as in RG 4 and should not be overlooked. The revised lists and the Introductory Notes of RG 4 and RG 8 were re-published by the List and Index Society in 1996.

The registers date from 1567 to 1970. The earliest registers belong to the foreign Protestant churches that were granted toleration in England well before any native dissent was made lawful. Registers of English dissenting congregations are very rare before active persecution stopped; the earliest English registers date from the 1640s. The last date, 1970, is something of an oddity, from the dissenting church of Cam, Gloucestershire: it is the last entry in a volume in almost constant use between 1776 and 1970 (RG 8/12C). Most of the registers come from the eighteenth and early nineteenth centuries. After 1754 they do not include marriages, although these do re-occur after 1837 in a few registers in RG 8.

Nonconformist registers often served a far wider area than the traditional Anglican parish because of the way the various denominations were organised. The paper list of RG 4 includes cross-references from outlying areas. Nonconformity was a very widespread movement in the eighteenth and nineteenth centuries: the 1851 ecclesiastical census showed that a quarter of the population regularly attended Nonconformist chapels.

Indications that you should investigate the Nonconformist registers and the large amounts of biographical material kept by some of the denominations might be:

- a long family history of Nonconformity;
- a number of Old Testament forenames in the family – Elijah, Ebenezer, Hezekiah, Rebecca and so on;
- a post-1837 marriage that took place in a Nonconformist chapel or in a register office;
- a parish register that has a suspiciously high number of marriages and burials of one surname in proportion to the number of baptisms.

On the other hand, known Nonconformist ancestors may need to be traced back to the parish registers, for pre-conversion events and occasional conformity, and the records of marriage and burial (if there was no local Nonconformist burial ground).

Having discovered a Nonconformist ancestor, it is worth digging a little deeper into his or her beliefs and the organisation and discipline of the particular denomination. A specialist guide that gives more detailed advice is Shorney's *Protestant Nonconformity and Roman Catholicism: A Guide to Sources in the Public Record Office*. Steel's *Sources for Nonconformist Genealogy and Family History* covers archive holdings in the National Archives and elsewhere. Another useful guide is Palgrave-Moore's *Understanding the History and Records of Nonconformity*. A general introduction to the beliefs and regional concentrations of the various Nonconformist denominations is *The Geography of Religion in England* by Gay.

Less extensive works can also be very useful; for Baptists, try *My Ancestors were Baptists* by Breed; for Quakers, *My Ancestors were Quakers* by Milligan and Thomas; and for Methodists, *My Ancestors were Methodist*, by Leary and Gandy. These also give indications as to the published works available in denominational libraries such as Dr Williams's Library.

5.6 The Protestant Dissenters' Registry of births, 1716–1837

The Protestant Dissenters' Registry at Dr Williams's Library, then in Redcross Street, London, was founded in 1742. It served the congregations of Baptists, Independents and Presbyterians in London and within a twelve-mile radius of the capital. However, parents from most parts of the British Isles and even abroad also used the registry. Almost 50,000 births were registered. Retrospective entries go back to 1716 and the registry continued to 1837 (RG 4/4658–4665, with indexes at RG 4/4666–4676).

The certificates used to compile the registers also survive (RG 5/1–161, with the same index as the registers). Parents wishing to register a birth had to produce two parchment certificates signed by their minister and by the midwife and one or two other people present at the birth. These gave the name and sex of the child, the name of the parents, the name of the mother's father and the date and place (street, parish and county) of birth. After 1828, paper certificates were required instead, which had to be signed by the parents as well; these signatures made them more acceptable as legal proof. On receipt of the two certificates, the registrar entered all the details, except the birth address, in the register, filed one of the certificates (now in RG 5) and returned the other to the parents with his certificate of registration.

The records are seen on microfilm and can be accessed at both the National Archives and the Family Records Centre.

5.7 The Wesleyan Methodist Metropolitan Registry of births, 1773–1838

The Wesleyan Methodist Metropolitan Registry was founded in 1818 at 66 Paternoster Row, London to provide for the registration of births and baptisms of Wesleyan Methodists throughout England, Wales and elsewhere, independently of any congregational records. Over 10,000 children were registered here. The registers continued till 1838, with retrospective registration of births going back to 1773 (RG 4/4677–4679, with an index at RG 4/4680).

One of two original certificates submitted by the parents was entered in the register and filed (RG 5/162–207, indexed by RG 4/4680) and the other was marked as entered and was returned to the parents. The certificates and the register entry have the name and sex of the child; the name and address of the father; the name of the mother and of both her parents; the date and place of birth; and the name of the Wesleyan circuit, with the signature (or name, in the register) of the parents, the witnesses to the birth and the baptising minister.

The records are seen on microfilm and can be accessed at both the National Archives and the Family Records Centre.

5.8 Quaker registers

The records and registers of the Society of Friends, or Quakers, 1613–1841, are very full and in excellent order. However, to understand and use them properly, you do need to get to grips with the rather complicated administrative structure of the Society. This is explained in *My Ancestors Were Quakers* by Milligan and Thomas, and also in Steel's *Sources for Nonconformist Genealogy and Family History*; the latter includes a full discussion of Quaker birth, marriage and death registers and practices. You also need to understand the distinctive Quaker dating practices (they used numbers for the names of months and days rather than the common names derived from pagan gods). For an explanation of these, and how they changed significantly over time, see Munby, *Dates and Time*, Appendix 11.

You can see these registers, together with original birth and burial notes, and original marriage certificates and copies, 1656–1834 in RG 6 ⑤, at both the Family Records Centre and the National Archives. They are arranged by (county) Quarterly Meeting and by Monthly Meeting. There are also a few registers and other records, 1761–1840, at RG 8/81 and 87–89. Most local meetings were under the Quarterly Meeting of their own county, but several are to be found with the records of unexpected quarterly meetings. There is a 'Key to Cross-Border Locations' filed with the paper list, which shows (for example) that the records of the meeting of Ringshall, Buckinghamshire are to be found in the Quarterly Meeting of Bedfordshire and Hertfordshire.

Quaker birth certificates were signed by any witnesses at the birth, who also had to give their own residence. The marriage certificates were signed by a large number of witnesses, not all of whom were Quakers. Some of the witnesses were identified as relatives. Marriage between two Quakers, conducted according to the Quaker usage, was accepted as legal from 1661 and was exempted from Lord Hardwicke's Marriage Act in 1753.

Outside the National Archives, indexes to (or rather alphabetical digests of) the registers, made in 1840–1842 and 1857, are kept at Friends House Library (address in 62): these can be consulted for a fee. Duplicate digests were also made, and sent to the county-based Quarterly Meetings in place of their registers. For more information on their present location, and on Quaker records in general, consult *My Ancestors Were Quakers*. The Introductory Note to RG 6, filed with the paper list, is well worth reading. The List and Index Society have published both the list and the Introductory Note.

5.9 Catholic registers

For various reasons, only 77 Catholic churches surrendered their registers to the commissioners in 1837. They are now in RG 4 and can be seen at both the National Archives and Family Records Centre. Of these, 44 came from Yorkshire, 13 from Durham, 10 from Northumberland, 2 from Lincolnshire and 1 each from Cumberland, Dorset, Hampshire, Lancashire, Nottinghamshire, Oxfordshire, Warwickshire and Westmoreland; however, some may have been personal to the priest, and thus cover events in other places as well. Most date from the mid- or late eighteenth century, but there are two or three dating from the late seventeenth century.

For the location of other Catholic registers, see the county volumes of the *National Index of Parish Registers* and *Sources for Roman Catholic and Jewish Genealogy and Family History* by Steel and Samuel. The latter also discusses the information in the registers.

5.10 Registers of foreign churches in England

The registers of several foreign churches are in RG 4 ⑤⑥, listed separately except for those of the Scottish churches, which are included in the county lists; there are also a few in RG 8 ⑤⑥. Most are Huguenot (French and Walloon Protestant) registers from the several churches of London, 1599–1840, and from Bristol 1687–1807, Canterbury 1590–1837, Norwich 1595–1752, Plymouth 1692–1807, Southampton 1567–1779 and Thorpe-le-Soken 1684–1726 (in RG 4); Huguenot registers from Dover, 1646–1731, are in RG 8/14. The Huguenot Society has published most of these registers: see **www.huguenotsociety.org.uk**. The other foreign registers are all from London; they are those of the French Chapel Royal 1700–1754, the Dutch Chapel Royal 1689–1754, the German Lutheran Chapel Royal 1712–1836, the German Lutheran churches 1694–1853, and the Swiss church 1762–1839, all in RG 4.

Two later French registers came from the French Episcopal Church of the Savoy, in Bloomsbury, London, 1843–1900 (RG 8/34), and from the Reformed French Church in Brighton, 1865–1879 (RG 8/94). The registers and papers of the Russian Orthodox church in London, 1721–1927, which are mostly in Russian, are at RG 8/111–304; they include registers of births, marriages and deaths. Marriages performed in the Greek Church in London, 1837–1865, can be found in J 166.

These registers can be seen at both the National Archives and the Family Records Centre.

5.11 Anglican registers in the National Archives

The National Archives does have quite a few Anglican registers – but these are from churches outside the parish system. Any with the code RG can be seen at the Family Records Centre and the National Archives; any with a different code can only be seen at the National Archives.

The commissioners for non-parochial registers collected some Anglican registers as well as Nonconformist registers in both 1837 and 1857. Most of these Anglican registers came from the custody of the Consistory Court of London in 1837, and are either from abroad (see 8.2) or relate to the so-called 'Fleet marriages' (see 5.13).

There is a varied collection from different chapels royal, but others remain in the custody of the Chapel Royal, St James's Palace:

- 1647–1709 chapels royal at St James's Palace, Whitehall and Windsor Castle (RG 8/110);
- 1755–1880 registers of the chapels royal (PRO 30/19/1);
- 1687–1754 and 1807 marriage licences for marriages in the Chapel Royal, Whitehall (not royal marriages) (RG 8/76–78);
- In addition, the National Archives has records in RG 4/4396 and 4328.

Other Anglican registers came from:

- Mercers' Hall, Cheapside, London (marriages, 1641–1754, and burials, 1640–1833, RG 4/4436);
- the Rolls Chapel, Chancery Lane, 1736–1892, with gaps (PRO 30/21/3/1);
- the chapel of God's House Hospital, Kingston-upon-Hull, marriage register 1695–1715 (RG 8/101);
- the Foundling Hospital (see 6.2).

From less charitable institutions, the prisons, there are a few records of births and burials. The Westminster Penitentiary has a register of baptisms, 1816–1871 (PCOM2/139), and another of burials, 1817–1853 (PCOM2/140). There is a register of deaths and inquests at the Millbank Penitentiary, 1848–1863 (PCOM2/165): in this case, most burials were in the Victoria Park cemetery, the records of which are discussed in 6.6. For other inquests, see 46, and for other prison records, see 47.

However, the bulk of the reputable Anglican registers in the National Archives came from the **military and Naval hospitals** as non-parochial registers. The birth, marriage and death registers of Greenwich Hospital (including the Royal Naval Asylum and the Royal Hospital Schools) cover 1705–1864 (RG 4/1669–1679 and RG 8/16–18). Those of the Army's Chelsea Hospital cover 1691–1856 (RG 4/4330–4332 and 4387). Although Greenwich Hospital and Chelsea Hospital were Navy and Army institutions, these registers appear to include local inhabitants as well. Another Anglican oddment is the long series of registers from the Dockyard Church of Sheerness, Kent covering 1688–1960 (ADM 6/429–433 and 438). We have recently received a large collection of **Naval baptism and marriage registers** from 1845–1998 (including banns and notice of marriage) from the Chaplain of the Fleet (ADM 338 ⑤). These come from Naval establishments all over the world. Most are from the twentieth century, but Malta and Chatham have runs from 1845 and 1867 respectively. For details of other Army registers, see 8.8 and 24.1. For details of Royal Marine registers, see 29.5.

5.12 The British Lying-In Hospital, 1749–1868

One of the National Archives' main hospital holdings is the series of records of the British Lying-In Hospital, Holborn, London. This was set up as a maternity hospital in 1749 to cater for the distressed poor (married women only), with special attention to the wives of soldiers and sailors. Admission was by recommendation: many women appear to have been the wives of servants, recommended by their husbands' employers. The baptismal registers, 1749–1830 (RG 8/62–66), are simply a list of names, parents and dates of birth and baptism composed by the hospital – until 1814, when proper Anglican baptismal registers appear and give the parents' address. However, they are supplemented by a fascinating source, the hospital's own record of the admission of the mother and the birth. This gives the names of the parents, the occupation of the father, the age of the mother, place of settlement (place of marriage after 1849), the expected date of delivery, the date of admission, the date of delivery, the name of the child and date of baptism, the date of discharge or death and the name of the person on whose recommendation the woman was admitted (RG 8/52–61). These hospital records cover 1749–1868 and give details of 42,008 admissions and about 30,000 baptisms, by no means all of Londoners; one woman at least came from the Cape of Good Hope, and others came from Yorkshire, Ireland, the Isle of Wight and Jersey.

5.13 Fleet marriage registers before 1753

In 1753, Lord Hardwicke's Marriage Act (26 George II c.33) ruled that the only lawful marriage was one celebrated by a beneficed Anglican clergyman in an Anglican church, after banns or with a licence. An exception was made for Jews and for Quakers. As a result, Nonconformists had to marry in the Anglican church; Catholics generally continued to marry in their own church. However, Lord Hardwicke's Marriage Act was not aimed directly at preventing Nonconformist marriages but at preventing clandestine Anglican ones. The main idea was to prevent people of property entering what their families considered ill-advised marriages, but in fact it took away an ancient right most used by the poor. Lord Hardwicke's Act brought to an end the legal basis of what became known as 'common law marriages', where couples could marry by an informal exchange of vows without any involvement of the church. It did not actually stop people entering into these relationships, but it removed their status as valid marriages.

Before it came into effect in 1754, clergymen without a parish were able to make a living by performing marriages on request, in places exempt from ecclesiastical jurisdiction. One of the most popular of these was the Fleet Prison and its precincts in London; the registers kept by the presiding ministers are known as Fleet registers. These registers from the Fleet and King's Bench Prisons, the Mint and the May Fair Chapel, 1694–1754, are now in RG 7 Ⓣ Ⓢ. In addition, there are two volumes covering 1726–1735 that were brought into court as evidence and are now in PROB 18/50. The RG 7 registers can be seen at the National Archives and the Family Records Centre; the PROB 18 register can only be seen at the National Archives. Herber has started producing a series of transcripts of the Fleet registers, called *Clandestine Marriages in the Chapel and Rules of the Fleet Prison 1680–1754*. Marriages for Hertfordshire couples have been indexed and published. There is an index to Fleet marriages for Sussex, south-west Kent and south-east Surrey, arranged chronologically within parish of residence of bride and groom.

The Fleet registers have entries from over the whole country, but with more from London and surrounding counties. About 200,000 marriages are thought to have been celebrated there. In general, the Fleet was frequented for marriages and for some baptisms by craftsmen and sailors, while professionals and the aristocracy went to the more salubrious May Fair Chapel. Such clandestine marriages could result in prosecution and there are records of many such cases among the ex officio Act Books of the Commissary Court of London in the Guildhall Library, and in the records of the Consistory Court of London in the London Metropolitan Archives. The information in the Fleet registers should be treated with caution, as the dates given are unreliable (particularly before 1714) and names or indeed whole entries may be fictitious. For more information see Herber's 'Sex, Lies and Crime', Brown's 'The Rise and Fall of the Fleet Marriages' or the chapter on clandestine marriages in Steel's *Sources of Births, Marriages and Deaths before 1837 (I)*.

5.14 Religious registration of births, marriages and deaths before 1 July 1837: bibliography

T Benton, *Irregular marriage in London before 1754* (Society of Genealogists, 1993)

G R Breed, *My Ancestors were Baptists* (Society of Genealogists, 1988)

R L Brown, 'The Rise and Fall of the Fleet Marriage', in *Marriage and Society*, ed. R B Outhwaite (London, 1981)

E Churchill, 'Percival Boyd Online' [Boyd's marriage index], *Ancestors* 24 (2004)

S Colwell, *The Family Records Centre: A User's Guide* (PRO, 2002)

Dr Williams's Trust, *Nonconformist Congregations in Great Britain: A list of histories and other material in Dr Williams's Library* (London, 1973)

J D Gay, *The Geography of Religion in England* (London, 1971)

J S W Gibson, *Bishops' Transcripts and Marriage Licences* (FFHS, 2nd edn, 1985)

J S W Gibson, *Bishops' Transcripts And Marriage Licences, Bonds and Allegations* (FFHS, 2001)

J S W Gibson, *Local Newspapers 1750–1920* (FFHS, 1987)

J S W Gibson and E Hampson, *Marriage and Census Indexes for Family Historians* (FFHS, 7th edn, 1998)

M Herber, *Clandestine Marriages in the Chapel and Rules of the Fleet Prison 1680–1754* (3 vols, London, 1998, 1999, 2001)

M Herber, 'Sex, Lies and Crime: Clandestine Marriage in the 17th and 18th centuries', *Family Tree Magazine*, vol 19 no 12 (2003)

Hertfordshire Family and Population History Society, *Fleet marriages of Hertfordshire people to 1754: An alphabetical index of grooms and brides* (1999)

C R Humphery-Smith, *The Phillimore Atlas and Index of Parish Registers* (Chichester, 1984)

International Genealogical Index, compiled by the Church of Jesus Christ of Latter-day Saints (also known as LDS and Mormons)

W Leary and M Gandy, *My Ancestors Were Methodists* (Society of Genealogists, 1982)

List and Index Society, *Non-Parochial Registers of Births, Marriages and Deaths (RG 4, 8)*, vol. 265 and 266 (1996)

List and Index Society, *Society of Friends' Registers (RG 6)*, vol. 267 (1996)

E H MILLIGAN and M J THOMAS, *My Ancestors Were Quakers* (Society of Genealogists, 1999)

L H MUNBY, *Dates and Time: A Handbook for Local Historians* (British Association for Local History, 1997)

National Index of Parish Registers (Society of Genealogists, 1968 continuing). For individual volumes, see the works listed under D J Steel

P PALGRAVE-MOORE, *Understanding the history and records of Nonconformity* (2nd edn, Norwich, 1989)

J PALMER, 'The Pallot Index: a route to the registers', *Ancestors* 18 (2004)

Parliament, *Report of the commissioners appointed to inquire into the state, custody, and authenticity of registers or records of births or baptisms, deaths or burials and marriages, in England and Wales other than parochial registers* (London, 1838: parliamentary paper presented to both Houses)

Parliament, *Report of the commissioners appointed to inquire into the state, custody and authenticity of certain non-parochial registers or records of births or baptisms, deaths or burials, and marriages in England and Wales (1857)* (London, 1858: parliamentary paper presented to both Houses)

D J STEEL, *Sources for Nonconformist Genealogy and Family History* (National Index of Parish Registers, vol. II, 1973)

D J STEEL and E R SAMUEL, *Sources for Roman Catholic and Jewish Genealogy and Family History* (National Index of Parish Registers, vol. III, 1974)

D J STEEL and others, *Sources of Births, Marriages and Deaths before 1837 (I)* (National Index of Parish Registers, vol. I, 1968)

M WALCOT, 'English Marriage Indexes', *Genealogists' Magazine*, vol. XIV, pp. 204–208

E WELCH, 'Nonconformist Registers', *Journal of the Society of Archivists*, vol. II, pp. 411–417

6 Illegitimacy, foundlings, divorce and burial

6.1 Illegitimacy
6.2 Foundlings, 1741 to present
6.3 Divorce and matrimonial disputes before 1858
6.4 Divorce, matrimonial disputes and separation from 1858:
the background
6.5 Divorce and matrimonial disputes from 1858: the records
6.6 Burial grounds and cemeteries
6.7 Illegitimacy, foundlings, divorce, and burial: bibliography

6.1 Illegitimacy

Illegitimacy is not easy to trace – often it is discovered by accident. For an exploration of the subject, see Paley and Fowler, *Family Skeletons*. Try Paley, *My Ancestors were Bastards*, for an overview of the sources, most of which are held locally (petty sessions, quarter sessions and poor law records). A2A should be helpful in locating these records.

At the National Archives, T 4 ⑦ (1680–1819) and TS 17② (1698–1981) are concerned with the transmission of property of illegitimate people who died without leaving a will. In these circumstances, any property went to the Crown. T 4 initially looks unpromising. In fact it includes quite a few eighteenth-century petitions from next of kin, asking for letters of administration to be granted to them instead of to the Treasury Solicitor.

6.2 Foundlings, 1741 to present

For London foundlings (abandoned children), try the records of the Foundling Hospital, London, set up by Thomas Coram in 1741. These are split between the National Archives, the General Register Office and the London Metropolitan Archives (addresses in 62). At the National Archives are the registers of baptisms and of all too many burials for 1741–1838 (RG 4/4396 and 4328). These continue from 1853 to 1948 in the keeping of the General Register Office (Corrections Branch). An index is available at the Family Records Centre and short birth certificates may be bought in the usual way. However, only the Thomas Coram Foundation (address in 62) will give details of parentage. It also holds a very affecting collection of tokens left by the mothers with their children. Similar tokens are among the records held by the London Metropolitan Archives, which holds the majority of the other records, including petitions from parents for the admission of their child (the system in operation from 1760), apprenticeship registers, minutes, etc. See also the recent articles by Clark and Lisle on the Foundling Hospital.

For registration of foundlings after 1 July 1837, look in the birth indexes under 'Unknown' (which appears after Z) at the Family Records Centre (or the microfiche copies at the National Archives). In 1977 the Abandoned Children Register was introduced: the children are indexed in the usual way under the name given to the child.

6.3 Divorce and matrimonial disputes before 1858

Before 1858 (except in Scotland) true divorce was rare and expensive and achieved by private bill in the House of Lords. There was only one divorce bill before 1670. The National Archives has a very few of these private acts for divorce, in c 89 ☑ and c 204 ☑, but they should be available at the House of Lords Record Office (see **www.portcullis.parliament.uk**). *The Times* newspaper online is a very good place to find out about these cases: you can access it free at the National Archives.

The church courts heard matrimonial disputes before 1858. Church court records, which are deposited in diocesan record offices, are largely unindexed and can be extremely difficult to interpret. The church courts could decree a legal separation, known as divorce *a mensa et thoro* (i.e., from board and bed), but the parties had to undertake not to remarry. Disputes over property rights and settlements after a divorce *a mensa et thoro* appear to have been heard in Chancery; for example, there are decrees from as early as 1538 in c 78 ☑. The Privy Council also appears to have had an interest in making sure that separation settlements were adhered to, and there are some entries in its registers in PC 2 about individual cases.

Some private separation agreements, apparently not involving the church courts, have been found enrolled on the Close Rolls in C54 ☑. They appear to have grown in popularity from the Interregnum, when church courts did not operate and private ingenuity filled the gap. Private separations restoring the wife to the status of a *feme sole*, responsible for her own debts, were not recognised by common law or equity; a married woman was in law treated as a *feme covert*, with her legal personality identical to that of her husband. Attempts to enforce such separations often led to much litigation in Chancery (see 58).

In order for the parties to remarry, the marriage had to be declared null from the beginning on the grounds of want of ability to marry (e.g., a precontract to marry another or want of consent to the marriage; for example, if the parties were under age and therefore incapable of consenting). This total dissolution of a marriage was described as a divorce *a vinculo matrimonii* (from the bond of matrimony). These uncommon procedures were abolished in 1754.

Appeals from ecclesiastical courts in matrimonial cases went to the High Court of Delegates between 1532 and 1832, and to the Judicial Committee of the Privy Council from 1833 until 1858. Copies of the proceedings of the lower, ecclesiastical courts for 1609–1834 are in DEL 1 ① (also indexed in DEL 11/7), and for 1834–1858 in PCAP 1 ②. The cases as presented to the appeal courts are in DEL 2 ①, DEL 7 Ⓕ and PCAP 3 ②: judgements are included. These records have been relatively little used, but can be very informative; they are currently being investigated further.

6.4 Divorce, matrimonial disputes and separation from 1858: the background

From 11 January 1858, the new Court for Divorce and Matrimonial Causes heard all divorce and matrimonial cases (e.g., restitution of conjugal rights, legitimacy, protection of earnings) until 1873, when it was reformed into the National Archives Probate, Divorce and Admiralty Division of the new Supreme Court. All divorce suits took place in London – a fact that served to restrict divorce to better-off couples. London lawyers had to be engaged, the petition had to be filed in the London registry, appearance in court was required – it all needed money and time that most people did not have.

From 1878, a different route was available for poorer women. Once a husband had been convicted of aggravated assault against her, the wife could apply to the local magistrate for a separation and maintenance order. By 1886, this route had been opened further: a husband who wilfully refused or neglected to maintain his wife and children, and deserted her, could be ordered to pay maintenance of up to £2 a week. By 1895, these various different possibilities had grown into a system to protect virtuous wives and their children from violent, cruel or neglectful husbands. Women seen as immoral were not covered: no husband could be obliged to maintain a wife who had already committed adultery, or who did so after separation. (Many law reformers condemned this kind of separation as a 'living death'.) Women flocked to the magistrates' courts to obtain these orders, partly because they were required to by some poor law authorities. By 1900, over 10,000 orders were issued each year. These separation orders continued in bulk for many years, until the advent of cheap and relatively easy divorce, at which point effectively only those with a religious objection to divorce used them. If the orders survive, they will be kept in local record offices.

If a husband or wife wanted a real divorce, with the chance to remarry, a judicial separation was a poor substitute. From 1914, poor petitioners were eligible for financial aid to seek a divorce under the Poor Persons

Rules, which helped a little. The real opening of divorce to all classes took place in the 1920s with the extension of legal aid and the provision of some local facilities. This was partly in response to the failure of many marriages during the First World War, and partly because in 1923 women were at last allowed to sue for divorce on the grounds of the husband's adultery alone. In 1922, ten assize towns were named as suitable for the hearing of certain kinds of divorce. From 1927, petitions could be filed in 23 district registries, while the case could be heard in 18 assize towns. This option proved increasingly popular: within 10 years nearly a quarter of all suits were started at district registries.

The Second World War caused so much dislocation of marriages that the rising torrent of divorce suits became a flood. The summer assizes in one town alone in 1946 had to process 320 divorce cases in a week, with the scenes outside the court being described as like the crowds at a racecourse. The county courts were finally able to hear divorce suits in the late 1960s. Most divorces now take place at county courts.

The Times online is a very good place to find out about divorce cases (and the only place to find the judgement in the first few years of the court, when many divorces were not granted). You can access it free at the National Archives and the Family Records Centre. In more recent years when divorces became more frequent, relevant local newspapers may be more helpful: see **www.bl.uk/collections/newspapers.html** or investigate **www.familia.org.uk/** for holdings in local libraries.

6.5 Divorce and matrimonial disputes from 1858: the records

If you are looking for legal proof of a divorce in any court, from 1858 to the present day, contact the Principal Registry of the Family Division, Decree Absolute Section (address in 62). For a fee, it will access a union index to the registered court copies of decrees absolute and either provide a copy of the information (if the divorce was granted by the Supreme Court) or arrange for a copy to be sent to you from the relevant county court. If you want the information on the cause of the divorce, you must specifically ask for the inclusion of details from the decree nisi as well. If the divorce took place within the last 5 years, you can also contact the county court where it took place for a cheaper service. If you can discover the case number from the public access indexes to cases at the National Archives or the Family Records Centre, you can order a copy of the decree at a reduced cost.

Case files were created for each suit, identified by year and a number. Surviving ones can be seen at the National Archives. The survival rate of these case files is excellent until 1927, not bad until 1937 and then disastrous. From 1938 onwards, only an absolutely minute sample has been kept.

These case files can give much more detail than the decrees. For a start, they include unsuccessful cases in which the petition was refused. They generally include the petition, copies of any relevant certificate, details of whether the plaintiff was suing as a poor person, affidavits – and copies of the decrees nisi and absolute after the first few years. If there is a previous or later petition, a cross-reference is given on the front of the file. Most have been stripped of further material, but a selection were kept complete to show all stages of a suit (these are identified in a list field with the paper list of J 77.) All the case files kept after 1938 are full case files.

The surviving case files are in J 77 (F until 1938, then 1), with what are kindly called indexes in J 78 7. The indexes can also be seen at the Family Records Centre. The dates given in the lists of both J 77 and J 78 are the dates of filing the initial petition, not the dates of the actual divorces (which are used by the index at the Principal Registry). The earlier divorce case files are likely candidates for digitisation in the next few years.

What does all this imply for the chance of finding a divorce case file?

1858–1927	All files should survive J 77	Indexed in J 78	A very few are known to be missing	Missing ones indexed in J 78 and noted as missing in J 77 list
1928–1937	About 80% of files should survive in J 77	Indexed in J 78	District registries divorce suits (about 20% of total) were destroyed on the recommendation of Lord Denning	District registry cases not indexed in J 78. Only decrees survive at the Principal Registry Index accessed by staff there
1938– date	No files survive except the sample in J 77	Principal Registry divorces indexed in J 78	Divorce files destroyed on the recommendation of Lord Denning	Only decrees survive, at the Principal Registry. Index to Principal Registry and District Registry divorces accessed by staff there

If there is no case file, you will have to try local newspapers for any further details. You may find this worth doing anyway, particularly before the mid-1920s, as divorce reporting was a staple fare of many newspapers (see 6.4).

Case files do not survive for the local district registries, which could handle divorce suits from 1927 (the first decrees absolute from suits started at district registries were issued in February 1928 by the Supreme Court). The district registries were increasingly popular: in their first three years, 17 per cent of divorce suits were filed in district registries, rising to 23 per cent in 1937. For these suits only the decree is left in official custody, at the Principal Registry. However, it is not easy to tell where a suit was filed. It seems that the only way you can find out if a divorce *granted between 1928 and 1937* will or will not have a case file at the National Archives is

- to buy a copy of the decree absolute from the Principal Registry, specifying

in your request that you wish to know if the suit was filed in a District Registry (no case file) or in the Principal Registry (case file);
- to do a speculative search in J 78.

THE INDEXES IN J 78

The indexes in J 78 are not in strict alphabetical order. They are more like entry books, with the parties entered in the relevant pages for surnames of the same letter, as the suit was filed. They are available on microfilm at both the National Archives and the Family Records Centre, but the files in J 77 can only be seen at the National Archives. (Copies of the 'indexes' for 1858–1903 can also be viewed for a fee at the commercial site **www. nationalarchivist.com/index01/about.cfm**.)

You will need to get the file number from the index and match it up in the list of J 77. The index is not very easy to use as each volume covers more than one year – and some years are in more than one series in J 77. Once you have found the entry, double check which year it is in: the turn of the year is usually marked within each letter-block, though not always very clearly.

1858–1937

For 1858 to 1937 almost all files filed in the Principal Registry survive, in J 77. The 20 per cent or so of divorce suits filed in the District Registries from 1927 do not survive. The files were closed for 75 years until recently, but have now all been made available. The files in J 77 are mostly arranged in blocks of 10,000: the series change when the number 10,000 is reached, so the series cover odd blocks of time.

Series	No of files	File references	Index
1858–1866	2547 files, listed by letter and number	J 77/1–63	J 78/1
1867–1884	10,000 files, listed by number	J 77/64–332	J 78/1–3
1885–1898	20,045 files, listed by number	J 77/333–657	J 78/3–5
1899–1909	10,000 files, listed by number	J 77/658–988	J 78/5–7
1909–1917	10,000 files, listed by number	J 77/988–1309	J 78/7–9
1917–1920	10,000 files, listed by number	J 77/1309–1611	J 78/9–10
1920–1922	10,000 files, listed by number	J 77/1611–1918	J 78/10–11
1922–1925	10,000 files, listed by number	J 77/1918–2234	J 78/11–12
1925–1928	10,000 files, listed by number	J 77/2235–2572	J 78/12–14
1928–1931	10,000 files, listed by number	J 77/2572–2908	J 78/13–15
1931–1934	10,000 files, listed by number	J 77/2908–3272	J 78/15–16
1934–1936	10,000 files, listed by number	J 77/3273–3546, J 77/3643–3704	J 78/16–17
1936–1938	7670 files, listed by number: 7671–10,000 (for early 1938) destroyed	J 77/3547–3642, J 77/3705–3864	J 78/17–18

The indexes also indicate the kind of petition, abbreviated as:

HD	Petition by husband for decree of divorce
WD	Petition by wife for decree of divorce
HN	Petition by husband for decree of nullity
WN	Petition by wife for decree of nullity
HJS	Petition by husband for decree of judicial separation
WJS	Petition by wife for decree of judicial separation
HRCR	Petition by husband for decree of restitution of conjugal rights
WRCR	Petition by wife for decree of restitution of conjugal rights
Legit	Petition for declaration of legitimacy
Div Ct	Appeal to Divisional Court from Justices
Prot	Application for order for protection of wife's earnings and property

For 115 cases between 1858 and 1934, representing the full range of disputes heard by the court, all documentation has been preserved. There is a list of these 115 cases in front of the paper list of J 77 – remember that you will have to match up the number given with the relevant block of years in the list.

If you find that a file from 1858–1882 is missing, try the court books in J 170. If you find that the file you are interested in does not include a copy of the decrees nisi and absolute (a common occurrence at first) try a search in *The Times.* This may be the only place to get proof of the failure of a petition – and the court did turn down many of the cases that came flooding in during the first few years. Divorce cases were reported in detail in the first years of the court, so it is well worth looking in all cases.

If the court suspected that the divorce was in collusion – by agreement of the parties, which was then illegal – the case was remitted to the King's Proctor for investigation. Try the indexed registers of investigated cases in TS 29 [7], although records dating from less than 75 years ago are still closed.

1938 ONWARDS

Unfortunately no case files survive for petitions *filed* in either the Principal or the District Registries after 31 December 1937. (If you are looking for a divorce *granted* in 1938 or even 1939 it may be worth looking for a case file in J 78, because of the time lag.) Case papers are now destroyed after about 20 years. If you are within the 20 year period, you can appear before a District Judge to request permission to see the case papers: contact the Principal Registry for details.

The sole exception is the small sample of full files in J 77 [1]. To see if you are lucky enough to have a case file included in this sample, try a search in the catalogue using the name and J 77. Few people will be lucky. If nothing is found, you will have to depend on the decrees alone, plus any reports in local newspapers.

However, the indexes to suits filed at the Principal Registry before 1 January 1959 still exist at the National Archives and FRC, and can at least provide evidence that a divorce or matrimonial suit took place.

☐ p. 566

This index is the only official place to find evidence of the existence of failed suits. (You may be able to find more details on failed suits in local newspapers.) For November 1946–1949, there are no indexes, only divorce receipt books. These have very little to recommend them: you would be far better off ignoring them and going for the Principal Registry material.

6.6 Burial grounds and cemeteries

Many people want to find out where a person is buried, as well as the date of their death. Start with the National Burial Index, described in 5.3, or look for a published obituary or death notice in the local newspaper. If these sources are fruitless, you may need to carry out a search in the original parish or cemetery registers. Of course, you have to have a reasonable guess as to where and when the person died. After 1837, the death certificate will provide this information (though not burial details).

Burials after 1853 could take place in either a parish or Nonconformist cemetery, or in one of the many local authority or privately run cemeteries that ringed Victorian cities. If you are looking for a city burial, you may need to consult maps of the area to find out which was the likeliest place. Burial records are generally held and maintained by local authorities: try the local phone book for addresses. For Greater London, consult Webb, *Greater London Cemeteries and Crematoria*. Records of one of these large cemeteries, the Victoria Park Cemetery in Hackney, London, 1853–1876, can be seen at the Family Records Centre and the National Archives (RG 8/42–51 ⑦; each volume is arranged in letter order).

If the death was before 1854, the most likely place of burial was in the local parish churchyard (and recorded in the parish register) or in the local Nonconformist burial ground. Although the Nonconformist registers do include details of deaths and burials, burials were usually in the parish churchyard and noted in the parish register until Nonconformist burial grounds were established. Some of these were small and local, such as the Protestant Dissenters' Burial Ground at Great Dunmow, Essex, 1784–1856 (RG 4/597), or the Dissenters' Ground at Boston, Lincs, 1789–1856 (RG 4/24–25). However, Nonconformists also established large burial grounds or cemeteries for dissenters; this practice later spread to all denominations. The main pre-1854 burial records in the National Archives and the Family Records Centre are those of these large cemeteries established in London. These are:

- Bethnal Green Protestant Dissenters' Burying Ground, or Gibraltar Burying Ground, 1793–1837 (RG 8/305–314 Ⓔ); index at the Family Records Centre (not at the National Archives);
- Bunhill Fields Burial Ground, City Road, 1713–1854 (RG 4/3974–4001, 4288–4291 and 4633, with indexes at RG 4/4652–4657). (Other records for

this cemetery, at the Guildhall Library, include an alphabetical list of burials, 1827–1854);

- Bunhill Burial Ground or Golden Lane Cemetery, 1833–1853 (RG 8/35–38);
- South London Burial Ground, East Street, Walworth, 1819–1837 (RG 4/4362);
- Southwark New Burial Ground, 1821–1854 (RG 8/73–74);
- Spa Fields, Clerkenwell, 1778–1849 (RG 4/4316–4322, 4366–4367).

In addition, the National Archives and the Family Records Centre have

- registers of burials at the Royal Hospital, Greenwich, 1705–1864 (RG 4/1669–1676 and RG 8 16–18);
- registers of burials at the Royal Hospital, Chelsea, 1692–1856 (RG 4/4330–4332 and 4387);
- registers of the Necropolis Burial Ground in Everton, Liverpool for all denominations, 1825–1837 (RG 4/3121). An index to these is available from **www.fhindexes.co.uk/everton.htm**.

Also worth consulting are the records of the removal of tombs and gravestones from churchyards, cemeteries and burial grounds of all denominations (including some Jewish ones) in order to develop the land for some other purpose (RG 37 ⑥). These are modern records of the actual removals and reinterments, but the tombs and gravestones themselves date from 1601 to 1980, with most coming from the later eighteenth and the nineteenth centuries. The files usually include a list of names, where these were discoverable, and frequently contain transcripts of the monumental inscriptions. They also indicate the place of reinterment. The Society of Genealogists has a significant collection of indexes to Monumental Inscriptions recorded from gravestones by many Family History Societies.

For London burials 1538–1853, you can search Boyd's London Burials Index of over 300,000 names at **www.britishorigins.com**.

6.7 Illegitimacy, foundlings, divorce and burial: bibliography

A BEVAN, 'Divorce 1858 onwards', *Ancestors* 10 (2002)

G CLARK, 'Records of Thomas Coram's Foundling Hospital', *Genealogists Magazine*, vol. 27 no. 5 (2002)

W R CORNISH and G DE N CLARK, *Law and Society in England 1750–1950* (London, 1989)

A HORSTMAN, *Victorian Divorce* (London, 1985)

C R HUMPHERY–SMITH, *The Phillimore Atlas and Index of Parish Registers* (Chichester, 1984)

N LISLE, 'Suffer the Children …' [Foundling Hospital], *Family History Monthly* 111 (2004)

O R MCGREGOR, *Divorce in England* (London, 1957)

E MCLAUGHLIN, 'The Name of the Father: tracing the paternity of illegitimate ancestors', *Ancestors* 20 (2004)

H Mellor, *London Cemeteries: Illustrated Guide and Gazetteer* (Godstone, 1985)

R Paley, *My Ancestor was a Bastard* (Society of Genealogists, 2004)

R Paley and S Fowler, *Family Skeletons: Exploring the lives of our disreputable ancestors* (The National Archives, 2005)

P Palgrave-Moore, *Understanding the history and records of Nonconformity* (2nd edn, Norwich, 1989)

P Park, 'Double dealing: matrimony and bigamy', *Ancestors* 24 (2004)

C Webb, *Greater London Cemeteries and Crematoria* (Society of Genealogists, 1999)

7 Births, marriages and deaths at sea

7.1 Civil registration at sea: an introduction

Records of births, marriages and deaths at sea were kept by the masters of British ships. From various dates in the nineteenth century, they were obliged to send on the information recorded relating to the birth or death at sea of English, Welsh, Scots and Irish people (or anyone else aboard – and seafarers came from all over the world) to the Registrar General of Shipping and Seamen (RGSS). The RGSS then forwarded the appropriate information to the separate General Register Offices of England and Wales, Scotland, Ireland (and Northern Ireland, from 1922). The registers kept by the RGSS (covering everyone) eventually came to the National Archives, while the General Register Offices keep their own Marine Registers (see 8.8, 13.1 and 14.1) covering only those people for whom they were responsible. The records at the National Archives therefore contain information about more people than the Marine Registers at the various General Register Offices.

These records have all been recently researched in depth, analysed and described by the Watts brothers, whose findings are published in *Tracing Births, Deaths and Marriages at Sea*. If you have a family who spent much of its time at sea, or if you have an intractable problem finding someone you suspect died at sea, you are advised to get hold of a copy of this immensely useful book. It covers not merely British merchant shipping sources but many colonial, foreign and Naval sources as well. It also includes a step-by-step section through the wide number of permutations of the location of these records.

7.2 Seamen: deaths, 1851–1890

By the Seamen's Fund Winding-up Act 1851, the masters of British ships were required to hand over the wages and effects of any seamen who had died during a voyage. Registers of wages and effects of deceased seamen

(BT 153 ☐F) were maintained until 1889–1890 (but 1882–1887 do not survive). They provide useful information:

- name and register ticket number;
- date and place of engagement;
- date and cause of the man's death;
- name, master's name and port of his ship;
- date and place of payment of wages, the amount of wages owed and the date they were sent to the Board of Trade.

The indexes to these registers (BT 154 for seamen ☐7, BT 155 for ships ☐7) give simple page references to BT 153. Associated with the registers are printed monthly lists of dead seamen giving name and age, rating, nationality or birthplace, last address and cause and place of death (BT 156 ☐7): they cover 1886–1890, and so fill part of the 1882–1887 gap in BT 153. There are also nine manuscript registers (BT 157 ☐7) containing half-yearly lists of deaths, classified by cause, for 1882–1888, which could with difficulty supply the rest of the gap.

7.3 Passengers: births, marriages and deaths, 1854–1891

Following the Merchant Shipping Act of 1854, registers were compiled (from the official ships' logs) of births, marriages and deaths at sea. All three are recorded from 1854 to 1883, births and deaths only from 1883 to 1887, and deaths only from 1888 (BT 158 ☐F): an index can be seen free at **www.nationalarchivist.com**, where you can also buy images of entries. Marriage entries in BT 334/117 (from as early as 1854 to 1972) record name of ship, official number, names of both parties, ages, whether single, widow or widower, profession or occupation, fathers' names, professions or occupations of fathers. This volume has been transcribed and can be seen at **www.theshipslist.com/Forms/marriagesatsea.html**.

From 1874 ship's masters had to separately report births and deaths aboard all ships registered in Britain or its colonies and on foreign-registered ships carrying passengers to or from the UK to the Registrar General of Shipping and Seamen, for forwarding as before. There is little evidence that foreign-registered ships bothered. The RGSS entered the data into two series of registers (BT 159 ☐7 and BT 160 ☐7) before forwarding it.

BT 159 contains entries of deaths of passengers at sea (1875–1888) and BT 160 of births to passengers at sea (1875–1891) in separate volumes for England, Scotland and Ireland. The registers for Scotland and Ireland contain details where the deceased or parent was a 'Scotch or Irish subject of Her Majesty'. The registers for England include all events not reported to the GROs for Scotland and Ireland and thus contain entries for foreign nationals, as well as those for English and Welsh subjects.

These are not duplicates of the Marine Registers held by the GRO at Southport, as those cover only the English and Welsh entries. The

BT registers contain much material on people of other nationality than English.

7.4 Passengers and seamen: births, marriages and deaths, 1891–1964

From 1891 a new series of registers (BT 334 F) begins, which includes records of the births, deaths and marriages of passengers at sea and the records of deaths and marriages of seamen at sea. For the period 1910–1918 there are also registers in BT 334 recording events specifically reported to one of the national Registrars General of births and deaths. One register of deaths and births at sea (1892–1918), first reported at Falmouth at an earlier stage in the process, has survived in CUST 67/74.

The registers in BT 334 include both UK and foreign subjects, passengers and seamen, and contain some entries related to the deaths of seamen ashore. The series also contains indexes to births and deaths; these are arranged both by ships' names and individuals' names. Although the Registrar General of Shipping and Seamen was required to report births and deaths to the appropriate Registrar General of Births and Deaths, over 50 per cent of the entries in BT 334 are blank in the column headed 'Which RG has been informed'.

- Birth entries (available 1891–1964, indexed to 1960) record: name of ship, official number, port of registry, date of birth, name, sex, name of father, rank or profession or occupation of father, name of mother, maiden surname of mother, father's nationality/birthplace and last place of abode, mother's nationality/birthplace and last place of abode.
- Death entries (available 1891–1964, indexed to 1960) record: name of ship, official number, port of registry, date of death, place of death, name of deceased, sex, age, rating [for seamen], rank or profession or occupation [for non-seamen], nationality and birthplace, last place of abode, cause of death, remarks. The death registers include entries for the *Titanic* and *Lusitania*
- Marriage entries (from as early as 1854 to 1972) are all in BT 334/117, and record: name of ship, official number, names of both parties, ages, whether single, widow or widower, profession or occupation, fathers' names, professions or occupations of fathers. This volume has been transcribed and can be seen at **www.theshipslist.com/Forms/marriagesatsea.html**.

Inquiries into deaths at sea can be found in BT 341 7, for 1939–1964. It includes passengers and crew of all nationalities: you need to know the name of the ship. For deaths of merchant seamen in the Second World War, use the rolls of honour in BT 339 7.

For records after 1964, use the General Register Office general indexes, available at the Family Records Centre and the National Archives (see 8.8).

7.5 Other sources for births, marriages and deaths at sea, from 1831 onwards

Details of some births and baptisms at seas (potentially from 1831) are included in RG 32/1–16 (indexed in RG 43/2). There are also registers of marriages aboard Naval ships, 1842–1889 (RG 33/156, indexed in RG 43/7). These often appear to be the marriages of people living in places where other methods of obtaining a valid British marriage may have been difficult, such as the Cayman Islands. (In the nineteenth century Naval captains could marry couples, but the master of a merchant ship could not do so. It appears that masters had to be reminded of this, so perhaps many had been marrying people illegally: see Watts, 'All's Well that Ends Well'.)

Deaths of British citizens on board French ships, 1836–1871, are in RG 35/16 (in French); deaths on board Dutch ships, 1839–1871, are in RG 35/17 (in Dutch): both are indexed by RG 43/4.

Registers of the deaths of British emigrants at sea, 1847–1869, are in CO 386/169–172.

7.6 Births, marriages and deaths at sea: bibliography

General Register Office, *Abstract of Arrangements Respecting Registration of Births, Marriages and Deaths in the United Kingdom and the Other Countries of the British Commonwealth of Nations, and in the Irish Republic* (London, 1952)

K SMITH, C T WATTS and M J WATTS, *Records of Merchant Shipping and Seamen* (PRO, 1998)

C T WATTS, 'All Aboard: births, deaths and marriages at sea', *Ancestors* 20 (2004)

C T WATTS, 'All's Well that Ends Well' [legality of marriage at sea], *Ancestors* 20 (2004)

C T WATTS and M J WATTS, *Tracing Births, Deaths and Marriages at Sea* (Society of Genealogists, 2004)

8 Births, marriages and deaths of Britons overseas or in the armed services

8.1 Overseas registers: an introduction

There are considerable numbers of sources available within Britain for births, marriages and deaths of Britons in other countries. Records are split between the various General Register Offices of England and Wales, Scotland, Ireland and Northern Ireland, the Guildhall Library and the National Archives. These sources do not cover births, marriages and deaths in the colonies, as these had their own registration systems and keep their own records: Yeo's *The British Overseas* gives addresses for the ex-colonies' official holdings. You can access registers from the old colonies (and elsewhere), however, by using the indexes on **www.familysearch.org** and the facilities provided by the excellent Family History Centres run by the Church of Jesus Christ of Latter-day Saints/The Genealogical Society of Utah (LDS). The LDS have filmed and indexed registers from all over the world; the films can be seen at their local centres for a small monthly fee. To find out the nearest centre, check on **www.familysearch.org**. (There are also microfiche copies of the indexes to the Australian registers, 1790–*c*.1900, at the Society of Genealogists.)

After 1949, and as colonies became independent, the United Kingdom High Commissions recorded registrations where relevant. Indexes to these are kept at the Family Records Centre (see 8.8). Some other exceptions are listed in 8.9.

Overviews of the records in the Guildhall and some other places, and in some of the Foreign Office records at the National Archives, are included in

The British Overseas. This lists the sources country by country but it does *not* include the overseas registers kept by the General Register Office of England and Wales, nor other records at the National Archives. This present chapter lists *only* the indexes of the General Register Office registers (8.8) and the holdings of the National Archives (8.9). As a result, you need to consult both *The British Overseas* and this book in order to get full information on what is available for a particular country. A copy of *The British Overseas* can be seen at both the National Archives and the Family Records Centre.

The Army also kept registers of births, marriages and deaths, whether at home or abroad. Most regimental registers and chaplains' registers before 1881 are kept by the General Register Office of England and Wales (although the National Archives has a few – see 24.1 for a fuller discussion). Armed service registers (for Army, Navy and later Air Force personnel and families) from about 1881 may be found in the relevant General Register Office. In addition, each General Register Office has indexes to War Deaths for the Boer War, First World War and Second World War. See 8.8 for a listing of these. These indexes can be seen in hard copy at the Family Records Centre, in microfiche at the National Archives, and online at **www.1837online.com**.

8.2 Religious registers, from the seventeenth century onwards

Religious registrations from English churches in foreign countries provide the earliest records. These records are split between

- the India Office Library and Records (at the British Library), which holds records of British and European baptisms, marriages and burials in churches across the Indian sub-continent, including Burma and Aden;
- the Guildhall Library, which has a large deposit of the Bishop of London's International Memoranda. These include details provided in many cases well after the event, perhaps with the intention of safeguarding inheritance. See Yeo, *The British Overseas* and Smith, 'Born or Buried Abroad?';
- the National Archives, which holds other church registers returned not to the Bishop of London but to the General Register Office of England and Wales. They (with other records) were later deposited in the National Archives in the RG code, and can be seen at both the National Archives and the Family Records Centre. See 8.5.

The Army also kept its own registers, whether at home or abroad. Regimental registers before 1881 seem to have ended up with the General Register Office of England and Wales (although the National Archives has a few – see 24.1). Armed service registers, from about 1881, and registers (or indexes) of war deaths may be found in the relevant General Register Office.

Heligoland, a favourite port of call for the North Sea fishing fleet, which was British between 1807 and 1891 (and has census entries for 1881 in CO 122/37) is thought to have birth, marriage and death registers in the local archives department of Kreis Pinneberg: see **www.kreis-pinneberg.de**.

8.3 Overseas civil registration from 1849: an overview

Registration records were kept by British consulates (in those foreign countries where there *was* a consulate) from various dates in the nineteenth century – some earlier than 1849. Statutory registration of English and Welsh citizens in foreign countries began in 1849, under the Consular Marriages Act, although on a voluntary basis. Registration of Scots abroad began in 1860 and of the Irish abroad in 1864. Since then, the Foreign Office has made annual returns from its own registers of births, marriages and deaths to the General Register Offices of England, Scotland, Ireland (1864–1921) and Northern Ireland (from 1922). The General Register Offices then compiled their own Overseas Registers and indexes from the information thus returned. These are the obvious place to start: see 8.8, 13.1 and 14.1.

The Overseas and Marine Registers kept by the General Register Office for England and Wales are not open to public inspection. The indexes can be consulted in volumes at the Family Records Centre, on microfiche at the National Archives and are also searched online at **www.1837online.com**: they are listed in 8.8. Certified copies have to be bought in the same way as home certificates (see 4 for more details, or look/order from **www.gro. gov.uk/gro/content/research/searchingforoverseasrecords**).

8.4 Foreign Office registers and related records in the National Archives

The embassy and consular records of the Foreign Office contain their registers from which information was returned annually to the General Register Office. They have the considerable advantage that you can browse through them: they are also known to contain information on more events. You should find that the consular registers include information otherwise distributed between the General Register Offices of Scotland, Ireland and Northern Ireland. In addition, the General Register Offices would only register births, marriages or deaths if the people involved fitted their strict criteria: the Foreign Office registers did not apply the same rules. If you are looking for someone who lived in a close-knit British community abroad, you may find all kinds of clues in the register about the life they led and the people they knew. For details of the various registers, listed by country, see 8.9. Later consular registers are still held by the Foreign Office.

There is also a 46-volume series of consular correspondence with the

☐ p. 566

Foreign Office on marriages abroad, covering 1814–1905. The series is split between FO 83 Ⓕ and FO 97 Ⓕ, with a register and index for 1814–1893 at FO 802/239. It includes information on some individual marriages. Also in FO 83 are covering despatches to certificates of marriages abroad giving the names of the parties, 1846–1890; general correspondence and circulars on consular marriages; and acknowledgements of receipt of certificates by the Bishop of London's Registry.

References to similar correspondence can be traced in the Foreign Office card index, 1906–1919, and in the printed index, 1920–1957; both these indexes are in the Research Enquiries Room at the National Archives. However, many of the documents they refer to no longer exist.

8.5 General Register Office records in the National Archives

The National Archives also holds miscellaneous non-statutory registers and records deposited by the Registrar General of England and Wales: these cover 1627–1958 (RG 32–RG 36 Ⓕ, with indexes of a sort in RG 43). They can now be seen at both the National Archives and the Family Records Centre. They relate to the births, baptisms, marriages, deaths and burials abroad, and on British and foreign ships, of British subjects and of nationals of the colonies, the Commonwealth or countries under British jurisdiction. Some foreign nationals are also included, together with material supplied by foreign governments (such as the First World War death certificates from the French and Belgian authorities: see 26.1.3).

References, by country, are given in 8.9; however, this includes only the most well represented countries in RG 32–RG 36, and there are many others besides (e.g., Uruguay and Gibraltar). You should check in the indexes in RG 43 even if the country you are interested in does not appear in 8.9, or if it does appear but with a wrong date range.

Other records of births, marriages and deaths abroad occur elsewhere among the public records; these are included in 8.9.

Two possible sources that are not listed in 8.9 are the Protestant Dissenters' Registry and the Wesleyan Methodist Metropolitan Registry. Both of these registered births abroad. For more details, see 5.6 and 5.7.

8.6 Commonwealth War Graves and other burial grounds

The Commonwealth War Graves Commission has details of servicemen who died overseas and on ships in the two World Wars. Try their excellent website, **www.cwgc.org.uk**, which is searchable by name. For details of military graves other than for the two World Wars, contact the Ministry of Defence, PS4 (CAS)(A). The addresses are in 62.

The British Association for Cemeteries in South Asia (BACSA) is a voluntary organisation dealing with the preservation, conversion and registration of European cemeteries in South Asia (Persian Gulf to Hong Kong), and in particular those that were formerly administered by the East India Company and the British government in India. It compiles records of both civilians and soldiers, and produces a twice-yearly magazine, *Chowkidar*. For more information see **www.bacsa.org.uk**.

8.7 Births, marriages and deaths of Britons overseas: bibliography

General Register Office, *Abstract of Arrangements Respecting Registration of Births, Marriages and Deaths in the United Kingdom and the Other Countries of the British Commonwealth of Nations, and in the Irish Republic* (London, 1952)

P SMITH, 'Born or Buried Abroad?' [overseas records at the Guildhall Library], *Ancestors* 33 (2005)

J WALL, 'The British Association for Cemeteries in South Asia', *Genealogists' Magazine*, XXIV, pp. 1–4

G YEO, *The British Overseas, A Guide to Records of Their Births, Baptisms, Marriages, Deaths and Burials Available in the United Kingdom* (Guildhall Library, London, 4th edn, 1994)

8.8 Indexes to the Overseas, Marine and Armed Forces Registers kept by the General Register Office of England and Wales

These indexes are to the Overseas Registers kept by the General Register Office of England and Wales: certificates have to be bought individually from the GRO. (See **www.gro.gov.uk/gro/content/research/searchingfor overseasrecords**.)

The indexes can be seen at the Family Records Centre in bound volumes and at the National Archives on microfiche. You can also search these indexes on a subscription basis at **www.1837online.com**: the cost is small for the convenience.

General Indexes, from 1966	
1966–date	**Registers of Births Abroad; and Marriages Abroad; and Deaths Abroad [Civilian and Armed Forces]** These registers took over from the Air, Consular, Marine, Miscellaneous, and Services series, and apparently from the marriage and death sections of the United Kingdom High Commission series (all below). The birth indexes give name, mother's maiden name, place of registration and date or year of birth. The marriage registers include the spouse's surname. The death registers give age.

Colonial and Ex-colonial Indexes, 1940–1981	
1940–1981	**UKHC Registers of Births Abroad 1950–1965; and Marriages; and Deaths** The United Kingdom High Commissions kept these registers in colonies and ex-colonies. Although the birth registers start in 1950, they do include a few births from the 1940s.

Civilian Indexes, 1837–1965

1849–1965	**Consular Registers of Births; and Marriages; and Deaths** Arranged alphabetically within a range of five or so years; no closer indication of date is given. Deaths were not registered with consuls until 1859. The indexes include name and consul's registration district: from 1906, the spouse's name is given in the marriage index, and the age in the death index. These are the statutory consular registers, kept as a result of the 1849 Act. Among the Foreign Office embassy and consular records at the National Archives are the duplicates kept by the consulates. You could use this index and then look at the consular register at the National Archives if you do not want to buy a certified copy. As the reference given in this index does not apply to the consular register, you would need to match up the place of registration with the right consulate, and then find that consulate's records from **8.9**.
1837–1965	**At sea: Marine Registers of Births; and Deaths** These give name and year of English and Welsh births and deaths at sea; after 1875, the name of the ship is given as well. The age is given for deaths. From 1837 to 1874 they relate to events occurring on British merchant and naval ships; from 1875, to other ships carrying passengers to or from the United Kingdom as well.
1947–1965	**Air Registers of Births; and Deaths** The index gives name, age (for deaths), place and year of births and deaths occurring in civil aircraft in flight.
1941–1965	**Protectorates of Africa and Asia: Registers of Births** The registers for 1895–1957, and the indexes up to 1940, are at the National Archives.
1956–1965	**Miscellaneous Foreign Registers of Births, Marriages and Deaths** The index gives name, place and year. Most entries appear to be from the Gulf States, Singapore, etc.
1818–1864	**Index to Registers of Births, Marriages and Deaths in the Ionian Islands** The index is to a military register, a civil register and a chaplain's register. It gives names only. See also **8.9**, under **Greece**.

Armed Forces Indexes, 1761–1965

1761–1924	**Regimental Registers of Births** These include events in the United Kingdom and abroad (from *c.* 1790). The indexes are arranged alphabetically, giving name, place, year and regiment. There are also marriage registers, but these are not indexed and cannot be inspected: see **24.1** for more information.
1796–1880	**[Army] Chaplains' Returns of Births; and Marriages; and Deaths** These all relate to events abroad. The index gives name, place and a date range of 2–3 years.
1881–1955	**Army Returns of Births; and Marriages; and Deaths** These all relate to events abroad. The indexes give name, station and date. From 1920, entries relating to the Royal Air Force are included.
1956–1965	**Service Departments Registers of Births; and Marriages** These relate to Army, Navy and Air Force births and marriages abroad. The indexes give name, station and year.

Armed Forces: Indexes to War Deaths, 1899–1948

1899–1902	*Natal and South Africa Forces*
1914–1921	*Army Other Ranks' War Deaths*
1914–1921	*Army Officers' War Deaths*
1914–1921	*Naval War Deaths*

1939–1948	*Army Other Ranks' War Deaths*	
1939–1948	*Army Officers' War Deaths*	
1939–1948	*Naval War Deaths: Ratings*	
1939–1948	*Naval War Deaths: Officers*	
1939–1948	*RAF All Ranks' War Deaths*	
1939–1948	*Indian Services' War Deaths*	

8.9 Table of overseas birth, marriage and death records in the National Archives

None of these are searchable online in our catalogue: you could use the GRO indexes above to find relevant entries. As many of these records appear partly to duplicate the records in the Guildhall, it is worth checking *The British Overseas* to find out which place has the more complete collection. The list in 8.9 indicates whether *The British Overseas* gives references to other sources outside the National Archives. Records at the Guildhall, as at the National Archives, are produced directly to the public, sometimes on microfilm.

African Protectorates	births 1911–1946; marriages 1912–1935; deaths 1911–1946	RG 36 [2]
Algeria	deaths 1840–1958	RG 35/14–15, 20–24 [2]
Angola		
Luanda	births 1865–1906; marriages 1871–1928; deaths 1859–1906	FO 375/1–4
Argentina [1]	(see http://homepage.ntlworld.com/jnth/)	
Buenos Aires	marriages 1826–1900	FO 446/3–6, 28–30
Ascension Island [1]	baptisms/births from 1858–1861 and onwards	RG 32 [2]
	deaths 1858–1920	RG 35 [2]
Austria [1]	deaths *c.* 1831–1920	RG 35/20–44 [2]
Vienna	marriages 1846–1890	FO 83 [3]
Vienna	marriages 1883–1891	FO 120/697
Vienna	baptisms 1867–1886 and onwards	RG 32 [2]
Belgium [1]	deaths 1831–1871	RG 35/1–3 [2]
(including Belgian Congo)	deaths 1871–1920	RG 35/20–44 [2]
	military deaths in hospital, etc., 1914–1920 (In alphabetical order, but not indexed in RG 43. There are no certificates for surnames beginning with C, F, P, Q or X.)	RG 35/45–69
Antwerp	baptisms and burials 1817–1852; marriages 1820–1849	RG 33/1–2 [2]

1 You may also need to consult Yeo, *The British* Overseas.
2 Entries in RG 32–RG 36 are largely indexed by RG 43: at both the National Archives and the Family Records Centre.
3 Indexed in FO 802/239.

Antwerp	baptisms and burials 1831–1836, 1841–1842; marriages 1832–1838, 1841–1842	RG 33/155 [2]
Antwerp	baptisms 1840 and onwards	RG 32 [2]
Antwerp	marriages and deaths: correspondence 1927–1951	FO 744
Brussels	marriages 1816–1890	RG 33/3–8 [2]
Brussels	marriages 1846–1890	FO 83 [3]
Ghent	marriages 1849–1850	RG 33/9 [2]
Bermuda [1]	naval dockyard baptisms, marriages and burials 1826–1946	ADM 6/434, 436, 439
Brazil [1]		
Bahia	marriages 1816–1820	RG 33/155 [2]
Maranhão	marriages 1844	RG 33/155 [2]
Pará	births and deaths 1840–1841	RG 33/155 [2]
Rio de Janeiro	marriages 1809–1818	RG 33/155 [2]
Rio de Janeiro	births 1850–1859	FO 743/11
Rio de Janeiro	baptisms 1850 and onwards	RG 32 [2]
Rio de Janeiro	marriages c. 1850 and onwards	RG 34 [2]
Rio de Janeiro	burials 1850 and onwards	RG 35/20–44 [2]
Rio de Janeiro	marriages 1870–1890	FO 83 [3]
São Paulo	births 1932; marriages 1933	FO 863/1–2
Brunei	births 1932–1950	RG 36 [2]
Bulgaria [1]		
Plovdiv	births 1880–1922; deaths 1884–1900	FO 868/1–?
Rustchuk	births 1867–1908; deaths 1867–1903	FO 888/1–2
Sofia	births 1934–1940	FO 864/1
Varna	births 1856–1939; deaths 1851–1929	FO 884/1–5
Burma		
Rangoon	marriages 1929–1942	RG 33/10 [2]
China [1]	births, marriages and deaths 1869–1876	FO 681/1
Amoy	births 1850–1950; marriages 1850–1949; deaths 1850–1948 (see also **China** FO 681/1)	FO 663/85–95
Canton	births 1864–1865, 1944–1950; marriages 1865, 1943–1949; deaths, 1865, 1944–1950 (see also **China** FO 681/1). For a list of British subjects in Canton, 1844–1951, see FO 694.	FO 681/2–9
Changsha	births 1905–1941; marriages 1906–1936; deaths 1906–1933	FO 681/10–12
Chefoo	births 1861–1943; marriages 1872–1940; deaths 1861–1942	FO 681/13–22
Chengtu	births 1902–1915; marriages 1904–1924; deaths 1904–1926	FO 664/3–5

1 You may also need to consult Yeo, *The British Overseas*.
2 Entries in RG 32–RG 36 are largely indexed by RG 43: at both the National Archives and the Family Records Centre.
3 Indexed in FO 802/239.

Chinanfu (Tsinan)	births and marriages 1906–1935; deaths 1906–1931, 1937	FO 681/23–27
Chinkiang	births 1865–1866, 1899–1926; marriages 1865–1866, 1896–1959; deaths 1865–1866, 1889–1927 (see also **China** FO 681/1)	FO 387/4–5, 7–11
Chungking	births 1888–1951; marriages 1891–1949; deaths 1891–1950	FO 681/28–34
Darien	births and marriages 1907–1940; deaths 1910–1940	FO 681/35–88
Foochow	births 1858–1866, 1905–1944; marriages 1909–1942; deaths 1858–1866, 1921–1945 (see also **China** FO 681/1)	FO 665/3–8
Formosa (Taiwan)	births, marriages and deaths 1866	FO 681/57
Formosa (Taiwan)	deaths 1873–1901 (see also **China** FO 681/1)	FO 721/1
Hankow	births 1863–1951; marriages 1869–1949; deaths 1861–1950 (see also **China** FO 681/1)	FO 666/2–22
Ichang	births 1879–1938; marriages 1881–1937; deaths 1880–1941 (damaged by fire)	FO 667/2–6
Kuikiang	births 1866–1929; marriages 1872–1928; deaths 1863–1929 (see also **China** FO 681/1)	FO 681/39–45
Kunming	births 1949–1951; deaths 1950	FO 668/2–3
Kwelin	births 1942–1944; deaths 1943	FO 681/46–47
Mukden	births and deaths 1949 (date of registration); marriages 1947–1948	FO 681/48–49, 79–80
Nanking	births 1930–1948; marriages 1929–1949; deaths 1930–1947	FO 681/50–53
Newchang	births, marriages and deaths between 1869 and 1876	FO 681/1
Ningpo	births 1858; marriages and deaths 1856–1858 (see also **China** FO 681/1)	FO 670/2–4
Peking	births 1911–1914; deaths 1911–1913 (date of registration) (see also **China** FO 681/1)	FO 564/13–14
Shanghai	births 1856–1864; marriages 1851; deaths 1851–1864	FO 672/1–3
Shanghai	marriages 1852–1951	RG 33/12–20 [2]
Shanghai, Union Church	marriages 1869–1951 (see also **China** FO 681/1)	RG 33/21–32 [2]
Shantung Province	marriages 1912–1914	RG 33/33 [2]
Swatow	births 1864–1865, 1947–1949 (date of registration); marriages 1865; deaths 1864–1865 (see also **China** FO 681/1)	FO 681/54–56
Taku	births 1862–1875; deaths 1871–1875	FO 673/9–10
Tengyueh	births 1904–1941; marriages 1913–1941; deaths 1906–1941	FO 681/60–62

1 You may also need to consult Yeo, *The British Overseas*.
2 Entries in RG 32–RG 36 are largely indexed by RG 43: at both the National Archives and the Family Records Centre.
3 Indexed in FO 802/239.

Tientsin	births 1864–1951; marriages 1862–1952; deaths 1863–1952 (see also **China** FO 681/1)	FO 674/297–327
Tsingtao	births 1911–1950; marriages 1923–1949; deaths 1921–1951	FO 675/7–10
Wei-hai-wei	births 1899–1929; marriages 1905–1940; deaths 1899–1929, 1938–1941	FO 681/63–71
Wei-hai-wei	births, marriages, deaths 1899–1930	RG 33/34 [2]
Wei-hai-wei	births, marriages, deaths 1899–1930	RG 36 [2]
Wei-hai-wei	index to births, marriages and deaths 1899–1930	RG 43/19 [2]
Whampoa	births and deaths 1865 (see also **China** FO 681/1)	FO 681/72–73
Yunanfu	births 1903–1948; marriages 1904–1949; deaths 1903–1950	FO 681/74–78
Colombia [1]	marriages 1824–1827	RG 33/155 [2]
	marriages 1846–1890	FO 83 [3]
Cartagena	births 1853–1924; deaths 1858–1927	FO 736/2–3
Denmark [1]	deaths 1842–1872	RG 35/4–7 [2]
Copenhagen	marriages 1846–1890	FO 83 [3]
Copenhagen	marriage affidavits 1853–1870	FO 211/236
Copenhagen	marriages 1853–1874	RG 33/35 [2]
Copenhagen	baptisms 1866–1870; marriages and burials 1869–1870 and onwards	RG 32 [2]

For Danish colonies,
see **West Indies**

Ecuador

Guayaquil	births, marriages and deaths 1879–1896	FO 521/2

Estonia see **Russia**

Falkland Islands [1]	births and baptisms [1853–1951]	RG 32 [2]
	marriages [1854–1951]	RG 34 [2]
	burials 1854–[1951]	
	RG 35/20–44 [2]	

Finland [1]

Helsinki	births 1914–1924	FO 753/19
Helsinki	deaths 1924	FO 768/5
Kristinestad	deaths 1928	FO 756/1
Raahe (Brahestad)	deaths 1930	FO 755/1
Tampere	births 1906–1923; deaths 1909–1934	FO 769/1–2
Turku (Abo)	births 1928; deaths 1929	FO 754/1–2
Vyborg	births 1924–1931; deaths 1929–1937	FO 751/1–3

1 You may also need to consult Yeo, *The British Overseas*.
2 Entries in RG 32–RG 36 are largely indexed by RG 43: at both the National Archives and the Family Records Centre.
3 Indexed in FO 802/239.

France [1]	deaths 1831–1871	RG 35/8–13 [2]
	deaths 1871–1920	RG 35/20–44 [2]
	military deaths in hospital, etc., 1914–1920 (In alphabetical order, but not indexed in RG 43. There are no certificates for surnames beginning with C, F, P, Q or X.)	RG 35/45–69
Boulogne	baptisms and burials 1815–1896; marriages 1829–1895 (index at RG 33/161)	RG 33/37–48 [2]
Brest	births 1842	RG 33/155 [2]
Calais and St Omer	baptisms 1817–1878; marriages 1818–1872; burials 1819–1878 (index at RG 33/49)	RG 33/50–55 [2]
Dieppe	births 1872–1892; deaths 1871–1894	FO 712/1–3
Le Havre	baptisms, marriages and burials 1817–1863	RG 33/56–57 [2]
Le Tréport	births 1917–1926; deaths 1899–1929	FO 713/1–2
Nantes	marriages 1851–1867	FO 384/1
Paris	baptisms, marriages and burials 1784–1789, 1801–1809, 1815–1869; marriages 1869–1890	RG 33/58–77 [2]
Paris	deaths 1846–1852	RG 35/11 [2]
Paris	marriages 1852–1890	FO 83 [3]
Paris	marriages 1935–1937	FO 630/1
Rouen	baptisms 1843–1844	RG 33/78 [2]
French colonies (Cochin China, Guadeloupe, Guyana, Haiti, India, Martinique, Mexico, New Caledonia, Réunion, Saigon, Shanghai, Senegal, Society Islands)	deaths 1836–1871	RG 35/14–16 [2]
(See also **Algeria, Réunion, Madagascar, Tahiti** and **West Indies**)		
Germany [1]	deaths c. 1831–1920	RG 35/20–44 [2]
Aachen	deaths 1925	FO 604/7
Bavaria	baptisms, marriages and death 1860–1861	FO 151/3
Bavaria	marriages 1860–1861	FO 149/99
Bavaria	marriages 1884–1897 (see also RG 32)	FO 601/2–6
Berlin	marriages 1846–1890	FO 83 [3]
Berlin	births 1944–1954; deaths 1944–1945	FO 601/2–6
Bremen	births 1872–1914; marriages 1893–1933	FO 585/1–5

1 You may also need to consult Yeo, *The British Overseas*.
2 Entries in RG 32–RG 36 are largely indexed by RG 43: at both the National Archives and the Family Records Centre.
3 Indexed in FO 802/239.

Bremerhaven	births 1872–1893	FO 585/1
Bremerhaven	marriages 1903–1914	FO 586/1
Cologne	births and marriages 1850–1866; deaths 1850–1866 and 1879–1881	FO 155/5–11, 17
Cologne	births 1880; marriages 1920–1934	FO 604/8–10
Darmstadt	births 1869–1898; deaths 1871–1905	FO 716/1–2
Darmstadt	marriages 1870–1890	FO 83 [3]
Dresden	births, baptisms and burials 1817–1836	RG 33/79 [2]
Dresden	marriages 1846–1890	FO 83 [3]
Dresden	births and deaths 1859–1866	RG 33/80 [2]
Dresden	births 1901–1907; marriages 1899–1900	FO 292/2, 4–5
Düsseldorf	births 1873–1884; baptisms 1903–1907; marriages 1873–1878, 1893–1898; deaths 1876–1884	FO 604/1–6, 8
Essen	births 1922–1927	FO 604/11
Frankfurt	marriages 1836–1865	FO 208/90
Frankfurt	marriages 1846–1869	FO 83 [3]
Hanover	baptisms, marriages, deaths and burials 1839–1859	RG 33/81 [2]
Hanover	marriages 1846–1869	FO 83 [3]
Hanover	births 1861–1866	FO 717/1
Karlsruhe	births 1860–1864; deaths 1859–1864	FO 718/1–2
Konigsberg	marriages 1864–1885	FO 509/1
Leipzig	marriages 1850–1865; deaths 1850–1860	FO 299/22
Munich	marriages 1846–1890	FO 83 [3]
Saxony	marriages 1850–1865; deaths 1850–1869	FO 218/3
Stuttgart	marriages 1847–1890	FO 83 [3]
(See also **Poland**)		
Greece [1]	marriages 1846–1890	FO 83 [3]
Ionian Islands, Zante	baptisms, marriages, deaths and burials 1849–1859. The registers for 1818–1848 are at Southport: see 4.5. The index covers both sets, and can be seen at the FRC (ONS) and at Kew: see 4.14 no. 8.	RG 33/82 [2]
Hawaii	births 1848–1893	FO 331/59
	marriages 1850–1853	RG 33/155 [2]
	registers of British subjects 1895–1944	FO 331/60–61
Hong Kong	deaths from enemy action in the Far East 1941–1945, indexed in RG 43/14 (see also **Indonesia** RG 33/132)	RG 33/11

1 You may also need to consult Yeo, *The British Overseas*.
2 Entries in RG 32–RG 36 are largely indexed by RG 43: at both the National Archives and the Family Records Centre.
3 Indexed in FO 802/239.

Hungary

Budapest	marriages 1872–1899	FO 114/1–5

Indian States [1]

Bikaner, Eastern Rajputana, Gwalior, Hyderabad, Jaipur, Madras States, Mysore, Punjab States, Travandrum and other states	births and deaths 1894–1947 (most from 1930s and 1940s) (indexed in RG 43/15)	RG 33/90–113
Jammu and Kashmir, Kolhapur and Deccan states, Udaipur	births 1917–1947 (indexed in RG 43/15)	RG 33/157–158, 160
Srinagar	deaths 1926–1947 (indexed in RG 43/15)	RG 33/159
Indian Sub-continent [1]	deaths c. 1831–1920	RG 35/20–44 [2]
French India	deaths 1836–1871	RG 35/16 [2]
Indonesia (Dutch East Indies) [1]	deaths 1839–1871	RG 35/17 [2]
	deaths 1871–1920	RG 35/20–44 [2]
Borneo	births 1907; deaths 1897–1907	FO 221/2–3
Borneo and Sarawak	deaths from enemy action 1941–1945	RG 33/132 [2]
Java	births 1869–1941; baptisms 1906; deaths 1874–1898 and 1912–1940	FO 803/1–3
Java	deaths 1839–1871	RG 35/20–44 [2]
Oleh Leh	births and deaths 1883–1884	FO 220/12
Sumatra	births and deaths 1883–1884	FO 220/12
Iran (Persia) [1]	births 1903–1950; marriages 1895–1950; deaths 1899–1950	FO 923/1–25
Bushire	births, marriages and deaths 1849–1895	FO 560
Isfahan	births 1829–1950; marriages 1893–1951; deaths 1892–1943	FO 799/34–37
Tabriz	births 1851–1951; marriages 1850–1950; deaths 1882–1931	FO 451/1–9
Iraq (Mesopotamia) [1]	births, marriages and deaths 1915–1931 (with marriage indexes in RG 33/138–139)	RG 33/133–137 [2]
	births, marriages and deaths 1915–1931 (indexed in RG 43/16)	RG 36 [2]

Israel see **Palestine**

Italy [1]	deaths 1871–1920	RG 35/20–44 [2]
Agrigento	births 1857–1904; deaths 1857–1885	FO 653/2–4

1 You may also need to consult Yeo, *The British Overseas*.
2 Entries in RG 32–RG 36 are largely indexed by RG 43: at both the National Archives and the Family Records Centre.
3 Indexed in FO 802/239.

Catania	births 1878–1939; deaths 1878–1904, 1919–1940	FO 653/5–7
Florence	marriages 1840–1855, 1865–1871	RG 33/114–115 [2]
Florence	marriages 1856	FO 352/43
Gela	births 1904–1930	FO 653/8
Licata	births and deaths 1871–1900	FO 720/1
Livorno (Leghorn)	births, baptisms, marriages and burials 1797–1824	RG 33/116–117 [2]
Marsala	births, 1847–1922; deaths 1847–1919	FO 653/9–11
Mazzara	births 1810–1911	FO 653/12–13
Messina	births and deaths 1854–1957	FO 653/14–17
Milazzo	deaths 1887–1903	FO 653/18
Naples	baptisms, marriages and burials 1817–1822	RG 33/118 [2]
Naples	baptisms, marriages and burials 1835–1836	RG 33/155 [2]
Palermo	births 1837–1891, 1932–1940; deaths 1850–1919	FO 653/19–21
Porto Empedocle	births 1906	FO 653/22
Rome and Tuscany	baptisms and marriages 1816–1852	FO 170/6
Rome	marriages 1870–1890	FO 83 [3]
Rome	marriages 1872–1889	RG 33/119 [2]
Sicily	births 1810–1957; deaths 1847–1957	FO 653/2–38 & FO 720/1
Sicily	baptisms 1838	RG 33/155 [2]
Syracuse	births 1909–1918; deaths 1912–1919, 1953–1957	FO 653/23–25
Taormina	deaths 1909–1922	FO 653/26
Trapani	births 1871–1906, 1924–1927	FO 653/27–28
Turin	marriages 1847–1869	FO 83 [3]
Turin	marriages 1858–1864	RG 33/120 [2]
Venice	marriages 1874–1947	RG 33/121 [2]
Japan [1]	marriage declarations and certificates 1870–1887	FO 345
Kobe	baptisms and marriages 1874–1941; burials 1902–1941	RG 33/122–126 [2]
Nagasaki	births 1864–1940; marriages 1922–1940; deaths 1859–1944	FO 796/236–238
Osaka	marriages 1892–1904	RG 33/127–130 [2]
Shimonoseki	births 1903–1921; marriages 1906–1922; deaths 1903–1921	FO 797/48–50
Tokyo	marriages 1870–1890	FO 83 [3]
Tokyo	marriages 1875–1887	FO 345/34
Yokohama	marriages 1870–1874	FO 345/34
Jordan		
Amman	births 1946; marriages 1927	RG 36 [2]

1 You may also need to consult Yeo, *The British Overseas*.
2 Entries in RG 32–RG 36 are largely indexed by RG 43: at both the National Archives and the Family Records Centre.
3 Indexed in FO 802/239.

Kenya (East African Protectorate)	births 1904–1924 (partly indexed by RG 43/18)	RG 36 [2]
Latvia see Russia		
Lebanon		
Beirut	marriages c. 1859–1939	FO 616/5
Libya		
Tripoli	marriages 1916, 1931–1940; deaths 1938–1939	FO 161/4–7
Lithuania see Russia		
Madagascar [1]		
Diego Suarez	births 1907–1921	FO 711/1
Tamatave	deaths 1935–1940	FO 714/1
Tananarive (Antananarivo)	births 1865–1868	FO 710/1
Malaysia [1]	births 1917–1949	RG 36 [2]
	births 1920–1948; deaths 1941–1945	RG 33/131–132 [2]
Borneo	births 1907; deaths 1897–1907	FO 221/2–3
Borneo and Sarawak	deaths from enemy action 1941–1945	RG 33/132 [2]
Johore	births 1924–1931	RG 36 [2]
Sarawak	births 1910–1948; marriages 1921–1935; deaths 1910–1948	RG 36 [2]
Malta [1]	marriages 1904–1936	FO 161/7
Mauritius see Réunion		
Mexico	marriages 1850 and onwards	RG 34 [2]
	deaths c. 1850–1920	RG 35/16, 20–44 [2]
Mexico City	burials 1827–1926	FO 207/58
Mexico City	marriages 1846–1869	FO 83 [3]
Mexico City	births and deaths 1854–1867	FO 723/1–2
Vera Cruz	births, deaths and burials 1858–1867	RG 33/140 [2]
Netherlands [1]	deaths 1839–1871 and 1871–1920	RG 35/17 & 20–44 [2]
The Hague	baptisms 1627–1821; marriages 1627–1889; births 1837–1839, 1859–1894; deaths 1859–1907 (These also include some church records; for others, see FO 259.)	RG 33/83–88 [2]
The Hague	marriages 1846–1890	FO 83 [3]
Rotterdam	baptisms and marriages 1708–1794	RG 33/89 [2]

1 You may also need to consult Yeo, *The British Overseas*.
2 Entries in RG 32–RG 36 are largely indexed by RG 43: at both the National Archives and the Family Records Centre.
3 Indexed in FO 802/239.

For Dutch colonies,
see **Indonesia,
Surinam** and
West Indies

Norway	deaths 1831–1920	RG 35/20–44 [2]
Bodo	births 1888–1890; deaths 1895	FO 724/1–2
Drammen	deaths 1906	FO 532/2
Kragero	deaths 1895	FO 725/1
Lofoten Islands	births 1850–1932	FO 726/1
Oslo (Christiania)	births 1850–1932; marriages 1853–1936; deaths 1850–1930	FO 529/1–14
Porsgrund and Skien	births 1885–1891	FO 531/2
Palestine [1]	births and deaths 1920–1935 (indexed in RG 43/17)	RG 33/141 [2]
	births 1923–1948; deaths 1941–1945 (partly indexed in RG 43/18)	RG 36 [2]
Jaffa	births 1900–1914	FO 734/1
Jerusalem	births 1850–1921; deaths 1851–1914	FO 617/3–5
Jerusalem	military baptisms 1939–1947	WO 156/6
Sarafand	military baptisms 1940–1946; banns of marriage 1944–1947	WO 156/7–8
Paraguay	births 1863 and onwards	RG 32 [2]
	deaths 1831–1920	RG 35/20–44 [2]
Peru [1]	births and deaths 1837–1841; marriages 1827 and 1836	RG 33/155 [2]
Poland [1]		
Breslau (Wroclaw)	births 1929–1938; deaths 1932–1938	FO 715/1–2
Danzig (Gdansk)	births 1851–1910; deaths 1850–1914	FO 634/16–18
Lodz	births 1925–1939	FO 869/1
Stettin	births 1864–1939; deaths 1857–1933	FO 719/1–2
Portugal [1]	deaths 1831–1920	RG 35/20–44 [2]
Azores	births, baptisms, marriages, deaths and burials 1807–1866	FO 559/1
Azores	baptisms, marriages and burials 1835–1837	RG 35/155 [2]
Azores	baptisms 1850–1857	RG 32 [2]
Azores	burials 1850–1857	RG 35/20 [2]
Cape Verde Islands	marriages 1894–1922	FO 767/6–7
Lisbon	marriages 1846–1890	FO 83 [3]
Lisbon	marriages 1859–1876	FO 173/8
Luanda see **Angola**		

1 You may also need to consult Yeo, *The British Overseas*.
2 Entries in RG 32–RG 36 are largely indexed by RG 43: at both the National Archives and the Family Records Centre.
3 Indexed in FO 802/239.

Oporto	baptisms, marriages and burials 1814–1874	RG 33/142 [2]
Oporto	baptisms, marriages and burials 1837	RG 33/155 [2]
Oporto	baptisms 1835 onwards	RG 32 [2]
Oporto	marriages 1835 onwards	RG 34 [2]
Oporto	burials 1835–1844	RG 35/20 [2]
Réunion (Mauritius)	deaths 1836–1871	RG 35/16 [2]
	marriages 1864–1921	FO 322/1–2
Romania [1]		
Braila	births 1922–1930; deaths 1921–1929	FO 727/1–2
Bucharest	births 1851–1931; baptisms 1858–1948; deaths 1854–1929	FO 625/2–4, 6
Bucharest	marriages 1870–1890	FO 83 [3]
Constanta (Kustendje)	births 1866–1873	FO 887/1
Galatz	marriages 1891–1939	FO 517/1–2
Lower Danube	baptisms 1869–1907	FO 625/5
Lower Danube	marriages 1868–1914	RG 33/143 [2]
Lower Danube	burials 1869–1870	FO 786/120
Sulina	births 1861–1932; deaths 1860–1931	FO 728/1–2 & FO 886/1–2
Russia [1]	births, baptisms, and deaths 1835–1870	RG 35/18–19 [2]
	births 1849–1909; marriages 1849–1861; deaths 1849–1915	FO 267/44–46
	deaths 1871–1920 [2]	RG 35/20–44
Archangel	births 1849–1909; marriages 1849–1861; deaths 1849–1915	FO 267/44–46
Batum	births 1884–1921; marriages 1891–1920; deaths 1884–1920	FO 397/1–6
Berdiansk (Osipenko)	marriages 1901	FO 399/1
Ekaterinburg (Sverdlovsk)	deaths 1918–1919	FO 399/5
Estonia, Pernau	births 1894–1930; deaths 1894–1930	FO 339/11–12
Estonia, Tallin (Reval)	births 1866–1940; marriages 1921–1939; deaths 1875–1940	FO 514/1–9
Konigsberg (Kaliningrad)	births 1869–1933; marriages 1864–1904; deaths 1857–1932	FO 509/1–4
Latvia, Libau	births 1883–1932; deaths 1871–1932	FO 440/10 & FO 661/4–5
Latvia, Riga	births 1850–1910; deaths 1850–1915	FO 377/3–4
Latvia, Riga	births 1921–1940; marriages 1920–1940; deaths 1921–1940	FO 516/1–9

1 You may also need to consult Yeo, The British Overseas.
2 Entries in RG 32–RG 36 are largely indexed by RG 43: at both the National Archives and the Family Records Centre.
3 Indexed in FO 802/239.

Latvia, Windau	births 1906–1909	FO 399/19
Lithuania, Kovno and Memel	births 1924–1940; deaths 1922–1940	FO 722/1–4
Moscow	births 1882–1918; marriages 1894–1924; deaths 1881–1918	FO 518/1–4
Nicolaiyev	births 1872–1917; deaths 1874–1915	FO 399/7–8
Novorossisk	births 1911–1920; deaths 1896–1920	FO 399/9–10
Odessa	births 1852–1919; baptisms 1893; marriages 1851–1916; deaths 1852–1919	FO 359/3–12
Poti	births 1871–1906; deaths 1871–1920	FO 399/13–14
Rostov	births 1891–1914; marriages 1904–1918; deaths 1906–1916	FO 398/1–9
St Petersburg (Petrograd, Leningrad)	baptisms 1818–1840; burials 1821–1840. Independent denomination. (Indexed in RG 43)	RG 4/4605 [2]
St Petersburg (Petrograd, Leningrad)	births, baptisms, marriages, deaths and burials 1840–1918 (with an index for 1886–1917 in RG 33/162)	RG 33/144–152 [2]
St Petersburg (Petrograd, Leningrad)	births 1856–1938; marriages 1892–1917; deaths 1897–1927	FO 378/3–9
St Petersburg (Petrograd, Leningrad)	marriages 1870–1890	FO 83 [3]
Sebastopol	births 1886–1898; marriages 1910; deaths 1893–1908	FO 399/3, 15–16
Theodosia (Feodosiya)	births 1904–1906; deaths 1907–1918	FO 399/17–18
Vladivostok	births 1911–1927; marriages 1916–1923; deaths 1908–1924	FO 510/1–10
Singapore	births 1922	RG 36 [2]
Somaliland (Somalia)	births 1905–1920 (partly indexed by RG 43/18)	RG 36 [2]
Spain [1]	deaths 1831–1920	RG 35/20–44 [2]
Aguilas	births 1875–1911; deaths 1874–1911	FO 920/1–2
Balearic Islands	births, marriages, deaths (1815–1880)	FO 214/51–53
Bilbao	deaths 1855–1870	FO 729/1
Cartagena	births 1847–1887; marriages 1858–1904; deaths 1855–1871	FO 920/3–6
Garrucha	births 1876–1890; deaths 1883–1905	FO 920/7–8
Madrid	marriages 1846–1890	FO 83 [3]
Madrid	registers of British subjects 1835–1895, 1906–1931	FO 445
Pormàn	births 1907; deaths 1911	FO 920/9–10
Seville	births, marriages and deaths 1948	FO 332/14–16

1 You may also need to consult Yeo, *The British Overseas*.
2 Entries in RG 32–RG 36 are largely indexed by RG 43: at both the National Archives and the Family Records Centre.
3 Indexed in FO 802/239.

Sudan [1]	births 1916–1950; marriages 1907–1950; deaths 1917–1946 (partly indexed by RG 43/18)	RG 36 [2]
Surinam (Dutch Guiana)		
Paramaribo	births 1897–1966; marriages 1922–1929; deaths 1889–1965	FO 907/1–32
Sweden [1]	deaths 1831–1920	RG 35/20–44 [2]
Gothenburg	marriages 1845–1891	RG 33/153 [2]
Gothenburg	baptisms 1881–1890	FO 818/15
Hudiksvall	deaths 1884	FO 730/1
Oskarshamn	deaths 1887	FO 731/1
Stockholm	marriages 1847–1890	FO 83 [3]
Stockholm	births, marriages and deaths 1920–1938	FO 748
Switzerland [1]	marriages 1816–1833	FO 194/1
	deaths 1831–1920	RG 35/20–44 [2]
Geneva	births 1850–1934; marriages 1850–1933; deaths 1850–1923	FO 778/13–22
Lausanne	births 1886–1948; marriages 1887–1947; deaths 1887–1948	FO 910/1–20
Montreux	births 1902–1939; marriages 1927–1933; deaths 1903–1941	FO 911/1–3
Syria [1]		
Aleppo	baptisms and burials 1756–1800	SP 110/70
Damascus	births, marriages and deaths 1932–1938	FO 684/16–17
Tahiti		
Papeete	births 1818–1941; marriages 1845–1941; deaths 1845–1936	FO 687/22–23
Raiatea	births, marriages and deaths 1853–1890	FO 687/34, 36–38
Taiwan see **China** *Formosa*		
Tristan da Cunha	marriages 1871–1951; deaths 1892–1949 (Registers of births and baptisms, 1867–1955, were returned to Tristan da Cunha in 1982.)	PRO 30/65
Tunisia		
Bizerta	deaths 1898–1931	FO 870/1
Djerba	deaths 1925	FO 871/1
Gabes	deaths 1925	FO 872/1
Goletta	births 1885–1888	FO 878/1–2
Monastir	deaths 1905–1908	FO 873/1
Sfax	deaths 1896–1931	FO 874/1
Susa (Sousse)	deaths 1894–1931	FO 875/1

1 You may also need to consult Yeo, *The British Overseas*.
2 Entries in RG 32–RG 36 are largely indexed by RG 43: at both the National Archives and the Family Records Centre.
3 Indexed in FO 802/239.

Turkey [1]	deaths 1831–1920	RG 35/20–44 [2]
Adana	marriages 1913, 1942 and 1946	FO 609/1–3
Adrianople (Edirne)	births 1888–1912; marriages 1887–1914	FO 783/3–7
Ankara and Konieh	births 1895–1909	FO 732/1
Constantinople (Istanbul)	marriages 1885–1958	RG 33/154 [2]
Constantinople (Istanbul)	marriages 1895–1924	FO 441/1–35
Dardanelles	births 1900–1914	FO 733/1
Smyrna (Izmir)	baptisms, marriages and burials 1833–1849	RG 33/155 [2]
Trebizond	registers of British subjects 1836–1913	FO 526
Uganda [1]	marriages 1904–1910 (partly indexed by RG 43/18)	RG 36 [2]
United States of America [1]		
Florida, Pensacola	births 1880–1901; deaths 1879–1905	FO 885/1–2
Hawaii see **Hawaii**		
Louisiana, New Orleans	births 1850–1932; marriages 1850–1881; deaths 1850–1932	FO 581/15–19
Massachusetts, Boston	births 1871–1932; deaths 1902–1930	FO 706/1–3
Michigan, Detroit	births 1910–1969; marriages 1936–1937; deaths 1931–1945, 1949–1968	FO 700/44–53
Minnesota, St Paul	births 1943–1966; deaths 1944	FO 700/71–74
Missouri, Kansas City	births 1904–1922, 1944–1966; marriages 1958–1961; deaths 1920–1926, 1943–1949, 1952–1965	FO 700/54–60
Nebraska, Omaha	births 1906	FO 700/61
Ohio, Cincinnati	births 1929, 1943–1948, 1951–1958; deaths 1947, 1950–1955	FO 700/31–35
Ohio, Cleveland	births 1914–1930, 1944–1969; deaths 1948–1969	FO 700/36–43
Oregon, Portland	births 1880–1926; deaths 1929	FO 707/1–2
Pennsylvania, Pittsburgh	births 1954–1956	FO 700/63
Rhode Island, Providence	births 1902–1930; deaths 1920 (date of registration)	FO 700/8–9
Texas, Dallas	births 1951–1954; deaths 1951	FO 700/24–25
Texas, El Paso	births 1916–1930; deaths 1914–1926	FO 700/26–27
Texas, Galveston	births 1838–1918; deaths 1850–1927	FO 701/23–24

1 You may also need to consult Yeo, *The British Overseas*.
2 Entries in RG 32–RG 36 are largely indexed by RG 43: at both the National Archives and the Family Records Centre.
3 Indexed in FO 802/239.

Washington, Aberdeen	births 1916; deaths 1914	FO 700/22–23
Washington, Tacoma	births 1896–1921; deaths 1892–1907	FO 700/20–21
Venezuela [1]	marriages 1836–1838	RG 33/155 [2]
West Indies		
Antigua	baptisms and burials 1733–1734, 1738–1745; marriages 1745	CO 152/21, 25
Barbados	baptisms and burials 1678–1679	CO 1/44
Cuba	baptisms 1847–1848; marriages 1842–1849	RG 33/155 [2]
Curaçao	births 1897–1966; marriages 1922–1929; deaths 1889–1965	FO 907/1–32
Danish (US) Virgin Islands i.e.,		
St Croix	deaths 1849–1870	RG 35/4 [2]
St John	deaths 1849–1872	RG 35/4 [2]
St Thomas	deaths 1849–1870	RG 35/4–7 [2]
Dominica		
Aux Caves	births 1870–1905	FO 376/1
Aux Caves	deaths 1870–1905	FO 376/2
Dominican Republic	births 1868–1932; marriages 1921–1928; burials 1849–1910; deaths 1874–1889	FO 683/2–6
Guadeloupe	deaths 1836–1871	RG 35/16 [2]
Guiana (Dutch) see **Surinam**		
Guyana (French)	deaths 1836–1871	RG 35/16 [2]
Haiti	births 1833–1850; marriages 1833–1893; deaths 1833–1850	FO 866/14, 21–22
Haiti	births 1870–1907	FO 376/1–2
Haiti	deaths 1836–1871	RG 35/16 [2]
Martinique	deaths 1836–1871	RG 35/16 [2]
Montserrat	baptisms and burials 1721–1729; marriages 1721–1729	CO 152/18, 25
Nevis	baptisms and burials 1726–1727, 1733–1734, 1740–1745	CO 152/16, 21, 25
St Kitts	baptisms and burials 1721–1730, 1733–1734, 1738–1745; marriages 1733–1734, 1738–1745	CO 152/18, 21, 25
Zanzibar	births 1916–1918; marriages 1917–1919; deaths 1916–1919	RG 36 [2]

1 You may also need to consult Yeo, *The British Overseas*.
2 Entries in RG 32–RG 36 are largely indexed by RG 43: at both the National Archives and the Family Records Centre.
3 Indexed in FO 802/239.

9 Inheritance: general advice on wills and probate

9.1 Wills and administrations
9.2 Who left wills?
9.3 Finding wills and administrations after 1858
9.4 Finding wills and administrations before 1858: an overview
9.5 Finding wills and administrations before 1858: where to look
9.6 Understanding a will
9.7 Death duty registers, 1796–1903: a useful short cut
9.8 Inheritance: general advice on wills and probate: bibliography

Important general advice is that when looking for a will you need to think first about probate, when the will is proved in court. Wills are usually stored and accessed by the date of probate, not the date of the making of the will, nor the date of death.

For probate records in the National Archives, see 10.

- Was the will proved in England and Wales? Or Scotland? (go to 13.1) Or Ireland? (see 14.1)
- Was the will proved after January 1858? (see 9.3)
- If before 1858, was it proved in the PCC? (see 10.3)
- If a will can't be found, what about looking for a grant of administration? (see 10.7)
- If there is nothing in the PCC, was a more local court used? (go to 9.5 and 9.7)
- Is there anywhere else to look? (see 9.2, 10.4 and 10.14)

9.1 Wills and administrations

Inheritance takes place with or without a will: a will just expresses the previous owner's intentions as to what should happen to his or her property. Different rules have governed inheritance over the centuries. If there was no will, the relevant rules of the time would apply, but because many people wanted to ensure that something different happened, they left wills. Wills are among the best sources for family history: on average, a will names about ten other people as well as giving details about the person whose will it is. You may have a collection of family wills already; if not, an official copy should exist. The executors named in a will took the original will (or a copy of it authorised by a notary to be an exact copy) to be proved as valid by a probate court; they then paid to have another copy written in the court's register. Administrations were granted by the court as an authority to proceed if the deceased left no will and there was property to dispose of or debts to sort out. They are not as informative, but are better than nothing.

The following vocabulary may be helpful before going any further:

- **Testator or testatrix:** the man or woman who left the will;
- **Executor or executrix:** the man or woman named in the will to 'execute' it – to put it into practice;
- **Probate:** the recognition by a court that the will was valid. Can also mean the copy of the will returned to the executors to use as their legal authority to act;
- **Intestate:** a man or woman dying without leaving a valid will;
- **Administrator or administratrix:** the man or woman appointed by the court to administer either the intestate's estate according to law, or the estate of a testator where the executor has failed to act;
- **Grant of administration:** the grant of a commission to the administrator to settle the estate according to the court's rules. Sometimes known as an 'admon'.

If possible, look for wills of relatives and executors or of other people mentioned in the will, or even other people from the same place and time. You may find references to your person that will help build up a rounded view of the circle of kinship, friendship and business contacts of their social world. This is becoming a much more feasible option as wills are becoming more accessible through good searchable indexes.

9.2 Who left wills?

There are no national figures for wills proved before 1858. In 1858, the new Court of Probate for England and Wales proved 21,653 wills – about 10 per cent of the 210,972 people who died that year. Of men who died that year, 21 per cent left a will or had an administration proved; for women, the figure was 8.6 per cent.

Not everybody needed to leave a will nor, if they did, to have their will proved by the court. Very small estates did not have to be submitted for probate. Many people left a will that was implemented informally, by agreement of all the family, without ever going near a probate court to prove the will. Effectively, this could only happen if everyone was agreed, the estate was simple and no debts were involved. If you are very lucky, you may perhaps find these unproven wills in personal papers, but they will not be in the probate court records. This informality seems to have dwindled as inheritance taxes became more common in the early nineteenth century; as the government became involved in what happened to any property, so the pressure to use the probate courts increased. Although wills disposing of a very small estate did not have to go through this procedure, many did. Surviving wills tend to be the ones that were proved before a court of probate (that is, judged by the court to be an accurate representation of the deceased's lawful intentions).

Poor people had very little to bequeath (although we do find at least some wills of pauper, for example, the rare 1840 will of Simon Bales, Cabinet Maker now an inmate in Saint Margaret's and Saint Johns Evangelist Poor House in the City of Westminster, Middlesex). Others may have been sufficiently well off, but not had the control of any property – for example, most wives during the life of their husbands (before the Married Women's Property Act of 1882). Yet even wives could leave a will with their husband's permission (Temperance Sawle, Wife of Tywardreth, Cornwall 18 June 1658) and women who were unmarried or widowed could and did leave wills freely (Elizabeth Wynne, Spinster of Mold, Flintshire 27 October 1750; Ann Oldman, Widow of Langwathby, Cumberland 07 May 1850). In fact, the records of one of the main will courts (the Prerogative Court of Canterbury or PCC) show that about 30 per cent of wills were left by women. (All the above examples come from this court (PROB 11): see 10 for how to find these and other wills in the PCC.)

But most wills were left by men with a reasonable amount of property (or those owed money by the government, for example, by the Army or Navy). Most were trying to alter the standard course of the inheritance laws of the country to suit the particular circumstances of their family. These laws originally meant that a fixed portion would go to a wife for her life and the rest would go to the eldest son. Over the centuries, these rules changed, but if anyone wanted to impose their own ideas on how the family should be catered for after their death, a will was the way to do it.

Many people of course died leaving no will but with affairs that needed settling. Others may have left a will, but one that was declared invalid by the probate court. In either of these cases, the probate court could be applied to for a grant of letters of administration. Administrations tended to be sought only if there were potential problems, such as underage children, no obvious heir, unsettled debts and so on.

For a specialist overview of using wills and many other (often under-used) probate records for family history, try Grannum and Taylor, *Wills and Other Probate Records*. Herber gives an excellent explanation in *Ancestral Trails* of the varying laws, customs and legal practices governing inheritance, and thus how wills were not an expression of a free choice as to the disposal of property. If you have managed to find an early will, you may find it illuminating to read *When Death Us Do Part: Understanding and Interpreting the Probate Records of Early Modern England* (edited by Arkell, Evans and Goose). As with all evidence from the past, the more you know about the context in which a document was made, the less likely you are to misunderstand it.

9.3 Finding wills and administrations after 1858

Wills were proved (and administrations granted) from 12 January 1858 onwards before the new national Court of Probate. This had a principal London registry and 40 district registries throughout England and Wales. A single printed index covering all wills and administrations in all registries was produced for each year from 1858. Its full title is the National Probate Calendar and it includes entries for both testators and intestates (in different sequences up to 1870). It can provide:

- Full name and address (and sometimes occupation);
- Full name of executors or administrators (and addresses 1858–1892): omitted after 1968;
- Relationship to the deceased (before 1892): omitted after 1968;
- Date and place of death;
- Date and place of probate or administration grant;
- Value of estate;
- For married women (not widows), the husband's name.

The National Archives and the Family Records Centre have copies of the National Probate Calendar for 1858–1943. Similar sets are held by the Guildhall, the Society of Genealogists and many other local record offices or libraries. So far, the National Probate Calendar is not available online, but the probate service has expressed an intention to put it online, so watch out for developments. It would be a fantastic resource, as the data included is so good. The Court has its own Probate Searchroom (address in 62) with a full set of copies of the National Probate Calendar where you can buy and receive a scanned copy of a will within an hour. You can also write to the Postal Searches & Copies Dept, York Probate Sub-Registry, 1st Floor, Castle Chambers, Clifford Street, York, YO1 9RG, giving the full name, address and date of death of the deceased and stating what you require. You can find the fees, and the relevant form, at **www.hmcourts-service.gov.uk/cms/1226.htm**.

If you want to know more about the actual procedure involved in getting a grant of probate or letters of administration, look at *Ham's Inland Revenue Yearbook*, which gives contemporary instructions. The National Archives' Library has copies of this annual work (under slightly varying titles) from 1875 to 1930.

9.4 Finding wills and administrations before 1858: an overview

Before 1858, wills were proved in over 200 church courts, whose records are scattered among many local record offices, with the National Archives holding the wills, administrations and other records of the top-level court, the Prerogative Court of Canterbury or PCC (see 10 for fuller advice on these). There is as yet no national union index to wills or administrations. A2A at **www.nationalarchives.gov.uk/a2a** is worth searching by name, as it contains many references to probate copies of wills in solicitors' papers and family papers, but it does not act as an index to the records of the church courts. However, the situation is slowly becoming much easier, as record offices start making wills searchable online. For some courts (such as the PCC or the Cheshire courts) you can search will indexes online by name, place, occupation or date, or any combination of these; for others you still have to rely on published or unpublished paper indexes.

Most wills in record offices now have published indexes, thanks to the work of the British Records Society and others. A record office will have indexes for the records they hold, but they may not have indexes for records held by other offices. The Society of Genealogists is probably the best place to search efficiently over a wide range of indexes, although the Library at the National Archives has a good collection of British Record Society publications. Another option is to use the services provided by the Family History Centres of the Church of Jesus Christ of Latter-day Saints at a number of locations across the world. You can investigate this option by searching their library database at **www.familysearch.com**.

The National Archives website contains a searchable index to, and images of, over one million wills proved in the Prerogative Court of Canterbury (the PCC – the only UK probate court records we hold) between 1384 and January 1858 (PROB 11 and PROB 1). Other archives are following, but with over 200 church courts proving wills before 1858, these are major and expensive projects, so we are really in a halfway house with wills. Some are so easy to search that you should just look on the off chance; others require the traditional family historian's skills of patient detective work.

9.5 Finding wills and administrations before 1858: where to look

The records of only one of the church courts, the Prerogative Court of Canterbury (PCC) are kept at the National Archives. This court was basically at the top of a hierarchy. As such it contains wills, in theory from wealthier people only, from all counties – in numbers ranging from under 1,000 from Westmorland to over 200,000 from Middlesex. Some executors chose to have wills proved in this court even though the will could quite easily have been proved in a lower court. As time went by, the definition of wealth (as fixed in 1604) became much less of a barrier, and so more people went to the PCC as a matter of course. Because PCC wills are now so easy to find in our Documents Online service, it is always worth trying a search on **www.nationalarchives.gov.uk/documentsonline/wills.asp** before looking anywhere else.

However, most people used the appropriate local church court, perhaps an archdeacon's court or a bishop's court. Even in the late 1850s, just before the national court was established, the PCC was only proving about 8,500 wills a year (compared to the national total of 21,653 in 1858). The courts did not follow county boundaries but ecclesiastical ones and it can be quite a problem to find out which is relevant. For 1796 onwards, the death duty records provide this information in many cases: see 9.7 for this short cut. Unfortunately A2A does not help here very much, as catalogues of wills seem to be either among the legacy data of record offices and have not yet been catalogued electronically or they have been catalogued as standalone applications. One single place to look for all wills before 1858 would be a wonderful boon for family, local and economic historians.

Maps of the areas covered by each church court and details of their surviving records are given in Gibson's very useful and inexpensive *A Simplified Guide to Probate Jurisdictions*. However, because more people know the county where a person lived rather than which archdeaconry they lived in, the following table is for English **counties**. It will give you an idea of where to look *after* you have tried the PCC wills. The second column gives you an indication of how many people from that county had wills proved in the PCC. (For a further discussion see 10.2.)

Contact details for these record offices are available in 62 and at **www.nationalarchives.gov.uk/archon**. In addition, many people have done a huge amount of indexing, transcribing, etc. The best place to find the results is under the probate section for the relevant county at **www. genuki.org.uk**.

County of residence	Wills from this county in the PCC	Where else to investigate	Any local indexes or records online?
Bedfordshire	5,805	Bedfordshire and Luton Archives	–
Berkshire	19,687	Berkshire Record Office; Oxfordshire Record Office; Wiltshire and Swindon Record Office	– – **www.wiltshire.gov.uk**
Bucking-hamshire	13,288	Centre for Buckinghamshire Studies; Oxfordshire Record Office; Hertfordshire Archives	– –
Cambridge-shire	9,191	Cambridgeshire Record Office; Cambridge University Library; Suffolk Record Office	– – –
Cheshire	3,938	Cheshire and Chester Archives	**www.cheshire.gov.uk** 130,000 entry index covering 1492–1940
Cornwall	7,466	Cornwall Record Office	–
Cumberland	2,085	Cumbria Record Office; Lancashire Record Office	– –

County of residence	Wills from this county in the PCC	Where else to investigate	Any local indexes or records online?
Derbyshire	4,722	Derbyshire Record Office; Lichfield Record Office	– **www.genuki.org.uk/ big/eng/DBY/ ProbateRecords/ about.html**
Devon	27,083	Devon Record Office; Cornwall Record Office; Dorset Record Office; Wiltshire and Swindon Record Office	– – – **www.wiltshire.gov.uk**
Dorset	14,838	Dorset History Centre	–
Durham	2,440	Durham University Library Archives	–
Essex	27,759	Essex Record Office; London Metropolitan Archives; Guildhall Library	– – –
Gloucester-shire	31,011	Gloucestershire Record Office	**www.gloucestershire. gov.uk www.bristol-city. gov.uk**
Hampshire	23,958	Hampshire Record Office	–
Herefordshire	6,636	Herefordshire Record Office; National Library of Wales	– Planned: **www.llgc.org.uk**
Hertfordshire	17,686	Hertfordshire Archives; Huntingdon Record Office; Essex Record Office; London Metropolitan Archives; Guildhall Library	– – – – –
Huntingdon-shire	3,358	Huntingdon Record Office	–
Kent	52,648	Centre for Kentish Studies; London Metropolitan Archives	– –
Lancashire	6,816	Lancashire Record Office	–
Leicestershire	6,980	Leicestershire Record Office	–
Lincolnshire	10,729	Lincolnshire Archives	–
London	86,233	London Metropolitan Archives; Guildhall Library; Lambeth Palace Library; City of Westminster Archives Centre	– – – –
Middlesex	201,133	As London	–
Monmouth-shire	2,947	National Library of Wales; Herefordshire Record Office	Planned: **www.llgc.org.uk**
Norfolk	14,366	Norfolk Record Office	–
Northampton-shire	11,068	Northamptonshire Record Office; Leicestershire Record Office	– –
Northum-berland	2,693	Durham University Library Archives	–

County of residence	Wills from this county in the PCC	Where else to investigate	Any local indexes or records online?
Nottingham-shire	3,172	Nottinghamshire Archives	–
Oxfordshire	15,042	Oxfordshire Record Office; Bodleian Library	– –
Rutland	1,796	Northamptonshire Record Office; Leicestershire Record Office	– –
Shropshire	12,537	Lichfield Record Office; Herefordshire Record Office; National Library of Wales	– – Planned: www.llgc.org.uk
Somerset	31,250	Somerset Archives; Bristol Record Office	– www.somerset.gov.uk www.bristol-city. gov.uk
Staffordshire	8,458	Lichfield Record Office	–
Suffolk	16,120	Suffolk Record Office; Norfolk Record Office	– –
Surrey	70,754	London Metropolitan Archives; Lambeth Palace Library; Hampshire Record Office	– – –
Sussex	19,147	East Sussex Record Office; West Sussex Record Office	– –
Warwickshire	15,581	Lichfield Record Office; Worcestershire Record Office; Shakespeare Birthplace Trust; Warwickshire Record Office;	– – – –
Westmorland	866	Cumbria Record Office	–
Wiltshire	19,830	Wiltshire and Swindon Record Office; Hampshire Record Office; Gloucestershire Record Office	– – www.wiltshire.gov.uk
Worcester-shire	11,841	Worcestershire Record Office; Herefordshire Record Office	– –
Yorkshire	13,600	Borthwick Institute;	www.britishorigins. com for indexes of 10,000 wills from the Prerogative and Exchequer Courts of York 1267–1500; and of 25,000 wills from the 54 peculiar courts of the Province of York 1383–1883
		Cheshire and Chester Archives; Cumbria Record Office; Durham University Library Archives; Nottinghamshire Archives; Lancashire Record Office; Leeds District Archives; West Riding Registry of Deeds	www.cheshire.gov.uk – – – – – –

County of residence	Wills from this county in the PCC	Where else to investigate	Any local indexes or records online?
Wales	12,894	(see 12) National Library of Wales; Herefordshire Record Office	Planned: **www.llgc.org.uk**
Ireland	4,537	(see 14)	
Scotland	3,879	(see 13)	
Channel Islands	1,842	(see 16)	
Isle of Man	164	(see 15)	

The rules on where the executors should take a will to prove it were:

- if the deceased held property in *one* archdeaconry, go to the archdeacon's court;
- if the deceased held property if in *more than one* archdeaconry but within one diocese, use the bishop's diocesan court;
- if the deceased held personal property worth over £5 in two distinct dioceses or jurisdictions, go to the archbishop's provincial court, known as the Prerogative Court of York (PCY) or the Prerogative Court of Canterbury (PCC);
- if the deceased held property in both provinces, use both the PCY and the PCC.

The province of York covered Yorkshire, Durham, Northumberland, Westmorland, Cumberland, Lancashire, Cheshire, Nottinghamshire and the Isle of Man; Canterbury covered the rest of England and Wales.

With the English Civil War, the situation grew complicated as there were two rival PCCs, one with the King at Oxford between April 1643 and March 1646 and one in London from November 1644. In the end, the London court took over the records of the Oxford court, destroyed its register but kept the wills brought before it: these are now searchable in PROB 10 on our catalogue (and may go into Documents Online). Some executors had the wills re-registered in London, others did not bother.

Between 1653 and 1660 a single court administered almost all probate business for England and Wales. (There may have been a falling off in the proving of wills from more distant parts of the country; some wills were later lodged with the restored Prerogative Court of York, for example.) The new national court was called the Court for the Proving of Wills and Granting Administrations. Its records are kept in unbroken series with those of the Prerogative Court of Canterbury. It was a much busier court than the PCC, proving 9,510 wills in 1658 (its busiest year) rather than the 2,000 or so that the PCC was proving in a good year on either side of the Civil War. The PCC did not achieve this amount of business again until just before it was abolished in 1858.

If someone (subject or foreign) died overseas leaving property in England and Wales (including Bank of England stock or stock in one of the great companies such as the East India Company) then all the usual rules were ignored and the will was proved at the PCC. See **www. originsnetwork.com** for an online index to Bank of England will extracts, 1717–1845. This dying overseas rule also brought in many soldiers and sailors (see 10.2 and 28.2.1).

9.6 Understanding a will

Once you have found a will and read through it, you may get the impression that you are reading, in your ancestor's own words, about his faith or his affections for different members of the family. Be careful here as this may be a false impression. Wills were often written in formulaic language by clerks or lawyers. Nevertheless, they did express the wishes of the testator (person leaving the will). For example, a declaration of faith is likely to have been one acceptable to the testator, even if not in his own words.

The evidence found in a will needs to be interpreted with caution. Wills were originally written to alter the normal course of inheritance law, which would otherwise be applied.

- The failure to leave a bequest to a near relative does not necessarily mean bad feeling. If an eldest son was to inherit the real estate (land), as his father's heir-at-law then his father's will did not need to mention him or his inheritance. Similarly, married daughters may not be men-tioned if they had had property settled upon them at the time of their marriages.
- The will might make no mention of real estate (usually land). Certain types of real estate, depending upon the terms of tenure, could be left by will after 1540; from 1660 the only exception to this is land held by copyhold, which was not devisable by will until 1815.
- There is no guarantee that all legatees would be still alive at the time probate was granted, or that the testator necessarily left sufficient property or money to cover all bequests.
- The words *father, brother* and *son, mother, sister* and *daughter* may be used to refer to in-laws as well as blood relatives. The term *cousin* was used for all types of kin.

9.7 Death duty registers, 1796–1903: a useful short cut

Death duty registers give different information to wills and much better information than administrations. (See 52.8 for more details of the tax.) They can also provide a good first place to look for further information on where to find wills and administrations between 1796 and 1858, when so many probate courts existed. This is a very helpful short cut to finding the actual will or administration. However, not all estates were subject to the death duties: current thinking is that about 25 per cent were from 1796 to 1805, going up to 75 per cent between 1805 and 1815.

These records are in registers in IR 26 (partly arranged by court of probate and indexed by IR 27). The registers can be seen for 1796–1858 on microfilm at both the Family Records Centre and the National Archives, and for 1858–1903 at the National Archives: the indexes are all at both sites. However, for 1796–1811 the main means of access is **www.nationalarchives. gov.uk/documentsonline**, where over 66,000 entries from the 'country courts' – the courts other than the Prerogative Court of Canterbury – are searchable by name. If you find an entry for someone you are interested in here you can download a copy of the death duty entry. You can also use the index to find court of probate. You can then get in touch with the local record office that holds those records to get a copy of the will.

Copy wills were also once among the death duty records but have largely been destroyed. Those for Devon and Somerset (from the major local probate courts but not from all) were sent to the county record offices to try to fill some of the gaps caused by the loss of local probate records in the bombing of Exeter in the Second World War. For information on Devon wills, see **www.devon.gov.uk/index/community/the_county/record_ office.htm**. For more on Somerset wills, see **www.somerset.gov.uk/ archives/Wills.htm**. The death duty copies of Somerset wills that were extracted from Inland Revenue records have been indexed by Hawkings: these indexes can be seen at the Family Records Centre and Somerset. (For information, there are 4,482 entries from Somerset and Devon in the country court death duty registers, 1793–1811, that are now searchable in Documents Online.)

9.8 Inheritance: general advice on wills and probate: bibliography

T ARKELL, N EVANS and N GOOSE, eds, 'When Death Us Do Part: Understanding and Interpreting the Probate Records of Early Modern England', *Local Population Studies*, Supplement (2000)

J COX, *Affection Defying the Power of Death: Wills, Probate and Death Duty Records* (FFHS, 1993)

J COX, *Hatred pursued beyond the grave* (HMSO, 1993)

A L ERICKSON, 'An Introduction to Probate Accounts', G H Martin and P Spufford, eds, *Records of the Nation* (British Record Society, 1990), pp. 273–286

J S W GIBSON, *A Simplified Guide to Probate Jurisdictions: Where to look for wills* (FFHS, 4th edn 1994)

K GRANNUM, 'Enduring Benefits', *Ancestors* 23 (2004)

K GRANNUM and N TAYLOR, *Wills and Other Probate Records: A practical guide to researching your ancestors' last documents* (The National Archives, 2004)

Ham's Inland Revenue Yearbook (annual: National Archives library has 1875–1930)

D HAWKINGS, *Index of Somerset Estate Duty Office Wills and Letters of Administration 1805–1811* (1995)

D HAWKINGS, *Index of Somerset Estate Duty Office Wills 1812–1857* (2 vols, 1995)

M D HERBER, *Ancestral Trails* (Society of Genealogists, 2004)

N NEWINGTON-IRVING, *Will indexes and other probate material in the Library of the Society of Genealogists* (SoG, 1996)

M OVERTON, *A Bibliography of British Probate Inventories* (Newcastle, 1983)

10 Inheritance: wills and probate records at the National Archives

10.1 Wills and administrations at the National Archives

The National Archives holds the records created or collected by the Prerogative Court of Canterbury (PCC), 1383–1858, including the wills of the Court for the Proving of Wills and Granting Administrations, 1653–1660. The PCC, despite its name, sat in London at Doctors' Commons near St Paul's Cathedral. It was the court covering the Archbishopric of Canterbury and had some jurisdiction over the Archbishopric of York, as Canterbury was the superior province in the church.

Administrations issued by the PCC date from 1559 to 1858. The main series of wills, PROB 11, is now searchable and viewable on Documents Online. The original wills of some famous people (put in an artificial collection called PROB 1) can also be seen online. These will be joined (we hope by the end of 2006) by PROB 6 and PROB 7, covering administrations. Administration data is not as full as that in wills, but making it easy to find will be a huge benefit. All the other series mentioned below have to be seen at the National Archives.

One thing you will not get from the registered wills or administrations is the date of death. The index gives date of probate, and the will gives the date of writing. From the mid-eighteenth century (and earlier if you are lucky) you may be able to find the date of death in PROB 14 (1657–1858 ☐)

if the executor or administrator could not travel to London to be sworn before the court. A commission was issued for him or her to be sworn locally: PROB 14 records these warrants. Where the deceased's estate was too small for the executor or administrator to be charged fees this fact is noted at the foot of the warrant, generally by the use of the term 'pauper'. In some cases, if the registered copy of the will in PROB 11 does not give information about marital status, occupation or place of residence it may be found in the probate act books, in PROB 8.

The huge project to make copies of all registered PCC wills available online started by indexing them from the original entry books of registered wills in PROB 11. The new index is searchable online free at **www.nationalarchives.gov.uk/documentsonline/wills.asp**. Having found a relevant index entry, you can download a copy of the will for a small fee. Don't bother to print the first page, which is just a cover sheet. You can still order copies in the traditional way by contacting the National Archives – and don't worry if you have a reference from a printed source in the old format such as 64 Fairfax or 28 Horne, as these can be translated.

Once you have your copy of a will from the registers in PROB 11, you may hit a snag – the writing. Entries were made in the court's register using a special form of handwriting, quite distinct from the everyday writing of the time. (Many courts had their own distinctive form of court hand for formal documents, based on medieval hands, which got more peculiar as the centuries passed.) If you find that the hand is just too much, you can hire one of the independent researchers from our list at **www.nationalarchives. gov.uk/irlist/** or you can order a copy of the original will, which should be in a more legible hand. See 2.6.

Remember too that death duty was imposed from 1796: records of this tax provide a reality check on the actual size of estates and also on what actually happened to property after death. See 9.7 and 52.8.

10.2 The Prerogative Court of Canterbury: who used it?

The index's major benefit (apart from reducing search times from hours to seconds) is that it includes the testator's description of himself or herself and place of residence when the will was written. We can at last begin to answer the question of who used the PCC. You can have a lot of fun discovering the answers to your own questions, such as who were the people in my ancestor's town or village or in his trade, or who had the same strange forename or surname.

I tried a few queries to give a flavour of what can be found and came up with the following:

- 3,725 wills of men in the Service of the Royal African Company of England of Cabo Corso Castle, Coast of Guinea, West Africa (high death rate there);
- 59 wills of inhabitants of the village of Trumpington, Cambridgeshire, from

1504–1855: bankers, butchers, gentlemen, husbandmen, innkeepers, clerics, professors, weavers, widows, wives, yeomen;

- 113,536 gentlemen; 70,463 Royal Navy men; 62,771 yeomen; 11,912 farmers; 10,494 husbandmen; 2,861 servants; 2,088 tanners; 1,665 men (and 2 spinsters) taking a voyage; 1,062 coachmen; 885 excise men; 738 periwig or peruke makers; 447 clockmakers; 384 pawnbrokers; 76 trumpeters; 61 duchesses; 47 policemen; 21 maids; 5 ferrymen; 1 diver.

It is hard to get numbers for the thousands of men in the Army because they don't describe themselves in set ways. For the Navy you can usually rely on some variant of His Majesty's Ship, or HMS. Unfortunately, we did not put in a marker for male or female: a lost opportunity, really, to find out about, say, women in business or male midwives.

The number of wills from each county makes clear the bias towards the south and south-west – but also shows that wills came to the PCC from all over England (see 12 for Wales).

200,000 +	Middlesex
50,000–100,000	London, Surrey, Kent
20,000–49,999	Somerset, Gloucestershire, Essex, Devon, Hampshire
10,000–19,999	Wiltshire, Berkshire, Sussex, Hertfordshire, Suffolk, Warwickshire, Oxfordshire, Dorset, Norfolk, Yorkshire, Buckinghamshire, Shropshire, Worcestershire, Northamptonshire, Lincolnshire
5,000–9,999	Cambridgeshire, Staffordshire, Cornwall, Leicestershire, Lancashire, Herefordshire, Bedfordshire
1,000–4999	Derbyshire, Cheshire, Huntingdonshire, Nottinghamshire, Monmouthshire, Northumberland, Durham, Cumberland, Rutland
Under 1,000	Westmorland

Figures for each county are given in 9.5. For breakdowns by Welsh, Scottish and Irish counties, see 12.3, 13.2 and 14.1 respectively.

Although the PCC records relate mainly to the wealthier sections of society in the province of Canterbury, the great prestige of the court attracted business to it that strictly speaking belonged to lower courts. As time went on, the declining value of money meant that the £5 barrier set in 1604 (to protect the income of the lower courts) became less of a restriction. In the eighteenth and nineteenth centuries the property of more and more peoples' estates came within its jurisdiction. From 1810, the Bank of England would not accept probate from any court except the PCC for holders of Bank of England stock. In the decade before the Court closed for business on 9 January 1858, it was proving about 40 per cent of all wills in England and Wales. In its last day, it proved 48 wills from England, 3 from Wales, 2 from Prussia and one each from Scotland, Belgium, France, Venice, Bermuda, Madras and Bengal.

Anyone who died *overseas* with property in England or Wales was supposed to have their estate handled by the PCC. The largest number of people affected by the 'dying overseas' rules were poor seamen. This brought into the PCC over 6,000 wills of seamen of slight value before 1815. In 1815, the rules changed, and the affairs of seamen dying with less than £20 wages owing were in theory directed to their local probate court. In fact, between 1816 and 1858 over 500 seamen had their wills proved by the PCC – men like *Philip Thomas Roza, Late Seaman on Board the South Sea Whaler Japan on her Voyage from the South Seas, 1834* or *Oliver Coxbury, seaman on board the Sir Stephen Lushington in Bombay Harbour, 1821*. Perhaps they all had over £20 owing.

As well as sailors, soldiers and merchants, some colonists or ex-colonists continued to hold property or debts in England and have their wills proved in the PCC. The wills are searchable online by place – try a term such as Africa, America, Australia, Bermuda, Canada, China, East Indies, New South Wales, New Zealand, Russia or West Indies. For America, see also Coldham's *American Wills and Administrations in the Prerogative Court of Canterbury, 1610–1857*: this has the benefit of covering administrations, which are otherwise hard to find.

10.3 PCC wills online: search tips

This index replaces the original indexes used by the court (which are in PROB 12). If you are familiar with the old printed indexes based on PROB 12, you may find that names are spelled slightly differently. Another point to note is that the will index online gives the domicile at the time the will was written, whereas the old indexes in (and based on) PROB 12 give the domicile of the testator at the time of death. These may be quite different, as a will could have been written decades before death.

In some cases, a name difference is a simple misreading (e.g., Sendamore for Scudamore), which we are happy to correct; in others, it is because the new index is done directly from the will. If a surname was not given in the will, it has not been supplied in the index. For example, you could not find Joseph Wilcocks from his index entry *Will of The Right Reverend Joseph Bishop of Rochester or Lord Bishop of Rochester, Dean of the Collegiate Church of Saint Peter Westminster 16 March 1756*. If you are looking for someone with a title, try treating the title as the surname. Again, we are happy to amend any entries.

Remember too that surnames can have all kinds of variant spellings: Taylor, Tayler, Tailor and Tailer can all appear and need to be searched separately. You can get round this by using wildcard searches, substituting an asterisk for letters, as long as you start with at least two letters. A search on Ta*l*r brought up several Taylours, as well as the four variants I had thought of. As a rule, if you are not successful try a less detailed search.

10.4 PCC original and other wills

So-called original wills are in PROB 10, arranged in alphabetic boxes by year and month of probate (which is given in the online index to PROB 11). Original wills survive in almost complete sequence from 1620: they are either the original will as drawn up and signed or a copy of that made before a notary. In either case, they are what the executor brought in to have proved. There is usually no factual advantage in looking at the originals if there are registered copies in PROB 11 – but there is a certain frisson in seeing them, and they can be easier to read. If you have the date of probate (given in Documents Online), you can search PROB 10, using an * in the 'Word of phrase' box and the year. You will have to browse through some pages to find the right month and letter. Here's an example – three John Smiths with wills proved in September 1818.

- From Documents Online (search on John Smith):
  - Will of John Smith, Merchant and His Britannic Majesty's Consul of Gothenburg, Sweden 23 September 1818 PROB 11/1608;
  - Will of John Smith, Cook of Christ Church in the University of Oxford, Oxfordshire 11 September 1818 PROB 11/1608;
  - Will of John Smith, Yeoman of Topsham, Devon 09 September 1818 PROB 11/1608.
- From the catalogue (search on * and 1818–1818):
  - PROB 10/4399 M–S 1818 Sept;
  - PROB 10/4400 S–W 1818 Sept.

This should be good enough to order a copy without coming in to the National Archives as the copying services factor in a small amount of time to locate documents in boxes.

Not all wills were registered in PROB 11 as executors had to pay extra for this service. Between 1383 and 1558 unregistered wills (now in PROB 10) are indicated in the old printed index by the letter F. Genuine cases of unregistered wills, particularly after 1660, are very rare. The exception here is during the Civil War, when there were two rival PCCs, one with the King at Oxford between April 1643 and March 1646 and one in London from November 1644. The London court in the end took over the records of the Oxford court and destroyed its register but kept the wills brought before it: these are now searchable in PROB 10 on our catalogue (and may go into Documents Online). Some executors had the wills re-registered in London; others did not bother.

Further collections of wills, usually copies or rejected wills, may be found in:

- PROB 20 ☑ 1623–1838. Most of these wills are contentious, generally having been brought into the court for a ruling as to its authenticity, and then rejected by the judge. PROB 20 includes a large number of precautionary wills made by sailors and others embarking on hazardous voyages;

- PROB 21 ⑦ 1623–1857. Copies of wills taken when the original was to be removed from the registry for exhibition in another court of law;
- PROB 22 ② 1782–1851. Wills lodged with the registry of the Prerogative Court of Canterbury for safe keeping. It is unlikely that any of the wills were proved. Most date from the 1820s–1850s;
- PROB 23 ② 1629–1827. Most of these are wills or relate to wills originally proved in inferior jurisdictions to the Prerogative Court of Canterbury.

10.5 Proving a will in the PCC

When a will was proved before the PCC the executors brought into court the original will or a notarised copy of it. A copy of the will was made by the court and a probate act (a commission, in the name of the Archbishop of Canterbury) was issued and attached by a seal to the copy will. These joined documents were then given to the executor as his authority to carry out the distribution of the estate according to the terms of the will. The whole thing was referred to as a 'probate'. You can often find these in other parts of our catalogue (e.g., C 109/406 Woodhead v Marriot: Probate of Martha Quincey 1830) or in the catalogues of other archives in A2A (e.g., from the East Sussex Record Office, Probate of the will of John Vinnall of Kingston, gent – ACC2327/48 – date: 1662).

The issue of the probate act was recorded in the probate act book (now in PROB 8 and PROB 9). The registry filed the will brought in by the executors, which is now in PROB 10 if it survives. If the executor paid a fee, a copy of the will would also be made in the Court's will registers, with a clause noting the granting of probate entered after the will (now PROB 11). The vast majority of wills proved before the Prerogative Court of Canterbury were registered.

Nuncupative wills (wills which were spoken before witnesses, not written down and signed) are in PROB 11, if registered. They are not identified as nuncupative in the online index. They usually start like this:

Memorandum that Anne Marshall of Bisham in the Countye of Berks Spinster beinge of good and perfecte mynde and memorie made her last will and Testament nuncupative in theis wordes followinge or the like effect PROB 11/135, fo. 266v.

Nuncupative wills are also identified as nuncupative in their probate clauses, and sometimes in the entries in the calendars of wills in PROB 12, PROB 13 and PROB 15.

The texts of proved wills were copied into large parchment registers (PROB 11) if the executors paid the fee. Almost all are in English; by the sixteenth century wills written in Latin are rare. Wills written in other modern European languages (usually Dutch and French) have an authenticated English translation. However, the probate clauses appended to the text of the wills and the texts of sentences (judgments) are in Latin until 1733, with the exception of those in registers for 1651 to 1660, which are in English. They generally follow a standard form, so this example should help make sense of others.

Probate clause of the will of William Christie
(prob 11/572, fo.212v)

Probatum fuit hujusmodi Testamentum apud London coram Venerabili viro Roberto Wood Legum Doctore Surrogato Venerabilis et Egregij viri Johannis Bettesworth Legum etiam Doctoris Curiae Praerogativae Cantuariensis Magistri Custodis sive Commissarij legitime constituti Vicesimo Secundo die Mensis Februarij Anno Domini Millesimo Septingentesimo Decimo nono Juramento Thomae Willisee Executoris unici in dicto Testamento nominati Cui commissa fuit Administratio omnium et Singulorum bonorum jurium et creditorum dicti defuncti De bene et fideliter administrando eadem ad Sancta Dei Evangelia Jurato. Examinatur.

English translation

This will was proved at London before the worshipful Robert Wood LL.D [Doctor of Laws] surrogate of the worshipful and wise John Bettesworth also LL.D Master Keeper or Commissary of the Prerogative Court of Canterbury lawfully constituted on the twenty-second day of the month of February 1719 [/20] by the oath of Thomas Willisee named sole executor in the said will to whom administration of all and singular the goods rights and credits of the said deceased was granted being sworn on the holy gospels to administer the same well and faithfully. Examined.

10.6 Complications with executors: various grants of administration

Once you have a copy of a registered will (from Documents Online) you may find that it has some unexpected notes about a grant of administration. Administration grants were not solely made if there was no will: they could be used to get round problems in executing a perfectly valid will.

- If the executor appointed in the will was unable (perhaps he had died before the testator) or unwilling to prove the will, letters of administration with will annexed were issued instead to someone else. This is noted in the probate clause, after the text of the will.

- If the executor died, or renounced the administration of the estate, before its distribution had been completed, letters of administration with will annexed of goods not administered (*de bonis non administratis*) were issued. This is noted in the margin of the register, alongside the text of the will.

- If more than one executor was appointed, and the executors sought probate at different dates (perhaps because one was abroad, or was underage) a subsequent grant of probate was made. This was called double probate and is also noted in the margin.

These marginal notes can be highly abbreviated, and often they are not as informative as the corresponding entries in the probate act books. These are arranged by date (PROB 8 ⑦ until 1781, PROB 9 ⑦ 1781–1858). If someone was appointed as an administrator with will annexed, they were required to enter into bonds for their proper administration of the estate, and such bonds are in the administration bond series (PROB 51 2 1541–1565, PROB 54 1601–1713 no list, PROB 46 7 1713–1858).

10.7 Intestates' estates, 1559–1858: grants of administration

If a person died leaving property or debts and no will, or a will that was declared invalid, a probate court could grant letters of administration to see the estate settled. The PCC, like other probate courts, granted letters of administration (where the estate came within the jurisdiction of the court) to people with a claim on an intestate's estate. Probate courts were normally required to grant administration of the estate to the deceased's widow or next of kin, as set down by statute in 1529. Administration of the estate of a married woman was granted to her husband. Sometimes administrations would be granted to creditors. The estates of illegitimate intestates who died unmarried and without issue were granted to the Crown; the Treasury received many letters from relatives asking if they could have letters of administration instead (now in T 4 7 for 1680–1819). The possessions of intestates with no next of kin reverted to the Crown: see TS 17 2.

Grants of administration were registered in the Administration Act Books 1559–1858 (PROB 6 7) or the Limited Administration Act Books 1810–1858 (PROB 7 7). These can be accessed at the National Archives or the Family Records Centre, by a particularly complicated set of finding aids. However, detailed advice on finding administrations is available at the National Archives and the Family Records Centre and as a research guide at **www.nationalarchives.gov.uk**.

The act book ordinarily records only the marital status and place of residence of the intestate, the name of the administrator and his or her relationship to the intestate and the date of the grant. From 1796, and in many cases before that date, a valuation of the deceased's personal estate is given in the margin. The court was required to grant administration to the deceased's next of kin, and the entry in the administration act book may therefore include the names of relatives who had ignored summonses to appear before the court, or who had renounced their claims to administer the estate. Be wary of assuming that a known relative (closer in blood than the person to whom administration was granted) had died by the time the grant was made merely because the known relative is not mentioned in the administration act book.

The information that the administration act books usually supply is:

- date of the grant of administration;
- name of the intestate;
- his or her parish of residence;
- name of the administrator;
- his or her relationship to the intestate;
- dates by which an inventory and an account had to be returned.

The administration act books may also give information about the marital status, occupations and places of death of the intestates. Information about intestates' occupations and places of residence becomes more frequent in later years. By the nineteenth century, administration act books often supply such details as the names of the regiment the intestate served in, or the name of street in which he or she lived at the time of death.

10.8 Understanding the administration act books

The administration act books in PROB 6 do not ordinarily give the complete texts of individual letters of administration; rather, they record the information unique to individual letters. The vast majority of the entries in the administration act books take the form of cursory formulaic summaries of the original grants. Except for the period 1651 to 1660, the act books are in Latin until 1733. From 1651 to 1660 and after 25 March 1733, the act books are in English, although certain technical phrases and abbreviations continued to be used in Latin.

Ordinary grant of administration
PROB 6/96, f 97^v

Johannes Bayly	_Tricesimo die Emanavit Commissio Elizabethae Bayly viduae Relictae Johannis Bayly nuper parochiae Sanctae Mariae Rotherhithe inComitatu Surriae sed in Nave Regia Le Dreadnought defuncti habentis &c [dum vixit et mortis suae tempore bona jura sive credita in diversis diocesibus sive peculiaribus jurisdictionibus sufficientia ad fundandum jurisdictionem Curiae Praerogativae Cantuariensis] ad Administrandum bona jura et credita dicti defuncti De bene &c [et fideliter administrando eadem ad sancta Dei evangelia] juratae_	_ultimus [dies] Novembris_ _ultimus [dies] Maij 1721_
John Bayly	On the thirtieth day a commission was issued to Elizabeth Bayly widow relict of John Bayly formerly of the parish of St Mary Rotherhithe in the county of Surrey but in the royal ship The Dreadnought deceased having etc [while he lived and at the time of his death goods rights or credits in different dioceses or peculiar jurisdictions sufficient to found the jurisdiction of the Prerogative Court of Canterbury] to administer the goods rights and credits of the said deceased having been sworn [on the holy gospels] to well and [faithfully administer the same]	last [day] of November last [day] of May 1721

- Letters omitted from the original texts on account of abbreviations have been supplied underlined. Words omitted from the original have been supplied underlined in square brackets.
- The first date in the right hand margin is the date by which the administrator was required to return an inventory of the intestate's personal estate. The second date is the date by which the administrator was required to return an account of his or her administration of the estate.

In some instances a grant was made limited to a particular part of the deceased's estate, or with special conditions attached. Limited grants of the estates of soldiers and sailors limited to their wages were commonly made to creditors of the soldiers and sailors who had advanced them money on the security of their wages. Grants limited to Bank of England and East India Company stock held both by foreign nationals whose property was otherwise held in their countries of residence and by trustees of married women become increasingly common in the eighteenth and nineteenth centuries. They may give detailed information about the relationship of the administrator to the deceased. Before 1744 limited and special grants of administration are generally to be found in PROB 6 at the front of the section for the month in which they were passed. From 1744 (PROB 6/120) they are entered either in one group at the beginning or end of the dif-ferent seat sections of the administration act books or at the beginning of the appropriate monthly sub-sections of the seat in question. Limited and special grants of administration made after 1809 are entered in PROB 7 ⑦.

10.9 What did administrators do?

Administrators had first to enter into a bond with the court to ensure that they fulfilled their responsibilities. Bonds generally give the names, marital status, occupations and places of residence of the administrator and his or her sureties. Those for 1714–1857 are in PROB 46 ⑦.

Administrators were required to collect the credits owed to the intestate and to pay the debts of the intestate and the expenses of the estate (such as medical fees, funeral bills and fees for the maintenance of dependants). Statute and custom regulated the distribution of the estate after the payment of expenses and debts. One third of the estate was to be distributed to the wife of the intestate and the remaining part was to be distributed in equal portions among the children of the intestate. Distribution of the estate could not be made until one year after the grant of administration was made. Beneficiaries were required to enter into bonds committing them to refund their portions or parts of their portions (should it be necessary for them to do so) if the administrator needed to settle unanticipated debts of the estate. Husbands of intestates received the whole of their wives' personal estates.

A person with a claim to a share in an intestate's estate could seek a judicial distribution of the estate twelve months after the grant of administration was issued. This meant asking for an order from the court that required the administrator to distribute the estate in accordance with the Statute of Distributions. Such causes can be traced in the litigation series of the Prerogative Court of Canterbury and provide valuable evidence of the distribution of estates. Orders for the distribution of estates are in PROB 16 ⑦.

10.10 Disposing of the estate: inventories and accounts

The executors or administrators had to prove to the court that they had carried out their functions properly. To do this, they had to submit inventories of the deceased's moveable property (including debts) and accounts of their expenditure (sometimes including expenditure on children over several years). When the goods have already been disposed of, there is sometimes a declaration in place of an inventory. These can be quite informative because they give the details of where the goods went. Accounts can be particularly valuable, as they may continue for some years and include all kinds of information – payments for the maintenance of dependants, details of funeral or nursing costs, etc. The rate of survival for all these documents is very poor before 1666 and erratic for the later seventeenth and early eighteenth centuries. After the mid-eighteenth century they were only exhibited if the estate was subject to litigation, if the administrator or executor renounced his or her responsibilities or if the beneficiaries of the estate were children.

Inventories and accounts are relatively poorly used by family historians, despite being easy to find if they do exist.

1417–1660	Inventories Series I	PROB 2	②⑤	
1642–1722	Cause Papers	PROB 28	①	
1653–1721	Exhibits pre-1722	PROB 36	②⑤	
1661–1720	Parchment Inventories	PROB 4	②⑤	
1661–1732	Paper Inventories	PROB 5	②⑤	
1662–1720	Filed Exhibits with Inventories	PROB 32	②⑤	
1683–1858	Indexes to Exhibits	PROB 33	⑦	original indexes to exhibits in PROB 31 and PROB 37
1702, 1718–1782	Inventories Series II	PROB 3	②⑤	
1722–1858	Exhibits, Main Series	PROB 31	Ⓕ	index of wills; card indexes of names and places to the inventories and other exhibits
1783–1858	Cause Papers, Later Series	PROB 37	②⑤	

PROB 31 and PROB 37 are also indexed by place of residence and include many people resident in the Americas and East Indies.

Inventories listing the deceased's personal property and accounts, and recording executors' and administrators' receipts and expenditure, may provide the most illuminating evidence about the deceased's social status, wealth and business activities. For example, the inventories of the goods, chattels and credits of Richard Tyacke of Godolphin, Cornwall, submitted in 1826, account for a total value of over £25,000 (PROB 31/1235/1030). They list leases for term of lives (one of which was worthless as the person on whom the lease depended was on the point of death), shares in pilchard fishing (worthless), tin mines and merchant trade, debts owing and the farm stock and furniture.

With an inventory, remember that what is listed will be what belonged to the deceased. This may not be the entire furnishings of a house, as some may have belonged to other people and so are not listed.

10.11 Litigation before 1858

Wills in general and the settlement of estates have created a huge amount of litigation. The main arenas were the courts of probate (for disputes on the validity of a will or on the claims of persons seeking letters of administration) and the court of Chancery (for disputes about the terms of the will). A single will may have led to lawsuits in both the PCC and in Chancery at the same time.

Chancery records are described in 58: there are a couple of search techniques that may help you find disputes about a will. One, from 1714 onwards, is to search for the names of the executors (usually as defendants) in C 11–C 16: many cases have only been described as 'Smith v Jones', and do not give any indication that a will is in dispute. The other, for 1574–1714, is to use Coldham's index to over 26,000 disputed wills litigated in Chancery (the Inheritance Disputes Index), which is searchable online for a fee at **www.originsnetwork.com/**.

There are four main ways to discover if there was a dispute in the Prerogative Court of Canterbury (a 'cause' in PCC language). Remember that before the mid-1700s causes were known by the name of the plaintiff and not by the name of the person whose estate was being disputed. The first clue, until about 1800, may be from the will in PROB 11: there may be a sentence (judgement) entered after the probate clause or as a separate entry, if the victorious party had paid for this to be done. The second and easiest way is to check the card index to the initial proceedings (1661–1858) in PROB 18 Ⓕ. This is arranged in two parts, by name of cause (e.g., Smith *contra* Jones) and by name of the deceased testator or intestate. Thirdly, if you go to the relevant act book (PROB 6–PROB 9) or the PROB 12 ⑦ calendar, you may find a marginal note saying *by decree* or *by sentence* (sometimes abbreviated). This means that the estate was the subject of a lawsuit or cause. Lastly, if there was a dispute about an estate on which death duty was payable (after 1796), details are likely to be noted in the death duty register (see 9.7 and 52.8).

The stages through which a cause passed are recorded in the acts of court (PROB 29, PROB 30). These records are concerned with procedure and you may find other series of litigation records more fruitful. The main series to check are allegations (the initial complaint, by the plaintiffs) in PROB 18 Ⓕ, answers by the defendants in PROB 25, depositions in PROB 24 and PROB 26, cause papers in PROB 28 and PROB 37 and exhibits in PROB 31 and PROB 311. Scott, in *Wills and Other Probate Records*, gives a step by step account of finding records in two testamentary disputes. The basic procedure was very similar to that used by the equity courts.

	Annotations of existence of a cause		
1559–1858	Act Books: Administrations	PROB 6	F
1810–1858	Act Books: Limited Administrations	PROB 7	F
1526–1828	Act Books: Probates	PROB 8	7
1781–1858	Act Books: Limited Probates	PROB 9	7
1384–1858	Registered Copy Wills	PROB 11	Online
1383–1858	Register Books	PROB 12	7
	Proceedings		
1661–1858	Allegations (i.e., the start of the cause)	PROB 18	F card indexes to causes, testators and intestates
1664–1854	Answers	PROB 25	8
1642–1722	Cause Papers	PROB 28	1
1783–1858	Cause Papers, Later Series	PROB 37	Index to testators and intestates. List and Index Society 184
	Depositions		
1657–1809	Depositions	PROB 24	F
1826–1858	Depositions Bound by Suit	PROB 26	1
	Exhibits		
1653–1721	Exhibits pre-1722	PROB 36	2 5
1662–1720	Filed Exhibits with Inventories	PROB 32	2 5
1722–1858	Exhibits, Main Series	PROB 31	F index of wills; card indexes of names and places to the inventories and other exhibits
	Procedural records		
1536–1819	Acts of Court Book	PROB 29	7
1740–1858	Acts of Court	PROB 30	F indexes to causes, testators and intestates

Sentences, the court's final judgement, were registered in PROB 11 if the successful party paid a fee for the registration until the end of the eighteenth century. They are listed in the calendars in PROB 12 7 in a separate section, which is to be found either adjacent to the section for surnames beginning with the letter S or at the end of the volume. Sentences will give you the names of the deceased testator or intestate, the name of the parties to the cause and the type of sentence.

Proctors (lawyers) for the opposing parties drafted the sentences. The judge in the cause then chose the sentence that accorded with his decision. The principal types of sentences were:

• *sententia pro concessione administrationis bonorum*	sentence granting letters of administration
• *sententia pro confirmatione administrationis bonorum*	sentence confirming the grant of letters of administration

• *sententia pro revocatione administrationis bonorum*	sentence revoking letters of administration
• *sententia pro valore testamenti*	sentence in favour of the validity of a will
• *sententia pro confirmatione testamenti*	sentence confirming a grant of probate
• *sententia pro revocatione testamenti*	sentence revoking a grant of probate

Other types of sentences related to the jurisdiction of the Court, the production of inventories and accounts and the validity of codicils.

10.12 Appeals before 1858

If probate was not granted by the PCC, it may be worth investigating to see if an appeal took place. Appeals before 1533 went to Rome: details are given in the *Calendars of Papal Registers*.

Between 1534 and 1834, appeals from the Prerogative Court of Canterbury and other church courts in testamentary causes went to the Court of Arches (whose surviving records are at Lambeth Palace Library) and to the High Court of Delegates. If either of these two courts granted probate, then the will may be found in their records, as well as in the PCC or the relevant lower court. Proceedings called before the Delegates can be seen at the National Archives (DEL 1 and DEL 2 ① and as 'testamentary cause', both indexed by DEL 11/7; DEL 7 Ⓔ, indexed by IND 1/10323; and DEL 8 ⑦). Wills and affidavits brought into court, 1636–1857, are in DEL 10 ②. The muniment books (DEL 9 Ⓔ) contain transcripts of documents and exhibits in appeals, 1652–1859, indexed in DEL 11/6 and DEL 11/7.

After 1834, appeals lay to the Judicial Committee of the Privy Council until 1858: see PCAP 1 ② and PCAP 3 ②.

10.13 Litigation after 1858

After 1858, testamentary causes were by the new Court of Probate (later part of the Probate, Divorce and Admiralty Division of the High Court), with appeal to the House of Lords. A 7 per cent sample of records (but still over 9,000 case files and papers) relating to contentious probates of wills from 1858 onwards is in J 121 ②. A very small sample of exhibits is in J 165 ②.

10.14 Other probate records at the National Archives

Other wills are found throughout the public records. Try searching the whole catalogue – use the surname plus 'probate' or 'will' or even 'personal estate'. Some manor court rolls include enrolled wills. An exceptionally good example is the manor of Newcastle-under-Lyme, part of the Duchy of Lancaster. This has a series of enrolment books of deeds and wills,

1810–1934, in DL 30/510/1–510/63, with indexes in DL 30/511/1–511/4. Other Duchy manors, such as Knaresborough, also enrolled wills. It may be worth checking in the National Archives' holdings of court rolls if you think that the person you are seeking was a tenant of a Crown manor: see 49.

The Paymaster General kept records of probates and letters of administration granted for Army and Navy personnel (it is not clear if they are for officers only) and their widows between 1836 and 1915. The registers can give clues to relationships, and the later ones give the address of the deceased (PMG 50 ⑦). Wills were deposited in the Navy Pay Office by naval ratings, Royal Marine other ranks and some warrant officers: see 28.2.1–2. Wills of some army officers, 1755–1881, may be found in WO 42 Ⓕ. Wills and copies of wills may be found, occasionally, among deceased soldiers' effects in the casualty returns, 1809–1910 (WO 25/1359–2410 and 3251–3471 ⑥).

The probate records of the Shanghai Supreme Court, 1857–1941, are in FO 917 ②. Other wills of some Britons in China, 1837–1951, are in FO 678/2729–2931 ③ or ②. The probate records of the British Consular Court at Smyrna, Turkey, 1820–1929, are in FO 626 Ⓕ.

10.15 Inheritance: wills and probate records at the National Archives: bibliography

T ARKELL, N EVANS and N GOOSE eds, 'When Death Us Do Part: Understanding and Interpreting the Probate Records of Early Modern England', *Local Population Studies*, Supplement (2000)

Calendars of Papal Registers (London and Dublin, 1896–1998)

A J CAMP, 'The Genealogist's Use of Probate Records', G H Martin and P Spufford, eds, *Records of the Nation* (British Record Society, 1990), pp. 287–298

P W COLDHAM, *American Wills and Administrations in the Prerogative Court of Canterbury, 1610–1857* (Baltimore, 1989)

P W COLDHAM, *American wills proved in London, 1611–1775* (Baltimore, 1992).

J COX, *Affection Defying the Power of Death: Wills, Probate and Death Duty Records* (FFHS, 1993)

J COX, *Hatred pursued beyond the grave* (HMSO, 1993)

A L ERICKSON, 'An Introduction to Probate Accounts', G H Martin and P Spufford, eds, *Records of the Nation* (British Record Society, 1990), pp. 273–286

K GRANNUM, 'Enduring Benefits', *Ancestors* 23 (2004)

K GRANNUM and N TAYLOR, *Wills and Other Probate Records: A practical guide to researching your ancestors' last documents* (The National Archives, 2004)

Ham's Inland Revenue Yearbook (annual: National Archives library has 1875–1930)

M D HERBER, *Ancestral Trails* (SoG, 2004)

R MILWARD, *A Glossary of Household, Farming and Trade Terms From Probate Inventories* (Derbyshire Record Society, *Occasional Paper* no. 1, 3rd edn, 1993)

M OVERTON, *A Bibliography of British Probate Inventories* (Newcastle, 1983)

'Wills and Administrations in the Court of Delegates', *The Genealogist*, new series 11 [1903], pp. 165–171, 224–227; 12 [1903], pp. 97–101 (Probate records in del 9)

11 Medieval and Early Modern sources for family history

11.1 Problems
11.2 Possibilities
11.3 Records searchable by name
11.4 Records searchable by place
11.5 Medieval and Early Modern sources for family history: bibliography

11.1 Problems

Before the parish registers started in 1538, births, marriages and deaths were not officially recorded, although the priest may well have kept notes. However, many series of records of use for family history start well before 1538 and continue long after. In general they contain information about the wealthier members of society, while most ordinary people were very sparsely documented. Information about ordinary lives does exist, but it occurs in records created for quite other purposes, such as land transfer or trials.

Medieval records are generally much more difficult to use than those from the sixteenth century and later as they are usually in a highly abbreviated form of Latin. English starts to become more common in informal documents in the late fifteenth century, but Latin was used in formal records until 1733 (except during the Interregnum). The handwriting and letterforms are very different from those of the present day alphabet. The use of surnames was general by about 1300, but there was no consistency in spelling. Surnames were not always used, nor always passed from parent to child. Different surnames could be used in different contexts. Even a fairly distinctive surname may be difficult to trace and may offer little guidance on family relationships.

Two invaluable books for tackling the problems presented by the language, palaeography (handwriting) and diplomatic (the form of documents) of medieval records are *Latin for Local History* by Gooder and *Latin for Local and Family Historians: A Beginner's Guide* by Stuart. Two useful and inexpensive guides to working with these records are *Examples of Handwriting 1550–1650* by Buck and *Simple Latin for Family Historians* by McLaughlin. For online learning, try the entertaining and instructive *Palaeography 1500–1800* tutorial on the National Archives website (**www.nationalarchives.gov.uk/palaeography/**); there is also a Latin tutorial at **www.nationalarchives.gov.uk/latin/beginners/**.

If you have a Latin document that you cannot understand, a useful tip is to look at a similar document from the 1650s, by which time all were in English. As so much of a formal document is common form, you may be able to use the English version to identify the whereabouts on the parchment of the crucial, unique pieces of Latin text that you need to concentrate on.

One further obstacle exists. Many of the surviving records come from the Exchequer, Chancery and the law courts, or relate to land law, and to fully understand them you need to be prepared to do some reading. Try *A Guide to English Historical Records* by Macfarlane and *English Local Administration in the Middle Ages* by Jewell.

11.2 Possibilities

If you are doubtful about going back into the sixteenth century and beyond, have a look at the friendly and very helpful **www.medieval genealogy.org.uk/** site, which includes many features and links that go beyond the scope of this chapter. A site for Early Modern historical resources (not just genealogy) is also worth using: **www.earlymodernweb. org.uk/emr/index.php**. You may also find Chambers' *Medieval Genealogy* to be a helpful guide.

Many of the most important medieval and Early Modern records have been published, or have detailed lists and indexes, and it is possible to go a long way using these published works. Most are available in the National Archives. Publications for any particular county (often produced by a county records society) can be seen in the Library, whereas those covering the whole country are in the Map and Large Document Room.

Because so many medieval documents are large, the Map and Large Document Room is the best place to use if you are looking at early records. If you need advice, ask at the desk, where there should be people with medieval knowledge available to give you general guidance. They will not be able to translate for you, nor to read documents on your behalf, although they can help with the odd word or two. You need to employ an independent researcher if you find you cannot cope with the original documents.

Possible sources for genealogical information fall into two kinds: those where information is arranged or has been indexed by name; and those where the arrangement is by place. Where you start depends on what you already know. You may have to look at all kinds of records, as none are obviously genealogical.

11.3 Records searchable by name

The advent of the online catalogue has transformed searching by name for medieval and Early Modern people, largely by providing a route via four main series:

- Prerogative Court of Canterbury wills in PROB 11 ②, ⑤, ⑥.
- Ancient Petitions in SC 8 ②, ⑤, ⑥.
- Early Chancery Proceedings in C 1 ②, ⑤, ⑥.
- Depositions in Exchequer law suits in E 134 ②, ⑤, ⑥.

The last three are searchable in the National Archives catalogue (**www.catalogue.nationalarchives.gov.uk/default.asp**) and the first in Documents Online (**www.nationalarchives.gov.uk/documentsonline/ wills.asp**). In all these series, the catalogue or index entries tend to use the original spellings. These could vary all the time, from one day to the next. You are strongly advised to use the following strategy when searching for surnames and place-names before about 1750.

- Collect all variant spellings as you find them – some of them you would never think of yourself.
- Identify the recurring letters in these variant spellings.
- Try substituting an * for the variant letters when searching (e.g. for the variant names Barber, Barbour, Barbar, Berber, try searching for B*rb*r).

You can often work out what likely variants exist even without seeing them. For example, Baldwin often appears as Baldwyn, Baldewyn or Baldewyne. A 'y' is substituted for an 'i' where the word contains a run of letters that looked very similar in early handwriting – letters formed of simple up or down strokes called minims, such as c, i, n, m, u, v, w. (The word 'minim' itself would be almost impossible to read accurately and I have spent hours pondering over 'minute'. 'Injunction' is pretty bad.) A good place to find variants is in the indexes to any of the calendar series published by the old Public Record Office, as these bring variants together.

Records from C 1 and E 134 crop up regularly when doing a name or place search. The records of these lawsuits can be very informative. Chancery, from *c.* 1380, tends to cover disputes over wills, marriage settlements, landed estates and other matters. Exchequer, from *c.* 1558, has a bias towards economic disputes – manorial customs, mills, weirs, common lands, etc. It seems also to have taken over disputes about land sold at the Dissolution of the Monasteries from the Court of Augmentations, which has its own set of fascinating cases. The lists of records of similar courts are not yet searchable online; although we are beginning to add the data, it is a very long job. For 'poor men's causes', try the records of the Court of Requests, from Henry VII to 1642. These contain cases concerning the title and ownership of property, dower and jointure and marriage contracts, allegedly of poor men against mighty suitors. The Court of Star Chamber, Henry VII to 1641, was concerned with the enforcement of law and order. There are many cases about the goods of suicides. For more information on using the records of these courts, and of the less informative common law courts, see 56–60.

Another source you can find by using the name as a search term online is the collection of inquisitions post mortem, from 1415–1485, and 1509–*c.* 1640 in a variety of series: see 49.7 for more detail. They are a fruitful source for people of some social status, and the actual document will give the name and age of the next heir on the death of a landowner. They are in Latin, but follow a standard form. Inquisitions from 1235–1432 and 1485–1509 have been published in English précis, as in the *Calendars of Inquisitions Post Mortem*. Many have also been published by local record societies.

Up until the late 1500s, it is easy to check documents issued from, or inspected in, the royal Chancery and recorded on parchment rolls, as most have been published and indexed. Although largely concerned with people of sufficient status to have direct dealings with central government, they contain many references to other people. The most important are the

- Patent Rolls (c 66 Ⓢ, Ⓕ), which contain, for example, grants of land, licences to alienate property held by tenure in chief and grants of wardship (see **www.uiowa.edu/~acadtech/patentrolls** for a searchable version of the patent rolls for 1348–1452);
- Close Rolls (c 54 Ⓢ, Ⓕ), which record, amongst other things, enrolments of private deeds and other useful information such as writs of livery and seisin;
- Fine Rolls (c 60 Ⓢ, Ⓕ), which include grants of wardship and marriage and writs of livery of seisin;
- Charter Rolls (c 53 Ⓢ, Ⓕ), which contain grants of property in the presence of witnesses.

Details of the calendars are given in 11.5; these series are not searchable online. The Patent and Close Rolls continue into the twentieth century, but after the late and early 1500s respectively have not been published.

The registers of the King's (Privy) Council (not all of which are in the PRO) have also been published and indexed. Because it is easy to do, it may be worth checking these if you have a person you wish to know more about. The medieval council registers have been published as *Privy Council Proceedings, 1386–1542*. The registers of the later Privy Council have been published as *Acts of the Privy Council of England, 1542–1631*. They continue after 1631 but have not been published. There is no guarantee that a person came to the attention of the council, but you may find something of interest.

Other possible sources that are easy to use and may contain something of interest start in the early sixteenth century and continue till the mid-eighteenth century. From 1509, large numbers of letters and papers relating to the government of the country and known as the State Papers, Domestic survive. These have been published (in brief) as *Letters and Papers … of*

Henry VIII and *The Calendar of State Papers, Domestic, 1547–1704* and are very well indexed. It may be worth checking the indexes on the off chance that someone you are researching is mentioned. There are similar series for Scotland and Ireland and for colonial and foreign affairs, which are listed in the bibliography. You may also wish to look among the records of the economic life of the nation in the various series of *Calendars of Treasury Books and Papers, 1557–1745*, which are also well indexed. These are partly replaced, up until about 1800, by the well-listed Treasury Papers in T 1 ☑, ⑤, ⑥, which is good to search online.

Apart from those deeds enrolled on the Close Rolls, the National Archives has deeds that came into the Crown's hands when it acquired property through purchase, forfeiture or other forms of escheat, or that were produced as evidence in law suits. Some of the National Archives' extensive holdings of medieval deeds have been calendared and indexed, and are even searchable online, but there is no cumulative index and it can be a lengthy job to look through all the lists (see 50.2).

There are many pedigrees on the Early Plea and Essoin Rolls (KB 26 ☑), the *Coram Rege* Rolls (KB 27 ☑) and the *De Banco* Rolls (CP 40 ☑): to find these, see Wrottesley, *Pedigrees from the Plea Rolls*. You may also find useful the copious extracts, mainly from the *De Banco* Rolls and similar legal records, made by General Plantagenet-Harrison in the late nineteenth century. There are several volumes, all hand-written with indexes, which are on the whole reliable (now PRO 66/3 ☑). His main interests were in Yorkshire and in all pedigrees, but you should be cautious in trusting the accuracy of the latter.

11.4 Records searchable by place

To use the other types of records, those arranged by place, you need to have some idea of where your ancestors lived, as it is then possible to trace fairly humble people through manorial records. These were the records kept by or on behalf of the lords of manors, who acted both as agrarian landlords and as local judicial and administrative authorities. Manor court rolls recorded, amongst other things, land transactions within the manor, minor lawsuits between tenants and minor breaches of the peace. It is sometimes possible to trace the inheritance of a peasant back through several generations. Rentals and surveys also name the tenants of the manor and describe their individual holdings. Ministers' and receivers' accounts were those rendered by officials responsible for the revenues of manors and other estates. Like rentals and surveys, they also include the names of tenants. The National Archives holds a considerable number of manorial documents, mostly from those manors, which formed part of the Crown lands. For further details about these documents see 49.

Many manorial documents are held in archives outside the National Archives: you can check whether there are any surviving records for a particular manor by consulting the Manorial Documents Register. So far only details for manors in Wales, the Isle of Wight, Hampshire, Norfolk, Surrey, Middlesex and the three Ridings of Yorkshire are searchable online at www.mdr.nationalarchives.gov.uk/mdr. For details of manors in other counties, you need to visit, write to or email the National Archives.

The feet of fines (CP 25/1–CP 25/2 ⑦) are the records of fictitious lawsuits entered into to evade conveyancing restrictions, and they run from 1190 to 1833 (see 50.4). A foot of fine was the bottom copy of a series of three or more copies of a final agreement between two parties. Until the fourteenth century, those made in the central common law court appear in the records of the Court of Common Pleas and Court of King's Bench. From then on, they were made in the Court of Common Pleas only. Other fines can be found in the palatinate jurisdictions. The fines are arranged by county. Many have been published by local record societies.

Muster rolls can be a valuable source of information, recording the names of able-bodied men liable for service in the militia. They do not list all men, only those between the ages of 16 and 60. Their principal value lies in the fact that they can establish the parish of a named male. In some cases it is possible to gain an indication of the status of the family from the valuation made of a man's lands and goods. Unfortunately, there is no separate list of muster rolls to be found in many different series in the National Archives or elsewhere. You will need to look at Gibson and Dell, *Tudor and Stuart Muster Rolls*. See also 25.1.

Taxation records can also be useful in tracing rich and poor, although the very poor were usually exempt. The series of Subsidy Rolls (E 179 ⑤) includes the surviving assessments and returns made for many different taxes from the twelfth to the seventeenth century. The best known are probably the hearth tax returns, which cover the years 1662–1674, providing the name of the householder and number of hearths for which he was responsible. There are even exemption certificates for paupers. There are records of many other taxes that can also be extremely useful. The terms of each tax are given in Jurkowski, Smith and Crook, *Lay Taxes in England and Wales, 1188–1688*.

The 1332 subsidy, for example, was the first for which assessments survive on any scale, although its catchment was primarily confined to prosperous householders. The poll tax returns of 1378–1380, which theoretically covered all male adults except the itinerant and the very poor, often give occupations and the relationships between members of the household. The subsidies of 1532–1535 again covered extensively the householders of middling and higher status. The lists are arranged by county, and the description of each document indicates the area covered (often by hundred or wapentake rather than parish or manor) and whether or not the names of assessed individuals are given (see 52).

Many of the records discussed in 11.3 are equally suitable for place-name searching – and the strategy used for coping with variant spellings is also relevant. Looking for information on the locality can bring you extra information about people who lived there. Maybe they gave evidence in lawsuits, for example. Think about looking at records not directly related to your family and you may find hidden gold: even if you don't find them by name, you will be visiting disputes and events they probably knew about.

11.5 Medieval and Early Modern sources for family history: bibliography

Published works: records

Acts of the Privy Council of England, 1542–1631 (London, 1890–1964)
Calendar of Charter Rolls, 1226–1516 (London, 1903–1927)
Calendar of Close Rolls, 1227–1509 (London, 1892–1963)
Calendar of Fine Rolls, 1272–1509 (London, 1911–1963)
Calendar of Inquisitions Miscellaneous, Henry III to Henry VII (London, 1916–1968)
Calendar of Inquisitions Post Mortem, Henry III to Henry VI, and Henry VII (London, 1898–2004)
Calendar of Patent Rolls, 1216–1509, 1547–1582 (London, 1891–1986) (for 1509– 1547, see Letters and Papers … of Henry VIII) [The series is being continued by the List and Index Society.]
Calendar of State Papers, Colonial, 1513–1738 (London, 1860–1969)
Calendar of State Papers, Domestic, 1547–1704 (London, 1856–1998)
Calendar of State Papers, Foreign, 1558–1589 (London, 1858–1950)
Calendar of State Papers, Ireland, 1509–1670 (London, 1875–1910)
Calendar of State Papers relating to Scotland, 1547–1603 (London, 1898–1969)
Calendar of Treasury Books, 1660–1718 (London, 1904–1961)
Calendar of Treasury Papers, 1557–1728 (London, 1868–1889)
Calendar of Treasury Books and Papers, 1729–1745 (London, 1898–1903)
Descriptive Catalogue of Ancient Deeds preserved in the Public Record Office (London, 1890–1915)
Inquisitions Post Mortem, Henry V–Richard III (List and Index Society, vol. 268–269, 1998)
Journals of the Board of Trade and Plantations, 1704–1782 (London, 1920–1938)
Letters and Papers … of Henry VIII (London, 1864–1932)
Privy Council Proceedings, 1386–1542 (London, 1834–1837)

Published works: guides

W S B Buck, Examples of Handwriting 1550–1650 (Society of Genealogists, 1996)
A J Camp, My Ancestor came with the Conqueror (Society of Genealogists, 1988)
P Chambers, Medieval Genealogy: How to Find Your Medieval Ancestors (Sutton, 2005)
E Churchill, 'Bridging the Gap; a guide to state papers and other 17th-century sources', Ancestors 11 (2002/3)
M Ellis, Using Manorial Records (Public Record Office, 1997)
P Franklin, Some Medieval Records for Family Historians (FFHS, 1994)
R E F Garrett, Chancery and other Legal Proceedings (Shalfleet Manor, 1968)
J Gibson and A Dell, Tudor and Stuart Muster Rolls (FFHS, 1991)

E A Gooder, *Latin for Local History* (London, 2nd edn, 1978)

J Guy, *The Court of Star Chamber and its Records to the reign of Elizabeth I* (Public Record Office, 1985)

R W Hoyle, *Tudor Taxation Records: A Guide for Users* (Public Record Office, 1994)

H M Jewell, *English Local Administration in the Middle Ages* (David & Charles, 1972)

M Jurkowski, C Smith and D Crook, *Lay Taxes in England and Wales, 1188–1688* (PRO, 1998)

A Macfarlane, *A Guide to English Historical Records* (Cambridge, 1983)

E McLaughlin, *Simple Latin for Family Historians* (FFHS, revised edition, 1991)

J Morris, *A Latin Glossary for Family and Local Historians* (FFHS, 1989)

P B Park, *My Ancestors Were Manorial Tenants* (Society of Genealogists, 1994)

J F Preston and L Yeandle, *English Handwriting 1400–1650* (Binghamton, USA, 1992)

D Stuart, *Latin for Local and Family Historians: A Beginner's Guide* (London, 1995)

J Titford, 'Pre–Parish Register Genealogy: English Sources in the Public Record Office', in K A Johnson and M R Sainty, eds, *Genealogical Research Directory 1998* (Sydney, 1998)

G Wrottesley, *Pedigrees from the Plea Rolls, 1200–1500* (London, c. 1906)

M L Zell, 'Fifteenth and Sixteenth Century Wills as Historical Sources', *Archives*, vol. XIV (1979), pp. 75–80

12 Welsh family history

12.1 General advice

Most Welsh family history is traced by exactly the same means as English family history – Wales and England have been one nation since the 1540s. However, the two societies did not grow similar until much later, especially with regard to language. Welsh was the native tongue of most inhabitants of Wales until well into the nineteenth century.

A major difficulty faced by family historians in Wales is caused by the late adoption of fixed surnames and the relatively small stock of names that evolved from the previous naming practices – Jones, Davies, Pritchard, Price, Williams, Parry, Bevan or Evans, Thomas, etc. For advice on understanding the patronymic system used until the seventeenth or eighteenth century, read Rowlands and Rowlands, *The Surnames of Wales* or Morgan and Morgan, *Welsh Surnames.*

12.2 Records and sources in Wales

There are two major websites that you will need to check for records and sources in Wales.

- The National Library of Wales' website (**www.llgc.org.uk**) contains an increasing number of really useful resources, which are in addition to its catalogues of printed works and archives. It contains the Crime and Punishment database (crimes, criminals and punishments in the Court of Great Sessions in Wales from 1730 to 1830) and the Welsh Biography Online, but you really need to check it to see what else is there and read its research advice. Some of its resources are not yet available online (such as indexes to wills and chapels), although there are plans to put will indexes online soon (check on **www.llgc.org.uk** for progress).
- The Archives Network Wales website at **www.archivesnetworkwales.info/**. This website (like A2A for England) is an index to sources rather than a source itself. It contains descriptions of the extent, type and scope of collections of documents held by record offices, universities and other bodies in

Wales, and provides links to further information and access details for the repositories.

Parish Registers of Wales is a useful guide to the whereabouts of original parish registers and copies in Welsh record offices and libraries and in the library of the Society of Genealogists. The National Library of Wales holds many parish registers and transcripts, as well as wills, tithe records, title deeds and personal and estate records. These are described in the *Guide to the Manuscripts and Records, the National Library of Wales*. Wills proved in Welsh consistory courts before 1858 have been indexed by the LDS in *Abstracts and Indexes of Wills*. Most of the Welsh record offices produce their own genealogical leaflets, as does the Welsh Tourist Board, and most can be accessed online. For a very useful printed directory of what is available where and when, see *Researching Family History in Wales* by Istance and Cann. A good survey of the available literature, and of where finding aids to records in Wales can be seen in England, is given by Herber in *Ancestral Trails*.

The records of Welsh courts before 1830, formerly held in the National Archives in the WALE series, have been transferred to the National Library of Wales. Relatively little survives before the introduction of the Courts of Great Sessions (similar to the English assizes) in 1540, but a lot thereafter is extant. For details, see Parry, *A Guide to the Records of Great Sessions in Wales*. Monmouthshire was not included in the Great Sessions circuits, but was added to the English Western assize circuit in 1543.

One famous source, which used to be in the National Archives, the Golden Grove Book of Pedigrees (an early eighteenth-century genealogical collection) is now in the care of the Dyfed Archives Service, Carmarthen Office (address in 62).

12.3 Records of Welsh people in the National Archives

Most of the records discussed in this book should be as helpful in tracing the history of Welsh families as they are for English families as England and Wales were governed and defended jointly after 1536. Censuses, civil registers, armed forces, service to the Crown, merchant seamen – all are relevant. However, one major source has only recently become easily available: Welsh wills proved in the Prerogative Court of Canterbury. A surprising 12,894 wills filed in PROB 11 can be identified as coming from Welsh counties, most from the border counties and the south coast, and can be searched for free and downloaded for a fee from **www. nationalarchives.gov.uk/documentsonline/wills.asp**. Far more were proved in church courts in Wales and are kept at the National Library of Wales. (Some wills proved in Monmouthshire, Montgomeryshire and Radnorshire are with the Herefordshire Record Office.)

Wales 12,894 wills in PCC	
Anglesey	382
Breconshire	1,024
Caernarvonshire	141
Cardiganshire	477
Carmarthenshire	963
Denbighshire	1,806
Flintshire	750
Glamorganshire	2,115
Merionethshire	573
Montgomeryshire	2,268
Pembrokeshire	1,354
Radnorshire	1,041

Some specific records may be particularly helpful because they relate solely to Wales or are arranged by place. The 1891 and 1901 censuses note whether people were Welsh speakers. Because of the strong Nonconformist tradition in Wales, the Nonconformist registers of births, marriages and deaths in RG 4 ⑤ and RG 8 ⑤ (for 1700–1858) are a very fruitful source (see 5). Going back even further, tax records in E 179 ⑤ are a good source, with the hearth taxes of the late seventeenth century being the most useful (see 52).

For an easy way into sixteenth- and seventeenth-century disputes in Wales and Monmouthshire, look at the several volumes published by the University of Wales, Board of Celtic Studies. These cover the courts of Star Chamber, Chancery, Augmentations and Exchequer: they are well indexed (details are given in the bibliography, where the relevant works are marked *). They can be seen in the Library at the National Archives, where there are also many works on Welsh history. For later Chancery records, see 58. The Exchequer equity depositions in E 134 are searchable by county as well as name and subject until 1760; they continue, listed by date, until 1841 (see 59).

The assize records for the Chester and North Wales circuit and the South Wales circuit (ASSI 57–ASSI 67, ASSI 71–ASSI 77, all ⑦) effectively continue the records of the courts of Great Sessions from about 1831 onwards. Unfortunately, they are nothing like as accessible as the Great Sessions records (**www.llgc.org.uk/sesiwn_fawr/index_s.htm**). The records of the Palatinate of Chester in CHES also cover Flintshire and other parts of North Wales. Probably the easiest way in after 1830 is to search using the old county name (see the table above) and then check out the documents in Criminal Registers in HO 27 from 1805–1892 or in the after-trial calendars of prisoners in HO 140 from 1868 onwards (see 48).

The records of the Army (see 23–27) are easy to search for Welshmen discharged to pension between 1760 and 1854: you can search in WO 97 and WO 121 using name or place of birth. There are registers of ex-soldiers and sailors living in Wales who were in receipt of a Chelsea or Greenwich out-pension, 1842–1862 (WO 22/114–117). Some of the entries relate to widows and children. Similarly, Naval ratings who joined the Royal Navy between 1853 and 1923 can be searched by name or place of birth in **www.nationalarchives.gov.uk/documentsonline/royal-navy-service.asp**; in this case you can download their service records in ADM 188. See 28 for details. Unfortunately, there is not a generic search for 'Wales'. Other records searchable by place of birth are the merchant seaman records for 1913–1972 in BT 372. However, for Welsh merchant seamen of an earlier period, try **www.welshmariners.org.uk**, an online index of 21,000 Welsh merchant masters, mates and engineers active from 1800 to 1945. See 35 for more advice.

12.4 Welsh marcher lordship and manorial records

Among the earlier records that stayed in the National Archives are those of some of the marcher lordships and of the principality. Because of the history of its conquest by the Normans and Plantagenets, medieval Wales was composed of the principality (basically Anglesey, Caernarvon, Merioneth, Cardigan and Carmarthen), run by the Crown, and several quasi-independent marcher lordships, some of which had fallen into the Crown's possession. In the 1530s and 1540s Wales was divided into shires and given a form of local government based on the English model. The marcher lordships were not actually abolished, and some of them continued to provide local courts. For more details, see the research guides under Wales at **www.nationalarchives.gov.uk**.

The National Archives has an unsurpassed collection of records from the marcher lordship of Ruthin or Dyffryn Clwyd, brought in for safe keeping from the leaking Ruthin town hall in the 1840s. They stretch between the thirteenth and the nineteenth centuries and include court rolls with lists of tenants, views of frankpledge, lists of freeholders and inhabitants and proceedings in the lordship court, which handled debt cases until the 1820s. The court rolls are in SC 2 ⑤; the other records are in WALE 15 ⑦.

There are also records from some other marcher lordships. Most are court rolls and surveys and are not as extensive as those of Ruthin. Records of marcher lordships held by the Duchy of Lancaster (Kidwelly, Ogmore, Monmouth, Brecon, Caldicot, Iscennen, etc.) are in DL 28–DL 30, DL 41–DL 42 and SC 2 (all ⑤). Records of marcher lordships that had fallen into Crown hands are in SC 2, SC 6, SC 11, SC 12, LR 2, LR 9, LR 11 and LR 13 (mostly ⑤).

Manorial records for Welsh manors are scattered through many archives and other places; their current whereabouts can be searched online on the Manorial Documents Register at **www.nationalarchives.gov.uk**/mdr.

12.5 Welsh family history: bibliography

An * shows that this work is in the University of Wales, Board of Celtic Studies, *History and Law* series.

I EDWARDS, *A Catalogue of Star Chamber Proceedings Relating to Wales* (Cardiff, 1929) *

G HAMILTON EDWARDS, *In search of Welsh Ancestry* (Chichester, 1986)

M HERBER, *Ancestral Trails* (Society of Genealogists, 2004)

D IFANS, *Nonconformist Registers of Wales* (National Library of Wales, 1994) [Lists Nonconformist registers deposited in public libraries and record offices in England and Wales.]

J ISTANCE and E E CANN, *Researching Family History in Wales* (FFHS, 1996)

E G JONES, *Exchequer Proceedings (Equity) Concerning Wales. Henry VIII– Elizabeth* (Cardiff, 1939) *

T I JEFFREYS JONES, *Exchequer Proceedings Concerning Wales in Tempore James I* (Cardiff, 1955) *

E A LEWIS, *An Inventory of the Early Chancery Proceedings Concerning Wales* (Cardiff, 1937) *

E A LEWIS and J CONWAY DAVIES, *Records of the Court of Augmentations relating to Wales and Monmouthshire* (Cardiff, 1954) *

S LEWIS, *Topographical Dictionary of Wales* (London, 1840)

G MORGAN, 'Welsh Names in Welsh Wills', *Journal of the Society of Archivists*, vol. XXV (1995), pp. 178–185

T J MORGAN and P MORGAN, *Welsh Surnames* (Cardiff, 1985)

National Library of Wales, *Guide to Genealogical Sources at the National Library of Wales* (National Library of Wales leaflet)

National Library of Wales, *Guide to the Manuscripts and Records, the National Library of Wales* (National Library of Wales, 1994)

G PARRY, *A Guide to the Records of Great Sessions in Wales* (National Library of Wales, 1995)

G PARRY, *Launched to Eternity Crime and Punishment 1700–1900* (National Library of Wales, 2001)

J ROWLANDS, *Welsh Family History; A Guide to Research* (Association of Family History Societies for Wales, 1993)

J ROWLANDS and S ROWLANDS, *The Surnames of Wales* (FFHS, 1996)

H WATT, *Welsh Manors and their Records* (National Library of Wales, 2000)

C J WILLIAMS and J WATTS-WILLIAMS, *Cofrestri Plwyf Cymru, Parish Registers of Wales* (National Library of Wales and Welsh County Archivists Group, 2000)

13 Scottish family history

13.1 Scottish family history: records in Scotland

Scottish family history is now very well served by some excellent websites, particularly

- **www.scotlandspeople.gov.uk** (General Register Office Scotland)
- **www.nas.gov.uk** (National Archives of Scotland)
- **www.scan.org.uk** (Scottish Archive Network), a single electronic catalogue to the holdings of more than 50 Scottish archives
- **www.scottishhandwriting.com** (online tuition in reading manuscript historical records written in Scotland in the sixteenth, seventeenth and eighteenth centuries).

You really need to use these websites for the most up-to-date advice.

Civil registration of births, marriages and deaths began in Scotland on 1 January 1855. The records, along with many parish registers (c.1700–1855), minor foreign registers from 1855 and the decennial census returns for 1841–1901, are held by the General Register Office (Scotland). Most can be searched online at **www.scotlandspeople.gov.uk** for a small fee; certificates are ordered from the General Register Office (Scotland) for a standard charge. You get access to

- indexes to the birth, marriage and death registers from 1 January 1855, including adoptions from 1930 and divorces from May 1984
- indexes of the Scottish Church Registers of births, baptisms and marriages, 1555–1854 (deaths and burials are not covered before 1855)
- censuses 1861–1901.

The General Register Office Scotland also holds various series of registers of births, deaths and marriages which took place outside Scotland but which relate to Scots or people normally resident in Scotland. These are similar to the registers for the English and Welsh abroad (see 8.1). They include births and deaths at sea (from 1855); returns from foreign countries (from 1860); armed services registers (from 1881); war registers (from 1899); and consular returns (from 1914). For more on births, marriages and deaths, see Sinclair, *Jock Tamson's Bairns*.

Wills, judicial records, deeds, etc. are in the National Archives of Scotland; see Sinclair's *Tracing Your Scottish Ancestry* and the *Guide to the*

National Archives of Scotland. Wills between 1500 and 1901 can be searched for free at **www.scotlandspeople.gov.uk** and downloaded for a small charge (you can no longer see the originals). After 1901, wills are consulted at the National Archives of Scotland. They also hold about 30,000 Scottish soldiers' and airmen's wills, 1857–1966.

13.2 Scottish family history: records in the National Archives

After the union of Scotland and England into the United Kingdom of Great Britain in 1707, Scots appear regularly in the main series of government records. They crop up in the records of the Army, Navy, Treasury, Customs, Excise, Merchant Navy, Foreign Office, Colonial Office, office of the Secretaries of State and so on. The legal systems remained different, so look in Scotland for anything to do with the courts or with legal affairs *within* Scotland.

Scots possessed of property in the form of goods, money and investments in England were supposed to have their wills proved in England as well as in Scotland. Before 1858, there are about 3,879 wills proved in the Prerogative Court of Canterbury and filed in PROB 11 from people resident in the following old Scottish counties. They can be searched for free, and downloaded for a fee, from **www.nationalarchives.gov.uk/ documentsonline/wills.asp.**

Aberdeenshire	503	East Lothian	141	Peebleshire	24
Angus	384	Fife (Fifeshire)	355	Perthshire	230
Argyllshire	75	Inverness-shire	114	Renfrewshire	139
Ayrshire	240	Kincardineshire	74	Ross-shire & Cromartyshire	56
Banffshire	83	Kinross-shire	7	Roxburghshire	113
Berwickshire	95	Kirkcudbrightshire	34	'Scotland'	91
Buteshire	13	Lanarkshire	377	Selkirkshire	21
Caithness	10	Mid Lothian	106	Stirlingshire	130
Clackmannanshire	22	Morayshire	7	Sutherland	19
Dumbartonshire	21	Nairnshire	14	West Lothian	75
Dumfriesshire	235	Orkney/Shetland	98	Wigtownshire	43

The Apprenticeship Books include details of Scottish apprentices (see 37) and the Scots are well represented in the records of the Merchant Navy (see 35), the Metropolitan Police (see 33) and, of course, the armed forces. The records of the Army are particularly fruitful (see 23–27). Try searching WO 97 and WO 121 for soldiers discharged to pension between 1760 and 1854, as they can be searched by county of birth as well as by name. For ex-soldiers and ex-sailors living in Scotland and in receipt of a Chelsea or Greenwich pension there are registers arranged by district pay office (e.g., Ayr, Paisley) for 1842–1862 (WO 22/118–140). Some of the entries relate to widows and children. Naval ratings who joined the Royal Navy between 1853 and 1923 can be searched by name or place of birth in **www.nationalarchives.gov.uk/ documentsonline/royal-navy-service.asp**; in this case you can download their service records from ADM 188; see 28. Other records searchable by place of birth are the merchant seaman records for 1913–1972 in BT 372 (see 35).

Of course, the Secretaries of State, based in London, conducted a stream of correspondence with Scotland. Much of this is included in the *Calendars of State Papers Domestic*, and in Panvel's excellent *Descriptive list of Secretaries of State: State papers Scotland, series two (1688–1782)* (SP 54 ④⑥②). This is published in three volumes with an index (which includes identifications of people, not given in the catalogue) by the List and Index Society. Sample entries give the flavour:

- Robert Farquharson, taken at Preston and awaiting transportation from Liverpool: petition for mercy; on his age and ill health. With affidavit of John Downy and William Charles of Aberdeenshire on Farquharson's age and situation; dated 18 June 1716 (SP 54/26/130);
- Inhabitants of the Perthshire villages of Crieff, Muthill, Ochterarder, Dunning, Blackford and the neighbouring country houses: petition concerning the losses they sustained during the 1715 rebellion, and on the compensation promised to them, from the assets of the forfeited estates. Undated (SP 54/22/18);
- James Hogg, minister and heritors, elders and other parishoners of Caputh, Perthshire: petition concerning the burning of the manse, in 1736, and the subsequent legal dispute. Undated (SP 54/23/63B).

Between 1745 and 1800, it may be worth searching T 1 ④⑥②, as the Treasury was deeply involved in Scottish affairs and this section of its papers is well listed. For example:

- SCOTLAND: Miscellaneous: William Nelthorpe encloses replies from Inverness and Wigtown Customs officers regarding emigration from the Highlands to the Americas. Rapacity of lairds and a notable deterioration in the climate, which destroyed many of their cattle, are the main reasons why so many have emigrated when the opportunity arose 1774 Jan 11 (T 1/500/231–235);

For Scottish emigrants to North America, see 18.4.

For the period before 1603, there are the separate Calendar of Letters and Papers Relating to the Affairs of the Borders of England and Scotland and Calendar of State Papers Relating to Scotland and Mary, Queen of Scots, 1547–1603.

The Society of Genealogists has a very extensive collection of Scottish materials, listed in *Sources for Scottish Genealogy in the Library of the Society of Genealogists*.

13.3 Scottish family history: bibliography

Calendar of Letters and Papers Relating to the Affairs of the Borders of England and Scotland (London, 1894–1896)

Calendar of State Papers, Domestic, 1603–1704 (London, 1857–1972)

Calendar of State Papers Relating to Scotland and Mary, Queen of Scots, 1547–1603 (London, 1898–1969)

K B CORY, *Tracing Your Scottish Ancestry* (Edinburgh, 2004)

J P S FERGUSON, *Scottish Family Histories* (Edinburgh, 1986)

G HAMILTON EDWARDS, *In search of Scottish Ancestry* (Chichester, 1986)

M D HERBER, *Ancestral Trails* (Society of Genealogists, 2004)

S IRVINE, *Scottish Ancestry; Research Methods for Family Historians* (2003)

S LEWIS, *Topographical Dictionary of Scotland* (London, 1846)

D MOODY, *Scottish Family History* (London, 1988)

M MOORE, *Sources for Scottish Genealogy in the Library of the Society of Genealogists* (SoG, 1996)

B PANVEL, *Descriptive list of Secretaries of State: State papers Scotland, series two (1688–1782). Pt. 1 (SP 54/1–23); Pt. 2 (SP 54/24–40); Pt. 3 (SP 54/41–48 and Index)* 3 vols (List & Index Society, vols 262–264, 1996)

Scotland, A Genealogical Research Guide (Salt Lake City, 1987)

Scottish Record Office, *A Guide to the National Archives of Scotland* (Edinburgh, 1996)

C SINCLAIR, *Jock Tamson's Bairns* (Edinburgh, 2000)

C SINCLAIR, *Tracing Your Scottish Ancestry: A Guide to Ancestry Research in the Scottish Record Office* (3rd edn, 2004)

A STEWART, 'Scotland by numbers' [statistical accounts], *Ancestors* 34 (2005)

D W WEBSTER, 'Records of life and death' [civil registration in Scotland], *Ancestors* 34 (2005)

14 Irish family history

14.1 Irish family history: records in Ireland
14.2 Irish family history: records in the National Archives
14.3 Irish family history: bibliography

14.1 Irish family history: records in Ireland

Many Irish records have been lost or destroyed (notably in the burning of the Irish Public Record Office in 1922). For a detailed recent overview of the surviving records and the availability of finding aids, and for general advice, read Herber, *Ancestral Trails*. Two indispensable works put out by the respective archives of Ireland and Northern Ireland are Grenham, *Tracing Your Ancestors in Ireland* and Maxwell, *Tracing Your Ancestors in Northern Ireland*. Very little in the way of documents or indexes has been made available online as yet. Detailed advice is given on **www.national archives.ie** (which links to many other useful sites), **www.groireland.ie** for ordering certificates and the website of the Centre for Irish Genealogical and Historical Studies at **http://homepage.tinet.ie/~seanjmurphy/nai/**.

A population census was taken in Ireland every ten years between 1821 and 1911, and those that survive are in the National Archives of Ireland in Dublin. The records from 1861–1891 were deliberately destroyed by the government and only a few of the 1821–1851 censuses survived the fire of 1922. For a list of survivals, and of transcripts or abstracts from lost censuses, see Gibson and Medlycott, *Local Census Listings, 1522–1930, holdings in the British Isles*. Unlike the early English censuses, these Irish censuses include names. Returns for 1901 and 1911 are fairly complete and are open. (The 1911 census can be seen on microfilm at the Family History Centre, Hyde Park, London.) A census was also taken in the republic in 1926 and is now open to public inspection. Records of applications for old-age pensions between 1908 and 1922 may have used census data as a proof of age, for these applicants were born before the introduction of civil registration in 1864. The applications survive at the National Archives of Ireland in Dublin and at the Public Record Office of Northern Ireland (PRONI) in Belfast. They have been indexed by name, and a copy of the index can also be seen at the Society of Genealogists.

The civil registration of all births, marriages and deaths in Ireland began on 1 January 1864, although the civil registration of marriages other than Roman Catholic had started in 1845. The records for the whole of Ireland until 1921, for the republic of Ireland from 1921 to date and of non-Roman Catholic marriages from 1 April 1845 are in the General Register Office of

Ireland in Dublin. Copy certificates can be bought online from **www.groireland.ie** but the index is not online. The records of births, marriages and deaths in Northern Ireland since 1 January 1922 are in the General Register Office in Belfast; an index to them is available there and at the Family Records Centre. Copy certificates can be bought online from **www.groni.gov.uk**; there is a computer index but it is not online. (Indexes for records kept by both offices can be seen on microfilm at the Family History Centre, Hyde Park, London.)

The two General Register Offices also hold various series of registers of births, deaths and marriages that took place outside Ireland, but which relate to people normally resident there. These are similar to the registers for the English and Welsh abroad (see 8). Those at Dublin include births and deaths at sea (from 1864); consular returns (from 1864); armed services registers (from 1883); and indexes to war registers (from 1899). After partition, the General Register Office of Northern Ireland kept similar series, with marine registers and consular returns from 1922 and armed service registers from 1927.

Irish parish registers have also suffered much destruction. The *International Genealogical Index* includes about 2,000,000 entries. To find out what survives and where it can be seen, use Mitchell's *Guide to Irish Parish Registers*. This lists what survives for each parish and also includes Presbyterian and Nonconformist registers. Very usefully, it includes references to copies held by the Society of Genealogists.

- Anglican Church of Ireland parish registers started in 1634, but few survive before the late 1700s. Only a minority of the population used them. About half had been deposited in the Irish Public Record Office for safe keeping; these were destroyed in 1922.
- Roman Catholic parish registers rarely date from before 1830. For maps of Roman Catholic parishes (which were usually bigger than Anglican parishes), see Grenham, *Tracing Your Irish Ancestors*.
- Presbyterian registers are either still with the congregations or with the Presbyterian Historical Society in Belfast. See Falley, *Irish and Scottish–Irish Ancestral Research*.

Wills were proved before church courts until 1858. Virtually all registered Irish probate records before 1904 were destroyed in 1922. Vicars' index to them is now the main clue to what was once there, but there are several attempts to reconstruct the lost data. We have a copy of the CD *Index of Irish Wills 1484–1858*. Many probate copies of wills survived, along with other material. For example, the Society of Genealogists has 18 volumes of abstracts from Irish wills, 1569–1909, and Herber gives details of abstracts of wills surviving in many locations. PRONI has copies and extracts of many Ulster wills and, for a fee, the Ulster Historical Foundation (at the same address) will undertake genealogical searches.

Over 4,500 Irish wills of people with property in England as well were proved at the Prerogative Court of Canterbury before 1858 and filed in PROB 11; they come from the following counties and can be searched for free and downloaded for a fee, from **www.nationalarchives.gov.uk/ documentsonline/wills.asp**.

Antrim	185	'Ireland'	200	Monaghan	32
Armagh	88	Kerry	32	Queens (Laois)	43
Carlow	38	Kildare	64	Roscommon	36
Cavan	31	Kilkenny	92	Sligo	35
Clare	17	Kings (Offaly)	29	Tipperary	136
Cork	743	Leitrim	18	Tyrone	74
Donegal	47	Limerick	143	Waterford	176
Down	60	Londonderry (Derry)	111	Westmeath	49
Dublin	1447	Longford	14	Wexford	109
Fermanagh	34	Louth	63	Wicklow	50
Galway	122	Mayo	42		

Calendars of all wills proved and administrations granted 1858–1922 may be seen in the *National Probate Calendar* at the Family Records Centre, National Archives of Ireland and PRONI. From 1922, try the National Archives of Ireland or PRONI. For records of land holding from 1708, try the Registry of Deeds in Dublin. These can include copies of wills that were used to prove entitlement.

Most of the historic archive was destroyed in 1922; fortunately, some volumes of calendars had been published beforehand (and can be seen in the National Archives Library). Particularly useful are the published versions of the *Patent and Close Rolls of Chancery in Ireland, Henry VIII, Edward VI, Mary and Elizabeth, and for the 1st to 8th year of Charles I*. For the full titles of other such publications, ask in the Library to see HMSO, *Sectional List 24: British National Archives*.

14.2 Irish family history: records in the National Archives

There are very many records in the National Archives at Kew that relate to Irish people; good example is set by Breem in his article 'Phoenix Records: how English archives can help trace Irish ancestors'.

Kings of England had claimed the title Lord of Ireland since 1169, although leaving much of the work to governors and viceroys. The establishment of English rule in Ireland in the late twelfth century involved the introduction not only of foreign settlers, but also of administrative practices based on those of England. In the thirteenth century a chancery, an exchequer and courts of law centred on Dublin developed, which produced written records of their operations. The fact that the lord of Ireland was also the king of England, and that every English subject in Ireland had the right to appeal directly to the king, meant that Irish affairs were also well represented in the records produced by the English government at Westminster. These two sets of records were created and kept independently by both administrations, but a series of disasters stretching from the thirteenth century to the twentieth means that almost all of the Irish archive has been lost. Fortunately, the National Archives of the United Kingdom continues to hold a wealth of material relating to Ireland in the medieval centuries. A guide to these medieval records has recently been produced by Dryburgh and Smith, which covers relations between natives and settlers, the church, life on the manor, trade and commerce, land-holding, Anglo-Irish relations and the operation of the law.

After the union of Ireland, Scotland and England into the single United Kingdom of Great Britain and Ireland in 1801, Irish people appear regularly in the main series of government records, until the union dissolved in 1922, leaving Northern Ireland as part of the UK. For generations, Irishmen came over as seasonal migrant labour and went back home with the money earned. Family migration from Ireland did not start until the dreadful famine of the 1840s forced people to leave. Because they were travelling within the same kingdom, there are no records treating the Irish as immigrants to the United Kingdom: they were internal migrants, within one country. The Irish crop up all over the census, in the records of the Army, Navy, Treasury, Customs, Excise, Merchant Navy, Foreign Office, Colonial Office, office of the Secretaries of State and pretty much everywhere else. The legal systems were distinct, so look in Ireland for anything to do with the courts or with legal affairs *within* Ireland. For example, the transportation of convicts described in 47 had an exact counterpart in Ireland (see **www.nationalarchives.ie/genealogy/transp. htm** for more information and for a searchable database of transported convicts). For records at Kew relating to Irish history, and only incidentally to Irish genealogy, see Prochaska's *Irish History from 1700: A Guide to Sources in the Public Record Office*.

Of course, thousands of Irishmen served in the Army and the Navy – indeed, by some estimates as many as 40 per cent of privates in the Army were Irish. Some records are obviously Irish, such as the muster rolls of the Irish militia, 1793–1876, in WO 13/2574–3393 ⑥. The records of discharges to pension 1760–1854 in WO 97 and WO 121, which can be searched by birthplace as well as name, show that enormous numbers of Irishmen took the king's shilling in English or Scottish (as well as Irish) regiments. Before the Union with the United Kingdom in 1801, Ireland had a separate Army with its own organisation and establishment. From 1801, Ireland remained a separate command, and the Irish regiments retained their Irish identity, but the Army was merged with the British Army. Records relating to the Army in Ireland, 1775–1923, are in WO 35 ⑦. Over 185,000 Irishmen served in the Army during the First World War – 50,000 in the regular Army, and 135,000 as volunteers (there was no conscription in Ireland).

The Royal Kilmainham Hospital, founded in 1679, acted as a permanent hospital for disabled soldiers (in-pensioners) and also distributed money to out-pensioners: see 25.4.2 and following sections for details of these records. Records of the payment of pensions, 1842–1862 and 1882–1883, are in WO 22/141–205 and 209–225, arranged by district; they are useful for tracing changes of residence and dates of death.

The only separate naval records for Irishmen are of nominations to serve in the Irish Coastguard, 1821–1849 (ADM 175/99–100), and the Coastguard establishment books for Ireland, 1820–1869 in ADM 175/13–21: see **www.coastguardsofyesteryear.org** for more on these, including lists of men. However, Naval ratings who joined the Royal Navy between 1853 and 1923 can be searched by name or place of birth in **www.nationalarchives.gov.uk/documentsonline/royal-navy-service.asp**: you can download their service records from ADM 188 for a fee. See 28 for other naval records. Other records searchable by place of birth are the merchant seaman records for 1913–1972 in BT 372 ⨆⑤; see 35.

The State Papers, Ireland (SP 60–SP 67⑧) contain despatches from the Crown's representative in Ireland – the Lord Deputy or Lord Lieutenant, his council and other officials to the Secretaries of State. They can contain letters sent in by soldiers, officials and private individuals; drafts and minutes of answers made to such letters; accounts of expenditure or requests for funds; instructions sent out to officials; projects for English colonisation or establishing new trades and industries; reports on the state of Ireland; etc. They are full of references to individuals and are relatively easy to use as they have been published in précis and indexed from 1509–1670 in the *Calendar of State Papers, Ireland*. The first volume in a new and fuller edition has just been published, covering 1571–1575. From 1670 to 1704, they have been included in the *Calendar of State Papers, Domestic*. In fact, the State Papers, Ireland continue up to 1782; for the later period there are brief lists in the online catalogue and much fuller lists in the Public Record Office of Northern Ireland. The same type of letters and papers continue in various Home Office and Colonial Office classes after 1782, but they are not fully listed, nor indexed, and so are not easy to use. If you want to investigate these, try Prochaska and the *PRO Guide*.

The records of the Royal Irish Constabulary, 1836–1922, are full and informative: see 33.7. For Irish Revenue Police, 1830–1857, who tried to prevent illicit distilling, try CUST 111 ⑦. For Customs officers in Ireland, 1682–1826, see CUST 20 ⑦. After this, try *Ham's Customs Year Book* and *Ham's Inland Revenue Year Book* which our Library has in a run from 1875 to 1930. These list Customs and Inland Revenue officials (up to 1923 for Ireland) and include a name index. For a general Irish directory to officials and people of status, see *Thom's Irish Almanac and Official Directory*, which the Library has from 1844 to 1928, with an odd volume for 1944. The Library also has runs of the *Dublin Almanac*, 1836–1849, and the *Dublin Directory*, 1840–1857.

The records of the Irish Tontines of 1773, 1775 and 1777 (see 53) cover 1773–1871, and list many people, with addresses. The records of the Irish Reproductive Loan Fund, in T 91 ⑤ may be helpful if you are looking for a family in Munster or Connaught in the mid-1800s. The fund provided loans at interest to the industrious poor, who had to provide some form of security. Records of the local associations, which administered the loans, survive for counties Cork, Clare, Galway, Limerick, Mayo, Roscommon, Sligo and Tipperary. In addition to the notes of security (signed by the debtor and two guarantors), there are loan ledgers, repayment books and defaulters' books. They do not give much detail other than place of abode and occupation. See Lawes' article for more details.

The Irish Sailors' and Soldiers' Land Trust was set up to provide cottages in Ireland, with or without gardens, for ex-servicemen (including airmen) after the First World War. In the 1920s and 1930s over 4,000 cottages were provided. Because of rent strikes in the republic, no further cottages were built there after 1932, but cottages continued to be built by the Trust in Northern Ireland until 1952. Provisions were later made to sell the cottages to the tenants or their widows. You will need to know the location of the cottage to use the records, as there are no name indexes. The tenancy files in AP 7 ⑦ are the place to start.

From 1925, there is a 'census' for the unions of Dungannon, Castlederg, Clougher and Omagh, in CAB 61/164–168. This was of political importance and gave the name of the head of each household and the number (no other details) of Catholic and non-Catholic persons in each household in these border areas on Ulster.

Maps of Ireland may be seen in the Map Room. The earliest date from the late 1500s (the Barony Maps in ZMAP 5). The Survey of 1655–1658 (ZOS 7) was the legal basis for the identification of Irish lands. The 1839 6-inch Ordnance Survey maps in ZOS 15 are the most detailed: they have a key sheet near the beginning of each county volume. The 1-inch Ordnance Survey maps in ZOS 14 date from 1851 to 1852. Lewis's *Topographical Dictionary of Ireland* is also useful in identifying places and filling out their history.

14.3 Irish family history: bibliography

D BEGLEY, *Handbook on Irish Genealogy* (Dublin, 1976)

D BEGLEY, ed., *Irish Genealogy; a Record Finder* (Dublin, 1982)

A BREEN, 'Phoenix Records: how English archives can help trace Irish ancestors', *Ancestors* 22 (2004)

B DE BREFFNY, *Bibliography of Irish Family History and Genealogy* (Cork and Dublin, 1974)

A CAMP, *Sources for Irish Genealogy in the Library of the Society of Genealogists* (Society of Genealogists, 1990)

B DAVIS, *An Introduction to Irish Research, Irish Ancestry; a beginner's guide* (FFHS, 1994)

P DRYBURGH and B SMITH, eds, *Handbook and Select Calendar of Sources for Medieval Ireland in the National Archives of the United Kingdom* (Dublin, 2004)

M FALLEY, *Irish and Scottish–Irish Ancestral Research: A Guide to the Genealogical Records, Methods and Sources in Ireland* (GPC, 1989: reprint of 1962 edition, 2 vols)

S FOWLER, *Tracing Irish Ancestors* (PRO, 2001)

J GIBSON and M MEDLYCOTT, *Local Census Listings, 1522–1930, holdings in the British Isles* (FFHS, 1994)

J GRENHAM, *Tracing Your Irish Ancestors* (Dublin, 1992)

S HELFERTY and R REFAUSE, *Directory of Irish Archives* (Dublin, 1993)

M D HERBER, *Ancestral Trails* (Society of Genealogists, 2000)

Irish Records Index, *Index of Irish Wills 1484–1858. Vol.1* Records at the National Archives of Ireland (CD-Rom)

Irish Roots Quarterly

A LAWES, 'The Irish Reproductive Loan Fund and its records', *Ancestors* 12 (2003)

S LEWIS, *Topographical Dictionary of Ireland* (London, 1846)

M MAC CONGHAIL and P GORRY, *Tracing Irish Ancestors* (Glasgow, 1997)

E MACLYSAGHT, *Bibliography of Irish Family History* (2nd edn 1982)

I MAXWELL, 'How to dig out your Ulster roots', *Ancestors* 36 (2005)

I MAXWELL, *Tracing Your Ancestors in Northern Ireland* (PRONI, 1997)

B MITCHELL, *A guide to Irish Parish Registers* (GPC, 1988)

J MORRIN, *Patent and Close Rolls of Chancery in Ireland, Henry VIII, Edward VI, Mary and Elizabeth, and for the 1st to 8th year of Charles I* (London, 1861–1864)

W NOLAN, *Tracing the Past. Sources for Local Studies in the Republic of Ireland* (Dublin, 1982)

A PROCHASKA, *Irish History from 1700: A Guide to Sources in the Public Record Office* (British Records Association and Institute of Historical Research, 1986)

Public Record Office, *Calendar of State Papers Ireland 1509–1670* (London, 1860–1910)

Public Record Office and Irish Manuscripts Commission, *Calendar of State Papers Ireland, Tudor Period, 1571–1575*, ed. M O'Dowd (London, 2000)

J RYAN, 'Irish Catholic Ancestors', *Ancestors* 12 (2003)

R SWIFT, *Irish Migrants in Britain, 1815–1914: a documentary history* (Cork, 2002)

A VICARS ed., *Index to the Prerogative Wills of Ireland, 1536–1810* (Dublin, 1897: reprinted, 1989)

15 Isle of Man family history

15.1 Manx family history: records on the Isle of Man

The Isle of Man, though subject to the English Crown since 1765, has its own Parliament, laws and courts. To find out more, see **www.gov.im/mnh/**. For a very useful gateway website for Manx family history, try **www.isle-of-man.com/interests/genealogy**. See also **www.manxroots.com**. See Narasimham, *The Manx Family Tree: A Beginners' Guide to Records in the Isle of Man* for details of all the following records and their indexes.

The civil registration of births and marriages on the Isle of Man began on a voluntary basis in 1849. It became compulsory for births and deaths in 1878 and for marriages in 1884. The original registers can be seen at the Isle of Man General Registry. Microfilm copies of the indexes up to 1964 can be seen at the Society of Genealogists, as can copies of some registers.

Parish registers survive for some parishes from the early 1600s. The *International Genealogical Index* is complete for Manx marriages, and refers to many baptisms. Microfilm copies of all parish registers can be seen at the Manx Museum, with some available at the Society of Genealogists.

Wills were proved in church courts until 1884, and then in the Manx High Court of Justice. Wills proved since 1911 are at the General Registry. Wills from the early 1600s to 1910 are kept in the Manx Museum. Wills of some wealthy Manx inhabitants before 1858 may be found in the Prerogative Courts of York, and 164 made it as far as the Prerogative Court of Canterbury (these can be searched for and downloaded from **www.nationalarchives.gov.uk/documentsonline/wills.asp**).

The Manx Museum has other records of interest to family historians, such as the militia records of the Manx Fencibles. Registers of ships registered in the Isle of Man 1824–1960 (CUST 114) have been deposited by the National Archives in the Manx Museum.

15.2 Manx family history: records in the National Archives

The position of the Isle of Man, as not part of the United Kingdom but a haven for smuggling, had long been a problem for the Customs service. Smuggling was a major cause of government worry about Man: a search in T 1 between 1746 and about 1800 will bring up references to Manx smugglers.

Negotiations for the Crown to buy the royalty and revenue of the Isle of Man from the Earl of Derby began as early as 1726 and continued until 1765, when the Duke and Duchess of Athol at last alienated the sovereignty of the Isle of Man to the Crown for £70,000. Haggling over compensation lasted until 1825, when the Isle of Man was entirely ceded to the British Crown. The island continued to have its own government and Parliament (the Tynwald) under a governor appointed by the Crown (see **www.gov.im/mnh**).

Because of this long struggle over property rights between the Athols and the Crown, it may be worth searching among the records in the CRES, LRRO and LR series. CRES 40/88–92 is a set of volumes containing a detailed valuation of the properties of the Duke of Athol on Man to be bought by the Crown, and of other Crown properties on Man, from 1826.

The censuses from 1841 to 1901 cover the Isle of Man and are obviously a prime source for family history (see 3). Of course, islanders may well turn up in any of the armed services and other records as described in this book. Topographically arranged records, such as the payments of pensions to ex-soldiers and sailors on the Isle of Man, 1852–1862 in WO 22/207, are particularly useful. Details of soldiers born in the Isle of Man and discharged to pension between 1760 and 1854 may be found by searching WO 97 and WO 121 in the catalogue using Isle of Man and the surname as keywords. Similarly, Naval ratings who joined the Royal Navy between 1853 and 1923 can be searched by name or place of birth in **www.nationalarchives.gov.uk/documentsonline/royal-navy-service.asp**. In this case you can download their service records. Other records searchable by place of birth are the merchant seaman records for 1913–1972 in BT 372. (See 23–27 for the Army, 28 for the Navy and 35 for the Merchant Navy.)

For correspondence between the Isle and the Secretaries of State, 1761–1783, see SP 48 ⑤⑦ (for 1761–1775, published in *Home Office Papers of the Reign of George III*)). The Privy Council was involved in the administration of the Isle of Man; some of its papers are in SP 48, but most are in PC 1 ⑥④ and PC 8 ⑥④. The Home Office has entry books of correspondence with Man, in HO 99 ⑦, from 1760 to 1921. These include lists of charitable bequests, by parish, in HO 99/22, dating from c. 1680 to c. 1825. An investigation into smuggling in 1791 produced numerous depositions from Manx office-holders and worthies: they are in HO 99/21.

15.3 Isle of Man family history: bibliography

R BELLERBY, 'Isle of Man Investigations', *Family History Monthly* 113 (2005)

M D HERBER, *Ancestral Trails* (Society of Genealogists, 2004)

J NARASIMHAM, N CROWE and P LEWTHWAITE, *The Manx Family Tree: A Beginners' Guide to Records in the Isle of Man* (Isle of Man, 3rd ed., 2000)

J REDINGTON and R A ROBERTS, eds, *Calendar of Home Office Papers of the reign of George III* (London, 1878–1899)

F WILKINS, *2,000 Manx Mariners: an eighteenth-century survey* (Kidderminster, 2000)

16 Channel Islands family history

16.1   Jersey

The portal website for Jersey family history is undoubtedly **http://user.itl. net/~glen/**, run by Alex Glendinning of the Channel Islands Family History Society. The Jersey Archive (**www.jerseyheritagetrust.org**) holds parish registers of baptism, marriage and burial before 1842, as well as much other material, such as wills, land transactions and legal records; it has an online catalogue. The Jersey Archive offers a paid research service. Some 953 Jersey wills were proved before 1858 in the Prerogative Court of Canterbury (in London): see 10.

Civil registers of births, marriages and deaths from 1842 are held by the Superintendent Registrar of Jersey and he can undertake fee-paid searches and issue certified extracts from those registers in his custody, which are not open to the public. The Superintendent Registrar cannot undertake genealogical research of a general nature. For general research, try contacting either the Société Jersiaise (**www.societe-jersiaise.org**) or the Channel Islands Family History Society; one of their members may be prepared to undertake paid research. Addresses are in 62.

The censuses also cover Jersey (see 3) and are obviously a main source. A few records of births, marriages and deaths in Jersey are in the National Archives, among the foreign registers in RG 32 Ⓕ, indexed by RG 43 Ⓣ. Details of soldiers born in Jersey and discharged to pension between 1760 and 1854 may be found by searching in WO 97 and WO 121 in the catalogue, using Jersey as the search criterion. Details of ex-soldiers and sailors in receipt of a Chelsea or Greenwich pension, or their widows and orphans, living in Jersey, 1842–1862, may be found in WO 22/205–206. Muster rolls of the Jersey militia, 1843–1852, are in WO 13/1055. For Army advice, see 23–27. Similarly, Naval ratings who joined the Royal Navy between 1853 and 1923 can be searched by name or place of birth in **www.nationalarchives. gov.uk/documentsonline/royal-navy-service.asp**; in this case you can download their service records in ADM 188. See 28 for fuller advice. Other records searchable by place of birth are the merchant seaman records for 1913–1972 in BT 372: see 35. After-trial calendars of prisoners, in HO 140, include Jersey prisoners: search HO 140 by Jersey to find the references (and see 47 for more information). Many of the other records described in this book will also include islanders.

The Association Oath Roll for Jersey (C 213/462) appears by its length to contain the signatures, or marks and names, of all the island's men in 1696. It has been published in facsimile, with full transcripts, by Glendinning as *Did Your Ancestors Sign the Jersey Oath of Association Roll of 1696?* There is also a petition of *c.* 1847 to Queen Victoria not to amend the island's constitution, which is signed by 5567 inhabitants (PC 1/4564), but this is not in any discernible order.

16.2 Guernsey, Alderney and Sark

The portal website for family history in these islands is also **http://user.itl.net/~glen/**, run by Alex Glendinning of the Channel Island Family History Society. La Société Guernesiase **www.societe.org.gg/sections/familyhistorysec.htm**) has indexed many of the major family history records for Guernsey, including the parish registers, the censuses, monumental inscriptions, obituaries, etc. They also offer a paid research service covering Guernsey, Sark and Alderney: you need to write (address in 62) as they cannot accept email enquiries. The website gives access to many other Guernsey family history websites. The Priaulx Library holds microfilm copies of most of the civil and ecclesiastical registers, and their indexes. Access to the microfilms is free of charge to personal callers; those unable to visit can ask for research to be done for a modest fee (**www.gov.gg/priaulx**; address in 62).

Civil registration of births, deaths and non-Anglican marriages began in Guernsey in 1840; in Alderney in 1850; and in Sark, of deaths in 1915. From 1919 all marriages and from 1925 all births and deaths in Guernsey, Alderney and Sark have been registered in Guernsey. The Priaulx Library do not have the civil marriage registers after 1901, although they do have the indexes: for these marriage certificates, and for the most modern events, you will need to contact the Greffe (address in 62). Copies of the nineteenth-century civil registration records for Guernsey can also be seen at the Society of Genealogists, where there are also indexes up to 1966.

Deeds, judicial records and wills may be consulted in person at the Greffe, Guernsey; all are indexed. Permission to consult wills of personalty from 1664 should be obtained from the Registrar of the Ecclesiastical Court. Some 863 Guernsey wills (and a handful from Alderney and Sark) were proved before 1858 in the Prerogative Court of Canterbury (in London): see 10.

Some records of births, marriages and deaths in Guernsey, Alderney and Sark are in the National Archives, among the foreign registers in RG 32, indexed by RG 43. Details of soldiers born in Guernsey and discharged to pension between 1760 and 1854 may be found by searching WO 97 and WO 121 using Guernsey as the search term. Details of ex-soldiers and sailors in receipt of a Chelsea or Greenwich pension or their widows and orphans living in the Channel Islands, 1842–1852, may be found in WO 22/205. Muster rolls of the Guernsey militia, 1843–1852, are in WO 13/887. See 23–27 for Army records, and 28 for the Navy. Naval ratings who joined the Royal Navy between 1853 and 1923 can be searched by name or place of birth in **www.nationalarchives. gov.uk/documentsonline/royal-navy-service.asp**; in this case you can download their service records from ADM 188. Other records searchable by place of birth are the merchant seaman records for 1913–1972 in BT 372; see 35. After-trial calendars of prisoners, in HO 140, include Guernsey prisoners: search HO 140 by Guernsey to find the references (and see 47 for more information). The Association Oath Roll of 1696 for Guernsey (C 213/463) is published in Glendinning's *Eye on the Past in Guernsey.*

16.3 The Channel Islands: general historical sources

The Channel Islands are subject to the Crown of England, but they are not part of the United Kingdom. Many of the records created there are in French, and relate to a different legal system. For Jersey historic records, contact the Jersey Archive (**www.jerseyheritagetrust.org**); for Guernsey historic (but not genealogical) records, the Island Archive Service (**http://user.itl.net/~glen/archgsy.html**). The addresses are in 62. Having said that, there is a huge amount of information available in the National Archives, which can now be accessed easily by searching the catalogue using Channel Islands, Jersey, Guernsey, Alderney or Sark as the search term. In fact, there is so much that you need to restrict the search by date as well: try blocks of 50 or 100 years. In general, records from before about 1840 are most likely to be found by searching on the island name; after that, 'Channel Islands' is more productive. A very large amount of material will be in HO, as the Home Secretary is responsible for relations with the local administrations and legislatures of the islands. Sample discoveries are:

- Indentures of apprentices 1846–1886. CUST 105/99;
- Register of fishing boats 1869–1900. CUST 105/94–95;
- Strandings in the Channel Islands. Vessels and lives lost between 1 Jan. 1872 and 11 Feb. 1887. MT 9/302;
- CHANNEL ISLANDS: Naturalisation of aliens and their acquisition of land in the Channel Islands: examples of earlier cases 1591–1821 cited by Bailiff of Guernsey 1848–1849. HO 45/2828;

For medieval records held in the National Archives relating to the Channel Islands, try the various accounts in E 101 and the Chancery miscellanea in C 47. For a survey of this material, an account of the medieval government of the islands and a list of wardens and sub-wardens, see Le Patourel, *The Medieval Administration of the Channel Islands, 1199–1399.*

For details of French refugees in Jersey, 1793–1796, see FO 95/602–603 and HO 98 (for all the islands).

For later papers in the National Archives relating to the administration and domestic affairs of the Channel Islands, see the series below. The papers can contain references to individuals, such as the lists of French Protestants living in Jersey in 1750 (in SP 47/4), but they are a historical rather than genealogical source. All may give you a perspective on life in the Channel Islands in the past. For example, the papers for Alderney in 1821 included the census return (no names given), explaining that the total decay in trade had caused much emigration to America, France and the other islands. (For Channel Island emigration to North America, see Turk's *The Quiet Adventurers in North America*.) Many are in French. Those with a calendar reference have been published and indexed.

Correspondence and papers between the Channel Islands and the Secretaries of State

1547–1625	SP 15 Ⓢ	Published in *Calendar of State Papers, Domestic, Addenda*
1625–1649	SP 16 Ⓢ	Published in *Calendar of State Papers, Domestic, Charles I*
1660–1670	SP 29 Ⓢ	Published in *Calendar of State Papers, Domestic, Charles II*
1670–1781	SP 47 Ⓢ⑦	1670–April 1704 Published in *Calendar of State Papers, Domestic, Charles II–Anne*; May 1704–1760 not calendared – use the manuscript précis in SP 130/63–64; 1760–1775 Published in *Home Office Papers of the Reign of George III*; 1776–1781 not calendared. The Introductory Note to SP 47 tells you how to translate any obsolete references you may find in these published works into modern references.
1782–1849	HO 98 Ⓕ	
1840–1979	HO 45 ⑥④	
1942–1977	HO 284 ⑦	

Entry books of the above correspondence (can give quick overview)

1748–1760	SP 111 ⑦	
1760–1921	HO 99 Ⓢ⑦	Published for 1760–1775 in *Home Office Papers of the Reign of George III*

Correspondence and papers between the Channel Islands and the Privy Council

18th–19th century	PC 1 ⑥④	
1860–1956	PC 8 ⑥④	

Other series relating mostly to Channel Islands

1806–1965	CUST 105 ⑦	Outport Records: Channel Islands

16.4 The Channel Islands in the Second World War

The National Archives holds material on the occupation of the Channel Islands by the Germans in the Second World War. For example, WO 208/

3741 includes accounts of life in occupied Jersey and Alderney, taken in October 1944. Ask at the Research Enquiries Desk to see the Press Packs 92D and 96F for further references. More information on other occupation records (including registration cards with photographs) is available from the local archives.

16.5 Channel Islands family history: bibliography

M AXTON and R AXTON, *Calendar and Catalogue of Sark Seigneurie Archives, 1526–1927*, List and Index Society, Special Series vol 26, 1991

M L BACKHURST, *Family History in Jersey* (Channel Islands Family History Society, 1991)

L R BURNES, 'Genealogical Research in the Channel Islands', *Genealogists' Magazine*, vol. XIX, pp. 169–172

Channel Islands Family History Society, *The 1851 Census of Jersey: An All-Island Index* (1996)

Channel Islands Family History Society, *The 1871 Census of Jersey: An All-Island Index* (1998)

Channel Islands Family History Society, *The 1891 Census of Jersey: An All-Island Index* (1994)

J CONWAY DAVIES, 'The Records of the Royal Courts', La Société Guernesiaise, *Transactions*, vol. XVI, pp. 404–414

A GLENDINNING, *Did Your Ancestors Sign the Jersey Oath of Association Roll of 1696?* (Channel Islands Family History Society, 1995)

A GLENDINNING, *Eye on the Past in Guernsey* (Channel Islands Family History Society, 1992)

M D HERBER, *Ancestral Trails* (Society of Genealogists, 2004)

J LE PATOUREL, J H LENFESTEY and others, *List of Records in the Greffe, Guernsey* (List and Index Society, Special Series Vols 2 and 11, 1969 and 1978). Additional lists may be consulted in typescript at the Greffe

J H LE PATOUREL, *The Medieval Administration of the Channel Islands, 1199–1399* (Oxford, 1937)

DAVID W LE POIDEVIN, *How to Trace your Ancestors in Guernsey* (Taunton, 1978)

J REDINGTON and R A ROBERTS, eds, *Calendar of Home Office Papers of the reign of George III* (London, 1878–1899)

M G TURK, *The Quiet Adventurers in North America* (Maryland, 1993)

17 Britons around the world

17.1 Foreign countries and British lands abroad

Many of us looking back now find it quite hard to believe that for several centuries the British had homes from home across the globe – and that people in the colonies were British subjects. From the reign of James VI and I, Britons conquered and colonised large areas across the world. Now we look at them and see foreign countries: then the distinction between foreign and colonial was quite distinct. And in the colonies, a Briton was at home. This distinction really only began breaking down in the latter half of the twentieth century, as the United Kingdom shrank back in on itself and began to cut old ties with its colonies.

If you can't find the information you want in this chapter, try the specialist guide by Kershaw, *Emigrants and Expats*. You may also be interested in the British Empire and Commonwealth Museum.

17.2 Travelling to, from and via Britain: ships' passenger lists

Ships' passenger lists were created for travellers on ocean-going merchant ships by order of a series of statutes stretching back to the 1830s and beyond. The master of a ship had to compile two lists of passengers and their destinations, and hand them both to the local customs official or emigration officer of the port of departure for checking. One was kept and passed up through the Customs for statistical purposes (the initial listing was only of emigrants in steerage, but cabin passengers were added later). The other was given back to the master to take with him. This one had to be kept up to date on the voyage, with details of any other passengers joining the ship and especially with details of any death or birth amongst the passengers. At the other end of the voyage, either this copy or a version of it in local format was handed in to the equivalent official. Any births or deaths then had to be certified back to the relevant General Register Office.

This system operated throughout the British Empire and with variations in foreign countries such as the United States. An outward passenger list thus became transformed into an inward passenger list at the end of the voyage. Both inward and outward lists should in theory exist in all colonies and in Britain, and at least lists of passengers arriving should exist for other countries.

Unfortunately, the passenger lists as handed to the local customs or emigration official do not survive for British ports in the National Archives before about 1890. It is not as yet clear why, but they were probably destroyed, considered of no further interest once statistical information had been extracted. It is fortunate that the colonial administrations took better care of the documents handed over by the masters.

- Australia. Earliest lists date from 1852: see **www.naa.gov.uk**
- Canada. A few before 1864, but the main collection starts from 1865. See **www.archives.ca**
- New Zealand. From the 1840s on: see **www.archives.govt.nz**
- South Africa. Unfortunately very few survive: the Pietermaritzburg Archives Repository does keep some shipping lists of European immigrants, 1845–1911. See **www.genealogy.co.za** for general advice
- USA. See **www.archives.gov/genealogy/immigration/#help**.

Similarly, much information exists in printed sources and on the internet and carries some wonderful examples of international cooperation by volunteers and interested parties. Try, for example, the excellent **www.theshipslist.com** and **www.immigrantships.net**. For an overview of what is available, and links to other sites, look at **www.cyndislist.com** and **www.port.nmm.ac.uk**. For a site offering indexes to passenger lists, see **www.passengerlists.co.uk**. Other strongly recommended sites are **www.portcities. org.uk/** covering London, Liverpool, Southampton, Bristol and Hartlepool, and **http://www.liverpoolmuseums.org.uk/maritime/**.

A few examples of passenger lists compiled by shipping companies survive in other archive repositories. The Public Record Office of Northern Ireland holds some passenger records for J. & J. Cooke, Shipping Agents, for sailings from Londonderry to USA and Canada, 1847–1871. These provide the names of 28,000 Irish passengers: see **www.proni.gov.uk/records/emigrate.htm**. Passenger lists for the Cunard Line, 1840–1853, are held at Liverpool University (with a copy available at the Merseyside Maritime Museum: **www.liverpoolmuseums.org.uk/maritime/archive/**). This museum also has many examples of souvenir passenger lists, either in shipping company collections or in ephemera collected by the passengers themselves, which date mainly from the 1880s onwards. For travellers to Britain before the 1890s, see 19.

Ships' passenger lists between 1890 and 1960 exist in the National Archives in vast quantity – and obviously include people from all over the world, not just from Britain and the British Empire. They are divided into two series, Inward and Outward – to Britain and from Britain. They cover all ports of the British Isles (and of what is now the Republic of Ireland up to 1923). These passenger lists are for long-distance voyages. They are no good for travel within Europe, unless

- the ship called at a European port en route, when any passengers picked up (on the way in) or dropped off (on the way out) were included on the list;
- transmigrants were among the passengers. These are people with a prepaid through ticket, travelling via Britain.

The Passenger Lists after 1960 have not been preserved centrally, though it may be worth getting in touch with the relevant shipping line to see if they have kept later ones. There are no passenger lists for air travel.

The **Inward Passenger Lists** (BT 26) can be a useful source of information for anyone arriving in or returning to the United Kingdom by sea as a paying passenger between 1890 and 1960. There are a very few lists surviving for 1878, also in BT 26. They give for each passenger name, age, occupation and address (in the United Kingdom) and the date of entry. Each ship provided separate lists for citizens of Britain and the British Empire and aliens (foreigners). The presence of passengers in transit (transmigrants) in a list is being included in the description (but not their names). Unfortunately, there are no name indexes as yet. However, we are part way through a major project to catalogue these records by ship, port of call and destination. (See the article by Burton and Harding for more information.)

The series is becoming increasingly searchable, but you may need to use different search strategies. The following catalogue entries give an indication of the information contained.

- New catalogue entry:
  BT 26/277/26 Southampton: RMS Kinfauns Castle (The Union-Castle Mail Steamship Company Ltd) travelling from Durban to Southampton. Embarking at Durban, East London, Port Elizabeth, Cape Town and Madeira. Official Number: 110173. List of passengers disembarking at Southampton. 1906 May 5.

  You could find similar entries by searching in BT 26 on the ship's name, or the company name or by any relevant port: it would be best to use a date range as there are many thousand such entries. You cannot search by country – Durban yes, South Africa no. Watch out for ports with potentially confusing names: Portland is in Ontario, not Dorset, and Halifax is in Nova Scotia, not Yorkshire. Kingston is Kingston, Jamaica.
- New catalogue entry with transmigrants:
  BT 26/948/4 Southampton: SS Homeric (White Star Line) travelling from New York to Southampton. Embarking at New York. Official Number: 146513. List of passengers disembarking at Southampton. [Passengers include transmigrants in transit to Russia, Belgium, Poland, Finland, Denmark and Yugoslavia.] 1930 Nov 15.
- Old catalogue entry:
  BT 26/725 Port: Southampton 1922 February to April.

You can search for these using port of arrival and year only.

Note that one ship on one voyage may have generated several passenger lists, as these were created to be handed in at each port of disembarkation.

After 1906, the Registers of Passenger Lists (BT 32) give, under each port, the names of the ships and their dates of arrival. It may be worth checking in *Lloyd's Register* for further clues: a copy is available at the National Archives.

Outwards Passenger Lists for 1890–1960 are in BT 27. These are lists of passengers leaving the United Kingdom by sea for destinations outside Europe and the Mediterranean area (they will include people disembarking en route at European or Mediterranean ports). Transatlantic vessels normally provide name, profession, sex, marital status, age and English/Scottish/Irish (later Welsh) classification. Vessels on other routes often provide just names and a vague destination, such as 'West Coast Africa'. Information is much fuller from 1922 onwards. Full addresses are given for British and alien non-transmigrants. For alien transmigrants (those with prepaid through tickets and not first class) no addresses are given, only the country, port of arrival and shipping line that brought them. The lists are arranged by year and by port of departure, and there are no name indexes. However, a bit of lateral thinking will show that ships leaving port must have arrived there first, and so you can use the better listing of BT 26 to work out where to look in BT 27. If you are looking for a ship that arrived in Durban from Britain in 1905, for example, but you do not know the ship or port of departure, try a search in BT 26 for 'Durban' restricted to 1906. Find out the port and date of arrival from Durban to estimate the date of departure to Durban.

The passenger lists may be digitised soon, which would allow for searching by name of passenger: if so, this will be clear on the National Archives website. In the meantime, we are finding out much more about passenger routes; lost knowledge is being regained. For example, some ships went on very roundabout routes: this one below curled right round the North Sea and English Channel to get to Liverpool from Canada (Portland being in Ontario, not Oregon).

- *BT 26/72/35 Liverpool: SS Labrador (Dominion Line) travelling from Portland to Liverpool. Embarking at Portland and Halifax. Official Number: 97889. List of passengers disembarking at Bergen, Christiana, Trondheim, Gothenburg, Malmo, Copenhagen, Esbjerg, Hamburg, Antwerp, Hull, London, Weston-super-mare, Bristol, Moville and Liverpool. 1895 Dec.*

17.3 Britons in foreign countries

For births, marriages and deaths of Britons in foreign countries (*not* in the colonies), see 8. Many of these records come from British consulates, others from British churches abroad. These records, taken as a historical source, can establish the existence of an expatriate community; the large number of burials in Oporto, for example, may lead to more about the British community there.

Under the Naturalization Act of 1870, Britons born in foreign countries (*not* in the colonies) could petition for a certificate of British nationality. This was only needed if their birth had not been registered at a British consulate. They submitted evidence to the nearest consulate, including their father's birth certificate, their parents' marriage certificate and their own birth certificate. The consul then forwarded the petition and documents to the Home Office, with the request that the documents be returned to their owner. However, some of the files do contain a brief précis of this information, which can be very useful. Others, alas, do not. Search in HO 45, using search 'origin AND *surname*'. You may then find it worthwhile to go back to the correspondence of the relevant consulate, which will be in the FO code (search by name of consulate in FO to get the series, and then look for the volume covering the right date).

Foreign Office (and the earlier State Papers Foreign) records may be worth investigation, although they can be difficult to find, but you still need to use the indexes and registers at the National Archives. A good guide exists to using Foreign Office and earlier records in Atherton's *Never Complain, Never Explain*. At the moment it is probably fair to say that these records in general take some dedication to access; they may contain treasure, but it can't be guaranteed.

However, the recent detailed cataloguing of FO 383 has opened up records about individual Britons interned in enemy countries during the First World War (see 31 for records of internment). A search on 'repatriation' in FO 83 brings up files on the relief and repatriation of pauper lunatics 1865–1905, of distressed Britons abroad 1886–1905 and of distressed Colonial and Indian subjects 1881–1905. (For the repatriation of mentally ill Britons from China, 1908–1932, see C 211/70–75 ②.) The probate records of the Shanghai Supreme Court, 1857–1941, are in FO 917 ②. Other wills of some Britons in China, 1837–1951, are in FO 678/2729–2931 ③ or ②. The probate records of the British Consular Court at Smyrna, Turkey, 1820–1929, are in FO 626 Ⓕ.

For people working for the Foreign Office, look at the *Imperial Calendar* or the *Foreign Office List* for information on postings.

17.4 Britons in the Empire

So far we have produced only one detailed guide to this subject area: Grannum's *Tracing Your West Indian Ancestors*. In fact, this includes information on many sources relevant for other parts of the colonies as well – more than can be given here.

Most colonial records are still where they were created – in the old colony or dominion. This applies particularly to records of birth, marriage and death. Any records described in this book may well have parallels in colonial archives. Probably the best way to explore them is to go via the national archives site of each ex-colony (try a search on the web), or by a family history site such as **www.cyndislist.com** (which will also give you links to relevant websites hosting much information).

However, there was a huge central administration of colonial and dominion affairs run from London, which received regular despatches, petitions, reports and publications from or about the colonies. These records are now in the codes CO, DO or FCO, for various periods. The annual *Colonial Office List* or the *Dominions Office*, available at the National Archives, gives a country-by-country guide and a staff list, which give brief career details of civil servants.

Early records have been published in précis in the *Calendar of State Papers, Colonial*. The volumes of this that cover America and the West Indies have recently been republished on CD-Rom and are now very easily searched. Other volumes, covering other parts of the world, still have to be seen in hard copy, but they do have reasonable indexes. Records after 1740 are not well catalogued, and you will need to use the original registers of correspondence at the National Archives to find your way around them: try a search by 'colony AND correspondence'. There are research guides available at **www.nationalarchives.gov.uk** to help you use the various indexes to these records. You may not find a direct reference to your ancestors, but you will find much about the institutions and events of where they were living. See the guides to these records by Pugh and Thurston for more detail.

The many series of Colonial and Dominions Original Correspondence may be worth exploring, but really need further cataloguing to open them up; they are arranged by name of colony. Recent cataloguing work has concentrated on correspondence from the Caribbean and has opened up much of interest about individuals. For example:

- 1860 Mar 7 Mr. Isaac Lindo, one of the Colonial Revenue Officers in Grenada; Memorial for an appointment at Sierra Leone or elsewhere; 'Mr Lindo is a Gentleman of colour, and a native of Barbados.' Both Hincks and Kortright recommend his application. Francis Hincks, Governor of Windward Islands, Grenada 10, Folios 102 – 107. CO 101/116/10;
- 1863 Oct 26: Forwards a petition from Matilda Cundy requesting financial assistance. Cundy was the widow of Convict Department Chief Warden Robert Cundy who died in 1851 while serving on the hulk Thames. Harry St. George Ord, Governor of Bermuda, No. 83, Folios 305–309. CO 37/187/49;
- 1916 July 20: Medical superintendent, Lunatic Asylum: submits applications for post from Dr W B Grannum and Dr J D Alleyne. With application

forms and copies of references. Leslie Probyn, Governor of Barbados, No. 138, folios 67–81. CO 28/289/11.

The colonies had their own legal systems, and most disputes were settled locally. However, there are many records of disputes from the colonies in the National Archives. Most involve shipping, and are to be found in the High Court of Admiralty records in HCA and PCAP (see 61). Some came as appeals from common law courts and ended up before the Privy Council. The Privy Council keeps these colonial appeals, both civil and criminal, and you will need to make an appointment to see them: see 62 for the address. However, the detailed listing of Caribbean correspondence has made available records such as:

- 1937 Dec 24–1938 Mar 12: Lutchmin Prashad Sukool, drug store proprietor of Blankenburg, Demerara: Privy Council appeal against conviction for murder of his store assistant; includes copies of trial papers, exhibits, and newspapers, 1935 to 1937. CO 111/753/1.

If you follow a Privy Council appeal, it is worth checking for related material in the correspondence from the relevant colony.

If a property formed part of a wider estate, a dispute may have been litigated in England, particularly in Chancery or in the Prerogative Court of Canterbury, which specialised in inheritance disputes (see 58 and 10). In some cases, the evidence brought into court as an exhibit was left behind. These exhibits are now in C 103–C 115, E 140 and J 90 (all ①④); and in PROB 31 Ⓕ, PROB 32 ②④ and PROB 36 ②④. These exhibits can contain letters and accounts from the colonies.

The government of each British colony or dominion published its own newspapers, known as government gazettes (or official or royal gazettes) for most of the nineteenth and twentieth centuries: to find out what exists, search the catalogue for '*colony* AND government gazettes'. Government gazettes usually have an index at the beginning of each volume; the names of individuals are usually listed in sub-sections. For instance, those appointed to positions in the colony will probably be listed in the 'appointments' category of the index. Some of the more common entries in which individuals appear are lists of immigrants and emigrants, voters' rolls, and notifications of appointments to positions in official bodies, the police and military services. Other items about individuals include notices concerning deaths and estates of the deceased, divorce, insolvency, and legal disputes and criminal cases. Frequently, the gazette will give valuable information about the person in question, including his or her address.

The majority of people named in the gazettes were settlers from Britain. However, members of colonised populations do appear in the records. This is especially true in countries where local people, at certain points, played a role in the workings of government – as policemen or clerks, for instance. Where people were legally property they might also appear in the records. Gazettes from the Caribbean, for example, carry advertisements for the return of slaves who had escaped. Some gazettes – depending on time and place – contain lists of Indian indentured labourers or of people applying for British citizenship. The records are also more likely to name male rather than female ancestors, but since women did own property, get divorced, leave wills and vote, their names appear from time to time.

If you are looking for individuals working for colonial governments, you *may* also find them listed in the Blue Books. These were books in which (mainly statistical) information on each colony was reported. They are usually arranged in the CO and DO 'miscellanea' series (search by '*colony* AND miscellanea') but occasionally they can be found in the supplements to the gazettes. In addition, there are series entitled 'public service lists' in several series for Australia (1902–1927), Canada (1887–1910), Iraq (1919–1920), New Zealand (1916–1920). To find these records, search the catalogue using 'public service lists' as the search term.

The National Archives also holds a small selection of newspapers published in the colonies, mostly covering the period *c.* 1830–*c.* 1860, although there are a few eighteenth-century examples. These are listed in the 'newspapers' section of the CO index at the National Archives. However, the British Library Newspaper Library (address in 62) has much more extensive holdings of colonial newspapers. You can search their catalogue by place as well as title at **www.bl.uk/catalogues/newpapers**. Other material of interest exists at the British Empire and Commonwealth Museum.

17.5 The British in India

The National Archives is not the place to trace Britons and Anglo-Indians in India. The central government body involved was not the Colonial Office but the India Office, whose records are now held at the British Library. However, the India Office catalogues are searchable from our website (**www.nationalarchives.gov.uk**), either on a site search or by going into A2A. The India Office Records include the archives of the East India Company (1600–1858); of the Board of Control or Board of Commissioners for the Affairs of India (1784–1858); of the India Office (1858–1947); of the Burma Office (1937–1948); and of a number of related British agencies overseas. More detailed information is available in Baxter, *India Office Library and Records: A Brief Guide to Biographical Sources.*

The India Office Records hold collections that cover the pre-independence history of present-day India, Pakistan, Bangladesh and Burma, on neighbouring countries of South and South-East Asia and on St Helena, South Africa, the Gulf States, Malaysia, Singapore, Indonesia, China and Japan. They are rich in biographical information on East India

Company servants, civil servants and Indian Army personnel, and on Europeans resident in pre-1947 India.

A biographical card index for the records (not included in A2A) is being compiled from a variety of sources. It currently contains 295,000 entries for civil and military servants and their families, and for non-official Europeans living in India. In addition, there are copy registers of births/baptisms, marriages and burials of European and Eurasian Christians in India, Burma and territories controlled from India, as well as wills, grants of probate and administration; inventories; and pension material. In addition, they hold the records of the Indian Army, the various naval forces, the Indian railway companies and the Civil Service.

The National Archives Library holds a run of the annual *East India Register*, continued by the *India List* (under various titles) from 1791–1947, as well as the separate *Indian Army List*. For other sources, see 27. For pension records of members of the East India Company Army, 1814–1875, try WO 23 ⑦. For Army pensioners in India between 1772 and 1899, taken from WO 120/35, 69 and 70, see Crowder, *British Army Pensioners Abroad, 1772–1899*. This is now also on the website of the Families in British India Society, **www.fibis.org**, which you should explore. Another source is *The Indiaman Magazine*, at **www.indiaman.com**, and yet another for family history in British India, **www.ozemail.com.au/~clday/**. The British Association for Cemeteries in South Asia is also worth checking out at **www.bacsa.org.uk**, and you may well be interested in the British in India Museum (address in 62).

For an overview of the problems of and sources for tracing Anglo-Indian families, see Charles, 'Anglo-Indian Ancestry'. See also *Sources for Anglo-Indian Genealogy in the Library of the Society of Genealogists*. For Indian families, see Husainy and Trumpbour's articles.

17.6 Britons around the world: bibliography

L ATHERTON, *'Never Complain, Never Explain'. Records of the Foreign Office and State Paper Office, 1500–c.1960* (PRO, 1994)

I A BAXTER, *India Office Library and Records: Brief Guide to Biographical Sources* (London, 1990)

V BRENDON, *Children of the Raj* (2005)

British Library, *India Office Records, Sources for Family History Research* (London, 1988)

J A BRYDEN, 'Genealogical Research in Gibraltar', *Genealogists' Magazine*, vol. XXIV, pp. 289–293

J BURTON and N HARDING, 'Bound for Britain', *Ancestors*, 37 (2005)

Calendar of State Papers, Colonial 1574–1738 (London, 1860–1970)

G CHARLES, 'Anglo-Indian Ancestry', *Genealogists' Magazine*, vol. 27 no. 3 pp. 104–110 (Sept 2001)

N K CROWDER, *British Army Pensioners Abroad, 1772–1899* (Baltimore, 1995)

East India Register (various titles)

D GILMOUR, *The Ruling Caste: Imperial Lives in the Victorian Raj* (2005)

G GRANNUM, *Tracing Your West Indian Ancestors* (2nd edn, PRO, 2002)

I V FITZHUGH, 'East India Company Ancestry', *Genealogists' Magazine*, vol. XXI, pp. 150–154

R HOLMES, *Sahib: the British Soldier in India* (2005)

A HUSAINY and J TRUMPBOUR, 'British Sources for South Asian ancestors', *Ancestors* 13 (2003)

A HUSAINY and J TRUMPBOUR, 'Military Sources for South Asian Ancestors', *Ancestors* 14 (2003)

India [Office and Burma Office] List, 1791–1947

Indian Army List, 1901–1939

R KERSHAW, *Emigrants and Expats: A guide to sources on UK emigration and residents overseas* (PRO, 2002)

M MOIR, *A General Guide to the India Office Records* (London, 1988)

Public Record Office, *The Records of the Foreign Office 1782–1939* (London, 1969)

R B PUGH, *The Records of the Colonial and Dominions Office* (London, 1964)

N C TAYLOR, *Sources for Anglo-Indian Genealogy in the Library of the Society of Genealogists* (SoG, 1990)

The Indiaman Magazine

A THURSTON, *Records of the Colonial Office, Dominions Office, Commonwealth Relations Office and Commonwealth Office* (London, 1995)

18 Emigration

18.1   Emigrants: general points

Large-scale emigration from Britain took place to the American colonies, the West Indies, Canada (British North America), the United States of America, Australia, New Zealand and southern Africa. According to the latest general history of British emigration (Richards, *Britannia's Children*) over 25 million people from Britain and Ireland emigrated between 1600 and 2000. For a specialist guide to the records of emigration in the National Archives, see Kershaw, *Emigrants and Expats*.

Much information about emigrants has been published over the years: the most useful items are listed in the bibliographies at 18.9 and 47.13 – and of course the internet offers a huge amount of material. The records of the countries receiving the travellers do tend to be fuller – and earlier in date – than those of the UK in bidding them goodbye. Similarly, much information exists in printed sources. Many of these are available on the internet, which carries some wonderful examples of international cooperation by volunteers and interested parties. Try **www.theshipslist.com** and **www.immigrantships.net**. For an overview of what is available, and links to other sites, look at **www.cyndislist.com** and **www.port.nmm.ac.uk**. There are some excellent specialist sites: for example, **www.warbrides.co.uk** is the place to look for **war brides** emigrating to join their husbands after the Second World War (based on passenger lists). This site is an offshoot of **www.passengerlists.co.uk/**. Other strongly recommended sites are **www. portcities.org.uk/**, covering London, Liverpool, Southampton, Bristol and Hartlepool, and **http://www.liverpoolmuseums.org.uk/maritime/**, the website of the Merseyside Maritime Museum.

No permission or passport was required to emigrate – if you could pay. If financial assistance was needed, approval had to be given and was usually confined to married couples and related family. Single women without family were discouraged. Some registers of emigrants asking for assisted passage survive for New Zealand and South Australia in the National Archives. However, most of our records on emigration tend to be about emigration rather than about emigrants. Involuntary emigrants are easier to trace: see 47 on the transportation of convicts.

If you are trying to trace ancestors coming back *into* the United Kingdom, there is little likelihood of finding a family before the censuses, or before the central registration of births, marriages and deaths (1837 in England and Wales, 1855 in Scotland) unless their place of origin is known or they were reasonably well off on emigrating. Emigrants who died with goods in England and Wales had their wills proved and inventories presented in the Prerogative Court of Canterbury, and so can be very easily found (see 10). However, the very useful *British 19th Century Surname Atlas* CD-Rom created from the 1881 census data (**www.archersoftware. co.uk/satlas01.htm**) may help you pinpoint at least a region or county to investigate.

18.2 Emigrants: general sources for most destinations, 1814–1960

The records of the Colonial Office include much material relating to emigrants. However, like so much of the records of nineteenth-century government, they have not been catalogued in detail and can be difficult to find. The ongoing cataloguing of Caribbean correspondence has turned up some wholly unexpected documents, such as:

- 1872 Dec 21 Reports on the recent immigration of 40 Swedes; encloses minutes of the Immigration Board, a list of applicants who desired to employ immigrants, a register that lists the immigrants' names, ages, birth places, occupations, salaries, and employers as well as examples of the kind of agreements that Swedish emigrants would have signed before leaving Sweden. John Henry Lefroy, Governor of Bermuda, No. 76, Folios 518–539. CO 37/202/91.

Who knows what stories will emerge when this material is catalogued properly? In the meantime, it will take dedication and good luck to track down any correspondence or petitions. Many letters from settlers or people intending to settle in British North America, Australasia, the West Indies and other places can be found in Emigration Original Correspondence, 1817–1857 (CO 384 ⑦). There are separate registers for British North America for 1850–1863 (CO 327 ⑦) and 1864–1868 (CO 328 ⑦). The Land and Emigration Commission was established in 1833 to promote emigration by providing free passage and land grants. The Emigration Entry Books, 1814–1871 (CO 385 ⑦) and the Land and Emigration Commission Papers, 1833–1894 (CO 386 ⑦) all bear investigation. CO 386 contains some jewels:

- registers of births and deaths of emigrants at sea 1854–1869 (CO 386/170–172);
- lists of ships chartered 1847–1875 (CO 179/185);
- registers of surgeons appointed 1854–1894 (CO 386/186–187).

Medical journals kept by the surgeons of 28 emigrant ships between 1825 and 1853 are included in ADM 101 ⑥.

Many poor emigrants were provided with assistance for the passage by their parish, under the provisions of the 1834 Poor Law Amendment Act. You may be able to find **parish lists of emigrants**, giving their occupation and destination. These are in MH 12 ⑦, among much other poor law material, and are not indexed. You need to know the likely poor law union the emigrants came from before starting this quest (see 41). Other records relating to parish-organised emigration will be found locally: see the article by Burchall, listed in the bibliography under North America and West Indies.

Passenger lists exist from 1890 to 1960: see 17.2 for more details and for information on earlier lists. Between 1836 and 1914, over 2.2 million people arrived from eastern Europe, Russia and Scandinavia at Hull, and left shortly after from Liverpool, London or Southampton on their way to a new world. Special trains were laid on to transport them across England. You should be able to find them leaving (but not entering) Britain by using the passenger lists. There is an interesting article on this on the site about Norwegian emigration at **www.norwayheritage.com/ships/**. But because these transmigrants used the same routes as British emigrants, the site can uncover a wide range of very useful sources. (You don't need to read Norwegian as most of those emigrants went to English-speaking countries.) See also the important site **www.passengerlists.co.uk/**.

18.3 Emigrants: possible sources for ex-soldiers and sailors, 1817–1903

Many ex-soldiers settled in the colonies. The awards of pensions to soldiers in British regiments stationed abroad or in native or colonial regiments, 1817–1903, are in WO 23/147–160 ⑦. These registers are arranged by the date of the board that granted admission to pension, but entries relating to a particular place (e.g., Canada, West Indies or the Cape) are fairly easy to find. These registers can provide a birthplace and details of service. Many of the entries relate to British soldiers who left the Army while their regiment was abroad, and who appear to have settled there.

Another potentially useful source for tracing people in receipt of a pension payable by the War Office (usually ex-soldiers and sailors, but also members of the East India Services) may be the registers of pension payments, 1842–1883, in WO 22 ⑦, which are arranged by place of payment. There are separate registers for places like Canada, New South Wales and

New Zealand, but also composite registers for miscellaneous colonies and for 'consuls' – who presumably had the responsibility for administering payments in foreign countries rather than colonies. The pensions were sometimes to widows or dependent children.

18.4 Emigrants to North America and the West Indies

The National Archives has a lot of material relating to early emigration to the West Indian and American colonies. Much of this has been printed in some form. Most of it is administrative in character, but it can include useful genealogical material. Main published sources include records of the Privy Council printed as *Acts of the Privy Council of England, Colonial Series*. Various useful classes of Treasury papers have been described and indexed in the *Calendar of Treasury Papers, 1557 to 1728* and the *Calendar of Treasury Books and Papers, 1729 to 1745*. The major early collections of papers relating to the West Indies and the American colonies are now searchable in the CD-Rom of *Calendar of State Papers, Colonial, America and West Indies*. This can also be accessed at the National Archives. Records relating to the West Indies are described in Grannum's *Tracing Your West Indian Ancestors*.

During the colonial era, some 200,000 to 300,000 indentured servants came to the British in America – about half of all emigrants. Indentured servitude was used to recruit and transport workers from England who could not otherwise afford the voyage. In return for their passage, maintenance during their service and certain rights at the end of their years of servitude, servants undertook indentures to work for their masters for a fixed number of years. Much has been written on this topic: see, for example, Coldham, *Bonded Passengers to America, 1615–1775*.

Registers of passengers bound for New England, Barbados, Maryland, Virginia and other colonies survive for 1634–1639, and for 1677 (E 157 ☑): the information in them, together with similar information (from CO 1) has been printed in Hotten, with more added by Brandow. For a further listing of passengers to America, 1618–1688, taken from the port books in E 190, see the typescript index available (by 'AMDG') at the National Archives (filed in the Map Room as 'refers to E 190 vol 3'). Port books (E 190 ☑) list the names of passengers transporting dutiable goods, but you need to have some idea of the port of departure or else be prepared for a very lengthy search after 1688. If you are researching an early emigrant, you may be interested in Alison Games' study of 5,000 travellers to America and the West Indies in 1635, *Migration and the Origins of the English Atlantic World*, which was based on the 1635 London port book.

There is a considerable amount of information on the inhabitants of Barbados, 1678–1680, including lists of property owners, their wives, children, servants and slaves, some parish registers and lists of the militia (CO 1/44 no. 47 i–xxxvii, CO 29/9 pp. 1–3). There is a descriptive list of the various records (with no names) in the *Calendar of State Papers, Colonial America and West Indies, 1677–1680*, no. 1236 i–xxxvii, which you should look at first. The white inhabitants of Barbados were listed in a census in 1715 (CO 28/16). (See Lane on Barbadian sources.)

A useful, though unfortunately short-lived, register (T 47/9–12 [F]) was kept of emigrants going from England, Wales and Scotland to the New World between 1773 and 1776. The information for England and Wales has been summarised in a card index, available at the National Archives, which gives name, age, occupation, reason for leaving the country, last place of residence, date of departure and destination. For 1815 only, there are details of 757 settlers enrolling in Edinburgh for emigration to Canada. Most came from Scotland, but some were from Ireland and England (AO 3/144).

Some information on colonists is contained in the correspondence and papers of the Colonial Office, which cover the West Indies as well as the continent of America and start in 1574: see the printed calendars listed in 18.9. The Chancery Town Depositions (C 24) contain interesting information about life in early colonial America, including much genealogical data, but they are not well listed: see the article by Currer-Briggs for reference to an index.

Details on tracts of land in West and East New Jersey, Pennsylvania, New England and elsewhere are in the records of the West New Jersey Society (TS 12 [7]), a company formed in 1691 for the division of land. There are many names in the correspondence, minute books, share transfers, deeds and claims. For the settlement of East Florida in 1763, and compensation for its handing back to Spain in 1783, see the records in T 77 [7] and the article by Foot. For employees and settlers of the Hudson's Bay Company, see BH 1 [7] and the article by Douglas.

In 1696, the mayor, recorder and commonalty of New York City swore the oath of association in support of William III: the resulting oath roll contains the signatures and marks of much of the male population of the city (C 213/470: see 20.2). During and after the American War of Independence, many people suffered losses on account of their loyalty to the British Crown and many subsequently migrated to Canada (British North America). They were entitled to claim compensation under the Treaty of Peace in 1783 and a new Treaty of Amity between Great Britain and the United States of America in 1794. See 34.8 for more details.

Records relating to slave owners in the West Indies, 1812–1846, are among Treasury, Audit Office and National Debt Office papers (T 71, AO 14, NDO 4). The surveys in T 71 may give the names of owners, plantations and even sometimes the slaves. Among the Chancery Masters' Exhibits, in C 103–C 114, are many private papers from West Indies plantations.

For ex-soldiers and sailors (or their widows and orphans) in receipt of a Chelsea or Greenwich pension who had settled in Canada, the registers of payment of the pension may be useful. There are separate volumes for

Canada, 1845–1862 (WO 22/239–242) and for Nova Scotia, 1858–1880 (WO 22/294–296). The composite volumes for several colonies, 1845–1875, may also be useful (WO 22/248–257). The muster rolls for Canadian militia and volunteers, 1837–1843, may be worth checking for ex-regulars (WO 13/3673–3717): earlier records are in Canada.

Emigrants from other countries to the American colonies can sometimes be traced through records in the National Archives. Lists of the names of Palatine subjects, who emigrated to America by way of Holland and England in 1709, occur in several classes: the easiest way to discover them is to use the published works by Knittle, MacWethy and the *New York Genealogical and Biographical Review*. (See also 19.2.)

Between 1740 and 1772, foreign Protestants living in the Americas could become naturalised British citizens by the act 13 George II, c. 7. This required seven years' residence, the swearing of oaths of allegiance (for Quakers, making an affirmation) and taking the sacrament according to the Anglican rite (this last requirement was waived for Quakers and Jews). Every year lists of those naturalised (now in CO 5 ⑦) had to be sent to the Commissioners for Trade and Plantations in London, where they were copied into entry books (CO 324/55–56). These provisions covered the West Indies as well as the American continent, but in fact only Jamaica (1740–1750), Maryland (1743–1753), Massachusetts (1743), New York (1740–1770), Pennsylvania (1740–1772), South Carolina (1741–1748) and Virginia (1743–1746) returned the lists to London. Over 7,000 foreign Protestants took advantage of this act: Giuseppi has printed their names in the Huguenot Society volume XXIV: see **www.huguenotsociety.org.uk/**.

Another method of naturalisation, used by hundreds rather than thousands, was by the expensive process of obtaining an act of the colonial assembly (CO 5 ⑦). To trace such a naturalisation it will usually be necessary to have a good idea of the date and also the colony of residence.

18.5 Emigrants to Australia and New Zealand

Microfilms of many relevant National Archives documents were made by the Australian Joint Copying Project and are available in Australia at the National Library in Canberra (**www.nla.gov.au**) and at the Mitchell Library in Sydney. Try accessing the National Archives website at **www.naa.gov.au**. For New Zealand, try **www.archives.govt.nz** and the Dictionary of New Zealand Biography database at **www.cultureandheritage.govt.nz/History/ DNZB**.

European settlement of Australia began with the penal colony of New South Wales in 1788. In the National Archives there are few records relating to voluntary emigrants to Australia and New Zealand until the Passenger Lists (BT 27), which survive from 1890: see 17.2. In Australia, however, there is material relating to British settlers who received assisted passages. For a good overview, and for access to many records and newspaper reports, see www.theshipslist.com/ships/australia for both Australia and New Zealand. In the National Archives there is far more extensive documentation of the transportation of convicts to Australia (see 47). However, to some extent the records of convict transportation also cover free emigrants as, in some cases, a convict's family would accompany him as voluntary emigrants and can be traced through some of the same records. A register of applications for passages to the colonies for convicts' families, 1848–1873, is in CO 386/154.

Censuses of convicts were conducted at intervals between 1788 and 1859 in New South Wales and Tasmania (HO 10): although primarily concerned with the convict population they do contain the names of those members of their families who 'came free' or who were 'born in the colony'. The fullest is that of 1828: see the edition by Sainty and Johnson, *New South Wales: Census ... November 1828*. The other editions by Baxter are also very useful: that for 1823–1825 gives a lot of background detail.

New South Wales Original Correspondence (CO 201 [F]) starts in 1784 and contains lists of emigrants. A microfiche index (the Deane index) to these settlers, military men and convicts is available at the National Archives. For registers to the correspondence before 1849, see CO 326 [7], and after 1849, see CO 360 [7]. For an indexed précis of correspondence see CO 714 [7].

The papers of the Land and Emigration Commission (CO 386 [7]) also contain correspondence and entry books of the South Australian Commission. They include three volumes of a register of emigrant labourers applying for a free passage to South Australia between 1836 and 1841, with a name index to the first two volumes only (CO 386/149–151, index at 152). The registers give name, trade, residence, age of children and an embarkation number if they were successful. The volumes contain over 9,422 entries – some relating to whole families or single people. A detailed list of those who died aboard emigrant ships arriving in South Australia between 1849 and June 1865 was published in the *South Australia Government Gazette* of 25 January 1866: see our copy at CO 16/20, pages 75–96.

New Zealand was not used as a penal colony. The first European settlement of New Zealand was around 1820. Details of early British emigrants may be found in the records of the New Zealand Company in CO 208 Original Correspondence, 1839–1858. Microfilm copies of CO 208 can also be seen at the National Library of Australia, the State Library of Victoria and the State Library of New South Wales, Mitchell Library, Australia. For lists of ships going to New Zealand from 1840 to 1885, see Brett's *White Wings*.

The New Zealand Company was formed in 1839 and incorporated in 1841 with power to buy, sell, settle and cultivate land in New Zealand. It surrendered its charter in 1850 and was dissolved in 1858. This series of records contains:

- registers of cabin passengers emigrating, 1839–1850, in CO 208/269–272;
- applications for free passage from emigrant labourers, 1839–1850, in CO 208/272–273 (indexed in CO 208/275), with original applications in CO 202/274;
- applications for land and lists of landowners, in CO 208/254–255.

Between 1846 and 1851, **Army pensioners** were encouraged to settle in New South Wales and New Zealand, although many of them failed as settlers. References to the settlement of ex-soldiers in Australia and New Zealand will be found in the National Archives' *Alphabetical Guide to Certain War Office and Other Military Records*, under *Australia and New Zealand*. There are also lists of ex-soldier emigrants, 1830–1848, to Australia (WO 43/542) and New Zealand (WO 43/543). Pensions from the Army and Navy were payable at district offices: records survive for offices in New South Wales, 1849–1880 (WO 22/272–275); in South Australia, Queensland, Tasmania and Victoria, 1876–1880 (WO 22/227, 297, 298 and 300); and in New Zealand, 1845–1854 and 1875–1880 (WO 22/276–293). Others deserted to settle: see *The Deserters* by Sexton.

18.6 Emigrants to South Africa

Registers of payments to Army and Navy pensioners (including some widows and orphans) at the Cape of Good Hope and elsewhere in South Africa, 1849–1858 and 1876–1880, are in WO 22/243–244. The muster rolls of the Cape Levies, 1851–1853, may prove useful (WO 13/3718–3725). The Genealogical Society of South Africa will give advice; see also Lombard's article.

18.7 Emigrants to Argentina

For a general history of emigration to Argentina, see Graham-Yooll, *The Forgotten Colony*. The best place for family historians to start is Jeremy Howat's excellent website *British Settlers in Argentina* at **http://homepage. ntlworld.com/jnth/**. This is an indexed collection of records from Argentina that document the presence of thousands of British and other English-speaking residents there. Records include baptisms, marriages, deaths and burials from the Anglican and Scots Presbyterian churches, transcripts from the National Archives of Argentina and the UK, Argentine census returns and contemporary publications.

According to Howat, the English were arriving in Buenos Aires in small numbers from as early as 1806, principally as businessmen and traders. Over the nineteenth century, many more English families with capital came and invested in large landed estates, founded banks and developed the export and import trade. Many of the Irish emigrants to the country came as sheep farmers, others to serve as agricultural labourers. The Scots arrived in contingents from 1825 on vessels sailing from Scottish ports. They founded great ranches, established Presbyterian churches and raised large families; many, through hard work, became wealthy.

The Welsh founded an idealistic Welsh-speaking community in Patagonia in 1865, hoping that its remoteness would preserve their language and customs. Between 1865 and the First World War, about 3,000 Welsh people emigrated to Patagonia in a conscious attempt to found a new Wales. Many of later generations migrated again, mainly to Canada and Australia, and some of them went back to Wales, but a significant Welsh-speaking community remains. For an overview of this community emigration, see Derrick, 'Welsh Emigration to Patagonia'. This gives references to passenger lists and many other documents in the National Archives, some in unexpected places. A passenger list of the *Mimosa* (which took the first Welsh emigrants to Patagonia), for example, can be found in FO 118/121 (dated 1866). For a Welsh Patagonian genealogy and oral history site, visit www.welsh-patagonia.com. For a full bibliography compiled by the National Library of Wales, try www.llgc.org.uk/lp/ lp0066.htm.

18.8 Children's emigration

Schemes to promote the emigration of poor children and orphans date back to the early seventeenth century. In the nineteenth century, emigration was encouraged by poor law legislation and by the activities of charities such as Dr Barnardo's. Most of the surviving papers at the National Archives on child emigration in the late nineteenth and the twentieth centuries are policy papers. MH 102 ⑥ contains records on child migration after the Second World War: some of the records are closed for 75 years but others, seen by the Child Migrant Trust, are now open after 30 years.

See Bean and Melville's *Lost Children of the Empire* for a useful overview of the subject. For child emigration to Australia, see *Good British Stock: Child and Youth Emigration to Australia* by the National Archives of Australia: this lists relevant National Archives series. For Canada, see the website (at **www.archives.ca**) of the National Archive of Canada.

18.9 Emigration: bibliography

General

Acts of the Privy Council of England, Colonial Series, 1613–1783 (London, 1908–1912)

L ATHERTON, *'Never Complain, Never Explain': Records of the Foreign Office and State Paper Office, 1500–c.1960* (PRO, 1994)

P BEAN and J MELVILLE, *Lost Children of the Empire* (1989)

Calendar of State Papers, Colonial, America and West Indies, 1574–1738 (London, 1860–1969) (Republished as a searchable CD-Rom, Routledge and Public Record Office, 2000.)

Calendar of Treasury Books, 1660–1718 (London, 1904–1962)

Calendar of Treasury Papers, 1557–1728 (London, 1868–1889)

Calendar of Treasury Books and Papers, 1729–1745 (London, 1898–1903)

J S W GIBSON, 'Assisted Pauper Emigration, 1834–1837', *Genealogists' Magazine*, vol. XX, pp. 374–375

Journals of the Board of Trade and Plantations, 1704–1782 (London, 1920–1938)

R C KERSHAW, *Emigrants and Expats: a guide to sources on UK emigration and residents overseas* (PRO, 2002)

Public Record Office, *Alphabetical Guide to Certain War Office and other Military Records preserved in the Public Record Office*, Lists and Indexes, vol. LIII (London, 1931)

R B PUGH, *The Records of the Colonial and Dominions Office* (London, 1964)

E RICHARDS, *Britannia's Children: Emigration from England, Scotland, Wales and Ireland since 1600* (Hambledon, 2004)

A THURSTON, *Records of the Colonial Office, Dominions Office, Commonwealth Relations Office and Commonwealth Office* (London, 1995)

North America and West Indies

'AMDG', 'Ships, Merchants and Passengers to the American Colonies 1618–1688' (unpublished MS, dated Purley 1982) [Taken from the Port Books in E 190.]

C M ANDREWS, *Guide to the Materials for American History to 1783 in the Public Record Office of Great Britain* (Washington, 1912 and 1914)

C E BANKS and E E BROWNELL, *Topographical Dictionary of 2885 English Emigrants to New England, 1620–1650* (New York, 1963, 1976)

C BOYER ed., *Ships' Passenger Lists: The South* (1538–1825); *National and New England* (1600–1825); *New York and New Jersey* (1600–1825); *Pennsylvania and Delaware* (1641–1825) (4 vols, Newhall, California, 1980)

J C BRANDOW, *Omitted Chapters from Hotten … Census Returns, Parish Registers and Militia Rolls from the Barbados Census of 1679/80* (Baltimore, 1983)

M J BURCHALL, 'Parish-Organised Emigration to America', *Genealogists' Magazine*, vol. XVIII, pp. 336–342

P W COLDHAM, *American Loyalist Claims* (Washington, 1980)

P W COLDHAM, *Bonded Passengers to America, 1615–1775* (Baltimore, 1983)

P W COLDHAM, *The Bristol Registers of Servants Sent to Foreign Plantations 1654–1686* (Baltimore, 1988)

P W COLDHAM, *The Complete Book of Emigrants, 1607–1776* (4 vols, Baltimore, 1987–1993)

P W COLDHAM, *Emigrants from England to the American Colonies, 1773–1776* (Baltimore, 1988)

P W COLDHAM, *English Adventurers and Emigrants, 1609–1660: Abstracts of Examinations in the High Court of Admiralty, with Reference to Colonial America* (Baltimore, 1984)

P W COLDHAM, *English Estates of American Colonists: American Wills and Administrations in the Prerogative Court of Canterbury, 1610–1699 and 1700–1799* (Baltimore, 1980)

P W COLDHAM, *English Estates of American Settlers: American Wills and Administrations in the Prerogative Court of Canterbury, 1800–1858* (Baltimore, 1981)

P W COLDHAM, *Lord Mayor's Court of London, Depositions relating to America, 1641–1736*, National Genealogical Society (Washington, 1980)

N CURRER-BRIGGS, 'American Colonial Gleanings from Town Depositions', *Genealogists' Magazine*, vol. XVIII, pp. 288–294

D DOBSON, *The Original Scots Colonists of Early America 1612–1783* (Baltimore, 1989)

D DOBSON, *Scottish Emigration to Colonial America 1607–1785* (Georgia, 1994)

A DOUGLAS, 'Genealogical Research in Canada', *Genealogists' Magazine*, vol. XXIII, pp 217–221

A DOUGLAS, 'Gentlemen Adventurers and Remittance Men' [Hudson's Bay Company], *Genealogists' Magazine*, vol. XXIV, pp. 55–59

R H ELLIS, 'Records of the American Loyalists' Claims in the Public Record Office', *Genealogists' Magazine*, vol. XII, pp. 375–378, 407–410, 433–435

P W FILBY, *American and British Genealogy and Heraldry* (Chicago, 2nd edn, 1975)

P W FILBY ed., *Passenger and Immigration Lists Bibliography 1538–1900* (Michigan, 1981)

P W FILBY and M K MEYER eds, *Passenger and Immigration Lists Index*, 13 volumes (Michigan, 1981–1995) (Lists *c*. 2,410,000 names of immigrants to USA and Canada, from the sixteenth to mid-twentieth centuries.)

W FOOT, 'That most precious Jewel' – East Florida 1763–83', *Genealogists' Magazine*, vol. XXIV, pp. 144–148

G FOTHERGILL, *A List of Emigrant Ministers to Australia 1690–1811* (London, 1904)

D W GALENSON, *White Servitude in Colonial America* (Cambridge, 1981)

A GAMES, *Migration and the Origins of the English Atlantic World* (Cambridge, Mass., 1999)

M S GIUSEPPI, *Naturalizations of Foreign Protestants in the American and West Indian colonies*, Huguenot Society, vol. XXIV, 1921

I A GLAZIER and M TEPPER, *The Famine Immigrants: Lists of Irish Immigrants Arriving at the Port of New York, 1846–1851* (Baltimore, 1983)

A C HOLLIS HALLETT, *Early Bermuda Records 1619–1826* (Bermuda, 1991)

J C HOTTEN, *Original Lists of Persons emigrating to America, 1600–1700* (London, 1874) [see also Brandow]

C B JEWSON, *Transcript of Three Registers of Passengers from Great Yarmouth to Holland and New England, 1637–1639*, Norfolk Record Society, vol. XXV (1954)

J AND M KAMINKOW, *A list of Emigrants from England to America, 1718–1759* (Baltimore, 1964)

W A KNITTLE, *Early Eighteenth Century Palatine Emigration* (Philadelphia, 1937)

A KULIKOFF, *From British Peasants to Colonial American Farmers* (Chapel Hill, 2000)

A H LANCOUR, *A Bibliography of Ships' Passenger Lists, 1538–1825* (New York, 1963)

G E LANE, *Tracing Ancestors in Barbados* (Baltimore, 2006)

G E MCCRACKEN, 'State and Federal Sources for American Genealogy', *Genealogists' Magazine*, vol XIX, pp. 138–140

M E MACSORLEY, *Genealogical sources in the United States of America* (Basingstoke, 1995)

L D MACWETHY, *The Book of Names especially relating to the Early Palatines and the First Settlers in the Mohawk Valley* (New York, 1932)

B MERRIMAN, 'Genealogy in Canada', *Genealogists' Magazine*, vol. XIX, pp. 306–311

National Archives and Record Administration, *A Guide to Genealogical Research in the National Archives* 3rd edn (Washington, 2001)

New York Genealogical and Biographical Records, vols. XL and LXI (New York, 1909 and 1910) (for Palatine emigrants)

L St Louis-Harrison and M Munk, *Tracing your ancestors in Canada* (National Archives of Canada, 1998)

G Sherwood, *American Colonists in English Records* (2 vols, London, 1932, 1933) (Lists passengers not mentioned in Hotten.)

C J Stanford, 'Genealogical Sources in Barbados', *Genealogists' Magazine*, vol. XVII, pp. 489–498

M Tepper, *American Passengers Arrival Records* (Baltimore, 1993)

M Tepper, *Passengers to America: A Consolidation of Ship Passenger Lists from the New England Genealogical Register* (Baltimore, 1988)

M Tepper ed., *New World Immigrants* (Baltimore, 1980) (a consolidation of passenger lists)

D Whyte, *A Dictionary of Scottish Emigrants to the USA* (Baltimore, 1972)

Australia and New Zealand

C J Baxter, *General Muster and Land and Stock Muster of New South Wales, 1822* (Sydney, 1988)

C J Baxter, *General Muster of New South Wales, 1823, 1824, 1825* (Sydney, 1999)

C J Baxter, *Musters and Lists New South Wales and Norfolk Island, 1800–1802* (Sydney, 1988)

C J Baxter, *Musters New South Wales, Norfolk Island and Van Diemen's Land, 1811* (Sydney, 1987)

G Bell, 'Convicts, colonists and colliers' [emigration to New South Wales], *Ancestors* 30 (2005)

H Brett, *White Wings. Vol. 1 Fifty years of sail in the New Zealand trade 1850–1900. Vol 2 Founding of the provinces and old time shipping: passenger ships from 1840 to 1885* (Auckland, 1924 and 1928, reprinted 1976)

A Bromell, *Tracing Family History in New Zealand* (Wellington, 1991)

P Burns and H Richardson, *Fatal Success: A History of the New Zealand Company* (Auckland, 1989)

M Chambers, *Finding Families: The Guide to the National Archives of Australia for Genealogists* (Canberra, 1998)

Y Fitzmaurice, *Army Deserters from HM Service* (Forest Hill, Victoria, 1988 continuing)

M Flynn, *The Second Fleet* (1993)

M Gillen, *The Founders of Australia, A Biographical Dictionary of the First Fleet* (Sydney, 1989)

D T Hawkings, *Bound for Australia* (Guildford, 1987)

H and L Hughes, *Discharged in New Zealand – Soldiers of the Imperial Foot Regiments who took their discharge in New Zealand 1840–1870* (Auckland, 1988)

D Hussey, 'Bound for Australia', *Ancestors* 6 (2002)

R Kershaw, 'Going Down Under: Migration to Australia and New Zealand', *Ancestors* 18 (2004)

L Marshall and V Mossong, 'Genealogical Research in New Zealand', *Genealogists' Magazine*, vol. XX, pp. 45–49.

J Melton, *Ship's Deserters 1852–1900* (Sydney, 1986)

A G Peake, *Bibliography of Australian Family History* (Dulwich, South Australia, 1988)

A G Peake, *National Register of Shipping Arrivals: Australia and New Zealand* (Sydney, 1992)

M R Sainty and K A Johnson eds, *New South Wales: Census ... November 1828 ...* (Sydney, 1980)

R Sexton, *The Deserters: Military and Naval Deserters as settlers in Australia and New Zealand 1800–1865* (1998)

P Stanley, *The Remote Garrison: the British Army in Australia 1788–1870* (Kenthurst, 1986)

N Vine Hall, *Tracing your Family History in Australia – A Guide to Sources* (London, 1985)

H Woolcock, *Rights of Passage: Emigration to Australia in the 19th Century* (London, 1986)

South Africa

E Bull, *Aided Immigration to South Africa, 1857–1867* (Pretoria, 1991)

R J Lombard, 'Genealogical Research in South Africa', *Genealogists' Magazine*, vol. XIX, pp. 274–276

E Mosse Jones, *Rolls of the British Settlers in South Africa* (Capetown, 1971)

P Philip, *British Residents at the Cape 1795–1819* (Capetown, 1981)

Argentina

B Derrick, 'Welsh Emigration to Patagonia', *Ancestors* 8 (2002)

A Graham-Yooll, *The Forgotten Colony: a history of the English-speaking communities in Argentina* (London, 1981)

A Hennessy and J King, eds, *The Land that England lost: Argentina and Britain, a special relationship* (London, 1992)

19 Immigration and nationality

19.1 Britons and aliens

Individual immigrants have been coming to Britain for centuries. If they came from Ireland and the British colonies across the world, they were Britons; if they came from elsewhere (including Scotland before 1707), they were called aliens. Aliens (to my sons' disappointment) were simply people from foreign countries (and not further away) who acknowledged another sovereignty. They were treated as a separate legal species, with fewer rights, because they were under no constraint of loyalty to the Crown. As a result, they are far better documented than migrants from Ireland and the colonies. However, the Crown only took real interest in documenting aliens at times of great political upheaval in Europe – during the French Revolution, during the revolutionary decade of the 1840s and throughout the twentieth century.

Once migrants had arrived and settled, they can be found in the normal ways, through registration of births, marriages and deaths, the census, etc. Watch out for how people describe themselves in the census: we find increasingly that many people call themselves naturalised British citizens when they were not. Who was to know? The census was guaranteed confidential and it has taken at least one hundred years to be able to compare the relevant records. Citizenship was a much less severe code before the twentieth century. Passports were little used, and Britons from across the world were British citizens. It was only from 1948 onwards that colonial Britons had to register British citizenship, with the door being closed behind them.

If you are interested in finding out more about nineteenth- and twentieth-century immigrants and immigration, explore the website www.movinghere.org.uk, where you can find out about the experiences of people from the Irish, Jewish, Caribbean and South Asian communities who moved to live in England. It is a joint resource created by writers, historians and curators using material from archives and museums all over England, and contains documents, photographs, sound and film clips. You can

- download (free) records, newspapers and photographs that tell the stories of migration;
- discover the different reasons why people came to England through case studies;
- listen to people's personal experiences of the different receptions they faced when arriving in England, and the struggle to create a new home;
- search the catalogue for associated material and get detailed advice on tracing your roots.

To get an even earlier view, try the web exhibition *Black Presence: Asian and Black History in Britain from 1500 to 1850* at www.nationalarchives.gov.uk/ pathways/blackhistory/. The Museum of Immigration is trying to save a unique house in East London that embodies so much of the immigrant history of this country from the Huguenots onwards (www. 19princeletstreet.org.uk). If the house is saved, its exhibition will reopen.

The National Archives publishes a specialist guide to immigration records, *Immigrants and Aliens* by Kershaw and Pearsall, which you could consult for more detailed advice. It includes a very useful list of relevant collections in local record offices, as well as a preface pointing out other potential sources of information.

19.2 Aliens arriving before 1793

Foreigners coming to settle were treated with some suspicion as a result of their supposed allegiance to another state. Medieval aliens had to pay double taxes, and there are separate lists of contributors to the 'alien subsidies' or taxes in E 179 (see 52). There are also three surveys of aliens living in London, taken in November 1571 (SP 12/82), December 1571 (SP 12/84) and [September] 1618 (SP 14/102) (published in transcript by the Huguenot Society).

Many French and Germans came to England to escape religious persecution of Protestants on the continent. The Huguenots were French Protestants fleeing from religious persecution from the 1550s onwards. They came in large numbers after the Revocation of the Edict of Nantes (which reversed the previous policy of toleration) in 1685. It is quite possible, however, for a Huguenot ancestor to appear in England some time after this, as many fled first to Holland or Germany and only later moved to England. The Central Bureau of Genealogy of Holland may be able to assist in these cases. There are often strong family traditions of Huguenot descent, and names with a French flavour are usually a good indication of such a background.

The main Huguenot settlements were in London (notably in Spitalfields and Soho), Norwich, Canterbury, Southampton, Rye, Sandwich, Colchester, Bristol, Plymouth, Thorney and various places in Ireland. In the late seventeenth century, it is estimated that some 45,000 Huguenots settled in Britain. There are no known records of any communities in the Midlands or the north of England and there is little on settlement in Scotland. It is of course more difficult to trace a family which struck out on its own to a new part of the country where no French church existed, and which used the local parish church for baptisms. Huguenot burial records are rare at all times and by the nineteenth century almost non-existent, except for the records of deaths of the inmates of the London Huguenot Hospital, which are in the Huguenot Library. For a fee, the Huguenot Library will undertake a brief search in their archive, which includes pedigrees and records about the administration of funds collected for the relief of the refugees. No personal callers can be seen, so you will need to write (address in 62).

Huguenot material is also to be found in other areas of settlement: for example, in the Guildhall Library of London, the Cathedral Library at Canterbury, the Norfolk Record Office at Norwich and the Archives Office at Southampton. Most of the sources for Huguenot genealogy in the National Archives have been published by the Huguenot Society in some form, and are available in the Library. See also **www.huguenotsociety. org.uk** for CD-Rom versions of its publications.

Thousands of Germans emigrating to the American colonies had to trans-ship in England. Among them, in 1709, was a sudden flood of Protestant exiles from the Rhine valley (sometimes known as the 'poor Palatines'), driven out by the ravages of a war and a desperately hard winter. They were aided onwards to England by the British Resident at The Hague, who sent embarkation lists back to the Treasury (now in T 1/119). Most of the Palatines were sent on to America, but many stayed behind in England and some even settled in Ireland. Many of the relevant sources have been published: see 18.4 and 18.9.

References before the eighteenth century may be traceable through the published *Calendars of State Papers Domestic*, as well as through the main series of Chancery enrolments (see 11.3). For the later seventeenth and the eighteenth centuries, try the published calendars of Treasury records, continued in the online catalogue to 1794 in T 1 ⬚. See Kershaw and Pearsall, *Immigrants and Aliens*, Chapter 8, for more detailed information.

For most of the eighteenth century, passes (for foreigners as well as natives) into and out of the country were issued by the Secretaries of State and noted in SP 44/386–411 Ⓔ for 1697–1784 and (in an overlapping book) in FO 366/544 Ⓔ for 1748–1794. These are included (and indexed) in the

Calendar of State Papers Domestic until 1704, and again in the *Calendar of Home Office Papers* for 1760–1775; for other years there is no index.

19.3 Aliens arriving 1793–1826

The French Revolution produced the next great influx of aliens. A registration system was first set up by the Aliens Act of 1793. On entering England, aliens were required to register with a Justice of the Peace and to give their name, rank, address and occupation. The JP then sent a certificate to the Aliens Office. These certificates appear to have been destroyed, although an index survives from 1826 to 1836 in HO 5/25–32 ⑦. However, the records of the Justices of the Peace may have survived in local record offices: see Kershaw and Pearsall, *Immigrants and Aliens*, Appendix 2, for more details. Some passes issued to aliens are included in the correspondence volumes of HO 1 ⑦, recording name, port of entry, nationality, religion, occupation, place of residence and intended destination. Aliens arriving in English ports, 1810–1811, may be traced in FO 83/21–22 ⑦.

The arrival of the émigrés provoked much government documentation (HO 69, PC 1, FO 95 and WO 1: try an initial search on these series using 'emigr?s OR emigr?'). For payments by the Treasury and by the French Refugee Relief Committee to French refugees, you need to explore T 50 ⑦ and T 93 ⑦. (Try Carpenter's book *Refugees of the French Revolution* first.) T 50 includes registers of allotments of pay from serving officers and men to their wives or families between 1795 and 1812, as well as pay lists of Breton and Norman refugees, ships' books, etc.

For entry books of correspondence about aliens, see HO 5 ⑦.

19.4 Aliens arriving 1836–1869

The political situation in Europe was in turmoil in the middle of the 1800s, with revolutions occurring or looking likely in several countries – including the UK. From 1836, a new Aliens Act required incoming aliens to sign certificates of arrival. They survive in HO 2 Ⓕ for aliens arriving in England and Scotland, 1836–1852 only. The certificates give nationality, profession, date of arrival, last country visited and, sometimes, other information. They are indexed to 1849 only (HO 5/25–32 ⑦).

The masters of ships sent lists of alien passengers, 1836–1869, to the Home Office (HO 3 ⑦Ⓕ). They are bound up in date order and there is no general index. However, if you are looking for a German, Pole or Prussian between 1847 and 1852, then try the Metzner index in the Research Enquiries Room. This covers both HO 2 and HO 3. For entry books of correspondence about aliens, see HO 5 ⑦.

We have records of annuities and pensions paid to some refugees for services to the Crown. These include

- allowances to Polish refugees, 1828–1856 (PMG 53 7, T 50 7 and T 1/409) and 1861–1865 (AO 3/1418);
- allowances to Spaniards, 1828–1829 (T 50 7) and 1855–1909 (PMG 53 7 and T 1/4285);
- Toulonese refugees, also Corsicans and Knights of Malta, 1834–1840, reports on applications and allowances (T 50 7);
- refugees from Holland, Malta and Santo Domingo, 1829–1841 (T 50 7).

19.5 Arriving by sea, 1878–1960: inwards passenger lists

The Inward Passenger Lists (BT 26 6 5) can be a useful source of information for anyone arriving by sea between 1890 and 1960 from places outside Europe and the Mediterranean area. (There are a very few lists surviving for 1878, also in BT 26.) These passenger lists are no good for travel within Europe, unless the ship had stopped at a European port on its inward voyage, when any passengers picked up were included on the list. This can include a surprising array of European and Scandinavian ports, however. The passenger lists give name, age, occupation and address (in the United Kingdom) and the date of entry; each ship provided separate lists for British citizens and aliens. To use these records, see 17.2.

Passenger lists of some ships bringing groups of Indian and Caribbean migrants between March 1948 and October 1960 are indexed by ship and person at **www.movinghere.org.uk**.

19.6 Aliens from *c.* 1914

Concerns about the increasing numbers of Jews arriving from Russian Poland led in 1905 to an Aliens Act to make aliens able to enter the UK only at the discretion of the authorities (see Lawes on this). For entry books of correspondence about aliens, see HO 5 7. Records do not seem to survive before the First World War.

Registration of aliens was tightened up in 1914 and again in 1919. Aliens had to register with the local police. Surviving registration cards for the London metropolitan area are in MEPO 35 2 – but only about 1,000 cases survive from the tens of thousands created since 1914. Most of the surviving cards are from the late 1930s. Some (but not all) police registration records have survived locally – for example, Bedfordshire and Luton Archives holds 25,000 record cards from 1919 until the 1980s (address in 62). For similar locally held collections, check Kershaw and Pearsall, *Immigrants and Aliens*, Appendix 2. See HO 213 7 for policy files of the Home Office Aliens' Department from 1914 onwards. Registration of aliens became a concern of MI5: some lists and addresses of suspected aliens are in KV 1 7.

Several thousand Belgians fled to the UK during the First World War. For these Belgian refugees, 1914–1919, there is a considerable amount of material entered on the 'history cards' in MH 8/39–93. Each card relates to a whole family, unless the refugee was single with no known relatives. The details given are name, age, relationships, wife's maiden name, allowances and the address for payment. Some hostel lists of refugees in 1917 are in MH 8/10. See the article by Fowler and Gregson for more details.

For Jewish refugees of the 1930s and 1940s, see 45. Records of the Czechoslovak Refugee Trust are in HO 294 (⬜, but also ⑦): they relate not only to Czechoslovak refugees, but also to German and Austrian refugees. The series includes some specimen personal files on families: these are closed for 50 years (some for 75 years) from the last date on the file.

During the two World Wars the British authorities interned enemy aliens: see 31 for details.

19.7 Poles in and after the Second World War

Poles had a particular welcome as immigrants. For details of war service in the Polish Free Forces, write to the Ministry of Defence, Polish Section (address in 62). The records of the Polish Resettlement Corps, set up in 1946 to ease their transition to civilian life in Britain and abroad, are in WO 315 ⑦. Other records relating to Polish resettlement are in AST 18 ⑦, with some in AST 7 ⑦, AST 11 ⑦, AST 1/23 and ED 128 ⑦. Many of these records are in Polish, and some are closed for 75 years. There are also some files on World War Two Polish pensions in PIN 15/2905–2917.

19.8 Deportations, 1906–1963

The power to expel aliens who had become paupers or criminals was given by the Aliens Act of 1905 (although monarchs had been expelling their own citizens and others for centuries – from the Jews expelled by Edward I in 1290 to the gypsies threatened by the Tudors). Common reasons for such expulsions were failure to register with or report regularly to the police, ignoring work restrictions and becoming a charge on public funds. Deported aliens were not permitted to return. The registers of deportees, 1906–1963, are in HO 372 ⑦. These tend to give name, nationality, date of conviction and offence, as well as whether (and when) the deportation order was revoked.

19.9 British passports

A passport now is seen as proof of citizenship, but this is a very recent development. Most Britons never had or needed a passport. The first passports were simply licences to travel overseas. For the late sixteenth and early seventeenth centuries, there are registers of people applying for licences before going overseas in E 157 ⑦. The earliest dates from 1572. There are lists of soldiers taking the oath of allegiance before going to the wars in the Low Countries, 1613–1624, and licences to go abroad, mostly to Holland,

1624–1632. For passes to go abroad between March 1650 and February 1653, see SP 25/111.

For most of the eighteenth century, passes (for natives as well as foreigners) into and out of the country were issued by the Secretaries of State and noted in SP 44/386–411 for 1697–1784 and (in an overlapping book) in FO 366/544 for 1748–1794. These are included (and indexed) in the *Calendar of State Papers Domestic* until 1704, and again in the *Calendar of Home Office Papers* for 1760–1775; for other years there is no index. The weekly emigration returns kept between 1773 and 1776 include Britons travelling for business or pleasure, as well as emigrants: see the card index to T 47/9–12.

From 1794, the issue of passports (or safe conducts) was regulated, but they were not a requirement for people leaving the country. It was rare for someone travelling abroad to apply for one: most holders of passports were merchants or diplomats. Until 1858, UK passports could be granted to people who were not British but who requested the protection of the UK while travelling. These passports were simple pieces of paper requesting that foreign powers should allow the holder to travel without hindrance. During the First World War, many European countries used passports to prove national identity, and Britain made them mandatory for British travellers in 1914. The first hard-cover passports were introduced in 1915.

If you have passports in the family, they should contain useful material. Unfortunately, the records of the *issue* of passports (which is what we hold) are disappointing, as they contain little information. The registers of passports issued, 1795–1948, are in FO 610 E: for March to May 1915, the register is in FO 613/2. The entries, in date order, show merely the date, the number of the passport issued and the name of the applicant. There are indexes for 1851–1862 and 1874–1916, but they give no more information (FO 611). A very miscellaneous collection of over 2,000 British and foreign passports, 1802–1961, is in FO 655 7; they are listed haphazardly, by date and place of issue. A small selection of case papers, 1916–1983, is in FO 737 7. For more detail, it may be worth checking in the correspondence of the Passport Office, 1815–1905 (FO 612/21–71 7). Records of British passports issued in foreign countries and British colonies may sometimes be found in consular and colonial records.

19.10 Aliens become Britons: denization and naturalisation

Foreigners wishing to become English (or later, British) had two options. They could apply for denization (which made them almost equivalent to native-born and granted them most of a free subject's rights and the protection of the king's laws) or naturalisation (which granted them all rights and made them a subject of the Crown). However, most foreign settlers did not bother to go through the legal formalities, and so do not appear in these records. In general, applications were only considered from people who had lived here for five years within the previous eight. The process itself was expensive and until the First World War did not bring many advantages. We get a surprising number of enquiries about people who described themselves in the census as naturalised but have left no trace in the naturalisation process. They obviously thought it was a good thing to make such a claim.

Denization took place when an alien was made a denizen by letters patent from the Crown. As a denizen, he could purchase land but could not inherit it. Any children born after the parents' denization appear to have been subjects: those born before could only be denizens. Denizens had the additional burden of paying a higher rate of tax, and were ineligible for government posts. Letters patent of denization were enrolled on the Patent Rolls (c 66) and the Supplementary Patent Rolls (c 67). Denizations before 1509 can be traced through the indexes to the *Calendar of Patent Rolls*; in the early volumes individual names are not given in the index, and it is necessary to look under 'Denizations' or '*Indigenae*'.

Naturalisation was more expensive than denization. It originally required a private act of Parliament, as well as the swearing of oaths of allegiance and supremacy and taking Holy Communion according to the Anglican rite, effectively disbarring Roman Catholics and Jews. It made the foreigner a king's subject, able to inherit land, and affected the children born before naturalisation as well. Naturalisations by private act of Parliament up to 1900 may be seen at the House of Lords Record Office (**www. portcullis.parliament.uk**). Between 1708 and 1711, all foreign Protestants who took the oaths of allegiance and supremacy in open court were deemed to have been naturalised (KB 24 ⑦, E 169/86). The information from these oath rolls has been published by the Huguenot Society. Between 1740 and 1773, foreign Protestants in the Americas were naturalised by the same process: see 18.4. Many Spanish Jews in Jamaica were also granted naturalisation, which was easier for a Jew to acquire in the West Indies than in England.

In 1844, the procedure for naturalisation was simplified and the Home Office began granting certificates of naturalisation. The Home Office only issued a certificate after initial investigations had been conducted satisfactorily. Access to these successful investigations (**naturalisation papers**) has recently been transformed by the Citizenship project involving many staff at Kew (see the article by Kershaw). The old indexes have been put online, thus getting rid of a very complicated process of working out modern references. Checking of the references then showed that many files had never been indexed at all, including those for alien soldiers serving in the First World War, who applied for naturalisation through a special procedure. All are now searchable online.

Naturalisation papers can be found in HO 1 ② for 1844 to 1871, HO 45 ② for 1872 to 1878, HO 144 ② from 1879 to 1934 and HO 405 ①I for 1934 to 1948. (Some famous people are in HO 382 ②.) A search before 1934 should provide the certificate number as well, which can then be used to find a copy of the certificate (see below).

Between 1934 and 1948, many thousands of individual foreign citizens (mostly European) arrived in the UK and applied for naturalisation. Personal files investigating them were kept by the Home Office. A selection of those relating to famous people was initially made: these are in HO 382. All the rest were scheduled for destruction. However, representations by historians and archivists about their value saved the 40 per cent of the correspondence files that survive: these are now in HO 405 ①. This is still a very large collection, so it may not all be available for several years (currently only surnames A to N have been transferred). All records dated after 1922 are closed for periods up to 100 years, though the Home Office will consider opening files on request. For files already transferred you can request a review by using the Request Review link in the Catalogue. For files not yet transferred, write to the Home Office, Departmental Records Officer (address in 62).

The actual **naturalisation certificates** were issued to the new citizens but the state kept copies between 1844 and 1969. For 1844 and 1873, the deeds of naturalisation were enrolled on the Close Rolls in C 54 Ⓕ. For 1870–1969, copy naturalisation certificates are in HO 334 Ⓣ. You need the certificate number to access them. You should be able to get this by searching for the naturalisation papers (above) for most of this period, but there are also indexes at the National Archives. The duplicate certificates end in June 1969. After this, the Home Office did not keep copies. If you need confirmation of naturalisation after this date, write to the Immigration and Nationality Department (address in 62), who will provide a letter suitable for legal purposes. The indexes do continue after 1969: if you want information rather than legal proof of naturalisation, the indexes give the same details as the letter would.

19.11 Registering British citizenship, from 1949

Under the British Nationality Act 1948, people from the independent Commonwealth countries had to register their citizenship in order to remain British citizens, and were issued with certificates of proof. People from the colonies that were not yet independent were still automatically British citizens and so did not need to register. However, as the African and Caribbean colonies became independent, their citizens too lost their British citizenship unless they registered as well. After 1968 this applied to all remaining colonies. There were certain restrictions: a father or grandfather had to have been a British citizen by birth or naturalisation.

Certificates show the name, address, trade or occupation, country of origin and the names of spouse and children if applicable. The Home Office kept a copy of the certificate (known as an R certificate) issued. These are in HO 334 Ⓣ, from 1949. If you are looking for the copy of a certificate issued less than 31 years ago, write to the Home Office, Departmental Records Officer: see 62 for the address. The National Archives has no name indexes for these certificates. If you do not already have the registration certificate number, you need to write to the Immigration and Nationality Department and ask for it: see 62 for the address.

19.12 Renouncing British citizenship

The Naturalization Act of 1870 allowed for the renunciation of British nationality by people born in the United Kingdom of foreign parentage. These 'declarations of alienage' can be found in HO 45 ☑, HO 144 ☑ and HO 344/259: most date from the first half of the twentieth century. The introduction of conscription in the First World War may well have caused an upsurge in these declarations. Some give proof of the entitlement to British citizenship.

19.13 Immigration and nationality: bibliography

Published works

K CARPENTER, *Refugees of the French Revolution: émigrés in London 1789–1802* (Basingstoke, 1999)

K CHATER, 'Taking French Leave' [Huguenots], *Ancestors* 33 (2005)

S FOWLER and K GREGSON, 'Bloody Belgians!', *Ancestors* 33 (2005)

G GRANNUM, *Tracing Your West Indian Ancestors* (Public Record Office, 2002)

Huguenot Society, *Publications* (now available on CD-Rom: see **www.huguenot society.org.uk/**)

Huguenot Society, *Returns of Aliens Dwelling in the City and Suburbs of London* (Publications of the Huguenot Society, vol. X)

A HUSAINY and J TRUMPBOUR, 'British Sources for South Asian ancestors', *Ancestors* 13 (2003)

R KERSHAW, 'Becoming a Brit: The Home Office Naturalisation Papers and the Citizenship Project', *Ancestors* 22 (2004)

E G KIRK, *Returns of Aliens in London, 1523–1603* (Huguenot Society, vol. X, London, 1900–1908)

R KERSHAW and M PEARSALL, *Immigrants and Aliens* (Public Record Office, 2000)

P LAIDLAW, 'Moving Here Earlier: Jewish Immigration before the 1880s', *Ancestors* 10 (2002)

A LAWES, 'Trying to close the door' [1905 Aliens Act], *Ancestors* 32 (2005)

R W PAGE, *Denization and Naturalisation of Aliens in England, 1509–1603* (Huguenot Society, vol. VIII, Lymington, 1893)

Registers of Churches, of Huguenots in London and elsewhere (Huguenot Society, London, 1887–1956)

W A SHAW, *Letters of Denization and Acts of Naturalisation for Aliens in England, 1603–1800* (Huguenot Society, Lymington, 1911, Manchester, 1923 and London, 1932)

R SWIFT, *Irish Migrants in Britain, 1815–1914: a documentary history* (Cork, 2002)

Published calendars

Public Record Office, *Calendar of Close Rolls, 1227–1509* (London, 1892–1963)

Public Record Office, *Calendar of Home Office Papers 1760–1775* (London, 1878–1899)

Public Record Office, *Calendar of Patent Rolls, 1216–1509, 1547–1582* (London, 1894–1986)

Public Record Office, *Calendar of State Papers, Domestic Series, 1547–1704* (London, 1856–1972)

Public Record Office, *Calendar of Treasury Papers, 1557–1728* (London, 1868–1889)

Rotuli Parliamentorum, Edward I to Henry VII (London, 1783, Index, London, 1832)

Unpublished finding aids

B LLOYD, 'List and Registers of Dutch Chapel Royal, 1689–1825'

Metzner index to German, Polish and Prussian aliens, 1847–1852, in HO 2 and HO 3

20 Signatures: oaths of allegiance, loyal addresses and petitions

20.1 Lists of signatories
20.2 Oath rolls
20.3 Loyal addresses
20.4 Petitions
20.5 Signatures: oaths of allegiance, loyal addresses and petitions: bibliography

20.1 Lists of signatories

Lists of signatories may not on the face of it be very useful to family historians, but they can provide evidence of existence, of neighbours and societies, and of matters of concern. They provide a context in which to build up knowledge, but are speculative: you may read hundreds of signatures and not actually get proof that the John Smith who signed was your John Smith. They are probably a better source if you are interested in the local history of your family.

20.2 Oath rolls

Between the sixteenth and nineteenth centuries, people were required on various occasions to swear oaths in support of the Crown and the Anglican church. Some of these oaths were sworn by those taking up or holding official positions and by lawyers on being admitted to the courts. Others were sworn by aliens in the process of becoming naturalised British subjects. Still others were taken by people to signify their loyalty to the Crown in times of political upheaval. Not all such oaths are recorded in the Oath Rolls held by the National Archives. The most notable exception is an oath in support of Crown, Parliament and the Protestant Religion, intended for all men over the age of 18 in 1641. These Protestation returns were sent into Parliament, and are now in the House of Lords Record Office (address in 62): they are listed by Gibson and Dell.

Anyone taking up any civil or military office was required by the Corporations Act of 1661 and the Test Act of 1672 to take the oaths of allegiance and supremacy. They also had to deliver a certificate into court stating that they had received the sacrament of the Lord's Supper according to the rites of the Church of England. These acts were not repealed until 1828. The Sacrament Certificates, signed by the minister and churchwardens of the parish, survive from 1672 to 1828 but are not easy to use (c 224, CHES 4, KB 22 (all 7) and E 196 4, 5).

The oath rolls are found in different places, depending on the occupation and place of residence of the person taking the oath. Oaths could be sworn before Justices of the Peace at Quarter Sessions or, if resident within 30 miles of Westminster, at one of the central courts of law in Westminster Hall. As a result, oath rolls may be found either in local record offices or in the National Archives. Oath rolls, including classes devoted to the oaths of lawyers (see 38), survive in the records of Chancery (c 193/9, c 184, c 214, c 215), Common Pleas (CP 10), Exchequer (E 169, E 200, E 3) and King's Bench (KB 24, KB 113) (all 7). Oath rolls of attorneys in the courts of Chester and Durham also exist (CHES 36/3, DURH 3/217) (all 7). Oaths of clergy (1789–1836) and of Roman Catholics after the conditions were relaxed (1778–1829) are in CP 37 7.

Between 1708 and 1711, all foreign Protestants who took the oaths of allegiance and supremacy in court, and who produced a sacrament certificate, were deemed to have been naturalised (KB 24, E 169/86 7). In its volumes XXVII and XXV, the Huguenot Society has indexed the rolls in the National Archives: other rolls, of oaths taken before the Quarter Sessions, may survive in county record offices. See 18.4 for oaths of allegiance on naturalisation in North America and the West Indies.

The Association Oath Rolls (c 213 4, 5 and c 214 7) contain the signatures or marks and names of people subscribing to the 'Solemn Association' of 1696, in support of William III after a Jacobite attempt to assassinate him. The oath of association was taken by everyone in a position of any authority – all members of Parliament, all military, Naval and civil office-holders of the Crown, the clergy and the gentry, freemen of the city companies and others besides. In some places, such as Jersey, Westminster and Suffolk, almost every adult male appears to have subscribed, and the returns approximate to a census of adult men: the Jersey and Guernsey rolls have been published in full by Glendinning. Transcripts are also appearing for other counties, such as Surrey and Wiltshire. C 213 also includes rolls from certain colonies and overseas settlements, such as Holland, Malaga, Geneva, Jamestown and New York.

20.3 Loyal addresses

Loyal addresses to the Crown were often subscribed with many names and published. For example, the editions of the *London Gazette* between September 1775 and March 1776 contain 150 loyal addresses supporting the war against America. The *London Gazette* can be seen at the National Archives in ZJ 1 7.

20.4 Petitions

Petitions to the Crown or to the government exist by the million among the public records. Most are from individuals, but there are several thousand from identifiable local groups. A good way to find them is to search the catalogue using petition AND inhabitant AND [place] as keywords.

For example:

- HO 44/35 Petition of inhabitants of the city of Gloucester, requesting abolition of the church rate and the freeing of John Thorogood, a Protestant dissenter gaoled for refusing to pay it. 1840;
- T 1/538/249–250 Petition from inhabitants of Mevagissy for Customs officer to 'clear and enter' vessels bringing salt and lumber for their important pilchard exporting trade, since at present they have to use Fowey 1777 July 31.

Petition AND householder brings up over 300 petitions to the Privy Council (PC) from the nineteenth and early twentieth centuries from a wide variety of 'new' towns about the issue of charters to those towns.

You may find petitions about local post offices, such as 'POST 14/70 Papers relating to the revision of rural posts under Ludlow, including petition from inhabitants of Orleton for establishment of a sub post office in the parish. 1855–1856'. Remember that these POST records are not held by the National Archives but by the British Postal Museum (address in 62).

20.5 Signatures: oaths of allegiance, loyal addresses and petitions: bibliography

A Supplement to Dr W Shaw's Letters of Denization and Acts of Naturalization (Huguenot Society, vol. XXXV, Frome, 1932)

J GIBSON, *The Hearth Tax, Other Later Stuart Tax Lists, and the Association Oath Rolls* (FFHS, 1996)

J GIBSON and A DELL, *The Protestation Returns 1641–42 and other contemporary listings: collection in aid of distressed Protestants in Ireland, subsidies, poll tax, assessments or grants, vow and covenant, solemn league and covenant* (FFHS, 1995)

A GLENDINNING, *Did Your Ancestor Sign the Jersey Oath of Allegiance Roll of 1696?* (Channel Islands Family History Society, 1995)

A GLENDINNING, *Eye on the Past in Guernsey* (Channel Islands Family History Society, 1992)

W A SHAW ed., *Letters of Denization and Acts of Naturalization for Aliens in England and Ireland 1701–1800* (Huguenot Society, vol. XXVII, Manchester, 1923)

C R WEBB, 'The Association Oath Rolls of 1695', *Genealogists' Magazine*, vol. XXI, pp. 120–23

21 Electoral registration

21.1 Poll books

Poll books are locally compiled lists of men who were entitled to vote (and sometimes of who they voted for) dating from the seventeenth to the nineteenth centuries. Until the late nineteenth century, only a minority of the male population (and none of the female) was normally entitled to vote in parliamentary elections. In the counties, the traditional qualification was ownership of freehold land worth at least 40 shillings a year, although in some boroughs all householders might have the right to vote. Electoral records need to be used with some knowledge as to the local qualification. The franchise was extended in 1832, 1867 and 1884 to cover most male householders, but not until 1921 did it cover all males over 21 normally resident in a constituency. Women over 30 who were householders or married to householders were also given the vote in 1921. Women did not receive voting rights equal to those of men until 1928.

There are large collections of poll books in the British Library, the Guildhall Library and the library of the Society of Genealogists. County record offices and local libraries have collections relating to their own areas. For a guide to their use and whereabouts, see Gibson and Rogers, *Poll Books c. 1696–1872*.

21.2 Electoral registers

After the 1832 Reform Act an annual register was kept of persons (still mostly male property-holders) entitled to vote. These registers were compiled every year (except for 1916–1917 and 1940–1944) and were deposited with the clerk of the peace. Most historic ones are now in local record offices or libraries, and are also at the British Library. For a useful guide, see Gibson and Rogers, *Electoral Registers since 1832 and Burgers Rolls*.

Those few electoral registers at the National Archives are listed here and may be seen in the National Archives Library. Most come from the early 1870s, but there are some for Norfolk from 1832–1833.

Current electoral registers for the locality can be seen in local public libraries: a national set is kept at the British Library. There are also several commercial websites where you can access information on the current electoral rolls: try a search on one of the standard search engines for 'electoral rolls UK'.

21.3 Electoral registers in the National Archives Library

England	
Bedfordshire	1874
Berkshire	1874; Wallingford 1874
Bristol City	1874
Buckinghamshire	1874; Aylesbury 1874; Buckingham 1874
Cambridgeshire	1872; Isle of Ely 1874
Cheshire	East 1874; Mid 1874; West 1874
Cornwall	1872–1875; East 1874; West 1874; Bodmin 1874; Helston 1874; Launceston 1874; Liskeard 1872, 1873; St Ives 1875
Cumberland	East 1874; West 1874; Carlisle City 1875; Cockermouth 1874; Whitehaven 1875
Derbyshire	East 1868–69, 1870; North 1870; South 1870
Devon	1875; East 1874; North 1874; South 1874; Barnstaple 1874
Dorset	1872, 1874; Poole 1870; Shaftesbury 1872; Wareham 1871
Durham	North 1874; South 1874; Hartlepool 1874; Stockton 1875
Essex	East 1875; South 1875; West 1875; Colchester 1874
Gloucestershire	1872, 1874; Cirencester 1872; Stroud 1873; Tewkesbury 1874
Hampshire	1874; North 1874; South 1874; Andover 1874; Petersfield 1874
Herefordshire	1874
Hertfordshire	1875
Huntingdonshire	1874; Huntingdon 1874
Kent	East 1874; Mid 1874; West 1874; Canterbury 1873
Lancashire	North 1874; North East 1874; South East 1874; South West 1874; Oldham 1873
Leicestershire	South 1874
Lincolnshire	Mid Lincs, Kesteven 1874; Mid Lincs, Lindsey 1874; North Lincs, Lindsey 1874; South Lincs, Kesteven 1874; Grantham 1874
Middlesex	1874
Monmouthshire	1874
Norfolk	East 1832–33; North 1874; South 1874; West 1832–33, 1874
Northamptonshire	North 1874; South 1874; Peterborough 1874
Northumberland	North 1874; South 1874; Berwick-upon-Tweed 1875
Nottinghamshire	North 1874; South 1874; East Retford 1872, 1874; Newark 1873
Oxfordshire	1874; New Woodstock 1873–74
Rutland	1874
Shropshire	North 1874; South 1874; Shrewsbury 1874; Wenlock 1874
Somerset	East 1874

Staffordshire	East 1874; North 1874; West 1874; Newcastle-under-Lyme 1873; Stafford 1874; Stoke-on-Trent 1871–72; Tamworth 1871–72; Walsall 1874; Wednesbury 1874; Wolverhampton 1874
Suffolk	East 1873, 1874, 1875; West 1874; Eye 1875
Surrey	East 1872; Mid 1872; West 1872; Guildford 1873
Sussex	1871, 1873; East 1874; West 1874; Chichester 1874; Horsham 1872; Midhurst 1871; New Shoreham 1871; Rye 1874
Warwickshire	North 1873, 1875; South 1874; Coventry City 1874
Westmorland	1872
Wiltshire	1872, 1874, 1875; South 1874; Calne 1874; Chippenham 1871; Cricklade 1873; Malmesbury 1871; Westbury 1874; Wilton 1874
Worcestershire	East 1874; West 1874
Yorkshire	East Riding 1874; North Riding 1874; West Riding, North 1874; West Riding, South 1874; Dewsbury 1874; Huddersfield 1875; Leeds 1874; Wakefield 1874; York City 1873
Wales	
Anglesey	1873, 1874, 1875; Beaumaris 1870, 1874
Brecon	1871
Caernarvon	1873, 1874, 1875; Caernarvon Borough 1873
Cardigan	1871–72, 1874; Aberystwyth, Cardigan and Lampeter 1871; Adpar 1871; Lampeter-Pontstephen 1871
Carmarthen	1872; Carmarthen Borough 1871
Denbigh	1874, 1875
Flint	1874; Flint Borough 1875
Glamorgan	1873, 1874, 1875; Loughor and Neath 1874
Merioneth	1874
Montgomery	1872, 1874; Montgomery Borough 1874
Pembroke	1871–72; Pembroke Borough 1875
Radnor	1875; New Radnor 1873

21.4 The Absent Voters' Register, 1918 and 1919

The 1918 Representation of the People Act allowed members of the armed forces and others connected with the war effort to have a postal or proxy vote in their home constituency. The national set of registers of absent voters can be seen at the British Library. Local copies are held in local record offices: try a search on A2A using 'absent voters' as the search term. If you have a name and a home address for a First World War soldier, sailor or airman, but no idea as to regiment or service details, these registers can provide a useful route to finding out more as they give brief service details. Men applying had to be over 19 (younger than other electors) and, obviously, to have survived up to 1918.

21.5 Electoral registration: bibliography

R H A CHEFFINS, *Parliamentary Constituencies and their Registers since 1832* (British Library, 1998)

N CONNELL, 'Absent Voters' Registers', *Family Tree Magazine*, December 1998, p. 5

J S W GIBSON and C ROGERS, *Electoral Registers since 1832 and Burgers Rolls* (FFHS, 1990)

J S W GIBSON and C ROGERS, *Poll Books c.1696–1872* (FFHS, 1994)

N NEWINGTON-IRVING, *Directories and Poll Books, including almanacs and electoral rolls, in the Library of the Society of Genealogists* (Society of Genealogists, 1995)

22 Changes of name

22.1 Change of name

It is perfectly legal for anyone simply to change his or her name without drawing any attention to the change, unless there is an intention to defraud. Many people who changed their name did not wish to draw attention to the fact. For example, in an age when it was almost impossible to divorce, some people simply took their new partner's name to give the appearance of marriage, and any children the appearance of legitimacy.

There were several ways to record the change of name, such as a statutory declaration before a Justice of the Peace or Commissioner for Oaths (which could not be enrolled on the Close Rolls for safe keeping); or an advertisement in the newspapers may have been used instead. (It may be possible to check local newspapers at the British Library Newspaper Library: address in 62.)

An alternative was just to assume an alias – with intention to defraud. For an index to habitual criminals and their aliases, from 1869, see 47.5.

22.2 Change of name by deed poll, 1851 onwards

For most people a deed poll means a change of name. Actually, a deed poll is the technical term for a deed involving only one party (poll meaning the parchment was smooth-cut, whereas an indenture or indented deed between two or more parties was cut in a zigzag way so each could be matched up with the other parts).

Changes of name by deed poll were (and are) made before a solicitor who could enrol them on the Close Rolls, for safe keeping. Relatively few changes of name were enrolled, as it was not a legal obligation and extra fees were payable. Most people who come to the National Archives looking for an enrolled change of name are disappointed. The original deed poll will have been given to the person who changed their name. Although the solicitor who prepared the deed poll may have kept a copy on file, it is unlikely to be a certified copy, nor is the file likely to have been kept for more than five years.

From 1851, the indexes to the Close Rolls (c 54 Ⓕ) include references to changes of name by deed poll that had been enrolled. In 1903, this function was taken over by the Supreme Court of Judicature Enrolment Books (J 18 Ⓕ), with indexes also in J 18. The indexes vary from time to time: until 1903 only the former name is given, but since then both are present, either as a note or a cross-reference. These records and indexes are seen in the Map Room. For a change of name in the last five years, apply to the Royal Courts of Justice, Room 81 (address in 62).

22.3 The *London Gazette*

From 1914, all deeds poll enrolled in the Supreme Court had first to be advertised in the *London Gazette* – but again, this does not mean all changes of name. However, for the duration of the Second World War, British subjects could only change their name if 21 days before doing so they had published in the *London Gazette*, the *Edinburgh Gazette* or the *Belfast Gazette* a notice giving details of the proposed change. These *Gazettes* are all being published on **www.gazettes-online.co.uk/**.

A supplementary index to both old and new names exists in the quarterly indexes to the *London Gazette* for 1938–1964: copies of the relevant pages are shelved by the J 18 indexes in the Map Room. The *London Gazette* itself may be seen in the National Archives under ZJ 1.

22.4 Changes of name by foreigners in the UK, 1916–1971

Enemy aliens resident in Britain had been forbidden to change their names in 1916: the ban was extended to all foreigners in Britain in 1919. The only exceptions made were when a new name was assumed by royal licence; or by special permission of the Home Secretary; or when a woman took her husband's name on marriage. In the first two of these cases, the change had to be advertised in the *Gazettes* (see above). These restrictions were removed in 1971, and anyone can now change their name.

22.5 Royal licences and private acts of Parliament: *c.* 1700 onwards

Royal licences to change a name appear very infrequently among the records from the late seventeenth century. The change is usually in response to a bequest conditional upon adopting the deceased's name, or a marriage settlement requiring the husband to adopt the wife's name or when a change to the coat of arms was also required. Warrants for such changes of name were entered into the current series of entry books; before 1782 in SP 44 ⑦; from 1782 to February 1868 in HO 38 ⑦; and from February

1868 in HO 142 ⑦. These last two series usually have internal indexes in each volume. Records of such changes of name were often advertised in the *London Gazette*. It may be worth also checking the records of the College of Arms (address in 62).

Private acts of Parliament were also used in the same kinds of instance (although only once since the 1880s): the originals are in the House of Lords Record Office (address in 62).

22.6 The Phillimore *Index to Changes of Name, 1760–1901*

This is a composite index from several sources, and does not claim to be an index to all changes of name. Its full details are An Index to Change of Name Under Authority of Act of Parliament or Royal Licence and including Irregular Changes from 1 George III to 64 Victoria, 1760 to 1901. A copy is shelved with the C 54 finding aids in the Map Room.

The sources covered are: private acts of Parliament; royal licences published in the *London* and *Dublin Gazettes*; notices of changes of name published in *The Times* after 1861, with a few notices from other newspapers; the registers of the Lord Lyon [king of arms], where Scottish changes of name were commonly recorded; records in the office of the Ulster King at Arms; and some private information.

It thus omits changes by royal licence not advertised in the *London Gazette*, and changes by deed poll enrolled in the Close Rolls but not advertised in *The Times*.

22.7 Changes of name: bibliography

H MEAD, *Change of Name* (London, 1995)

W P W PHILLIMORE and E A FRY, *An Index to Change of Names, 1760–1901* (London, 1905)

23 The Army: an overview

23.1 Introduction to Army research

For many people, tracing a father, grandfather or great-grandfather who fought in the First World War is the first step in researching their family history. Others come to Army research after finding a census entry, or a certificate, describing a man as a soldier in a particular regiment or as an Army pensioner. For some researchers, the organisation of the Army is familiar from their own direct experience; for others, it is all new and strange. Some people want to know as much as they can about a soldier's time in the Army, while others want to concentrate on the family tree.

Researching in Army records is not always easy but can be very rewarding. One thing that often surprises people is how much time soldiers spent abroad: the British Army was involved in colonial defence and conquest since the time of Charles II, even when not fighting wars in Europe.

Researching among Army records can cover such an enormous number of sources that this book has five chapters on the subject, outlined below. You may have to follow cross-references from one to another, as the Army constitutes a series of interrelating subjects.

- 23: background information on the Army
- 24: records of most use for the family tree
- 25: service records up to 1914
- 26: service records from 1914 onwards
- 27: linked services

Service records tend to be those papers that document the soldier's professional life rather than his personal one. There is some overlap, however, particularly as soldiers' families gradually became entitled to more long-term consideration from the state (in the form of pensions) and so next of kin were recorded. One thing to remember is that very many series of military papers simply no longer exist. We know, for example, that soldiers' wives could be sent back to their husbands' parish of origin, but finding any military paperwork on this is very unlikely.

The service records have been split into two chapters, before and after

1914. This is because 1914 saw the beginning of the great twentieth-century militarisation of the British people. Because so many men (and women) served after 1914, Army service records were in many ways simplified but in other ways made more complex. Before 1914, you may have to look in many places, with no guarantee of finding a record because the Army was not particularly interested in the individual soldier's family situation. From 1914, information was carefully recorded – but may no longer survive for 1914–1918 because of enemy bombing in 1940. However, what survives does provide information on a giant cross-section of the men of the United Kingdom, and a smaller one of women. Service records for soldiers who continued to serve after 1920 (1922 for officers) are not yet at the National Archives, but are already of interest to huge numbers of families.

Within both chapters, the next division is between officers and other ranks. Non-commissioned officers are other ranks. Officers tend to have fuller records, and pensions were provided for their families from a much earlier date: they were wealthier and socially more important. This does not mean that you cannot find out quite a lot about an ordinary British soldier. If you are prepared to trawl through some of the less popular series mentioned here, you may be able to find out detailed information on particular individuals.

23.2 Background information on the Army

Some understanding of the organisation of the Army is helpful. Garrisons and barracks (after an initial period of quartering troops on local people) were established for the quartering of troops throughout the country. In times of war, when the garrison troops were needed elsewhere, special battalions of veterans (ex-soldiers given a pension to be subject to recall) were raised to take their place in order to safeguard order in Britain itself.

The basic unit of the Army was the regiment, under the command of a lieutenant-colonel. The regiments were of various types: cavalry, infantry, artillery and engineers. In peacetime, a regiment usually consisted of two battalions, each split into several companies (troops or squadrons in the cavalry). One battalion was usually posted abroad to guard the Empire or to take part in whatever war was going on. The other battalion was based at home – that is, anywhere in the British Isles or Ireland or in the relevant colony if it was a colonial regiment – and was responsible for recruiting and training, as well as home defence. From about 1870, each regiment had a permanent regimental depot (at a third location); before then, the depot was wherever the home battalion happened to be. Before 1870, recruitment was to the regiment, and was usually from the locality where the home battalion happened to be posted at the time (they moved about quite a lot). However, recruiting parties did range quite widely. After 1870, regiments could still recruit directly, but a man had the option of joining 'the Army' and being assigned to any regiment.

More battalions were created in times of need, particularly during the two World Wars, when one regiment might easily have 10 battalions or even more. The Middlesex Regiment had over 40 between 1914 and 1918. The First World War was really the first period of mass enlistment into local battalions, such as the famous 'Pals' battalions. Before then, each regiment had men from across the United Kingdom.

The Army was manned by commissioned officers (usually wealthy men: commissions were generally purchased before 1871), and other ranks (drawn from the poorer classes). Until 1914 there was voluntary enlistment into the other ranks. Conscription was used in 1916–1918 and again in 1939–1961. The First World War considerably improved the social status of soldiers, as more families became personally involved.

As well as the Regular Army, each county had its own militia regiments from 1757. These made up a conscripted part-time force; in wartime they acted as full-time soldiers. Other ranks in militia regiments had a better public reputation – were more respectable – than the common soldiery of the regular Army. From 1881, each militia regiment was attached to a regular Army regiment as its third battalion.

Volunteer forces were raised in the Napoleonic wars, and again from 1859. In 1908, they were formed into the Territorial Force, which provided much of the manpower of the First World War before conscription in 1916. It was renamed the Territorial Army in 1920.

23.3 Regimental name changes and the *Army Lists*

Each basic unit of the British Army, the regiment, formed its own social family. Regimental museums are the place to find out about this world: many have collections of paintings and photographs as well as records. The National Army Museum also holds much regimental material. A regiment is likely to have had several name changes and amalgamations over its history. These can make it complicated to match up the regiment you know a soldier belonged to with a list of records arranged by a completely different regimental name. A quick way round this is to ask at the enquiry desk for Swinson, *A Register of the Regiments or Corps of the British Army*. You can also find regimental name changes by using the search facility on the online catalogue: select subjects, places and prominent people, put in the regimental name you have, and you will get a cross-reference to variant names of the same regiment. An alternative is the site **www.regiments.org**, which covers not just British land forces, but also Empire, Indian and Commonwealth ones. It is well worth spending time exploring this site: you may find that someone has pulled out all kinds of information from the records already.

For the First World War, try **www.1914-1918.net**, which has good information on units and a whole host of extra information: again, it is a site to use and re-use. If you need more information on units, you could order up and look at WO 380/17, which is a register of the formations, amalgamations, disbandments and changes of title of infantry regiments, 1914–1919.

Another cause of confusion can be 'regimental order of precedence'. Each regiment had its own known place in the hierarchy. This was something all members of the Army would have known about, and it often made sense to the War Office to order their records in this way, even during the Second World War. For example, an entry book of payments to officers' widows might have all the surnames beginning with A entered together – but within the As the widows would not be entered in alphabetical order but in the order of the regiment's place in the hierarchy. To find out where your regiment sat in the order of precedence, look in any *Army List*.

The *Army List* defined the regimental order of precedence. For 300 years, the Army has produced regular editions of the *Army List*. Although we talk about **the** *Army List*, there are in fact several series with that name. The first official *Army List* was published in 1740. For each year between 1798 and 1951, there are two (and sometimes three) series of *Army List* available, which can be seen in the National Archives. The different series vary in format and content: some are just lists of officers, others (the monthly lists) contain a lot of detail about the organisation of regiments. For more information, see the research guide to *Army Lists* available at the National Archives (and on the website).

The Monthly *Army Lists*, 1798–June 1940, cover the officers of the Regular Army *plus* those of the Militia, Territorial and Colonial forces. These are arranged by regiment, and give some idea of where the regiment was. This can be very useful if you want to find out more, or if you have little information – for example, a man described on a certificate as a soldier but with no other details. You may be able to work out what regiments were in that area from looking at the relevant monthly *Army List*. However, you can also use records of where regiments were stationed in WO 379 and WO 380 ⑦.

23.4 Printed works, websites and other places

Each chapter on the Army has its own brief bibliography. If you have any free moments in the National Archives, it would be a good idea to spend them exploring our library holdings and noting books to order from your own library. The National Archives Library is a reference library with a large collection of works on military history. You can search its catalogue online at **www.library.nationalarchives.gov.uk**. It has several general histories of the British Army and of specific wars or campaigns that can help you to make sense of the military world in which your ancestor lived. It also holds an excellent collection of regimental histories, which can often be the easiest way to find out more about where a soldier was likely to have served. You may also want to spend some time in the National Archives bookshop, looking at its excellent range of military history books.

Most of the series you will be using will be from the War Office, in the wo code. If you want to explore further in the War Office, among the records that relate to warfare and Army administration and not to individuals, you will need to use Roper's *The records of the War Office and Related Departments, 1660–1964*. These records *may* (sometimes) be of interest in discovering more about a soldier's life.

There is a growing number of websites for military history. See Christian, *The Genealogist's Internet*, for a good guide. The two previously mentioned, **www.regiments.org** and **www.1914–1918.net**, are exceptionally good starting places. There are also many other places to look for information about soldiers. The most obvious are the Imperial War Museum (**www.iwm.org.uk**), the National Army Museum (**www.national-army-museum.ac.uk**) and the various regimental museums: these specialise in the life of the Army, and you should be able to discover some general idea of how your ancestor lived as a soldier. Most regiments have their own museums, some of which also have archival collections: for more details see Wise's *Guide to Military Museums*, or look to see if there is a website.

To see if any private papers exist (and where to find them), try a search on the National Register of Archives (**www.nationalarchives.gov.uk/nra/**).

23.5 The Army: an overview: bibliography

Army List (London, annually from 1754)

D ASCOLI, *A Companion to the British Army, 1660–1983* (London, 1983)

P CHRISTIAN, *The Genealogist's Internet* (PRO, 2001)

S FOWLER and W SPENCER, *Army Records for Family Historians* (PRO, 1998)

M ROPER, *The records of the War Office and related departments, 1660–1964* (PRO, 1998)

J SLY, 'A Rough Guide to the British Army', *Ancestors* 22, 23, 24 and 25 (2004)

J SLY, 'Medals for Family Historians', *Ancestors* 19 (2004)

A SWINSON ed., *A Register of the Regiments and Corps of the British Army: the Ancestry of the Regiments and Corps of the Regular Establishments of the Army* (London, 1975)

A S WHITE, *A Bibliography of the Regiments and Corps of the British Army* (London, 1965)

T WISE, *A Guide to Military Museums* (1999)

24 Army sources for family history

Most War Office (Army) records don't give details of parentage, marriage or children of officers and men. But some do and many of them are in the National Archives. As with so much of Army life, officers and men were treated differently when it came to marriage and family.

The Army was not very interested in other ranks' wives and children until the Crimean War, which attracted on-the-spot journalists and also many tourists. The presence of these amazed and concerned onlookers and the extensive press coverage drew attention not merely to the low standards of medical care, but also to the problems of other ranks' families. Reform was not immediate, but when it came it set the tone for the Army's continued concern for the wives and children of its men.

24.1 Army registers of births, marriages and deaths, 1761–1987

The most relevant records are kept elsewhere. These are the various Army registers of births, marriages and deaths. The General Register Office of England and Wales holds the largest number, but some regiments apparently still hold copies. As they have never been analysed as a series (and most are not available for public inspection), we do not know what percentage of Army marriages and births are covered. The National Archives holds a few of these registers.

24.1.1 Army registers of births, marriages and deaths at the General Register Office

Army registers of births, marriages and deaths are kept in the General Register Office of England and Wales. Although you cannot see the registers themselves, you can buy certificates of the events they include in the normal way at the Family Records Centre, by telephone to the General Register Office or online at **www.gro.gov.uk/gro/content/research/searchingforoverseasrecords**).

The registers do sometimes contain extra information that will not be included in the certificates as supplied. For instance, in the regimental registers there is quite often a single page per family, with all children entered on the one page. You need to identify and order certificates for each one separately. It would be very helpful for family historians if these registers could be made fully available, as was done with the Nonconformist registers in the 1950s. At the moment, only the indexes are freely available to the public. All the indexes can be seen as volumes at the Family Records Centre, as microfiche at the National Archives and online at **www.1837online.com**. However, even the indexes can be helpful.

- Indexes to the Regimental registers of births/baptisms and marriages, covering both at home (from 1761) and abroad (from *c.* 1790) to 1924
  - There is an index to the births (giving name, place, year and regiment)
  - There is no index to the marriages in the regimental registers. To find out details of a marriage, you have to know the husband's regiment and a rough date. (At the Family Records Centre, ask at the enquiry desk to be put in touch with the Overseas Section, which may conduct a search for you. You can also do this online at **www.gro.gov.uk/gro/content/research/searchingforoverseasrecords**
- Indexes to the Religious registers. Army chaplains' registers of births, baptisms, marriages, deaths and burials abroad, 1796–1880
  - These are indexed. Unfortunately, the indexes do not give the regiment, simply name, place and date range
- Indexes to the Civil registers from 1881
  - From 1881 the religious registers appear to be continued by the Armed Forces returns, 1881–1955, of births, marriages and deaths overseas
  - From 1956–1965, there are combined service department registers of births and marriages overseas
  - From 1965, separate service registers were abandoned, and entries were made in the general series of overseas registers

These various sets of indexes can be used to cross-refer to each other (you may pick up some extra information this way) and to the usual civil registers. There are often duplicate entries, and sometimes unexplained absences. For example:

- *Alice Abbott*, born Bangalore 1885 appears in both the Chaplains' index *and* the Regimental index. The latter gives her father's regiment – the Royal Artillery;

- *Mabel Louisa Abbott*, born Jersey 1883, appears in the Chaplains' index but not in the Regimental index;
- *Amelia Aaron*, born Aldershot 1859, appears in the Regimental index (father's regiment, 12th Foot) and also in the civil index – September quarter, registration district Farnham.

At the moment, finding the discharge record for a soldier between 1855 and 1882 can be difficult if you do not know his regiment (see 25.4.2.1). It may be worth checking the regimental indexes to see if you can match information about the family and find the father's regiment.

Similar armed services registers (from 1881) and war registers (from 1899) exist in the keeping of the General Register Offices of Scotland, Ireland and Northern Ireland (from 1927). These contain returns for people who were born, or who were normally resident, in Scotland, Ireland and Northern Ireland. We think that these people would *also* appear in the records of the General Register Office of England and Wales, as the registers were normally sent there first, but this is not yet clear.

Records for the military while on the Ionian Islands appear to have been kept separately. The General Register Office has registers of births, marriages and deaths, 1818–1864: the index is to a military register, a civil register and a chaplain's register. It gives names only and can be seen at the Family Records Centre and National Archives and online at **www.1837 online.com**. (See also 8.8.)

24.1.2 Army registers of births, marriages and burials at the National Archives

The National Archives has a small number of regimental registers of births, baptisms, marriages and burials of the kind kept by the General Register Office. Some of these are annotated with information on discharge and others have the baptismal entries of children entered on the same page as the marriage certificate of the parents. The National Archives has baptism and marriage registers for:

	Former militia name			
King's Own Yorkshire Light Infantry, 3rd battalion	1st West Yorkshire Militia	1865–1904	WO 68/499	7
Rifle Brigade, 6th battalion	114th West Meath Militia	1834–1904	WO 68/439	7
Royal Horse Artillery		1817–1827, 1859–1883 (most are) 1860–1877	WO 69/63–73, WO 69/551–582	7 7

	Former militia name			
Somerset Light Infantry, 3rd and 4th battalions	Somerset Militia	1836–1887, 1892–1903	WO 68/441	⑦
West Norfolk Regiment		1863–1908	WO 68/497	⑦
West Yorkshire Rifles, 3rd battalion	2nd West Yorkshire Militia	1832–1877	WO 68/499	⑦

In addition, there are Army registers of baptisms for Dover castle, 1865–1916 and 1929–1940; Shorncliffe and Hythe, 1878–1939; Buttervant, 1917–1922; and Fermoy, 1920–1921 (WO 156 ④). This series also includes burial registers for the Canterbury garrison, 1808–1811, 1859–1884 and 1957–1958, and baptisms and banns of marriage for Army personnel in Palestine, 1939–1947. The National Archives does not currently know the whereabouts of the registers of other garrison churches: we would be glad to hear of any.

The baptism, marriage and burial registers of the Royal Chelsea Hospital, 1691–1856, are in RG 4/4330–4332 and 4387 ⑦.

24.2 Military wills

Officers' wills are likely to be found by following the advice given in 10. For registers of powers of attorney, see 24.3.1. If a private soldier died abroad before 1858 and left assets over a certain amount, grants of probate or administration were issued in the Prerogative Court of Canterbury: see 10 for how to find them. There are 337 wills of this kind for men describing themselves as privates, but there may be many more who just described themselves as 'of' their regiment: over 6,000 wills give the testator's regiment. (Between 1800 and 1858, they are usually indexed in a separate section at the end of each letter in the indexes in PROB 12⑦. This is still worth checking for administrations, even though the wills can now be found online.)

However, military wills of smaller estates did not have to be proved in court, so there is no record of these unless they have survived among casualty returns in the War Office records: see 25.4.3 for more details. Soldiers going into active service wrote brief wills: those for England and Wales are now kept by the Principal Probate Registry, but they are not accessible. Collections of similar wills for some Scottish and Irish soldiers are at the National Archives of Scotland and Ireland. See Clarke, 'Scottish soldiers' wills, 1857–1965' for more details.

24.3 Army officers: sources for family history

Officers were not supposed to marry before the age of 30, and then only with their colonel's permission. Reports by officers of their marriage were made between 1830 and 1882; some of the marriages date from about 1799. Of course, if the officer or his wife did not survive until 1830 there will be no report. These reports are in wo 25/3239–3245 ⑤. They are indexed up to 1851 by maiden name of wife, giving place and date of birth and marriage, and witnesses (Miss Fairbrother's index). This is not helpful if the maiden name is what you are looking for. Miss Fairbrother also indexed the 1829 return of serving officers by wife's maiden name, also giving date and place of birth, marriage, children's birth and sometimes death. The 1829 return, in wo 25/780–806, is discussed in 25.3.2. There are also certificates of marriage and birth of children, 1755–1908, in wo 42 ⑤, which is indexed. The various military registers of births, marriages and burials (see 24.1) may include references to officers' families if they followed the regiment. After 1882, information about the wife should be found in the officer's service record: see 25.3.3.

Provision of an authentic baptism certificate was required for commissioned officers, as membership of the established church implied loyalty to the Crown. As a result, there are many baptism certificates for Army officers in the War Office records. There are two main caches: for the regular Army, 1755–1908, in wo 42 ⑤; and for militia officers, 1777–1868, in wo 32/8903–8920 ⑤. There are indexes to both. When applying for a commission, many officers would give some statement about their family background: see the Commander–in–Chief's memoranda in wo 31 ⑦, discussed in more detail at 25.3.2.

24.3.1 Army officers: letters of attorney

Registers of letters of attorney for Army officers exist in several series. Many of these letters were made in favour of the wife or other close relative, or were granted by the probate courts to the widow as executrix.

1755–1783	Registers of letters of attorney	WO 30/1	⑦
1756–1827	Registers of letters of attorney	PMG 14/142–164	⑦
1759–1816	Entry books of powers of attorney, apparently arranged by date	PMG 14/104–125	⑦
1802–1821	Registers of letters of attorney granted by officers' widows	PMG 14/165–167	⑦
1811–1814	Alphabetical entry books	PMG 14/126–137	⑦
1836–1899	Registers of letters of attorney: includes Ordnance officers from 1858	PMG 51	⑦

There is also a series of indexed registers of letters of attorney, 1699–1857, relating to Ordnance (Royal Artillery and Royal Engineer) officers, civilian staff and creditors who expected to receive payments of any kind from the Ordnance Office (wo 54/494–510 ⑦).

24.3.2 Pensions to officers' widows and dependants

Other than this, more information is only likely to be found in military records if the officer died leaving his family in want. From 1708 pensions existed for the widows of officers killed on active service; from 1720, pensions were also paid to the children and dependent relatives (usually indigent mothers over 50) in similar cases out of the Compassionate Fund and the Royal Bounty. These pensions were not an automatic right, and applicants had to prove their need.

OFFICERS' WIDOWS' PENSIONS 1713–1920

(See 24.3.3 for First World War widows' pensions.)

These records can be very useful. You can find out where the family was settled, as they often give place of payment. If it is through the Post Office, no location is mentioned. If it is through a government office, a particular place is mentioned, such as the I. R. (Inland Revenue) at Athlone, the Comm^t (Commissariat) at Toronto, the Cust[oms] at Bristol. You should be able to find the officer's death date – the date when the warrant *started*, not when it was granted. You can also find the date of the widow's death.

1808–1920	Ledgers of payments of widows' pensions: these give name, address, other details and where paid	PMG 11	[7]
1755–1908	Application papers for widows' pensions and dependants' allowances: these can include proofs of birth, marriage, death, and wills, etc.	WO 42	[7]
1815–1895	Registers of payments	WO 23/105–123	[7]
1815–1892	Lists of widows receiving pensions	WO 23/88–92	[7]
1713–1829	Lists of widows receiving pensions	WO 24/804–883	[7]
1808–1825	Abstracts of applications: there is an index in the Research Enquiries Room	WO 25/3073–3089	[F]
1760–1818?	Application papers, as above, of uncertain date, arranged alphabetically	WO 25/3089–3197	[7]
1764–1816	Correspondence relating to widows' pensions: the volumes are internally indexed, and contain details on many widows	WO 4/1023–1030	[7]
1735–1811	Registers of payments	WO 25/3020–3058	[7]
1748–1811	Indexes to pensions	WO 25/3120–3123	[7]

Selected correspondence on widows' pensions is also in WO 43 ([1], [F]). There is a card index in the Research Enquiries Room. A search in the catalogue within WO 43 may identify interesting material for some widows – for example, the widow of army surgeon Daniel Davies, 18th Foot, who was left to support five deaf and dumb children in the 1850s (WO 43/913).

COMPASSIONATE ALLOWANCES, 1773–1915

These can be detailed, giving the names and birth dates of children.

1812–1915	Ledgers of payments	PMG 10	7
1805–1895	Summary of those placed on the Compassionate List	WO 23/120–123	7
1858–1894	Registers of those placed on the Compassionate List	WO 23/114–119	7
1822–1885	Ledgers of pension payments for the widows of foreign officers	PMG 6 and PMG 7	7
1803–1860	Correspondence relating to the Compassionate Fund	WO 4/521–590	7
1812–1813	About 2,000 'compassionate papers' – affidavits by widows and children in receipt of a compassionate pension that they received no other government income. In rough alphabetical order. Give details of the officer, often the age of the children, and sometimes the name of the guardian, as well as some indication of county or country of residence (they were sworn before local justices)	WO 25/3110–3114	7
1773–1812	Registers of compassionate allowances awarded to dependants	WO 25/3124–3125	7
1779–1812	Ledgers of payments	WO 24/771–803	7

Registers of pensions to the widows of Royal Artillery and Royal Engineer officers, 1833–1837, are in WO 54/195–196 ⑦, with ledgers of payments, 1836–1875, in PMG 12 ⑦. For pensions and compassionate allowances to the widows and dependants of commissariat officers, 1814–1834, see WO 61/96–98 ⑦.

24.3.3 First World War: pensions to dependants of deceased officers, all services

This section covers all armed services, not just the Army. It is placed in this chapter because the Army had by far the most casualties. Widows of men who served in the First World War were able to claim even if their husbands had died many years after 1918.

Pension etc.	Date	Information	Reference	
deceased officers: pensions paid to relatives	1916 Apr – 1920 Mar	Name and address of the claimant, rank and name of officer, date of birth and date of payment. Some volumes indexed	PMG 44/1–7	7
missing officers: pensions to relatives	1915 Mar– 1920 Mar	Name and address of relative receiving pension, relationship to missing officer and name and rank of officers, dates of payment	PMG 47/1–3	7
officers' children: allowances	1916–1920	Child/children's name; name, rank and regiment of father; record of payments and who collected the money	PMG 46/1–4	7

Pension etc.	Date	Information	Reference	
officers' widows' pensions	1917 Sept–1919 July	Name and address of widow, officer's name, rank and date of birth, date of payments	PMG 45/1–6	7
officers' widows and dependants: special grants and supplementary allowances	1916–1920	Name and address of claimant, rank and name of officer, date of birth and payment: indexed	PMG 43/2	7
all services, all ranks	1920–1989	See 26.1.7. Names are given as Smith John	PIN 26	2

An 8 per cent sample of widows' and dependants' pension case files, for all services, is in PIN 82 2. It is arranged in alphabetical order of serviceman's name, with his regiment (often in abbreviated form) or ship and cause of death. Names are usually given the form Bain Thomas – but sometimes as Bain T or Bain Thos. A typical entry might read 'SMITH Fred G RFA Disability: Killed in action'.

24.4 Army other ranks: sources for family history

Before the reforms of the 1850s, other ranks could marry at 26. If their wives were allowed 'on the strength' of the regiment as part of the married establishment, they could live in barracks among the soldiers and were entitled to draw half-rations free and quarter-rations for children. Wives married without permission lived in lodgings or in the various shanties that grew up around garrison towns, and were not supported in any way by the regiment.

When regiments were ordered abroad, only 4 or 6 wives per company (of 100 men) were allowed to travel with their men – to act as nurses, cooks and washerwomen for the regiment. The wives were chosen by ballot (practically on the quayside), drawing papers marked 'to go' or 'not to go'. Almost no documentary evidence remains of this practice. The Army did not provide for those left behind. If they had no means of subsistence, they had to go back to the soldier's parish of origin to draw poor relief there. (This is one reason why the Army was interested in the soldier's parish of origin, recorded in the description books: see 25.4.6.) You may find some trace of a soldier's family in the overseers' accounts for the parish, which are kept in local record offices. With a great deal of hard work you may even be able to track them in the accounts of the parishes they passed through on the way (see 41 on poor law records). Of course, rules were made to be bent and these ones were: other wives were often smuggled aboard ship. Again, in their travels around the world (and it is amazing how frequently regiments were moved across the globe) soldiers married – or failed to marry – local women. These camp followers had no rights: to avoid becoming a camp follower, a soldier's widow would marry another soldier fast.

Sufficient public concern was raised by the Crimean War for a govern-

☐ p. 566

ment-backed charity, the Royal Patriotic Fund, to become involved in supporting Army and Navy widows, orphans and other dependants. The Fund presented two reports to Parliament, in 1860 and 1871, listing respectively all the dependants it had helped and those whose pleas were rejected (because the man's death had not been caused by the Crimean War). Indexed hard copies of these Parliamentary Papers (*Parliamentary Paper* microfiche 66.322–323) are also available at the National Archives. They give the names of wife, children, date of marriage, date of birth of children, place of wife's residence and an indication of what happened to the children.

After the reforms of the late 1850s, married quarters began to be built and allotted to the families 'on the strength'. Colour sergeants were now all permitted to marry on the strength, as were 50 per cent of other sergeants. Up to 40 per cent of other ranks were allowed to marry on the strength, but permission was only granted after seven years' service, two good conduct badges and savings of £5. Women did not follow the Army on campaign, although they could go if a regiment was ordered to the colonies – to the West Indies or India. From 1868–1883 marriage rolls, containing information of those wives and children who were on the regimental books, were sometimes included with the muster books in wo 12 and wo 16 (both ⑦) (see 25.4.6).

References to next-of-kin are sometimes found in the casualty returns and registers of effects (see 25.4.4).

There is a selection of over 1,000 personal files on the widows of Army other ranks and Naval ratings whose service was between about 1880 and 1914 in PIN 71 ②. This is searchable by widow's surname followed by forenames (such as Andrews Mary Ann Priscilla) but it does not say whether the man was Army or Navy. It only includes some Boer War widows. However, it is well worth a look. The dates given in the list are the date of the man's enlistment and the date the widow's pension stopped. There are also over 5,000 disablement pension files of the same period in PIN 71, searchable as *surname, forename* (Sandwell, William Henry).

Another source for the families of British and colonial armed forces who died in the South African or Boer War is the 1901 report to Parliament by the Royal Patriotic Fund of widows, children and close dependants supported by the Fund up to 14 February 1901. This can be seen at the National Archives in *Parliamentary Paper* microfiche 107.348–349: an indexed hard copy is also available. This report does not give details of service: see 25.7.4 to discover more on the Boer War.

24.5 Army other ranks: schools for orphans and other children

The Royal Hibernian Military School was founded in Dublin in 1769 for the children of soldiers on the Irish establishment; in 1924 it merged with the Duke of York's Military School. Unfortunately, enemy bombing in 1940 destroyed most of its records: what survives is a boys' index book (wo 143/27 ☑) drawn up in 1863 with retrospective entries from about 1835 and with annotations up to about 1919. This gives name, class, references to petitions and registers now lost, corps and remarks (e.g., volunteered 16th Foot 5 August 59). A further index, from 1910, is in wo 143/26 ☑. See O'Reilly for a history of the school.

The Royal Military Asylum was founded at Chelsea in 1801 as a boarding school for children of serving or dead soldiers. There was a branch at Southampton, which seems to have existed between 1825 and 1840 (wo 143/61–63 ☑). Girls were admitted to the female branch until 1840, which was abolished in 1846. The Royal Military Asylum was renamed the Duke of York's Royal Military School in 1892, and moved to Dover in 1909.

At first, many of the children were not orphans, but most later entrants appear to have lost at least their father and quite frequently both parents. Children appear to have been admitted between the ages of 2 and 10, and were discharged in their mid-teens. Most of the girls not claimed by their parents were apprenticed, often as servants; the boys went into the Army, or were apprenticed if they were not fit for military service.

The boys' admission and discharge registers, 1803–1956, are very informative, although unfortunately they are arranged only by date of admission (wo 143/17–23 and 70 ☑). One of the boys' registers, for 1804–1820, is in letter order. The information for the girls (in wo 143/24–25 ☑) is the fuller. It includes number, name, age, date of admission; from what regiment, rank of father (P, T, S etc., for private, trooper, sergeant); parents' names and whether dead; their parish of settlement; when dismissed, and how disposed of (e.g., died, retained by parents while on pass, apprenticed). The boys' admission register gives the same information except for parents' names. The discharge registers give more information on apprenticeship, regiment or other fate.

If you find a child in the records of the Royal Military Asylum, try going beyond the admission and discharge registers to see if you can find out more. For example, there are registers of boys' offences, 1852–1879, in wo 143/53–58 ☑; an apprenticeship book, 1806–1848 (wo 143/52 ☑); correspondence, reports and memoranda from 1805–1917 (wo 143/37–45, with a subject index in wo 143/46 ☑); and records of the Normal School, 1847–1872 (wo 143/47–51 ☑).

Many other military orphanages were built during the nineteenth century, such as the Royal Victoria Patriotic Asylum and the Royal Caledonian Asylum. Their records are not in the National Archives (for the Royal Caledonian Asylum archive, email admin@rcst.org.uk). However, the Royal Patriotic Fund supported many children through these and other schools or orphanages. For a list of children of Crimean War soldiers and sailors who were supported in this and other ways, see the Royal Patriotic Fund 1860 report to Parliament (*Parliamentary Paper* microfiche 66.322–323: also available in an indexed hard copy at the National Archives).

24.6 Army sources for family history: bibliography

V BAMFIELD, *On the Strength: the story of the British Army Wife* (London, 1974)

T CLARKE, 'Scottish soldiers' wills, 1857–1965', in *Scottish Archives* vol 10 (2004)

S FOWLER and W SPENCER, *Army Records for Family Historians* (Public Record Office, 1998)

G H O'REILLY, *History of the Royal Hibernian Military School Dublin* (Genealogical Society of Ireland, 2001)

D J ODDY, 'Gone for a soldier: the anatomy of the nineteenth-century army family', *Journal of Family History*, 25 (2000), pp. 39–62

F C G PAGE, *Following the drum: women in Wellington's wars* (London, 1986)

N T ST J WILLIAMS, *Judy O'Grady and the colonel's lady: the army wife and the camp follower since 1660* (Oxford, 1988)

W SPENCER, *Army Service Records of the First World War* (Public Record Office, 2001)

A VENNING, *Following the Drum: the lives of army wives and daughters past and present* (London, 2005)

25 Army service records before 1914

25.1 Soldiering before the Restoration

Before the Civil War there was no regular standing army in Britain. Although some records of soldiers do exist before 1660, it is extremely unlikely that they will provide any useful genealogical material on individuals.

The most useful are not Army but militia (local forces) records. Able-bodied men aged between 16 and 60 were liable to perform military service within their counties, and occasionally outside them, in times of need. From the 1540s, the records of musters of this militia were returned to the secretaries of state and many of these, with some earlier ones from 1522 onwards, are scattered among various series in the National Archives. The deputy lieutenants of the counties, however, retained some muster books, and these are now in private collections or county record offices. See Gibson and Dell's *Tudor and Stuart Muster Rolls* for a county-organised analysis and directory of surviving muster rolls.

From the sixteenth century, regiments were raised to meet special requirements and were usually known by the names of colonels who commanded them: there was no central administration. Such few references as there are to individual soldiers should be sought among the State Papers Domestic and Foreign (sp Ⓢ) and the Exchequer and Audit Office Accounts (AO 1–AO 3 Ⓖ). The regimental index in the *Alphabetical Guide to War Office Records* is a good place to start. Other places to look are:

- for the payment of military wages – Exchequer Issues (E 403 Ⓩ) and Exchequer Accounts (E 101 Ⓩ);
- for officers' commissions and widows' pensions – the *Calendars of State Papers, Domestic;*
- for oaths of allegiance taken by soldiers going to the Low Countries, 1613–1624 – the licences to pass beyond the seas (E 157 Ⓩ).

The establishment of the Army is given for 1640 in sp 41/1. All officers serving in the Civil War and Commonwealth period are listed in Peacock's book *The Army List of Roundheads and Cavaliers*. The Commonwealth did keep a standing army and there is much documentation about it in the Commonwealth Exchequer Papers (sp 28 Ⓩ).

Individual parliamentary soldiers who were owed arrears of pay after 1649 might be given certificates known as debentures. These certified what they were owed and, secured on property confiscated by Parliament, could be used to purchase such properties, which could then in turn be sold to pay off their debts. The Certificates for the Sale of Crown Lands, in E 121 ④, contain thousands of names of officers and men who had served in the parliamentary forces. However, this series is arranged by the county in which the confiscated Crown lands were situated and is not indexed, either by name or regiment; moreover, a particular regiment might be assigned several properties in more than one county. It only covers England and Wales.

Similar debentures were issued to parliamentary soldiers who had served in Ireland, where confiscated lands were to be divided by lot. Fewer than 12,000 debentures were subsequently returned for certificates of possession. Most soldiers did not settle but probably sold them on to their officers. About 7,500 grants were confirmed after 1660. Unfortunately these debentures, which were held in Dublin, have not survived. Calendars of some grants that were confirmed after 1660, indexed by personal name, are in the *Fifteenth Report* of the Irish Record Commission (1825). The Books of Survey and Distribution, held by the National Archives in Dublin (some counties in print), record the final land settlement. References to troops serving in Ireland (mainly to officers) can also be found in the *Calendars of State Papers, Ireland*.

Records of the Committee for Indemnity (SP 24 ☑), which was set up to indemnify parliamentary soldiers and officials from legal liability for acts committed during the civil war, contain many references to individual soldiers. Cases are arranged alphabetically.

Muster rolls for the Scots Army in England in January 1646, unindexed but arranged by regiment and company, are in SP 41/2.

25.2 The Army, 1660–1914

There are few personnel records for the late seventeenth-century Army, but very large amounts over the next three centuries, when the British Army was a relatively small, professional organisation composed disproportionately of Scots and Irish. The eighteenth-century Army that founded the British Empire changed over time: the Peninsular and Crimean Wars brought many changes, culminating in the Army reforms of the 1870s and 1880s.

The growth of the British Empire saw the Army fighting, living and dying in every continent. (There are registers covering the embarkation of troops for foreign service, the roster of regiments serving in Ireland and regiments stationed in the colonies, in WO 379/13–14, for 1859 to 1914.) As well as the British Army, the Indian Army and the colonial regiments absorbed men from all over the Empire.

In long wars, a revived domestic militia was called up to reinforce the Regular Army (see 25.5 for more on the militia). On occasion, volunteers swelled the professional troops, particularly during the Napoleonic Wars when invasion was likely, in the mid-nineteenth century when revolution was feared and during the South African (Boer) War.

25.3 Army officers before 1914

In this book, 'officer' means a commissioned officer who held his rank by virtue of a royal commission. The other kind of officer, a non-commissioned officer, held his rank by a warrant instead and is a senior member of

☐ p. 566

the 'other ranks'. Sergeants did not hold their office by warrant, and could be reverted to the ranks.

There are four sorts of commissioned officer. General officers and regimental officers (major and above) were sometimes called Field Officers – that is, able to take command on a field of battle.

General officers	Coordinated the efforts of the whole Army: field marshal, general, lieutenant-general, major-general
Regimental officers	Colonel (in command of a regiment), lieutenant-colonel, major
Company officers	Captain (in command of a company) and his subalterns, lieutenant, cornet (cavalry), ensign (infantry). In 1871 cornets and ensigns became second lieutenants
Others	Paymaster, adjutant, quartermaster, surgeon and chaplain

There were also many other ranks or titles, such as brigadier-general, colonel-commandant, brigade-major, etc. Officers were graded by seniority, which ruled promotion within the regiment; if an officer was promoted out of sequence he was given brevet rank, e.g., as a brevet-major. Some officers held two ranks at the same time – the regimental rank, which was higher and usually a special appointment and the Army rank, which was the actual rank of his commission.

25.3.1 Army officers: *Army Lists* and biographical dictionaries

Brief biographies of eminent soldiers may be found in the *Dictionary of National Biography* and the *British Biographical Archive* (see 1.13). Hart's unofficial *Army List* (1839–1915) includes many professional biographical details of eminent and less eminent officers, giving far more information than the official *Army Lists*. It covers both the British Army and the Indian Army. Although the first volume dates from 1839, it contains details of (living) officers' services going back many decades before then. An incomplete set covering 1840 to 1915 is on open access at the National Archives: a full set is included in wo 211 ⑦.

Hart's working papers are in the National Archives. They include many letters from Army officers between 1838 and 1873, giving details of their service history, correcting errors and adding to entries: most of these are filed in alphabetical ranges such as A–C. Some include extra material such as extracts from military journals or from newspapers. These are also in wo 211 ⑦.

Hart was compiling a biographical dictionary of Army officers when he died; the text of the entries for many officers of senior rank is also in wo 211 ①. Most of the officers covered are great names from the wars with revolutionary and Napoleonic France.

The official *Army List* can be used to trace the broad outline of an officer's career. It includes British Army officers and some Indian Army officers. The first official *Army List* was published in 1740; since 1754 it has been published regularly. There are complete record sets, with manuscript amendments, of the annual lists (1754–1879) and the quarterly lists (1879–1900) in wo 65 ⑦ and wo 66 ⑦; incomplete sets are on open access. Large reference libraries may also have a set. Manuscript lists of Army officers were kept from 1702–1752 (wo 64 ⑦); there is an index at the National Archives.

The *Army List* was arranged in order of regiment, with a name index from 1766 (Engineer and Artillery officers were included in the index only from 1803). From 1879 it included a gradation list of officers – that is, a list in order of seniority, giving dates of birth and promotions and, from April 1881, details of service. For later *Army Lists*, see Spencer, *Army Records for Family Historians*. The *Army List* did not include militia officers before the mid-nineteenth century. For more information on other printed sources for militia officers, see Spencer, *Militia and Volunteer Forces 1757–1945*.

Details of officers granted commissions before 1727 can most easily be traced in Dalton's *English Army Lists and Commission Registers, 1661–1714*, in his *Irish Army Lists, 1661–85* and in his *George I's Army, 1714–1727*, all available at the National Archives. The *Royal Military Kalendar* has details of officers of field rank (major) upwards. It was compiled in 1820 of officers then alive, so that the service covered goes back well into the eighteenth century. Announcements of all commissions were made in the *London Gazette* (ZJ 1 ⑦).

Officers of the Honourable East India Company Army, the Indian Army and of British regiments stationed in India are given in the *India List* and the *Indian Army List*: the Library at the National Archives has incomplete sets of these.

25.3.2 Army officers before 1871

There are many regimental publications of officers' services: it may be worth checking the Library at the National Archives. You can access the library catalogue on the website at **www.library.nationalarchives.gov.uk**: try a search on 'regiment'.

At first only the regiments kept officers' service records, although the War Office undertook sporadic surveys from 1809. There are joint indexes at the National Archives covering both series (wo 76 Ⓕ and wo 25 Ⓕ): one is to names and the other to regiments.

The main source for an officer's service record is in the regimental records of officers' services, in wo 76. These start in 1755 and continue until 1914. Not all regiments are represented, and the records of some were lost. The information kept by the regiments varies a great deal but it usually gives the ranks held, service details and some personal particulars – sometimes including the names of wife and children.

The War Office conducted five surveys between 1809 and 1872. Officers were supposed to return various pieces of information – but of course not all did.

☐ p. 566

1809–1810	1st	Arranged alphabetically. Details of military service only	WO 25/744–748 [7], [F]
1828	2nd	Arranged alphabetically. Covers only officers retired or on half-pay (and therefore refers to service completed some years before). Age at commission, date of marriage and date of children's birth	WO 25/749–779 [7], [F]
1829	3rd	Arranged by regiment. Covers only serving officers. Age at commission, date of marriage and date of children's birth. *Wives* indexed separately, by maiden name, giving date and place of birth of the husband, date and place of marriage, names of children, with date of birth and place of baptism and sometimes death (Miss Fairbrother's manuscript index, at the National Archives)	WO 25/780–805 [6], [F]
1847	4th	As the 2nd	WO 25/808–823 [7], [F]
1870–1872	5th	Arranged by year of return and then by regiment Personal details	WO 25/824–870 [7], [F]

Remember that if you cannot find an officer in the card index to wo 25 and wo 76 it may be because he slipped through the net: the regimental records may be incomplete or he may have missed the War Office survey years. Try looking at Hart's papers in wo 211 [7], particularly for officers who served between 1838 and 1875.

Until 1871, most cavalry and infantry officers purchased their commissions; a number of commissions were also granted without purchase. Cadets could attend the Royal Military College (at Great Marlow from 1802 and at Sandhurst from 1812) but attendance at the RMC was not compulsory. Commissions in the Engineers and Artillery were not bought but granted on merit: cadets had to be trained at the Royal Military Academy at Woolwich (see below 25.3.4).

Most of the information in commission purchase records is formal and can be got from the *Army List* or the *London Gazette*. Hart's *Army List* is especially useful as it notes purchased commissions by adding a 'p' to the entry. There is a Research Guide on Army Commissions available on the National Archives website. For more information about the purchase system, see the books by Spiers and Bruce. The most fruitful sources are:

1704–1858	Indexed Letter Books: correspondence about the purchase and sale of commissions. A good source for details of fees paid. Later volumes can include addresses of officers – either where the regiment was stationed or their own private address	WO 4/513–520 [7]
1780–1874	67 original commissions: listed by name	WO 43/1059 [1]

1793–1870	Commander-in-Chief's Memoranda: applications to purchase and sell commissions. Arranged (usually in monthly bundles) by the date of commission as announced in the *London Gazette* (this date is given in the *Army Lists*). They often contain statements of service, certificates of baptism and letters of recommendation	WO 31	7

In 1871, the old system of purchasing commissions was replaced by promotion based on selection and professional qualification. The current holders of commissions were eligible for compensation on their retirement. Registers were drawn up of all officers holding a commission on 1 November 1871, with the dates and estimated value of their commission; later annotations show the date of retirement and the sum granted in compensation. These registers (in wo 74/177–182 7) do not give personal details.

25.3.3 Army officers, from 1871

The regimental records of service in wo 76 F continue until about 1914 and are the first place to look for an officer's service record. (The records of the Royal Garrison Regiment, 1901–1905, are in wo 19.) There are some oddments in wo 25 F for officers whose service ended before 1914. Look in the card indexes to wo 25/wo 76. For officers who retired before 1914 but who came back to serve in the First World War, look in both wo 339 (3) and wo 374 (3).

For officers commissioned after 1901, look in wo 339 (3) and wo 374 (3) and wo 76. Unfortunately, the records in wo 76 do not survive for officers who served *after* 1914, as they were destroyed by enemy bombing in 1940.

At the same time, the War Office introduced a new system of keeping personal records, as promotion was now to be by merit. A confidential report on each officer's ability was completed each year by the Commanding Officer of the unit, and sent to the Military Secretary. Sad to say, these were destroyed in the bombing of 1940.

From 1877, examination for a cadetship at the Royal Military College, Sandhurst (by now incorporating the India Military Seminary previously at Addiscombe) or the Royal Military Academy, Woolwich became the normal route of entry. Details of examination results are in csc 10 7. If the candidate failed the exam, another route in was to get a commission in the Militia and then sit the Civil Service Exam, results for which are also in csc 10. The papers in csc 10 are more interesting than they sound: they often give details of a likely career.

There are two other sources that might be worth investigating.

1871–1891	Original applications for compensation (for abolition of sale of commissions) from officers of the British and Indian establishment, with certificates of service attached, related correspondence and memoranda as to sums awarded.	WO 74/1–176 ☐F☐ Indexed (by regiment) in WO 74/177–182
1803–1914	Original submissions and entry books of submissions to the Sovereign of recommendations for staff and senior appointments, rewards for meritorious service and for commissions and appointments. Block submissions only after c. 1900	WO 103 ☐7☐

25.3.4 Officers of the Royal Engineers and Royal Artillery

Commissions in the Royal Engineers and Royal Artillery were granted to those men who had been selected to attend (and successfully pass) a course of instruction at the Royal Military Academy at Woolwich. Royal Artillery and Royal Engineer officers were the responsibility of the Board of Ordnance until 1855, when they were transferred to the War Office; before 1855, there are separate and extensive records. Only the most obvious have been described here: look through the wo 54 list for others. After 1855, look in the various series for commissioned officers described above.

1670–1855	RA	RE	Original warrants and patents of appointment	WO 54/939–945	☐7☐
1743–1852 with gaps	RA	RE	Commission books	WO 54/237–247	☐7☐
1727–1751	RA	–	Artillery officers' service records	WO 54/684	☐7☐
1751–1771	RA	–	Artillery officers' service records: these seem to be missing		
1771–1914	RA	–	Artillery officers' service records	WO 76	☐F☐
1786–1850	–	RE	Returns of Engineer officers	WO 54/248–259	☐7☐
1796–1922	–	RE	Engineer officers' service records: each volume has its own index	WO 25/3913–3920	☐7☐

For Royal Artillery officers, check the List of Officers of the Royal Regiment of Artillery, 1716–June 1914. Hart's personal copy of John Kane's List of Officers of the Royal Regiment of Artillery as they stood in 1763, with a continuation to the present time [1805] has his own annotations up to 1839 (in wo 211/69). You could also try a speculative search in wo 18 ☐7☐ for an officer serving between (or before) 1770 and 1820. This series consists of bound volumes of original warrants for payments on various accounts (cadets, pensions, recruiting, hospitals and effects of deceased men), together with the original receipts, certificates of existence, letters petitioning for allowance, etc., from the individuals concerned. They are only arranged by year, but a trawl may be profitable.

For Royal Engineer officers, consult the Roll of Officers of the Corps of Royal Engineers from 1660 to 1898.

A search in WO 54 should turn up many items of interest, such as the Royal Artillery Married Society register of officers and widows, 1788–1816 (WO 54/312).

25.3.5 Non-regimental Army officers

Not all officers were regimental officers. For other officers, see:

Staff	1792–1830	Pay index	WO 25/695–699	⑦
	1802–1870	Lists of staff officers, some with addresses	WO 25/700–702	⑦
	1782–1854	General returns of staff in British and foreign stations	WO 25/703–743	⑦
Commissariat	1798–1842	General returns of service	WO 61/1–2	⑦
Commissariat and Transport	1843–1889	Register	WO 61/5–6	⑦
War Office		Senior staff	*Army Lists*	
	1809–1819	Registry of officers, clerks, etc., of the War Office	WO 381/4	⑦
	1852–1857	War Office establishments	WO 381/10	⑦

25.3.6 Officers: half-pay and pension records before 1914

Before 1871 there was no general entitlement to a retirement pension; an officer either moved off the active list on to half-pay or sold his commission. Half-pay officers are included in the *Army List* but sometimes do not appear in the index. Records of half-pay do not contain much genealogical information. The most useful are probably the ledgers of payment, 1737–1921, in PMG4 ⑦. These give dates of death or of sale of the commission (which ended entitlement to half-pay); from 1837 they also give addresses. Later ledgers give date of birth as well. From 1737 to 1841, the ledgers are arranged by regiment and are unindexed; from 1841 they are in one alphabetical sequence of names.

Pensions were available for wounded officers from 1812. Registers of such pensioners, 1812–1892, are in WO 23/83–92 ⑦; correspondence on such claims, 1812–1855, can be found in WO 4/469–493 ⑦. Further correspondence, 1809–1857, can be found in WO 43 Ⓕ: there is a card index. Actual records of payments are in PMG9 ⑦ (including First World War payments) and PMG12 ⑦.

25.3.7 Army officers: courts martial

For courts martial, see the free research guide on *British Army: Courts Martial, 17th–20th Centuries*, available at **www.nationalarchives.gov.uk/catalogue/researchguidesindex.asp** and at the National Archives.

25.4 Army other ranks before 1914

In the Army, the 'other ranks' were the privates (infantry) and troopers (cavalry), trumpeters and drummers, supervised by corporals and sergeants who were non-commissioned officers promoted from the ranks. Specialist regiments and corps used different names.

The information kept on each soldier reappears in different permutations in many different types of document (even so, this is only a fraction of the original documentation). This basic personal information you may be able to piece together includes name, age, trade on enlistment, place of enlistment, place of birth, physical description, state of health and date of death or discharge. Some records contain information on wife, children or other next of kin. Parents are not recorded as a matter of course, unless as next of kin.

Surviving Army records on other ranks before 1914 are of four kinds:

Becoming a soldier	• joining up (attestation) papers – surviving ones are filed with discharge papers. Many do not survive	25.4.2.1–2
	• description books (includes place of birth)	25.4.6
Being a soldier	• regimental muster books and regimental pay lists – these only survive until 1897	25.4.6
	• These provide a fairly complete guide to a soldier's Army career from enlistment, through movements with the regiment throughout the world, to discharge	
	• Each muster book and pay list covers a short space of time. It can take a long time to collect information. Try discharge papers unless you know your soldier died in service or deserted	
Leaving the Army	• discharge papers, for soldiers who survived their service	25.4.2.1–2
	• This is the place we recommend to start your search, unless you know your soldier died in service or deserted	
	• casualty returns, for soldiers who died or deserted	25.4.4
Drawing a pension	• pension records	25.4.2.1–4
	• payment registers	25.4.2.4

You may be surprised to find such a concentration on pension records, but they are by far the easiest way to access accumulated information on a soldier. We usually recommend researchers to start looking for discharge to pension papers (if they know their soldier was not killed), as this can be the quickest way to find information. (If you are looking for a sapper or miner before 1856, go to 25.4.8 first.)

The discharge papers have been the focus of enormously valuable indexing projects by the Friends of the National Archives, which (as well as identifying individuals) have added greatly to our knowledge of Army pensions. Much of this gained knowledge has been published in Hore's two articles on Chelsea Pensioners.

25.4.1 An overview of Army pensions for other ranks, to 1913

Before 1806, enlistment was technically for life – but only the soldier made this commitment. The Army authorities could discharge him at any point. Many fit soldiers were discharged from their regiments at the end of a war and sent to serve in the 'invalid' or garrison battalions, before being eventually discharged as 'worn out'. Other soldiers were discharged direct from the line regiments of the 'fighting' Army as 'worn out' (and therefore entitled to a pension). These worn-out pensioners could be recalled at any time to serve, usually in an invalid or garrison battalion – but even in a line regiment if they were fit enough. If medical evidence was not produced as to why a soldier could not serve, the pension was stopped. The pension rate was 5d a day. Sergeants who had over 20 years' service and a good record qualified for 1s a day: to receive this they had to have a letter from the king (and were thus known as 'lettermen'). You may find records of both discharges (from the line regiment and later from the garrison/invalid force) in wo 97: see 25.4.2.1 below for details.

Invalid and garrison battalions have muster books and pay lists in the usual series: see 25.4.6.The garrisons tended to be at coastal forts or in Ireland or the Channel Islands. The 'invalids' were subject to recall into the fighting Army at any time (subject to a medical examination). Invalid battalions were sent to Australia to police the convicts and guard the colony. Soldiers could continue to serve in invalid or garrison forces for up to another 20 or 30 years before they were actually discharged to pension as 'worn out' to make way for a new wave of 'invalids' at the end of another war.

Soldiers who enlisted under the liberal 1806 regulations were entitled to discharge after 21 years' service (25 years for Cavalry), with a pension of 1s a day plus an extra 1/2d a day for each year's service after that. After 1817, soldiers could also take a reduced pension at or after 14 years' service. Soldiers wounded or maimed in the course of duty also qualified for pension. Relatively few served their full term of 21 years and even fewer continued on for the further 5 years needed to claim the pension equivalent to full pay.

However, according to a War Office report by Charles Babbage in 1832, very many men were still being discharged as 'worn out' before completing their 21 years' service. Babbage presented two opposing explanations for this: either the severity of Colonial Service rendered soldiers useless; or commanding officers thought younger men made a regiment look smarter (wo 43/610, f. 90). Babbage thought the latter more plausible.

For most of the nineteenth century, most soldiers who did not die through disease, accident or war were discharged before or by the age of 41. Many of these received a pension. In the 1840s, according to the War Office, there were about 73,000 Army pensioners living in the UK, nearly half of them under 55 and now recovered from the illness or disability that had earned them the pension.

What does all this mean for anyone researching a soldier?

- It is well worth looking among the records of men discharged to pension. Although only a minority earned the full pension after 21 years' or more service, many soldiers received a smaller pension.
- If you find an Army pensioner in the censuses, with his age, you can make a rough estimate as to his likely years of service. Most soldiers were recruited between the ages of 18 and 25, with a very few enlisting up to the age of 30; the average age of men completing 21 years' service was 41. With likely start and end dates, you can try the muster lists and pay books.
- If you know the rate of pension, you can make an estimate as to the length of service that earned it.
- Service at Waterloo counted as 2 years' service.
- 2 years' service in the East and West Indies counted as 3 years for soldiers enlisted between 1806 and 1818 (but not after). A similar regulation was introduced later in the century, when service in the East and West Indies counted as double time.
- You may need to look later than you expected, for a final discharge from a garrison regiment or invalid battalion or from the reserve.

The pension system was revised slightly by the Miller report of 1875. After 1883, soldiers discharged after completing one of the new limited engagements, or who had bought their discharge, were also eligible for a reduced pension. A further round of reforms took place in 1900 to 1905. What follows is a snapshot of the situation in the late 1870s.

Permanent pensions (as at late 1870s)

	European: daily rates	Black (native soldiers in the colonies): daily rates
After 21 years' service NCOs received extra, for every year of service as an NCO	8d–1s	6d
Aggregated pensions not to exceed	3s	1s 4d
On reduction of the Army Soldiers discharged after 14 years' service	As above: deduct 1/2d for each year short of 21 years	As above: deduct 1/2d for each year short of 21 years
On premature discharge Soldiers discharged after 18 years' service (on regiment being posted abroad, or if considered to be comparatively inefficient)	As above: deduct 1/2d for each year short of 21 years	As above: deduct 1/2d for each year short of 21 years
Wounds or injuries * Totally incapable of earning livelihood	1s 6d–3s 6d 6d–3s	9d–1s 6d–10d
Incapable of service	1s–2s 6d	9d–1s
Blindness – total	6d	6d
Blindness – 1 eye – allowance added to discharge pension		

* Could be applied for retrospectively

	European	Black daily rates
Unfitness caused in or by Army service Less than 7 years' service	6d, for no more than 18 months	11/2d, for no more than 2 years
7–18 years' service If still disabled at the end of the period, the pension could be extended or made permanent. In some cases, a gratuity of £30 could be made instead: it was only to be paid when the soldier was settled in his intended place of residence	An extra 3 months' pension for each year of service	An extra 4 months' pension for each year of service

GOOD CONDUCT AND ROYAL BOUNTY PAYMENTS

Good Conduct Pay	The amount of good conduct pay received daily at the time of discharge (or at the time of promotion to NCO) could be added to the pension. Not added to pensions for wounds, injuries or blindness	
Royal Bounty For gallant conduct For extreme suffering from wounds	Europeans 6d n/a	Blacks 3d 3d

Men who did not have the requisite number of years or wounds to qualify for a pension could apply to the monarch via the War Office for a pension: these letters are in wo 246 ⑦.

Pensioners who also received poor relief had their pension paid to the parish: see 41. Pensions could be forfeited for felony, gross fraud or gross misconduct, or for failing to serve in a regiment of the line or in support of the civil power when called upon. Papers on reinstatement of pension on appeal are in wo 121 ②. For more details, see Hore's two articles on Chelsea out-pensioners.

25.4.2 Army other ranks: Chelsea and Kilmainham pensions

Before (and after) the founding of the Royal Hospitals, disabled ex-soldiers were often granted places as almsmen in royal church foundations: petitions for such places, often giving details of service and wounds, for 1660 to 1751, are in so 5/31.

The main system of Army pensions to other ranks was operated by the Royal Hospital Chelsea (London, founded 1681) and the Royal Hospital, Kilmainham (near Dublin, founded 1679). Chelsea and Kilmainham supported both in-pensioners who lived in the hospitals and a much larger number of out-pensioners. The out-pensioners remained under military discipline to some extent: they formed a reserve pool to be called on in case of wartime emergency or domestic crisis.

Soldiers in the British Army on what was called the British Army Establishment received pension payments from the Royal Hospital Chelsea.

 ☐ p. 566

Some regiments were on the Irish Establishment (this means paid for by money from the Irish Exchequer, *not* Irish regiments as is often stated) and received pensions from the Royal Hospital Kilmainham before 1823. The distinction between the two is confusing, as regiments moved on and off the Irish Establishment. After 1823, Chelsea paid all pensions but Kilmainham continued to provide the medical examinations for soldiers discharged in Ireland.

If you cannot find a soldier in the pension records, you really do need to know which regiment he served in, as most records before 1873 are arranged in order of regiment. If you do not know the regiment, turn to 25.4.7. Pension records, by their very nature, refer to service often begun many years before the date of the pension award. Do remember this when looking at the covering dates given below – they do *not* refer to the dates of service but to date of *discharge*.

See also 25.4.2.4, for records relating to the actual payment of the pension to your soldier, which can provide information on his life after leaving the Army.

25.4.2.1 Discharge to Chelsea pension, 1760–1913

The National Archives holds an enormous number of Chelsea records. Current advice (if you are looking for a soldier who you know survived his service) is to start with the Royal Hospital Chelsea Soldiers' Documents in wo 97, 1760–1913. These comprise the attestation and/or discharge papers of soldiers discharged to pension (and of some who were rejected for pension).

From 1883 to 1913, this series also includes the discharge papers of men discharged after the new short service of 7 years in the regular Army, followed by 5 years in the reserve. The discharge documents will appear after the 5 years in the reserve: there will not be any if the man died in that period, although these may appear after about 1895. Similarly, if he was called up in 1914 while in the reserve, his papers will have been moved into wo 364, where they may not survive (see 26.1.6). However, it's fair to say that after 1883 most soldiers are in wo 97 *if they survived their service*. Some have even been found for men who died in service.

The Soldiers' Documents in wo 97 give age, birthplace, trade or occupation on enlistment, a record of service including any decorations, the reason for discharge to pension and, in some cases, place of residence after discharge and date of death. From 1883, they also contain details of next of kin, marriage and children.

The discharge papers in wo 97 are arranged as follows:

Date of discharge	Arrangement		
1760–1854	By regiment: searchable in the online catalogue. You can search by name, regiment and birthplace. The dates given are either of enlistment, or of discharge or of both: you will need to check the document itself to find out which *Does not include regiments 'on the Irish establishment' before 1823*	WO 97/1–1271	⬚1, ⬚6
1855–1872	By regiment and range of surname. Not searchable online by name. The Friends of the National Archives are currently indexing these. See 24.1.1 for a possible way to find the regiment	WO 97/1272–1721	⬚7⬚P
1873–1882	By cavalry, artillery, infantry or corps. Not searchable online by name	WO 97/1722–2171	⬚7
1843–1899	By name: misfiled papers. Not searchable online by name, as description is by range of surnames. See below for more detail	WO 97/6355–6383	⬚7⬚P
1883–1900	By name. Not searchable online by name, as description is by range of surnames	WO 97/2172–4231	⬚7⬚P
1900–1913	By name. Not searchable online by name, as description is by range of surnames	WO 97/4232–6322	⬚7⬚P
1900–1913	By name: misfiled papers. Not searchable online by name, as description is by range of surnames	WO 97/6323–6354	⬚7⬚P

The 'misfiled' papers for 1843–1899 in wo 97/6355–6383 are not in fact all misfiles. Some are the papers of soldiers who joined up under assumed names and later admitted to their real names. Their records were altered to give the real names, which is what they are now filed by. Some are misfiles, however, as are all the later ones for 1900–1913.

There are other, similar, records, which may be worth checking if you find nothing in wo 97 – or even if you do find material there.

- For soldiers who joined up about **1880** onwards, try a *surname* search on the online catalogue in pin 71 ⬚6, which includes over 6,000 detailed disability pension and widows' pension files. The list of this series has its quirks, but if you find something it will mean a lot of material – including the papers *not* in wo 97. Don't be put off if you find a suitable one but it is for a widow and you know the soldier was discharged: the widow could be applying years after her husband left the Army for the continuation of her now-dead husband's disability pension. The widows' pensions are listed by widow's name only, with no indication as to husband's name or service (Naval ratings are also included). The date range given against each description runs from date of enlistment to date the pension ceased.
- For **1823–1913**, try the registers of pensions paid for length of service in wo 117 ⬚7 for 1823–1913. They are in date order, and then by Chelsea number (given in wo 97): even without the number, you can make a guess

☐ p. 566

as to date of discharge and then trawl through the registers. From 1857 they give regiment, rank, age, years of service, rate of pension, details of foreign service, regimental surgeon's report, character reference, cause of any disability, place of birth, trade, height and physical description. From 1874 you may also find intended place of residence, date of discharge and number of good conduct badges. From 1903 you will also find date of enlistment, and from 1905 details of medals.

- For Kilmainham pensions before 1823, see 25.4.2.2.
- For **1787–1813**, try the Discharge Documents of Pensioners 1787–1813 in WO 121/1–136 [1]: these are searchable online by name in the online catalogue. They include approximately 20,000 certificates of soldiers awarded pensions. (The Friends of the National Archives' estimate is that over half are also in WO 97 and that these papers are more informative.)

Further material also exists:

1782–1833	Discharge documents, mostly of men previously discharged to pension, who have come back for garrison duty, and are being discharged again. Also includes petitions of men whose pensions have been stopped, asking successfully for restoration of pension. The Friends of the National Archives are working their way through these to make them searchable by name, place and regiment	WO 121/137–180; [1] WO 121/181–222	[7] becoming [1]
1735–1868	Correspondence on out-pensions	WO 246/97–101	[7]
1816–1817	Discharge Documents of Pensioners, Foreigners' Regiments	WO 122	[7]
1838–1896	Deferred pension records	WO 131	[7][P]

Disability pension records exist from 1715 to 1914, although only those of the last 50 years are easy to find.

1715–1882	Disability pensions, arranged by date of admission to pension	WO 116/1–124, 252	
1882–1913	Disability pensions, arranged by date of admission to pension	WO 116/186–251	[7]
1877–1914	Personal files on over 5,000 disabled soldiers and Naval ratings who served between 1877 and 1914 and received disability pensions; this is searchable in the online catalogue by name in reverse order, e.g., Bloggs Frederick (but it does not say whether the man was Army or Navy). The dates given are the date of the man's enlistment and the date the pension stopped. Includes medical records, accounts of how injuries were incurred and the man's own account of the incident and conduct sheets. The conduct sheets give place of birth, age, names of parents and siblings, religion, physical attributes, marital and parental status	PIN 71	[2]

You could also try the Chelsea Regimental Registers, 1715–1857, in WO 120 [F] and [7], although these are really about ex-soldiers in receipt of a pension who were liable to be called back to serve. They give a brief description, age, place of birth, particulars of service and reason of discharge for the period *c.* 1715–1843. For 1843 to 1857, they give only the date of award, rate of pension and the district pay office where the pension was paid. From about 1812 the dates of death have been added, the last in 1877. There is a partial index for 1806–1838, available on request.

There are other possibilities as well. From 1810 soldiers were able to purchase their discharge: this gave good men the chance to leave, as well as a way of shedding those the regiment wished to be rid of. Men with good conduct awards (medals or pay) were entitled to discounts on the purchase of their discharge. These discharges were:

1817–1829	By purchase	WO 25/3845–3847 [7]
1830–1838	By own request	WO 25/3848–3849 [7]
1830–1856	With modified pension	WO 25/3850 [7]
1838–1855	Free or free deferred pension	WO 25/3851–3858 [7]
1856–1861	Free permanent pension	WO 25/3859–3861 [7]
1861–1870	Free permanent pension, modified/ deferred pension, or purchase	WO 25/3863–3868 [7]
1852–1870	First period, incorrigible, ignominy, penal servitude or 21 years with militia	WO 25/3869–3878 [7]
1856–1857	Regiment under reduction	WO 25/3879–3882 [7]
1866–1870	Limited service act	WO 25/3883–3893 [7]
1863–1878	On return from India (at the Royal Victoria Hospital, Netley)	WO 12/13077–13105 [7]
1871–1884	General register	WO 121/223–238 [7]
1882–1883	Gosport discharge depot musters: men returning from overseas	WO 16/2284 [7]
1883–1888	Gosport discharge depot musters: men returning from overseas Index available	WO 16/2888–2916 [7] [F]
1884–1887	Without pension (gives address to which discharged)	WO 121/239–257 [7]

25.4.2.2 Discharge to Kilmainham pension, 1706–1822, and at Kilmainham, 1823–1863

The Royal Hospital Kilmainham dealt with pensions for regiments on the Irish Army Establishment from 1679 until 1800, when the British and Irish Army Establishments were united in principle, if not in practice. Regiments seem to have been placed on the Irish Establishment when they were sent to Ireland: some of them seem to have remained on it even if they were then sent off to America or elsewhere. The Irish Establishment also included many Irish regular and militia regiments. Kilmainham continued to issue and pay pensions until 24 December 1822, when all payments of pensions were taken over by Chelsea (by the statute 7 George IV *c.* 16). However, after 1822 soldiers discharged in Ireland had to be examined at Kilmainham until at least 1863, and any recommendation (including refusals of pension) forwarded to Chelsea. The related discharge certificates of soldiers who were granted or refused pensions were also sent, and filed in WO 97.

The earliest record of Kilmainham pensions is a survey conducted in 1744 of all pensioners thought to be still alive (some are marked as dead); the earliest grant seems to be about 1706 (WO 118/45). All the men in this register seem to be from or settled in Ireland, but the regiments are from across the British Isles. Later registers show that many of the men are neither from nor settled in Ireland, but were simply discharged while serving in Ireland.

You need to access these records by using the indexes, which cross-refer to three series: the brief admission books (by page); the admission registers (by number); and the certificates (by the same number). The indexes are actually alphabets, grouping soldiers by first letter of surname.

		In	Indexed by	
Admission Books (brief details only)	• 1759–1809 • 1809–1816 • 1816–1819	WO 118/36 WO 118/46 WO 118/38	WO 118/39 WO 118/40 WO 118/41	[F]
Admission Registers (fuller data)	• Series A 1807–1819 • Series B 1819–1822	WO 118/2–12 WO 118/42–43	WO 118/39–41 WO 118/44	[F]
Certificates (other data)	• Series A • Series B • Series GB	WO 119/7–55 WO 119/56–66 WO 119/67–69	WO 118/39–41 WO 118/44	[F]

Each type of document can give different information, so it is worth checking all of them. Other registers record alterations to pensions in 1807, when Kilmainham pension rates were made equivalent to Chelsea rates in 1806. It seems that this was done in two sections. Pensioners apparently resident in Ireland in 1807 are recorded in WO 118/1 and 2 (up to entry 2127), with the original A certificates in WO 119/1–8. Pensioners resident in Great Britain (not Ireland) are recorded in WO 118/35, with the related original GB certificates in WO 119/67–69.

For soldiers with Kilmainham pensions but living in British colonies who were transferred to Chelsea between 1819 and 1822, see WO 118/13 and WO 119/70.

Soldiers discharged in Ireland after 1822 continued to have entry to pension administered by the Kilmainham board. Medical examinations took place there every month, and certificates recording the Kilmainham decision on acceptance or rejection of the claim to pension were sent on to Chelsea, where they will be found in WO 97. These examinations are recorded for 1823 to 1863 in WO 118/15–34: it is not clear whether they stopped then or whether the paperwork simply no longer survives. The information given in the examination registers includes name, regiment, residence, service details, birthplace, trade, description and conduct, as well as fairly detailed medical notes.

25.4.2.3 Chelsea and Kilmainham in-pensioners

In-pensioners had to give up claims to out-pension rates and take a more modest pension plus accommodation at Chelsea or Kilmainham. If they wished, they could move out of the hospital and back onto an out-pension. Out-pension records tend to be more detailed, so you need to look at both.

Kilmainham records are rather sparse: there are two registers of in-pensioners covering 1839–1922 in WO 118/47–48, and giving details of previous admission to out-pension. Pensioners were transferred from Kilmainham to Chelsea in 1929. Chelsea records are much fuller. The main collection of muster rolls (1702–1865) and admission books and rolls (1778–1917) are in WO 23 ⏹, with separate indexes of admissions for 1837–1872 and for 1858–1933 in WO 23/146 and 173 respectively. The report of the 1894 Belper Committee into Chelsea and Kilmainham contains minutes of evidence from in-pensioners and a list of inmates (WO 32/6296). The evidence is very interesting, showing how men were forced to part from their wives, often leaving them destitute. In addition, there are the burial, marriage and baptism registers of the Chelsea Hospital for 1691–1856 in RG 4/4330–5332 and 4387. For later records, see 26.1.6.

25.4.2.4 Army pensioners

Army pensioners formed a significant proportion of the population. In 1894, there were just over 74,000 Army pensioners in the UK, with another 8,000 living abroad: over half of them were under 55. This is remarkably similar to the number in the 1840s, when there were about 73,000 Army pensioners living in the UK, nearly half of them under 55 and now recovered from the illness or disability that had earned them the pension. However, the greatest number of pensioners occurred in the late 1820s and 1830s, when men who had fought in the (first) Great War – against France – were coming out of the Army and into the pension lists. The needs of Empire kept the figures high after that.

No. of out-pensioners in the UK	
1782	11,907
1806	21,689
1816	39,217
1828	85,515
1840s	73,000
1894	74,000

Army pensioners were strongly encouraged to emigrate to the colonies in the early part of the nineteenth century: this applied especially to those discharged in a relatively close colony. Pensioners were not awarded land after 1831, but they were able to receive their commuted (lump sum) pension in the colony, and got part of it in advance to kit out themselves and their families for the journey. (See wo 247/79 for more information directed at would-be emigrants. This includes at the back a list of commuted pensioners residing in Canada in 1839 to whom Chelsea had agreed to give some extra assistance.)

Before 1842, pensioners who lived more than 25 miles from London, but still in England, Scotland or Wales, received their pension from the local excise man, from locally raised excise duties. In Ireland, the postmaster paid out the pensions. Pensioners living within 25 miles of Chelsea were paid at Chelsea. Records of the excise and postmaster payments from before 1842 do not seem to have survived. (For details of the payment system, see wo 26/40 pp. 157–179.)

For 1842 to 1883, out-pensions were paid through district pension offices, including many overseas offices. (After this, pensions were paid through the Post Office and records do not seem to survive.) The records are arranged by place of the district pension office (large town or name of colony), which can be very useful if you know only the area or country in which the man, or his dependants, resided and not his regiment (wo 22 ⑦, or PMG8 ⑦ for payments made in Hanover). There are separate registers (wo 23/147–160) of men admitted to pension from colonial regiments, 1817–1903, who did not have to appear in person to collect their pensions. In many of these cases, details of service and birthplace are given. Some of these entries relate to men from the British Army who retired while their regiment was overseas and who were given permission to receive their pension there. There are separate volumes for black and colonial soldiers.

The main series of service records of those soldiers who were discharged to pension are described in 25.4.2.1. There are many other records from Chelsea Hospital that can be very useful. In particular, the Chelsea registers, etc., 1702–1917 (wo 23 ⑦) contain a vast amount of information. The series includes:

- pension claims from soldiers in colonial regiments, 1836–1903;
- East India Company Army pensioners, 1814–1875;
- Chelsea registers of pensioners by regiment, 1805–1895;
- pensions for the Victoria Cross, wounds or other merit;
- bounty.

25.4.3 Army war dead before 1914

Nominal rolls of the dead were kept for many of the campaigns fought during the second half of the nineteenth century:

China	1857–1858	WO 32/8221, 8224, 8227	⑦
	1860	WO 32/8230, 8233, 8234	⑦
New Zealand	1860	WO 32/8255	⑦
	1863–1864	WO 32/8263–8268, 8271, 8276–8280	⑦

South Africa	1878–1881	WO 25/3474, 7770, 7706–7708, 7727, 7819	[7]
Egypt	1882, 1884	WO 25/3473	[7]
Sudan	1884–1885	WO 25/3473, 6123, 6125–6126, 8382	[7]
Burma	1888	WO 25/3473	[7]
Sierra Leone	1898	WO 32/7630–7631	[7]
South Africa	1899–1902	WO 108/89–91, 338	[7]
China	1914	WO 32/4996B	[7]

Some of these have been published: check the bibliography. These rolls do not include the normal occurrences of death in peacetime or outside the war zone.

25.4.4 Army other ranks before 1914: soldiers who died

Each regiment made regular returns of its casualties, in which the usual round of one or two deaths from sickness is suddenly broken by long lists of men killed in action. If you know your soldier's regiment, try the casualty returns. The main collection of monthly and quarterly regimental casualty returns covers 1809–c. 1875, with a few entries and annotations in the indexes continuing up to 1910 (WO 25/1359–2410, 3251–3260 [F], indexed in WO 25/2411–2755, 3261–3471). There is also a series of entry books of casualties, 1797–1817, from the Muster Master General's Office (WO 25/1196–1358 [7]).

These can provide quite a lot of personal information. Despite their title, the casualty returns also refer to absences, desertions and discharges, not just to the dead and wounded. The information given is name, rank, place of birth, trade at enlistment; the date, place and nature of the casualty; any debts or credits; and the next of kin or legatee. Wills, inventories of effects, letters from relatives and accounts have also been found, but *very* infrequently.

If a soldier died in service, this will also be recorded in the regimental muster books and pay lists. It can be difficult to find records of soldiers who died in service after 1898, when the muster books and pay lists no longer survive. For married men after 1898, it may be easiest to look at the over 1,000 widows pension records in PIN 71 ([1]: widows' names in reverse order – e.g., Langford Blanche Mary: no further detail given) as widows' pensions became available to all other ranks' widows on the married roll in 1903. However, before this widows and children were apparently dealt with by the Royal Patriotic Fund. This body presented Parliament with three detailed reports on aid given to widows and orphans of the Crimean War and of the South African War: see 24.4. Records of *some* dead soldiers have been found in WO 97, so it may be worth looking there on the off chance.

If you do not know the regiment, try the records relating to payments to next of kin of dead soldiers. There are long gaps in these records but they are arranged alphabetically and are easy to use.

1810–1822	Registers of authorities to deal with the effects (possessions) of dead soldiers. Give name, regiment, period of death, amount of effects and credits, date of order to agent, agent's name, person applying (usually next of kin) and their address	WO 25/2966–2971	7
1830	Index of deceased soldiers' effects: gives the regiment	WO 25/2974	7
1830–1844	Register of deceased soldiers' effects and credits: gives the regiment	WO 25/2975	7
1862–1881	Record books of deceased soldiers' effects	WO 25/3476–3490, indexed by WO 25/3491–3501	F
1882–1899	Do not appear to survive		
1900–1913	Records of deceased soldiers' effects	National Army Museum	

25.4.5 Army other ranks before 1914

If a soldier deserted, this will be recorded in the regimental muster books and pay lists: see 25.4.6. It can be difficult to find records of soldiers who died in service after 1898, when the muster books and pay lists no longer survive. However, information on deserters was forwarded to the Army authorities by means of the casualty returns, 1809–1910 (see 25.4.5).

Deserting			
1811–1852	Registers of deserters, giving descriptions, date and place of enlistment and desertion, and outcome. • 1811–1827 by cavalry, infantry and militia (militia 1811–1820) • 1827–1852 by regiment	WO 25/2906–2934	7
1828–1845	Details of 36,578 deserters, giving name, parish and county of birth, regiment, date and place of desertion, a physical description and other relevant information, were published in the police newspapers Hue and Cry and the Police Gazette. These have been indexed by the Manchester and Lancashire Family History Society, and the indexes published in hardcopy and CD-Rom (can be seen at the National Archives)	HO 75/1–18	F

1689–1830	An incomplete card index (by deserters, county of capture and regiment) to captured deserters. Compiled from bounty certificates of rewards (paid out of locally collected taxes) to the informant. • Rewards paid out in Bedfordshire, Berkshire, Buckinghamshire, Cambridgeshire and Cheshire • Rewards paid out in London and Middlesex (You will get one or more large boxes of tax documents, with no obvious clue as to where the bounty certificates will be. Look for a bundle wrapped up in a stiff brown paper. If there is not one wrapped up, look for a bundle of paper, not parchment)	E 182/2–114 E 182/594–673	F
1803–1815	Deserters who surrendered themselves under proclamation	WO 25/2955	7
1813–1848	Registers of captured deserters, giving name, regiment, date of capture and place of confinement, whether discharged from the Army or returned to his regiment, and to whom the reward (if any) was paid. • Indexes 1813–1833 in WO 25/2952–2954	WO 25/ 2935–2951	F

Punishment

1799–1823	Unindexed registers for the *Savoy* hulk, in which some deserters were sentenced to imprisonment	WO 25/2956–2961	7

You may be able to find correspondence on individual deserters, 1744–1813 and 1848–1858, in WO 4/591–654 F. These are indexed in each volume by the deserter's name. For deserters in Australia (HO 75), consult Fitzmaurice, *Army Deserters from HM Service.*

For courts martial, see the free research guide on *British Army: Courts Martial, 17th–20th Centuries*, available at **www.nationalarchives.gov.uk/ catalogue/researchguidesindex.asp** and at the National Archives.

25.4.6 Army other ranks before 1914: regimental records: muster books, pay lists and description books

The basic regimental service records were the muster books, pay lists and description books: these were used for the day-to-day administration of the regiment. (See 25.4.9 for other records of the Guards regiments.)

1732–1878	Main series of muster books and pay lists	WO 12	7
1710–1878	Artillery	WO 10	7
1816–1878	Engineers	WO 11	7
1780–1878	Militia and volunteers	WO 13	7
1877–1898	Main series, artillery, engineers: coverage is incomplete and information given is very limited	WO 16	7

In general, each muster book and pay list occupies one volume per year, and you may therefore have to search through several volumes. The first entry for a recruit in the muster generally gives his age, place of enlistment and trade, but does not give birthplace. Remember, recruitment is not usually into the 1st (the overseas) battalion, so look in the records of the 2nd battalion or the regimental depot for this first entry. You may find in the margin or by the name a number written like a fraction, such as 3/1566: this is a reference to the man's previous service in another regiment – in this case the 3rd Foot, with the regimental number there of 1566.

If the soldier died in service or was discharged, you should find an entry to that effect in one of the quarterly lists of men becoming non-effective: however, these lists are not always present. Where one does exist, it should give the birthplace of the man discharged or dead, his trade and his date of enlistment.

Muster books should contain details of remittances of pay back to families at home. From about 1868 to about 1883, the musters also contain marriage rolls, which sometimes give information about children as well as wives, if they occupied married quarters.

DESCRIPTION BOOKS

There are two main series of description books.

1768–1908	Depot description books. Compiled as recruits were assembled at the regimental depot. Give a description of each soldier, his age, place of birth and trade	WO 67	[7]
1778–1878	Regimental description and succession books. Give a description of each soldier, his age, place of birth and trade and successive service details • Not all start in 1778 or go to 1878 • Only a small percentage of all soldiers are included • Some are arranged alphabetically, others by date of enlistment	WO 25/266–688	[7]

The depot rolls or description books, 1768–1908 (WO 67) are usually the fuller of the two series. Men were usually allotted a number (this number does not appear on any forms until the 1830s). Depot rolls, however, do not list soldiers who enlisted where the regiment was stationed. Neither do they list soldiers who transferred from one regiment straight into another.

The regimental description books in WO 25/266–688 can contain these details, but they are not books containing details of every man in the regiment who served between the covering dates. They were started in 1825, or slightly earlier, after an investigation into the fraudulent claims of service. Regiments had to write down the services of every man in the regiment who was still serving at that time, and to list the men in chronological order of enlistment (or alphabetically). Consequently, the further back one goes, the fewer the men from that period. Most books would appear to have between 1,000 and 1,500 names (some have a lot more), but considering that regimental strength was 1,000 and the regiments had been through 22 years of war and wastage, this is a small percentage of the total number.

25.4.7 Army other ranks before 1914: how to find the regiment

If you do not know the soldier's regiment, and have been unable to find him in WO 97, there are still possible ways to find it out. Unfortunately, you can't assume that he would have joined the regiment that by its name appears to have been local. Before 1870, each regiment recruited its own soldiers, usually from the locality where the home battalion happened to be posted at the time (they moved about quite a lot). However, recruiting parties did range quite widely. After 1870, regiments could still recruit directly, but a man had the option of joining 'the Army' and being assigned to regiment.

If you have a photograph, you could try to identify the uniform: see the article by Barnes on this subject.

The regimental registers of births, 1761–1924, kept by the General Register Office are indexed, and the indexes can be seen at the Family Records Centre and the National Archives. The index gives the regiment and place of birth of children born to the wives of serving soldiers, if they were attached to the regiment. If you have some knowledge of offspring or areas of service, this can be an easy way to narrow the field. To identify the correct child, parent and regiment, you may have to buy more than one certificate (see 24.1.1).

If you know the county or country in which your soldier was living between 1842 and 1862 for England and Scotland, or between 1842 and 1882 for Ireland and abroad, you may be able to find the regiment fairly easily. Between these dates there are records of payment of pensions, arranged by the district pay offices, which name the regiment served in (WO 22 ⑦ and PMG8 ⑦ for payments in Hanover). For nearly 9,000 pensioners in India, Canada and South Africa between 1772 and 1899, taken from WO 120/35, 69 and 70, see Crowder, *British Army Pensioners Abroad, 1772–1899*.

Another possibility, if the soldier died in service, is to check the records of deceased soldiers' effects: see 25.4.4. These are arranged by initial letter of surname and give the regiment, which opens up the regimental records. However, if the soldier died owing money to the Army, instead of vice versa, you are unlikely to find a reference to him here.

If you have any information on place of service, you may be able to identify the regiment from Kitzmiller's *Guide to British Army Units and their Whereabouts*.

There are also two series of early nineteenth-century Army-wide returns of service of non-commissioned officers and men, arranged by regiment, and then alphabetically. One contains statements of periods of service and of liability to serve abroad as on 24 June 1806 (WO 25/871–1120 ⑥). The other contains returns of the service of non-commissioned officers and men not known to be dead or totally disqualified for service, who had been discharged between 1783 and 1810 (wo 25/1121–1131 ⑦). Looking through these without knowing the regiment is a long shot, but may work.

25.4.8 Army other ranks before 1914: Artillery and Engineer (Sapper and Miner) service records

Because the Royal Artillery, the Royal Engineers and the Royal Corps of Sappers and Miners were the responsibility of the Ordnance Office (and not of the War Office) until 1855, they have a different set of records. Until 1772, the Royal Engineers were officers only, using casual labour for physical work: after this a Corps of Royal Military Artificers, composed of other ranks only, was raised. In 1811, it became the Royal Corps of Sappers and Miners, with both officers and other ranks. This was amalgamated with the Royal Engineers after the abolition of the Ordnance Office in 1856.

However, many documents relating to Sappers and Miners are described in the lists as relating to Royal Engineers. Description books for 1793–1833 are in wo 54/313–316 ⑦. Entry books of discharges, casualties and transfers of Artillery and Engineer (Sapper and Miner) soldiers, 1740–1859, are in wo 54/317–337⑦. A register of deceased Sappers and Miners, 1824–1858, gives date and cause of death and to whom any effects went (wo 25/2972). Service records of the Royal Artillery, 1791–1855, and for the Royal Horse Artillery, 1803–1863, are in wo 69 ⑦. These include attestation papers and show name, age, description, place of birth, trade and dates of service; of promotion; of marriage; of discharge; and of death. They are arranged under the unit in which the soldier last served: to find this, use the indexes and posting books (wo 69/779–782 and wo 69/801–839 ⑦). This series also contains records of Royal Horse Artillery births and marriages (see 24.1.2). Laws' guide to the location of Artillery batteries may be useful if you know only the area of service. After 1856 (RA) or 1863 (RHA) look in wo 97 for discharge papers (see 25.4.2.1).

There is a miscellaneous collection of records of service for soldiers in the Artillery, Sappers and Miners, etc., and for civilian subordinates of the Board of Ordnance, arranged alphabetically in the Ordnance Office In-Letters (wo 44/695–700 ⑦). Also for the Artillery from before 1770 to 1820, try wo 18 ⑦. This consists of bound volumes of original warrants for payments on various accounts (pensions, recruiting, hospitals, deceased soldiers' effects, etc.), together with the original receipts, certificates of existence, letters petitioning for allowance, etc., of the individual concerned. Unfortunately, the list is only by year: you may have to spend a long time looking.

Registers of Artillery and Sapper and Miner pensioners, compiled in 1834 but dating back to the Napoleonic wars, are in wo 23/141–145 ⑦; they include descriptions. Royal Artillery registers of pensions for long service and disability, 1833–1913, are in WO 116/125–185 ⑦. There is an incomplete series of registers recording the deaths of soldiers in the Artillery, 1821–1873, in WO 69/583–597 ⑦. Papers relating to Artillery and Engineer (Sapper and Miner) deaths and personal effects, 1824–1859, are in WO 25/2972–2973 and 2976–2978 ⑦.

Musters and pay lists for the Royal Artillery, 1708–1878, are in WO 10 ⑦; for the Royal Sappers and Miners and the Engineers, 1816–1878, in WO 11 ⑦. Musters for both Artillery and Engineers, 1878–1898, are in WO 16 ⑦.

The Army Works Corps was a short-lived body, existing actively only for service in the Crimea. Its records are in WO 28 ⑦ and include paymaster's ledgers, receipts for wages and gratuities, pay and cash books, registers of officers, clerks, foremen and men, etc., for 1855–1864.

25.4.9 Army other ranks before 1914: Guards regiments

The various Guards regiments kept their own regimental records for longer than the rest of the Army. Records of soldiers and non-commissioned officers discharged from the five Footguards Regiments (Grenadiers, Coldstream, Scots, Irish, Welsh) are in the custody of their respective Regimental Headquarters at Wellington Barracks, Birdcage Walk, London SW1E 6HQ.

Records of the Life Guards, the Royal Horse Guards and the Household Battalion for men who enlisted between 1799 and 1919 have recently been transferred to the National Archives as WO 400 ⑦. This series contains surviving records of service for non-commissioned officers and other ranks who served in the Life Guards, the Royal Horse Guards and the Household Battalion, and whose Army service *ended* in these regiments. (If a man moved on to another regiment, his Army service record went with him.) The Household Cavalry Museum at Combermere Barracks in Windsor holds an extensive range of related material, including regimental order books, rolls, returns, etc.

25.5 Militia regiments, volunteers, the Royal Garrison Regiment and the Territorial Force

For an in-depth study, see Spencer, Militia and Volunteer Forces 1757–1945.

By the 1757 Militia Act, **militia regiments** were re-established in all counties of England and Wales, after a period of dormancy. A form of conscription was used: each year, the parish was supposed to draw up lists of adult males and to hold a ballot to choose those who had to serve in the militia. The militia lists (of all men) and the militia enrolment lists (of men chosen to serve) should in theory provide complete and annual censuses of all men aged between 18 and 45 from 1758 to 1831. The surviving lists, held locally, can be very informative, giving details about individual men and their family circumstances. However, the coverage of the country, for various reasons, is not complete. For more information, see the article by Medlycott or the book by Gibson and Medlycott. Records of the militia once formed are also usually in county record offices. Other sources held locally are the poor law records, which can include orders for the maintenance of the children of militia men.

There are some major records relating to the militia in the National Archives. Muster rolls (in wo 13 ☑) are the main source, although they were only kept when the militia was 'embodied' (this means serving in a military capacity, not in aid to the civil power). The sergeants (often ex-regular soldiers) and drummers were the only full-time staff of the militia, so information can usually be found on them (discharges are in wo 121 ☑). The muster rolls cover militia regiments for 1780–1783; for 1793–1814; and intermittently in the 1830s, 1840s and 1850s. In most cases, these muster rolls do not indicate place of origin. These muster rolls in wo 13 also include those of the supplementary militia, 1798–1816, and local militia, 1808–1816, together with those of other volunteer forces such as the fencibles, the yeomanry and the volunteers.

More useful for family history are the Militia Attestation Papers, 1806–1915 (wo 96 ☑), which were filled in at recruitment and, in most cases, were annotated to the date of discharge to form a record of service. They include the date and place of birth. Most date from the mid-nineteenth century. These attestation papers are arranged in the order of precedence of the regular Army unit to which the militia regiments were attached after the reorganisation of the Army in 1881. The list of wo 96 gives the name of the regular unit as at 1881, not the earlier militia unit. The way round this problem is to consult the *Army List* of 1882 or after, and to find out from there which militia regiments were attached to which Army regiment.

The Militia Records, 1759–1925 (wo 68 ☑) include records of some militia regiments in Great Britain and Ireland, and consist of enrolment books, description books, pay lists, returns of officers' services, casualty books, regimental histories, etc., and also registers of marriages, births and baptisms (see 24.1.2). The Military Correspondence, 1782–1840 (ho 50 ☑), and the Military Entry books, 1758–1855 (ho 51 ☑), contain much material on the militia.

A few militia soldiers qualified for pensions as a result of service in the French Revolutionary and Napoleonic wars, and their discharge certificates among the ordinary Soldiers' Documents (wo 97 ☑) give their place of birth and age on enlistment: see 25.4.2.1. Many Irish militia soldiers qualified for pension: see 25.4.2.2. Other details of militia pensioners, admitted to pension between 1821 and 1829, may be found in a peculiar register drawn up in 1858 and arranged first by year of admission, then by age on admission (wo 23/25).

The National Archives has some sources for local payments of subsistence from the Land Tax to families of conscripted soldiers (and other militia payments) in E 182 (☒: arranged by county where the payment was made). They can be very difficult to find, as the records include many other items and there are no indexes.

In 1901 the **Royal Garrison Regiment** was raised to relieve regular battalions of garrison duty for the Boer war. It was disbanded in 1906. Attestation papers are in WO 96 ☒ and other service records in WO 19 ☒ as follows:

- Officers' services, 1901 to 1905, including particulars as to the age, qualifications and marriage of each officer, with the dates of birth of his children. They also contain succession lists;
- Digests of services and diaries of proceedings of the 3rd and 4th Regiments, 1901 to 1905;
- Casualties, 1904 to 1906;
- Posting book, 1903 to 1906: alphabetical index of men posted to other regiments from the Royal Garrison Regiment, giving the dates of enlistment and the corps to which posted.

In 1908 the militia was restyled. Volunteer units of infantry, yeomanry (cavalry) and artillery, etc., were formed into the **Territorial Force**, which was renamed the Territorial Army in 1920. Most of the records are held locally: the muster rolls of some London and Middlesex Volunteer and Territorial regiments (1860–1912) are in the National Archives (WO 70 ☒). Very many of the men who served in the First World War served as Territorials, and their records are described in 26.1.6. For more information on the Territorials, see **www.1914-1918.net/tf.htm.**

25.6   Military medals before 1914

The considerable number of records relating to the creation and award of military medals generally only give the barest details about the recipient. Because medal records contain little genealogical information, they are not discussed at length here. You may wish to investigate instead our specialist guide, Spencer's *Medals*. If you are interested in tracing the history of a medal's creation and design, consult the records of the Royal Mint, particularly MINT 16, which is searchable by medal name. This series also contains a little correspondence from a few recipients of medals.

There were three main types of military medal: for a particular campaign; for gallantry and meritorious service; and for long service and good conduct.

Campaign medals began with the Waterloo Medal. There was a medal for earlier service, mostly in the Peninsular War and America, 1793–1814, called the Military General Service Medal, but in fact this was not issued until 1847, and then only to men who had survived until that date: see the books by Mullen and Challis.

The Waterloo Medal Book records the corps and regiments engaged in the battle, giving the name and rank of officers and men (MINT 16/112). Wellington's despatch of 29 June 1815, listing the officers killed and wounded, was printed as a supplement to the *London Gazette* of 1 July 1815: copies can be found in ZJ 1 ⑦ and also in MINT 16/111. After Waterloo, medals were awarded for most major campaigns – for example, the Indian Mutiny Medal of 1857. Clasps were often awarded for particular battles within a campaign, such as a Sebastopol clasp for a Crimea Medal. The medal rolls for campaign medals, 1793–1913, are in WO 100 (seen on microfilm), arranged by ranges of regiment. Correspondence and papers relating to some of the actual medals are in MINT 16. The India Office Library and Records hold the medal rolls for some campaigns that took place in India.

Gallantry medals were first awarded during the Crimean War. All gallantry awards bestowed upon members of the British army were announced in the *London Gazette* (ZJ 1). Awards announced in the New Year or Birthday Honours (January and June) were not accompanied by citations.

Records of Long Service and Good Conduct Medals for other ranks who had served at least 18 years run from 1831 (WO 102 ⑦). The records of the Meritorious Service Medal, for non-commissioned officers, run from 1846 (WO 101 ⑦). The records include details of candidates for, as well as recipients of, these awards. A register of annuities paid to recipients of the meritorious or long service awards, 1846–1879, is in WO 23/84. For sergeants, corporals and privates awarded the Distinguished Conduct Medal for distinguished service and gallant conduct in the field between 1855 and 1901, search WO 146 ①.

25.7 Records of specific wars

Beyond the general runs of records already discussed, you may find some other sources useful for soldiers engaged in particular conflicts.

25.7.1 American War of Independence, 1776–1783

Headquarters Papers in WO 28 ⑥① have been listed in detail for this period, and can contain letters and mentions of individual officers and men. The muster books and pay lists of many regiments involved in this war may be found (see 25.4.6), but the certificates of men discharged in North America, which should give the age and place of birth, can seldom be traced. It is unlikely that you will find anything but a man's name, rank and date of discharge in the musters. There are some pay lists and account books for Hessian troops, but they provide few personal details. Muster rolls of the Hessian troops in British pay in North America are held in West Germany: there is an index available at the National Archives. The Loyalist Regiment Rolls for provincial troops are in the National Archives of Canada.

25.7.2 The wars with France, 1793–1815

Before 1914, the wars with France were known as the Great War. It has been calculated that as many as 10 per cent of the eligible male population were involved in the fighting. Unfortunately, there is no simple way of finding the soldiers of this period. You need to use the normal procedure of regimental registers in WO 75 for officers, and a combination of the pension papers (in WO 97, WO 121, WO 118 and WO 119) and the musters in WO 12 for other ranks. However, there are a couple of shortcuts.

For officers, try Hart's papers in WO 211. The first part of this contains Hart's biographies of senior officers of the Peninsular War. Later pieces contain reports by officers who survived into the late 1830s of their time in the French wars. Try also Hall's *The History of the Peninsular War, vol. 8: Biographical Dictionary of British Officers Killed and Wounded, 1808–1814*.

For other ranks, try the 1806 regimental service returns in WO 25/871–1120 ⑥. If you are interested in any of the Guards regiments, or the 1st–4th regiments of Foot, try the regimental indexes to these records published by Barbara Chambers. She also offers access to other French Wars material, mostly on the Guards regiments, from both the National Archives and the regimental museums: see 62 for the address.

For soldiers in general, you could try the prize registers in WO 164 ⑦. Soldiers were eligible for prize money from the proceeds of their victories; if they had died, their dependants could claim it. The Royal Chelsea Hospital was given the right to administer the unclaimed prize monies in 1809, but the records of claims go back to actions well before then. The registers in WO 164 are divided by action, and by which regiments had a claim: they were annotated for several years after with details of who had claimed the money and who did not. For some of the major actions of the Peninsular War, and of the battle of Waterloo, the lists of original payments are included.

A sample entry would be that for the prize money of John *Hainsley*, gunner in the Royal Artillery, who was due prize money for action on Martinique, St Lucia and Guadeloupe in 1794. The prize money was claimed by his widow, Janet *Ainslie*, on a certificate by Captain Colebrooke in 1799 and again in 1800 (WO 164/57, p 22 and WO 164/71, p 22).

The series also includes the Peninsula letter books (WO 164/1–16 Ⓕ) and the Waterloo letter books (WO 164/17–19 Ⓕ) of claimants who believed they were entitled to prize money: many were the parents, widows, uncles and so on of the soldier. They are indexed by both claimant *and* soldier. The dates of the letters range from 1816 to 1831: obviously, many of the soldiers were dead if relatives were making the claim. For example, Catherine Graham of Blackwater Town, County Tyrone was awarded £7 17s 7d Peninsular Prize money due her late brother Sergeant John Cooper of the 3rd Foot in 1829 (WO 164/16, p 138).

The Waterloo Medal Book records the corps and regiments engaged in the battle, giving the name and rank of officers and men (MINT 16/112).

Wellington's despatch of 29 June 1815, listing the officers killed and wounded, was printed as a supplement to the *London Gazette* of 1 July 1815: copies can be found in ZJ 1 and also in MINT 16/111.

25.7.3 Crimean War, 1854–1856

Beyond the general runs of records already discussed, you may find these sources useful for soldiers engaged in this conflict. For the Crimea, there are two series of special muster rolls, in addition to the standard series:

1854–1856	the troops at the Scutari depot	WO 14	7
1854–1856	British, German and Swiss legions	WO 15	7

The reports of the Royal Patriotic Fund of aid given to the widows and orphans of soldiers who served in the Crimea, and of similar petitions rejected, are very interesting: the rejected petitions include details of the soldier's service after the Crimea. See 24.4 for more details.

However, there are certain problems with using the Crimean War Medal Rolls in wo 100: they were disarranged and bound out of order. You may find that the most cost effective way to find service and medal records is to consult **www.crimeanwar.info**, described by Oldham in 'The Great Crimean War Index', which brings together a huge array of records for over 100,000 men.

25.7.4 South African (Boer) War, 1899–1902

Beyond the general runs of records already discussed, you may find these sources useful for soldiers engaged in this conflict.

Death registers of British soldiers who died in South Africa, 1899–1902, are kept by the General Register Office: indexes can be seen at the Family Records Centre and the National Archives (see 8.8). See also the *South Africa Field Force Casualty List, 1899–1902*, available at the National Archives. This is a published version of the casualty returns in wo 108/89–91 and 338. There is also Watt's *In Memoriam: Roll of Honour, Imperial Forces, Anglo-Boer War 1899–1902*.

At the National Army Museum, the Soldiers' Effects Ledgers for 1901–1913 are in alphabetical order of surname. These cover soldiers who died, and give full name, regimental number, rank, date and place of death, place of birth, date of enlistment, trade on enlistment, next of kin as stated either by the regimental record or by the soldier's will, the name of the legatee and the record of payment of wages, etc., owed. It is worth looking for a will in the National Probate Calendar as well, as soldiers were required to make a will before going on active service: see 9.3.

Officers' service records may or may not survive, depending on how long they served. Unfortunately, records of many officers commissioned about 1901 no longer survive, thanks to weeding of supplementary files in the

1930s and enemy bombing of the main series of records in 1940. Read 26.1.5 for more detail.

The service records of British regular soldiers (as at the time of discharge to pension or death) are in WO 97 ⑦ℙ, in alphabetical order. There are two sequences for this date, so make sure you order the right box of both: see 25.4.2.1. If they re-enlisted for the First World War, their earlier records *may* have been added to their later records: you may need to check both (see 26.1.6). See **www.roll-of-honour.com/Databases/BoerDetailed/index. html** for an ongoing index to men who served in the Boer War.

Very many men volunteered for the Boer War and served in the volunteer force, the Imperial Yeomanry. These soldiers' documents of the Imperial Yeomanry, 1899–1902, are in WO 128 ⑦ℙ. The easiest way into these records is to use the published index, Asplin's *Roll*, which is available at the National Archives, or on his own website at **http://hometown.aol.co. uk/kevinasplin/home.html**. Both give details of nearly 40,000 men. Then you can match up the details with the list of WO 128 in order to access the record. Further details about the records of the Imperial Yeomanry can be found in Spencer, *Militia and Volunteer Forces 1757–1945*. Other forces were raised locally in South Africa: enrolment forms and nominal rolls of these local armed forces, 1899–1902, are in WO 126 ⑥ and WO 127 ⑥. Some records of the City Imperial Volunteers are at the Guildhall Library.

The Medal Rolls for the Queen's and King's South African Medals (in WO 100 ⑥) may sometimes contain a few personal details, such as the date of discharge or death and the home address.

Personal files on over 5,000 disabled soldiers and Naval ratings, who served between 1877 and 1914 and received disability pensions, are in PIN 71 ② (search on surname AND forename); many will be Boer War soldiers. This series is searchable on the online catalogue by name (but it does not say whether the man was Army or Navy). The dates given are the date of the man's enlistment and the date the pension stopped. The information contained includes medical records, accounts of how injuries were incurred and the men's own account of the incidents, and conduct sheets. The conduct sheets give place of birth, age, names of parents and siblings, religion, physical attributes, marital and parental status. There are also over 1,000 personal files on the widows of Army other ranks and Naval ratings whose service was between about 1880 and 1914 in PIN 71 ②. This series is searchable online the same way.

The reports of the Royal Patriotic Fund of aid given to the widows and orphans of the British and colonial forces are very interesting. See 24.4 for more details.

For the 7,800 Canadian forces that served in the Boer war, try out the relevant database at the excellent **www.genealogy.gc.ca**.

25.8 Army service records before 1914: bibliography

Army lists, etc., of personnel

Army List (London, annually from 1754)

K J ASPLIN, *The roll of the Imperial Yeomanry, Scottish Horse & Lovats Scouts: 2nd Boer War, 1899–1902; being an alphabetical list of 39,800 men of these volunteer forces who enlisted for the 2nd Boer War. Listing regimental details, clasps to Queen's South Africa Medal and casualty status* (2 vols. Salisbury, 2000) (This is also searchable online at **http://hometown.aol.co.uk/kevinasplin/home.html**)

British Biographical Archive (London, 1984 continuing)

L S CHALLIS, *Peninsula Roll Call* (London, 1948)

F AND A COOK, *The Casualty Roll for the Crimea* (London, 1976)

C DALTON, *English Army Lists and Commission Registers, 1661–1714* (London, 1892–1904)

C DALTON, *George I's Army, 1714–1727* (London, 1910–1912)

C DALTON, *Irish Army Lists, 1661–1685* (London, 1907)

C DALTON, *Waterloo Roll* (London, 2nd edn 1904)

M G DOONER, *The 'Last Post': being a Roll of All Officers (Naval, Military or Colonial) who gave their lives for their Queen, King and Country, in the South African War, 1899–1902* (1903, reprinted 1980)

E DWELLY, *Waterloo Muster Rolls: Cavalry* (Fleet, 1934)

H G HART, *Army List* (London, 1839–1915)

List of Officers of the Royal Regiment of Artillery, 1716–June 1914 (London, 1914)

A L T MULLEN, *Military General Service Medal, 1793–1814* (London, 1990)

A L T MULLEN, *Military General Service Roll, 1793–1814* (London, 1990)

E PEACOCK, *The Army List of Roundheads and Cavaliers* (London, 2nd edn, 1874)

A PETERKIN, W JOHNSTON and R DREW, *Commissioned Officers in the Medical Services of the British Army* (London, 1968)

Roll of Officers of the Corps of Royal Engineers from 1660 to 1898 (London, 1898)

Royal Military Kalendar (London, 1820)

South Africa Field Force Casualty List, 1899–1902 (1972)

S WATT, *In memoriam: Roll of Honour, Imperial Forces, Anglo-Boer War 1899–1902* (University of Natal, 2000)

Overviews

H BICHENO and R HOLMES, *Rebels and Redcoats: The American Revolutionary War* (2004)

S FOWLER and W SPENCER, *Army Records for Family Historians* (National Archives, 1998)

R HOLMES, *Redcoat: The British Soldier in the Age of Horse and Musket* (2002)

R HOLMES, *Sahib: the British Soldier in India* (2005)

W SPENCER, *Medals: The Researcher's Companion* (National Archives, 2006)

W SPENCER, *Records of the Militia and Volunteer Forces 1757–1945* (National Archives 1997)

E M SPIERS, *The Army and Society 1815–1914* (Longman, 1980)

General works

D J BARNES, 'Identification and Dating: Military Uniforms', in *Family History Focus*, eds, D J Steel and L Taylor (Guildford, 1984)

A Bruce, *An Annotated Bibliography of the British Army, 1660–1714* (London, 1975)

A Bruce, *The Purchase System in the British Army, 1660–1871* (Royal Historical Society, London, 1980)

Calendar of State Papers, Domestic (London, 1856–1972)

Calendar of State Papers, Ireland (London, 1860–1912)

M Croft, 'William Murphy, Chelsea Pensioner, aged 15' [Army children], *Ancestors* 4 (2001)

N K Crowder, *British Army Pensioners Abroad, 1772–1899* (Baltimore, 1995)

C Firth and G Davis, *The Regimental History of Cromwell's Army* (Oxford, 1940)

Y Fitzmaurice, *Army Deserters from HM Service* (Forest Hill, Victoria, 1988)

J S W Gibson and A Dell, *Tudor and Stuart Muster Rolls* (FFHS, 1991)

J S W Gibson and E Hampson, *Specialist Indexes for Family Historians* (FFHS, 1998)

J S W Gibson and M Medlycott, *Militia Lists and Musters, 1757–1876* (FFHS, 1989)

J Hall, *The History of the Peninsular War, vol. 8: The Biographical Dictionary of British Officers Killed and Wounded, 1808–1814* (London, 1998)

L Hore, 'Family or country: Chelsea out-pensioners in the late eighteenth century', *Ancestors* 13 (2003)

L Hore, 'Life after the Army: Chelsea out-pensioners in the late eighteenth century', *Ancestors* 12 (2003)

A Husainy and J Trumpbour, 'Military Sources for South Asian Ancestors', *Ancestors* 14 (2003)

J M Kitzmiller, *In Search of the 'Forlorn Hope': a Comprehensive Guide to Locating British Regiments and their Records* (Salt Lake City, 1988)

M E S Laws, *Battery Records of the Royal Artillery, 1716–1877* (Woolwich, 1952–1970)

W Lenz, *Manuscript Sources for the History of Germany since 1500 in Great Britain* (German Historical Institute in London, *Publications*, vol. 1). This has many references to German troops in British service in the eighteenth and nineteenth centuries.

M Medlycott, 'Some Georgian 'Censuses': the Militia Lists and 'Defence' Lists', *Genealogists' Magazine*, vol. XXIII, pp. 55–59

B Oldham, 'Letter from the Crimea', *Ancestors* 11 (2002/3)

B Oldham, 'The Great Crimean War Index', *Ancestors* 14 (2003)

Public Record Office, *Alphabetical Guide to certain War Office and other Military Records preserved in the Public Record Office* (Lists and Indexes, vol. LIII)

Public Record Office, *Lists of War Office Records* (Lists and Indexes, vol. XXVIII and Supplementary vol. VIII)

E E Rich, 'The Population of Elizabethan England', *Economic History Review*, 2nd series, vol. II, pp. 247–265 (Discusses the Elizabethan muster rolls.)

J Sly, 'Stars of Remembrance' [World War campaign medals] *Ancestors* 35 (2005)

A Swinson ed., *A Register of the Regiments and Corps of the British Army: the Ancestry of the Regiments and Corps of the Regular Establishments of the Army* (London, 1975)

A S White and R Perkins, *Armies Of The Crown* [CD-Rom containing two bibliographies of all the published Corps and regimental histories of the British Army and of the published histories of the armed forces of the British and Indian Empires.] (Naval and Military Press)

26 Army service records, from 1914 onwards

For the fifty years after 1914, most British families had direct experience of military life among at least some of their members in a way that was entirely new. Millions served in the First and Second World Wars, and national service continued until 1961. So many men and women served, so many died and so many carried mental and physical wounds for the rest of their lives that these two Wars made a huge mark on the British people. In many ways, this experience combined with universal suffrage to produce a new personal and political perception that Britons were not subjects but citizens, with all the rights of citizens to a better life. Both the national provision of decent housing in the 1920s and the health and education reforms of the 1940s owe much to the feeling that 'we all fought – we all deserve better'.

26.1 The First World War

The First World War saw mass mobilisation of soldiers for the first time in the United Kingdom. Conscription started in 1916. We don't know exact figures, but historians think that about 7.2 million men served in the Army between 1914 and 1919. Because so much was destroyed in the Second World War, there is no single complete set of service records for the First World War, only an enormous jigsaw with (we fear) many pieces missing. Information is scattered and needs to be pieced together. Proposals are currently being discussed to create a huge database of all service records and other personal data for the First World War. With some luck, much of the detailed advice given here may become increasingly unnecessary. If at some point you can find all the information you need in a matter of minutes, this chapter can stand in testimony to how complicated the searching was beforehand.

There is an existing online resource that gives outstanding advice and information on how to trace individuals and on the experience of the Army in the First World War. This is Chris Baker's *The Long, Long Trail: The story of the British Army in the First World War* at **www.1914–1918.net**. For a fuller explanation of all the records relating to service in the Army during the First World War, see Spencer, *Army Service Records of the First World War*.

With so many men serving, it can be quite difficult to track down a particular man, especially as so many of the service records were burned when the War Office record store at Arnside Street in London caught fire as a result of enemy action in September 1940. A full list of the many *types* of documents destroyed – but not of each document destroyed – can be seen on Documents Online. Its reference is wo 32/21769, but the easiest way to find it is just to search for Arnside. (Like all documents in Documents Online, this can be seen free at the National Archives.) However, it is still worth looking at the National Archives: even if you can't find a service record, you may be able to piece together quite a lot of information from other sources.

Many people know the man's Army number: this can help in finding the records of the award of medals, and thus the regiment he served in. It does help if you know which regiment and battalion a man served in, especially if he had a common name. If you don't already know regiment and battalion, there are two ways to proceed. If he survived, or if you don't know what happened to him, look at the medal roll index and the medal roll itself (see 26.1.1). If you know the man died, look at the Commonwealth War Graves database (see 26.1.3). If you find several likely people, you will have to follow them all and do some detective work on the results.

26.1.1 First World War: the campaign medal index

The card index to the campaign medal rolls at the National Archives is the nearest thing we have to an index to the Army in this period. The index records awards of campaign medals to officers and other ranks of the Army and Royal Flying Corps – and also to many civilians – who saw service overseas. The index also includes cards for some gallantry and long service awards: see 26.1.8 for more details. You may also wish to investigate our specialist guide, Spencer's *Medals*.

These index cards are now searchable (free) and viewable (for a fee) online at **www.nationalarchives.gov.uk/documentsonline**. It can be easy to find the right card if you know the Army number (for other ranks) or the regiment, but difficult if you are looking for a common name and have no other information.

Although the medal index includes over 5.5 million cards, this still leaves nearly 2 million men without entries. Only those men who served abroad were eligible for campaign medals. If you do not find an entry, it may be worth looking at the (incomplete) National Roll of the Great War (see 26.1.4) for any published record of home service and, of course, trying for a service record. Officers had to apply for their campaign medals: many did not and will therefore not appear in the index. (However, officers' service records have a higher survival rate than those of other ranks: see 26.1.5.)

Those who served abroad during the Great War were awarded one or more campaign medals – all too often after their death. Those who only served in the United Kingdom did not receive awards, unless they were discharged as a result of sickness or wounds contracted or received during the War and were then given the Silver War Badge. Their index cards look different.

1914 Star	Instituted in 1917 for service ashore in France and Flanders between 5 August and 22 November 1914. In 1919 a clasp was awarded to those who had been under fire between these dates
1914–1915 Star	Instituted in 1918 for those who saw service in France and Flanders from 23 November 1914 to 31 December 1915, and to those who saw service in any other operational theatre of war from 5 August 1914 to 31 December 1915
British War Medal 1914–1920	Instituted in 1919 for eligible service personnel and civilians alike. The basic requirement for Army personnel and civilians was that they either entered a theatre of war, or rendered approved service overseas between 5 August 1914 and 11 November 1918. Service in Russia in 1919 and 1920 also qualified for the award
Victory Medal 1914–1919	Instituted in 1919 for all eligible personnel who served on the establishment of a unit in an operational theatre
Territorial Force War Medal 1914–1919	Awarded only to members of the Territorial Force who had been a member of the Territorial Force on or before 30 September 1914, *and* had served in an operational theatre outside of the United Kingdom between 5 August 1914 and 11 November 1918
Silver War Badge	Awarded from September 1916 to all of those military personnel who were discharged as a result of sickness or wounds contracted or received during the War, either at home or overseas

A very few of the index cards have extra data written on the back – usually the address to which the medals were sent. The backs of the cards have not been filmed or digitised by the National Archives. However, the Ministry of Defence has now finished using the original cards, and has passed them on to the Western Front Association: for more information, see **www.western-front.co.uk.**

The index is actually to the 3,273 volumes of medal rolls, arranged by regiment in WO 329 [6]: it contains almost all the information to be found on the actual rolls. The exception is that cards for regular Army soldiers tend not to show the battalion (a sub-division of a regiment) in which he served, though cards for men in the Territorial Force often do give the battalion. (For more information on the Territorials, see 25.5 and **www.1914-1918.net/tf.htm.**) If the battalion is not shown on the card, you can therefore pick this up from the medal roll. You will need to know the battalion if you want to extend your research to the war diaries, which provide a daily record of each battalion's activity (see 26.1.10).

Cards may include a note, such as KR 392. This is a reference to King's Regulations and a paragraph number. 392 is the most common paragraph, and lists 27 causes of discharge. The most used one is KR 392 (xvi) – 'No longer physically fit for service'. Copies of the King's Regulations can be seen in the Library at the National Archives. If you have a really detailed enquiry about the King's Regulations, however, try the specialist advice of the National Army Museum.

The medal roll is also marked to show whether the medal had actually been received or not. If there is a tick against the name, the medal had been received by the soldier or next of kin, by registered post. If there was a cross, either the delivery had failed or the medal had been deliberately returned. After ten years, these medals were melted down. Many people look at the medal roll in the hope of asking for the medal to be issued now. However, the Medal Office cannot now issue First World War medals, as they are no longer produced. Instead they will tell you to look for a private source, such as a military tailor or a medal dealer.

We do get a lot of enquiries from people who have bought a medal and would like to restore it to the original holder's family. Unfortunately, this is not a realistic wish: we do not hold details of all the descendants of medal holders. Perhaps the best thing to do would be to present it to the relevant regimental museum.

26.1.2   First World War: using the medal rolls index

The best way to access the index is to use the name search on the National Archives' website at **www.nationalarchives.gov.uk/documentsonline.** (Incidentally, if you have a 'problem' surname that could conceivably be spelled a different way, you can assume that the Army used the spelling given in the medal index, or in the *Army List*.) Some men were listed by surname and initials, others by surname and forename. The index cards are displayed six to a page, so if you pay to see one card, you will see five others as well. The cards were arranged (and were therefore filmed) in alphabetical order of surname, and then by alphabetical order of forename *initials*. Men with only one initial are placed before men with two. (For example, Buckland P[hilip] comes before Buckland P[ercy] C[lifford].) Very often there are several men of the same name: in this case their index cards are filed or displayed according to the regimental order of precedence (cavalry before infantry).

If you have any family tradition as to regiment, this may help you identify your Brown G among the many others. You may need to do some investigation here, as family tradition and official records often express the same information in different ways. For instance, my grandfather Percy Buckland always told me that he had served in the Queen's Westminsters. There was no index card giving this as a regiment. A search in the sources given in 26.1.11 showed that the Queen's Westminsters was also known as 16th (County of London) Battalion of the London Regiment, Queen's Westminster Rifles, a Territorial Force battalion – and there was a card for him giving the 16/London Regiment. It would have been an awful lot quicker to have checked the known regimental details first.

Remember that the medal roll index contains almost all the information to be found on the actual medal rolls themselves – except sometimes the battalion a man served in. If you don't already know which battalion you are looking for, make sure you go beyond the index to look at the medal roll itself. You need to note down the old reference on the card (e.g., TP 16/101/B/2 p. 139) and, at the National Archives, convert it to a modern wo 329 reference, so you can order the actual medal roll. Pick up the *How to* leaflet at the National Archives to find out how to do this.

26.1.3 First World War: accessible information on the war dead

Information on men who died in the War is often much easier to trace than information on men who survived. For a start, there is the Debt of Honour Register on the website of the Commonwealth War Graves Commission (**www.cwgc.org**). This is accessible from the National Archives. You can find here a record of all Army personnel who died in the First World War, with date of death, place of burial, regiment and sometimes a mention of parents or wife. If you are looking for a really common name, you may have some problems, as quite often only an initial is given instead of a forename. However, you can combine it with a search of *Soldiers [and Officers] Died in the Great War*. This 81-volume publication covers both soldiers and officers and lists all the men who died between 1914 and 1919. There is an online searchable version at **www.military-genealogy.com** (pay per view). You can also access it on CD-Rom at the National Archives. To use the books you had to know the regiment: now you can search the website by several categories of information.

Search terms for *Soldiers Died in the Great War*			
surname	place of birth (town)	died	rank
forename	place of birth (county)	died of wounds	regiment
initials	place of enlistment (town)	killed in action	battalion
date of death	place of enlistment (county)	theatre of war of death	regimental no.

Gallantry medals he may have won are also listed.

There are also published obituaries, apparently written by relatives, in De Ruvigny's *Roll of Honour*, which can be seen at the National Archives. Many other obituaries will have been published in local newspapers, professional journals, staff magazines and school magazines: these can be well worth seeking out.

You should be able to order a death certificate from the General Register Office: there are indexes to the death registers for Army war dead, 1914–1921, at both the Family Records Centre and the National Archives (see 8.8). At the National Archives, there are many French and Belgian certificates of the deaths for British soldiers. These are for men who died in civilian hospitals or elsewhere outside the immediate war zone, or who were killed in action and their bodies picked up later by the French and Belgian authorities after the front had moved on. They are arranged by first letter of surname and date from 1914 to 1920 (RG 35/45–69 ☑): certificates for surnames beginning C, F, P, Q and X are missing. We do not know how complete the collection is.

The National Army Museum has the records of deceased soldiers' effects for the First World War, and will search them for a fee. These give next of kin as stated either by the regimental record or by the soldier's will, the name of the legatee and the record of payment of wages, etc., owed. It may be worth looking for a will in the National Probate Calendar: see 9.3.

26.1.4 First World War: the National Roll of the Great War

The National Roll of the Great War was a publishing venture of the post-War years, designed to provide a brief description of the War service of individual subscribers. It contains details of over 100,000 men and women whose entries were written and paid for by themselves or their family. As such, it is often considered untrustworthy. Most entries refer to combatants, but is also contains men and women who did not serve overseas, and some entries for people who worked in related areas, such as the munitions industry or the Merchant Navy. The publishers began to compile the volumes in 1920, but had gone into liquidation by 1922, having produced only 14 volumes covering some of the major cities. They have been reprinted by the Naval & Military Press (who have also produced a 15th volume containing an index) and been published on CD-Rom by S & N Genealogy Supplies.

All the volumes are available in the Library at the National Archives:

• Section I – London	• Section VIII – Leeds
• Section II – London	• Section IX – Bradford
• Section III – London	• Section X – Portsmouth
• Section IV – Southampton	• Section XI – Manchester
• Section V – Luton	• Section XII – Bedford & Northampton
• Section VI – Birmingham	• Section XIII – London
• Section VII – London	• Section XIV – Salford

The Manchester volume, containing details of about 10,000 men and women, can be searched and seen free online at **www.spinningtheweb. org.uk** – just type the surname and National Roll into the search box on that page.

26.1.5 First World War: officers' service records

Service records as originally maintained by the Army do not survive for officers whose service ended after 1914 as they were destroyed by enemy bombing in 1940. However, in addition to the main service record, there was a correspondence file, which, depending on length of service, could become very bulky. These did survive the bombing, and are now the main source for officers who fought in the First World War and who left the service between 1914 and 1922. These correspondence files are arranged in two series WO 339 (③: mostly regular Army and emergency reserve) and WO 374 (③: mostly Territorial Force). For more information on the Territorials, see **www.1914–1918.net/tf.htm**. In total some 217,000 individual files can be found in these two series. There are also a few files of notable individuals in WO 138 – mostly top brass, but also the poet Wilfred Owen.

These files can contain medical records, reports made by repatriated prisoners of war, details relating to pensions and in fact almost anything, not necessarily about his ability. Unfortunately many correspondence files of regular Army officers who obtained their commissions before 1901 were weeded or destroyed in the 1930s. You may therefore find a lot of information, or you may find very little.

The quickest way to access WO 339 is to search in the online catalogue, using the surname. If this turns up several people of the same name, you will need to go to WO 338 ⑦, the index to WO 339, which gives more detail to help you identify the right person. WO 338 also contains references to officers who served after 1922 (see 26.2), as well as to those officers whose correspondence files were weeded and for whom no service papers therefore survive. WO 338 gives the 'long number' used by the Army registry system: if you are unfortunate enough to be looking for an officer whose papers were weeded to extinction, it may be worth using the long number to check in the original register to the correspondence files in WO 340 ⑦.

You may find many Indian Army officers in WO 338 (with IA instead of regiment), WO 339 and WO 374. These were officers on leave or retired, who became officers in short-staffed regular Army or new Territorial Force regiments.

Records of British Army other ranks who were later commissioned into the Indian Army have been added to wo 339 (as wo 339/139092–139906): you will need to use these pre-commission records with post-commission records at the India Office Library and Records (address in 62).

For more detailed information, see Spencer's *Army Service Records of the First World War*. Brief details of an officer's career can also be found in the *Army List*: see 24.3.3.

26.1.6 First World War: other ranks' service records

Army service records for men who fought in the First World War are incredibly popular. We know that only about 40 per cent survive after the warehouse they were kept in was bombed in 1940. We also know that a lot of people look at the paper catalogue, or search the online catalogue, for a specific name. Many of them find similar names, but not the one they want. They give up and go away at this point, convinced that their man's papers must have been among the 60 per cent destroyed. This is a pity. When this particular catalogue was created by the Ministry of Defence as part of the transfer of these records to the National Archives, they used a standard archival practice of giving just the first and last name in each box of documents/microfilm – to indicate the *range of contents*. So if you are looking for a Philip Abbott, you may find an entry reading Abbott, John – Abbott, Robert and wrongly conclude that no record survives for Philip.

Surviving service records for soldiers discharged after 1913 are in two series. In general we say that you are likely to find a man in either but not both of these series: as ever, the exception proves the rule and a few men have been found in both.

WO 364	For *c.* 750,000 men medically discharged as a result of sickness or wounds, contracted or received 1914–1919	In alphabetical order on 4,915 reels of micro-film	*The unburnt documents –* a complete set	
WO 363	For *c.* 2,000,000 of the men who died or who were demobilised at the end of the War, up to 1920 – both regular soldiers and 'duration of the War servicemen only'	In alphabetical order on *c.* 20,000 reels of microfilm	The *burnt documents –* about 40 per cent of the set	[7] [P]
WO 363, WO 364	Misfiled service records from both series. These are indexed on the online catalogue, and are searchable by 'surname AND forename'			[2]

The surviving records of service in wo 363 were those that were damaged, but not destroyed, as a result of bombing in 1940. At the time, the records of other ranks were stored in regimental order: the infantry regiments were in the main path of the fire and bore the worst casualties. This means that you are quite likely to find service records for a soldier in a cavalry regiment, or in the Labour Corps, but less likely to find one in an infantry regiment. Unfortunately, we don't know which regiments took a direct hit, as it were, although work done to date shows that the records of the Royal Sussex Regiment, the Essex Regiment, the West Kent Regiment, the Warwickshire Regiment and the Wiltshire Regiment were badly affected.

The condition of the surviving records can be very good or very bad: they can sometimes be difficult to read. They were sorted into alphabetical order, and filmed, through the financial support of the Heritage Lottery Fund.

Here in wo 363 (if you are lucky), you can find the records of men who were killed in action or who died of wounds, men who were prisoners of war, men who survived the War and even men executed for desertion. However, you may well find that you are unlucky. Unfortunately there is no index to all these records: the only way to find out if a service record survives is to check the relevant microfilm. The only exception here is if the service record was misfiled out of alphabetical order. These have been refilmed and entered onto the online catalogue: a search on wo 363 and wo 364 therefore does need to be done, using 'surname AND forename'. It's a good idea to do this first, in case you are lucky – but be aware that if you do not find an entry in the catalogue, you may still find a service record on the microfilm.

To sum up, you cannot tell from our catalogue whether a file still exists for a particular person or not: the only way to find out is to read through the relevant microfilms. You can do this at the National Archives. You can also do this around the world for wo 363 via the Family History Centres run by The Church of Jesus Christ of Latter-day Saints, as they have a copy of the microfilm. If you have never used this more local option, go to the page on Family Search Questions at **www.familysearch.org** and then choose the questions for 'Family History Centers'. (We hope that all these problems will be solved by getting the Soldiers' Documents searchable and available online reasonably soon.)

Records of men who enlisted in the Life Guards, the Royal Horse Guards and the Household Battalion before 1919 have recently been transferred to the National Archives as wo 400 7. This series contains surviving records of service for non-commissioned officers and other ranks whose Army service *ended* in these regiments. (If a man moved on to another regiment, his Army service record went with him.) Records of soldiers and non-commissioned officers discharged from the five Footguards Regiments (Grenadiers, Coldstream, Scots, Irish, Welsh) are in the custody of their respective Regimental Headquarters at Wellington Barracks, Birdcage Walk, London SW1E 6HQ.

26.1.7 First World War: disability and other pensions: all services

This section covers all armed services: it is placed in this chapter because the Army had by far the most casualties.

PENSIONS TO DISABLED OR INVALID OFFICERS AND MEN

Pension, etc.	Date	Reference	Information	
Officers: half pay	Up to 1921	PMG 4/270–277		[7]
Disabled officers and men		PMG 9/53–65	Registers of payments of pension	[7]
Army officers and nurses; RAF, Navy and Marine officers	1917–1920	PMG 42/1–12; PMG 42/13–16	Registers of temporary retired pay and of gratuities granted for disability: give rank, name, address, date of warrant, amount paid	[7]
All services, all ranks	1920–1989	PIN 26	See below	[3], [2]

Pension case files are in PIN 26. This series contains 22,756 personal files on people awarded (or refused) pensions, from all services. Although large, this represents only 2 per cent of the pensions awarded. PIN 26 is easily searched by 'surname AND initial' or 'surname AND forename' in the online catalogue. Hits look like: FRANKLIN John Nature of Disability: Gassed or CHAPLIN C Nature of Disability: Defective Teeth. This may not be enough to identify whether you have the right person. Make sure that you check which sub-series you have found (see below for details). The files can contain fascinating material, some medical, some social, and can cover many years, with claims being raised a good four decades or more after the end of the War. Earlier documents than 1920 also exist in the files.

PENSION CASE FILES, ALL SERVICES

PIN 26	Sub-series of types of pensioner (all searchable by surname in the online catalogue)
1–203	All services, all ranks. Not in alphabetical order
204–16374	[Army: other ranks], disability
16375–16683	[Army: other ranks], disability (with some out of alphabetical order at the end)
16684–17178	Navy, disability
17179–19523	Widows (by name of husband) (See also PIN 82)
19524–19720	Alternative widows pensions (by name of husband) (See also PIN 82)
19721–19820	Mercantile Marine, death and disability
19821–19853	Dependants (by own name)
19854–19923	Men (DM series)
19924–19954	Officers (DO series)
19955–19984	Alternative disabled pensions

☐ p. 566

19985–20286, 22744	Nurses, disability
20287–21065	Overseas, death and disability
21066–22756	Officers, death and disability

For soldiers who served before 1914, were discharged to a disability pension and then re-enlisted during the First World War, try a surname search in PIN 71.

For soldiers admitted to the Royal Hospital Chelsea as in-pensioners before 1933, see 25.4.2.3. In addition, you should check the selection of personal files of deceased pensioners, 1923–1980, in WO 324 ①. Some will still be closed.

26.1.8 First World War: gallantry medals

You may wish to investigate our specialist guide, Spencer's *Medals*. Index cards for the award of the Distinguished Conduct Medal (DCM); Military Medal (MM); Meritorious Service Medal (MSM); Territorial Force Efficiency Medal (TFEM); Territorial Efficiency Medal (TEM); and for Mentioned in Despatches (MiD) can be searched and seen online at **www.nationalarchives.gov.uk/documentsonline/medals.asp**. All gallantry awards bestowed upon members of the British Army were announced in the *London Gazette* (ZJ 1⑦). The indexes of the *London Gazette* for the First World War are available on the open shelves in the Microfilm Reading Room. They can also be seen online at **www.gazettes-online.co.uk**. Citations for all awards granted for gallantry during the First World War can also be found in the *London Gazette*. Awards announced in the New Year or Birthday Honours (January and June) were not accompanied by citations.

Name indexes of recipients of the Distinguished Conduct Medal (DCM) and Military Medal (MM) awarded for gallant service in the First World War are available on microfiche. Very few citations were published for the Military Medal. A further register of the DCM can be found in WO 391 ⑦. A name index for the Military Cross (MC) awarded during the First World War is in WO 389 ⑦. The register of Distinguished Service Order (DSO) is in WO 390 ⑦.

Records of Long Service and Good Conduct Medals for other ranks who had served 18 years are in WO 102 ⑦. The records of the Meritorious Service Medal, for non-commissioned officers, run from 1846 to 1919 (WO 101 ⑦). The records include details of candidates for, as well as recipients of, these awards.

26.1.9 First World War: courts martial

Death sentences were passed by the British Army in courts martial between 1914 and 1924 for offences such as sleeping on duty, cowardice, desertion, murder, mutiny and treason on over 3,000 British soldiers, on members of

Dominion, Colonial and foreign forces and on several British and foreign civilians. Over 90 per cent of these sentences were later changed to other punishments – hard labour or penal servitude. For an introduction for family historians, see O'Neill, 'To discourage the others'. Other works debating the justice of death sentences are given in the bibliography.

To find the records for all offences except mutiny, start with Oram and Putkowski, *Death Sentences Passed by the Military Courts of the British Army, 1914–1924*. This gives a list by surname and a list by date. Each entry gives a reference number. Add wo to the front of this number and you have the full National Archives reference. Most records of courts martial are in wo 213, wo 92 or wo 90 (all Ⓢ). For death sentences carried out, see Putkowski and Sykes, *Shot at Dawn* for full listings.

Over 2,000 men were charged with mutiny between 1914 and 1922. Start with Putkowski, *British Army Mutineers, 1914–1922*. This gives a list by surname; a list by unit; a list by date for mutinies at home; and a list by date for mutinies abroad. Each entry gives a full National Archives reference, including the internal page number. (When ordering one of these documents, leave out the page number; if you are ordering a copy, put the page number in as extra information.) Most records of courts martial of mutineers are in wo 86, wo 90, wo 92 and wo 213 (all Ⓢ).

For courts martial that did not pass a death sentence, you need to track down the records of the court in the National Archives or perhaps in the regimental museum: see the free research guide on *British Army: Courts Martial, 17th–20th Centuries*, available at the National Archives and at **www.nationalarchives.gov.uk/catalogue/researchguidesindex.asp**.

26.1.10 First World War: war diaries

Once they have found which battalion their man served in, many people go on to look for the war diary of that battalion. A war diary is a daily record of operations, intelligence reports and other events kept for each battalion by an appointed junior officer. It is *not* a personal diary (try the Imperial War Museum for a collection of those). Specialist units, such as military hospitals, also kept war diaries. One copy was sent into the War Office, and is now in the National Archives. Other copies were kept by the unit, and may now be with the regimental records. Copies of the War Diaries for Dominion, Indian and Colonial forces are also kept at the National Archives.

As war diaries were written in carbonised form, with duplicates sent to various places, you may find that some may be difficult to read. Many were scribbled hastily in pencil. Some use obscure abbreviations. Some diaries will record little more than daily losses, map references, etc.; others will be much more descriptive. It is unusual for diaries to mention the names of ordinary soldiers. You can *sometimes* find details in the diaries about awards of the Military Medal and the Meritorious Service Medal.

Regimental museums *may* hold copies of their war diaries, but you will probably find it easier to look at the National Archives. The National Archives holds the duplicates sent to the Medical Historians' Department of the War Office, in the series wo 95 ⑥; the main copy was destroyed in the bombing of Arnside Street in 1940, along with so many service records. War diaries containing confidential information (often concerning courts martial) were kept back for years by the Ministry of Defence. These are now in wo 154 ⑥, and can be read. A large number of maps were extracted for safe keeping and are in wo 153. However, some war diaries can't be found in the National Archives (particularly for Home Forces): it seems that the Medical Historians did not have a full set.

Some war diaries of Royal Flying Corps are in AIR 1 ⑦. Royal Naval Division war diaries are in ADM 137 ⑦ until 1916, and then in wo 95 ⑦.

There are several ways to find a war diary in wo 95. Using the online catalogue, you can do a keyword search in wo 95, giving (part of) the unit name and battalion number (15 *not* 15th) as keywords. If this is not successful, try a variant of the name. If this is not successful, try browsing the list of wo 95 to see what kinds of terms are used. You can always use the paper catalogue at the National Archives, which is arranged in order of battle, with several indexes. If it is not in wo 95, try wo 154.

War diaries of smaller units, such as medical, engineer and service units, can be difficult to find. Keyword searches can be helpful – try several variants. Try the list of Royal Artillery, Army Service Corps, Machine Gun Corps and Medical Units, giving the Division, Corps or Army they fought with, in wo 95/5494. You can also consult the *Orders of Battle*, which list month by month the location of each unit, and the Division or Army to which they were attached. Ask at the Reference Desk at the National Archives for the set of the *Orders of Battle* for Belgium, France and Germany, arranged by Division (not by unit).

There are also some related sources you may wish to look at to conduct really detailed research:

• Correspondence and Papers of Military Headquarters	WO 158	⑥
• Miscellaneous Unregistered Papers	WO 161	⑥
• Intelligence Summaries	WO 157	⑥
• Gallipoli, Palestine, and Italian Campaigns: Photographs	WO 317, WO 319, WO 323	⑥
• Campaign Maps	WO 153, WO 297, WO 298, WO 300, WO 301, WO 302, WO 303	⑥

At the National Archives Library you can see the official *History of the Great War*. This multi-volume, multi-author work was written from official documents (still then closed to the public) directly after the War. Some copies are marked up with document references, so you can go back to the sources easily. See the bibliography for further details.

26.1.11 First World War: identification and embarkation of regiments

The easiest way to identify units in the First World War is to use the excellent **www.1914–1918.net** or James, *British Regiments, 1914–1918*. A slower way would be to consult wo 380/17 for a register of the formations, amalgamations, disbandments and changes in title of infantry regiments, 1914–1919. For cavalry regiments, ask at the enquiry desk for Swinson, *A Register of the Regiments or Corps of the British Army*. For details of change of uniform and colours, try the various registers in wo 380, indexed by wo 380/11.

For the dates of embarkation of units going overseas, 1914–1918, see wo 379/16.

26.1.12 First World War: tracing wounded soldiers back from the front

Mentions of men wounded on the front line can sometimes be found in the war diaries of the various medical units they were passed through, especially during the quieter periods of the War when more time could be spent on the diaries. The route was via the Regimental Aid Post, Advanced Dressing Station, Field Ambulance, Casualty Clearing Station, General and Stationary Hospitals, Ambulance Train or Hospital Ship, back to dear old Blighty and one of the many military hospitals that had sprung up over Britain. For more information, see **www.1914–1918.net/wounded.htm**, which includes an example, much useful information and the locations of casualty clearing stations and military hospitals in France and Britain (which you may otherwise be able to get from MH 106/2389). You may be able to track down hospital records in Britain via **www.nationalarchives. gov.uk/hospitalrecords** if you are very fortunate indeed.

The early stages of this route were particular to each division, and if you have the soldier's battalion, you should be able to find the war diary of the related Casualty Clearing Station or Field Ambulance. (Realistically you would be lucky to find any relevant entries for earlier stages.) An easy way to do this, once you have the battalion, is to find the relevant war diary in wo 95 in the catalogue, click on the description and then choose 'full details'. This will give you the name of the division – 2 Division for example. You can then search on the division number and unit (2 AND Casualty Clearing Station) to find the relevant war diary. This does not always work, especially in the later stages of the War.

We do have a representative selection only of several types of medical records from various theatres of war in MH 106 ⑥⑦. They were brought together during and immediately after the War for use in statistical studies of the treatment for injuries sustained, and diseases contracted, by British troops. The original studies made on these records were published in Mitchell and Smith *(Medical Services) Casualties and Medical Statistics of the Great War.* The records were later used by the Ministry of Pensions, which inherited them, and subsequently by the War Pensions Branches of its successor departments, to verify claims for war disability pensions.

The series MH 106 includes admission and discharge registers from a sample of hospitals and casualty clearing stations, field ambulances, an ambulance train and a hospital ship. There are also medical sheets, selected to illustrate the diversity of diseases contracted, injuries received and treatments prescribed, and medical cards relating to individuals in selected regiments. The regiments covered are the Leicestershire Regiment (all other ranks in alphabetical order and a sample of officers, MH 106/2130–2139 and MH 106/2158–2173) and the Royal Field Artillery (all other ranks in alphabetical order and a sample of officers, MH 106/2140–2157 and 2174–2183). Both are for 1916 to 1920 only. There are smaller samples for the Grenadier Guards, Hussars, Royal Flying Corps and the women's services. Earlier records are arranged by type of wound. There is some good material in this series, but it is not listed by individual.

26.2 Soldiers' records: between the World Wars

The service records of officers who served after 1922 and of other ranks who were discharged after 1920 are still held by the Ministry of Defence (for whom they are still an active set of records). They are not open to public inspection, but next of kin can request a précis of the service record for a fee. Write to the Ministry of Defence (see 62).

Records of soldiers admitted to the Royal Chelsea Hospital as Chelsea Pensioners after 1933 are still kept by the Hospital: the address is in 62. For those admitted before 1933, see 25.4.2.3. In addition, you should check the selection of personal files of deceased pensioners, 1923–1980, in WO 324 ①: some will still be closed.

At the National Army Museum you can see the records of deceased soldiers' effects for soldiers who died in service (or who were discharged insane) after 31 March 1921. These give details of money owing, and to whom it was paid: contact the National Army Museum to arrange access (see 62).

26.3 Second World War: soldiers' records

Service records for the Second World War are still held by the Ministry of Defence (for whom they are still an active set of records). They are not open to public inspection, but the individual concerned can request a précis of the service record, which will be provided for a fee. The only other people who can do this are those who have been given the living individual's written consent or (if the individual has died) that of the official next of kin. Write to the Ministry of Defence (see 62).

The *Army Roll of Honour for the Second World War* contains details for men who were killed or died while in the Army between 1 September 1939 and 31 December 1946. This includes men who died from natural causes, but excludes those who died 'dishonourable deaths' – by execution for a capital crime while in the Army, for example. There is an online searchable version at **www.military-genealogy.com** (pay per view). You can also access it on CD-Rom at the National Archives. The Roll of Honour was originally compiled in 1944–1949, on coded punch cards, and has been in the National Archives for some years as wo 304. It can only now be easily searched. The information given is:

• Surname and forenames	• Unit serving in at time of death
• Army service number	• Place of birth
• Date of death	• Place of domicile
• Rank	• Place of death
• First unit served in	• Decorations

You can find out about burials from the Commonwealth War Graves Commission database, the Debt of Honour register (which can be accessed on their website at **www.cwgc.org**). This register can also supply personal details, such as the name and address of parents or wives. The indexes to the registered death certificates for the Army War dead, 1939–1948, can be seen at both the National Archives and the Family Records Centre and online at **www.1837online.com**: see 8.8. You have to buy the certificates from the General Register Office, and these should give cause of death. There are also retrospective registers of deaths from enemy action in the Far East, 1941–1945 (RG 33/11 and 132, indexed in RG 43/14). At the National Army Museum you can see the records of deceased soldiers' effects for soldiers who died in service (or who were discharged insane) during the Second World War. These give details of money owing, and to whom it was paid: contact the National Army Museum to arrange access (see 62).

At the National Archives Library you can see the official *History of the Second World War*: see the bibliography for more details. This multi-volume, multi-author work was written from official documents (still then closed to the public) directly after the War. Some copies are marked up with document references, so you can go back to the sources easily.

Recommendations for awards for **gallantry** or meritorious service made during the Second World War are in the series wo 373 ②,⑦. It is arranged by operational theatre (where the award was won) and then in *London Gazette* date order. Part of the series (awards gained in North West Europe) has been catalogued in detail, and is now searchable by *Surname AND forename* to get a result such as Name: Powell, Arthur Reginald. Rank: Cpl (L/Sgt). Number: 5626530. Regiment: 7th Bn The Hampshire Regt. Award: MM. Theatre of War: North West Europe. Folio(s): 539. For other theatres of war, you have to know the type of award, the operational theatre and the date the award was announced. (This series will soon all be searchable and

☐ p. 566

available online.) WO 373 also contains recommendation for most awards made to members of the Army up to 1982, including those serving in Korea, Malaya and the Falklands. You may wish to investigate our specialist guide, Spencer's *Medals*.

For records of Long Service and Good Conduct Medals (for other ranks who had served 18 years) see WO 102 ☷.

If you know details of the battalion or unit in which your man served, you may want to look for the **war diary** to discover what that battalion or unit was actually up to. A war diary is a daily record of events, often with appendices of signals and orders. For the Second World War, the war diaries are in several series, so you may need to know in which areas of the world the battalion served. If you don't know this, try a search on the unit name restricted to WO and 1939 to 1945, and browse through the results. Most units can now be searched for by unit name. (We have an ongoing programme to replace the original highly contracted description provided when the records were accessioned with something more obvious to use as a search term – to replace *A. & S. Hgh* with *Argyll and Sutherland Highlanders*, for example.) For some smaller or specialist units you may need to browse or ask advice.

British Expeditionary Force	WO 167	Military Missions	WO 178
British North Africa Force	WO 175	North-West Europe	WO 171
Central Mediterranean Forces	WO 170	North-West Expeditionary Force	WO 168
Dominion Forces	WO 179	Ships Signals Sections	WO 257
GHQ Liaison Regiment	WO 215	South-East Asia Command	WO 172
Home Forces	WO 166	Special Services	WO 218
Madagascar	WO 174	Various Smaller Theatres	WO 176
Medical Services	WO 177	War Office Directorates	WO 165
Middle East Forces	WO 169	West Africa Forces	WO 173

Records of soldiers admitted to the Royal Chelsea Hospital as Chelsea Pensioners after 1933 are still kept by the Hospital: the address is in 62. In addition, you should check the selection of personal files of deceased pensioners, 1923–1980, in WO 324 ☐.

The *Home Guard List*, 1939–1945, was arranged by Command (area) and included name indexes. The lists are available in the National Archives Library.

26.4 Soldiers' records: after the Second World War

Service records are still held by the Ministry of Defence (for whom they are still an active set of records). They are not open to public inspection, but next of kin can request a précis of the service record for a fee. Write to the Ministry of Defence (see 62).

Recommendations for most gallantry or meritorious service awards made to members of the Army up to 1982, including those serving in Korea,

Malaya and the Falklands, are in WO 373 ☑. This series, which is available on microfilm, is arranged by operational theatre (where the award was won) and then in *London Gazette* date order. You therefore have to know the type of award, the operational theatre and the date the award was announced, unless you are prepared to spend some time looking. You may wish to investigate our specialist guide, Spencer's *Medals*. You can also find operational records of later wars in the National Archives: a research guide is available at the National Archives or on the National Archives website.

Records of soldiers admitted as Chelsea Pensioners to the Royal Chelsea Hospital after 1933 are still kept by the Hospital: the address is in 62. In addition, you should check the selection of personal files of deceased pensioners, 1923–1980, in WO 324 ☑.

At the National Army Museum you can see the records of deceased soldiers' effects for soldiers who died in service (or who were discharged insane) up to 1960. These give details of money owing, and to whom it was paid: contact the National Army Museum to arrange access (see 62).

26.5 Army service records, from 1914 onwards: bibliography

Army lists, etc., of personnel
Army List (London, annually)
Army Roll Of Honour – World War II (CD-Rom, Naval and Military Press)
British Biographical Archive (London, 1984 continuing)
Dictionary of National Biography (London, 1909 continuing)
H G HART, *Army List* (London, 1839–1915)
Soldiers Died in the Great War 1914–19 (CD-Rom, Naval and Military Press)

Official histories
History of the Great War (HMSO: also available on CD-Rom from the Naval and Military Press)

Western Front
1914 – Vol I: Mons, the retreat to the Seine, the Marne and the Aisne (Sir James Edmonds)
1914 – Vol II: Antwerp, La Bassée, Arnetieres, Messines and Ypres (Sir James Edmonds)
1915 – Vol I: Winter 1914–15: Battle of Neuve Chapelle: Battles of Ypres (Sir James Edmonds and G C Wynne)
1915 – Vol II: Battles of Aubers Ridge, Festubert, and Loos (Sir James Edmonds)
1916 – Vol I: Sir Douglas Haig's Command to the 1st July: Battle of the Somme (Sir James Edmonds)
1916 – Vol II: 2nd July 1916 to the end of the Battles of the Somme (W Miles)
1917 – Vol I: The German Retreat to the Hindenburg Line and the Battle of Arras (C Falls)
1917 – Vol II: Messines and Third Ypres (Passchendaele) (Sir James Edmonds)
1917– Vol III: The Battle of Cambrai (W Miles)
1918 – Vol I: The German March Offensive and its Preliminaries (Sir James Edmonds)

1918 – Vol II: March–April: Continuation of the German Offensives (Sir James Edmonds)

1918 – Vol III: May–July: The German Diversion Offensives and First Allied Counter-Attack (Sir James Edmonds)

1918 – Vol IV: The Franco-British Offensive (Sir James Edmonds)

1918 – Vol V: 26th September – 11th November. The Advance to Victory (A F Becke)

Other theatres of war

Campaign in German South West Africa 1914–1915 (J J Collyer)

East Africa (C. Holdern)

Egypt and Palestine (Sir George Macmunn and C Falls)

Gallipoli (C E Aspinall-Oglander)

Italy 1915–1919 (Sir James Edmonds and H R Davies)

Macedonia (C Falls)

Mesopotamia Campaign 1914–1918 (F J Moberly)

Togoland and the Cameroons (F J Moberley)

Medical history

Defence of the United Kingdom, B Collier, 1957

Grand Strategy, N H Gibbs and others (6 vols, 1956–1976)

History of the Second World War (HMSO)

(Medical Services) Casualties and Medical Statistics of the Great War (T J Mitchell and G M Smith)

The Campaign in Norway, T K Derry, 1952

The Mediterranean and Middle East (6 volumes, 1954 –1988), I S O Playfair and others, 1954

The War in France and Flanders, 1939–40, L F Ellis, 1953

Victory in the West, L F Ellis and others, 1962 –1968

War Against Japan, K S Woodburn and others (5 vols, 1957–1969)

General works

G Beech, 'Military Maps of the Western Front', *Ancestors* 8 (2002)

C M Corns and J Hughes-Wilson, *Blindfold and Alone: British Military Executions in the Great War* (London, 2005)

P Dennis, *The Territorial Army 1907–1940* (Royal Historical Society, 1987)

N Hanson, *The Unknown Soldier: the story of the missing of the Great War* (London, 2005)

R Holmes, *Tommy: the British Soldier on the Western Front 1914–1918* (London, 2004)

A Husainy and J Trumpbour, 'Military Sources for South Asian Ancestors', *Ancestors* 14 (2003)

E A James, *British Regiments, 1914–1918* (Heathfield, 1998)

W Moore, *The Thin Yellow Line* [execution of British soldiers during the First World War] (Ware, 1999)

J O'Neill, 'To discourage the others' [execution of British soldiers during the First World War], *Ancestors* 41 (2006)

G Oram and J Putkowski, *Death Sentences passed by the Military Courts of the British Army, 1914–1924* (London, 1998)

J Putkowski, *British Army Mutineers, 1914–1922* (London, 1998)

J Putkowski and J Sykes, *Shot at Dawn: Executions in World War One by Authority of the British Army Act* (London, 2003)

Marquis de Ruvigny's *Roll of Honour* (London, n.d.)

I Slocombe, 'The Reluctant Recruits' [military conscription tribunals in the First World War], *Ancestors* 34 (2005)

J Sly, 'Medals out of Africa' [Boer War], *Ancestors* 32 (2005)

W Spencer, *Army Service Records of the First World War* (National Archives, 2001)

W Spencer, *Medals: The Researcher's Companion* (National Archives, 2006)

W Spencer, *Records of the Militia and Volunteer Forces 1757–1945* (National Archives, 1997)

I Swinnerton, *Identifying your World War I Soldier from Badges and Photographs* (FFHS, 2001)

A Swinson ed., *A Register of the Regiments and Corps of the British Army: the Ancestry of the Regiments and Corps of the Regular Establishments of the Army* (London, 1975)

R Van Emden, *Boy Soldiers of the Great War* (London, 2005)

A S White and R Perkins, *Armies Of The Crown* [CD-Rom containing two bibliographies of all the published Corps and regimental histories of the British Army and of the published histories of the armed forces of the British and Indian Empires] (Naval and Military Press)

27 Army: linked services

27.1 The Yeomen of the Guard and the Yeomen Warders of the Tower of London

Despite the similarities of title, these were two quite distinct bodies. The Yeomen of the Guard are part of the Royal Household, protecting the monarch since 1485. The Yeoman Warders are a force created for the defence of the Tower of London.

Unfortunately, most of the records of the Yeomen of the Guard were destroyed in a fire at their headquarters in St James's Palace in 1809. For any survivals, and for modern records, write to the Exon of the Queen's Bodyguard at the address in 62. At the National Archives there are some sporadic references: the fullest is a set of quarterly pay lists from 1784 to 1812 in AO 3/106. In 1696 the Yeomen of the Guard took the Association Oath: the roll of oath-takers is at C 213/370.

The Yeoman Warders are better represented in the National Archives. Many were ex-Army. Muster rolls from 1690–1887 are in WO 94/37–39 ⑦; and pay records from 1715 to 1911 (with a gap for 1834–1874) in WO 94/24–35 ⑦. Pension records, 1873–1941, are in PMG35/1–16 ⑦.

To find sporadic references to individual yeomen, try a search in the catalogue using 'Yeomen AND guard' or 'Yeomen AND warder'. Try also the published material in the various calendar series (see 11.3).

27.2 Army chaplains

Until the end of the eighteenth century, chaplains were employed on a regimental basis, but after 1796 one chaplain served three or four regiments. The first Presbyterian chaplains were appointed in 1827; Catholic chaplains in 1836; Wesleyans in 1881; and Jewish chaplains in 1892. As chaplains were commissioned officers, they are found in the *Army List* and through the normal routes for finding officers. Try also the sources in 43.

In addition, there are certificates of service, 1817–1843, in WO 25/256–258 ⑦. Records of payment, 1805–1842, are in WO 25/233–251 ⑦. The registers of retired pay, 1806–1837 (WO 25/252–253 ⑦), give details of chaplains who saw service in the eighteenth century. Letters from chaplains, 1808–1836, are in the Chaplain General's Letter Books (in WO 7/60–72 ⑦).

27.3 Army medical services

Before the 1850s, British Army medical services were organised on a regimental basis. Each regiment had its own medical officer and the male orderlies who staffed the regimental hospital were seconded from the regiment. The orderlies received no medical training but often acquired some knowledge through length of service. The easiest way to start looking for officers is to consult *Commissioned Officers in the Medical Services of the British Army* by Peterkin, Johnston and Drew. There is a series of records of service of officers of the Medical Department, 1800–1840, in WO 25/3896–3912 ⑦, which includes details of the professional education of surgeons. These records are indexed. There is a certain amount of information for 1811–1818 in WO 25/259–263 ⑦; for 1809–1852, there are casualty returns of medical staff (WO 25/265, 2384–2385 and 2395–2407 ⑦). For the period 1825–1867, there are registers of the qualifications of candidates for commissions in the Medical Department (WO 25/3923–3944 ⑦).

During peacetime the problems of this decentralised local system were not apparent. It was well suited for dealing with minor skirmishes and policing duties in scattered locations throughout the world. Most medical officers' experience was also limited, both in medical and organisational terms. There were only three military general hospitals (Chatham, Dublin and Cork). Even where more than one regimental hospital occupied the same buildings, as at Aldershot, they tended to be staffed and administered separately. In addition, the medical officers were part of the civil establishment of the Army and had no authority over the orderlies, who were classified as combatants.

The experience of nursing by women in the Crimean War did not convince the Army Medical Department of their worth in this capacity. The Department had argued for a trained and stable nursing staff, but not necessarily female and civilian. In 1855 the Medical Staff Corps was created, to be renamed the Army Hospital Corps in 1857. In 1884 it reverted to its previous name. Volunteers (men able to read and write, of regular habits, good temper and a kindly disposition) were recruited from regiments of the line and were to be trained and permanently appointed. Musters for this corps, under both names, sent in from military hospitals all over the British Empire between 1855 and 1888, will be found in WO 12 and WO 16. Discharges to pension are in WO 97/1698 and 1702 for 1855–1872 and in

WO 97/2154–2157 for 1873–1882. After 1882 they are in a single alphabetical sequence with all Army other ranks, still in WO 97.

In 1898, regimental officers and men from the Medical Staff Corps were formed into the Royal Army Medical Corps (RAMC). The archives of the Royal Army Medical Corps and several collections of private papers of officers and men of the RAMC are kept by the Wellcome Library. The Army Medical Services Museum has collections showing life in the various medical services. Addresses are in 62. The Royal Army Medical Corps has a medal book, 1879–1896, which may be worth a look (WO 25/3992).

Records of regular RAMC officers who served before and in the First World War will be found in WO 339 or WO 374: there is a separate index in WO 338/23, covering 1871–1921. Service records of the very many doctors recruited into the RAMC for the duration of the First World War, and given temporary commissions – identified as RAMC(T) – have unfortunately been destroyed. You may be interested in Whitehead, *Doctors in the Great War* to find out more. For more on the First World War, see 26.1.12.

27.4 The women's Army nursing services

The disastrous experience of the Crimean War (1854–1856) highlighted the difficulties of the peacetime organisation. The inadequacies of equipment and supplies, and the problems caused by poor communications, were compounded by the lack of medical experience of many of the orderlies and by poor management of resources. The call for female nurses was popularised by *The Times'* war correspondent W H Russell. Florence Nightingale was offered the command of a scheme to send a nurses' expedition to Scutari: various religious sisterhoods were also keen to be involved. The first party sent out was made up of representatives from the Anglican and Catholic orders and secular nurses. Testimonials of women wishing to nurse in the Crimea, c.1851–c.1856, may be found in WO 25/264.

Despite the mixed reaction to female nurses in the Crimea, the draft Regulations for Inspectors General of Hospitals, 1857, allowed for female nurses to be employed in General Hospitals. In 1861 Jane Shaw Stewart was appointed the first Superintendent of a female nursing service, with a staff of six nurses, at Woolwich. In 1863 Miss Stewart was also appointed Superintendent General of Female Nurses at the new (and enormous) Victoria Hospital at Netley, thus becoming the first woman to appear in the British *Army List*. In 1883 the Army Hospital Services Committee recommended an expansion of the female nursing corps. The much larger Army Nursing Service was established in 1884, and renamed Queen Alexandra's Imperial Military Nursing Service (QAIMNS) in 1902. Two reserve military nursing services were also established. In 1894 Princess Christian's Nursing Reserve was set up, to be renamed Queen Alexandra's Imperial Military Nursing Service Reserve (QAIMNS(R)) in 1908. The Territorial Force Nursing

Service (TFNS), established in 1908, became in 1921 the Territorial Army Nursing Service.

The records of professional qualifications and recommendations for appointment of staff nurses in QAIMNS, 1903–1926, are in wo 25/3956. There are some pension records, but few nurses served long enough to qualify for a pension. Pension records for nurses appointed before 1905 are in wo 23/93–95 and 181 ⑦; pensions for QAIMNS nurses, 1909–1928, are in pMG34/1–5 ⑦. There are some service records for National Aid Society Nursing Sisters, 1869–1891, in wo 25/3955.

The Royal Red Cross medal (see Spencer, *Medals*) was instituted especially for military nurses in 1883 (wo 145 ⑦). Nurses were also awarded medals for service in Egypt, 1882, and South Africa, 1899–1902 (wo 100 ⑦). For women's service in the latter, see Gray, *The South African War 1899–1902: Service Records of British and Colonial Women*.

The First World War saw thousands of women serving in the established nursing services, in the new Women's Army Auxiliary Corps (also called Queen Mary's Army Auxiliary Corps) or as volunteers in many organisations (e.g., Voluntary Aid Detachment, Scottish Women's Hospital, YMCA, British Field Hospital for Serbia). The quickest way to find details is to search the medal card index online by name: it contains cards for around 44,000 women who served overseas. This should give you details of which service or volunteer unit was involved. (See 26.1.2 for the medal card index. The original medal cards for women's service have been passed to the Imperial War Museum.) After that, the actual service records are held in different archives, depending on the service. Try a search in the National Register of Archives at **www.nationalarchives.gov.uk/nra** or in A2A at **www. nationalarchives.gov.uk/a2a**.

First World War service records of 15,792 Army nurses are in wo 399 ② in two series: one for the QAIMNS (Queen Alexandra's Imperial Military Nursing Service) and the QAIMNS(R) (the reserve) and one for the TFNS (Territorial Force Nursing Service). (Search as Smith AND Mary, not Mary Smith.) If a nurse married, her record may be under her married name. Although dated 1914–1922 in the catalogue, the records actually cover the careers of nurses whose service finished before 1939. Registers of First World War disability pensions for nurses are in pMG42/1–12, with a selection of case files in pin 26/19985–20826 (② as Smith AND Mary). Details relating to some awards granted to members of the QAIMNS can be found in wo 162/652.

The Womens' Auxiliary Army Corps was established in 1917. By November 1918, over 57,000 women had enrolled with non-military titles, as officials (officers), forewomen (sergeant), assistant forewomen (corporals) or workers (privates). No officers' service records are known to survive, but those of other ranks for 1917 to 1920 are in wo 398 (② on Documents Online). Details relating to some awards granted to members of the WAAC can be found in wo 162/65.

Records of the volunteer nursing services, the First Aid Nursing Yeomanry Corps (FANYs) and the Voluntary Aid Detachments (VADs) are held by the British Red Cross (address in 62). There is a detailed history of the FANYs in HO 322/451. Some admittance and discharge registers of VAD hospitals do survive in local archives. Records of the many volunteer organisations are scattered and not always easy to find: you may need to look for both the full title and the abbreviation if searching online (both on the National Archives website and elsewhere).

27.5 Military hospitals and other medical units in the First and Second World Wars

War diaries for the Army Medical Services (including military hospitals, convalescent depots, ambulance trains, casualty clearing stations, field ambulances, etc.) for the First World War are scattered throughout the general series WO 95 ⑦; for the Second World War they are in their own series, WO 177 ⑦. You can search for these by unit name, but watch out for abbreviations.

Details of the whereabouts of various medical units in the First World War are given in MH 106/2389. MH 106 as a whole contains a representative *selection* of medical records: admission and discharge registers from hospitals and casualty clearing stations, field ambulances, an ambulance train and a hospital ship. There are also medical sheets, selected to illustrate the diversity of diseases contracted, injuries received and treatments prescribed, and medical cards relating to individuals. See 26.1.12 for more details. A similar set of records from both the First and Second World Wars is in WO 222.

27.6 The Indian Army and the British Army in India

There was an Army in India that was maintained by the East India Company until 1859. This Army consisted of separate divisions of European and Indian troops, which were both officered by Europeans. After 1859 the Company's Indian troops became the Indian (Imperial) Army. The European Regiments became Regiments of the Line, and the Company's Artillery and Engineers became part of the Royal Artillery and Royal Engineers: these formed the British Army in India. Details of regiments and of officers of the Honourable East India Company Army, the Indian Army and of British regiments stationed in India are given in the *India List* and the *Indian Army List*: the PRO Library has incomplete sets of these. Officers from the various Indian Armies are given in *Hart's Army List*, with some officers in the *Army List* as well.

The service records of the British Army in India will be found with the other Army records in the National Archives. There are musters of regiments in India from 1883 to 1889 (in WO 16/2772–2786 ⑥). A soldier's discharge on his return home was recorded in the depot musters of his regiment (WO 67 ⑥), in the musters of the Victoria Hospital, Netley, 1863–1878 (WO 12/13077–13105), or in the musters of the Discharge Depot, Gosport, 1875–1889 (in WO 16/2284 and 2888–2905).

British officers after 1859 were trained at Sandhurst (cavalry and infantry) before beginning their careers in India. Their records of service are with the India Office Library and Records. These can be consulted up to 1947.

The service records of European officers and soldiers of the Honourable East India Company's service and of the Indian (Imperial) Army are mainly preserved at the India Office Library and Records, but there are some records in the National Archives. Lists of officers of the European Regiments, 1796–1841, are in WO 25/3215–3219. Compensation for the sale of Indian Army commissions, 1758–1897, is recorded in WO 74. Alphabetical lists of East India Company Army pensioners (other ranks) for 1814–1866 are in WO 23/21–23; there are more detailed registers for 1849–1868 in WO 23/17–20 and for 1824–1856 in WO 25/3137.

Registers of the death of officers in all the Indian services for the Second World War are kept by the General Office, as well as being recorded in the Commonwealth War Graves Commission's database (see 8.8 and 26.1.3). The National Army Museum has Hodson's Index, a very large secondary source card index of British officers in the Indian (Imperial) Army, the Bengal Army and the East India Company Army (but not the British Army in India). Many of the entries go beyond bare facts to include colourful stories of life. Civilians and government staff are included if they had seen Army service. The cards from this index relating to the Bombay Marine, the East India Company's Navy, are to be passed to the National Maritime Museum: the main deposit of Bombay Marine records is in the India Office Library and Records.

27.7 Army: linked services: bibliography

Army lists, etc., of personnel
Army List (London, annually from 1754)
British Biographical Archive (London, 1984 continuing)
Dictionary of National Biography (London, 1909 continuing)
H G HART, *Army List* (London, 1839–1915)

General works
S BIDWELL, *The Women's Royal Army Corps* (London, 1977)
E CROSTHWAIT, 'The Girl Behind the Man Behind the Gun' : The Women's Army Auxiliary Corps, 1914–1918', in L Davidoff and B Westover, eds, *Our work, our lives, our words: women's history and women's work* (Totowa, NJ, 1986), pp. 161–81.
M HOWARD, *Wellington's doctors: the British army medical services in the Napoleonic Wars* (Staplehurst, 2002)

A HUSAINY and J TRUMPBOUR, 'Military Sources for South Asian Ancestors', *Ancestors* 14 (2003)

S GRAY, *The South African war 1899–1902: Service records of British and colonial women: a record of the service in South Africa of military and civilian nurses, laywomen and civilians* (Auckland, New Zealand, 1993)

L MCDONALD, *The Roses of No Man's Land* (London, 1993)

J PIGGOTT, *Queen Alexandra's Royal Army Nursing Corps* (London, 1990)

H POPHAM, *F.A.N.Y.: the story of the Women's Transport Service 1907–1984* (London, 1984)

H POPHAM, *The FANY in War and Peace* (Barnsley, 2003)

D SHAW, 'The forgotten army of women: Queen Mary's Army Auxiliary Corps', in H P Cecil and P H Liddle, eds, *Facing Armageddon: the First World War experienced* (Barnsley, 1996)

G D SHEFFIELD, *The Redcaps: a history of the Royal Military Police* (London, 1994)

J SHEPHERD, *The Crimean doctors: a history of the British medical services in the Crimean war*, 2 vols (Liverpool, 1991)

W SPENCER, *Medals: The Researcher's Companion* (National Archives, 2006)

28 The Royal Navy

28.1   Naval records: introduction

Naval records can appear complex because of the large numbers of different ranks (reflecting the specialist work of so many of the men in the Navy). However, in many ways they are simpler than Army records: the Navy kept good in-service records from the 1840s/1850s, so pension records are not as important. Also, the First World War records were not affected by later destruction to anything like the same extent as the Army records.

Naval service records are also becoming available online on the National Archives website at www.nationalarchives.gov.uk. Currently, over half a million service records for men joining between 1873 and 1923 can be seen online (see 28.4.3). The Trafalgar database (**www.nationalarchives.gov.uk/ trafalgarancestors/**) can give the vital information needed to trace the careers of the 18,000 or so men who fought at Trafalgar (see 28.4.1). Online sources outside Admiralty records can also be used; for example, the online index to wills kept by the National Archives refers to over 70,000 Naval seamen before 1858 (see 28.2.1).

However, not all Naval service records are suitable to go online: in many cases basic details, or further information, have to be sought out. We do publish two detailed specialist guides to Naval records. Pappalardo's *Tracing Your Naval Ancestors* is the most up to date, covering records up to the 1920s. My colleague Bruno Pappalardo has a habit of continuous production of new catalogues, which open up long held but inaccessible service records. Having created the Trafalgar Ancestors database, he is now moving on to investigate a wide range of other Naval records, such as payments home by sailors (see 28.2.7).

Rodger's *Naval Records for Genealogists* concentrates on the earlier Naval archive. It is quite a complex book to use, but it has a comprehensive index. The information given here is only a small selection of the immense range of records that Rodger and Pappalardo list. Even Rodger and Pappalardo cannot cover the entire wealth of Naval records; there is much to discover among correspondence classes, for example (see 28.8.1).

Of course, there are other places to discover more about life in the Navy, notably the National Maritime Museum at Greenwich, which has a huge collection of Naval artefacts, records, etc., the Royal Naval Museum (see the article by Trotman) and the museum ships, HMS *Victory* and HMS *Belfast*. Addresses are given in 62. There are also too many online resources to mention: a good place to start is with the National Maritime Museum's portal at www.port.nmm.ac.uk. Try also www.battleships-cruisers.co.uk/. This site takes a little exploring, but you will find much of interest. Probably the best place to learn in detail and gain an overview is from Rodger's acclaimed books on Naval life and history: see 28.9 for details of these and other cited works.

28.2 Sources for Naval families

This is not really the place to start but more a place to come back to once you have some firm data to investigate further. The exception is if you are looking for someone whom you know or suspect died in service before 1853, when the Naval wills discussed in 28.2.1 could act as an easy starting-point.

Family historians need to go for service records to find out career details of Naval ancestors. However, few early records will give any family information, although later service records tend to give brief family details. Officers' passing certificates may include details of parents: see 28.3.3. We have recently received a large collection of Naval baptism and marriage registers from 1845–1998 (including banns and notice of marriage) from the Chaplain of the Fleet (ADM 338 ⑤). These come from Naval establishments all over the world. Most are twentieth century, but Malta and Chatham have runs from 1845 and 1867 respectively. See also the indexes to the registers of Naval births, marriages and deaths abroad, 1881–1965, mentioned in 8.8. Pension records are a prime source of family details (see 28.3.9 for officers and 28.4.5 for ratings).

There are some other places you can look. The following sources are not as widely known as they should be. You may need to do quite a lot of work before investigating them (for example, if you discover that your seaman was killed in action, there are further places to look for possible payments to his family). See 28.8.3 for more records on Naval dead and casualties, 1742–1948, and Pappalardo or Rodger for more detail.

28.2.1 Probate court wills, 1554–1858, and Naval wills, 1784–1861: an easy route

Wills can be an easy way to find men before the Navy started to keep individual service records in 1853. Before this date you need to know the name of at least one ship on which a man served. Almost all seamen's wills give the name of the ship and very many give the man's number in the ship's muster book. With this information you can go straight to the muster book (see

28.4.2) and follow the man back from ship to ship. Wills can also provide the link between Jack aboard and Jack ashore, confirming and extending family details. This is a new method only made feasible by the creation of the easily searched indexes to the main set of wills registered for probate before 1858. Wills after 1858 are kept elsewhere (see 9.3) but by 1858 Naval men are much easier to find among the Admiralty records.

Seamen were reasonably likely to make wills as they were paid in arrears by an institution that kept close track of its money. Until 1815, seamen who died with over £20 of back wages owing to them (a frequent occurrence) had their wills proved (or administration granted, if they died intestate) in the Prerogative Court of Canterbury (PCC). These PCC wills are now searchable online (see 11 for how to do this). I found the wills of 70,463 Royal Navy men by searching the PCC wills index, so this can be a very good place to start for someone who died in service.

If you have not found your man from the online PCC index and you *know* that he died in service, it may be that he was owed less than £20 of back wages. In such a case, his will would have been proved in the relevant local probate court and will not be so easy to find. After 1815, wills were all proved in the relevant local court until 1858. Many wills of Naval seamen may be found in the records of the Commissary Court of London (London division) at the Guildhall Library. Before investigating probate records further (see 9 and 10 to do so), there is any easier source from 1784 onwards – the collections of Naval wills among the Admiralty records.

The Naval wills are not just for men who died in service, as claims could also be made after the death of pensioners long retired from the Navy. Also, many men deposited wills but never had call to use them. Wills of ratings, Royal Marine other ranks and some warrant officers were sent in to the Navy Pay Office either as a matter of practical forethought or, in some less provident cases, straight after being written on the deathbed. Most are very simple (generally written on pre-printed forms and witnessed by the captain and officers as required) and bequeath any pay or prize money owing (usually to a parent, wife or sibling, but sometimes to a friend) and appoint an executor. The parish at least is usually given – a piece of information that can help enormously with research on dry land.

From 1786, the depositing of wills in the Navy Pay Office was strongly encouraged as part of a fight against fraudulent claims for back pay and prize money (26 George III, c 63). Not all men did so, but enough did so to make this a very useful source both for family history and for finding a man's ship before 1853 (see 28.4.1 on why you need to know this).

Wills from 1786 to 1861 are in ADM 48/1–105 E, with registers that give name, date of will ('executed' here simply means 'made' – not the execution of the will, but the making of the will), the ship, the man's number in the ship's muster, current residence and the name, address and relationship or occupation of the executor. These Naval will registers (that also act as indexes) are in ADM 142/1–14 7. When the will was registered, a cheque (i.e., a certificate) was sent to the executor, to be produced back to the Navy Pay Office when the time came to prove the will. If a note was made that the cheque was then sent on to Doctors' Commons for the Prerogative Court of Canterbury, or to another probate court, this means that the man was dead and probate procedure had started. Comparing the various dates should give you an idea of date of death. (There is also a card index that currently indexes surnames A–H, but the registers are worth consulting, even with an A–H name, to work out a date of death.)

Before you try to use the will registers in ADM 142/1–14, you need to understand their odd system of alphabetisation. From the surname you are looking for:

- take the first letter
- add to it the next vowel (Y is treated as a vowel)
- then add the first consonant (whether that appears before or after the vowel).

You should end up with three letters. For example, Pritchard would be found under PIR, Evans under EAV, Whyte under WYH, Carter under CAR. Cross-references are given for variant spellings (e.g., Towel/Tole).

The Navy Pay Office received **applications for back pay** from the executors and next of kin of officers, ratings, Marines and dockyard employees. Although the actual applications do not seem to survive, between 1800 and 1860 the Pay Office kept notes that sometimes have wills, birth, marriage or burial certificates or other documents proving the applicant's relationship attached to them (in ADM 44 and ADM 45 F). Because applications were often made some time after the date of death (and the Navy Pay Office's investigations to prove the claim often took several years after the application), you may end up with a date of death far earlier, or an application far later, than you expected when you first started to investigate these records.

| 1800–1860 | Notes on applications from executors of ratings and Marine other ranks who died in service | ADM 44 | Use registers in ADM 141 ⑦: gives ship, date of claim, date of death [DD = discharged dead] and date of order to pay [Cas = cashier] |
| 1830–1860 | Notes on applications from executors of officers, dockyard employees and pensioners (ratings) | ADM 45 | Card index |

To access these notes, you need to use the same abbreviations system described above for ADM 142. These letters will appear at the top of the page in ADM 141. You then need to pick up the initial letter and the number given in the relevant entry to make a letter/number sequence to look up in the ADM 44 list. The notes on the applications in ADM 44 are more difficult to read than the register entries, so write down as much as you can from the register.

 ☐ p. 566

We also have a register of wills made at the Naval hospital, Gibraltar 1809–1815 (ADM 105/40).

28.2.2 Naval wills, 1862–1901

In 1862 a new series of Naval wills was started, this time apparently filed after death. Very few actual wills survive (but they should be found in the National Probate Calendar: see 9.3). There is a remnant from 1862 to 1882 in ADM 48/106–107. However, the registers for this series survive from 1862 to 1901 in ADM 142/15–19, and these give name, ship, date of registering the will and date of death. ADM 154, registers of men discharged dead, 1859–1878, may also be worth a look.

28.2.3 Killed in action, 1675–1832: the Royal Bounty to families

The widows, dependent children or indigent widowed mothers aged over 50 of officers and ratings killed in action were entitled to a lump sum of one year's wages, known as the Royal Bounty. This was paid out by the Navy Pay Office. Although many people applied for the Bounty, not all were successful. The Navy Pay Office was very concerned to find out whether the death was actually caused by wounds received in action, or whether the widowed mother was of the right age or sufficiently indigent. Many mothers applied who were not widowed, for example. It seems that the public's perception of the Royal Bounty was more generous than that of the Navy Pay Office.

Proof had to be sent to support applications for the Bounty: this consisted mainly of marriage and death certificates, with other documents attesting the age, relationship or poverty of the applicants. There is a broken series of these very useful papers (both those accepted and those rejected) running from 1675–1822 (ADM 106/3021–3034 [F]), with a manuscript index, at the National Archives.

For those who were successful in their claim, there are pay lists of the Royal Bounty, 1739–1787 and 1793–1832, which give the name, address and relationship of the dependent, the name, quality and ship of the dead man, and the amount paid (ADM 106/3018–3020 and ADM 30/20). Unfortunately these are not indexed. Applications for bounty, 1798–1821, are in ADM 106/3021–3022, with particulars for bounty, 1806–1817, in ADM 106/3033.

28.2.4 Naval officers: pensions to widows, etc.

The pension records described here are only the most important of those available: all are listed in detail in Rodger's book, *Naval Records for Genealogists*.

The **Admiralty's own pensions** included pensions to the widows and orphans of commissioned officers and masters, dating from 1673, and of other warrant officers from 1830. There is an application book for widows' pensions, 1809–1820, in ADM 22/238.

1673–1781	ADM 18/53–118	7
1694–1832	ADM 7/809–822, indexed by ADM 7/823	F
1708–1818	ADM 181/1–27	7
1734–1835	ADM 22/56–237	7
1830–1860	ADM 23/55 Register of Widows' Pensions	7
1834–1880	ADM 23/29–31 Widows of officers killed in action	7
1836–1839	ADM 23/45–46	7
1836–1870	PMG 16	7
1836–1929	PMG 19	7
1867–1880	ADM 23/47–52	7
1870–1919	PMG 20 Widows, etc. of officers killed on duty	7
	For First World War pensions to dependants, see 24.3.3	

Widows of warrant officers killed in action or on service were also eligible for pensions paid by the Chatham Chest: the registers of payment 1653–1799, were shared with the pensions to wounded men (ADM 82, described in 28.4.5). Greenwich Hospital also provided a school for children of officers and men, to which orphans had priority of admission (see 28.2.6).

The **Charity for the Relief of Officers' Widows** paid pensions to the poor widows of commissioned and warrant officers. Pay books, 1734–1835, are in ADM 22/56–237 7; for 1836–1929 they are in PMG 19/1–94 7. The papers submitted by officers' widows to the charity applying for pensions between 1797 and 1829 include many marriage and death certificates (ADM 6/335–384 F): there is an index at the National Archives. Similar papers for 1808–1830, referred for further consideration in doubtful cases, are in ADM 6/385–402 7. Entry books of sworn statements in place of marriage certificates, 1801–1818, are in ADM 30/57.

From 1809, the Admiralty administered the **Compassionate Fund**, voted by Parliament. It dealt with pensions and grants to orphans and other dependants of commissioned officers killed in action or who had died in service, who were not otherwise eligible for assistance. The registers of applications for relief give the officer's rank, date of death, length of service and ship, date and place of marriage, the applicant's age, address and relationship to the dead officer and other circumstances: they run from 1809 to 1836 (ADM 6/323–328 7). Pay books for the Compassionate List run from 1809 to 1921, giving the names and ages of recipients and their relationship to the dead officer: from 1885 warrant officers' next of kin were eligible. For 1809–1836, use ADM 22/239–250 7; for 1837–1921, use PMG 18 7.

28.2.5 Naval ratings: pensions and other benefits to widows and orphans

Dependants of ratings killed in action were entitled to one year's pay, known as the Royal Bounty: see 28.2.3 for 1765–1832. The Chatham Chest also paid pensions to the widows of warrant officers, ratings and dockyard workers killed in action or on service; the registers of payment were shared with the pensions to wounded men (ADM 82, described in 28.4.5). Before the mid-nineteenth century, Greenwich Hospital paid no widows' pensions as such but employed seamen's widows in its infirmary. They may be traceable through the establishment books (ADM 73: see 28.7.3). Greenwich Hospital also provided a school for children of officers and men, to which orphans had priority of admission (see 28.2.6).

For ratings serving from about 1880 on, try PIN 71, which contains over 1,000 personal files on the widows of Naval ratings and Army other ranks. This is only a selection of such files, but it is alphabetically arranged and very informative (see 28.4.5). For some widows' pensions, 1921–1926, see PMG 72/1–2. For First World War pensions, see 26.1.7.

28.2.6 Royal Hospital School, Greenwich and the Royal Patriotic Fund

The School, which was attached to the Royal Greenwich Hospital, was established for the sons of seamen shortly after the hospital was founded. In 1805 it was joined by a similar school for younger orphans (boys and girls), the Royal Naval Asylum. Orphans of officers and ratings killed in action or who had died in service had the prior claim for admittance, but entry was not restricted to them. The school admission papers, 1728–1870, include certificates of birth or baptisms for the children applying for entry, together with the marriage certificate of the parents, and details of the father's Naval service (ADM 73/154–389 ⑦: see also 28.4.1 for entry books). They are arranged by initial letter of surname. The registers of applications, which are mostly indexed, include the same information, 1728–1883 (ADM 73/390–449 ⑧). Registers of later claims of Naval orphans or other Naval children are in ADM 161, ADM 162 and ADM 163 (all ⑦, 1865–1961). There are apprenticeship registers for children leaving the Royal Hospital School, 1808–1838, in ADM 73/421–448 ⑦. The church registers, including many burials, for the Royal Hospital School and the Royal Naval Asylum are in RG 4/1669–1679 and RG 8/16–19: see 5.11.

The Royal Patriotic Fund presented two reports to Parliament, in 1860 and 1871, listing respectively all the Army and Navy dependants it had helped and those whose pleas were rejected (because the man's death had not been caused by the Crimean War). These reports can be seen at the National Archives as *Parliamentary Paper* microfiche 66.322–323 and 77.362–363: indexed hard copies are also available at the National Archives. They give the names of wife, children, date of marriage, date of birth of children, place of wife's residence and what happened to the children.

28.2.7 Payments home 1795–1852

Between 1795 and 1852 we have registers of payments home (known as *allotments*) made by some warrant officers and seamen in ADM 27. Those for 1795–*c*. 1812 should be searchable by name of the ship, but later ones are in numerical allotment numbers, which correspond to the ships' names. If you know when someone was serving on a particular ship, this can be an easy way to find family information. You may find the record of payments from wages indicating the relationship of the receiver (wife, mother and so on), their name and where they lived. The entry will also give the seaman's number on the ship's muster roll. If you want to find out more, there is an interesting 'History of the Allotment system in the Navy' from 1858 at ADM 7/719.

28.3 Naval officers

The fighting officers of the Royal Navy hold office by virtue of a royal commission and are therefore known as **commissioned officers**. They are, in descending order of rank, admiral of the fleet, admiral, vice-admiral, rear-admiral, commodore, captain, commander, lieutenant-commander, lieutenant and sub-lieutenant. Midshipmen and masters mates were technically not officers but ratings, although they were treated as very junior officers.

The initial promotion to the commissioned rank of lieutenant from midshipman or master's mate was for many by examination: however, passing the examination did not guarantee a commission. Subsequent promotions were by merit and luck as far as the rank of captain, and by seniority above that. The names of the ranks changed their meanings somewhat over time, and in particular 'captain' was often used as the title for the officer in command of a vessel, whether he was a captain or a lieutenant.

The **senior warrant officers** were the master, purser, boatswain, gunner, carpenter and surgeon (see 28.7.1 for surgeons); engineers were added later. These were all experts in their own field, who held their authority by a warrant and who were examined by and answerable to other authorities. For example, masters were examined by Trinity House and returned their accounts to the Navy Board. However, masters became commissioned officers from 1808, as did pursers and surgeons in 1843 and engineers in 1847. Many more warrant officers were able to rise to commissioned rank in the late nineteenth and twentieth centuries.

Junior warrant officers (i.e., those who did not have to keep accounts) were the armourer, chaplain, cook, master at arms, sailmaker and schoolmaster. Rodger gives much more detail, particularly of the expansion of the warrant officers from three branches in 1867 to twenty-four in 1945, of which all but one could proceed to commissioned rank. His book contains many additional references to scattered sources relating to the junior warrant officers.

There are some sources that cover the whole of the eighteenth to twentieth centuries, which are described first, although they are not necessarily the best place to start research. Genuine service records do not exist before the mid-nineteenth century. Instead, information has to be pieced together from a variety of sources. From the mid-nineteenth century, the Navy began to keep systematic records on individual officers. As well as the records described below there are many other possible sources of information in the National Archives on an officer's career. Examples are records of candidates for promotion and registers of officers unfit for service. These records are numerous and have become scattered among many different National Archives series. The easiest way to locate them is to use the reconstructions of the original series in Rodger's *Naval Records for Genealogists*. (The correct ordering of the records was lost when they were transferred, and so related records can be found in different ADM series: Rodger investigated the mistakes and has produced a list of how they should have been arranged.)

Sometimes commissioned and warrant officers can be found in the same sources, other times they appear in different series. A reference here to 'Naval officers' or 'officers' means both are covered, otherwise 'commissioned officers' or 'warrant officers' will be specified.

28.3.1 Naval officers: published sources

There are no systematic records listing men serving in the Navy before the Restoration (1660). After 1660, printed sources are also available: all these mentioned below can be seen in our Library. For 1660–1815, the main one is Syrett and DiNardo's *The Commissioned Sea Officers of the Royal Navy*. For 1691–1902, try also Pappalardo, *Royal Naval Lieutenants: Passing Certificates*. For 1793–1815, try Marione's *The Complete Navy List of the Napoleonic Wars*. Admirals' and captains' services may be described in Charnock's *Biographia Navalis* (up to 1798), Campbell's *Lives of the British Admirals* (up to 1816), Marshall's *Royal Naval Biography* (up to 1835) and in the *Dictionary of National Biography* (the new edition is also online at www.oxforddnb.com: this can be accessed free at the National Archives and through many libraries). O'Byrne's *Naval Biographical Dictionary* gives the services of all commissioned officers alive in 1846. See also the *British Biographical Archive*. Chaplains can be found in Kealy's *Chaplains of the Royal Navy, 1626–1903*.

From the end of the eighteenth century, it is fairly easy to trace the outlines of a commissioned officer's career in the Royal Navy. Start with the printed *Navy Lists*, which began as *Steel's Navy List* in 1782 and were updated quarterly from 1814. These contain seniority lists of officers, from lieutenant upwards, which are keyed to lists of ships with the officers appointed to them. Warrant officers appear in the *Navy Lists* at varying later dates. The *Navy Lists* are available on open shelves at the National Archives, including the wartime confidential editions of 1914–1918 and 1939–1945 in ADM 177. The *New Navy List*, compiled by Haultain, covers February 1841–February 1856. It contains similar information to the *Navy List*, but with the addition of details of war service going back even to the 1780s. This too can be seen at the National Archives.

However, the National Archives does *not* hold the officers' newspaper, the *Naval Chronicle*, which should be available at the British Library Newspaper Library. We do have Tracy's abridged version for 1793–1798, and also Hurst's *Naval Chronicle, 1799–1818: Index to Births, Marriages and Deaths.*

28.3.2 Naval officers: full pay and half-pay registers, 1668–1920

These full and half-pay registers were used for the issue of certificates of service, needed as a passing qualification for a commission or to establish entitlement to a pension. Kept by the Navy Pay Office, they were the authoritative records of an officer's service. However, the full pay registers are not the best place to start, as the information included is brief. The Registers of Officers' Half-pay (a retainer for the services of unemployed officers, also used as a kind of pension for 'retired' officers) can provide addresses and other information over a much longer period: PMG 15 would be a good place to start as each volume has an index.

1795–1830	Full pay	Separate indexed registers for each rank (including surgeons and chaplains): give name, rank and successive appointments	ADM 24/1–92	[8]
1830–1872	Full pay	General register of officers: gives name, rank and successive appointments Separate registers for surgeons stop at 1858. Separate indexes	ADM 24/93–170	[8]
1847–1874	Full pay	Warrant officers and engineers	ADM 22/444–474	[7]
1668–1689	Half-pay	Not indexed – entered in no particular order with many other entries	ADM 18/44–67	[7]
1693–1836	Half-pay	In seniority order	ADM 25/1–255	[7]
1836–1920	Half and retired pay	Also Royal Marine officers (1859–1873) With indexes or in alphabetical order	PMG 15	[8]
1867–1900	Half-pay		ADM 23/33–140	

For 1837, there is an address book for commissioned officers, mates, masters, surgeons, pursers and chaplains on half-pay (PMG 73/2).

28.3.3 Naval officers' passing certificates, 1660–1902, and certificates of service

The Navy was a force that needed expert professional skills. As a result, progress through the early stages of an officer's career was regulated by examination from the 1660s. There are several series of passing certificates for the different ranks: they often include certificates of previous service, and sometimes baptismal certificates.

LIEUTENANTS' PASSING CERTIFICATES, 1691–1902

Most senior commissioned officers had to qualify as lieutenant at some point in their career. The passing certificates of master's mates and midshipmen qualifying as lieutenants often include certificates of service up to the day they took the examination, and sometimes include baptismal certificates proving membership of the Church of England. The easiest way to access these is to use Pappalardo, *Royal Naval Lieutenants: Passing Certificates 1691–1902*, which acts as an index to the following records.

1691–1832	Passing certificates and supporting documents	ADM 107/1–63
1854–1902	Passing certificates	ADM 13/88–101 and 207–236
1744–1819	Original passing certificates (an incomplete collection)	ADM 6/86–116
1788–1818	Passing certificates issued abroad	ADM 6/117–118

There are a few records relating to the examinations that are not in Pappalardo's index. These include registers of the examination of prospective lieutenants, 1795–1832, which give name, age, qualifying service and remarks for each candidate (ADM 107/64–70). Registers of certificates of service of prospective candidates, 1802–1848, are in ADM 107/71–75. There are even records of young gentlemen failing to pass for lieutenant (sometimes with the reasons given) for 1801–1810 (ADM 30/31).

MASTERS' PASSING CERTIFICATES, 1660–1850

Masters were supreme professionals in the knowledge of their ship and in their seamanship. They tended to stay longer with a ship than the fighting officers, and were re-examined if they moved on to a different type of ship. Passing certificates for qualifications in seamanship date from c.1660–1830 (ADM 106/2908–2950); they may include certificates of baptism and service. One master may have had several certificates, as promotion to a different rate of ship required a different qualification. The certificates are arranged alphabetically.

There is also an unusual series of service records for masters, compiled in the 1830s and 1840s but covering the period 1800–1850 (ADM 6/135–168 [7]). Records were kept in individual files, containing passing certificates, certificates of service and a variety of other certificates and correspondence; the files are in alphabetical order of surname.

GUNNERS' PASSING CERTIFICATES

1731–1812 (with gaps)	Passing certificates	ADM 6/123–129
1856–1863	Passing certificates	ADM 13/86–87
1864–1867	Passing certificates	ADM 13/249–250

PURSERS' AND PAYMASTERS: PASSING CERTIFICATES

Pursers, later renamed paymasters, oversaw the supply and issue of the ship's stores, and also of the seamen's pay, and they had to be men of some financial substance to be appointed. Pursers became commissioned officers from 1843.

1803–1804	Notes on candidates for promotion	ADM 6/121
1813–1820	Passing certificates	ADM 6/120
1847–1854	Notes on candidates for promotion	ADM 11/88
1851–1867	Passing certificates	ADM 13/79–82
1868–1889	Passing certificates	ADM 13/247–248

Boatswains' passing certificates

1810–1813	Passing certificates	ADM 6/122
1851–1855	Passing certificates	ADM 13/83
1856–1859	Passing certificates	ADM 13/85
1860–1887	Passing certificates	ADM 13/193–4

Examination results from the Royal Naval College, Greenwich, 1876–1957, are in ADM 203 [7].

Certificates of previous service

These had to be produced to prove qualification for commissions, warrants or pensions. The dates of service always predate the certificate, often by very many years. Some will be found with the passing certificates (see above), others with records relating to entitlement to pension (see 28.3.9). Still others were bound up to form the first service registers (see 28.3.6). Outside these areas are many other sub-series, mostly in ADM 29. See Rodger, *Naval Records for Genealogists* for more details.

28.3.4 Naval officers: surveys, 1816–1861, and various lists, 1660–1815

The series of surveys conducted between 1816 and 1861 are the most convenient records of officers' service, but they do not cover all officers and are not always to be trusted. The end of the Napoleonic wars in 1815 meant that the Navy shrank in operational strength from 145,000 to 19,000 men. Because there was no means of retiring officers, there were ten times as many as were required. In order to discover which officers had the best claims to be employed the Admiralty sent out circular letters to officers asking them to provide dates of birth or details of service. The replies were bound up and used for reference by the Admiralty. However, the coverage is by no means complete as it depended on the officer receiving and replying to the letter. Many replies were lost, and the accuracy of some of them is doubtful. The exercise was repeated on several occasions.

Survey date	Coverage	References	Indexes
1816–1818	General returns	ADM 9/2–17; strays at ADM 6/66	ADM 10/2–5 Also printed indexes at the National Archives
1816–1818	Boatswains, gunners and carpenters	ADM 11/35–37	7
1822	Commissioned officers including masters: age	ADM 6/73–83	7
1828	Admirals	ADM 9/1; strays at ADM 6/66	ADM 10/1
1831	Commissioned officers including masters: age	ADM 6/84–85	7
1833–1835	Masters	ADM 11/2–3	7
1846	Commissioned officers: age, address and previous service	ADM 9/18–61	ADM 10/6–7 Also printed indexes at the National Archives
1851	Masters: age, address and previous service	ADM 11/7–8	ADM 10/6–7
1852, 1859	Pursers	ADM 11/42–44	7
1855, 1861	Masters	ADM 11/9	

There are also various versions of an early list of all admirals, captains and commanders, with notes of their service, death or fate. The easiest to use are probably the alphabetical lists, 1660–1685 (ADM 10/15), 1660–1688 (ADM 10/10, which continues to 1746 arranged by seniority) and 1688–1737 (ADM 7/549). The first two also include lieutenants.

There are **black books** of commissioned officers not to be employed for future service, 1759–1815 (ADM 12/27B–27E), and another of warrant officers, 1741–1814 (ADM 11/39).

28.3.5 Naval officers: succession books, 1673–1849

Succession books were a type of officers' service record arranged by ship, not by individual officer. However, most are indexed by name as well as ship, so they can provide a fairly easy way of tracing a commissioned or warrant officer from ship to ship. In the usual form, a page was devoted to each ship, and the successive appointments to each position in the ship were listed.

1673–1688	Commissioned and warrant officers	ADM 6/425–426
1688–1725	Admirals, captains and commanders only	ADM 7/655
1699–1824	Junior officers appointed by Admiralty warrant or order, e.g., midshipmen, volunteers per order, chaplains, masters at arms, schoolmasters and scholars of the Royal Naval Academy	ADM 6/427 and 185
1733–1763, 1771–1807	Masters, surgeons, surgeon's mates, sailmakers and some others	ADM 106/2896–2901

1764–1831	Pursers, gunners, boatswains, carpenters and some dockyard officers	ADM 106/2898 and 2902–2906
1780–1849	Captains, commanders and lieutenants	ADM 11/65–72
1800–1839	Pursers, gunners, boatswains, carpenters and some dockyard officers	ADM 6/192 and ADM 11/31–33

Boatswains and carpenters could and did transfer between sea service and dockyard work: records relating to dockyard employees are discussed in 28.6.

28.3.6 Naval officers: service registers from c. 1840–1917/1931

In the mid-nineteenth century, the Navy began to create a central record-keeping system for officers. In the earliest registers, information was added about previous service, so that the data can go back many years. Finding service records is relatively straightforward.

Engineers were the first officers to whom this system of record keeping was applied, from 1837 (see ADM 196/71 followed by ADM 29/105–111 for engineers entering 1837–1879).

For c. 1840 to May 1917 (for commissioned officers) and up to 1931 (for warrant officers) there are registers of service, mostly in ADM 196 Ⓕ, with indexes on open access at the National Archives. For officers serving when the new system was introduced, these registers contain much earlier data. The dates given in the list are of entry: data was added to these registers up to the death or pension, and so can continue for many years beyond 1917 or 1931 – in some cases, until the 1950s.

In these registers, each officer has a page to cover his entire career, noting date of birth, marriage and death, home address, names of parents and wives (but almost never of children), names of ships served on, details of pay and pension, and assessments of character and ability. Several different departments kept these registers, and an officer's career may be entered in three or four almost identical registers. This can be useful, as there are frequent gaps in the various series.

Records of officers in the Royal Naval Air Service, 1914–1918, are in ADM 273: see 30.2 for more details.

28.3.7 Naval officers: confidential reports, 1884–1943

For 1885–1943, there are several series of confidential reports on officers, giving their commanding officer's (often brutally candid) view of suitability for promotion. These are also in ADM 196. You may need to get the officer's date of entry or promotion from the *Navy List* to access these easily.

Entry/ Promotion	Confidential Reports on	Reference	Indexes
1884–1939	Assistant Clerks, Paymaster Cadets and Paymasters	ADM 196/171	Includes index

☐ p. 566

1885–1928	Lieutenants and Sub-Lieutenants	ADM 196/141–151	Indexed by ADM 196/138–139
1893–1943	Captains and Admirals	ADM 196/86–94	Include indexes
1900–1912	Gunners	ADM 196/166	Includes index
1908–1931	Commanders	ADM 196/125–128	Include indexes. Union index in ADM 196/129
1913–1930	Acting Mates and Mates promoted to Lieutenant, and recording service as far as Lieutenant Commander	ADM 196/154–155	Include indexes

28.3.8 Naval officers: all branches after the First World War

As discussed in 28.3.6, service registers in ADM 196 record details of commissioned officers entering the Royal Navy up to May 1917 and of warrant officers entering up to 1931. There is however another source for commissioned officers, of which only a small part has as yet come to the National Archives.

During the First World War the Admiralty switched to a new method of record keeping, with each officer having a separate file or card rather than his details being entered into huge books or registers referring to many officers. This made it possible for the Ministry of Defence to rearrange these individual records of former Naval officers by date of birth, regardless of the arm of service. As a result, the records of commissioned officers of the Royal Navy, the Royal Naval Reserve, the Royal Naval Volunteer Reserve and the Women's Royal Naval Service have all been filed together. They are being released to public viewing in batches according to the officer's date of birth.

So far we have these individual records of all officers in all arms of the Naval services only for those who were born before 1900 – in fact, between 1860 and 1899. These 10,000 or so records are in ADM 340 ⑦℗, in one sub-series of record-of-service cards (ADM 340/1–150) and another of files (ADM 340/151–456). You must check both sub-series to make sure you have found everything. Unfortunately the catalogue lists them only by range of names, so that the cards are catalogued in the format 'ABBOTT – ALDER' and the files as 'ABBEY H J – ADAMS Thomas Henry'. It is probably easier to browse these in the paper list at Kew.

Some of these records detail service as far back as 1880 and others go as far forward as 1960. The earlier material is often a copy of that recorded elsewhere, particularly for the Royal Naval Reserve (28.5.2) and the Women's Royal Naval Service (28.5.7), but also in the service registers in ADM 196.

For officers born from 1900 onwards, you still need to contact the Ministry of Defence to apply for the equivalent record: see 62.

28.3.9 Naval officers: pensions

Until well into the nineteenth century, provision of pensions within the Navy was haphazard. There was no general entitlement to a pension for long service, although half-pay was used to provide a kind of pension for officers, eventually merging into retirement pay. At various dates from 1836, officers became eligible for a retirement pension, or superannuation, either automatically on reaching a certain age or upon application. See 28.3.2 for registers of half-pay and retirement pay up to 1920.

Extra pensions were available for particularly deserving cases, and there is usually a certain amount of personal information recorded in support of claims to these pensions. Pension records for officers are extensive and are fully listed by Rodger. A few commissioned officers received Greenwich Hospital out-pensions: there are registers covering 1814 (ADM 22/254–261), 1815–1842 (ADM 22/47–48) and 1846–1921 (PMG 71 ☑). Warrant officers, and the civil establishment of the Navy, were paid pensions out of the Navy estimates. There are registers for 1694–1832 (ADM 7/809–822, indexed by ADM 7/823). See also 28.4.5 for pensions for wounds paid out of the Chatham Chest, 1653–1799.

28.4 Naval ratings

28.4.1 Naval ratings before 1853: strategies to find ratings

The standard way of tracing a Naval seaman or rating, before the introduction of continuous service in 1853, is to use the muster books and pay books (see 28.4.2). However, this can take a very long time. It is also so dependent on getting the right ship that it is sensible to investigate easier sources; if you are lucky, you will save yourself considerable time. Bruno Pappalardo has spent years on this problem, so take advantage of his work.

The first place to look, as the easiest, is the **Trafalgar Ancestors Database** at **www.nationalarchives.gov.uk/trafalgarancestors** based on Pappalardo's researches in a wide range of ADM sources. This database commemorates the 18,000 or so men and one woman (Jane Townshend) who served under Nelson in the Battle of the Trafalgar on 21 October 1805. It covers commissioned and warrant officers, ratings, supernumeraries and Royal Marines. In 1805, the Royal Navy employed around 110,000 individuals. So if your ancestor served in the Royal Navy in 1805 there is a fair chance that he served in the Battle of Trafalgar. Trafalgar Ancestors can be searched by surname: use its advanced search facility for searching by first name, by age, by birthplace, by ship's name, by rating or by rank. Searching on birthplace shows that the Navy recruited from Africa, America, the West Indies, India and most countries in Europe, as well as from the home countries. (The database will be added to over time, so you may find it worth rechecking.)

Another easy route created recently by Pappalardo is to search the detailed catalogue entries for ADM 29/1–96 ② and then check the document found. These records are large entry books of **certificates of service**, giving details of service compiled by the Navy Pay Office from its records (musters and other pay records). They were created in response to a whole series of applications for certificates of service made by ratings (and some warrant and commissioned officers) or on behalf of their dependants if they had died, for a variety of reasons. These include:

- pensions, gratuities, medals;
- admittance of orphaned children into the Greenwich Hospital School;
- removal of erroneous entries of the term 'run' (indicating desertion) from the musters;
- discharge from the Navy for foreigners or apprentices wrongly press ganged (certificates of freedom).

These applications were made not merely by or for men in the Navy, but also by or for men who had left the Navy to serve (many) in the Coastguard and (a few) in the Royal Marines, the Sea Fencibles, the Royal Dockyards or as convict guards. The dates given as covering dates are those of the application, not of the service itself. Some of the service details go back as far as the 1740s. Names of ships served on are given in the documents themselves, though not in the catalogue. (See Pappalardo, 'Indexing the Admiralty' for more details.)

The actual certificates issued by the Navy Office (as opposed to the record of issue it kept in the entry books in ADM 29) can sometimes be found

- for men applying for entry to Greenwich Hospital as in-pensioners in ADM 73/1–35 ⑦;
- for men whose orphans applied for entry to the Greenwich Hospital School in ADM 73/154–389 (together with supporting documentation such as baptismal and marriage certificates).

In case the sailor died in service, or even if he did not, try the wills and relative's applications for back pay described in 28.2.1, as these provide an index for many seamen, 1786–1861. This may give you the name and date of at least one ship served on.

Another route to find the ship is to investigate pension payments. If your seaman received a Chatham or Greenwich pension (for which there are indexed registers) you may be able to discover the ships he worked in quite easily (see 28.4.5).

If you still have not found any trace of your seaman's ship, you will need great luck and hard work to proceed – or perhaps simply to wait for Pappalardo's next effort.

28.4.2 Naval ratings before 1853: ships' musters and pay books

Because there was no centralised record of ratings' services until 1853, the main sources for tracing a seaman before then are the individual ship's muster book and pay book. To use these, you need to know at least one of the ships on which he served, and when. With this information, you should be able to work your way slowly from muster to muster, and from ship to ship. Be aware that you may be in for some lengthy research.

A ship's muster lists the names of all the crew serving on board a ship at a particular time. For the ship's crew (but not usually for officers and Royal Marines), a muster provides place of birth and age when joining the ship. They can also indicate from which ship a person joined and which ship they were discharged to.

Musters, or lists of the ship's company, are available from 1667 to 1878 (ADM 36–ADM 40, ADM 41, ADM 115 and ADM 117: all ⑥ – don't use HMS as a search term). (After 1878 the few surviving ships' ledgers are in ADM 117, but these muster-like records were mostly destroyed by enemy action in 1941.) The musters can be found very easily by searching the catalogue using the ship's name and the date range you want (this will also bring up logs). If you are unsuccessful, try checking variant spellings of a ship's name as the catalogue is not always consistent – you may find references to both the *Weasel* and the *Weazle*, for example. Look in the *Navy List* (see 28.3.1) of a suitable date for variant spellings.

The musters followed a standard format, described by Rodger and Pappalardo, who give the various abbreviations used. There were general musters, held annually, and eight-week monthly musters, which contain extra information on various deductions from pay, such as for treatment for venereal disease.

Within each muster were separate sections: the ship's company, the Marines, supernumeraries for wages and victuals and supernumeraries for victuals only. In the latter case, these were men actually on the ship but who technically belonged to (and were paid on) another ship. To find out if a man was actually present on board or not, look at the columns 'mustered' and 'chequed' – if there is an entry in the latter, then the man was absent with leave, perhaps on another ship for victuals only! If you are trying to track a man from ship to ship, take care to look right through these categories, as men recently turned over are likely to be found among the supernumeraries.

Information on each member of the ship's company was entered into the following columns in both general and monthly musters:

- Number
- Entry & Year
- Appearance (i.e., arrival on board)
- Whence & Whether Prest (pressed) or not (this is where you may find the name of the previous ship)

- Age (from 1764: it means age at first entry to the ship, not at the time of the muster)
- Place & Country of Birth (from 1764)
- No. and Letter of Ticket (for wages)
- Men's Names
- Qualities (rank or rating)
- D DD or R (discharged, discharged dead or run; also DS, discharged to sick quarters)
- Time of Discharge & Year
- Whither or for What Reason (this is where you may find the name of the ship to which he was turned over).

From about 1800, **description books** may (rarely) be included with the musters. These give age, height, complexion, scars and tattoos.

The **pay books**, 1691–1856 (ADM 31–ADM 35 all ⑥), which duplicate much of the information of the musters, have one big advantage. They contain 'alphabets' (indexes of surnames in alphabetical order of first letter only) from about 1765, some fifty years before the musters had them. It may be worth checking through the alphabets in the pay lists before going on to look at the musters, 1667–1878 (ADM 36–ADM 41). The pay books were copied from the musters and may contain more errors; in some cases, they may also include information about next of kin to whom remitted wages were paid.

When tracing men from ship to ship, it may be useful to consult the **hospital musters**, particularly if the name was marked DS (discharged to sick quarters): see 28.7.2.

28.4.3 Naval ratings, 1853–1923: service records

The first centralised registration of ratings began in 1853 with the introduction of 'continuous service' instead of the previous uncertain length (i.e., discharged when no longer needed). This means that it is easy to find seamen's service records, listing personal details and the ships they served on; to find out more about what the ships did and where they went, see 28.8.

From 1853 on, as ratings entered the Navy they signed up for ten years' service if they were 18 or over; existing ratings could sign up for seven years' service. It took some time before most existing ratings were on the new system. Both new and existing ratings (and boys under 18) were given a continuous service number. Their details were entered in a register – date and place of birth and physical characteristics on entry. (For those who entered as boys, there is a form giving parental consent.) Further details were added throughout their career, to form a summary of their service. The registers between 1853 and 1872 are not yet online, although we hope they will be soon. They are in ADM 139 Ⓕ, with separate indexes, also in ADM 139. Be careful to note from the index whether the service number has an A or B at the end, or no letter at all. Make sure you look at the top of the page, as this often says Series A or Series B. When you go to the list of ADM 139 to match up the number, take care to look for the right series – plain A or B – or you may get the wrong document.

The system was modified for entrants from 1873 onwards, when a different numbering system was started. Between 1873 and 1894 service numbers were issued to new entrants on a next man, next number basis. Men who were still serving were also transferred from the old registers in ADM 139. These new registers of men are in ADM 188: they are fully searchable, not in the catalogue but at **www.nationalarchives.gov.uk/ documentsonline/royal-navy-service.asp.** Records of over 500,000 Naval seamen in the Navy at 1873, or joining between 1873 and 1923, can be searched by forename, surname, place of birth, date of birth (use the format DD/MM/YYYY) or official number. The register will give date and place of birth, physical characteristics on entry and a summary of service, compiled over the years. From 1892 you can find greater detail in the records: occupation, any badges awarded, 'character' and 'ability', physical appearance such as hair and eye colour, height and tattoos, and a note of any wounds received. As with Nelson's Navy, ratings in the Victorian Navy came from all over the world, not just from the home countries and the British Empire.

Despite the simplicity of searching ADM 188, there are still a few useful tips.

- The covering dates 1873–1923 of the ADM 188 registers relate to the opening of the registers, not to the information in them. However, entries can continue for many years, according to the length of service of each seaman. While the last entrants were ratings entering the Navy in 1923, further entries were made to existing registers up until 1928. Sometimes you will find a stamped entry saying something like 'Records transferred to card'. This refers to the next registration system, started in 1928, when the Navy switched to using an index card for each man. These records are not yet in the National Archives. Write to the relevant address in 62 under Ministry of Defence: Royal Navy.
- If a man entered the Navy before 1873, he will have an additional service record in ADM 139, which is not yet online. Also, some men may have in effect two accounts of service within ADM 188; firstly in the register and then continued in the Continuation Books ('new register'). These have been linked together online, so both are attached to the same man's entry.
- The date produced by the online search is date of birth not date of entry to the Navy. If you are not sure that you have the right person, you can find date of entry without looking at the actual document (which you would have to pay to do outside the National Archives) by checking the reference in the Catalogue. The easiest way to do this is to copy the ADM 188 reference

for any man that you are interested in, go through the website to the Catalogue, and paste the reference into the 'Go to reference' box. This will give you the year of entry for all new entrants (but not for the ratings continued from the old system). If the date of entry is after 1908 you can then click on 'Full details' to get the branch of the Navy as well.

These complications reflect the changes in OFFICIAL SERVICE NUMBER SYSTEMS over time. These changes can be so complicated that a search in ADM 188 in Documents Online by service number is probably best avoided. The earliest service numbers were allocated in three sequences, so that ADM 139 and ADM 188 may refer to three men numbered, for example, 1234, 1234A and 1234B. From 1873 an 'Official Number' was allocated to all Royal Navy ratings. The General Number (or 'O' number) was used from 1873 to 1907, and service numbers between 40,001 and 366,000 were issued (the jump in numbers to 40,001 was deliberate to avoid confusion). As the Royal Navy became a more complex service, it was decided to group service numbers together to identify which branch of the service a man served in. Between 1894 and 1907 blocks of service numbers were issued to the branches, to be allocated as a new man joined that branch. It is therefore possible to find two men who joined the service on the same day with wildly differing service numbers.

In 1903 the Royal Navy started a short service (SS) system. The SS papers are also in ADM 188. Those men with SS numbers 1–12000 served as seamen; those with numbers 100001–126000 served as stokers. In 1908 the service number system was changed again. Rather than have a plain numeric service number, alphabetical prefixes denoting the branch of the service were used:

J for Seamen
K for Stokers
L for Domestics
M for Miscellaneous.

The prefix F was given to the Royal Naval Air Service (RNAS) when it was formed in July 1914. Records of 55,000 ratings serving in the RNAS will be found in ADM 188 with the F prefix. When the RNAS became part of the RAF, any rating who transferred had the F prefix replaced by a 2 prefix (see 29.2).

If you have from elsewhere a service number starting with Y, this would be for a man who enrolled under the deferred scheme – the Royal Naval Volunteer Reserve. He will not have been called on to serve and there will be no service record under that number. However, he may have had another number, so try a name search in ADM 188 as usual.

28.4.4 Naval ratings, after 1923

These service records are not yet in the National Archives. Write to the relevant address in 62 given under Ministry of Defence: Royal Navy. You will need to prove entitlement to buy a précis of the record – you must either be the rating, or next of kin or have written permission from the rating or next of kin.

28.4.5 Naval ratings' pensions

Until the late nineteenth century, there was a varied collection of Naval pensions to ratings. For example, disabled seamen were often petitioners to the Crown for places as almsmen in the royal church foundations: there is a register of such petitions, 1660–1751, in SO 5/31.

The **Chatham Chest** was set up about 1590: its records cover 1653–1799. It was funded by a deduction from seamen's wages and paid pensions to wounded warrant officers (including midshipmen and surgeons), ratings and dockyard workers killed in action or on service. The earliest payments are in the account books, 1653–1657. There are registers of payments to pensioners, 1675–1799, with alphabetical lists of the pensioners at Lady Day in each year. The indexes of pensions, 1744–1797, give names, amount of pension, particulars as to wounds, names of ships in which they served and other information. All these records are in ADM 82 ⑦.

The **Royal Greenwich Hospital** was founded in 1694 as a home for infirm Naval seamen and Royal Marines: **in-pensioners** lived there until 1869. There are entry books of these in-pensioners, 1704–1869, which give very full particulars and are mostly indexed. Admission papers, although dating from 1790–1865, relate to service going back to at least 1750; they give descriptions, with details of service and the nature of disablement. Both entry books and admission papers are in ADM 73 ⑦ (see 28.4.1 for more on certificates on service). Papers of candidates for admission, 1737–1859, are in ADM 6/223–266 Ⓕ, with a card index covering 1737–1840. The church registers of the hospital, 1705–1864 (RG 4/1669–1679 and RG 8/16–18), can be interesting: most entries relating to in-pensioners are of deaths and occasionally include some comment as to manner of death.

However, most Greenwich pensioners were **out-pensioners** who lived elsewhere. They received out-pensions as a form of superannuation, but were often still in full employment elsewhere. If pensioners re-entered the Navy, their pension would lapse until their discharge. Registers of candidates for out-pensions, 1789–1859 (with gaps), are in ADM 6/267–320 ⑦. Pay books of out-pensions, 1781–1809, are in ADM 73/95–131 ⑦. For 1814–1846 they are in ADM 22/254–443 ⑦, arranged alphabetically. From 1842–1883 pensions were paid by the War Office through district pension offices, including many abroad: these records are arranged by place (WO 22 ⑤). After this they were paid by the Paymaster General through the Post Office.

In 1853 continuous service for ratings was introduced, with the aim of rewarding long service with a pension after 20 years. Seamen who achieved

▢ p. 566

and kept the character marking 'very good' were entitled to a higher pension. The majority of ratings entered as boys, signed their first continuous service engagement at 18, and therefore retired at 38 (many retired at 43, after signing on for a further five years). This left a man with much of his working life remaining. The Navy employed pensioners in many duties in dockyards and Naval establishments: see 28.6. Few records of pensions to continuous service ratings survive. From the late nineteenth century, other departments became involved, such as the Paymaster General (PMG) and the Ministry of Pensions (PIN). Payments to seamen and Marines living abroad, 1879–1921, are in PMG 71/5–13 ⑦. For First World War pensions, see 26.1.7.

Disabled pensions for Naval ratings who served before 1914 can be found in PIN 71 ② – but with no further identification than name. This contains the personal files on over 5,000 disabled ratings and soldiers (with some who returned to serve in the First World War, perhaps as Royal Fleet Reserve men). The information contained includes medical records, accounts of how injuries were incurred, the men's own account of the incident and conduct sheets. These conduct sheets give place of birth, age, names of parents and siblings, religion, physical attributes, marital and parental status. The series is unfortunately a selection only and does not cover all disabled soldiers and sailors of that date.

28.5 Naval reserve forces and the Wrens

The Navy was backed up in time of need by a pool of expert seamen formed into a formal reserve, and by volunteers, in a series of reserve forces. For a catalogue of the many reserve forces, see Rodger, *Naval Records for Genealogists*, Appendix III. The most important are described below.

28.5.1 Sea Fencibles, 1798–1810

The Sea Fencibles was a part-time organisation of fishermen and boatmen commanded by Naval officers formed for local defence, especially against invasion. Musters and pay lists, 1798–1810, are in ADM 28 ⑦, with a list of officers 1798–1810 in ADM 28/145 and records of appointments and a widows' charity in ADM 28/146–147. Entry book of orders appointing officers to Sea Fencibles, cutters, tenders, signal stations, the Impress Service and other shore appointments are in ADM 11/14–17 for 1804–1815.

28.5.2 Royal Naval Reserve, 1859 onwards

The Royal Naval Reserve was established in 1859 as a reserve force of officers and men of deep-sea merchant ships. By 1890 there were 20,000 men in the RNR. In 1911, it was decided that trawlers should be employed in wartime as minesweepers and patrol vessels, so the Royal Naval Reserve Trawler Section was set up, enrolling fishermen. Also in 1911, the Royal Fleet

Auxiliaries were established, with RNR officers (until 1921, when they were ranked with other Merchant Navy officers). From 1914 to 1921, a separate organisation of the RNR operated on the Shetland Islands – the Shetland Royal Naval Reserve. This was effectively a coast-watching and local defence organisation. In 1914 the Royal Naval Reserve provided some 20–30,000 more men than the Navy required. These officers and ratings of the RNR were hastily formed into the Royal Naval Division: see 28.5.6.

Records of **Royal Naval Reserve officers** who served between 1862 and 1920, and of honorary officers from 1862 to 1960, are in ADM 240 ⒡. These show details of merchant as well as Naval service and are arranged in numerical order of commission. There are no separate indexes, but some of the pieces can be used as indexes. In particular, ADM 240/84–88 serves as an index to the records of service between 1914 and 1921, which are in ADM 240/37–50. In addition, RNR officers are indexed in ADM 196/26. It is not known, however, to which set of service records this index referred. For later service records, see 28.3.8.

RNR officers were first included in the *Navy List* in 1862: entries give name, rank, date of commission and seniority. During the two World Wars much of the usual information was omitted from the published editions of the *Navy List* and confined to confidential editions for service use only. These are available as ADM 177 ⒎. There is a complete set of published *Navy Lists* in the Microfilm Reading Room.

For **Royal Naval Reserve ratings** serving between 1860 and 1913, try BT 164 ⒡, with indexes in BT 377/1–6. The index refers to all ratings who served, but only a selection of service records were kept, so you may be unlucky. The records in BT 164 are volumes and cards. Each page or card represents five years' service, with successive terms indicated by A, B, C, etc. For any one seaman you may therefore need to look in several places. For RNR ratings who served in the First World War and entered up to *c.* 1921, try BT 377 ⒡, indexed by BT 377/1–6. The records are in service number order; you can also pick up the service number from the ratings' First World War medal rolls in ADM 171/120–124.

For RNR ratings who entered 1922–1958, records are still with the Ministry of Defence, CS(R)2a; for men who entered after 1958, records are with HMS *Centurion*: addresses are in 62 under Ministry of Defence: Royal Navy.

Long Service medal records are in ADM 171/70–72, covering 1909–1949. For other records of merchant seamen, see 35.

28.5.3 Royal Fleet Reserve, 1901 onwards

The Royal Fleet Reserve was composed of ex-Naval seamen: the equivalent for officers was the Emergency List. Records of service in the Royal Fleet Reserve, 1914–1918, will be found as further entries on the original service record in ADM 188 (see 28.4.3).

28.5.4 Royal Naval Volunteer Reserve, 1903 onwards, and Mine Clearance Service

The Royal Naval Volunteer Reserve was founded in 1903. It was composed of men from all walks of life – except merchant seamen and fishermen, who formed the Royal Naval Reserve, and Naval short service men, who formed the Royal Fleet Reserve. RNVR officers' records for 1903–1919 are in ADM 337/117–128 Ⓔ, accessed by a card index. You will get an old reference: look at the list of ADM 337/117–128 to convert it. RNVR ratings records for 1903–1919 are also in ADM 377 Ⓔ. A few have indexes, but to find most you have to know the rating's service number. You can get this from the RNVR ratings' medal roll in ADM 171/125–129. The records in ADM 377 are arranged by division and then by service number. Each division had its own 'distinguishing letter':

Letter	Division	Volumes	Index
AA	Anti-Aircraft	ADM 337/93–94 ADM 188/1155–1177	ADM 337/92
B or BZ	Bristol Division	ADM 337/1–18	
C or CZ	Clyde Division	ADM 337/19–32	
E	Birmingham Electrical Volunteers	ADM 337/95	
KP, KW, KX	Crystal Palace (entered from Kitchener's Army)	Try the Fleet Air Arm Museum	
L or LZ	London Division	ADM 337–33–48	
M or MZ	Mersey Division	ADM 337/49–61	
MB	Motor Boat Reserve	ADM 337/96–99	ADM 188/1155–1177
MC	Mine Clearance Service	ADM 337/101–108	ADM 337/100: see below
PZ	Crystal Palace (entered from civil life or from the Royal Navy)	ADM 337/62–67	
R	Royal Naval Division	Try the Fleet Air Arm Museum (see also 28.5.6)	
S or St	Sussex Division	ADM 337/68–69	
SWS	Shore Wireless Service	Try the Fleet Air Arm Museum	
T or TZ	Tyne Division	ADM 337/70–84	
WZ	Wales Division	ADM 337/85–91	
Y	Allocated when a man volunteered, to be replaced by a service number when called up		

If only a Y number is found, the implication is that the man was not called on to serve.

The Fleet Air Arm Museum holds Engagement Papers (the contract). For some divisions, this is all you can expect to find. Other divisions sometimes have gaps in their records. If you can't find a service record, write to the Fleet Air Arm Museum (address in 62).

The Mine Clearance Service (MCS) was created at the end of the First

World War to clear all sea mines. It was manned by the Royal Navy but administered by the RNVR. The service records are in ADM 337 Ⓕ, in RNVR MC number order (see the table above). However, the index in ADM 337/100 gives only the men's old Royal Navy service numbers. In such cases the medal roll index is of no help, as members of the Mine Clearance Service did not receive campaign medals for this post-war work. It is therefore very difficult to find an MCS service record unless you know the number from a private source.

RNVR Records from 1919–1958 have not yet been transferred to the National Archives: contact the Ministry of Defence, CS(R)2a (address in 62). In 1958, the RNVR was amalgamated with the RNR.

28.5.5 Mercantile Marine Reserve and Commissioned Chartered Ships, 1914–1918

The Admiralty also hired armed or unarmed vessels in the First World War. Crew lists and agreements for these vessels are held by the Maritime History Centre at the Memorial University of Newfoundland: see www.mun.ca/mha/holdings/crewlist.php for information. Some men of the Mercantile Marine Reserve (merchant seamen serving on merchant vessels requisitioned by the Admiralty for wartime service) may also have been part of the Royal Naval Reserve. Service details can therefore be sought from BT 377; see 28.5.2. Although there is no separate sequence of service records, it may be possible to trace an individual who received the Mercantile Marine Reserve medal in BT 351. It is also possible that records of service may be found among the merchant seamen's records of service: see 35.

28.5.6 Royal Naval Division, 1914–1918

In 1914 the Royal Naval Reserve provided some 20–30,000 more men than the Navy required. These officers and ratings of the RNR were hastily formed into the Royal Naval Division and served ashore in Flanders as soldiers. By the time the war ended, the Division had suffered nearly 48,000 casualties, so many men must have joined the Division who had no connection at all to the sea or the Navy. In 1916, the Division was actually transferred to the Army as the 63rd (Royal Naval) Division. War diaries of the Royal Naval Division are in ADM 137 until 1916, and then in WO 95.

Service records are in ADM 339 Ⓔ in three alphabetical sequences: ratings who survived; ratings who were killed in action; and officers (both survivors and dead). Names beginning with Mc or Mac are filed at the end of M. For RNVR entrants only, there are engagement papers at the Fleet Air Arm Museum (address in 62). Some RND officers joined from the Royal Marines: their records do not seem to be in ADM 339. Try looking in ADM 196 instead (see 29.2–3).

Royal Naval Division war diaries and operational orders are in WO 95/4290–4291 (for Gallipoli) and ADM 137/3063–3088D Ⓖ. Army campaign medals awarded to men in the Royal Naval Division can be found easily at www.nationalarchives.gov.uk/documentsonline/medals.asp.

28.5.7 Women's Royal Naval Service, 1916–1931

The Royal Navy was the first of the armed forces to recruit women. The Women's Royal Naval Service (WRNS) was founded in 1916 to release men from acting as cooks, clerks, electricians, signallers, storekeepers, telegraphists and many other shore-based posts. By 1919, over 6,000 women were 'Wrens'. For more detail, see Fletcher, *The WRNS: A History of the Women's Royal Naval Service.* Personal Files of Short Service Officers, 1916–1931, are in ADM 318 ②. Registers of appointment for Short Service Officers, 1917–1919, are in ADM 321 ⑦. Ratings' service records are in ADM 336 Ⓕ for 1918–1919.

28.6 The Royal Naval Dockyards

28.6.1 Royal Naval Dockyards: general and employment records

The Royal Dockyards were the first great industrial enterprises of the British Empire. The great English dockyards were strung round the south coast from Deptford, Woolwich, Chatham, Sheerness and Portsmouth to Plymouth. Other Naval dockyards were situated all round the world. Some of the most important were Halifax in Nova Scotia, Gibraltar and the West Indies. For a very interesting collection of photographs and reproductions of detailed articles written about the dockyards in 1902, have a look at www.battleships-cruisers.co.uk/. The site takes a little exploring, but you will find much of interest, including message boards on dockyard ancestors. We also have photographs of work in dockyards, 1857–1961, in ADM 195 ⑤.

Officers at the dockyards were appointed by the Board of Admiralty, but otherwise yards were under the administration of the Navy Board, represented at the yard by a resident commissioner. However, there was considerable movement between the two branches of the service. The commissioners and the masters attendant were usually retired sea officers. Dockyard shipwrights, having served their apprenticeship, often became carpenters in the Navy and might return to be master shipwrights, and in the same way the other master tradesmen and the boatswain were normally recruited from the sea service. The career of any skilled man may therefore have to be traced in the records of both services: Naval pensioners often began a second career in the dockyards.

The principal officers at each yard were:

Master shipwright: responsible for most workmen and all construction and repair work;
Master attendant: managed the ships in harbour and saw to the maintenance of the ships in Ordinary, i.e., when the ship was laid up;

Clerk of the cheque: mustered the workmen, looked after expenses and kept accounts of earnings;

Clerk of the survey: checked the details of all stores received and issued and surveyed materials;

Clerk of the ropeyard (at Woolwich, Chatham, Portsmouth and Plymouth): mustered the men, and received and issued stores.

In 1822 a number of posts were abolished, including clerks of the survey and ropeyard. In 1832 the Navy Board was abolished and the yards came under the principal officers of the Navy at the Admiralty. Resident commissioners were discontinued in favour of a captain or admiral superintendent.

Correspondence between the seventeenth- and eighteenth-century dockyards and the Navy Board (from records split between the National Archives and the National Maritime Museum) is being listed in full onto the National Archives catalogue by volunteers from the Naval Dockyards Society. Try a name search in both ADM 106 ② (our material) and ADM 354 ② (their material). Please note that records in ADM 354 have to be seen at the National Maritime Museum.

Records of the dockyards in general are split between the National Archives and the National Maritime Museum: we tend to have the staff records. For records held at Greenwich, see the Museum's research guide on Naval dockyards at **www.port.nmm.ac.uk/research/b5.html**; for a research guide to ours, see **www.catalogue.nationalarchives.gov.uk/RdLeaflet.asp?s LeafletID=50**.

Our main sources are the Yard Pay Books, 1660–1857 (ADM 42 ⑤). For minor yards, treated as ships, try the pay books and musters in ADM 32, ADM 36 and ADM 37 (all ⑤). In addition, ADM 106 contains some other interesting sources, particularly the description books of artificers, 1748–1830 (ADM 106/2975–3005 and 3625 ⑦): these include physical descriptions of the men in the main English yards (intended to prevent theft and fraud). The Chatham Chest paid pensions to the widows of dockyard workers (and others) killed in action or on service: the registers of payment were shared with the pensions to wounded men (ADM 82, described in 28.4.5). Pensions for dockyard workers (including many ex-seamen) for 1836–1928 are in PMG 25 ⑦; for earlier records, see ADM 23 ⑦. For baptisms, marriages and burials, 1826–1946, in the Naval dockyards in Bermuda, see ADM 6/434, 436 and 439.

Information about dockyard and other Naval apprentices may be found in ADM IV by using the Admiralty Digest (a subject index in ADM 12, relating to ADM 1 and other series): look under the heading 'Apprentices in Dockyards'. Examination results for dockyard and artificer apprentices, from 1876, are among the records of the Civil Service Commission (CSC 10 ⑦). See also CSC 6 ⑦ for the regulations on applications for dockyard apprentices, 1885–1956. The information for candidates included with these csc documents can give you a good idea of what the life and expected career pattern was like. For dockyard police, see 33.4.

28.6.2 Royal Naval Dockyards: slaves and convicts

In the eighteenth and nineteenth centuries the dockyards used both free and unfree labour – a highly skilled workforce plus convicts and slaves. The great English dockyards of Deptford, Woolwich, Chatham, Sheerness, Portsmouth and Plymouth used a mixture of very skilled artificers and convict labour – it was no accident that the convict hulks were moored by the dockyards. From 1777, convicts were used to dredge the Thames, to develop the Arsenal and the nearby London docks and to work as unskilled labour – as muscle power – in the Naval dockyards. (To find out more about the hulks and conditions of work, see the very interesting pages on prison hulks on the Thames at **www.portcities.org.uk/london**: see also 47.3.)

In the West Indies' dockyards many of the skilled artificers (as well as the labourers) were black slaves originally sold or loaned to local Naval dockyards by West Indies merchants: search ADM 106 and ADM 354 for many references to the 'King's Negroes' or 'negros' as both skilled and unskilled labour. There are separate pay books for black dockyard workers (slavery and payment could go together) in Antigua for 1785–1824 (ADM 42/2114) and in Jamaica for 1787–1825 (ADM 42/2310). After this, they should appear in the standard records.

Guy Grannum has been investigating slavery in the Navy, and has provided some information from work in progress. Outside of the dockyards he has not come across the Navy owning slaves (unlike the Army). Slaves do sometimes appear on Naval ships in the Caribbean – as local pilots or as skilled labour, perhaps hired from their owners. In the cases he has found that the slaves disappear from the musters when the ship leaves the Caribbean but reappear when the ship returns there. Many black men served in the Navy: there were certainly people from the Caribbean and Africa at Trafalgar (see 28.4.1) but we don't know if any were slaves. It would have been unlikely because slaves could not volunteer for the Navy as they were someone's property and they could not be pressed because that would be theft.

Male convict labour shipped from Britain was more important in the development of Bermuda as the 'Gibraltar of the West' as a bulwark against the United States. Construction of the Royal Naval Dockyard at Bermuda was carried out by convicts between 1824 and 1863. Of 9,000 convicts sent to the hulks in Bermuda, approximately 2,000 perished during construction, many from yellow fever. Others were trained in the skilled labour needed to build ships. For more information, see **www. bermuda-online.org/rnd.htm** and the many relevant articles in the *Bermuda Journal of Archaeology and Maritime History*. Some convicts were released on the island, but many were shipped to Tasmania to start a new life after serving their sentence (CO 37 ⑦). Other male convicts were sent from Britain to hulks at Gibraltar, 1842–1870, for similar purposes: see Dr Baly's report 1854 on the Convict Establishment at Gibraltar in CO 91/219. (There is more on health records of convict and black dockyard workers at 28.7.2 and more on convicts in 47.)

28.7 Naval medical services

28.7.1 Naval surgeons and male nurses

Surgeons and their mates were the only medical help available on individual ships, although female nurses worked in Naval hospitals and hospital ships from the seventeenth century. Male nurses were later called sick berth staff, and records were kept with the usual ratings records.

Until 1796, surgeons qualified by examination at the Barber-Surgeons' Company in London and were then warranted to ships by the Navy Board. There is an incomplete collection of surgeons' passing certificates, c. 1700–1800, issued by the Barber-Surgeons or by examining boards of surgeons at the outports or overseas (ADM 106/2952–2963, arranged alphabetically ⑤). There is an index to these at the National Archives, giving dates and texts of the certificates, but no references to the documents.

There are several series of service registers for surgeons: the longest covers 1774–1886 (ADM 104/12–29 ⑤, indexed in ADM 104/11). Separate full pay registers of surgeons run from 1797 to 1858, before merging with the general series (ADM 24: see 28.3.2). One particularly interesting series of registers of service contains correspondence on the merits of individual officers, 1829–1873 (ADM 104/31–40). Another interesting series of reports on questions of pay, half-pay and promotion of surgeons, 1817–1832, includes much personal information about named officers (ADM 105/1–9 ⑧). See also the memoranda and reports on surgeons (individually and collectively), 1822–1832, in ADM 195/10–19. For other sources, consult Rodger's book.

The SURGEONS' medical journals for Naval ships and Naval hospitals, 1785–1963 (ADM 101: early part ⑥, later ⑦) and for convict ships, 1858–1867 (MT 32 ⑦) are well worth a look. Unfortunately, only a selection survives, and logs from 1946 onwards are closed for 75 years. Surgeons on board ship were required to keep a general journal on the health of the ship's company. Such journals contain accounts of the medical or surgical treatment of men, daily sick lists, statistics on diseases and comments on the state of health of the crew: quite often in the eighteenth and nineteenth centuries they include more general information as well. The Navy was always keen to preserve the health of its men and these journals, often written by educated men with acerbic and independent opinions, are usually the most accessible and informative source for the history of a voyage.

There are full pay books of surgeons (and nurses) at Haslar Hospital (near Portsmouth), 1769–1819 (ADM 102/375–397), and at Plymouth Hospital, 1777–1819 (ADM 102/683–700).

You may wish to explore the full range of records of the Admiralty's Medical departments in ADM 97–105, 132–133 and 304–305: these are well worth checking out.

28.7.2 Naval hospital records

Until the mid-eighteenth century, the Royal Navy had no dedicated hospitals on land (Greenwich Hospital was the grandest kind of almshouse). Instead it converted ships to hospital ships as needed, or sent seamen ashore for a cure. However, death and desertion rates were unacceptably high. Three major hospitals were then built by the Navy Board, all accessible by water, at Haslar (for Portsmouth) from 1745, at Stonehouse (for Plymouth) from 1758 and at Chatham from 1827. Like so many Navy enterprises, they were done on a grand scale: the Haslar hospital could house 1,500 patients and was the largest brick building in Europe. If you are interested in these and other Naval and military hospitals, you may like to find out more at **www.britarch.ac.uk/projects/ dob/deflin5/hosparch.html**. We also have correspondence from the Haslar and Stonehouse Hospitals to the Admiralty from 1793–1839, nicely identified in ADM 1/3533–3541 [7]; other such correspondence will exist in ADM 1 but will have to be found using ADM 12 [F].

There are extensive muster lists of patients in Naval hospitals and *stationary* hospital ships dating from 1740 to 1880 (ADM 102 [6],[5]). These come from the three main hospitals (see below) and from Antigua, Ascension Island, Bermuda, the Cape of Good Hope, Deal, Gibraltar, Halifax in Nova Scotia, Jamaica, Madras, Malta, Woolwich, Yarmouth and many other hospitals and hospital ships as well. There are separate records for black patients for Barbados (ADM 102/54 'Barbadoes (servants & Negroes)' 1814–1816) and for the Cape of Good Hope (ADM 102/130 'Negroes' 1812–1816). It was rare for the Navy to make any colour distinction in its record keeping: this may reflect the extensive number of black dockyard slaves ('King's Negroes') in those places. Likewise, convict dockyard workers at Bermuda seem to have received separate care 1824–1848: after this they were looked after on the convict hospital ship Tenedos moored at Boaz Island (search HO 8 by Tenedos or Boaz for records 1848–1863). To see what there is for 1824–1848, try a search on Bermuda in ADM 101, ADM 102 and ADM 104. Admission and discharge registers of the Royal Naval Hospital Malta, 1836–1879, are in ADM 304, together with inpatient records.

Haslar (Portsmouth)			
Deaths of seamen	1755–1765	ADM 102/374	7
Pay lists of surgeons and nurses	1769–1828	ADM 102/375–398, 921	7

Musters of sick and wounded seamen	1792–1855 1856–1859 1860	ADM 102/271–334 ADM 102/876–879 ADM 102/915	7
Musters of sick and wounded Marines and others	1785–1824 1805–1809	ADM 102/335–347 ADM 102/862	7
Musters of lunatics	1818–1854	ADM 102/356–373	7
Musters of sick and wounded soldiers	1809–1816	ADM 102/351–355	7
Others (private quarters 1791–1801, Russians 1808–1812, servants 1814–1815)		ADM 102/348–350	7

Stonehouse (Plymouth)

Pay lists of surgeons and nurses	1777–1827	ADM 102/683–781	7
Musters of sick and wounded seamen	1792–1855 1856–1859 1860	ADM 102/601–662 ADM 102/894–897 ADM 102/919	7
Musters of sick and wounded Marines and others	1793–1824	ADM 102/665–676	7
Musters of sick and wounded soldiers	1809–1810	ADM 102/678	7
Others (private quarters 1774–1801, Revenue Cruisers 1818–1824, servants 1815, 1822–1824)		ADM 102/663–664 681–682 679–680	7

Chatham (watch out: *Chatham* hospital ship 1793–1802 moored at **Plymouth**)

Musters of sick and wounded seamen	1828–1854 1855–1857 1858–1859	ADM 102/133–157 ADM 102/872 ADM 102/914	7

As well as the Haslar musters of lunatics, there are also several musters of lunatics at Hoxton House, 1755–1818 (ADM 102/415–420). Yarmouth too was a major hospital for Naval lunatics. Reports on the treatment of Naval lunatics, 1812–1832, are in ADM 105/28.

The musters of *sea-going* hospital ships will be found with the other musters in ADM 36 6 and ADM 37 6. These are not identified in the catalogue as hospital ships, but you will probably have their name already if you are following a man through a series of muster books.

28.7.3 Naval female nurses

Greenwich Hospital, in its original form, paid no widows' pensions, but it employed the widows of seamen in its infirmary, with records as follows:

1704–1864	Alphabetical lists of nurses	ADM 73/87–88
1704–1865	Registers of service. Give name, date of entry and date of and reason for leaving	ADM 73/83–86

1783–1863	Registers of nurses. Give name, age at time of entry, date of entry, where born, husband's forename, husband's date of death and in which service employed, amount of pension, husband hurt or wounded and on what service, whether number of children and ages at time of entry. (Details of husband and family are not completed for the early entries)	ADM 73/85
1817–1842	Applications of ratings' widows for admission to Greenwich Hospital as nurse	ADM 6/329 ADM 6/331

There are also full pay books of nurses at Haslar Hospital, 1769–1819 (ADM 102/375–397), and at Stonehouse (Plymouth) Hospital, 1777–1819 (ADM 102/683–700). Hospital musters give details of patients, not staff.

During the later nineteenth century the Navy ceased to employ women as nurses, until the establishment of the professional Naval Nursing Sisters in 1883. They were employed first at Haslar (Portsmouth) and Stonehouse (Plymouth), from 1897 at Chatham and Malta and from 1901 at all Royal Naval Hospitals. In 1902 they were renamed as Queen Alexandra's Royal Naval Nursing Service (QARNNS). From 1884, Head Nursing Sisters were included in the *Navy List*: other nursing officers were included from 1890. Naval nurses were eligible for the Royal Red Cross Medal from 1883, and bars from 1917: see WO 145/1–3.

1884–1909	Nursing sisters. Gives name, rank, dates of birth, entry and discharge. Indexed.	ADM 104/43
1890–1908	Annual reports on nursing sisters. For each year staff are listed in order of seniority, with name, age, hospital, dates of service and very brief comments on character and work.	ADM 104/95
1894–1929 [1959]	Nursing sisters. Dates are of appointment – the register includes service and other details up to 1959. Gives name, rank, dates of birth, entry and discharge, next of kin, annual report marks, sick leave, comments of character and ability, training qualifications and medal awards. Indexed.	ADM 104/161
1914–1919	QARNNS Reserves, signed up for wartime service only. Gives civil hospital, Naval hospital, service details, brief reports of conduct and ability, recommendations for Royal Red Cross. No personal information given.	ADM 104/162–164

Succession books, listing nursing sisters and wardmasters by hospital and barracks, are available for 1921–1939 (ADM 104/96). Staff are listed in rough date order, name, rank, date and cause of appointment and discharge.

Later records are not in the National Archives. Write to Navy Search (address in 62 under Ministry of Defence: Royal Navy).

28.8 Life and death in the Navy

Having found details of a Naval forebear, many people want to investigate the records of the ships in which their ancestor served. This really means looking at operational records.

28.8.1 Logs and reports of proceedings, 1669–1967

Naval logs recorded the ship's position, movements and weather but they rarely provide personal information on the officers and crew of a particular ship. However, they do provide a reliable record of a ship's voyages.

1669–1852	Captains' logs	ADM 51	6
1672–1871	Masters' logs	ADM 52, ADM 54	6
1757–1904	Explorations logs	ADM 55, ADM 51	6
1799–1967	Ships' logs	ADM 53	6
1914–1967	Submarines' logs	ADM 173	6
	Lieutenants' logs	At the National Maritime Museum	

For the Second World War, the logs of ships smaller than cruisers do not appear to have survived, apart from for 1939 and the early months of 1940.

The logs in the National Archives can be found very easily by doing a search in the catalogue using the ship's name and the date range you want, and restricting the search to ADM (this will also bring up musters and pay books). Try it both with and without HMS – much early cataloguing of ADM records did not include HMS as part of the ship's name. If you are unsuccessful, try checking variant spellings of a ship's name as the catalogue is not always consistent – you may find references to both the *Weasel* and the *Weazle*, for example. Look in the *Navy List* (see 28.3.1) of a suitable date for variant spellings.

The surgeon's journal may give a glimpse of daily life on board ship from a less official perspective: it is well worth looking to see if one exists for a ship that you are interested in. See 28.7.1.

Another set of records is less easy to find but may be much more interesting, as they were intended to be (and are) very informative. These are the letters and reports of proceedings from the captain of each ship, reporting back to the Admiralty from all parts of the world. To use them, you have to discover the name of the ship's captain (from documents you have already looked at or from the *Navy List*). You will not be able to find them on the catalogue but through original indexes at the National Archives.

For 1698–1839, they are in ADM 1/1435–2738 in a sub-series of Captains' Letters, filed by the initial letter of the captain's name. For a subject index from 1793 onwards, use the indexes in ADM 12, looking under the ship's name and picking out *Captain's Letters* or *R of P* (reports of proceedings); then go back to the ADM 1 list.

For 1839–1938, you will need to use the indexes in ADM 12 to find similar letters in ADM 1 (for the First World War, in ADM 137).

For 1939 on, they may be found in ADM 1 or ADM 199, but there is as yet no ADM 12 to help you.

Once you have learned how to use ADM 12, you will discover that it is a detailed index to Admiralty letters and can contain references to almost anything. It is certainly worth exploring for officers, and can be for men.

Lieutenants' letters to the Admiralty can also be found in the same way, although letters before 1791 were destroyed by enemy action in 1941.

28.8.2 Naval operational records

Operational records are extensive and can be complicated. There are free research guides available at the National Archives and at **www.national archives.gov.uk** giving guidance on Naval operational records for 1660–1914, 1914–1918 and 1939–1945. If you are interested in the World Wars, try looking in the National Archives Library for the two detailed official histories written directly after the wars from the documents – the *History of the Great War* and *History of the Second World War*. Each of these has volumes on the war at sea.

28.8.3 Naval (war) dead and casualties, 1742–1948

There are various collections of material on Naval dead: see also the early records discussed in 28.2, many of which related to Naval dead.

1742–1782	Names of seamen slain	ADM 106/3017	[7]
1787–1809	Dead men's wages: alphabetical list of seamen; no. 4 gives name and ship, no. 5 also gives date of death	ADM 80/4–5	[7]
1798–1831	Register of dead men's wages	ADM 80/6–12	[7]
1854–1929	Registers and indexes of killed and wounded: several sub-series are included here	ADM 104/14–149	[8]
1859–1878	Ratings discharged dead	ADM 154	[7]
1893–1950	Index to registers of reports of death	ADM 104/102–108	[7]
1900–1941	Registers of reports of deaths	ADM 104/122–126	[7]
1903–1933	Naval officers died	ADM 10/16	[7]
1915–1929	Index to registers of killed and wounded	ADM 104/140–143	[7]
1914–1919	Card index of Naval officer casualties, giving date and cause of death, next of kin and place of commemoration or burial	ADM 242/1–5	[F]
1914–1919	War graves roll for Naval ratings and Royal Naval Reserve, giving date and cause of death, next of kin and place of commemoration or burial	ADM 242/7–10, 15	
1939–1948	Registers of reports of deaths: Naval ratings	ADM 104/127–139	[7]

If you know the name of the ship on which a man served, try searching on it in ADM 1 (restrict the dates to 1914–1918) and you may well get casualty or survivor lists for that ship.

Information on men who died in the First and Second World Wars can be easily accessed from the Debt of Honour Register on the free website of the Commonwealth War Graves Commission (**www.cwgc.org**). You can find here a record of all Navy personnel who died in the First and Second World Wars, with date of death, place of burial, ship and sometimes a mention of parents or wife. If you are looking for a really common name, you may have some problems, as quite often only an initial is given instead of a forename.

See also the indexes to the registers of Naval war deaths, 1914–1921 and 1939–1948, and to Naval births, marriages and deaths abroad, 1881–1965, available at the Family Records Centre and National Archives mentioned in 8.8. Death certificates can be bought in the usual way.

Another possible source for more information is the *National Roll of the Great War*: see 26.1.4 for more details.

28.8.4 Naval medals

Medal rolls do not give detailed information about individuals. Campaign medal rolls for the Navy are in ADM 171. Before 1914 they are arranged by ship, with no name indexes. For 1914–1920, they are in alphabetical order, with separate sequences for the Royal Navy, the Royal Naval Reserve and the Royal Naval Volunteer Reserve. The award of the following, and some other, campaign medals are recorded in ADM 171:

1793–1840	Naval General Service Medal. Lists of recipients, 1793–1840, are given in the book by Douglas-Morris
1840, 1857 and 1900	China Medal
1854	Crimea Medal
1857	Indian Mutiny Medal
1873	Ashanti Medal
1875–1876	Arctic Medal
1899	Queen's South Africa Medal
1901	King's South Africa Medal
1902	Africa General Service Medal
1911	Delhi Durbar Medal
1914–1920	British War Medal and Victory Medal and Stars

Gallantry medals are discussed in detail by Pappalardo. They were first instituted during the Crimean War and others were added later, particularly during the First World War. Some surviving recommendations are in ADM 1 and ADM 116 (search by 'surname AND (85)' in both). Registers of gallantry awards to Naval officers during the First World War are also in ADM 171 Ⓔ; there is an index available, which gives the dates of entries in the *London Gazette*. The *London Gazette* can be searched online at **www.gazettes-online.co.uk**. You may also wish to investigate our specialist guide, Spencer's *Medals*.

28.9 The Royal Navy: bibliography

LISTS, ETC., OF PERSONNEL

British Biographical Archive (London, 1984)

J CAMPBELL and W STEVENSON, *Lives of the British Admirals* (London, 1917)

J CHARNOCK, *Biographia Navalis* (London, 1794–1798)

Dictionary of National Biography (London, 1909 continuing)

K DOUGLAS-MORRIS, *The Naval General Service Medal, 1793–1840* (Margate, 1982)

N H G HURST, *Naval Chronicle, 1799–1818: Index to Births, Marriages and Deaths* (Coulsdon, 1989)

A J KEALY, *Chaplains of the Royal Navy, 1626–1903* (Portsmouth, 1905)

P MARIONE, *The Complete Navy List of the Napoleonic Wars, 1793–1815* (CD-Rom, 2003)

J MARSHALL, *Royal Naval Biography* (London, 1823–1830)

National Maritime Museum, *Commissioned Sea Officers of the Royal Navy, 1660–1815* (London, 1954 and later)

Navy List (London, 1814 onwards)

W R O'BYRNE, *Naval Biographical Dictionary* (London, 1849)

D STEELE, *Steele's Navy List* (London, 1782–1817)

D SYRETT and R L DINARDO, *The Commissioned Sea Officers of the Royal Navy 1660–1815* (Navy Records Society, 1994)

GENERAL WORKS

Calendar of State Papers Domestic, Charles I (London, 1858–1897)

Calendar of State Papers Domestic, Charles II (London, 1860–1947)

Calendar of State Papers Domestic, Commonwealth (London, 1875–1886)

History of the Great War (HMSO)

History of the Second World War (HMSO)

The Royal Navy

A BROOKE and D BRANDON, 'Surgeons at Sea' [Naval surgeons on convict ships], *Ancestors* 40 (2005)

S R BROWN, *The Age of Scurvy* (2005)

M H FLETCHER, *The WRNS: A History of the Women's Royal Naval Service* (1989)

B PAPPALARDO, 'A Record of Merit' [passing certificates], *Ancestors* 8 (2002)

B PAPPALARDO, 'Indexing the Admiralty', *Ancestors* 15 (2003)

B PAPPALARDO, *Royal Naval Lieutenants: Passing Certificates 1691–1902* (List and Index Society, vol. 290, 2002)

B PAPPALARDO, 'Surgeons at Sea' [Naval surgeons on all ships], *Ancestors* 13 (2003)

B PAPPALARDO, *Tracing Your Naval Ancestors* (PRO, 2002)

B PAPPALARDO, 'Trafalgar: Men who won the victory', *Ancestors* 38 (2005)

P PARL, 'Naval Quota-Men of 1795 and 1796', *Ancestors* 17 (2003/4)

G J PRENDERGHAST, 'Pressed into Service', *Ancestors* 38 (2005

N A M RODGER, *Naval Records for Genealogists* (PRO, 1988)

N A M RODGER, *The wooden world: an anatomy of the Georgian navy* (London, 1986)

N A M RODGER, *The safeguard of the sea: a Naval history of Britain, 660–1649* (London, 1997)

N A M RODGER, *The command of the ocean: a Naval history of Britain, 1649–1815* (London, 2004)

J SLY, 'For service at sea' [Naval General Service Medal], *Ancestors* 38 (2005

W Spencer, Medals: The Researcher's Companion (National Archives, 2006)

J Thompson, The War at Sea 1914–1918 (Imperial War Museum, 2005)

P Tomaselli, 'Naval and Royal Marine Records at the Fleet Air Arm Museum', Family History Monthly 102 (2004)

N Tracy, The Naval Chronicle: the contemporary record of the Royal Navy at war. (London, 1998)

A Trotman, 'The Royal Naval Museum, Portsmouth: Genealogy at the King Alfred Library and Reading Room', Genealogists' Magazine, vol. XXIV, pp. 197–199

The Royal Dockyards

Bermuda Journal of Archaeology and Maritime History

K V Burns, The Devonport Dockyard Story (1984)

J G Coad, The royal dockyards, 1690–1850: architecture and engineering works of the sailing Navy (Aldershot, 1989)

J D Crawshaw, History of Chatham Dockyard (1999)

W Davey, The Royal Marines and the dockyards 1755–1949 (Royal Marines Historical Society, 1986)

B H Patterson, (comp) A dictionary of dockyard language (Portsmouth Royal Dockyard Historical Society, 1984)

C F E Hollis Hallett, Forty Years of Convict Labour: Bermuda 1823–1864 (Bermuda 1999)

P MacDougall, Royal Dockyards (Newton Abbot, 1982)

R Morriss, The Royal Dockyards during the Revolutionary and Napoleonic Wars (Leicester, 1983)

D V Nicholson, The King's Negroes: The Journal Of Boatswain Fox, Antigua Navy Yard, 1820–1823 (Museum of Antigua and Barbuda)

D V Nicholson, The Story Of English Harbour (Museum of Antigua and Barbuda)

B H Patterson, Giv'er a cheer boys': the great docks of Portsmouth dockyard 1830–1914 (Portsmouth: Royal Dockyard Historical Society, 1989)

P H Watson, The two hundredth anniversary of the Halifax dockyard (Maritime Museum of Canada, 1959)

J Webb, An early nineteenth century dockyard worker (Portsmouth Museums Society, 1971)

29 The Royal Marines

29.1 History of the Royal Marines

The first British military unit to be raised specifically for sea service was the Lord Admiral's Regiment, formed in 1664. From 1690 additional Marine Regiments were raised in wartime for sea service and disbanded at the end of the war, when the soldiers were discharged and the officers went on half-pay. Oath rolls exist for the oath in support of William III taken by the First and Second Marine Regiments in 1696 (C 213/290–291).

Though intended for and usually employed in the sea service, these early Marine Regiments were part of the Army and were organised like other foot regiments. Parties serving at sea came under Naval discipline and were borne on their ship's books (on a separate list) for wages and victuals (see 28.4.2). In other respects their administration and records did not differ from those of other foot regiments. Marine Regiments sometimes served ashore as ordinary infantry.

These Marine Regiments were disbanded for the last time in 1749. At the approach of war again in 1755, a new Corps of Marines was formed under Admiralty authority. This was not part of the Army and it had no regimental structure, though it continued to use Army ranks and uniform. The 50 companies were divided for administrative and recruiting purposes between three divisions, with their depots at Portsmouth, Plymouth and Chatham. From 1805 to 1869 there was a fourth division, based at Woolwich. Both divisions and companies were purely administrative entities and not fighting formations; officers and other ranks were drafted for sea service without regard to them, and each ship's party of Marines commonly included men of several companies. The Marine depots maintained records similar to those of foot regiments, while Marine detachments at sea were borne on the ships' books as before. Marines sometimes served ashore, particularly as landing parties, organised into companies and battalions. If serving under military command in such circumstances they came under military discipline, but otherwise they were responsible solely to the Admiralty.

The duties of Marines afloat were in action to lay down musketry on the enemy's decks and otherwise to mount sentries and contribute to the unskilled labour of working the ship. From time to time they continued to be supplemented in these roles by infantrymen lent by the Army. Until the twentieth century the duties of the Royal Marines were almost entirely to provide detachments for ships. In 1914, however, a large force of Marines was landed to defend Antwerp, and some subsequently fought on the Western Front. In the 1930s the Marines developed a new role as part of the Mobile Naval Base Defence Organisation, and from 1942 they contributed units known as Commandos that operated under Combined Operations Headquarters and specialised in raids on enemy coasts. After the Second World War this became the principal duty of the corps.

Another category of troops serving afloat were artillerymen, who manned the mortars carried by bomb vessels. Disciplinary and other problems led the Admiralty in 1804 to form companies of marine artillery to man the bomb vessels. This led to a formal division in 1859 between the Royal Marine Artillery (the Blue Marines with barracks at Eastney, near Portsmouth) and the Royal Marine Light Infantry (the Red Marines), which lasted until the two corps were amalgamated in 1923.

Correspondence and papers on policy matters, including the raising and deployment of marine companies, may be found in several series of records. The In-Letters of the Admiralty include a special section for letters from marine officers 1787–1839 (ADM 1/3246–3357 ⑦) and the Out-Letters also include a section for letters to, or concerning, marines for the period 1703–1845 (ADM 2/1147–1251 ⑦).

There is a specialist guide to the National Archives' holdings by Thomas, *Records of the Royal Marines*. Other records (usually less formal records and personal material) are held by the Royal Marines Museum at Eastney. Their archives contain manuscripts, letters, documents, diaries and administrative material dating back to the eighteenth century, plus a photo, tape and video collection. They also have a library that contains *Navy Lists* from 1783 and *Marine Officer Lists* from 1755, supplemented with *Army ists*, for tracing the service of any Marine officer. The collection includes biographical, campaign and uniform sections along with various regulations, laws, orders and reports. Sets of professional journals are also available. Of particular interest is the Marines' own magazine, *The Globe and the Laurel*, from 1892 to date, which contains obituaries of officers and other ranks. A card index to officers' obituaries exists, and one is being created for the other ranks. These collections can only be made available for research by appointment. For more information, try the Museum's website (**www.royalmarinesmuseum.co.uk**) or write to the address in 62.

29.2 Royal Marines: commissioned officers appointed up to 1925

The scattered nature of Marine forces meant that a considerable number of junior officers was required. Commissions in the Marines, unlike Army commissions, were not sold but were free appointments. As a result, a large number of Marine officers came from the poorer gentry families of the remoter parts of Ireland and Scotland who could not afford to buy commissions but still sought honourable employment. There was little chance for promotion within the Marines as the number of senior officers needed was so small. Some Marine officers went on to buy further promotion in the Army.

Commissions and appointments for 1703–1713 are recorded in ADM 6/405; those for 1755–1814 are in ADM 6/406. There is no index, and they contain no genealogical information. There are some lists of officers' services, 1690–1740, in ADM 96/1–2. Apart from these, no original service records of officers appointed before 1793 have survived. You can discover the outline of an officer's career from the *Marine Officers Lists*, 1757–1850 (ADM 118/230–336 ⑦ Ⓕ) and 1760–1886 (ADM 192 ⑦ Ⓕ): they are indexed from 1770. You could also use the *Army Lists* from 1740 onwards. The *Navy List* (from 1797) and *Hart's Army List* (from 1840) also include Marine officers. A register of commissions between 1849 and 1858 is in ADM 201/8.

Service records for Marine officers commissioned between 1837 and 1925, with some from 1793 onwards, will be found in ADM 196/58–65, 83 and 97–114, Ⓕ ⑧. These give full service details and in some cases the name and occupation of the officer's father. For officers appointed up to 1883, use the composite index in ADM 313/110; after that the ADM 196 volumes are each indexed. There is a separate service register for officers of the Royal Marine Artillery, 1798–1855, in ADM 196/66.

There are some other sources that may be worth investigation. Pay records in ADM 96 ⑦ can give some extra information. There are lists of half-pay officers for 1789–1793 and 1824–1829 in ADM 6/410–413. The survey of officers conducted in 1822 (as for the Navy: see 28.3.4) can provide details of age (ADM 6/73–83 and 409 ⑦). There was a further survey in 1831 (ADM 6/84–85). For 1837, there is an address book for Marine officers on half-pay (PMG 73/2). Confidential letters on officers' affairs, 1868–1889, are in ADM 63/27–30 ⑧; they are indexed. The general administrative papers in ADM 193 ⑦ and ADM 201 ⑦ may provide more information on individuals.

Very comprehensive obituary material may be found in *The Times* online (www.timesonline.co.uk), as well as in *The Globe and the Laurel* (held by the Royal Marines Museum).

All enquiries concerning officers commissioned after 1925 should be sent to the Royal Marines at the address given in 62 under Ministry of Defence.

29.3 Royal Marines: warrant officers appointed up to 1920

For Woolwich division, 1812, there is an alphabetical list of warrant officers and ratings, entered for limited service (ADM 6/407).

Dates of entry	Latest date of discharge		
1875–1903	1946	ADM 196/34	Ⓕ
1873–1907	1946	ADM 196/35	Ⓕ
1904–1912	1923	ADM 196/67	Ⓕ
1890–1920	1944	ADM 196/102	Ⓕ

There is a name index of Royal Marine warrant officers and references for their records filed with the ADM 196 list. Many warrant officers went on to become commissioned officers.

29.4 Royal Marines: other ranks enlisting up to 1925

Records relating to Royal Marines other ranks are abundant. Marines aboard ship (provided that their ship is known) can be found in the ship's muster books and pay lists: see 28.4.2. There are three main series of records relating to a marine's service (attestation forms, description books and service registers), each arranged by Division. A marine usually stayed in the same Division throughout his career. If you do not know the Division, try the following methods to discover it:

- Look in the card index to the attestation records in ADM 157;
- If you know any of his medal entitlements, look at the campaign medal rolls in ADM 171;
- If you know the name of a ship he served on, and the date, use the *Navy List* (these are on the open shelves at the National Archives) to establish the ship's home port (Plymouth, Portsmouth, Chatham or Woolwich). Before 1947, marines who were to serve on board a ship were drawn from the same RM Division as the home port of the ship;
- If you know his Company number, and a date, consult the table in Appendix 1 of Thomas's *The Records of the Royal Marines*. Or try the tables of allocation of Company Numbers to Divisions as set out in the *Lists of Officers of the Royal Marines* in ADM 118/230–336 and ADM 192;
- If your man was a war casualty in the First World War consult ADM 242/7–10. These are documents similar to a war graves roll. For the Second World War, see the Royal Marines Museum book *A Register of Royal Marine Deaths, 1939–1945*, available at the National Archives;
- If you have an address where he lived, from a birth or marriage certificate or from the census, you may assume with some certainty that he would have joined the nearest Division to that address. He would have belonged to that Division's 'catchment area'.

The attestation forms, 1790–1925 (ADM 157 Ⓕ, Ⓩ) were completed at the time of enlistment but are now filed in order of discharge date (except for those of the Chatham division) up to 1883. They can include details of

☐ p. 566

discharge or death. There is a card index covering the first 659 pieces of ADM 157 – that is, up to 1883. The cards use the following abbreviations:

- 16/170: this number means the entry for this man will be found in ADM 157/16 on folio 170. (Sometimes these numbers are reversed – check in the class list, against the date)
- a.c. 1823: this means the attestation was at Chatham in 1823. (Other Divisions are given as Pl – Plymouth, Po – Portsmouth, W – Woolwich.)
- 84co.: this is the Company number
- d. 1844: this is the discharge date.

Division	Dates	Arrangement	Document References
Chatham	1790–1883	Enlistment	ADM 157/1–139
Chatham	1842–1912	Discharge	ADM 157/1276–1851
Plymouth, Portsmouth, Woolwich	1820	Enlistment	ADM 157/140
Woolwich	1839–1869	Discharge	ADM 157/665–1275
Plymouth	1842–1883	Discharge	ADM 157/141–337
Plymouth	1884–1900	Discharge	ADM 157/1852–1868
Portsmouth	1804–1836	Enlistment	ADM 157/338–352
Portsmouth	1837–1883	Discharge	ADM 157/353–615
Portsmouth	1884–1904	Discharge	ADM 157/1869–2057
Portsmouth	1904–1923	Discharge	ADM 157/2471–2847
Portsmouth R M Artillery	1834–1835	Indexed	ADM 157/664
R M Artillery	1861–1918	Enlistment	ADM 157/2848–2849
R M Artillery	1899–1925	Discharge	ADM 157/3247–3269
R M Artillery	1860–1923	Discharge	ADM 157/2850–3246
Miscellaneous Short Attestations	1869–1883	Enlistment	ADM 157/616–659
Miscellaneous Short Attestations	1884–1901	Discharge	ADM 157/660–663
Ranks Without Official Numbers	1884–1925	Enlistment	ADM 157/2058–2303
R M Engineers	1914–1919	Discharge	ADM 157/3467–3625
RM Labour Corps (Chatham)	1915–1919	Enlistment	ADM 157/3459–3466
RM Labour Corps (Deal)	1914–1922	Enlistment	ADM 157/3270–3458

Each Division also kept its own discharge books:

- Woolwich ADM 81 7 (includes an alphabetical list of warrant officers and ratings who had entered for limited service, dated 1812 ADM 6/407);
- Chatham ADM 183 7;
- Plymouth ADM 184 7;
- Portsmouth ADM 185 7.

The description books, c. 1750–1940 (ADM 158 7), consist of several different, though related, types of register arranged by division, date of enlistment and then by first letter of surname. They provide age on enlistment, parish of birth and a brief physical description. They do not give details of service.

The service registers cover 1842–1936 but are subject to a 75-year closure rule: they are in ADM 159Ⓔ, arranged by service number. In 1884, a system of divisional numbers was introduced, with each man having a unique number in his Division: it was applied retrospectively, so each Division has a different starting date for the numbers. Men who had served with the Woolwich Division (disbanded in 1869) were numbered among their new Division from 1869. If you do not have the service number, order the index for your man's surname in ADM 313 Ⓣ. This should give you the service number. If you have not been able to identify his Division, you will have to order each piece within ADM 159 that contains his service number, regardless of Division. However, the information contained in these registers is worth looking at for date and place of birth, trade, religion, date and place of enlistment, physical description, a full record of service and comments on conduct, promotions, etc. The registers so far available cover some men who served up to the Second World War.

For records of service of men enlisted after 1925, write to the address given in 62 under Ministry of Defence: Royal Marines.

Registers of Service for the Royal Marines Band, 1903–1918, are in ADM 159/103–112. Those for the Medical Unit, 1914–1918, are in ADM 159/209–210.

29.5 Royal Marines: records of families

Each division of the Royal Marines kept its own registers of births, marriages and deaths, of children and wives borne on the strength – that is, entitled to some form of maintenance out of division funds. These registers give the Marine's rank and some information on posting from the Division to a ship or station under the heading 'disposal'.

Chatham	1830–1913	ADM 183/114–120
Portsmouth (marriages only)	1869–1881	ADM 185/69
Plymouth	1862–1920	ADM 184/43–54
Woolwich (marriages only)	1822–1869	ADM 81/23–25
Royal Marine Artillery	1810–1853 1866–1921	ADM 193 ADM 6/437

29.6 Royal Marines: casualty and pension records

Marines casualties from 1893–1956 are listed alphabetically in ADM 242/7–10 Ⓣ, giving name, rank, number, ship's name, date and place of birth, cause of death, where buried and next of kin. Try also the Commonwealth War Graves Commission (see 26.1.3). There are also many registers of killed and wounded in ADM 104 Ⓣ, 1854–1941, although the later ones are closed for 75 years. For more information on other possible sources, see Thomas's

Records of the Royal Marines or the research guides at **www.national archives.gov.uk**.

Pension records for the Royal Marines and their families are fairly extensive, but in general the records are the same as those for Naval pensions: the Royal Hospital Greenwich was founded to aid both the Navy and the Marines. For more details, see 28.4.5. There are two alphabetical registers of Marine officers receiving Greenwich pensions, 1862–1908, which give considerable details (ADM 201/22–23).

Pensions to the widows of Marine officers will be found in ADM 196/523 (1712–1831), PMG 16 (1836–1870), PMG 20 (1870–1919) and PMG 72 (1921–1926) – all ⑦. The last series, PMG 72 ⑦, appears to relate to other ranks as well. For pensions to officers' children, 1837–1921, see PMG 18 ⑦. More information on families may perhaps be found in the registers of powers of attorney, 1800–1899 (PMG 51 ⑦).

For details of pensions and other help provided to families by the Royal Greenwich Hospital, which catered for the Marines as well as the Navy, see 28.2.6 and 28.4.5.

29.7 Royal Marines: wills

There is a collection of Royal Marines wills and administrations, 1740–1764, in ADM 96/524. Wills were later deposited in the Navy Pay Office by Royal Marines other ranks, 1786–1909, and are discussed in 28.2.1 and 28.2.2. There is also a register of probates affecting the payment of pensions, 1836–1915, in PMG 50 ⑦.

29.8 Royal Marines: medals

Medal records for the Royal Marines are the same as those for the Navy: see 28.8.4. Many Marines also received Army gallantry medals. For correspondence on good conduct medals and gratuities, 1849–1884, which includes individual service records, see ADM 201/21.

29.9 The Royal Marines: bibliography

J A GOOD, *A Register of Royal Marine Deaths, 1914–19* (Royal Marines Historical Society, 1991)

J A GOOD, *A Register of Royal Marine War Deaths, 1939–1945* (Royal Marines Historical Society, 1991)

A J LOWE (ed.), *Records of the Portsmouth Division of Marines, 1764–1800* (Portsmouth Record Series 7, 1990)

Royal Marines, *The Globe and the Laurel* (1892–)

P C SMITH, *Per Mare Per Terram: A History of the Royal Marines* (St Ives, 1974)

C C STADDEN and others, *Uniform of the Royal Marines* (Romford, 1997)

G THOMAS, *Records of the Royal Marines* (PRO, 1995)

P TOMASELLI, 'Britain's Sea Soldiers', *Family History Monthly* 95 (2003)

P TOMASELLI, 'Naval and Royal Marine Records at the Fleet Air Arm Museum', *Family History Monthly* 102 (2004)

30 The Royal Air Force and earlier air services

30.1　History of the air services

The first air service was the Royal Flying Corps (RFC), created by royal warrant in 1912 to counter the potential threat of German airships. It was composed of the Military and Naval Wings, the Central Flying School and the Royal Aircraft Factory and came under the control of the War Office. A brief biography of those airmen whose service number was between 1 and 1400 (i.e., those men who joined the RFC between 1912 and August 1914) can be found in *A Contemptible Little Flying Corps* by Webb and McInnes. In July 1914, the Naval Wing was detached to become the Royal Naval Air Service (RNAS), controlled by the Admiralty. The services were reunited as the Royal Air Force (RAF) on 1 April 1918 by the amalgamation of the Army's Royal Flying Corps and the Navy's Royal Naval Air Service.

The official histories of both the First and Second World Wars, in the National Archives Library, give accounts of events. Spencer's *Air Force Records for Family Historians* is a specialist guide to the records, to consult for more detail. Research guides at **www.nationalarchives.gov.uk** give advice on medals and on using operational records to track down individuals.

For war dead, see 26.1.3 on the Commonwealth War Graves Commission. The Family Records Centre has indexes to RAF war deaths, 1939–1948, and also to RAF births, marriages and deaths abroad, from 1920: these indexes can also be seen at the National Archives. The actual certificates have to be bought from the General Register Officer at Southport. See 8.8.

The RAF has its own historical website, which is well worth a look, at **www.raf.mod.uk/history**. The RAF Museum at Hendon has planes, photographs, air logbooks and a huge collection of privately deposited officers' records. Its archive includes a card index of every aircraft that flew in the RAF. The Imperial War Museum at Duxford is another place to see early RAF planes. The addresses are given in 62.

30.2 Officers in the RFC, RNAS or RAF

Service records of RFC officers who died or were discharged before 1 April 1918 will be found with the usual run of Army officers' records in WO 339 ③ or WO 374 ③ and are subject to the same warnings that some may not survive or may still be with the Ministry of Defence (see 26.1.5). RFC officers still alive at the creation of the RAF took their records with them, and these will now be found filed in alphabetical order with their later records in AIR 76 ⑦.

Royal Naval Air Service registers of officers' service records from July 1914 to March 1918 are in ADM 273 Ⓕ, with a card index of names at the National Archives. The RNAS registers include confidential reports on the officer's ability, some combat details and brief accident or sickness reports. They should (but don't always) give birth date and next of kin.

Once the RAF was formed, it created its own records of service rather than using those created by the Admiralty or War Office. These new records, mainly for officers discharged before 1920, are in AIR 76 ⑦ in alphabetical order.

The card index to medals awarded for First World War service to members of the RFC and the RAF is searchable online at **www.national archives.gov.uk/documentsonline/**. Campaign medals awarded to the RNAS are in ADM 171 ⑦. Disablement pensions and gratuities for the First World War may be found in PMG 42 ⑦. Pensions paid to the dependants of deceased officers are in PMG 44 ⑦. See also PMG 43 for supplementary payments to officers and dependants.

Service records after the early 1920s (it is difficult to be exact) are still kept by the Ministry of Defence. The officer or next of kin, or someone else with their formal permission, can ask for brief details by writing to the address in 62 under Ministry of Defence: RAF. They also have details about campaign and gallantry medals for the same period, and their file reference can provide a clue to locating recommendations in AIR 2 at the National Archives that would otherwise be very difficult to find.

Officers' careers can also be traced in the *Air Force List*, available at the National Archives. The *Air Force List* starts in 1918: before that you will need to use the *Army List* or *Navy List*. For 1939–1954 the *Confidential Air List* is kept separately (in AIR 10 ⑦). Correspondence with officers, recommendations for awards and promotions, confidential reports and combat reports are found in AIR 1: indexes are available. For records of RAF prisoners of war, see AIR 20/2336, and 31.5.

30.3 Airmen in the RFC, RNAS or RAF

The card index to medals awarded for First World War service to 26,314 members of the RFC and to 26,946 men of the RAF is searchable and viewable online at **www.nationalarchives.gov.uk/documentsonline**. Campaign medals awarded to the RNAS are in ADM 171 ☑. The service records of RNAS other ranks (in ADM 188) are also searchable and viewable online in the same site, as 'Royal Naval Seamen'. They contain information on service up to 31 March 1918. Service records of RFC airmen who were killed or discharged before 1 April 1918 may be found in WO 363 or WO 364 – subject to the usual warnings that many no longer survive because of bomb damage in 1940 (see 26.1.6).

Service records of RAF airmen with a service number up to 329000 are in AIR 79 ☑, arranged in service number order. A quick way to find the service number is to check the medal index online: if it is not there, use the index in AIR 78. The service records usually give date and place of birth, physical description, religion, next of kin, wife and children, date of joining, promotions, units served in, award of medals and date of discharge.

However, if a man within this number range (1–329000) went on to see service in the Second World War, his record will not be in AIR 79 as it is still kept by the Ministry of Defence. Details for these men (and of men whose service number was 329001 or higher) can be obtained by the airman, his next of kin or someone with their formal permission from the address in 62 under Ministry of Defence: RAF.

A muster of all other ranks serving in the RAF on formation can be found in AIR 1/819/204/4/1316 and also at AIR 10/232–237. The muster can provide the man's rate of pay, his trade, the date of his last promotion and whether he was on an open engagement or was serving for the duration of the war only.

Pensions to disabled airmen and gratuities for the First World War may be found in PMG 42 ☑.

30.4 Operational records

Operational records of the RFC during the First World War are in AIR 1, AIR 23, AIR 25 and AIR 27–AIR 29 (all ⑥). Operational records of the RNAS can be found in ADM 1, ADM 116 and ADM 137 ⑥.

Operations Record Books (AIR 24–AIR 29 ⑥) are the diaries of the RAF and do not contain much personal detail, apart from promotions, transfers and awards. Crashes and casualties incurred during operations are recorded here. For those that happened on non-operational flights, apply to the Ministry of Defence, Air Historical Branch (address in 62).

30.5 Women's Auxiliary Air Force

By 1917 the Royal Flying Corps had all-women companies to ease the labour shortage. The Women's Auxiliary Air Force was founded with the RAF on 1

April 1918. Over the next nine months alone 9,000 women were recruited to work as clerks, fitters, drivers, cooks, armourers, radio operators, parachute packers, balloon operators, flight mechanics, instrument mechanics and pigeon women. Women were divided into those who could only work locally (because of domestic responsibilities) and 'mobiles'. In March 1919, 'mobiles' were sent to France and Germany to replace demobilised airmen. Approximately 500 women served abroad between 1919 and 1920. The WAAF finally disbanded on 1 April 1920, only two years after it had been formed. There is a very interesting website at **www.raf.mod.uk/history/wraf.**

Service records for the Women's Auxiliary Air Force officers are not known to survive. Service records for airwomen, 1918–1920, are in AIR 80 [7], [P], [F], in alphabetical order by blocks of names. There is also an index in AIR 78. They give name, age, home address, marital status, details of dependants, appointments and promotions, and whether the woman was mobile or not. These records are likely to be viewable on Documents Online soon.

The service was reformed on 28 June 1939 and renamed the Women's Royal Air Force on 1 Feb 1949. Records from 1939 onwards are still kept by the RAF: write to the address at 62 under Ministry of Defence: RAF.

30.6 Royal Air Force Nursing Service

This service began in January 1919; in 1923 it became Princess Mary's Royal Air Force Nursing Service. Service records remain with the Ministry of Defence (address in 62).

30.7 The Royal Air Force and earlier air services: bibliography

Air Force List (from 1918)

P G COOKSLEY, *The RFC/RNAS handbook 1914–18* (Stroud, 2000)

B E ESCOTT, *Women in Air Force blue: the story of women in the Royal Air Force from 1918 to the present day* (Wellingborough, 1989)

C G JEFFORD, *Observers & navigators, and other non-pilot aircrew in the RFC, RNAS & RAF* (Shrewsbury, 2001)

G PITCHFORK, *Shot Down and in the Drink: RAF and Commonwealth aircrews saved from the sea, 1939–1945* (National Archives, 2005)

G PITCHFORK, *Shot Down and on the Run: RAF and Commonwealth aircrews who got home from behind enemy lines, 1940–1945* (National Archives, 2003)

Q J REYNOLDS, *They fought for the sky: the story of the First War in the air* (1960)

W SPENCER, *Air Force Records for Family Historians* (PRO, 2000)

I TAVENDER, *The Distinguished Flying Medal Register for the Second World War* (Savannah, 2000)

P TOMASELLI, 'The Royal Naval Air Service', *Family History Monthly* 91 (2003)

J V WEBB and I McINNES, *A Contemptible Little Flying Corps* (London, 1989)

D W WRAGG, *Wings over the sea: a history of naval aviation* (Newton Abbot, 1979)

31 Prisoners of war and internees

31.1 Introduction
31.2 Prisoners of war before 1793
31.3 Prisoners of war, 1793–1914
31.4 Prisoners of war and internees, 1914–1919
31.5 British and Commonwealth prisoners of war, 1939–1945
31.6 Merchant seamen prisoners of war, 1939–1945
31.7 Prisoners of war and internees in British hands, 1939–1945
31.8 Prisoners of war, 1950–1953
31.9 Prisoners of war and internees: bibliography

31.1 Introduction

Information on individual prisoners of war and internees is not always easy to find, although a search of the catalogue reveals a vast array of documents. However, before the Second World War most of these files concern administrative or policy matters; individuals may be mentioned, but only as they come to official attention in some way or another. There are no registers of all prisoners or internees, for example. Prisoners of war in British hands for the First and Second World Wars are almost impossible to trace. Given enough time, it should be possible to find something about earlier prisoners and British prisoners.

31.2 Prisoners of war before 1793

These records mainly relate to the American Revolutionary War, and to the wars with France. Other records relating to prisoners of war from these conflicts can also be identified from Andrews, *Guide to the Materials for American History, to 1783, in the Public Record Office of Great Britain*. The few records available relate largely to French or American prisoners in British custody. These include:

- In-Letters of the Admiralty Medical and Prisoners of War Department in ADM 97 ☑;
- Correspondence and Miscellaneous Papers in ADM 105 ☑, which contain the petitions and complaints of prisoners from 1703;
- State Papers Naval in SP 42 ☑.

Lists of American seamen made prisoners of war and removed from the ports to Shrewsbury in the 1770s are in SP 42/57.

Records concerning the exchange of British prisoners can be found in ADM 97 ☑, WO 1/11 and 13 and WO 34/67 and 170. A list of names of both

British and American officers who were prisoners of war was drawn up in 1781 with a view to an exchange. The list gives the name, rank and corps/regiment of British and German officers who were to be exchanged with American officers of the same rank. They can be found in WO 40/2. Reference to this can also be found among Treasury files in T 64/23–24.

31.3 Prisoners of war, 1793–1914

There is a lot of material for the period of the Revolutionary, French and American wars, but it is not easy to access. Very little is indexed and catalogue entries are poor.

For Britons in enemy hands, there are lists and accounts of prisoners of war in France and elsewhere, in ADM 103 ⑦. The agent in charge of each prison transmitted these and recorded, in a numbered sequence, the names, origins and eventual disposal of all the prisoners under his charge. They mainly cover Naval and civilian prisoners.

More information exists for prisoners of war in British hands. French Army prisoners held in the Low Countries, 1793–1796, were the responsibility of the Commissary of Prisoners. There are lists in AO 11/1–4 and in AO 3/875–877 (officers and NCOs only). The letter books of the Commissary for this period are in AO 16/146–148. All other prisoners, and all prisoners from 1796 whatever their service or nationality, were the responsibility of the Admiralty's Sick and Hurt Board, later called the Transport Board. The correspondence of these Boards is in ADM 105/44–66 ⑦. Medical and Prisoners of War Departments In-Letters for this period are in ADM 97/98–131 ⑦. Out-letters are in ADM 98 ⑦, which also includes Out-Letter books of the Transport Board and Victualling Board concerning prisoners of war. Transport Board minutes relating to prisoners are in ADM 99/92–263 Ⓕ (with an index in ADM 99/264–265), and various accounts are in ADM 100/4–5 and ADM 10/14.

The Transport and Sick and Hurt Board's main series of records, the Registers of Prisoners of War, is in ADM 103. These contain many lists of prisoners, usually arranged by nationality or by place of confinement or parole. A search for an individual prisoner will be difficult. The majority of the Registers consist of the General Entry Books kept by the agents in charge of each depot, prison ship or parole town (if you know the relevant place or ship, try a search in ADM 103 by that name to identify particular registers). The agent was in most cases also required to record the circumstances of the prisoners' capture and their eventual disposal.

There is no general index to American prisoners. However, there is an alphabetical list of American prisoners compiled by the University of Virginia, available at the National Archives. This supplements a general alphabetical register of American prisoners compiled in 1813, in ADM 6/417. Paroled prisoners can be found both in ADM 103 (by place of parole) and in the lists of enemy prisoners on parole in Britain, which were sent to the Home Office (HO 28 ⑦).

For the Crimean War from 1853 to 1855, there is some official material relating to Russian prisoners in British hands in the headquarters papers in WO 28/182. The records of the Russian Orthodox Church in London in RG 8/180 include lists of Russian prisoners (in Russian) with correspondence in Russian, English and French relating to the distribution of money to them. Britons captured during the Crimean War are listed in the *London Gazette* (available in the National Archives as ZJ 1 ⑦). These lists are incomplete, arranged by regiment, and usually give officers only.

For the South African or Boer War from 1899 to 1902, there are registers of Boer prisoners, recorded in prisoner number order and arranged by area of confinement (e.g., Natal, Transvaal) in WO 108/303–305 and 368–369. Correspondence about their confinement in Ceylon, St Helena and elsewhere can be found in CO 537/403–409 and 453, with transport details (apparently including lists of people) in MT 23 (search this using 'prisoner' as the keyword). Correspondence concerning Dutch, German and French prisoners is in FO 2/824–826.

Britons captured by the Boers during the South African War are listed in the *London Gazette* (available in the National Archives as ZJ 1 ⑦). These lists are incomplete, arranged by regiment, and usually give officers only.

31.4 Prisoners of war and internees, 1914–1919

The National Archives holds no comprehensive lists of British and Commonwealth prisoners of war. However, the International Red Cross Headquarters in Geneva keeps a list of all known POWs and internees of all nationalities for the First World War. Searches are only made in response to written enquiries and an hourly fee is charged. You can write to the International Council of the Red Cross (address in 62).

During the First World War, both sides set up internment camps to hold enemy aliens – civilians who were believed to be a potential threat and have sympathy with the enemy's war objectives. Internees were treated differently to prisoners of war as they were given privileges inside their camps. Records here cover Britain, Austria–Hungary, the Balkans, Belgium, Egypt, France, Germany, Italy, Netherlands, Russia, Scandinavia, Spain, Switzerland, Turkey, America and Portugal, with reference to prisoners and internees in various other countries as well. These include British dominions and colonies in which there were prisoner camps (in particular Australia, Canada, India and South Africa) or internment issues (for example, in Ceylon, New Zealand, Gibraltar, Malta), but also German colonies in Africa and the Pacific, together with other countries in Europe, the Far East, North and South America, Africa and the Middle East.

In the United Kingdom, the Aliens Registration Act was introduced on 5 August 1914. This and subsequent legislation required that enemy aliens of military age should be interned and others repatriated. The legislation required thousands of enemy aliens who were living and working in the United Kingdom to register with their local police station. People had to supply personal and employment details. From 28 November, it was decreed that everybody (British or foreign) must register with the police when moving into hotels or boarding houses. Internment camps (in addition to prisoner of war camps) began to be set up across the United Kingdom in a variety of locations, including an old wagon factory at Lancaster, the racecourse at Newbury and in London at Alexandra Palace and Islington. Other makeshift camps, such as those at York and Frimley, were set up and internment ships were moored at Southend, Portsmouth and elsewhere.

A number of these were unsatisfactory, and the bulk of the internees came to be housed on the Isle of Man, at Knockaloe and a smaller camp at Douglas. The alien civilian camp at Knockaloe, near Peel, was originally intended to house 5,000 internees, but by the end of the War some 24,500 were held there (effectively over half of the island's population). They were in wooden huts covering 22 acres, split into 23 compounds, divided between four camps, each of which had its own hospital, theatre, etc. The wealthier men were allowed to live together in a special camp at Lofthouse Park near Wakefield in Yorkshire and in 'privileged' sections of other camps (for this they paid the Government a weekly sum, and in addition they were able to add many improvements to the official quarters provided). Officers were held at Donington Hall, a former stately home near Derby. (Two specimen lists of German subjects interned as POWs in 1915–1916 survive in WO 900/45–46. The list is divided into Army, Naval and civilian prisoners, and gives the regiment, ship or home address of each prisoner.)

In Germany, on 5 November 1914, all British males within Germany became subject to internment. These individuals came from all aspects of society and included merchant seamen, individuals from the professional classes and business community, as well as academics, students, sportsmen and even travellers and holidaymakers. A racecourse near Berlin named Ruhleben became the principal prison camp for the men, who were then interned *en masse*. During the First World War, the camp at Ruhleben had over 4,000 internees.

With no systematic records surviving here, by far the easiest place to start is with the Prisoners of War and Aliens Department of the Foreign Office in FO 383, which was responsible for the treatment of both British and enemy prisoners, including interned civilians. FO 383 [2][5][6] has recently been catalogued to display the contents more fully (see the articles by Stembridge, who has supplied much of the information given here). Each document consists of a number of files relating to different subjects, which have been catalogued in detail as they first appear; but a related file appearing later on in the document will have to be traced by using the correspondence numbers in the 'Last Paper' and 'Next Paper' boxes given on that file's cover. Some of these 'docket numbers' have been included in some descriptions. (If you want to order copies without checking the document, you will need to include an instruction on your order form to pick up any related papers indicated by the 'Last Paper' and 'Next Paper' boxes.)

Sample entries can give an idea of the riches contained:

- Hugh Jefferson Stokes, British subject interned at Ruhleben: representations made by his father, Edward D Stokes of Ealing, regarding his son's wife and infant children reported to be at Nijmegen, Netherlands, in great financial distress (in FO 383/25);
- Alois Brunnthaler, Austrian subject, interned at Knockaloe, Isle of Man: claims compensation for loss of personal effects; refused (in FO 383/117);
- Jaya Krishna Rau, British subject in Vienna, wishes to return to India, but meanwhile requests increase of funds transmitted monthly through the United States embassy (in FO 383/117);
- Mrs A Gauge of Biggleswade, Bedfordshire, enquires about sending supplies to her son, Private S Gauge, 10th Hampshire Regiment, prisoner in Bulgaria; and on behalf of Mrs Greenhood of Aspley Guise, Bedfordshire, about her son, Private C A Greenhood, 10th Hampshire Regiment (in FO 383/131);
- Pastor Richard Handmann, Georg Wilhelm Wagener and other German missionaries taken from the steamship *Golconda* at Tilbury, Essex, and interned at Alexandra Palace. All repatriated in June 1916 with exception of Geppart and Farrenkopf (in FO 383/144).

The previous means of access to the records of the Prisoners of War and Aliens Department was by the card index to Foreign Office correspondence at the National Archives. This may still be worth searching for references to correspondence that no longer exists: all Foreign Office material tends to have been heavily weeded.

Home Office records dealing primarily with policy relating to internees and internment camps can be found in HO 45 and HO 144: try a search on 'aliens' restricted to 1914–1919. There is a classified list of interned enemy aliens in HO 144/11720/364868; further lists of male enemy aliens aged 45 and upwards, submitted to the Secretary of State by commandants of internment camps, are included in HO 45/11522/287235. Other material on enemy internees is in MEPO 2/1796–1799.

For other ways to trace **prisoners of war** (rather than internees), ask at the National Archives for the guide by Bowgen, 'Researching British and Commonwealth Prisoners of War: World War One'. This will give you

- the National Archives sources most likely to provide personal details;
- copies of name indexes of British, Irish, Colonial and Indian POWs extracted from WO 161/101;
- references to lists of names of Military and Merchant Navy POWs;

- a list of POW camps in Germany and Enemy territory;
- an indexed map of the main POW camps in Germany and Austria.

The primary source for personal information is the collection of narrative reports made by officers, medical officers, other ranks and occasionally merchant seamen and civilians. These have been indexed online in the *Behind the Wire* database at **www.1914–1918.net/POW/index.php**. They are held in wo 161/95–100 Ⓕ. There is an index in wo 161/101, and some of the references from this index refer to reports which were sent on to the Foreign Office and are now in FO 383, not in wo 161/95–100. The reports can include details of unit, home address, when and where captured, wounds suffered, transfer between camps, comments on treatment and conditions and escape attempts. Some other reports may be found with the officers' service records (see 26.1.5, 28.3.6, 29.2 or 30.2). If you are looking for an officer, ask in the National Archives Library for *List of British Officers taken prisoner in the various Theatres of War between August 1914 and November 1918*. The military agents Cox and Co. compiled this in 1919. It has a name index at the back, and is arranged by theatre of war and then by regiment. The list covers the British Army, Royal Air Force, Royal Naval Air Service and Royal Naval Division, and gives the name and rank of the officer, the date when he went missing, where and when he was interned (but not the specific camp/s) and the date of his repatriation. If the officer died while a prisoner, the list gives the date and place of death.

There are no known official sources to help discover whether an ordinary serviceman or NCO was made a POW. It should be recorded on their service record, usually giving only dates of capture and release (see 26.1.6, 28.4.3, 29.4 or 30.3). You may like to read the personal accounts of the last-surviving British prisoners of war in *Prisoners of the Kaiser* by Van Emden for an understanding of their experience.

Other Merchant Navy POW records (for both sides of the conflict) can be found in MT 9 (use 'code 106' as the search term). In addition, for Royal Navy, RNAS, RNR and RNVR POWs try searching the ADM 12 Ⓩ registers of correspondence. For the RAF, RFC and RNAS try the Air History Branch indexes at the National Archives, which refer to AIR 1 Ⓕ.

Records concerning POW camps can also be found. The most comprehensive are the reports held in wo 161/95–100 Ⓕ, which can be accessed by using the place and subject indexes in wo 161/101. Individual camps can also be searched for by name in FO 383 ④⑥. Further records relating to POW camps, administration and policy are found in CO 693 Ⓕ, with related registers in CO 754 Ⓩ and CO 755 Ⓩ. Records of the Committee on the Treatment by the Enemy of British POWs (1914–1919) are in HO 45/10763/270829 and HO 45/10764/270829, with additional policy and administrative material in wo 162/341 (Prisoner of War Information Bureau) and wo 106/45 (Prisoner of War Directorate).

Prisoners of war and internees in British hands were guarded by special units: the easiest way to find men in these is to search the campaign medal index at **www.nationalarchives.gov.uk/documentsonline/** by the keyword 'prisoner'. The same search in the catalogue of wo 95 will bring up 52 war diaries of prisoner-of-war camps and hospitals, many scattered across the various theatres of war, particularly in the Eastern Mediterranean.

For war crimes, see ts 26 ⑦.

31.5 British and Commonwealth prisoners of war, 1939–1945

There are no central lists of British servicemen who were prisoners of war. However, the National Archives Library holds alphabetical registers of British and Dominion POWs of all ranks who were held in Germany and German occupied territories, available on the shelves at the National Archives. They give details of name, rank and service/Army number as well as regiment/corps, prisoner of war number and camp location details. The lists are corrected generally up to 30 March 1945 and are in three volumes:

- *Prisoners of War: British Army 1939–1945;*
- *Prisoners of War: Naval and Air Forces of Great Britain and the Empire 1939–1945;*
- *Prisoners of War: Armies and other Land Forces of the British Empire 1939–1945.*

The books were compiled both from the lists of POWs in wo 392 ⑦ and other sources so that they are more comprehensive than wo 392.

The Red Cross in Geneva keeps an incomplete list of POWs and internees of all nationalities for the Second World War: searches are only made in response to written enquiries, and an hourly fee is charged. Write to the International Council of the Red Cross (address in 62).

There were an estimated 192,000 British prisoners of war in enemy hands during the Second World War: 142,000 held by Germany and 50,000 held by Japan. Searching for details of individuals can be difficult. There are three main sources, which are relatively easy to use:

- For those who survived imprisonment, try the liberation questionnaires in wo 344 ⑦ made during repatriation;
- For those who escaped or evaded imprisonment (very few in the Far East) try the escape and evasion reports in wo 208 Ⓕ and elsewhere;
- For prisoners of the Japanese, try also the index cards and registers in wo 345 Ⓕ and wo 367 ⑦.

These are each described in more detail below.

The 140,000 **liberation questionnaires** in wo 344 were completed by mainly British and Commonwealth prisoners of war of all ranks and services, plus a few other Allied nationals and merchant seamen. While the plans to question all liberated POWs never materialised, these records nevertheless represent a large percentage of those still in captivity in 1945 (about 172,000 British servicemen survived captivity). Watch out when using WO 344: the records are arranged in alphabetical order but the catalogue only gives them by blocks of names. You cannot be sure that a questionnaire will exist for your POW, as we know that not all completed one. You can search WO 344 by using the first couple of letters of the surname as a wildcard search term (such as Br*): remember there are two separate sequences, one for Germany (1–359) and one for Japan (361–410), so check you have the right reference. If you wish to do this from a distance, try ordering a copy once you have the reference: the copying process allows a little time for identification within the document, so you can find out quite cheaply whether a report exists for your person or not. There is one oddment: questionnaires described as 'Miscellaneous A–W including Army, Navy, RAF, air personnel other than RAF, Marines, Merchant Navy and Civilians' are in WO 344/360.

Although the questionnaires for those held by Germany or Japan differ in appearance and format, the information they might provide is very similar. As well as giving personal details, name, rank, number, unit and home address, these records can include date and place of capture; main camps and hospitals in which imprisoned and work camps; serious illnesses suffered while a prisoner and medical treatment received; interrogation after capture; escape attempts; sabotage; suspicion of collaboration by other Allied prisoners; and details of bad treatment by the enemy to themselves or others. In addition, individuals were given the opportunity to bring to official notice any other matters, such as courageous acts by fellow prisoners or details of civilians who assisted them during escape and evasion activities. Consequently, additional documentation is sometimes attached. Both questionnaires also enquire if the prisoner had witnessed or had any information about war crimes. If so, they were required to complete a form 'Q'. These forms contained information about behaviour of enemy captors that could constitute illegal acts.

The **escape and evasion reports** in WO 208 🖹, made by officers and men of the armed forces and the Merchant Navy, are invaluable sources of personal information. They usually include service details, when and where captured, home address and civilian occupation. For RAF personnel they also give details of where based, type of aircraft, when, where and how the aircraft was lost and the presumed fate of the rest of the aircrew. Every report has a narrative, of variable length, which describes an individual's experiences as an escaper, evader or prisoner of war. In addition, many include appendices that can provide the names and addresses of civilian helpers, nature of help given and relevant dates; details of the escape method and allied personnel who assisted in an escape; details of the usefulness of officially provided escape aids, which ones were used, and suggested improvements and/or additions. The reports mostly relate to the

European, Mediterranean or North Africa theatres of war. There were very few successful escapes and evasions in South-east Asia.

These reports are in three sequences in WO 208 ⒡ and are accessed by a card index. Make sure you check the user's guide by the card index, as it explains the various references on the cards. Additional escape and evasion reports are also in WO 208 and AIR 40/1545–1552, AIR 14/353–361 and AIR 14/461–465, but are not included in the index.

For **prisoners of war and internees held by the Japanese**, try first the index cards in WO 345 ⒡ and the registers in WO 367 ⑦. The index cards are some 56,000 pre-printed cards in English and/or Japanese that appear to have been compiled by a central Japanese authority, with some degree of Allied assistance. Despite the title of the series, they seem to be prisoners of war rather than internees.

The three registers in WO 367 record the names of some 13,500 allied prisoners of war and civilian internees of British and other nationalities. They give minimal information about each prisoner, apparently compiled for the Japanese camp administration, although the majority of the information is given in English. Further details and an index by nationality are held with the paper list of WO 367. The registers refer to camps numbered 1–4, the identity of which has recently been established in the work of John Brown as

- No. 1 camp – Changi;
- No. 2 camp – Serangoon Road Camp;
- No. 3 camp – River Valley Road Camp;
- No. 4 camp – Adam Road Camp.

John Brown has also compiled a name index to these registers, the *Malay Volunteers Nominal Roll*, which he has deposited at the National Archives Library and the Imperial War Museum on CD-Rom.

If you are unlucky in these sources, you need to use the Research Guides available at **www.nationalarchives.gov.uk**. For other records about prisoners of war and civilian internees, try FO 916 ⑥ and CO 980 ⑥ (as well as FO 371 ⒡). You should find general files relating to reports on internment camps and a number of lists of British (and enemy) internees, some arranged by location, name and number of camp.

31.6 Merchant seamen prisoners of war, 1939–1945

There is an extensive collection of records in BT 373 ①⑥, giving the circumstances of capture and the eventual fate of UK and Allied Asian merchant seamen captured during the Second World War. Details of ships captured or lost due to enemy action are in BT 373/1–359, searchable by ship's name. These contain miscellaneous papers relating to the circumstances of loss or capture. There are document pouches for individual seamen in BT 373/360–3716: these are searchable by surname and sometimes by forename as well. Each pouch typically contains the name of the ship lost; a card or form containing circumstantial details (including POW camp, POW number, surname, forenames, date of birth, place of birth, Discharge A number, rank or rating, name of ship, ship's official number, date of loss of ship, next of kin, relationship, address and country of detention); Prisoner of War Branch PC 96 (postal censorship) forms vetting messages to and from family and friends; Envelope RS3, which usually has notes of release from captivity/ repatriation written on it where appropriate, containing many of the details from the POW card and additionally a National Service AF Account Number. Some of the pouches may also contain personal letters to and from prisoners of war.

Collective alphabetical listings of prisoners of war (as opposed to individual pouches) are contained in BT 373/3717–3722. For details of prisoners of war who died in captivity in Japan and Germany, try BT 373/3720–1.

31.7 Prisoners of war and internees in British hands, 1939–1945

Individual prisoners of war in British hands are very difficult to trace, if not impossible. The best sources for Axis prisoners are local archives, libraries, newspapers and local history groups. See the detailed Research Guide on this subject available at **www.nationalarchives.gov.uk**.

We do hold records about the internment of aliens during the Second World War. Fears of invasion led to a general feeling of hostility towards all 'enemy' aliens. Internees primarily consisted of enemy aliens, but other aliens were also interned, including refugees who had fled Nazi Germany to escape persecution.

Internment began immediately before the outbreak of war in 1939 with a small number of Germans considered to be potentially hostile; tribunals were set up to decide who should be detained and who should be allowed to remain at liberty. Internment of German and Austrian nationals was later expanded dramatically from 12 May 1940 onwards; Italian nationals were interned after Italy's declaration of war on 10 June 1940. By mid-1940, 8,000 internees had been gathered into camps to be deported to the colonies and the dominions. However, this policy was later reversed and from autumn 1940 to the end of 1942 most internees were released, with many of the remainder being repatriated from 1943 onwards. It was not until late 1945 that the last internees were finally released.

The main records are indexes that cover both aliens considered for internment but still at liberty in the UK and those actually interned. The index cards are in HO 396, and cover 1939 to 1947. The index cards are in several sub-series:

- Internees at liberty in UK: searchable by name at **www.movinghere.org.uk** with free images. These will be picked up (perhaps more easily) on a site search of **www.nationalarchives.gov.uk**;

- Canada internees ☷;
- Australia internees ☷;
- German internees released in UK ☷;
- Italian internees released in UK ☷;
- Dead index (wives of Germans, etc.) ☷;
- Germans interned in UK ☷;
- Italians interned in UK ☷.

The cards are in alphabetical order within each sub-series and are now seen on microfilm. They are either the original slips, giving personal details on the front and sometimes details of the individual's case on the reverse (for those interned this information is closed for 85 years) or copy slips within the sets, particularly those listing internees shipped out to Canada or Australia, which give name, date of birth, reference and the name of the internee ships with dates of embarkation. Individual internees may have more than one card. For example, if one person was interned in the UK, shipped to Canada, released from internment and returned to this country, there will be cards in several different pieces.

Only a very small sample of personal case files of internees survives, in HO 214 ②. The files were created whenever the Home Office became involved in a personal case for whatever reason. Aliens' personal files, 1934–1948, in HO 405 ① also include internment papers: see 19.6.

Many internees were sent to other parts of the British Empire; passenger lists will be in BT 26 (see 17.2). Many ships carrying internees were destroyed at sea by enemy torpedoes: you should be able to find survivors' reports of lost vessels searching ADM using the ship's name. Similarly, official inquiries into such losses may be found in CAB 66. The sinking of the SS *Arandora Star* (with the loss of 800 internees) by a German U-boat in July 1940 led to protests about the internment policy, which changed in 1942 to internment of *enemy* aliens in camps in Britain only.

Internment camp records can be found in HO 215 ⑤. These are arranged by name of internment camp, but can include lists of internees, giving name, date of birth and (if applicable) date of release. This series also contains general files relating to internment, conditions in camps, visits to camps, classification and segregation of internees and the movement of internees abroad. During the Second World War, Home Office records dealing primarily with policy relating to internees and internment camps can be found in HO 45 and HO 144: try a search on 'aliens' restricted to 1939–1945. HO 213 also contains a selection of files relating to internment camps: you can find these by searching on 'internm* OR interne*'.

References to individual internees and internment camps may be found in FO 371 Ⓔ but before ordering any documents you need to convert the old Foreign Office reference recorded in the printed index to a modern reference: guidance is available on how to do so. Other Foreign Office records on enemy aliens interned by the British are in FO 916 ☷. The series includes general files relating to reports on internment camps and a number of lists of alien internees, arranged by location, name and number of camp.

31.8 Prisoners of war, 1950–1953

There are lists of British and Commonwealth servicemen who were known or believed to be prisoners of war in Korea. Men captured between January 1951 and July 1953 are listed in WO 208/3999. For a list of Commonwealth prisoners of war, compiled in January 1954, see WO 308/54. Correspondence with returned Korean War POWs, and on personnel missing or presumed dead, is in WO 162/208–264 ⑦ (in alphabetical order), WO 32/19273 and DO 35/5853–5863 ⑦.

31.9 Prisoners of war and internees: bibliography
Unpublished works
A BOWGEN, 'Researching British & Commonwealth Prisoners of War: World War One' (2000: available at the National Archives Research Enquiries Desk)

A BOWGEN, 'British Prisoners of War, World War Two' (available at the National Archives Research Enquiries Desk)

Published works
C M ANDREWS, *Guide to the Materials for American History, to 1783, in the Public Record Office of Great Britain* 2 vols (Washington D.C. 1912–1914)

A BOWGEN, 'British army POWs of the First World War', *Ancestors* 6 (2002)

A CRAWLEY, *Escape from Germany* (Stationery Office, 2001)

I DEAR, *Escape & Evasion* (Cassell, 1997)

M R D FOOT and J M LANGLEY, *MI 9: Escape and Evasion 1939–1945* (London, 1979)

O HOARE, *Camp 020: MI 5 and the Nazi Spies: the official history of MI 5's wartime interrogation* (PRO, 2000)

B MACARTHUR, *Surviving The Sword* (Time Warner, 2005)

S P MACKENZIE, *The Colditz Myth* (Oxford, 2004)

B MOORE and K FEDOROWICH, eds, *Prisoners of War and their Captors in World War II* (Berg, 1996)

A NEAVE, *Saturday at MI 9* (London, 1969)

J NICHOL and T RENNELL, *The Last Escape* (London, 2002)

Prisoners of War: Armies and other Land Forces of the British Empire 1939–1945 (Polstead, 1990)

Prisoners of War: British Army 1939–1945 (Polstead, 1990)

Prisoners of War: Naval and Air Forces of Great Britain and the Empire 1939–1945 (Polstead, 1990)

P STEMBRIDGE, 'First World War prisoners see the light' [cataloguing of FO 383], *Ancestors* 35 (2005)

P STEMBRIDGE, 'FO 383 Cataloguing Project', *Prophile*, vol. 16 no 1, April 2005

R VAN EMDEN, *Prisoners of the Kaiser: The Last POWs of the Great War* (Barnsley, 2000)

32 Preventive services and the Coastguard

32.1   Preventive services

During the eighteenth century, three armed preventive services were created for the prevention of smuggling goods in and out of the country to avoid paying customs duty. These were the Revenue Cruisers, the Riding Officers (both dating from 1698) and the Preventive Water Guard, set up in 1809. These three services were part of the Customs, although from 1816 the Admiralty appointed the officers and men of the Revenue Cruisers, and the Riding Officers were often appointed from the Army. The Riding Officers operated in Kent and Sussex. The Revenue Cruisers were largely confined to the Kent, Sussex and East Anglian coasts and the Thames estuary until the end of the eighteenth century, when they then covered the English and Welsh coasts. Scotland had its own fleet.

Confusingly, the Board of Excise also had its own Revenue Cruisers and its own officers called Riding Officers. These covered the entire country, not just the coasts of Kent and Sussex, and were concerned with the collection and evasion of excise duty (a tax on goods made within the country, not imported).

32.2   Preventive forces: service records

For information relating to the (Customs) Riding Officers and the Preventive Water Guard, try the records of the Board of Customs (see 34.2). For the (Excise) Riding Officers and (Excise) Revenue Cruisers, try the Excise records (see 34.2 again). For the Coastal Blockade, try the Admiralty records (see 28). For the Revenue Cruisers, try both the Admiralty and the Customs records.

A good place to start may be with the published reports made to

Parliament about the operation of the various preventive services. Ask in the National Archives' Library about access details – they vary from online to CD-Rom and microfiche. The reports can include information such as name, age, place of birth, date of appointment, etc. Examples include:

- *A Return of Officers and Men appointed to the Preventive Boat Service between November 1816 and March 1819* (House of Commons Sessional Papers 1819 (569) XVII, 77; provides name, age, place of birth, trade, length of time at sea, salary, other allowances or appointments;
- *Names of Commanders of Revenue Cruisers in Scotland 1822–1823* (House of Commons Sessional Papers 1823 (94) XIV, 293;
- *Names of Men Killed on the Kent and Sussex Coasts in Conflicts between the Coast Blockade and Smugglers 1821–1825* (House of Commons Sessional Papers 1825 (95) VXIII, 385.

Later reports on the Coastguard can give details of earlier service in the preventive services. Pension records for *c.*1818–1825 are in CUST 40/28. See 32.5 for more suggestions.

Administration of the Revenue Cruisers was split between the Customs and the Admiralty, with the latter appointing the officers and men after 1816. This system continued when the Revenue Cruisers were merged into the Coastguard in 1822. Officers serving in Revenue Cruisers are given in the *Navy List* from 1814. Admiralty appointments to Revenue Cruisers of lieutenants, masters and boatswains for 1816–1831 are in ADM 6/56; for later appointments see 32.4.

Some pension records for the Preventive Service, 1818–1825, are in CUST 40/28.

32.3 The Coastguard

The Coastguard was formed in 1822 by the amalgamation of the three services described above. In 1831 another preventive service, the Coastal Blockade (set up by the Admiralty in 1816) became part of the Coastguard. The four preventive forces employed nearly 6,700 men at the time of amalgamation.

The Board of Customs had overall control of the Coastguard from 1822 until 1856, when the Admiralty was granted control by the Coastguard Service Act. Most members of the Coastguard were in fact ex-Navy men. After 1856, many people from the Bengal Marine entered the Coastguard after the East India Company gave up its Navy. The Coastguard as run by the Admiralty consisted of three distinct bodies: the Shore Force, the Permanent Cruiser Force and the Guard Ships, Naval ships at major ports acting as headquarters of Coastguard districts. After 1856, the duties of the Coastguard were the defence of the coast, the provision of a reserve for the Navy and the protection of the revenue against evasion by smuggling. Over the next seventy years new responsibilities were added, stressing assistance to shipping, supervision of the foreshore and life-saving. Volunteer Life Saving Apparatus Companies were set up in the 1860s, attached to each Coastguard Station around the coasts of Britain and Ireland (see 32.6).

The First World War showed that the Coastguard could not act as a reserve for the Navy; instead, the Navy and the Marines had to provide manpower for the Coastguard to maintain adequate coastal defences.

In 1925, the Coastguard's duties were split, into a Naval Signalling Force (run by the Admiralty); a Coast Prevention Force (run by the Customs); and a coast watching force (run by the Board of Trade), which was allowed the name of the Coastguard. Its focus was on saving life, the salvage of wrecks and the foreshores. From 1923, responsibility for the Coastguard moved around between departments: see BT 166/39 for a brief history of the Coastguard (up to 1954) and for a report into the efficiency of the Coastguard in 1931. For the Coastguard's own version, see **www.mcga.gov. uk/c4mca/mcga-hm_coastguard.htm.**

Coastguard records for the twentieth century are widely scattered in the National Archives. If you want to do a search in the catalogue, remember to use the variants 'coast guard' and 'coastguard'.

32.4 The Coastguard: service records

Because so many departments have administered the Coastguard, documents relating to the service are widely scattered. There is no single index of names of persons or places. You may have some trouble understanding the abbreviations used in the various Coastguard personnel records; the most common are:

- Boatn = Boatman
- Chf Btman; Chief Boatn; Chief Bn = Chief Boatman
- Chf Officer = Chief Officer
- Comd Bn; Comd Btman = Commissioned Boatman
- Permt Extn = Permanent Extraman
- Tempoy Extn = Temporary Extraman

Nominations		Records	Indexes
1819–1866	Nominations of officers and rating: England	ADM 175/74–80	ADM 175/97–98: 1819–1862 only
1831–1850 1851–1856	Nominations of boatmen	ADM 6/199 ADM 175/101	
1820–1849	Nominations of officers and ratings to stations in Ireland. Indexes give a lot of detail.	ADM 175/74, 81	ADM 175/99–100
1820–1824	Nominations of officers and ratings to stations in Scotland	ADM 175/74	

Service records		Records	Indexes
1886–1947	Coastguard officers: indexes	ADM 175/103–107, 109–110	
1900–1923	Coastguard ratings (apparently including Naval and Marine ratings): service record cards – alphabetical	ADM 175/82A–84B	
	First World War Medals	ADM 171 Ⓕ	
1919–1923	Naval ratings serving with the Coastguard	ADM 175/85–89	ADM 175/108
1919–1923	Royal Marines serving with the Coastguard	ADM 175/90	
1921–1929	Naval Shore Service Signal Service	ADM 175/111	
Discharge			
1858–1868	Index to discharges	–	ADM 175/102
1919	Reduction of Coastguard 1919: registers of discharges, all self-indexed, except 96	ADM 175/91–96	ADM 175/107 for ADM 175/96

The main nineteenth-century 'personnel' records were actually a kind of succession book, recording the officers and ratings serving at the various stations; these can give personal details. They are arranged by place or type of ship, or by name of ship: see the table below for details. To use these books, you need to have some idea of where your man was serving at a particular time; if you don't already have this, you may be able to get it from the records in the table above.

Place 1816–1866		
British Isles	1816–1822	ADM 175/1
England and Wales	1816–1866	ADM 175/2–10
Ireland	1820–1862	ADM 175/13–19
Scotland	1817–1827	ADM 175/3
	1822–1866	ADM 175/22–23
Type of ship 1822–1868		
Cruisers	1822–1863	ADM 175/24–25
Tenders	1858–1868	ADM 175/26
Districts 1858–1879		
English and Welsh districts		
Falmouth	1858–1878	ADM 175/31–33
Harwich	1858–1878	ADM 175/34–35
Hull	1861–1875	ADM 175/36–38
Liverpool	1858–1878	ADM 175/56–60
Milford	1860–1869	ADM 175/62–63
Newhaven	1858–1879; 1886–1894	ADM 175/64–68 and 11
Weymouth	1858–1868	ADM 175/71–73

Irish districts		
Kingstown	1858–1879; 1862–1866	ADM 175/39–45 and 20
Limerick	1867–1876; 1866–1869	ADM 175/52–55 and 21
Lough Swilly	1868–1869	ADM 175/61
Queenstown	1859–1868	ADM 175/69–70 and 20
Scottish districts		
Clyde	1861–1878	ADM 175/27–30
Leith	1858–1878	ADM 175/46–51
South of England	1904–1918	ADM 175/12

There is a specialist website for the Irish Coastguard at **www.coastguards ofyesteryear.org**. It includes lists of men taken from records in ADM 175.

A good place to start may be with the published reports made to Parliament about the operation of the various preventive services. Currently there is a CD-Rom index to these in the National Archives Library, and the reports can be seen on microfiche in the Microfilm Reading Room; however, they are being put online, so ask for further details. See, for example:

- *A Return of Captains and Commanders in the Preventive or Coastguard Service and Revenue Cruisers on 1 July 1833* (House of Commons Sessional Papers 1833 (744) XXIV, 285; provides name, rank, date of appointment, salary and other emoluments);
- *Return of Names, Age, Date of Appointment, Gross Pay and Allowances of all Chief Officers of the Coastguard, with Previous Service* (House of Commons Sessional Papers 1857 XXVII, 253).

Officers serving in Revenue Cruisers (part of the Coastguard since 1822) are given in the *Navy List* from 1814. Admiralty appointments to Revenue Cruisers of lieutenants, masters and boatswains for 1816–1831 are in ADM 6/56 with related letters for 1822–1832 in ADM 2/1127. Quarterly musters of Coastguard and Revenue Cutters, 1824–1857, are in ADM 119 ⑥. For the establishment of the Revenue Cruisers between 1827 and 1829, try CUST 19/52–61 ⑦. Men serving on the Revenue Cruisers can also be traced in the ship's Establishment and Record Books, 1816–1879 (ADM 175 ⑥).

Among the Customs records are other items relating to the Coastguard. Coastguard minute books, 1833–1849, are in CUST 29/40–42; Coastguard statistics are in CUST 38/32–60; and CUST 39/173 contains the salaries and incidents of the Thames Coastguard, 1828–1832.

32.5 The Coastguard: pension records

1855–1935	Civil Coastguard	PMG 23 ⑦
1866–1884	Coastguard	ADM 23/17–21
1870–1928	Greenwich pensions for chief officers of Coastguard	PMG 70 ⑦
1884–1926	Civil Coastguard	ADM 23/71–75 and 194–199

As many of the Coastguard were ex-Navy men, they can be found among Naval pension records. An easy place to look is ADM 29 ②; see 28.

Pensions were normally notified to the Treasury by the Board of Customs (before 1856) or by the Admiralty (after 1856). Annual lists of names of those superannuated appear in the Treasury registers under 'Public Offices' (T 2 ☷). Only rarely do the papers to which they refer survive among the Treasury Board Papers (T 1 ☳). The text of the Customs letters to the Treasury can usually be obtained from the Out-Letter Entry Books: Extra-Departmental (CUST 30 ☷); these often given information about a man's career and his grounds for retirement.

32.6 Coastguard stations and cottages

A series of registers giving information about repairs to Coastguard buildings and the supply and replacement of equipment, 1828–1857, are in ADM 7/7–39 ☷. These volumes are internally arranged by the name of the Coastguard station. There is an 1856 return showing the buildings, cottages and land held by the Coastguard in CUST 147/2A, with a schedule of deeds and leases of Coastguard premises in Great Britain in 1857 in CUST 42/66. Information about cottages erected or leased by the Admiralty between 1856 and 1863 can be obtained from a series of Parliamentary Papers (House of Commons, 1860 XLII 275; 1861 XXXVIII 133 and 1863 XXXV 157), which can be seen on microfiche at the National Archives. Papers about the station at Pett, Sussex, 1870–1923, are in WO 55/270.

Some plans of Coastguard stations, officers' houses, cottages, gun batteries, watchrooms and other structures, 1844–1908, are in WORK 30/3143–3233 ☷. References to Coastguard properties may also be traced in the Treasury Board Papers in T 1 ☳ and the Admiralty and Secretariat Papers in ADM 1 ☳, using registers in T 2 and ADM 12.

32.7 The Coastguard: volunteers

The volunteer Life Saving Apparatus Companies, set up in the 1860s, were composed of sets of up to 25 local men. From 1911 they were eligible for the Rocket Life Saving Apparatus Long Service Medal: a register for 1911–1935 is in BT 167/84. In 1932, the Coast Life Saving Corps of about 6,000 civilians was set up to coordinate the work of the Life Saving Apparatus Companies, plus the Watchers and the Intelligence Section (general volunteers). Annual lists of enrolled volunteers for 1920 to 1937 are in BT 167/87–97. Some were very elderly, having been volunteer life-savers since the 1860s. The records can give name, date of birth, date of enrolment and residence.

32.8 Preventive services and the Coastguard: bibliography

N A M RODGER, *Naval Records for Genealogists* (PRO, 1998)
B SCARLETT, *Shipminder: The Story of Her Majesty's Coastguard* (London, 1971)
G SMITH, *Something to Declare! 1,000 Years of Customs and Excise* (London, 1980)
W WEBB, *Coastguard: An Official History of HM Coastguard* (London, 1976)

33 Police forces

33.1   Introduction

Police forces in the sense that we now understand the term did not exist until the mid-nineteenth century. Before then, the day-to-day work of policing was carried out by a number of local forces such as watchmen, constables, headboroughs and magistrates. The records they created are almost always held in local record offices. The first modern police force in the UK mainland was the Metropolitan Police Force. Although there were some earlier local experiments, provincial police forces did not begin until after the County Police Act of 1839, and no part of England and Wales could be compelled to provide a police force until the County and Borough Act of 1856. Storch's 'The policeman as domestic missionary' and Emsley's *The English Police* tell more about the social context within which the early police forces acted, and why there was so much opposition to them.

33.2   London

The Metropolitan Police Force was created in 1829. Its jurisdiction was initially defined as an area of about seven miles' radius from Charing Cross (excluding the City of London), but this was extended in 1839 to a fifteen mile radius. In 1835 the Bow Street Horse Patrol was incorporated into the force, followed by the Bow Street Foot Patrol and the Thames Police Office in 1839. The Metropolitan Police also had responsibility for the police of the royal dockyards and military stations at Portsmouth, Chatham, Devonport, Pembroke, Rosyth and Woolwich from 1860 to 1934 (see the article by Jephcote).

Some records of the Bow Street Horse Patrol are included in MEPO 2/25. An unindexed service register for the Bow Street Foot Patrol, 1821–1829, is in MEPO 4/508. This gives name, place of residence, age, place of birth, height, marital status, number of children, name of recommender, military service and date of appointment, together with date and reason for discharge.

The City of London Police is quite separate from the Metropolitan Police and its records are not held in the National Archives. Surviving personnel records are good. They include a complete series of registers listing everyone who has ever served in the force together with personal files on about 95 per cent of City of London police officers. For further information, write to the City of London Police Records Office (address in 62).

33.3 The Metropolitan Police Force: service records

From the beginning, the Metropolitan Police Force attempted to recruit young men who were well built, physically fit, literate and of good character. Women were not recruited until 1919. Service records of policewomen do not survive.

Many recruits came from outside the metropolitan area, partly because poor living conditions meant that young Londoners often failed to meet the required standards of health but also because there was prevalent belief that standards of moral fitness were higher in the provinces than in London. There was a high turnover of staff, especially in the very early years of the force.

Full certificates of service records survive only for the period from January 1889 to November 1909 (MEPO 4/361–477). They are arranged by warrant number and give a description of the recruit, date of birth, trade, marital status, residence, number of children, name and place of last employer, previous public service, surgeon's certificate, postings to divisions, dates of promotion or demotion and causes of removal. However, there is a wealth of other material that can be used to reconstruct basic personal information about most Metropolitan Police officers, except that no records survive for the period between May 1857 and February 1869. Annual Police Orders (MEPO 7 [7]) can be used to try to trace officers who were pensioned, promoted, dismissed and transferred during the 1857–1869 gap in the records.

In order to gain maximum information you may need to use more than one type of record. The easiest source to use is the alphabetical register of joiners, covering September 1830–April 1857 and July 1878–1933 (MEPO 4/333–338). This normally gives name, rank, warrant number, division and dates of appointment and removal. The earliest volumes also supply the names and addresses of referees. The registers of leavers, March 1889–January 1947 (MEPO 4/339–351), are also relatively easy as each volume is indexed; they too will give name, rank, warrant number, division and dates of appointment and removal.

Other useful sources, each providing name, rank, warrant number, division and dates of appointment and removal, are:

- alphabetical register, 1829–1836 (HO 65/26), which also gives dates of promotion or demotion;
- numerical registers (arranged by warrant number), September 1829–March 1830 (MEPO 4/31–32), which also give the officer's height and cause of removal from the force;
- attestation ledgers, February 1869–May 1958 (MEPO 4/352–360), which include signatures of recruits and witnesses. There is a section at the back for police stationed at the royal dockyards and military stations, arranged by warrant number;
- returns of death whilst serving, 1829–1889 (MEPO 4/2), with an index (MEPO 4/448), which also gives cause of death.

Annual Police Orders (MEPO 74) can also be used to trace officers who were pensioned, promoted, dismissed and transferred, but they are subject to a 50-year closure.

Papers relating to the service of certain distinguished officers are held in the Special Series of correspondence and papers from the Commissioner's Office (MEPO 3/2883–2921); they are closed for at least 75 years.

Some name indexes are available at the National Archives. The most extensive is a general alphabetical index of former serving officers, mainly based on information in police orders (MEPO 7 ⑦), supplemented by the joiners' ledgers, leavers' ledgers, records of service ledgers and attestation ledgers (MEPO 4). There is also an index to officers who joined the Metropolitan Police, 1880–1889, and an index to pensioners who left the force between 1852 and 1889 (see below).

33.4 The Metropolitan Police Force: pension records

Pension records are an excellent source of family history information. Before the Police Pensions Act was passed in 1890, pensions were awarded on a discretionary basis, but after that date they were granted as of right to officers who had served for 25 years and a modified pension/gratuity was paid to those who were discharged as medically unfit. Pensions and gratuities granted between 1829 and 1859 are mentioned in correspondence and papers (MEPO 5/1–90 Ⓕ).

Records of pensioners who retired or resigned between 1852 and 1932 are in MEPO 21 Ⓕ. They contain detailed personal information, including physical description, date and place of birth, marital status and dates of service. Until 1923 they also give details of promotions and postings, intended place of residence after retirement and names of parents and next of kin. After 1923, they include date and place of marriage, together with a physical description of the wife and her date and place of birth. The records are arranged by pension number (which approximates to a chronological order of resignation: you may get this from the indexed registers of leavers in MEPO 4/339–351 ☷ for 1889–1947). Pension records after 1932 are still held by the Metropolitan Police.

A register of pensions to widows of officers killed on duty, 1840–1858, is in MEPO 4/33.

From 1867 to 1894, pensions to members of the Metropolitan Police who were previously employed in the old Admiralty Dockyard Police are included in PMG 25 ☷.

33.5 The Metropolitan Police Force: other records

Records relating to the duties and administration of the Metropolitan Police officers are held in MEPO 3 ☶ and HO 287 ☶. There is an unindexed register of local constables sworn to act within the Metropolitan Police district, 1839–1876 (MEPO 4/3–5).

The Metropolitan Police District was divided into several divisions each under the charge of a superintendent: maps of the divisions and their changing boundaries can be found in MEPO 15 ☷. Divisional records have not been transferred to the National Archives. Incomplete divisional records are held by the Metropolitan Police Museum, and those of the Thames division are held at the Wapping Police Museum. Neither of these is open to the public, but both will try to answer written enquiries: the addresses are given in 62.

Other information on the early years of the Metropolitan Police can be found in *Hue and Cry* and the *Police Gazette*, 1828–1845 (HO 75). Records of investigations conducted by the Metropolitan Police are mainly to be found in MEPO 2 ☶, MEPO 3 ☶ and MEPO 4 ☶.

For information concerning gallantry awards to Metropolitan Police officers, see below 33.11.

33.6 Other police forces in England and Wales

The Metropolitan Police Force is the only British police force to be directly controlled by the central government (its chief officer, the Commissioner, reports directly to the Home Office). Its records are therefore held in the National Archives. Local government runs other police forces in the UK. Their records are not public records and are not held in the National Archives, although our library does hold some published histories of local forces. To find out more, try **www.policehistorysociety.co.uk**, which has links to police museums and archives and other resources. Full details of a good, but now dated, guide to local police records by Bridgeman and Emsley are given in the bibliography below.

33.7 Ireland

The work of Jim Herlihy has transformed searching for Irish policemen: see his *The Royal Irish Constabulary: a complete alphabetical list of officers and men 1816–1922*, and *The Royal Irish Constabulary: a short history and genealogical guide with a select list of medal awards and casualties*. These are both available at the National Archives. See also Brewer's *The Royal Irish Constabulary: an oral history*.

Until 1836, there were a number of local forces of constables in Ireland. Some information about the careers of superannuated constables can be found in Parliamentary Papers: House of Commons Sessional Papers, 1831–1832, vol. XXVI, p. 465 (list of superannuations of local Irish forces). The list gives name, period of service, amount granted and the nature of the injury that was the cause of the superannuation. Copies of Parliamentary Papers are readily available at the British Library and good local reference libraries; they are also available at the National Archives. In 1836, these local groups were united into a single force known as the Irish Constabulary, which was renamed the Royal Irish Constabulary (RIC) in 1867. The RIC was responsible for the whole of Ireland with the exception of Dublin (policed by the Dublin Metropolitan Police, founded in 1786) and so was disbanded in August 1922 when Ireland gained its independence.

The service records of members of the Royal Irish Constabulary are held in HO 184 Ⓕ. The registers are arranged by service number, but there are separate alphabetical indexes. They normally give name, age, height, religious affiliation, native county, trade, marital status, native county of wife (but not her name), date of appointment, counties in which the man served, length of service and date of retirement or death, but no information about parentage. The same series (HO 184 Ⓕ) also includes separate registers, with integral indexes, for officers and for members of the auxiliary forces (colloquially known as the Black and Tans) who helped suppress unrest in Ireland in the period immediately before independence. Further information about the activities of the Black and Tans is held in WO 35 Ⓩ.

Pensions and allowances granted to officers, men and staff, and to their widows and children, are recorded among the Paymaster General's records (PMG 48 Ⓩ) and usually give the recipient's address. This series also includes registers of deceased pensioners (1877–1918) and of awards of pensions made on the disbandment of the force. Files on pension options at the time of disbandment, arranged by county are held amongst the records of the Colonial Office (CO 904/175–176).

Records relating to appointments to the Irish Revenue Police, 1830–1857, are in CUST 111 Ⓩ. This force, initially under the control of the Board of Excise but from 1849 controlled by the Board of Inland Revenue, was formed to combat the making of malt and distillation of spirit in Ireland in contravention of the Irish (Illicit distillation (Ireland)) Act of 1831.

33.8 South Africa

The National Archives has the original correspondence and registers of in- and out-letters of the Colonial Office relating to the South African Constabulary, 1902–1908 (CO 526 F, CO 639 7 and CO 640 7). A large proportion of this correspondence relates to individuals: however, much of the correspondence that is noted in the registers has in fact been destroyed. The registers have name indexes and can provide some information even if the correspondence noted has not survived.

Although there are no service records, information on individuals can be found. The general orders give appointments, postings, leave on medical grounds and resignations. Some pension returns are there, supplying the name of the widow and place of payment (Britain or South Africa). There are also nominal rolls of various kinds: casualties, men taken on (sometimes supplying the name and address of next of kin), men placed on the married establishment and men taken off the strength. In addition, individuals are sometimes mentioned in correspondence.

There appears to have been some confusion between the South African Constabulary and the various local armed forces: men who joined the Constabulary sometimes served with other forces. See 25.7.4 for local forces.

33.9 Palestine

As explained below (33.10), personnel records of officers serving overseas do not normally survive amongst the records of the British government. However, service records for the Palestine police (and other Palestine government servants, such as dockyard and railway workers) for the period of the British mandate (1920–1948) have been kept in this country for pension purposes. They are split between the British Empire and Commonwealth Museum and St Antony's College Oxford (addresses in 62).

Some records relating to medal entitlement for members of the Palestine police are held by the Foreign and Commonwealth Office, Records and Historical Service Unit (address in 62). These consist of a card index for awards of the Defence Medal, 1939–1945, and rolls for awards of the Defence and General Service medals. The card index entries always include the surname and initial of the first name of the recipient and whether the Defence or General Service Medal was awarded. The entries may also contain further information, such as rank and number, full name and address together with file number and the date of issue of medals, but it is extremely unusual for all these details to be present on a single card. The medal rolls are not arranged in alphabetical order, but by rank and list number, so it can be difficult to identify individual entries. They are also fragile. The Records and Historical Services Unit is not open to the public but is prepared to answer written enquiries concerning the issue of medals. However, you should note that the cards cannot be used to prove whether someone was or was not a member of the police force at any time, and that they will not establish length of service of any individual nor whether there was any entitlement to a pension.

Colonial Office records held in the National Archives sometimes contain information about the activities of the Palestine police. For the most part, however, they relate to political aspects of operations, major disturbances (involving large numbers of deaths or extensive damage to property) and enquiries into corruption. They do not contain material on recruitment, promotion, resignations or routine administrative detail, nor information on day-to-day work. Details of an excellent (although now dated) guide to records relating to Palestine by Jones are given in the bibliography.

33.10 Other colonial police forces

As a general principle, you are unlikely to find personnel records for individuals who served in colonial police forces or information about the day-to-day activities of colonial police forces in the National Archives. Nor is it likely that the Foreign and Commonwealth Office or any other government department holds such information for future transfer to the National Archives. This is because such forces were administered by the government of the colony concerned, rather than directly by the Colonial Office (later Foreign and Commonwealth Office) in London. Any files created would therefore have been in the possession of the relevant colonial government. They would have remained in that colony even after independence because they would have been essential to the day-to-day administration of policing in the newly independent country. However, as noted above for South Africa and Palestine, it is possible that some personal information is included in files that were created by the Colonial Office for other purposes. Such information is likely to be incidental to the main purpose of the file and is unlikely therefore either to be indexed or even indicated in the lists. Conducting a search of this kind would require considerable determination, a lot of time and a willingness to accept that it may not be successful. If you wish to undertake such a search, you would be well advised to consult a good guide to colonial records such as the one by Thurston listed below.

33.11 Police honours and decorations

Although the National Archives does hold Home Office files relating to recommendations for the award of the King's Police Medal from its introduction in 1909, all the information of substance in those files appears in Farmery's *Police Gallantry*. Farmery's book also uses information from the *Police Review* and the *Police Chronicle*, as well as other sources, and often includes a photograph of the individual concerned. It gives direct references to the Home Office files in HO 4 𝔽. Awards were notified in the

London Gazette but entries before 1960 do not include a citation. The National Archives holds copies of the *London Gazette* in series ZJ 1, and there is a copy of Farmery's book in the National Archives Library, but as both are published works copies should be available to you at a good local reference library or via the inter-library loan system.

Records relating to awards of the King's Police Medal to Metropolitan Police officers are:

- 1909–1951 register of Metropolitan Police Officers under consideration for the award, MEPO 22/2;
- 1909–1912 list of awards, MEPO 2/1300.

An indexed register of decorations, honours and awards to Metropolitan Police officers, 1945–1988, is in MEPO 22/1.

33.12 Police forces: bibliography

D ASCOLI, *The Queen's Peace: the origins and development of the Metropolitan Police 1829–1979* (London, 1979)

V BAILEY, *Policing and punishment in nineteenth century Britain* (London, 1981)

J D BREWER, *The Royal Irish Constabulary: an oral history* (Belfast, 1990)

I BRIDGEMAN and C EMSLEY, *A guide to the archives of the police forces of England and Wales* (Police History Society, 1990)

C EMSLEY, *The English Police: apolitical and social history* (Hemel Hempstead, 1991)

J P FARMERY, *Police Gallantry, The King's Police Medal, the King's Police and Fire Service Medal and the Queen's Police Medal for Gallantry 1909–1978* (Periter, Sydney, 1995)

F FEATHER, 'Looking for a Policeman', *Ancestors* 12 (2003)

F FEATHER, 'Tracking Down The Part-time Police', *Ancestors*, 26 (2004)

J HERLIHY, *The Royal Irish Constabulary: a complete alphabetical list of officers and men 1816–1922* (Dublin, 1999)

J HERLIHY, *The Royal Irish Constabulary: a short history and genealogical guide with a select list of medal awards and casualties* (Dublin, 1997)

C J JEFFRIES, *The colonial police* (London, 1952)

J R JEPHCOTE, 'The Metropolitan Police Dockyard Division', *The Peeler*, 1 (2002), pp. 25–27

P JONES, *Britain and Palestine* (Oxford, 1979)

S H PALMER, *Police and Protest in England and Ireland, 1780–1850* (Cambridge, 1988)

S PETROW, *Policing morals: the Metropolitan Police and the Home Office, 1870–1914* (Oxford, 1994)

D PHILIPS and R D STORCH, *Policing Provincial England 1829–1856: The Politics of Reform* (Leicester, 1999)

Police History Society, *Journal of the Police History Society* (1986 onwards)

Police History Society, *Notes for Family Historians* (Police Historical Memo No. 1, 1987)

A SHERMAN, *My ancestor was a policeman: how can I find out more about him?* (Society of Genealogists, 2000)

C STEEDMAN, *Policing the Victorian community: the formation of English provincial police forces, 1856–80* (London, 1984)

R D STORCH, 'The policeman as domestic missionary: urban discipline and popular culture in northern England, 1850–1880', *Journal of Social History* (Summer 1976)

M B TAYLOR and V L WILKINSON, *Badges of office: an illustrated guide to the helmets and badges of the British police 1829 to 1989* (Henley-on-Thames, 1989)

A THURSTON, *Records of the Colonial Office, Dominions Office, Commonwealth Relations Office and Commonwealth Office* (London, 1995)

R WHITMORE, *Victorian and Edwardian Crime and Punishment from Old Photographs* (London, 1978)

34 In the service of the Crown

34.1   Civil servants

Sources for civil servants are not as helpful as might be expected. There are few personal details about civil servants in the public records, so it is quite difficult to trace them. If you know the office or department, it is worth looking through its records to find establishment lists, etc., which may possibly be useful. To discover where to find the establishment records of a particular office, including defunct offices, use a keyword search on the catalogue (staff lists or establishments are useful keywords), limiting it to the relevant code if you can. As an example of what can be found, a search on MAF 39 will give you

- staff lists for 1892–1947, with ranks and salaries;
- registers of service 1854–1929;
- lists of those serving in the armed forces in the two World Wars for the Board of Agriculture (up to 1903), the Board of Agriculture and Fisheries (1903–1919), and the Ministry of Agriculture and Fisheries.

After 1855 entry to the Civil Service was by competition. Even posts as lowly as lady telegraph learners or post sorters had examination as the means of entry. The Civil Service Commission administered examinations for the Army, Navy and India services (civil, forestry, etc.), as well as for the Civil Service. Surviving records are mostly about the qualifying examinations (CSC 8 ⑦ and CSC 10 ⑥), and contain little personal information except clues to a person's educational and social status, and ability. In these terms, the examination results can be quite interesting, especially when matched up with the regulations in CSC 6 ⑥. As well as specifying how the candidates were to be examined, these regulations often give an idea of the nature of their work and of any potential future career. You do need an idea of likely date of entry in order to use the regulations, but they are well worth looking at to set people in context.

Individual application papers have been destroyed, although a selection of those of famous or infamous people can be found in CSC 11 ②. The evidences of age submitted by candidates between 1855 and 1880, often applying for quite lowly jobs, are now kept by the Society of Genealogists (CSC 1). The Society has plans to make their index available online. The proofs of age tend to come from areas where civil registration did not exist at the time of birth – from Scotland and Ireland, for example (see the interesting articles by McDougall and Mynott).

For information about nineteenth-century departments, another possibility is to explore the *Parliamentary Papers*, which contain annual reports from the various branches of the civil service and also include many reports on aspects of its work. These may give you details of the work actually done, as well as establishment lists. From the indexes it is not clear if some of the returns are statistical or if they contain personal information of some kind. If you do find useful lists as a result of exploring the *Parliamentary Papers*, the National Archives would be interested to know so that the information can be shared.

Many senior civil servants are best sought not in the records but in such publications as the *Dictionary of National Biography* or the *British Biographical Archive* (see 2.8). For 1883–1977, try *Kelly's Handbook to the Titled, Landed and Official Classes*, which gives a potted biography (available at the National Archives Library).

A number of official printed sources are available at the National Archives on the postings of senior civil servants, but they do not provide personal information. The main one is the *British Imperial Calendar*, which runs from 1810 to 1972, when it became the *Civil Service Year Book*. From 1852 there is the *Foreign Office List* and from 1862 the *Colonial Office List*. You can also find people through a search in the online *Parliamentary Papers*. Try also Sainty and Collinge's lists of *Office Holders in Modern Britain*, which cover the period 1660–1870. They include officials of the Admiralty, the Board of Trade, the Colonial Office, the Foreign Office, the Home Office, the Navy Board, Royal Commissions of Inquiry, the Secretaries of State, the Treasury and the Lord Chamberlain's and Lord Steward's Departments of the Royal Household. These can be seen online at **www.british–history.ac.uk/**.

Other possible sources outside the particular department's own records may be among the records of the Treasury (e.g., the Departmental Accounts in T 38 ⑦) or the pension records of the Paymaster General (PMG 27 ⑦ and PMG 28 ⑧). In the indexed pension records in PMG 28, you can find details about people who worked in prisons at home and in the colonies, or in the 'public departments' of England, Scotland and Ireland. The later registers generally give name, office held, age on retirement, length of service, salary, pension, cause of retirement, pension start date and a reference to the Treasury letter authorising the pension. Some include annotations, which can provide clues to past or future life – or to death. For instance, the tragic entry for Magnus Fea Ogilvy shows that on his retirement (for ill-health) at the age of 34 in June 1869 he was the chief clerk of the Scottish Board of Lunacy with a salary of £300 a year. He had served for 11 years 8 months and was granted an annual pension of £55. In November 1869 a note was added that payment should be made to his mother, Mrs Martha Ogilvy, while he was detained in James Murray's Lunatic Asylum. A further note recorded his early death, in October 1871 (PMG 28/15).

Pension or injury compensation awards for public servants (in Britain, the colonies and Naval dockyards), 1893–1970, in T 164 ① can also be fruitful:

- Campbell, M., ex-Constable, Royal Irish Constabulary, who emigrated to Canada; resumption of payment of pension after a lapse and authority to pay arrears after a further lapse and proof of his death to legal personal representative 1923–1925. T 164/36/7;
- Bloomburgh, Capt. J.H., Assistant Commandant of Police and Director of Prisons in Somaliland; service in the Camel Constabulary to count for pension from Protectorate Funds 1914–1921. T 164/8/8.

The Royal Bounty could be paid out to public servants and other loyal citizens in cases of particular need or virtue:

- Grant from the Royal Bounty Fund to the mother of Petty Officer Evans, Scott's Antarctic Expedition. 1914 T 1/11608;
- Grant from the Royal Bounty Fund to the sister of Walter Pater; Miss F.M. Sloan, teacher at Roye, France, responsible for the rescue of British soldiers; W.H. Shrubsole, geologist. 1915. T 1/11886.

If you want details of payments of wages and pensions before 1834, try looking in E 403 ⑦ (a huge class with lots of little-used material). Colwell's *Dictionary of Genealogical Sources in the PRO* has two pages of references to appointments and payments, which you may find helpful.

34.2 Customs, Excise and the Inland Revenue

Customs officers were responsible for collecting duty on imports and preventing smuggling, and Excise men were responsible for collecting taxes levied on home products. For indexed directories of customs officers, Excise men and Inland Revenue officials, 1875–1930, see *Ham's Customs Year Book* and *Ham's Inland Revenue Year Book*, in the National Archives Library. Entry was by civil service competition at this period: see 34.1.

Warrants for the appointment of Customs officers, 1714–1797, are in c 208 Ⓕ, indexed by c 202/267–269. The Customs Board minute books, in cust 28 Ⓩ, contain information on the first and later postings of Customs officers, with any praise or censure; they contain no family information, but they can be used to work out the details of a man's career. For Ireland, there are registers of officers' appointments, 1761–1823, in cust 20/154–159.

For the Customs, there are pay lists and staff lists, arranged by place: in general these give little personal information, although very occasionally details of marriage might be given.

1671–1970	Staff lists	CUST 39
1673–1689	Quarterly bills of salaries	PRO 30/32/15–29
1675–1813	Quarterly bills of salaries for England and Wales (and Isle of Man from 1810)	CUST 18
1684–1826	Ireland: salary and establishment books, some	CUST 20
1714–1829	Scotland: quarterly returns of staff	T 43
1716–1847	England: quarterly returns of staff	T 42
1814–1829 1829	Quarterly bills of salaries for England, Wales, Isle of Man. Scotland is for 1829 only. Includes revenue cruisers in UK from late 1827–1829	CUST 19

Some family details can be found in the pension records in cust 39/ 145–151, which cover 1803 to 1922. For Ireland, there are pension records covering 1785–1851 in cust 39/161. The most useful for family historians are, as always, the sections relating to widows' pensions, which give details of any children. Applications for pensions can be found in t 1 Ⓕ, using the indexes in t 2 and t 108. Other family details may be found among the correspondence of the individual ports ('outports' in the Customs service) with the Customs Board: look among the various cust series for these.

Excise men, employed by the Board of Excise, were responsible for collecting the payments for internal indirect taxes on consumable goods. In 1849 the Board of Excise was amalgamated with the Board of Stamps and Taxes to form the Board of Inland Revenue, but in 1909 it went back to join with the Customs instead.

The best research route is via the Excise Entry Papers, 1820–1870 (cust 116 Ⓕ). The Entry Papers usually consist of two letters, folded together. The first is a letter of recommendation, giving the name of the applicant, his age, place of birth, marital status (but no details of his wife), and a character reference. The second letter is from the Excise officer responsible for the applicant's training: this states whether he is proficient in writing, spelling and arithmetic. There is a card index to cust 116/1–36 (about half the series).

Many of the other sources for tracing Excise men are similar to the Customs records. The Excise Board minute books, 1695–1867 (cust 47 Ⓩ) contain information on the first and later postings of Customs officers, with any praise or censure. They contain no family information, but they can be used to work out the details of a man's career. Excise pension records, 1856–1922, can include some family details (CUST 39/157–159). This series also contains some information on senior officers up to 1970. There are pay lists for the English Excise, 1705–1835 (T 44 ⑦) and the Scottish Excise, 1708–1832 (T 45 ⑦). It is always worth investigating such records as extra material can turn up. For example, in 1796 nearly all Excise officers signed local petitions for an increase in their salary. The petitions show the problems they had managing on their pay, give details of the cost of living and point out the difficulties that arose for their families from being frequently moved from post to post (T 44/38).

Records relating to the Irish Excise men, 1824–1833, and the Irish Revenue Police, 1830–1857, are in CUST 110 ⑦ and CUST 111 ⑦. There are a few papers relating to the Irish Revenue Police in CUST 116/41. For later brief details, see *Ham's Customs Year Book* and *Ham's Inland Revenue Year Book*, in the National Archives Library.

For both Excise men and **Inland Revenue** employees, you could try the archive of the Excise (later Inland Revenue) Life Assurance and Benevolent Fund Society, in IR 92 ⑦. This was set up in 1845 to grant annuities to widows and orphans of its members. Its register of members in IR 92/15 (1843–1966) can be used to trace a taxman's career, movement round the country, date of birth and death, even if he left no widow or orphan.

34.3 The Post Office

Post Office administrative and staff records appear in the National Archives catalogue in the POST series. However, they are not actually held by the National Archives and so we cannot supply copies or answer questions about them. Instead you will need to contact the British Postal Museum and Archive (**www.postalheritage.org.uk/**; address in 62). For reading matter, try Farrugia, Browne and Perry.

A general history can be helpful, especially as the Post Office was so important in the paying out of government money locally. It was established in 1635 by Charles I, with a number of main routes from London to and from the provinces. Postmasters on the routes collected and distributed mail and also collected revenue. The General Post Office (set up by statutes of 1656 and 1660) was based in the City of London and composed

- the Inland Office, which handled all internal letters;
- the Foreign Office, which handled all overseas mails;
- the Penny Post Office, which dealt with all locally posted mail for London.

This building and most of its records were destroyed by the Great Fire of London in 1666.

The postal network spread across the country in the eighteenth century, when there was much development of routes and post towns; and regional officers (surveyors) were appointed from 1715. The Post Office expanded enormously in the nineteenth century. Postal rates were subject to a reform that resulted in the introduction of penny postage and the adhesive postage stamp, with a dramatic increase in the amount of mail. From the 1850s on, a network of post offices sprang up over the country, often in response to local petitions. Many petitions about getting a local post office or altering its services can be found by searching POST 14 by place-name: for example:

- POST 14/70 Papers relating to the revision of rural posts under Ludlow, including petition from inhabitants of Orleton for establishment of a sub post office in the parish. Min No 5658 1855–1856;
- POST 14/165 Papers relating to Post Office rejection of an application to restore the recently discontinued Sunday post between Ferry Hill post town and Sedgefield, including petitions from Sedgefield inhabitants in favour of discontinuance, Nov 1855, and in favour of restoration, February 1856. 1856.

Some even tell a story:

- POST 14/129 Papers relating to improvement of the Marazion and Relubbas rural post, under Truro post town, and reprimand of the messenger for improper conduct, including letters of complaint against the messenger from Thomas and William Pascoe of St Hilary vicarage near Relubbas, report by the messenger and petition from the inhabitants of Marazion, Relubbas and Goldsithney in support of the messenger. 1855–1856.

As well as transforming communications, this network of local post offices became the conduit for payments between individuals and the government – and in particular of pensions to the armed forces and later of old age pensions and other benefits.

34.4 Loyal servants of the Crown: confiscation of royalists' lands, 1642–1660

Major confiscation of royalists' lands took place during the Civil War and Interregnum. Royalists' estates were generally forfeited until their owners paid a hefty fine to the Committee for Compounding, when their lands were returned. These papers have been well described in the *Calendars of the Committee for Compounding*. Those who refused or were not permitted to compound had their estates remitted to the treason trustees (or Drury House trustees); these papers have largely disappeared. For an interesting introduction to these records, see Churchill.

Sales of such lands may be traced via the close rolls (C 54: use the calendar in IND 1/17353 and index in IND 1/17354). The names of the new owners were notified to the Committee for Compounding and are given in the *Calendar*. Watch out: some 'owners' were the agents of the real purchasers and others were prospective buyers who failed to proceed further.

There is an entry book of payments by the treasurers in E 164/60; and IND 1/17349 is an abstract of claims of the forfeited estates of delinquents, made in 1652.

For more information on land confiscation during and after the Civil War, see the Research Guide *Crown, Church and Royalist Lands: 1642–1660*, available at **www.nationalarchives.gov.uk**.

34.5 The Royal Household after 1660

The responsibilities of the two departments of the household could be broadly divided between above stairs (Lord Chamberlain's) and below stairs (Lord Steward's). The Royal Archives has a comprehensive card index of people employed in the Lord Chamberlain's and Lord Steward's departments, 1660–1837, and is prepared to answer postal enquiries. The address is in 62. There are published lists by Sainty and Burcholz of *Officials of the Royal Household, 1660–1837*, which you should consult first: they are available at the National Archives and online at **www.british-history.ac.uk/**. Payments relating to salaries and retirement allowances of the royal household and of people on the Civil List, 1834–1929, are in PMG 27, but these are not usually informative. In addition to the household records described below, there are many other sources for royal household servants, such as the accounts in E 101, E 351, LC 9, LS 1, LS 2, LS 3 and T 38.

The **Lord Chamberlain** was broadly responsible for 'upstairs': the chambers, the wardrobe, the office of robes, ceremonies, revels, musicians, chapels, housekeepers, messengers, yeomen of the guard, watermen, physicians, artists, craftsmen and other offices such as Librarian, Latin Secretary, Poet Laureate, Examiner of Plays and Keeper of Lions at the Tower. A good place to start for 1660–1784 is the Glencross Index to many of the establishment records in LC 5 (filed with the LC 5 paper list). This includes the entry books of wills and letters of attorney of household servants, 1750–1784 (LC 5/104–106).

There are records of appointments, 1660–1851 (LC 3/61–71) and 1851–1901 (LC 5/237–241). LC 3/56–60 is a less complete series for various dates between 1685 and 1838. Established servants are named in LC 3/1–23 for various dates between 1641 and 1849. Records of payments, 1516–1782, are in LC 5/11–83. Officers are not usually named in the Salary, Livery and Pension Books, LC 3/37–52 (1667–1857), except pensioners, holders of offices about to be discontinued and widows. LC 3/37 is a book of arrears for 1667 to 1685, where the names of both salaried and waged servants appear. Servants appointed to the Office of Robes appear in the Letter Books of that office, LC 13/1–5 (1830–1901).

Servants' names are given in respect of various payments and appointments in the Warrant Books of the Treasurer of the Chamber, LC 5/11–26 (1660–1800), the Comptroller, LC 5/27–30 (1754–1781), and the Wardrobe, LC 5/31–83 (1516–1782). LC 5/247 concerns officers and servants,

1864–1897. Warrants of Several Sorts, LC 5/248–251 (1820–1866), include some appointments, among payments, general instructions and grants of 'grace and favour' lodgings. Several of these are indexed by the Glencross Index, filed with the LC 5 paper list. There is material relating to servants among the Correspondence Books in LC 1, while servants at various royal palaces appear in the Palaces Ledgers, LC 9/367–374 (1806–1846). Messengers' travelling expenses can be found in LC 10/1–9 (1784–1838).

Records about royal mourning may include lists of people receiving mourning clothes. The servants of royal households other than those of the monarch and consort rarely appear, but the records of funerals in LC 2 may list the households of deceased royal persons. The household of the later Duke of York in 1827 is listed in LC 2/56. Housemaids are named in connection with mourning in the Bill Books for sundries, LC 11/144–5 (1846–1857).

The **Lord Steward** was responsible for 'downstairs' until 1854, when his office was abolished and its functions were taken over by the Master of the Royal Household, whose records are not public but are held by the Royal Archives. The Lord Steward, and later the Master, had responsibility for the kitchen offices (almonry, ewery, bakery, pastry, confectionery, buttery, spicery, poultry, larder, pantry, wine cellar, scullery), the counting house, the wood and coal yards, the gardens and stables and a whole host of other offices, such as keeper and repairer of the buckets. Warrants of appointments, 1660–1820, are in LS 13/246–267. The names of servants, including purveyors, extraordinary staff and the higher officers of the stables, appear in the Cheque Rolls, LS 13/6–13 (James I–George II). Certificate Books of Admission, LS 13/197–204 (1672–1820), include servants of the Steward's department, stables, chapels and the Secretaries of State. Special duties and leaves of absence are recorded in LS 13/205–208 (1766–1811).

In the Middle Ages household servants had been entitled to eat at the board as part of their remuneration. By the seventeenth century the entitlement had often been translated into money payments, or boardwages, the responsibility of the Lord Steward's Department and paid by the Board of Green Cloth. The Kitchen Ledgers, LS 9/60–77 (1660–1729), show these payments to the Steward's staff, staff of the Chamber and Wardrobe, including the Lord Chamberlain himself, the Secretaries of State and chapel staff. Other expenses are recorded, including travelling expenses, pheasant keeping and payments to widows and for burials. Receipt books for wages and allowances, LS 13/154–167 (1761–1816), contain the signatures of many servants for receipt of boardwages and other payments, including 'carpet and cushion money'. These chronological entries are not indexed.

The Creditors also record the payment of boardwages, LS 8 (1641–1854). The Creditors of two minor royal households survive in LS 8/315–316 (Princess Charlotte, 1814–1815) and LS 8/317 (Prince of Hesse-Homburg, 1818). The households of royal princesses and the Duke of Clarence are mentioned in LS 8/237 (1805). LS 13/321 records pensions for members of

Princess Charlotte's household. Stable Creditors, LS 13/210–230 (1761–1781), show Creditors and salary bills for the stables, Chamber and chapels. LS 13/295–299 (1815–1834) records allowances in kind, including 'pitchers and platters'. The names and often the signatures of clerks, housemaids, footmen, laundresses, coachmen and postilions appear among those of servants of all household departments.

Records of the royal gardens, which provided produce for the table, appear in LS 10, LS 11 and LS 12 (1796–1854, all ⑦) but staff, other than head gardeners, are rarely named. Garden labourers at Kew, Windsor and Hampton Court, 1834–1835, are named in LS 11/19–20. Gamekeepers are rarely named in the royal household records, although four gamekeepers at Richmond are named in LC 3/23 (1846–1849). There are detailed records relating to the employment of estate staff, such as gamekeepers, park and gatekeepers and fishermen, at Windsor Great Park in the records of the Crown Estate Office, in CRES 4 (1766–1958).

In 1854 the office of Lord Steward was abolished, and its functions were taken over by the Master of the Royal Household, whose records are not public. Contact the Royal Archives (address in 62) for more information.

34.6 The Royal Household before 1660

There is a break in the series of Royal Household during the Interregnum, but some bills of the 1650s for the Lord Protector's Household have been preserved in series of Bills and Vouchers LC 9/377–390 (1622–1843).

Names of members of the Royal Household are separately listed for 1523–1696 in the E 179 taxation returns (see 52.4). For the lower household answerable to the Lord Steward there is an entry book for 1627–1641, LS 13/251. An index to the members of Charles's household from LC 3/1 (1641) is filed with the paper list of LC 3.

34.7 Royal warrant holders

Today the Royal Household carefully controls the issue of royal warrants to tradesmen. The grant of such a warrant entitles the holder to use the phrase 'By Appointment', and to display the royal coat of arms. For a general view, see Heald's *By Appointment: 150 Years of the Royal Warrant and its Holders*.

From 1900 lists of royal warrant holders are published annually in the *London Gazette* (ZJ 1 ⑦). False claims to possession of royal warrants became a prosecutable offence under the Patents Act, 1883 and the Merchandise Marks Act, 1887. The issue of royal warrants to tradesmen was recorded systematically from the 1830s. Warrants to tradesmen supplying ceremonial items (e.g., peruke makers) and to those supplying more personal items (e.g., combs, perfumes and corset stays) to the office of robes, 1830–1901, are in LC 13/1–5. Warrants to tradesmen supplying such items as furnishings, linens and stationery for Queen Victoria are in LC 5/243–246. Each volume has an internal index. The original bills presented by tradesmen, whether warrant holders or not, are in LC 11 ☐.

Before the 1830s the situation was not so well regulated. Tradesmen's appointments, 1660–1837, appear with the appointment of household servants in LC 3/61–70. Unfortunately, no appointments were recorded between 1767 and 1773. Orders to tradesmen and for court mourning, 1773–1827, are in LC 5/197–199. Suppliers of all kinds of goods are named in the series of Warrant Books LC 5/132–163 (1628–1810). The Accounts (LC 9 ☐) and Bill Books (LC 10 ☐ and LC 11 ☐) may also reveal suppliers of goods to the household between 1600 and 1900. Office of Robes accounts can be found in LC 12 ☐ (1860–1901).

The Lord Steward's Department was responsible for the royal kitchens, cellars, stables and gardens. Suppliers to the department were appointed as purveyors. They were often appointed in the place of a previous purveyor, not to a salary or wage but to enjoy 'rights, profits, privileges and advantages'. Some original warrants to purveyors survive in the series of Original Warrants, LS 13/246–250 (1761–1782). Other tradesmen also received this kind of warrant – such as, cork cutter, wine chest maker and cake maker. Copies of these warrants were recorded in the Warrant Books, LS 13/251–267 (1627–1820). From 1674 they are divided into two series, Royal and Steward's. Warrants to purveyors appear in the Steward's series. Grocery, poultry, wines and wax candles are among the goods to be purveyed. Tradesmen's warrants do not appear to have been recorded in the Lord Steward's records after 1820, but there is a volume showing fees for warrants, which includes fees for purveyor's warrants, from 1838–1850 (LS 13/306).

The Kitchen Ledgers LS 9/60–77 (1660–1729) include the names of suppliers of such items as beer, glasses, bottles and toothpicks among others. Suppliers are also named in the Mensils, LS 9/227–290 (1761–1814), monthly lists of the consumption of foodstuffs and wines, and also of coals and brushes.

Orders to tradesmen are recorded in LS 13/134–153 (1763–1851). The tradesmen are not always named, especially in the earlier period, where often only the trade is given; for example, the Brazier, the China and Glassman. There are orders for food, wine, beer, fuel, lights, china, cutlery, turnery, ironmongery, linen, floor coverings and stationery. Tradesmen's bills appear in the Accounts Books in LS 2 (1761–1854). The Creditors in LS 8 ☐ show amounts owed to various suppliers. LS 8/1–98 (1641–1760) are a single series, while those for 1761–1815 are divided into three series (LS 8/100–270): Kitchen Creditors for foods; Household for foods, fuel, lights and laundry; Incidental for stationery, hardware and cartage. There are also separate Creditors for Hampton Court Palace for 1795–1799. A new system, where quarterly accounts were arranged according to palaces, recorded the names of goods, suppliers and costs and is in LS 8/271–314

(1815–1854). Suppliers to the stables appear in the Stables Creditors, LS 13/210–230 (1761–1781).

34.8 Loyal Servants of the Crown: American Loyalists, 1776–1841

Americans (both black and white) who had suffered hardship as a result of their loyalty to the Crown during the War of Independence were entitled to claim compensation. The American Loyalists' Claims Commission heard claims amounting to nearly £5,000,000, of which £1,420,000 was allowed to be good.

Claimants' papers are in T 79 F, 1777–1841. Papers on American refugees, Loyalists' temporary allowances, pensions lists and accounts are in T 50 F, 1780–1835. Evidence of witnesses, reports and other communicated documents, the examinations and decisions of the commissioners, lists of claims, etc., are in AO 12 F and AO 13 F, 1776–1835. These are published in précis by Coldham in *American Loyalist Claims*.

Much has been published on loyalist claims, including directories of names: to find out more, use the excellent online bibliography at **www. rhs.ac.uk/bibl/**. Two useful sources explaining the records are by Ellis and Palmer. See also Locker, 'Exiles to England'.

34.9 Coronation and Jubilee medals, 1935–1977

Lists of people who received the following medals can be found in the National Archives Library:

- King's Silver Jubilee Medal 1935
- Coronation Medal 1937
- Coronation Medal 1953
- Queen's Silver Jubilee Medal 1977.

For other similar civilian awards, try the *London Gazette* (ZJ 1).

34.10 The National Fire Service and the Air Raid Precaution Service, 1939–1945

We are sometimes asked about records of the National Fire Service and the Air Raid Precaution Service. Unfortunately, no personnel records survive for either service.

34.11 The Women's Land Army 1939–1950

The Women's Land Army was set up in June 1939 to help increase the amount of food grown within Britain. By 1941, its numbers had risen to 20,000 and, at its peak in 1943, over 80,000 women were 'Land Girls'.

Numbers did not rise after that, as women were needed to make aircraft and were encouraged to take up factory work instead. However, women did continue to join and in fact many served until it was disbanded in 1950.

Women joined the Land Army from all backgrounds, a third coming from London and other large cities. About a quarter were employed in milking and general farm work. 6,000 women worked in the Timber Corps, felling trees and running sawmills. The Women's Land Army had a uniform, but as the Land Army was not a military force it was not compulsory. Some women lived in hostels but most lived on individual farms. Conditions were often poor and pay was low. See the books by Mant and Tyrer for more detail.

The original service records of the Women's Land Army have not survived. However, the index cards were used for pension purposes and the National Archives has them on microfiche only in MAF 421/1, for 1939 to 1945 only. The cards give name, change of name on marriage, address, date of birth, previous occupation, WLA service number and dates of service. Some cards have photographs and remarks on suitability for the service. Watch out when selecting your fiche, as only the first five letters of the start and end surnames are given on the fiche label. The final fiche is a compilation of mis-sorted cards.

The original cards are kept by the Imperial War Museum (address in 62): if you want to see them, you must allow at least a week's notice as they are stored off-site. The MAF 421 reference is not needed, as they are kept in alphabetical order.

34.12 In the service of the Crown: bibliography

To find more publications, please use the excellent online bibliography at **www.rhs.ac.uk/bibl/**.

M K BANTON, 'Taking up the white man's burden' [Colonial Service], *Ancestors* 30 (2005)

British Imperial Calendar (London, 1810–1972)

C BROWNE, *Getting the message: the story of the British post office* (Sutton, 1993)

Calendars of the proceedings of the Committee for Compounding with Delinquents, 1643–1660, M A E Greene (5 vols, London, 1889–93)

E CHURCHILL, 'Bridging the Gap; a guide to state papers and other 17th century sources', *Ancestors* 11 (2002/3)

P W COLDham, *American Loyalist Claims* (Baltimore, 1980)

Colonial Office List (London, annually from 1862)

Court & City Register (London, 1742–1808)

R H ELLIS, 'Records of the American Loyalists' Claims in the Public Record Office', *Genealogists' Magazine* vol. XII, 1958

J FARRUGIA, 'The archives of the Post Office', *Prophile*, 7:2 (1996), pp. 12–21

Foreign Office List (London, annually from 1852)

E B FRYDE ed., *Handbook of British Chronology* (London, 3rd edn, 1986) (Lists monarchs, officers of state, archbishops and bishops, dukes, marquesses and earls, in chronological sequence.)

Ham's Customs Year Book (annual: the National Archives library has 1875–1930)

Ham's Inland Revenue Year Book (annual: the National Archives library has 1875–1930)

T HEALD, *By Appointment: 150 years of the Royal Warrant and its Holders* (London, 1989)

Kelly's Handbook to the Titled, Landed and Official Classes (annual: the National Archives Library has 1883–1977)

B LOCKER, 'Exiles to England: The War of Independence and the American Loyalists', *Family History Monthly* 52 (2000)

J MANT, *All Muck, No Medals: landgirls by landgirls* (Lewes, 1994)

E McDOUGALL and D MYNOTT, 'A Man of a Certain Age: the strange story of Walter Bourke', *Ancestors* 22 (2004)

E McDOUGALL and D MYNOTT, 'Irreplaceable Evidence of Age for the Civil Service Commission', *Genealogists' Magazine* 27 (2002)

G PALMER ed., *A Bibliography of Loyalist source material in the United States, Canada and Great Britain* (American Antiquarian Society/Meckler, 1982)

C R Perry, *The Victorian Post Office: the growth of a bureaucracy* (Woodbridge, 1992)

Royal Kalendar (London, 1746–1849)

J C SAINTY and others, *Office Holders in Modern Britain* (London, 1972–1998; also at **www.british-history.ac.uk**). So far, comprises:

I	*Treasury Officials 1660–1870*, J C Sainty, 1972	
II	*Officials of the Secretaries of State 1660–1782*, J C Sainty, 1973	
III	*Officials of the Boards of Trade 1660–1782*, J C Sainty, 1974	
IV	*Admiralty Officials 1660–1870* J C Sainty, 1975	
V	*Home Office Officials 1782–1870* J C Sainty, 1975	
VI	*Colonial Office Officials 1794–1870* J C Sainty, 1976	
VII	*Navy Board Officials 1660–1832* J M Collinge, 1978	
VIII	*Foreign Office Officials 1782–1870* J M Collinge, 1979	
IX	*Officials of Royal Commissions of Enquiry 1815–1870*, J M Collinge, 1984	
X	*Officials of Royal Commissions of Enquiry 1870–1939*, E Harrison, 1995	
XI	*Officials of the Royal Household 1660–1837: Department of the Lord Chamberlain and associated offices*, J C Sainty and R O Bucholz, 1997	
XII	*Officials of the Royal Household 1660–1837: Department of the Lord Steward and the Master of the Horse*, J C Sainty and R O Bucholz, 1998	

G SMITH, *Something to Declare!: 1000 years of Customs and Excise* (London, 1980)

D STARKEY ed., *The English Court from the Wars of the Roses to the Civil War* (London, 1987)

N TYRER, *They fought in the fields, the Women's Land Army: the story of a forgotten army* (London, 1996)

C YOUNG, 'Staying in Touch' [Post Office], *Ancestors* 19 (2004)

35 Merchant seamen

35.1 Introduction

The Britain of the past was a great maritime nation. Its island status and the widespread nature of its empire meant that merchant shipping was of huge importance, and many more families relied on the sea for a living than is conceivable now. Given that merchant shipping was privately owned and manned, it is quite surprising to find that the Victorian government took such a keen – but sporadic – interest in recording details of merchant seamen. Records of officers exist from 1845, and are currently available up to approximately 1969. Accessible records of merchant seamen survive in bulk for 1835 to 1857, and again from about 1918. Ship-based records also exist and can be used to fill the 1858–1918 gap, but these records are not easy to access, and you do need to know what ship to look for.

The records relating to merchant seamen have been fully examined in two specialist guides: Smith, Watts and Watts, *Records of Merchant Shipping and Seamen* (this is also the best guide for fishing vessels and fishermen) and Watts and Watts, *My Ancestor was a Merchant Seaman*. Try these, if you want more detail. The Society of Genealogists has a useful collection on merchant seamen; see Hailey, *Maritime Sources in the Library of the Society of Genealogists*.

35.2 Looking for merchant seamen and officers before 1835

This is not easy. There is a lot of recorded information but most of it is about ships. Before 1835 there are no systematic records of merchant seamen, so you have records only where the path of a seaman crosses with officialdom. The most likely records relate to trade, taxation, legal disputes and the Royal Navy. Such material, by its very nature, will contain many more references to the masters of ships than to the ordinary seamen who sailed in them. The chances of finding information on a particular seaman are very slim. Make sure you consult one of the two specialist guides (above) on the topic.

The Society of Genealogists has copies of the 8,000 petitions to Trinity House from merchant seamen or their families requesting charitable support, 1787–1854 (the originals are at the Guildhall). The index is searchable online at **www.originsnetwork.com**.

There are interesting lists of Dorset seamen, fishermen and mariners, taken in 1665, in PRO 30/24/7/550–564 from the divisions of Blandford, Bridport, Dorchester, Lyme Regis, Shaftesbury, Sherborne and Whitchurch. Many give details of age, family size, address and status.

There are many wills of merchant seamen from the late seventeenth century to 1857 among the records of the Commissary Court of London (London Division) at the Guildhall Library (address in 62). The Prerogative Court of Canterbury wills, at the National Archives, include wills of at least 1,500 merchant seamen who died abroad before 1858: see 10.

A register of apprentices from all over England, bound to fishermen in the south-east, survives for 1639–1664 (HCA 30/897). For 1710–1811, there was a general tax on apprenticeship indentures: try looking for references to seamen both as apprentices and as masters in the Apprenticeship Books (IR 1) and their modern indexes (see 37). For the port of Colchester, there is a register of seamen's indentures covering 1704–1757 and 1804–1844 (BT 167/103). A list of children apprenticed to the sea from Christ's Hospital, 1766, survives in T 64/311. There is also a list of indentures for apprentices on ships bound for the West Indies from Newcastle upon Tyne, 1815–1823, in CUST 84/380.

From 1747, the masters or owners of merchant ships had to keep muster rolls for each voyage. These can give the names of officers and seamen employed on the ship, their usual place of abode, dates of engagement and discharge, and the name of the ship in which they last sailed. They exist for the following ports (not London). Unfortunately, there are no indexes, although the musters for Dartmouth and Plymouth are currently being indexed by the Maritime History Archive at the University of Newfoundland (see **www.mun.ca/mha/holdings/crewlist.php**).

Aberdeen–Cardigan (A–C)	1800–1850	BT 98/1–2
Bristol	1831–1837	BT 98/90
Dartmouth	1770–1948	BT 98/3–17
Drogheda, Montrose, Newport	1838	BT 98/28
Dundee	1835–1857	BT 98/18–27
Greenock	1800–1851	BT 98/29
Lancaster	1800–1851	BT 98/30–31
Leith	1835	BT 98/32
Liverpool	1772–1850	BT 98/33–89, 91–104
Lynn	1850–1851	BT 98/105
Montrose	1838	BT 98/28
Newport	1838	BT 98/28
Plymouth	1761–1833	BT 98/106–118, CUST 66/227
Portsmouth	1835–1848	BT 98/119–120
Scarborough	1747–1765	CUST 91/111–112
Shields	1747–1793	BT 98/121–135

Other series that may yield useful information include:

- Registers of Protection from being Pressed, 1702–1815 (ADM 7/363–376);
- Registers of Protection for fishermen and the coasting trade from being Pressed, 1755–1815 (ADM 7/381–388, 650);
- Registers of Ship's Passes, 1683–1845 (ADM 7/73–164) (these give the destination and duration of voyages);
- Accounts of the Receiver of Sixpences for the Thames, 1725–1830 (ADM 68/194–219) and the port of Exeter, 1800–1851 (BT 167/38–40);
- Navy Board: Registers of Payments to masters of merchant ships for giving passage home to shipwrecked mariners, etc., 1729–1826 (ADM 30/22–25).

35.3 Merchant seamen apprenticeships, 1824–1953

Regular records start in 1824: for earlier apprentices, see 35.2. The Merchant Seamen Act of 1823 required that merchant ships of 80 tons and over had to carry indentured apprentices. The indentures had to be enrolled with local customs officials. Under the Merchant Seamen Act of 1835, these local officials had to make quarterly returns of the indentures' register to the General Register and Record Office of Seamen in London. Registration of London indentures was done directly into the General Register. From 1844, copies of the actual indentures were sent up to London. These statutory apprenticeships were abolished in 1849, but registers were still maintained of those who were apprenticed after that date. Later apprenticeships seem to have been intended as a route to becoming an officer: it is not clear if this was so for the earlier period. Certainly fishing apprenticeships were often used to clear out pauper boys from workhouses: see Horn's article.

The Indexes of Apprentices registered in the General Register between 1824 and 1953 will be found in BT 150 ⑧, in three sequences:

- BT 150/1–14: London and parish 1824–1879;
- BT 150/15–46: outports 1829–1879;
- BT 150/47–57: London and outports 1880–1953.

The indexes all give the apprentice's name, age, the date and terms of his indenture and the name of his master: from BT 150/15 onwards they include also the port where he first signed on and the name of his first ship. From 1845, they are actually an index to the original indentures. Samples only of these survive (including some indentures for fishing vessel) in BT 151 ⑥ for merchant apprenticeships 1845–1950 and BT 152 ⑥ for fishing apprenticeships 1895–1935, from months in years ending 0 or 5.

Some of the local registers do still survive amongst the Customs records:

Aldeburgh	1856–1879	CUST 98/87
Belfast	1827–1846	CUST 113/9
Bideford	1857–1880	CUST 69/224
Cardigan	1859–1896	CUST 76/138
Carlisle	1840–1888	CUST 83/135
Fowey	1825–1925	CUST 67/81
Littlehampton	1856–1897	CUST 57/28
Newhaven	1893–1908	CUST 56/89
Ramsgate	1893–1908	CUST 52/112
Scarborough	1884–1894	CUST 91/121
Scilly Isles	1857–1878	CUST 68/185
Teignmouth	1853–1893	CUST 64/205
Wisbech	1857–1875	CUST 96/127
Workington	1875–1907	CUST 83/125

The collection of Crisp's Indentures, preserved at the Society of Genealogists, contains some original indentures of seamen from the north-east of England, dated between 1845 and *c.* 1861.

35.4 Officers' certificates of competency and service, 1845–1969

If you are looking for a Welsh officer, go straight to **www.welshmariners. org.uk**, an online index of 21,000 Welsh merchant masters, mates and engineers active from 1800 to 1945. If not, you will need to work your way through the following information.

By an order of 1845, the Board of Trade authorised a system of voluntary examinations of competency for men intending to become masters or mates of foreign-going and home-trade British merchant ships. Masters and mates passing the voluntary examination before 1850 should be found in BT 143/1 and BT 6/218–219, with a register of names at BT 143/1. *Lloyd's Register of Shipping* contains as an appendix, 'An Alphabetical List of all the Masters and Mates in the Merchant Service, who have voluntarily passed an Examination'. Copies can be seen at the National Archives.

Certificates gradually became compulsory and could be obtained by proving long service (service) or by examination (competency). The certificate registers give name, place and year of birth, date and place of issue of the certificate and rank examined or served in. Deaths, injuries and retirements have often been noted. Up to 1888, the registers record details of the ships served in, and this may be followed up in the crew lists in a similar way to that described above for ordinary seamen.

Certificates for masters and mates are to be found, up to 1921, in BT 122–BT 126 and BT 128 for colonial certificates, all F. All these series are well indexed by BT 127: there is guidance available at the National Archives on converting the index reference. From 1862 there are certificates for engineers (BT 139–BT 142, with colonial engineers in BT 140 F and indexes in BT 141) and from 1883 for skippers and mates of fishing boats (BT 129 and BT 130, with indexes in BT 138 F).

Applications for certificates issued in the UK up to 1928 are preserved at the National Maritime Museum – these often record voyage details prior to the issue of a certificate. Later applications are believed not to have survived.

From 1910, a combined index to masters, mates and engineers, and to the skippers and mates of fishing boats, was started to replace those formerly kept in registers (above). The term 'index' for this collection is a slight misnomer in that it is not an index to any other records: in effect it replaced the earlier registers and indexes and became a self-indexing register. It was kept in card form for the period 1910 to approximately 1969, covering home and foreign trade, and each card gives name, date and place of birth, certificate number, rating, date of passing and port of examination. The index is available on microfiche as BT 352 7.

From 1913, voyage details of officers can be found in the registers of seamen: see 35.7 and 35.8.

35.5 Registration of seamen, 1835–1857

The Merchant Shipping Act 1835 ordered the registration of merchant seamen (with the aim of creating a reserve for manning the Royal Navy in time of war). Registers of seamen, and associated indexes, were created and information was entered in them from crew lists, the filing of which was also required by the same Act (see 35.10). This form of registration of seamen lasted from 1835 to 1857.

There are three series of Registers of Seamen, which were compiled directly from the crew lists. In addition, there is a Register of Seamen's Tickets (1845–1854), which contains personal information, supplied by each seaman on applying for his register ticket, as well as that gleaned from the crew lists. All these registers give the seamen's age and place of birth and contain cross-references to the crew lists (see 35.10).

The first (BT 120 ☒) consists of entries in five alphabetically arranged volumes, 1835–1836. The second series (BT 112 ☒) covers 1835 to 1844 in two distinct parts covering 1835 to February 1840 (Part 1) and December 1841 to 1844 (Part 2). There appears to be no material covering the gap March 1840–November 1841. Part 1 consisted of some 19 volumes in which the entries were arranged according to a numeric scheme within alphabetical segments (initial two letters of a seaman's surname). Part 2 consisted of some 71 volumes arranged essentially alphabetically. An index to surnames for Part 1 is in BT 119. Use BT 119/28 to find the location of surnames within Part 2.

At some stage during its administrative use, the volumes of Part 1 and Part 2 were disassembled and an attempt was made to recombine them in a single alphabetical series. This resulted in 79 volumes, of which 78 survive today. Some pages from the indexes to registers have also become embedded in these volumes.

In 1845 the ticket system was introduced and lasted until October 1853; the registers give date and place of birth and a physical description. Coastguards and Royal Navy, as well as merchant seamen, were often issued with a register ticket. The registers (BT 113 ☒) are arranged in order of ticket number: there is a name index in BT 114. We know that the index contains references to some ticket numbers for which there is no entry in the ticket registers. The last series, started in 1853 after the ticket system was abolished, lists seamen alphabetically (BT 116 ☒). All these series are seen on microfilm. See also 35.10, on agreements and crew lists.

35.6 No registration of seamen, 1857–1913

Registration of seamen was abandoned in 1857 and, until its reintroduction in 1913, there is no easy way to discover the career of a merchant seaman. If you are lucky, you may have some idea of the ship served on, so you could check the ship-based crew lists that continue throughout this period. For advice on using ship-based sources, see 35.10 and onwards. Apprenticeship records may perhaps help find some men (35.3).

The Royal Naval Reserve, which was established in 1859, was officered and manned by deep-sea merchant seamen, and there are some service records: see 28.5.2. The Modern Records Centre at the University of Warwick has some National Union of Seamen material: the address is given at 62.

35.7 Registration of seamen, 1913–1941

The Central Indexed Register (sometimes referred to as the Fourth Register of Seamen) was started on index cards in October 1913 and maintained until 1941. About 1.25 million cards survive.

However, there is very little for 1913 to 1920. It seems that CR 1 and CR 2 index cards for these years were destroyed in error in 1969. Try instead the index of 133,135 seafarers awarded the Mercantile Marine War Medal for service during the First World War in BT 351 ⑦. This index does not give ships served on, but does give personal data: see 35.14.

There is also a special index surviving covering the period 1918–1921 (CR 10 cards in BT 350), so it may be possible to find at least some early records there, or perhaps in the fourth index in BT 364. Another possibility is to look at the seamen's pouches in BT 372, as these can include men who served as far back as 1913, as long as they were still serving in 1941: see 35.8.

The Register consists of four large card indexes, seen on microfiche.

- The CR 1 cards, 1921–1941 (BT 349 ⑦), are arranged alphabetically by surname and so provide the starting point for a search. They record place and date of birth, discharge number, rating and a short description of the seaman. A few of these cards also have a photograph of the seaman.
- The CR 2 cards, 1921–1941 (BT 348 ⑦), are arranged numerically by discharge number and include a brief record of the ships on which the seaman served (by ship's number) and the dates of his signing on.
- The CR 10 cards, 1918–1921 (BT 350 ⑦), form a special index and (as well as including similar information to the CR 1 cards) bear a photograph of the seaman. This index, made by a 1918 Order under the Defence of the Realm, seems to have been intended to record the issue of seamen's identity certificates.
- The fourth index (BT 364 ⑦) we think was compiled by extracting cards from the other three indexes, for reasons that are unclear. It is arranged numerically, with the CR 1 card leading, and there are usually three cards (CR 1, CR 2 and CR 10) for each seaman. You may be able to find the number from BT 382 (see 35.8).

The Southampton Archives Office now has the original index cards and are able to provide better copies of the cards and particularly of any photos attached to them (address in 62).

35.8 Seamen's pouches, 1913–1972

In 1941 the Essential Work (Merchant Navy) Order created a Merchant Navy Reserve Pool to ensure that men would always be available to man vessels. The government paid officers and seamen to remain in the Reserve Pool when they were ashore. For the first time continuous paid employment (instead of casual employment) was available to all seamen (and women), and comprehensive registration became possible.

All those who had served at sea during the previous five years were required to register and a new Central Register of Seamen (sometimes referred to as the Fifth Register of Seamen) was established and maintained until 1972: the registers or docket books are in BT 382 [7] and give details of service. An envelope or pouch was assigned to each seaman or woman, to contain other records. Any CR 1 and CR 2 cards of seamen who were still serving in 1941 were removed from the old Central Indexed Register and placed in the new pouches (most in BT 372 [1]). The pouches can therefore contain records of men who served as early as 1913, and of others who served beyond 1972.

The seamen's pouches are in three main series:

- Main series in BT 372 [1], easily found by a surname search. The date and place of birth is shown in the description, which helps in sorting out people with the same initials. It is also very useful in showing the whole range of merchant seamen, who came from all over the British Empire and beyond;
- Merchant seamen who served on Special Operations (the liberation of Europe) June 1944–May 1945 in BT 391 ([2]: catalogued as BT 372 but in the format 'Smith, John');
- Merchant seamen (British and Asian) who served on Royal Navy ships 1939–1946 in BT 390 [7] (but being re-catalogued slowly in the same way as BT 391).

In the pouch were placed records relating to the individual (often including small loose photographs) at the time of discharge. The pouches can contain documents going back to 1913 for those who transferred from the Fourth Register. Unfortunately, there is no longer a pouch for every seaman or woman. It seems that pouches with discharge numbers below 95,000 were destroyed sometime before 1988. In other case, pouches were not created, or do not survive. However, the docket books in BT 382 [7] cover any gap. If you do not find anything in these three series, a useful tip would be to use BT 382 to get the number, than go and look at the old fourth index (BT 364: see 35.7). This odd collection of index cards does look like an early forerunner of the pouch system, and people have been found this way.

From BT 372, BT 390 or BT 391 you should get place and date of birth, discharge number, rank or rating (with certificate numbers for officers), details of other qualifications and details of ships served on. This has various abbreviations – F for Foreign, H for Home and MNRP for Merchant Navy Reserve Pool – i.e., ashore.

The catalogue entry for each seaman's pouch includes (for BT 372 and BT 391 so far) surname or patronym, initials or forename, discharge number with prefix code where appropriate (see below), place of birth and date of birth. The place of birth information is catalogued as it was given on the outside of the pouch. Sometimes both parish and county are given, but often only one or the other is present. Similarly, for non-British place names the country may not have been included. For example, Halifax may be Yorkshire or Nova Scotia.

Key to meaning of prefix in the seamen's numbers			
[No prefix]	mostly British	K/O	India or Pakistan
A	India and Pakistan	M or Malta	Malta
BAR	Barbados	Mau	Mauritius
BG	British Guyana	Nig	Nigeria
B/HT	British – born in India	R	British
C/O	Bangladesh citizens	S	Various (mainly British)
C or CAN	Canadian	SA	South Africa
E	Eire	SE	Western Isles, Northern Ireland
F	Falkland Islands	SEY	Seychelles
G	Ghana	SI	Singapore
HK	Hong Kong	SL	Sierra Leone
I, Ind or India	Indian	St L	St. Lucia
J or Jam	Jamaica	T & T	Trinidad and Tobago
K	Tanganyika	Z or Zan	Zanzibar

The major sub-series in BT 372 relate to seamen mainly of European origin, 1941–1946 and 1946–1972. Although described as 'mainly of European origin', these do include many individuals from British colonies outside Europe and the date ranges should only be considered as a guide. Separate, smaller sub-series exist for

- Asiatic Seamen, mainly of Indian origin (1941–1965);
- Asiatic Seamen, mainly of Indian origin (1966–1972);
- seamen of Indian, Chinese and Foreign Nationalities – Unnumbered Series (1941–1972);
- allied Prisoners of War and Internees (1941–1945);
- service on Royal Navy Ships: Auxiliary War Vessels (T124, T124T, T124X, etc.) (1939–1945);
- deaths of Merchant Seamen recorded for pension purposes (1944–1951).

We also hold indexes to the registers of cooks' certificates of competency and service, 1913–1956. The indexes give surname, forename, year and place of birth, plus sometimes discharge 'A' number, certificate number and remarks. The actual registers are held at the National Maritime Museum, Greenwich. You may need to use our indexes to get the Certificate Number before approaching the National Maritime Museum.

35.9 Registration of officers and seamen, from 1973

The current, Sixth Register, called the 'UK Register', dating from 1973, is kept by the Registry of Shipping and Seamen (address in 62). In it are recorded details of when the seafarer joined, the granting and renewal of certificates and any disciplinary matters; voyage details are not given. Information is only released to the individual or, if deceased, the next of kin. Both ordinary seafarers and officers are included in this register, which has a supporting alphabetical index.

35.10 Ship-based sources: crew lists and agreements (and some log books), 1835–1860

In 1835 a new system of crew lists and agreements was introduced, by the Merchant Shipping Act 1835: records are in BT 98/140–6944 🅕. The crew lists should provide name, age, place of birth, quality (i.e., rank), previous ship, date and place of joining and time and date of death or leaving the ship. Thus you can work backwards from them but not forwards (in theory – it is not easy).

Masters of any ships belonging to UK subjects undertaking a foreign voyage, and masters of any British registered ships of 80 tons or more employed in the coastal trade or the fisheries, had to enter into a written agreement with every seaman on conditions of service. On return to the home port, the master of a foreign trade vessel had to deliver a list of the crew and the original agreements to the Registrar General of Shipping and Seamen.

The date given in the catalogue refers to the year in which they were handed in. This should be the *end* of the voyage for foreign trade voyages, and for home trade voyages at the end of June or December of the appropriate year. Documents for home trade vessels were delivered half-yearly at the end of June or December.

A few of the official log books survive with the crew lists from about 1852, but it was not until 1854 that masters were required to deposit them at the end of the voyage with the agreements. Many were subsequently destroyed: the log books that were kept are chiefly those containing entries of a birth or death at sea, or log books of smaller vessels printed on the same form as the crew list and agreement.

Before 1857 crew lists and agreements are arranged by port of registry and then alphabetically by ships' names. For 1851 (a date chosen, as the census of 1851 does not include these seamen) indexes for ports of Ireland, Scotland and Wales (covering men from all over the country) can be obtained from **www.fhindexes.co.uk**; others will become available.

From 1857 crew lists and agreements are arranged by the ship's official number. To find the official number, use *Lloyds Register of Shipping* or the *Mercantile Navy List*; there are only incomplete sets of *Lloyds Register* and the *Mercantile Navy List* at the National Archives but there are full sets at the Guildhall Library and National Maritime Museum (addresses in 62).

If you want to trace an individual seaman in the crew lists, you must first refer to the appropriate seamen's register (see 35.5) to get the ship's port of registration and name. Between 1835 and 1844, make a note of the number of the port and the name of the ship given in the register entry (ignore the port rotation number). There is a key to the port numbers in the paper list for BT 98, and the crew lists are arranged by port of registry of the ship and then by ships' names.

Between 1845 and 1854, you will still need to start with the appropriate seamen's register, but the procedure is more complicated and differs for foreign and home trade. A full explanation is given in Smith, Watts and Watts, *Records of Merchant Shipping and Seamen* or Watts and Watts, *My Ancestor was a Merchant Seaman*. The key feature is that at this period ships' names are not given, only the port number and a port rotation number – to which there is no key. Crew lists are organised annually (in BT 98) according to port of registry and ships' names, not port rotation numbers. Also, during this period it is known that not all details of voyages were actually entered into the registers: those for 1849, 1850 and 1852–1854 appear never to have been entered at all, even though the crew lists do survive.

From 1853 to 1857 details of voyages are to be found in the appropriate seamen's register, but now ships' names and port of registry are given, so the crew list should be readily located in BT 98, where they are arranged by year, port of registry and ship's name.

After 1857 you can no longer go through the seamen's registers to use the crew lists in BT 98. Since there is no longer an index of seamen indicating which ship they were on, it can take a great deal of hard work and good luck to trace individual seamen through the crew lists.

35.11 Ship-based sources: crew lists and agreements and log books, from 1861

These are the agreements and crew lists of British Empire vessels, containing the names of officers and seamen; their date and place of birth; the date and place of joining and leaving the vessel; the previous vessel; wages, rank and reason for leaving the vessel; ports of call and a description of the vessel. They have an obvious value for the period when registration of seamen stopped (1857–1913) but can be difficult to use because they are scattered. See the work of the Crew List Index Project at **www.crewlist. org.uk/** for access to a growing number of really useful finding aids for 1861–1913.

1861 is really an artificial date: the system continued from 1857, but what has altered is the location of the records. Only a sample of agreements, crew lists and log books (which were generally filed together with the crew lists) are preserved at the National Archives. Many have been preserved at other archives.

- About 70 per cent of the archive is held at the Maritime History Archive (MHA) at the Memorial University of Newfoundland. The MHA took all those crew lists not taken by any other institution for the years between 1863 and 1976, and offers a paid copying and research service in the material. See their website at **www.mun.ca/mha/index.php**. The MHA has published guides to their holdings and those of local repositories in the UK. Copies of all these are available at the National Archives.

- The National Archives holds 10 per cent of all Crew Lists 1861–1938 and 1951–1992. These are in
  - BT 99 ☐F 1861–1974 (this is becoming searchable by ship's number, thanks to the Crew List Index Project)
  - BT 100 (famous ships, e.g., *Great Eastern, Great Britain, Cutty Sark, Lusitania, Waratah, Titanic, Queen Mary, Queen Elizabeth II*) ☐6 1835–1999
  - BT 144 (fishing vessels) ☐F 1884–1929
  - BT 165 ☐F logs 1857–1972 detached from crew lists.
- The National Maritime Museum (NMM) holds the remaining 90 per cent of crew lists for the years 1861, 1862 and all years ending in 5 (except 1945). No list is available of these holdings. Those for 1975 and 1985 have not been arranged, and so access to them is restricted.
- Various county record offices, libraries and other repositories hold those crew lists not at the National Archives or the NMM for the period 1863–1912. See **www.crewlist.org.uk**.

The crew lists for the period 1939–1950 (the Second World War) were retained for longer than for other years (for pension and medal purposes). For some reason, they did not go into the main series of BT 99 or BT 100 when they arrived at the National Archives, but instead were placed in BT 381, with some in BT 380 and BT 387:

- most ships, BT 381;
- allied and commandeered ships, BT 380;
- requisitioned or chartered allied foreign ships, BT 387.

The result is a mess. For example, crew lists of the *Durban Castle* (official number 166617) are in BT 100 in 1938, in BT 381 for 1939–1946, in BT 99 for 1947, missing for 1948 and in BT 380 for 1949–1950. To make the best of it, try a search by the ship's official number in all of BT 99, BT 380 and BT 381. If there are gaps, look at BT 387, which is listed by range of ships' names: you will have to find the right range and then look at the documents. If there are still gaps, look at the BT 385 card index, just to see if the documents survive. The index cards record all logbooks and crew agreements received at the Registrar General of Shipping and Seamen for 1939 to 1950; they are arranged in alphabetical order of ship's name. This is effectively an index to all British merchant ships active during the Second World War. (Similar index cards from before 1939 and after 1950 have been transferred to the National Maritime Museum.)

During the war, details of ports called at, or other voyage details, were recorded on Ships' Movement Cards, together with the location of any sinking. These cards are now in BT 389 ☐7, arranged in alphabetical order of ship's name. For further details of captured or sunk ships, see BT 373 ☐6.

This series contain miscellaneous papers relating to the circumstances of loss or capture, and can be very informative, mentioning the actions of individuals.

After 1976 only the 10 per cent sample of agreements and crew lists held by the National Archives has been preserved (with the exception of 90 per cent of those for 1975 and 1985 at the National Maritime Museum); the rest of these records, up to 1994, have been destroyed. The Registry of Shipping and Seamen (address in 62) holds all crew lists from 1995 onwards.

35.12 Merchant seamen: births, marriages and deaths at sea

For births, marriages and deaths at sea, see 7 and 8.8.

35.13 Medals for gallantry at sea

Records of medals awarded for saving lives at sea, 1839–1882, are in FO 83/769. The Albert Medal was awarded for gallantry at sea: the medal registers, 1866–1913 (BT 97 ⑦), also include awards to sailors in the Royal Navy until 1891. Records of other awards for gallantry at sea, 1856–1981, are in BT 261 ⑦, BT 339 ⑦ (each volume is in alphabetical order) and MT 9 (search for 'code 6' to get medal references: some are also searchable by name).

For the many gallantry awards made for wartime service, start with the official gazettes at **www.gazette-online.co.uk**: the *London Gazette* is kept at ZJ 1. There is a research guide available at the National Archives and on the National Archives website, which gives more details of gallantry medals and honours. See also our specialist guide, Spencer's *Medals*.

35.14 First World War

If you are tracing a relative who died, the Commonwealth War Graves Commission's 'Debt of Honour Register' should be your starting point: you can search it at **www.cwgc.org**. It includes both British and Commonwealth merchant seamen for the First World War. Most seamen will have lost their lives when their vessel sank, and there will be no known grave. Many are remembered on the Merchant Marine Memorial at Tower Hill in London. The Memorial Register may be consulted close by at Trinity House Corporation (address in 62). Another possible source for more information, particularly for seamen from London or Southampton, is the *National Roll of the Great War*: see 26.1.4 for more details.

The Mercantile Marine War Medal was awarded to those 133,135 members of the Merchant Navy who had made at least one voyage through dangerous waters during the First World War. An index to recipients is kept at BT 351 ⑦. As recipients of this medal were automatically entitled to the British War Medal, this index also records the issue of that medal. The index generally gives a full name, year and place of birth, certificate of competency number for masters, mates and engineers, identification number, and address at the time the medal was issued.

For prisoners of war, see 31.4. Otherwise, use the seamen's (35.7) and ship-based records (35.11) as far as possible. This may not be very far, as seamen's records were accidentally destroyed and ship-based records are scattered.

35.15 Second World War

At the outbreak of the Second World War in 1939, the British merchant fleet and its resources came under the control of the Ministry of Shipping. It is difficult to do sufficient justice to the contribution of the Merchant Navy. It has been estimated that one in every three died – a rate higher than any of the armed services. If you are tracing a relative who died, the Commonwealth War Graves Commission's 'Debt of Honour Register' should be your starting point: you can search it at **www.cwgc.org**. It includes both British and Commonwealth merchant seamen. Most seamen will have lost their lives when their vessel sank, and there will be no known grave. Many are remembered on the Merchant Marine Memorial at Tower Hill in London. The Memorial Register may be consulted close by at Trinity House Corporation (address in 62).

Fuller records have been preserved for this period, including all crew lists, ships' movement cards and an index of ships (see 35.11). For seamen's pouches for the Second World War, see 35.8. Many seamen of British, colonial and allied origin became prisoners of war: there are records of over 3,000 in BT 373 ①. These are described in more detail in 31.6. BT 373 ⑥ also gives details of the capture or destruction of their ships. Carr's article 'The Red Ensign at War' pulls all this information together.

For gallantry medals, see 35.13. Service medals were not automatically issued, but had to be claimed by the veteran. BT 395 contains a record of medals as claimed by and issued to merchant seamen from 1946 to 2002. (If someone is not listed in the index, it may be because they have not yet claimed their medal entitlement. Medals can still be claimed, but entitlement has to be proved: contact the Registry of Shipping and Seamen for further details on this at the address in 62.) These records are all searchable and viewable (for a small sum) online at **www.nationalarchives. gov.uk/documentsonline/seamens-medals.asp**, where you will find detailed advice on how best to search.

Eight medals were awarded to British merchant seamen who met the qualifications for each.

War Medal (1939–1945)	Generally awarded if the service period qualified for one of the Stars and if terminated by death, disability due to service or capture as a prisoner of war. A merchant seaman had to have served a minimum of 28 days at sea.
Atlantic Star (1939–1945)	Awarded after the Battle of the Atlantic for service between 3 September 1939 and 8 May 1945 and if the service period was terminated by their death or disability due to service. The qualifying service period for the Atlantic Star could only begin after the 1939–1945 Star had been earned by 6 months' service. A merchant seaman had to serve in the Atlantic, home waters, North Russia Convoys or South Atlantic waters. The Atlantic Star was also awarded to those awarded a gallantry medal, with no minimum qualifying period.
1939–1945 Star	Awarded for service between 3 September 1939 and 2 September 1945 and if the service period was terminated by death or disability due to service. A merchant seaman could qualify after 6 months' service with at least one voyage in an operational area. The 1939–1945 Star was also awarded to recipients of a gallantry medal, with no minimum qualifying period.
Africa Star (1940–1943)	Awarded for service between 10 June 1940 and 12 May 1943, serving in the Mediterranean. A merchant seaman might also qualify serving in operations off the Moroccan coast between 8 November 1942 and 12 May 1943. The minimum qualifying period was one day.
Pacific Star (1941–1945)	Awarded for service in the Pacific Ocean, South China Sea or the Indian Ocean between 8 December 1941 and 2 September 1945. Generally the qualifying service period for the Pacific Star could only begin after the 1939–1945 Star had been earned by 6 months' service.
Burma Star (1941–1945)	Awarded for service in the Burma Campaign between 11 December 1941 and 2 September 1945. A merchant seaman qualified serving within a restricted area in the Bay of Bengal. Generally the qualifying service period for the Burma Star could only begin after the 1939–1945 Star had been earned by 6 months' service.
France & Germany Star (1944–1945)	Awarded for service between 6 June 1944 and 8 May 1945, in direct support of land operations in France, Belgium, Holland or Germany, in the North sea, the English Channel or the Bay of Biscay (service off the coast of the south of France could qualify for the Italy Star, see below). There was no minimum time qualification for a Merchant Seaman.
Italy Star (1943–1945)	Awarded for service between 11 June 1943 and 8 May 1945, in the Mediterranean and the Aegean Sea. Operations in and around the Dodecanese, Corsica, Greece, Sardinia and Yugoslavia after 11 June 1943 would also qualify. Generally the qualifying service period for the Italy Star could only begin after the 1939–1945 Star had been earned by 6 months' service. There were no clasps awarded with the Italy Star.

Following the War, medal papers were raised including details of a seaman's service. These were sent to ports for the veteran to sign, confirming the accuracy of the information, and were then returned to the Registrar General of Shipping and Seamen. Each entry in BT 395 gives details of the seaman's name and the medals, ribbons and clasps issued, together with a reference to the medal papers file, which is still held at the Registry of Shipping and Seamen. Usually, his discharge book number and date and place of birth are listed too.

35.16 Merchant seamen: bibliography

A Guide to the Crew Agreements and Official Logbooks, 1863–1913, held at the County Record Offices of the British Isles published by the Maritime History Archive, Memorial University of Newfoundland

J Carr, 'The Red Ensign at War' [Merchant Navy in the Second World War], *Ancestors* 23 (2004)

Guide to the Agreements and Crew Lists: Series II (bt 99), 1863–1912 (in three volumes) at the Memorial University of Newfoundland

Guide to the Agreements and Crew Lists: Series II (bt 99), 1913–1938 at the Memorial University of Newfoundland

J Hailey, *Maritime Sources in the Library of the Society of Genealogists* (SoG, 1997)

P Horn, 'Pauper apprenticeship and the Grimsby fishing industry, 1870 to 1914'. *Labour History Review*, 61 (1996)

Index to Crew Lists, Agreements and Official Logs at the Memorial University of Newfoundland, microfiche

Lloyds Register of Shipping (London, annually from 1764)

K Matthews 'Crew Lists, Agreements and Official Logs of the British Empire 1863–1913, now in possession of the Maritime History Group, Memorial University', *Business History*, vol. XVI, pp. 78–80

Mercantile Navy List (London, annually from 1857)

K Smith, C T Watts and M J Watts, *Records of Merchant Shipping and Seamen* (PRO, 1998)

W Spencer, *Medals: The Researchers' Companion* (National Archives, 2006)

C T Watts and M J Watts, *My Ancestor was a Merchant Seaman* (Society of Genealogists, 2nd edn, 2002)

C T Watts and M J Watts, 'Unravelling Merchant Seamen's Records', *Genealogists' Magazine*, vol. XIX, pp. 313–321

36 Railway workers

36.1   Railway records

The records of the nationalised railway companies were collected by the British Transport Historical Commission. They include the records of several hundred railway, canal and dock companies taken over by larger companies. These records were formerly housed in London, York and Edinburgh. The Edinburgh collection has now gone to the National Archives of Scotland and the York and London collections have come to the National Archives at Kew. Local and other record offices also have extensive collections relating to the impact of the railways.

The National Archives has produced a specialist guide, Edwards' *Railway Records*, which gives valuable advice on railway staff records, among many other types of record.

36.2   Railway staff records

Staff records of a kind do exist, and those companies whose staff records are in the National Archives are listed in 36.5. Some give only names, wages and positions; others may give a full record of service. Railway staff records are hard to use.

- They are arranged by company, or successor company.
- Within each company, staff registers are divided up in ways which are now unclear, such as
  - Locomotive Carriage and Wagon Department
  - Electrical Engineer's Department
  - Traffic Department
  - Weekly staff
  - Salaried clerical positions.
- There are no union indexes.

Almost no one knows that their great-grandfather worked for the Traffic Department, for example, but just that he worked on the Great Western

Railway. So be prepared to spend a long time looking. For help, try the Railway Ancestors Family History Society: see **www.railwayancestors. fsnet.co.uk/** (address in 62).

The covering dates given in 36.5 and in the lists themselves can be very misleading. For example, the dates given in the list for RAIL 426/14 are 1923–1937: in fact, the documents are history sheets for clerical staff retiring between 1923 and 1937, so the information in them actually goes back into the nineteenth century. Another problem is that covering dates for a staff register often seem improbably long, because the first date was taken to be the earliest date on the first page (usually a birth date) and the last date was the latest date given on the final page (usually a death date). The actual years that the register covers are often much shorter, but difficult to discover.

Hawkings' *Railway Ancestors* gives detailed information on the content of record types and lists (for each company) of the surviving records, which may be useful for family history.

36.3 Other sources of information

The Railway Benevolent Institution was a general cross-company body: railwaymen had to subscribe to become eligible for its benefits. Subscribing railway staff or former staff and their families who applied for its aid could be granted money. Its records are in RAIL 1166. The Annual Reports for 1881–1959 (RAIL 116/1–80 ☐) mainly consist of lists of supporters, but they do include reports from the railway's orphanage at Derby, often with letters back from grown-up orphans (identified by initials). Minutes are in RAIL 1116/87–149 ☐, for 1858 to 1982. However, for a wonderful source of information about railway families try the books of grants for 1888–1919 (but also covering much earlier railway involvement) in RAIL 1166/81–86 ☐. These detail approved grants and give information about individual railwaymen and their wives and families who were in difficulties through accident, sickness, old age or death. If the grant is to the widow or family, the railwayman himself is not named but his company and job are given. Each volume has its own index.

Another possible source of information on individuals may be the large collection of railway periodicals at the National Archives. The British Transport Historical Collection Library, which we hold as ZPER, has a number of these and is worth exploring by anyone with an interest in railway history.

36.4 Railway police

Records for the railway police of the various railway companies do not appear to be amongst the railway staff records in the National Archives. Information about the numbers and organisation of the railway police *c.* 1900 can be found in RAIL 527/1036. The occasional references to 'Police Department' in the railway staff records relate to signalmen, etc.

36.5 Staff records at the National Archives, arranged by name of railway company (all ⑦)

Barry Railway Company	1886–1922	RAIL 23/46–60, 64–65
Brecon and Merthyr Tydfil Junction Railway Company	1880–1922	RAIL 65/31–35
Cambrian Railways Company	1898–1944	RAIL 92/142–148
Cardiff Railway Company	1869–1923	RAIL 97/32–44
Chester and Holyhead Railway Company	1862	RAIL 113/53
Cleator and Workington Junction Railway Company	1879–1923	RAIL 119/13
Furness Railway Company	1852–1922	RAIL 214/97–104
Great Central Railway Company	1857–1949	RAIL 226/193–235, 637
Great Eastern Railway Company	1855–1930	RAIL 227/445–490
Great Northern Railway Company	1848–1943	RAIL 236/727–745
Great Western and Midland Railway Companies Joint Committee	1865–1915	RAIL 241/28
Great Western Railway Company	1835–1954	RAIL 264/1–463
Hull and Barnsley Railway Company	1885–1927	RAIL 312/77–81
Hull and Selby Railway Company	1845–1875	RAIL 315/30
Isle of Wight Central Railway Company	1860–1963	RAIL 328/16–18
Lancashire and Yorkshire Railway Company	1853–1941	RAIL 343/827–845
Lancashire, Derbyshire and East Coast Railway Company	1904–1906	RAIL 344/56
Liverpool and Manchester Railway Company	1845	RAIL 371/23
London and Birmingham Railway Company	1833–1847	RAIL 384/284–291
London and North Eastern Railway Company	1920–1942	RAIL 397/1–11
London and North Western and Great Western Railway Companies Joint Committee	1871–1897	RAIL 404/177–180
London and North Western and Midland Railway Companies Joint Committee	1861–1911	RAIL 406/16
London and North Western Railway Company	1831–1927	RAIL 410/1217–1218, 1797–1986
London and South Western Railway Company	1838–1944	RAIL 411/483–537
London Brighton and South Coast Railway Company	1837–1925	RAIL 414/750–796
London Midland and Scottish and London and North Eastern Railway Companies Joint Committee	1891–1938	RAIL 417/16
London Midland and Scottish Railway Company	1923–1946	RAIL 426/1–15
London, Tilbury and Southend Company	1871–1923	RAIL 437/44–57
Manchester, Sheffield and Lincolnshire Railway Company	1847–1926	RAIL 463/177, 210–215

Midland and Great Northern Railways Joint Committee	1879–1893	RAIL 487/115
Midland and South Western Junction Railway Company	1891–1921	RAIL 489/21
Midland Railway Company	1864–1924	RAIL 491/969–1081
Neath and Brecon Railway Company	1903–1921	RAIL 505/13
Newcastle upon Tyne and Carlisle Railway Company	1845–1848	RAIL 509/96
North and South Western Junction Railway Company	1883–1916	RAIL 521/19
North Eastern Railway Company	1843–1957	RAIL 527/1895–1965
North London Railway Company	1854–1920	RAIL 529/130–138
North Staffordshire Railway Company	1847–1923	RAIL 532/58–67
North Sunderland Railway Company	1893–1948	RAIL 533/75–76
North Union Railway Company	1841–1856	RAIL 534/29
Otley and Ilkley Joint Line Committee (Midland and North Eastern Railway Companies)	1865–1901	RAIL 554/24–25
Port Talbot Railway and Docks Company	1883–1918	RAIL 574/13
Rhondda and Swansea Bay Railway Company	1882–1922	RAIL 581/36–37
Rhymney Railway Company	1860–1922	RAIL 583/41–65
Sheffield District Railway Company	1897–1916	RAIL 611/25–26
Shropshire Union Railways and Canal Company	1844–1897	RAIL 623/66–68
Somerset and Dorset Joint Line Committee	1877–1928	RAIL 626/44–53
Somerset and Dorset Railway Company	1863–1877	RAIL 627/6
South Eastern and Chatham Railway Companies Managing Committee	1850–1944	RAIL 633/343–382
South Eastern Railway Company	1845–1944	RAIL 635/302–310
South Wales Railway Company	1844–1864	RAIL 64/45, 47, 52, 55–56
Southern Railway Company	1923–1957	RAIL 651/1–10
Stockton and Darlington Railway Company	1835–1856	RAIL 667/1283–1291
Stratford upon Avon and Midland Junction Railway Company	1873–1923	RAIL 674/11
Taff Vale Railway Company	1890–1924	RAIL 684/94–120
Trent Valley Railway Company	1845–1946	RAIL 699/5
Wirral Railway Company	1884–1926	RAIL 756/10–11
York and North Midland Railway Company	1848, 1843–1850	RAIL 770/77–81
York, Newcastle and Berwick Railway Company	1845	RAIL 772/106

36.6 Railway workers: bibliography

Published works

H V Borley, *Chronology of London Railways* (Railway & Canal Historical Society, 1982)

E Carter, *An Historical Geography of the Railways of the British Isles* (Cassell, 1959)

C Edwards, *Railway Records: A Guide to Sources* (PRO, 2001)

F Hardy, 'Railway Records for Family Historians', *Genealogists Magazine*, vol. XXIII, pp. 256–260

D Hawkings, *Railway Ancestors* (1995)

T Richards, *Was Your Grandfather a Railwayman?* (FFHS, 3rd edn, 1995)

Unpublished finding aids

Card index of subjects to British Transport Historical Commission Records

37 Apprentices

37.1 Civilian apprenticeships

Apprentices were traditionally bound by indentures to serve their master for the space of seven years; the master was equally bound to teach the apprentice his trade. Indentures often name the apprentice's parents, as the apprentice would be under-age and unable to enter such an agreement alone. In its early years the system was policed by the guilds, to which the master had to belong. Later apprenticeships were not necessarily with guild members but they were still established by means of the legally enforceable indentures. Many disputes about apprenticeship can be found in the Chancery pleadings (see 58).

Formal indentures involved some trouble and expense. By the eighteenth century apprenticeships were often undertaken without any formal indenture, especially in common trades such as weaving. In many trades it was expected that men would bring up their sons or nephews to the trade. Further, it was ruled that the Statute of Apprentices did not extend to trades that did not exist when it was passed in 1563; this excluded many eighteenth-century industries, most notably the cotton industry. In many areas the Statute was not enforced, and in the Yorkshire woollen industry formal apprenticeship hardly existed by the end of the eighteenth century. In 1814, compulsory apprenticeship by indenture was abolished, although apprenticeship continued into the twentieth century.

The actual indentures of apprenticeship were private documents. If they survive at all they will normally be in private hands, or in local record offices. There is the Crisp collection of about 1,500 indentures, from the seventeenth to nineteenth centuries, at the Society of Genealogists (address in 62). Many records of apprenticeship survive with guild or with parish records, usually in local record offices; many have been published. London livery companies often kept full records of membership, which give places of birth, previous residences and other details. For these, apply to the Guildhall Library, London (address in 62).

However, between 1710 and 1804 apprenticeship indentures were subject to stamp duty – except for pauper apprenticeships. The payment registers for this duty are kept in the National Archives.

The apprenticeship stamp duty registers, 1710–1811, are in IR 1 🄴, with separate indexes (made on behalf of the Society of Genealogists and copied from their originals in the Guildhall Library). These Apprenticeship Books record the names, addresses and trades of the masters, the names of the apprentices and dates of their indentures. Until 1752 the names of apprentices' parents are given, but rarely after that year. There are indexes of masters' names from 1710 to 1762, and of apprentices' names from 1710 to 1774. Where the stamp duty was paid in London, entries will be found in the 'City' registers in IR 1; where it was paid elsewhere, entries will be found in the 'Country' registers.

As the tax could be paid up to one year after the completion of the apprenticeship, the records continue until 1811, eight years after the end of the tax in 1804. As a general rule, you may need to search the records of several years' payments in order to find a particular entry, even if you know the date of the indenture. Duty was payable by the master at the rate of 6d for every pound under £50, which he received for taking on the apprentice, and 1s for every £1 above that sum.

Apprentices were protected against the press gang: for registers of protection 1740–1806, see ADM 7/393–399.

37.2 Pauper apprenticeships

It was not only parents or guardians who arranged for apprenticeships. Pauper children (like Oliver Twist) were often apprenticed to provide them with a trade and to save rate-payers the expense of maintaining them. At first these were usually local apprenticeships, but with the growth of mills and factories during the Industrial Revolution many pauper children were taken far from home to work for long years with no one to look out for their interests. In some cases, it was little more than slavery.

Masters did not have to pay stamp duty for apprentices taken on at the common or public charge of any township or parish, or by or out of any public charity (by the statute 8 Anne c.5 s.59). This means that very many apprentices were never subject to the duty and were therefore not mentioned in the IR 1 registers. In such cases local (borough or vestry) or charity records, if they survive, are likely to be the only source of information on individuals: many record offices have good indexes and a search in A2A may help. The Foundling Hospital also kept apprenticeship registers, which are now at the London Metropolitan Archives (address in 62).

37.3 Military and merchant seamen apprenticeships

The National Archives has records of the apprenticeship of children from the Royal Naval Asylum, Greenwich and the Duke of York's Military School, Chelsea: see 28.2.6 and 24.5 respectively. For Royal Navy apprenticeships, see 28.6.1. Among the War Office records there is a list of apprentices who enlisted in the Army but had to return to their masters until their indentures expired, 1806 to 1835 (WO 25/2962 ☑).

For merchant seamen and fishing apprenticeships, see 35.3.

37.4 Apprentices: bibliography

For apprenticeship lists from the Stationers' Company, 1701 to 1800, check the *Biography Database 1680–1830* in the National Archives Library. Some local history societies have published apprenticeship registers, often in combination with material extracted from the IR 1 registers: try a search on 'apprentice' or 'apprenticeship' in the National Archives Library catalogue (**www.library.nationalarchives.gov.uk** or in **www.rhs.ac.uk/bibl/**).

Biography Database 1680–1830 (Newcastle, 1998 ongoing)

E CHURCHILL, 'Apprentice Records at the Society of Genealogists', *Ancestors* 21 (2004)

I MAXTED, *The British Book Trades, 1710–1777: an index of Master's and Apprentices' Records in the Inland Revenue Registers at the PRO, Kew* (Exeter, 1983)

Public Record Office, *Alphabetical Guide to War Office & Other Material* (Lists and Indexes, vol. LIII)

W B STEPHENS, *Sources for English Local History* (Manchester, 2nd edn, 1981)

D L THOMAS, 'Dungeons of despair' [Newgate prison], *Ancestors* 41 (2006)

University of Warwick, *Trade Union and Related Records* (Coventry, 1988)

C WEBB, 'The City Boys: Records of London Apprentices', *Ancestors* 21 (2004)

38 Lawyers

38.1   Introduction

Holborn's *Sources of Biographical Information on Past Lawyers* is a specialist guide to finding out about lawyers.

The published *Law Lists*, produced annually from 1775, are the easiest place to start. There is a set running from 1799–1976 in the National Archives, and the Guildhall Library, London also has a good, but incomplete, set, including *Law Lists* for 1787 and 1795. However, they can be difficult to use effectively. Between 1775 and 1789 they contain the names of some men never actually admitted to a court, whereas from 1790 they only give the names of those who had taken out the annual certificate to practise that year. Until 1861 they do not give the date of admission. The entries also give the name of the firm for which the solicitor or attorney worked, together with an indication of its address.

Lists of attorneys and solicitors admitted in 1729 and 1730 were printed for presentation to Parliament; a copy is available at the National Archives.

Papers of many lawyers have been deposited in archives across the country: the easiest way to find them is to search the National Register of Archives on our website **www.nationalarchives.gov.uk.**

38.2   Judges and serjeants-at-law

The National Archives does hold some records of the appointment of judges and of the creation of serjeants-at-law (who had the monopoly of pleading in the court of Common Pleas until 1846 and from whom, for several centuries, judges were selected). However, these are widely scattered and not very informative. As there is a great deal of biographical information in print on the judges and the serjeants-at-law, you would be well advised to investigate the published sources first: the main ones are listed in 38.8.

38.3 Barristers

The term barrister is used, in England and Wales, to describe someone admitted to practise in the superior courts and who is entitled to act as an advocate in those courts. Traditionally, barristers have had a higher level of education and higher social status than solicitors and attorneys. The National Archives is not the place to look for records relating to barristers: entry to the profession is controlled by the Inns of Court (Lincoln's Inn, Gray's Inn, the Inner Temple and the Middle Temple). The Inns of Court have published many of their records of genealogical interest: see the printed sources listed in 38.8. For the Inner Temple see **www.innertemple. org.uk/archive/itad/index.asp**. For further information, contact their libraries; addresses are in 62.

However, the National Archives does have records of the oaths of allegiance sworn by barristers; swearing of this oath was required before a barrister could practise in the courts. Signatures to the oath, 1673–1944, are in KB 24 ⑦ and 1858–1982, in KB 4 ⑦.

38.4 Solicitors and attorneys: the central courts

The words attorney and solicitor have had a changing meaning not only over the centuries, but also in different parts of the English-speaking world. The word attorney, strictly defined, means a person appointed by another to act in his/her place: often but not necessarily a person who is legally qualified. In the USA and other countries that have a unitary bar, the term attorney-at-law has thus become virtually synonymous with legal practitioner. This was not (and is not) the case in England and Wales, where the term was used for lawyers who were admitted to practise in the superior courts of common law and whose function was to deal with the procedural steps of litigation rather than advocacy. Attorneys were officers of court and subject to the discipline of the court. Solicitors performed similar procedural functions in courts of equity. Many individuals combined both roles, and in 1873 under the terms of the Judicature Act all solicitors and attorneys became 'Solicitors of the Supreme Court'.

Until 1838, solicitors and attorneys had to be admitted to each of the courts in which they wished to practise. The various central and regional courts regulated the admission of new solicitors and attorneys, and each court kept its own records relating to such admissions. In 1728 an act of Parliament required attorneys and solicitors to have served five years as clerks under articles before they could be admitted to a court. Then in 1749 a further act required that a statement to the effect that the articles had actually been carried out (an 'affidavit of due execution') should be filed in the court within three months of admission. Articled clerks were effectively apprentices and so it is also sometimes possible to trace them by using the apprenticeship books in IR 1 (see 37.1 for further details).

If you are trying to trace a man who describes himself as an attorney, then you should try the records of the common law courts first. Since many attorneys practised in both the King's Bench and the Common Pleas, and were therefore admitted to both courts, start your search by checking the name index to CP 5 filed with the paper list in the reading rooms. The series CP 5 🗈 relates to the Court of Common Pleas and contains original articles of clerkship and related papers from about 1725 (with a few earlier items going back to 1713) to 1838. The articles of clerkship provide the names and places of residence of the trainee attorney or solicitor, his parent or guardian and the attorney to whom he was articled. They also supply the parent's occupation, and sometimes the premium paid for the articles. Some documents are endorsed with the name of the judge who authorised admission. Registers of articles are in CP 71 🗈, but they are difficult to use as they are arranged by date of admission rather than by name.

If you do not find your man in the CP 5 index, try the King's Bench Registers and indexes of affidavits of due execution of articles in KB 170 🗈. They cover the period 1749–1875. In practice these registers contain most of the details that are in the actual affidavits, so a search of the registers may well be enough. The affidavits themselves survive only from about 1775 to 1875 and are in KB 105–KB 107 and KB 109 🗈. They usually contain the following details: the name of the clerk; the name, address and occupation of his parent or guardian; the name and address of the master to whom he was bound; and the date of the articles and length of the term of the articles. Occasionally they also give the age of the clerk.

Registers of affidavits of due execution for the Exchequer of Pleas survive for 1833–1855 only in E 4/3.

The admission rolls or books themselves are likely to be less useful for family history purposes since they give at most simply a name, date of admission and address. Rolls of attorneys for the King's Bench are in KB 172 🗈 (1729–1875); for the Common Pleas in CP 11 🗈 (1730–1750); and for the Exchequer of Pleas in E 4 🗈 (1830–75). Admission books for the Common Pleas are in CP 70 🗈 (1729–1848) and CP 72 🗈 (1740–1853).

Attorneys' admission rolls for Common Pleas are in CP 8 🗈 (1838–1860). They record the signatures of attorneys and solicitors who had originally enrolled in other courts; and they also give the court to which the individual was originally admitted, together with the date of admission and place of residence both at the time of the original admission and at the time of signing the roll. A contemporary index covering these rolls and others that have not survived is now in CP 72 🗈 (1838–1875). A supplementary admission register is in CP 69/1.

The admission roll and registers of town and country solicitors, 1832–1883, for the Court of Bankruptcy are in B 2/8–11 🗈.

If your man was described as a solicitor then you probably need to look at the records of the equity courts. For Chancery (the main equity court) the main records are the Petty Bag Office Solicitors Rolls 1729–1875 in C 216 🗈. Nominal rolls that partially duplicate the 1729–1858 material are in

☐ p. 566

IND 1/4613–4614. Various affidavits of due execution of clerkship and other admission papers are also in C 216 ⑦. There are certificates of admission, giving names and dates of admission and addresses in C 203/7 (1730–1787), which sometimes include admissions to the King's Bench, and also in C 217/21, 22, 181–187 (c. 1804–1843). Some affidavits of due execution, 1730–1839, are in C 217/23–40, 181–187. Other admission papers are also in C 217/40–54, 182–187. Alphabets of solicitors taking out certificates, 1785–1842, and an address book of attorneys, c. 1849–1860, are in C 220/11.

Admission papers after 1874 have not survived but some information can be gained from the indexes to affidavits of due execution in KB 170/13, IND 1/29729–29733 and indexes to articles of clerkship, 1875–1889, in IND 1/29712–3.

For the equity side of Exchequer there are Solicitors' Certificate Books in E 108 ⑦ (1785–1843), Rolls of Books of Solicitors in E 109 ⑦ (1729–1841) and oath rolls for solicitors and commissioners for oaths (1730–1841) in E 200 ⑦.

38.5 Solicitors and attorneys: the Chester, Durham, Lancaster and Welsh courts

Affidavits of due execution and registers of affidavits of due execution for attorneys admitted to the courts of the Palatinate of Chester, 1728–1830, together with oath rolls, 1729–1830, are in CHES 36 ⑦. There is also an admission roll (1697–1728) in CHES 35/3/1 and a further admission roll (1777–1806) for the Chester court of Exchequer in CHES 36/3/7.

Affidavits of due execution for those admitted to the courts of the Palatinate of Durham, 1660–1843, are in DURH 9 ⑦, with petitions for admission and admissions of attorneys 1660–1723 in DURH 3/218 and a register of certificates to practise, 1785–1842, in IND 1/10152.

Records of attorneys admitted to the Palatinate courts of Lancaster, 1730–1875, are in PL 23 ⑦. They include affidavits of due execution, 1749–1814, registers of affidavits, 1749–1823, rolls of attorneys, 1730–1785, an oath roll, 1730–1793, a register of certificates to practise, 1785–1871, and minutes of attorneys' assize dinners, 1790–1805.

Before 1830, solicitors and attorneys practising in the Courts of Great Sessions in Wales were enrolled in the records of those courts. These are now at the National Library of Wales (address in 62). For more information, see Parry, *A Guide to the Records of Great Sessions in Wales.* After 1830, attorneys practising in the assize courts in Wales were allowed to enrol in the courts at Westminster (see above). This privilege was also extended to attorneys and solicitors working in the courts of the Palatinate of Lancaster and the Palatinate of Durham.

38.6 Solicitors and attorneys: records kept by the Law Society

The Law Society has the records of the Registrar of Attorneys and Solicitors, established in 1843. These include lists of admissions from 1845 onwards, with additional lists of admissions back to about 1790. They also have some registers of articles of clerkship from about 1860 onwards. These records are kept at the Law Society, Ipsley Court (address in 62).

38.7 Civil lawyers

For civil lawyers (i.e., those who practised the civil law used in the church courts and the High Court of Admiralty and the High Court of Delegates) there is a selective index of advocates and proctors attached to the paper list for PROB 39 ②. Civil lawyers were also listed in *Law Lists* (38.1). There are short biographies of London advocates (the civilian equivalent of barristers) in Squibb's *Doctors' Commons*. The admission of proctors (the civilian equivalent of attorneys) in London – that is, those practising from Doctors' Commons – is recorded in the registers of the Archbishop of Canterbury at Lambeth Palace Library. Records of civil lawyers who practised in provincial church courts are best sought locally, in diocesan record offices. Some papers relating to the admission of proctors to the High Court of Admiralty are in HCA 30/539, for 1727–1841, and warrants relating to their appointments are included with other warrants in HCA 50 ⑦.

38.8 Lawyers: bibliography

R L ABEL, *The Legal Profession in England and Wales* (Oxford, 1988)

J H BAKER, *The Order of Serjeants at Law*, Selden Society, Supplementary Series vol. V (London, 1984)

E H W DUNKIN, C JENKINS and E A FRY, *Act Books of the Archbishop of Canterbury, 1663–1859* (British Record Society, Index Library 1929)

E FOSS, *A Biographical Dictionary of the Judges of England* (London, 1870)

J A FOSTER, *Men-at-the-Bar: A Biographical Handlist of the Members of the Various Inns of Court including Her Majesty's Judges etc.* [as at 1885] (London, 1885)

J A FOSTER, *The Register of Admissions of Gray's Inn, 1521–1889* (London, 1889)

G HOLBORN, *Sources of Biographical Information on Past Lawyers* (British and Irish Association of Law Librarians, 1999)

J HUTCHINSON, *A Catalogue of Notable Middle Templars* (London, 1902)

F A INDERWICK and R A ROBERTS, *A Calendar of Inner Temple Records, 1505–1800* (London, 1896–1936)

Law List (London 1775, continuing)

Lincoln's Inn, *Admissions, 1420–1799* (London, 1896)

Lincoln's Inn, *The Black Books, 1422–1914* (London, 1897–1968)

G PARRY, *A Guide to the Records of Great Sessions in Wales* (Aberystwyth, 1995)

Parliament, *List of Attorneys and Solicitors Admitted in Pursuance of the Late Act for the Better Regulation of Attorneys and Solicitors, 1729–1730* (London, 1729–1731)

J SAINTY, *A List of English Law Officers, King's Counsel and Holders of Patents and Precedence*, Selden Society, Supplementary Series vol. VII (London, 1987)

J SAINTY, *The Judges of England 1272–1990: a list of Judges of the Superior Courts*, Selden Society, Supplementary Series vol. X (London, 1993)

G D SQUIBB, *Doctors' Commons* (Oxford, 1977)

C TRICE MARTIN, *Minutes of Parliament of the Middle Temple, 1501–1703* (London, 1904–1905)

39 Education

39.1   Introduction

The National Archives holds the central records of the Department of Education and its predecessors, not records of teachers, pupils or the daily life of schools. Where these exist, they will be held locally. The records held at Kew do cover individual schools but are mostly purely administrative. They are described in a series of detailed research guides available from **www.catalogue.nationalarchives.gov.uk/researchguidesindex.asp** under the titles

- Education: Elementary (Primary) Schools
- Education: Inspectorate and HMI Reports
- Education: Records of Special Services
- Education: Records of Teachers
- Education: Secondary Schools
- Education: Sources for the History of
- Education: Technical and Further Education.

These are based on Morton, *Education and the State*, which you should see for a full discussion.

Try the normal routes for checking local holdings: the National Register of Archives or A2A (see 1.12–1.13)

39.2   Teachers' records

The National Archives holds policy papers on teacher training and registration, rather than staff records themselves. Information about staff of individual schools may sometimes be found in the appropriate local record office. In the National Archives, there are some records of teachers' pensions available for teachers in England 1899–1930 (PMG 68 ⑦). Other pension records relate to Army schoolmasters and schoolmistresses, 1909–1928, in PMG 33 ⑦ and PMG 34 ⑦.

The Society of Genealogists (address in 62) now keeps the registers of the Teachers Registration Council for 1902 to 1948. They are not open to public inspection, but a search can be made on your behalf. See also *School, University and College registers and histories in the Library of the Society of Genealogists*.

39.3 School and pupil records

If you know which parish a person lived in, it may be worth checking the Victorian and later school records for that parish, both in the National Archives and locally. You can gain an interesting perspective on an ancestor's early days by looking at school records, although he or she will not be mentioned by name in the National Archives records. Try a search on A2A or the NRA for the school records. In the local record office, ask for school logbooks and admission registers, which will name individuals. Some are still held by the schools.

At the National Archives, the most likely series are:

ED 49	Elementary endowed schools (schools with charitable foundations – often very old)	1853–1945	5, 6
ED 21	Elementary schools set up or taken over by the state after 1870: includes inspection reports	1870–1945	5, 6
ED 27	Secondary endowed schools (schools with charitable foundations – often very old)	1850–1945	5, 6
ED 35	Secondary schools set up or taken over by the state	c. 1900–1945	5, 6
ED 109	Secondary schools: inspector's reports	c. 1900–1945	5, 6

For more detailed advice, use Morton, *Education and the State*.

Deeds relating to the foundation of schools, and to other charitable foundations, were enrolled in Chancery (c 54 F) until 1902 and then in the Supreme Court (J 18 F). There are indexes to these trust deeds, arranged by place, covering 1736 to 1904; although most relate to Nonconformist chapels, very many concern schools.

39.4 Education: bibliography

Published works

R Burlison, 'Ragged Reading, 'riting and 'rithmetic' [ragged schools], *Ancestors* 36 (2005)

A Morton, *Education and the State from 1833* (PRO, 1997)

R Ratcliffe, 'The Education Revolution', *Ancestors* 21 (2004)

School, University and College registers and histories in the Library of the Society of Genealogists (Society of Genealogists, 1996)

Unpublished finding aids

Indexes to trust deeds, by place, 1736–1904

40 Hospitals and the medical professions

40.1 Sickness before the National Health Service

'Pain and discomfort were accepted as part of life to be endured with stoicism ... Working class people did not expect to be comfortable. Most went hungry and their undernourished children showed evidence of rickets ... Successful treatment by the family doctor was accepted with gratitude and the many failures were tolerated without rancour or recrimination. Patients' expectations were not high. The death of children from infectious disease was the way of the world ...' This interesting quote (taken from Geoffrey Rivett's website on the history of the National Health Service at **www.nhshistory.net/nhs_inheritance.htm**) is a reminder of how much changed in the second half of the twentieth century.

40.2 Hospital records

Hospitals immediately before the founding of the National Health Service in 1948 were either voluntary or public (municipal). The voluntary hospitals provided quality care to a limited number of in-patients and a larger number of out-patients. Elderly people, the poor and those with chronic diseases were expected to use the public hospitals.

The thousand plus voluntary or charitable hospitals varied from prestigious teaching hospitals such as Guy's to small cottage hospitals for rural or suburban areas. Many of the cottage hospitals were founded in the nineteenth century, with more built as memorials after the Boer War or the First World War. Fundraising for these frequently cash-strapped hospitals was an integral part of community life.

The public hospitals developed from the Poor Law Board infirmaries set up to cope with poor people who were chronically sick or just old, and who entered the workhouse to survive (see 41). By the 1920s, the infirmaries of workhouses in cities often overshadowed the original function and the institutions had become hospitals. Under the Local Government Act 1929, these hospitals were taken over from the Poor Law Board by local authorities – and so were often called county hospitals.

Hospital records are now quite widely scattered, but are easy to locate using the HOSPREC database at **www.nationalarchives.gov.uk/hospital records/**. If you find a relevant entry, you will need to contact the archive that holds the records. Administrative records are normally closed for 30 years, and patients' records are closed for 100 years.

40.3 Doctors and dentists

In general, the National Archives is not the place to look for records of doctors or dentists except as they were engaged upon government service. Papers of many doctors and dentists have been deposited in archives across the country: the easiest way to find them is to search the National Register of Archives (see 1.12).

Appointments of medical staff to workhouses can sometimes be traced in MH 9 ⑦ and MH 12 ⑦. Records of doctors in the Army and Navy, however, are quite extensive: see 27.3 and 28.7.1. For a guide to the subject, see Bourne and Chicken, *Records of the medical professions: a practical guide to the family historian.*

The *Medical Directory* lists names and addresses from 1845; the Library at the National Archives has copies from 1895 to 1987. From 1858, all doctors had to be registered, with details published in the annual *Medical Register.* The Library has this from 1915 to 1973. For the eighteenth century, look at Wallis and Wallis, *Eighteenth-Century Medics (Subscriptions, Licences, Apprenticeships)*, which lists many thousands of individuals, including physicians, surgeons, apothecaries, dentists and midwives.

The Royal College of Physicians was established in 1518 and holds records on its members. Some records of the Barber-Surgeons Company are at the Guildhall Library, including registers of Naval surgeons, 1705–1745. Physicians and surgeons had to have a licence from a bishop from 1580 to 1775: records will be in local record offices, or at Lambeth Palace Library for licences from the Archbishop of Canterbury. The Bishop of London's records of licensing doctors are at the London Metropolitan Archives and the Guildhall Library.

40.4 Civilian nurses

There was no central registration of civilian nurses before 1921. In the second half of the nineteenth century, charitable movements for the care of the sick began to develop into a profession. The Nightingale Fund, set up as a result of the Crimean War, enabled the Nightingale Training School to be opened in 1860. There were two tiers of entry: the ordinary probationer

□ p. 566

who received free training and the lady-pupil who paid for her training (and who often became a matron). By the end of the nineteenth century most of the larger, voluntary hospitals had their own nurse training schools. Before 1919, the individual nurse training schools kept records: these are often still with the hospital records (see 40.2). The London Metropolitan Archives holds records of some London training schools, including Guy's Hospital, the Nightingale Training School and the Nightingale collection (address in 62).

In contrast, the workhouse infirmaries largely relied upon the older, mainly female, pauper inmates to act as unpaid nurses. It was difficult to attract trained nurses as the pay and conditions of work were unfavourable in comparison to those of the voluntary hospitals. In Liverpool and London experiments to introduce paid and unpaid nurses into infirmaries were eventually successful. Some of these infirmaries established their own nurse training schools, but many continued to use pauper nurses. Paid workhouse nurses can sometimes be found among the Registers of Paid Staff in MH 9 ⑦. Appointments of workhouse matrons and nurses may also be found among the correspondence and papers in MH 12 ⑦. You need to look for the papers relating to a particular poor law union and then read through unlisted correspondence, so this is not an easy option (see 41.2). If you want to follow up workhouse infirmaries and care of the poor sick, have a look at Geoffrey Rivett's site **www.nhshistory.net/poor_law_ infirmaries.htm**.

Quite often, nurses appear as such in the censuses – although of course anyone could call themselves a nurse. Other frequent descriptions are:

- Subordinate or Subsidiary Medical Services (abbreviated to SMS)
- Poor Law Official
- Monthly Nurse
- Sick Nurse
- Attendant or Ward Attendant.

The use of partially trained and untrained women as nurses in the First World War in Voluntary Aid Detachments (VADs) renewed the profession's fears about lack of qualification and led to calls for state registration. In 1916 the Royal College of Nursing was formed and maintained its own register (excluding male nurses and mental nurses). The Nurses Act 1919 established the General Nursing Council, with responsibility for approving training schools and for setting up a register of nurses. The register covered general nurses, male nurses, mental nurses and sick children's nurses. No provision was made for the entry of nurses with a lower standard of training. The registration of civilian nurses began in 1921.

From 1921 to 1973, State Registered Nurses were entered on the Register of Nurses (DT 10 ⑤ – the register is in number order, but the series includes alphabetical indexes to it). As the Register included nurses who were currently active, it includes people who qualified well before 1921. From

1947 to 1973, State Enrolled Nurses, with only two years' training, were entered on the Roll of Nurses (DT 11 Ⓕ – the register is in number order, but the series includes alphabetical indexes to it). From 1973 to 1983, information on both registered and enrolled nurses can be found in DT 12 Ⓩ. The information given in the Registers and Rolls includes name and maiden name, qualifications and training, address, change of name, date of marriage and date of death.

The Royal College of Nursing maintains its own archive and welcomes queries from family historians: see their factsheet at **www.rcn.org.uk/ resources/historyofnursing/factsheets-tracingnurses.php**. Papers of several nursing associations and individual nurses have been deposited in archives across the country: the easiest way to find them is to search the National Register of Archives on (see 1.12).

40.5 Midwives' records

For eighteenth-century midwives, see Wallis and Wallis. There are registration records of midwives from 1872–1888 and 1904–1983 in DV 7 Ⓩ: many of these are too damaged to be seen. Papers of several midwives have been deposited in archives across the country: the easiest way to find them is to search the National Register of Archives (see 1.12). The Royal College of Nursing maintains its own archive (address in 62) and welcomes queries from family historians about midwives: see their factsheet at **www. rcn.org.uk/resources/historyofnursing/factsheets-tracingnurses.php**.

40.6 District nurses

Training of district nurses was carried out by voluntary organisations, the chief among them being Queen Victoria's Jubilee Institute for Nurses, later the Queen's Institute of District Nursing and now the Queen's Nursing Institute. Its functions were to train district nursing associations and to supervise the county and district nursing associations. Administrative records of the nursing associations are in PRO 30/63, arranged by county. Some records of the nursing associations are largely held in local record offices: the easiest way to find them is to search the National Register of Archives (see 1.12). Some material on district nursing associations is also at the National Archives in LAB 23/49–52.

Other records of the Queen's Institute of District Nursing (under the name of The Queen's Nursing Institute) are held at the Wellcome Library (address in 62). These include registers of district nurses.

40.7 Medicine: bibliography

B ABEL-SMITH, *A history of the nursing profession* (London, 1975)

P ALLAN and M JOLLEY, eds, *Nursing, midwifery, and health visiting since 1900* (London, 1982)

E Bendall and E Raybould, *A history of the General Nursing Council for England and Wales, 1919–1969* (London, 1969)

S Bourne and A H Chicken, *Records of the medical professions: a practical guide to the family historian* (1994)

J Cassidy, 'Endangered Lives: Health and the Victorians', *Ancestors* 17 (2003/4)

J Cassidy, 'The Health of the Nation: Medicine, Money and Patients in Eighteenth-Century England', *Ancestors* 27 (2004)

J Harvey Bloom and R Rutson Jones, *Medical Practitioners in the Diocese of London, Licensed Under the Act of 3 Henry VIII, c.11: An Annotated List 1529–1725* (Cambridge, 1935)

C Hillam, *Brass Plate and Brazen Impudence: Dental Practice in the Provinces 1755–1855* (Liverpool, 1991)

W Munk, *The Roll of the Royal College of Physicians of London, 1518–1825* (London, 1861–1878)

R Porter, *Bodies Politic: Disease, Death and Doctors in Britain, 1650–1900* (London, 2001)

J H Raach, *A Directory of English Country Physicians, 1603–1643* (London, 1962)

G C Rivett, *From Cradle to Grave: fifty years of the NHS* (London, 1998)

School, University and College registers and histories in the Library of the Society of Genealogists (Society of Genealogists, 1996)

M Stocks, *A Hundred Years of District Nursing* (London, 1960).

C H Talbot and E A Hammond, *The Medical Practitioners of Medieval England: A Biographical Register* (London, 1965)

A Tanner, 'For the love of the children' [Great Ormond Street Hospital database], *Ancestors* 36 (2005)

P J Wallis and R V Wallis, *Eighteenth Century Medics (Subscriptions, Licences, Apprenticeships)* (Newcastle-upon-Tyne, 2nd edn, 1988) – lists about 35,000 individuals

41 Poor Laws and friendly societies

41.1   The old Poor Law of 1601

Paupers have attracted the active interest of the state since the Elizabethan Poor Laws were codified in 1601. Most pre-1834 records (such as those discussed in this section) will be found in the local county or borough record office, as paupers were a charge on their parish of settlement and local taxes or 'poor rates' were raised for their support.

The various accounts kept by the parish Overseers of the Poor and Churchwardens will usually give the names of people who paid the rates and those who received relief. These are the key family history records. The parish of settlement was generally the parish of birth, although this could change for married women, apprentices or those working in another parish for long periods. It was important for the parish authorities raising and spending these local rates that only those with a right to relief from their particular parish received aid. Many parishes did not act straight away to implement the 1601 Act and so it is not the case that parish Poor Law records/accounts begin in that particular year. Those parishes who believed they had very few or no problems in terms of poverty may have just continued as before, perhaps periodically raising an amount of money either through charity or by adopting a proportional rate on the land.

People with doubtful settlements were examined by local Justices of the Peace with a view to determining which parish was responsible for them. The written and sworn statements, referred to as examinations, are in effect brief biographies of the poor that may supply concise details of place of birth, marriage, movement across the county (following work) and their recent employment. Many disputes of individual settlements between parishes can be found in the records of Quarter Sessions. The records produced in the course of proving settlement can be very informative for family history. For a brief and lucid guide to the poor relief system, the various Poor Laws and the idea of settlement, see Herber, *Ancestral Trails*.

There is very little detailed and consistent family history material in the National Archives about the operation of the Elizabethan Poor Law and its system of outdoor relief for the deserving poor, or about Houses of

Correction established for the undeserving poor. You will find much more material by searching A2A (see 1.13). See Cole, *An Introduction to Poor Law Documents before 1834* or Fowler, *Using Poor Law Records*.

41.2 The new Poor Law of 1834 and the workhouse system

Workhouses to supply indoor relief in as repulsive a way as could be designed (in order to put people off from applying for help) were established by the Poor Law Commission under the Poor Law Amendment Act of 1834. The act required parishes to be grouped together into 'Poor Law unions'. These unions were managed by 'guardians of the poor', who were elected by the ratepayers of the constituent parishes. The guardians then appointed permanent staff to run the union workhouse on a day-to-day basis. Although the new Poor Law underwent various changes throughout their existence, the Poor Law unions continued until 1930. You need to know which union your people may have belonged to before you begin your search. To find out in which union a particular parish belonged, see Gibson and Youngs, *Poor Law Union Records: 4 Gazetteer of England and Wales*. The three previous pamphlets in this excellent series give advice on the range of records to be found, and references to documents in local record offices and in the National Archives.

For the records created under the New Poor Law you will need to search both local record offices and the National Archives. For family history purposes the local material will be of the most use. Where records survive you should expect a wide variety of material for particular Poor Law unions, including rate books, guardians' minute books, punishment books, admissions and discharge books.

The records of the Poor Law Commission (and later the Poor Law Board and Local Government Board) are in MH. They are not particularly easy to use for family history, and searches are likely to be lengthy but could be ultimately very rewarding. MH 12 ⑥, the main class of correspondence, is known to contain the names of thousands of individuals but will not contain the names of all (or even most) of those claiming poor relief. The records contained in MH 12 begin in 1834 and end around 1900, as most of the twentieth-century material was destroyed by enemy action and fire during the Second World War. There is no name index to these records. They are listed by Poor Law union and the covering dates of each volume are provided. However, there is no indication as to subject matters covered in these volumes. There are subject indexes in MH 15 ⑦, but only to correspondence that created a precedent and which the Poor Law Commission would thus have needed reference to in the future. The Assistant Commissioners (and other inspectors) Reports in MH 32 ⑦ will also provide a great deal of information of the Poor Law unions under their remit, but have only a small number of references to individual relief claimants. Many of the records in MH 12 and MH 32 are in a poor condition.

Work has been started to list at least some of these MH 12 volumes. We are working with the Southwell Workhouse Research Group (based at the National Trust's Southwell Workhouse property in Nottinghamshire) to list all the Southwell Poor Law Union correspondence in MH 12 for the nineteenth century. The records for 1834 to 1871 should be catalogued by early 2007, when the digitised images of the records themselves will also be made available. The remaining Southwell material will be also be catalogued but not digitised. Some of the early volumes for the Manchester Poor Law Union are listed in detail in our catalogue. A single volume for Bradford, Yorkshire covering the setting up of the new system has been transcribed and published by Paul Carter, who is leading all the above projects.

Local records are easier to use, particularly with Gibson and Youngs to hand.

Remember that there was intense local interest in making sure that locally taxed money was not spent too liberally on the workhouses. As a result, meetings of the Board of Guardians might be reported quite fully in local newspapers. Individuals are not usually mentioned by name, unless they have done something to bring attention to themselves – for example, complained about the food.

41.3 Poor Law union staff

For workhouse staff, 1837–1921, you should consult the registers in MH 9. The registers include information on the wide variety of staff, including workhouse mistresses and masters, nurses and work instructors. The entries are brief and to the point; dates of appointment and salary are given and the date of death is sometimes noted. Personal details of people appointed, up to c. 1900, may be found in various forms among the mass of papers in MH 12. The forms often give full name, age, address, details of previous jobs and reasons for appointment to the present post, and salary. Names of wives and number of children are sometimes given, as are details of religion and qualifications. MH 12 can also contain references for applicants and correspondence on dismissal.

You may find it worth looking at *Parliamentary Papers* to check on returns of Poor Law union officials made to Parliament: these can give personal details. They can be accessed online at the National Archives.

41.4 Friendly societies

Friendly societies abounded across the country in the eighteenth and nineteenth centuries, sporting such wonderful titles as the Amalgamated Independent Order of Total Abstinent Sons of the Phoenix, or the Confederated Thespian Brotherhood. Some of these were purely local, others local branches of national organisations. You may well find reference to them among family papers, or even have some insignia if you are lucky (see Dennis on badges and regalia).

Weinbren's interesting article on using friendly society records sets the context very well. 'Friendly societies were founded as mutual aid organisations, to protect individuals and their families in times of hardship. By paying in money every month, members were eligible for payments in case of sickness or death. Most of these societies were formed in the eighteenth and nineteenth centuries as people left the countryside with its community support networks and moved to urban areas, and they felt the need for an organisation to support them when family and friends were unavailable. Fearful of falling into poverty and ending their days in the workhouse and being buried in a pauper's grave, they also enjoyed the companionship that friendly societies offered, where everyone was a "brother" or a "sister".

Most friendly society records are kept locally (try a search in A2A: see 1.13), but large numbers of regulations are kept at the National Archives, from 1784 on. The government was always suspicious of any meeting of working people, and doubly suspicious if life insurance was involved: it was always seen as having too much of a tang of incitement to murder about it. The friendly societies covered much more than burial expenses though – such as help with emigration, sick benefit and trade support. Even quite small places could support several friendly societies.

Friendly society records at the National Archives are mostly in the several FS series. They are not always easy to find. Some can be found by an online search in FS, but most are listed solely by county and have to be found by using indexes at the National Archives.

41.5 Poor Laws and friendly societies: bibliography

A Brundage, *The English Poor Law, 1700–1930* (Basingstoke, 2002)

R Burlison, 'No destitute child ever refused' [Dr Barnado], *Ancestors* 37 (2005)

A Carter ed., *Little Melton – the story of a Norfolk village* [shows what can be found from MH 12], (Little Melton, 2004)

P Carter, *Bradford Poor Law Union: Papers and Correspondence with the Poor Law Commission, October 1834 to January 1839* (Yorkshire Archaeological Society, 2004)

A Cole, *An Introduction to Poor Law Documents before 1834* (FFHS, 1993)

S Cordery, *British Friendly Societies, 1750–1914* (2003)

V S Dennis, *Discovering Friendly and Fraternal Societies: Their Badges and Regalia* (2005)

S Donnelly, 'Mapping London's Rich and Poor', *Ancestors* 9 (2002)

S Fowler, *Using Poor Law Records* (PRO, 2001)

D Fraser, ed., *The New Poor Law in the nineteenth century* (London, 1976)

J S W Gibson, C Rogers and C Webb, *Poor Law Union Records: 1. South-East England and East Anglia* (FFHS, 1993)

J S W Gibson and C Rogers, *Poor Law Union Records: 2. The Midlands and Northern England* (FFHS, 1997)

J S W GIBSON and C ROGERS, *Poor Law Union Records: 3. South-West England, The Marches and Wales* (FFHS, 2000)

J S W GIBSON and F A YOUNGS, *Poor Law Union Records: 4. Gazetteer of England and Wales* (FFHS, 1997)

P GOSDEN, *The Friendly Societies in England, 1815–1875* (Manchester, 1961)

P GOSDEN, *Self-help: voluntary associations in the 19th century* (1973)

M HERBER, *Ancestral Trails* (Society of Genealogists, 2000)

D HEY, 'A Burden on the Parish', *Ancestors* 9 (2002)

L HOLLEN LEES, *The Solidarities of Strangers: the English Poor Laws and the People, 1700–1948* (Cambridge, 1998)

E HOPKINS, *Working-Class Self-Help in Nineteenth-Century England* (1995)

J KNOTT, *Popular opposition to the 1834 Poor Law* (London, 1986)

A MORTON, 'Contracting out Cruelty' [pauper children], *Ancestors* 29 (2005)

S PEARL, 'Charities: the forgotten poor relief', *Family Tree Magazine*, May 1991

G REDMONDS, 'Scenes from Ordinary Life' [quarter sessions and the enforcement of the Poor Law], *Ancestors* 17 (2003/4)

K D M SNELL, *The Annals of the Labouring Poor* (Cambridge, 1985)

W TATE, *The Parish Chest* (Cambridge, 1969)

K THOMPSON, 'Workhouse Days', *Ancestors* 9 (2002)

D WEINBREN, 'Mutually Beneficial: using the records of friendly societies', *Ancestors* 22 (2004)

R WILTSHIRE, 'Asylum for London's Poor and Sick', *Ancestors* 31 (2005)

T WOOD, 'Workhouse Ancestors', *Family Tree Magazine*, October and November 1995

42 Lunacy

42.1   Lunacy: an introduction

For most of the past, the state has had little interest in the mental health of its subjects, unless they had a sufficient amount of property to require the intervention of the Crown as a feudal lord. Pauper lunatics were dealt with locally.

For a guide for family historians, see Faithfull, *Basic Facts about Lunatics*. Lappin's thesis, 'Central Government and the supervision of the treatment of lunatics 1800–1913' is a detailed guide to records on lunacy. Copies are available in the National Archives Library and at the Wellcome Library. For the historical background, try Porter, *A Social History of Madness*.

42.2   Chancery lunatics: royal interest in the property of lunatics and idiots

The custody of the lands and persons of idiots ('natural fools from birth') and lunatics ('sometimes of good and sound memory and understanding and sometimes not') belonged to the Crown. Idiots and lunatics were the responsibility of the Lord Chancellor, although the Court of Wards took this over for 1540–1646: they were sometimes known as the 'Chancery lunatics'. The king was entitled to administer the lands of an idiot during his life, but of the lunatic only during periods of insanity. The lands or possessions were not generally retained in Crown hands, but granted out for the term of the lunacy or idiocy to 'committees' (i.e., those to whose care the lunatic or his estate was committed – possibly the next of kin).

Although the Crown's interest was at first paramount, over time the priority appears to have become the proper administration of the lunatic's estate, an issue often of vital importance to the next of kin. The whole point of getting a person declared of unsound mind by a Chancery inquisition was to take away his or her power of independent legal action in the disposition of property; it had nothing to do with committal to an asylum, which was a separate medical procedure. In many cases the alleged lunatic was already in an asylum when the inquisition took place; the only requirement for committal was for two doctors to issue a certificate. From

1900 to 1983, we have a two-per-cent sample of the working papers of the Court of Protection in J 92 ☑, selected to illustrate both the administration of patients' estates and their medical histories.

Lunatics and idiots were brought to the Chancellor's attention by several routes. Concerned relatives could submit a petition to the Chancellor. So could solicitors or others who were acting as the executors of a will or as trustees, where one of the beneficiaries was thought to be a lunatic. Creditors could petition for someone to be declared a lunatic, as they could claim payment of the debt from the Master in Lunacy. Lunacy Commissioners themselves, fearing that the money of an asylum inmate was being misappropriated, could petition for an investigation. All petitioners had to support their request for a commission of inquiry with at least two sworn affidavits supporting their opinion of the state of mind of the supposed lunatic. These affidavits do not generally survive, but the gist is given in the abstract of the petition in C 211. About 1,000 surviving affidavits in support of petitions for a lunacy commission are to be found in C 217/55, dating from 1719 to 1733: they are as yet not listed individually nor indexed.

The Lord Chancellor had first to order commissioners to hold an inquisition into whether a person was of sound mind or not; second, to commit the custody of the lunatic and his estate to suitable persons (called 'committees'); and third, to examine the accounts, etc., of the committees.

Commissions and inquisitions are in Latin until the Interregnum, and between 1660 and 1733; for the Interregnum and from 1733 they are in English. Inquisitions of lunacy produced before 1540 are with the inquisitions post mortem in C 132–C 141 ☑ and C 142 ☑ (see 49.7). From 1540 to 1648 they are in WARD 7 ☑. Petitions and inquisitions from about 1648 to 1932 are in C 211 (or in PL 5 ☑ for Lancashire). The C 211 inquisitions are fully searchable by name, forename or place in the catalogue from 1853 onwards; from 1648 to part way through 1853, there is a manuscript index. Disputes ('traverses') on the validity of an inquisition may be found in the common law side of Chancery: see 57.1. There are few lunacy commissions for England in the twentieth century. The later records, however, do contain copies of inquisitions taken in Ireland and in some British colonies; the latter are specifically concerned with the mental health of the person and with getting them transported back to Britain.

Information about the estates and possessions of a lunatic was sent to the Clerk of the Custodies, who granted out the custody of the persons and estates of lunatics and idiots by the issue of letters patent to the committees. These were not generally enrolled on the patent rolls, but in a separate series of rolls, which unfortunately appear to have been destroyed in the later nineteenth century. However, there is register of bonds by committees, 1817–1904, in J 103 ☑. Some bonds given by committees, 1876–1919, are in J 117/123.

Accounts were supposed to be submitted annually by the committee to the Chancery Masters: these are easy to find (if they survive) by checking c 101 ☐, the Chancery Masters' accounts. There are just over 400 accounts for lunatics, described as (for example) 'Smith, a lunatic'. They often give more detail about the tenants than they do about the lunatic, but they can provide some extra information.

The most informative records may be found among the Chancery Masters' reports and exhibits, but there is no guarantee of finding anything (see 58.8–58.9. You can pick out lunatics from Chancery litigation if they are described as *In re Smith, a lunatic*. The reports are in c 38 ☐: there are indexes in IND 1, which can be identified from the c 38 list. Some exhibits from cases relating to lunatics will be found in c 103–c 115 ☐; in fact, the whole series c 115 exists because of the lunacy of Frances Scudamore, Duchess of Norfolk. Later exhibits will be found in J 90 ☐.

If you find that exhibits exist, you may have struck lucky. For example, the exhibits in *Re Freeman: a lunatic*, in c 110/164, include extracts from the parish register of St Peter's, Antigua, 1719–1728 and 1752. They relate to the lunatic Thomas Freeman's family – several letters from his brother Arthur, and the original letter patent sent out to the family's lawyer committing Freeman to his custody; as well as a further 50 or so papers detailing a legacy of £1,500 by his godfather and namesake to Freeman as an infant, and the difficulty of deciding if it was going to be paid in Antiguan or British currency.

Decrees and orders relating to lunatics should be found in c 33 ☐ and J 79 ☐ (records from this latter series need to be ordered three days in advance).

Official visitors' reports on Chancery lunatics, from 1879 (with a 75-year closure) are in LCO 10 ☐: they give name, address, age, income and allowance.

42.3 Lunatic asylums

People of means had to make private arrangements for any lunatics in the family. The private madhouses were licensed by the justices of the peace, and were examined by several series of government commissioners. One register of admissions to private asylums outside London, for 1798 to 1812, is in MH 51/735: it includes the names of 1,788 patients, and is indexed by both lunatics (at the front) and keepers of licensed houses (at the back).

Pauper lunatics were dealt with locally under the Poor Law, vagrancy law or criminal law and were therefore likely to end up in workhouses, houses of correction or prisons before the establishment of county lunatic asylums in the mid-nineteenth century. These records would be kept locally, but we have returns of insane inmates in workhouses and asylums from 1834 to 1909 (MH 12 ☐). These give name, age, type of disability and whether considered dangerous. Unfortunately, they are arranged by county and Poor Law union, and there are subject indexes only (MH 15 ☐). Correspondence with asylum districts in MH 17 may be worth looking at. See 41 on how to identify the Poor Law union and on guides to the records that exist.

There are also returns of insane prisoners in prisons and houses of correction, submitted in March 1858 (MH 51/90–207 ☷).

From the early nineteenth century, justices of the peace were encouraged to build county lunatic asylums to house any pauper lunatics in their county; in 1845, this became compulsory. The 1890 Lunacy Act gave asylums a wider role, and patients with means began to be admitted. Records of the county asylums are likely to be kept locally, as may those of the private asylums: check the HOSPREC database at **www.nationalarchives.gov.uk/ hospitalrecords/**, or A2A (see 1.13).

Most patient files have been destroyed. A very few survive in MH 85 ☑, MH 86 ☑ (with 75-year closures on descriptions as well as documents) and MH 51/27–77 ☑ (these look very interesting). However, the registers to the patient files survive in MH 94 ☷ for various categories of inmates from 1846 to 1960. This series contains registers kept by the Lunacy Commission, 1846 to 1913, and the Board of Control, 1913 to 1960. They record the name and sex of the patient; the name of hospital, asylum or licensed house; and the date of admission and of discharge or death of each patient. Further information on the medical and legal circumstances of each patient was entered in the diaries, 1937–1957, also preserved in this series. These note the receipt of medical statements and action to be taken; the receipt of a patient's right to see a judicial authority; the urgency of the case; and further remarks. Temporary and private patients' diaries vary a little in the information they provide.

A union card index to all patients admitted (possibly from as early as 1774) was destroyed in 1961: apparently it covered over 2.5 million names.

42.4 Naval and military lunatics

There are several musters of lunatics at Hoxton House, 1755–1818 (ADM 102/415–420 ☷) and at Haslar Hospital, 1818–1854 (ADM 102/356–373 ☷). Yarmouth too was a major hospital for Naval and military lunatics. Reports on the treatment of Naval lunatics, 1812–1832, are in ADM 105/28. Reports on the Royal Military Lunatic Asylum, Yarmouth (1848–1852) are in MH 51/42.

42.5 Lunacy: bibliography

P FAITHFULL, *Basic Facts about Lunatics* (FFHS, 2002)

J H LAPPIN, 'Central Government and the supervision of the treatment of lunatics 1800–1913: a guide to sources in the Public Record Office' (unpublished MA thesis, 1995). Available in the National Archives Library

W PARRY-JONES, *The trade in lunacy: a study of private madhouses in England in the eighteenth and nineteenth centuries* (London, 1972)

R PORTER, *A Social History of Madness* (1989, reissued 1999)

43 Churches and chapels

43.1 The established church

Until the break with Rome in 1534, the established religion of England and Wales was (Roman) Catholic. After this (with the brief exception of Mary I's reign, 1553–1558), the established religion was that of the Church of England, covering a wide range from high church to low church, Anglo-Catholic to Calvinist.

The National Archives is not the obvious place to look for ecclesiastical records: see Owen's book on the records of the established church and Bourne and Chicken's guide to Anglican records. In fact, the National Archives does have considerable holdings on the administration of the church in relation to the state, and particularly on the monasteries, but relatively little of this contains information of interest to family historians. However, there are some sources in the National Archives that can provide information on the clergy and the lay members of the church before and after the Reformation.

43.2 Excommunicates from the established church, 1280s–1840s

Excommunication was a punishment imposed by the church for a wide variety of offences, both religious and moral. The National Archives holds the requests (technically, known as *significavits* or significations) from the bishops for the 'secular arm' (i.e., the power of the state) to be used against people excommunicated by the church. These significations survive from the 1220s to 1611 (c 85 Ⓔ), and again from George II to the 1840s (c 207 Ⓩ). It is not clear what has happened to the intervening requests. The later excommunications are often for contempt of court.

The earliest significations usually provide little more than the name of the person excommunicated, but the later ones in c 85 can include reference to occupation, place of residence, father, nature of the offence, etc. About 7,600 significations survive from c 85, and its card index is arranged first by diocese and then alphabetically by name of the person excommunicated. The documents themselves are in Latin. The significations in c 207 are in English, but have not yet been indexed: as a result, they are less easy to use than the earlier ones.

Significations for the county palatine of Chester were issued by Chester officials and are in CHES 38/25/4–25/6 for 1378–1396, 1551, 1663–1668 and 1671–1690. Those for Flint, Henry VIII to Elizabeth I, and for Pembroke-shire, George II, have been transferred with the rest of WALE 28 to the National Library of Wales.

43.3 Anglican clergymen

Searching for Anglican clergy between 1540 and 1835 is being transformed by an ongoing project, the Clergy of the Church of England Database, which will document the careers of all Church of England clergymen between 1540 and 1835 – **www.kcl.ac.uk/humanities/cch/cce/**. Not all dioceses are covered yet, but the site is very clear about what is available and what is forthcoming.

After 1835, and before using any documentary sources, you should consult the following printed works, which should be available in a good reference library (and are also in the National Archives Library). *Crockford's Clerical Directory*, published annually from 1858, is the place to start, followed by the lists of Oxford and Cambridge *Alumni* [students]. The National Archives Library also holds:

- *Clerical Guide* of 1836, which is almost a snapshot of the state of the national church in 1836;
- *Clergy List* for 1842–1917, which includes some details of the higher clergy of the Anglican church worldwide;
- *Clergy Directory* for 1872–1916 (an annual alphabetical list of beneficed clergy and their positions).

The ordination records in the appropriate diocesan archives can be a very useful source of genealogical information: they usually include a certified copy of the baptismal entry or a letter explaining why there was none, details of education and character references. There were several life insurance companies catering solely for the clergy: the Guildhall Library has a collection of London insurance company records, which can provide a wealth of personal details.

Most National Archives documents relating to the appointment of Anglican clergymen to benefices are very formal and do not include any information of great use to family historians. The bishops' certificates of institutions to benefices, 1544–1912 (E 331 ⊞), are usually approached through the Institution Books, 1556–1838 (IND 1/17000–17015). These are arranged firstly by county (1556–1660) or diocese (1661–1838), then by place: they give the name of the clergyman instituted to the benefice, the date, and the name of the patron of the benefice. They can be useful for tracing the ecclesiastical career of the clergyman but they do not provide any personal details. The Composition Books record payments due by the cleric on taking up his benefice, 1535–1795 (IND 1/17016–17028 [7]) and refer to the records in E 334.

For the Commonwealth period, there are returns in C 94 [7] made by parish juries to a commission of inquiry of 1650–1651 that investigated church livings in England and Wales. These provide the name and character of the incumbent, the amount, source and nature of his maintenance, the nearness or otherwise of the parochial chapelries and the advisability of parochial unions or divisions. Matthews' *Calamy Revised* is a useful source of information about clergy appointed during the Interregnum.

If you are researching someone who was a clergyman in 1801 or 1851, you may like to investigate two series of records composed of returns made by the parish clergy on conditions in their parish. The Acreage Returns of 1801 (HO 67 [7] – arranged by diocese), although intended to provide factual information on the state of agriculture at a village level, can include some very individualistic comments made by the parish priest on his parishioners. The Ecclesiastical Census of 1851 (HO 129 [4], [5]), although a survey of places of worship, can also provide an interesting picture of life at the parish level and sometimes personal details on the clergy as well.

43.4 Roman Catholics

Elizabeth I, coming to the throne in November 1558, was queen of a country at risk of division on religious lines between Protestant and Catholic. In 1559, an Act of Uniformity imposed fines on all men who refused to attend Church of England services at their parish church; in 1563, the death penalty was imposed on priests who said mass. Later laws imposed numerous penalties and fines for non-attendance at Anglican services, and Catholics were effectively barred from inheriting land, entering the professions or taking up civil or military office: because they could not accept the monarch as Head of the Church, it was feared they would not be loyal subjects. In the eighteenth century, active discrimination was largely allowed to lapse, although formal Catholic emancipation was not to come until 1829.

In the National Archives, records of Catholics are largely the records of their persecution and the bulk of these accordingly varies with fluctuations in anti-Catholicism. Many records relate to the attempts of Catholics to demonstrate their loyalty. There are lists of Catholic solicitors and attorneys for the period 1790–1836 (CP 10 [7]), 1791–1813 (C 217/180/5) and

1830–1875 (E 3 ⑦). The 'Papists' oaths of allegiance, etc. in E 169/79–83 give names and addresses for 1778–1857 (with gaps).

However, most relate to the imposition of fines or seizures of land for failure to attend Protestant services (and could actually apply to Protestant Nonconformists as well as Catholics). The fines laid down in the 1559 Act of Uniformity for failure to attend church were collected by churchwardens and so do not appear in the central government records. After 1581, recusancy (refusal to attend the Anglican church) became an indictable offence, so fines levied were accounted for at the Exchequer by sheriffs of each county. These fines were initially recorded in the Pipe Rolls (E 372 ⑦) but would be very difficult to find among all the other data recorded there. After 1592 they are in two series of Recusant Rolls (E 376 ⑦ and E 377 ⑦). These are annual returns of dissenters (Protestant and Catholic) who had property forfeited or were fined, 1592–1691. However, they are large, mostly in Latin and difficult to use. It is a good idea to check one of the published editions first in order to understand the format of the rolls. Entries are arranged by county, and they record convictions, fines, rentals for forfeited lands and details of chattels seized.

There are several 'returns of Papists' in the State Papers and records of the Privy Council. For example, there is a printed return for 1625–1642 in SP 16/495 and a return for 1708 in SP 34/26. Try also the manuscript indexes to the Privy Council registers in PC 2 ⑧ under 'Church affairs'. Accounts for the forfeited estates of recusants, 1625–1684, are in E 351/414–452 ⑦. Most Catholics supported the King in the Civil War, so their estates may be referred to in *Calendars of the Committee for Compounding with Delinquents*. There are many inventories of Catholic possessions in the State Papers for the Interregnum (SP 28 ⑦).

From the reign of George I and the Jacobite risings, there are lists of Catholics who forfeited their estates (E 174 ② ⑤, KB 18 ⑦, FEC 1 ② ⑤ and FEC 2 ⑦). These are easy and useful sources – at last!

County record offices hold much material on persecutions of Papists. Between 1715 and 1791, Catholics were required to register their estates with the local Clerk of the Peace: these are likely to be with quarter sessions records.

The baptism, marriage and burial registers of Catholic churches are either in the National Archives (see 5.9) or still with the church concerned. The relevant diocesan archivist or the Catholic Central Library may be able to assist in tracing them. The *English Catholic Ancestor* aims at acquiring and disseminating information about Catholic families. The Catholic Record Society has published a great deal of useful record material, but does not handle enquiries. Burials of Catholics often took place in the parish churchyard and are therefore recorded in the parish registers. For much fuller information on Catholic genealogy, see Steel and Samuel. For an overview of being a Catholic in England from 1558 to 1778 see Rowlands, *Catholics of Parish and Town*.

□ p. 566

The National Archives has published a specialist guide, *Protestant Nonconformity and Roman Catholicism* by Shorney, as well as the useful *Tracing Catholic Ancestors* by Gandy.

43.5 Protestant Nonconformists

Nonconformists (like Roman Catholics) were initially thought to be of suspect loyalty. The Recusant Rolls, 1592–1691 (E 376 ⑦ and E 377 ⑦) are annual returns of both Protestant Nonconformists and of Catholics who had property forfeited or who were fined for dissenting from the Church of England.

There are a number of oath or affirmation rolls for Nonconformists in the National Archives. The Association Oath of 1696, in support of William III, was sworn or affirmed by London and Hampshire dissenters (C 214/9–10), Quakers in Colchester (C 213/473), Nonconformist ministers in Cumberland (C 213/60–61) and Baptist ministers in London (C 213/170). There are also affirmation rolls for Quaker attorneys, 1831–1835 (E 3 ⑦) and 1836–1842 (CP 10⑦). For Huguenots, see 19.2.

Under the Toleration Act of 1689, Justices of the Peace were made responsible for licensing Nonconformist meeting houses: these licences may be found among the quarter sessions records in local record offices. From 1736, deeds involving the inalienable transfer of land for charitable purposes had to be enrolled on the Close Rolls (C 54 🖻 and, from 1902, J 18 🖻). The great majority of these deeds involved the establishment of Nonconformist chapels, schools, burial grounds and charities: between 1736 and 1870 over 35,000 deeds were enrolled. There are two indexes to these deeds, both to places: for 1736–1870 there are volume indexes to trust deeds and for 1870–1904 there are card indexes. In addition, C 54 and J 18 also have annual indexes to their whole contents. These deeds are a very valuable source for local history and for the involvement of individual Nonconformists in establishing their chapels and setting up schemes for self-improvement.

The National Archives holds the majority of Nonconformist registers of births or baptisms, marriages and deaths or burials for the period before 1837, and also a considerable number after that date (see 5.4). However, in some cases, these registers contained other records of the church or chapel as well. The General Register Office, to whom they had been surrendered, adopted the practice of tearing out the other records where this could be done easily and returning them to the church. To discover their present location, you need to consult a guide to the particular denomination's archives (see 43.8). In a few cases, the information was spread throughout the volume and escaped such archival vandalism, so that some of the registers discussed in 5 still include more general records.

The National Archives has published a specialist guide, *Protestant*

Nonconformity and Roman Catholicism by Shorney, as well as the useful *Tracing Nonconformist Ancestors* by Gandy.

43.6 Sacrament certificates: a proof of membership of the Church of England

From 1672 onwards, various statutes required that office-holders (and aliens seeking naturalisation) should take certain oaths in support of the Crown and against papal supremacy. In addition, the swearer was required to take the sacrament of the Lord's Supper according to the Anglican rites, to prove that he was a member of the Church of England and neither a Roman Catholic nor a Protestant Nonconformist. Evidence of this was provided by a certificate completed and signed by the minister and church-wardens of the parish with the signatures of two witnesses appended. The certificates were presented when the oath was sworn, at one of the central courts if within 30 miles of Westminster and at the quarter sessions if further away. As a result, the majority of sacrament certificates in the National Archives are from Middlesex, Hertfordshire, Surrey and Kent, within the 30-mile radius of Westminster.

Certificates presented to Chancery, 1673–1778, are in c 224 ⑦; those presented in the Exchequer, 1700–1827, are in e 196 ⑦. Certificates presented in King's Bench survive from 1676 and from 1728–1828 (kb 22 ⑦). Certificates presented in the Cheshire courts, 1673–1768, are in ches 4 ⑦: many of them date from the 1715 Jacobite Rising. Sacrament certificates presented to the quarter sessions should be in local record offices: see A2A (1.13).

43.7 Orthodox churches in London

The archive of the Russian Orthodox Church in London (sometimes known as the Orthodox Greco-Russian Church), 1721–1951, is in rg 8/111–304 ⑦. Most of the archive is in Russian, with some documents in Greek, English, French and German; the catalogue entries are in English and are descriptive but not detailed. The records are of various kinds to do with the organisation of the church and the Russian community in England, including Russian prisoners of war during the Crimean War. There are also registers and other records of baptisms, marriages and deaths, as well as communicants and conversions, dating from 1721 to 1927. Some of these relate to Greeks and other non-Russians.

For the Greek orthodox community, there is the register of marriages solemnised by the Greek Church in London between 1837 and 1865 in j 166.

43.8 Churches and chapels: bibliography

R W Ambler, 'Enrolled Trust Deeds – A source for the History of Nineteenth Century Nonconformity', *Archives* vol. XX (1993), pp. 177–186

D Annal, 'Movers and Quakers; Nonconformist Registers at the FRC', *Ancestors* 14 (2003)

D A Bellenger, *English and Welsh priests 1558–1800: a working list* (Bath, 1984)

S Bourne and A H Chicken, *Records of the Church of England: A Practical Guide for the Family Historian* (Maidstone, 1988)

G R Breed, *My Ancestors were Baptists* (Society of Genealogists, 1995)

J Bossy, *The English Catholic Community, 1570–1850* (London, 1975)

Calendar of State Papers, Domestic, Committee for Compounding with Delinquents, 1643–1660 (London, 1889–1893)

Catholic Directory (London, annually from 1837)

Catholic Record Society, *Bibliographical Studies*, vols I–III, changed to *Recusant History*, from vol. IV (Bognor Regis, 1951 to date)

Catholic Record Society, *Publications* (1905, continuing)

K Chater, 'Taking French Leave' [Huguenots], *Ancestors* 33 (2005)

Clergy Directory (1872–1916)

Clergy List (1842–1917)

Clerical Guide (1836)

Crockford's Clerical Directory (Oxford, annually from 1858)

N Currer-Briggs and R Gambier, *Huguenot Ancestry* (Chichester, 1985)

Dr Williams's Trust, *Nonconformist Congregations in Britain* (London, 1973)

The English Catholic Ancestor (Aldershot, 1983–1989; Ealing, 1989 continuing)

J Foster, *Alumni Oxonienses, 1500–1886* (Oxford, 1891)

M Gandy, *Catholic Family History: A Bibliography* (4 vols, 1996)

M Gandy, *Catholic Missions and Registers* (6 vols, 1993)

M Gandy, *Catholic Parishes in England, Wales and Scotland: An Atlas* (1993)

M Gandy, *Tracing Catholic Ancestors* (PRO, 2001)

M Gandy, *Tracing Nonconformist Ancestors* (PRO, 2001)

R M Gard, *Directory of Catholic archives in the United Kingdom and Eire* (Newcastle upon Tyne, 1984)

N Graham, *The Genealogists' Consolidated Guide to Nonconformist and Foreign Registers in Inner London, 1538–1837* (Birchington, 1980)

R D Gwynn, *Huguenot Heritage: the History and Contribution of the Huguenots in Britain* (London, 1985)

D Hey, 'The Rise of Protestant Nonconformity', *Ancestors* 14 (2003)

Huguenot Society, *Publications* (1885 continuing: many now available as CD-Rom)

J Le Neve and others, *Fasti Ecclesie Anglicanae* (London, 1716). There is a revised and updated version, covering 1066–1857 (London, 1962 continuing)

W Leary, *My Ancestors were Methodists* (Society of Genealogists, 1999)

F D Logan, *Excommunication and the secular arm in medieval England* (Toronto, 1968)

A G Matthews, *Calamy Revised* (Oxford, 1934)

E H Milligan and M J Thomas, *My Ancestors were Quakers* (Society of Genealogists, 1999)

M Mullett, *Sources for the History of English Non-Conformity 1660–1830* (British Records Association, 1991)

D M Owen, *The records of the established church in England, excluding parochial records* (British Records Association, 1970)

P Palgrave-Moore, *Understanding the History and Records of Nonconformity* (Norwich, 2nd edn, 1989)

M B Rowlands, ed, *Catholics of Parish and Town 1558–1778* (Catholic Record Society Monographs, 1999)

A Ruston, *My Ancestors were English Presbyterians/Unitarians* (Society of Genealogists, 1993)

L F Salzman, 'Sussex excommunicates', *Sussex Archaeological Collections*, vol. LXXXIII, pp. 124–140

D Shorney, *Protestant Nonconformity and Roman Catholicism: A Guide to Sources in the Public Record Office* (PRO, 1996)

S Smiles, *The Huguenots: Their Settlements, Churches, and Industries in England and Ireland* (London 1867, reprinted 2003)

D J Steel, *Sources of Nonconformist Genealogy and Family History* (London, 1973)

D J Steel and E R Samuel, *Sources for Roman Catholic and Jewish Genealogy and Family History* (London, 1974)

J Venn and J A Venn, *Alumni Cantabrigienses, from the Earliest Times to 1900* (Cambridge, 1922–1927)

R Wiggins, *My Ancestors were in the Salvation Army* (Society of Genealogists, 1997)

J A Williams, *Sources for Recusant History (1559–1791) in English Official Archives* (1983)

44 Jews

44.1   Jewish genealogy

Most of the techniques and sources for researching Jewish ancestors who settled in the United Kingdom are the same as those for tracing anyone else who has lived here. However, there are some sources specific to the Jewish community and others which can be particularly valuable. If you can, do try the very helpful online guide to Tracing Jewish Roots by S Isroff (giving excellent advice on how to start, and further links) at **www.moving here.org.uk/galleries/roots/jewish/jewish.htm**. For published guides to Jewish genealogy, see the bibliography.

44.2   Jewish settlement

There were Jews in England in the early Middle Ages, but no line of descent has been traced from members of this early community, which was expelled in 1290. The Jewish community developed from Sephardic (Portuguese, Spanish and Italian) Jews, arriving from 1656 onwards, and from Ashkenazi (Central and East European) Jews, first coming in the 1680s from Holland and Bohemia. By 1800, there may have been 15,000 to 20,000 Jews in England. Three-quarters of these were in London, with significant communities in Bristol and Exeter, often involved in trade and appearing in all the usual business and legal records.

This relatively small number was suddenly expanded by the influx of about 120,000 Russian and Polish Jews in the 1880s, 1890s and 1910s, fleeing Tsarist persecution to find a new life wherever they could, despite their new destitution. The 1930s and 1940s saw the arrival of more Jews seeking a refuge – all too many of them the sadly unaccompanied children of the Kindertransport.

To explore Jewish history, culture and religion in Britain and beyond, have a look at **www.jewishmuseum.org.uk/index.asp**.

44.3 Records elsewhere: earlier sources

The birth, marriage and death registers of synagogues before civil registration started in 1837 are often still held by the congregations concerned. For help, apply to the Board of Deputies of British Jews (**www.bod.org.uk/bod/index.jsp?page=extra&address=archives/archive. jsp**). The Hartley Library at Southampton University has part of the Anglo-Jewish Archive, which used to be in the Mocatta Library, University College London. However, the main genealogical collections are now at the Society of Genealogists. These are the collections of Sir Thomas Colyer Fergusson, Ronald D'Arcy Hart and A M Hyamson. Addresses are given in 62.

Don't forget to try a search on A2A for records held in local archives: see 1.13.

44.4 Records elsewhere: later sources

The London Metropolitan Archives has a large and growing collection of archives on Jewish life in London and the UK, including the records of the Jewish Temporary Shelter. The records, which start in 1886, include files on Jewish immigrants and give name on arrival, age, town of origin, destination after leaving the shelter and trade or profession.

The London Metropolitan Archives also has the records of the Jews Free School, London. Between 1880 and 1900, one third of all London's Jewish children passed through its doors – by 1900 it had some 4,000 pupils and was the largest school in Europe. They also house administrative records of the Jewish Refugees Committee from the 1930s, as well as some personal files on the children who came on the Kindertransport programme.

Other personal files on Jewish refugees from the 1930s and 1940s (including children) are still kept by the Jewish Refugees Committee: these give date and place of birth, nationality, profession, home address, date of arrival and address in Britain. Access to all of these different records may be restricted: at the Jewish Refugees Committee, for example, to the person on whom the file was kept or to their proven next of kin if they have died (write first or see **www.worldjewishrelief.org/projects/?id=50**). The Hartley Library at the University of Southampton also holds material on individual refugees: you need to write to them first. All these addresses are in 62.

44.5 Sources for daily life in the National Archives

Sources here are too numerous to cover adequately but the following examples may be useful:

- Poor Law Board and Local Government Board correspondence with local Poor Law authorities in areas of Jewish settlement may be expected to yield information on local conditions (see 41). Indeed the Clerk to the

Whitechapel Guardians was in the late 1880s the chief source of such information for both the Home Office and the Metropolitan Police (see MH 12/7941–7947⟨7⟩);

- For Jewish schools and Jewish educational problems, try a search in ED using Jew* as the search term;
- For the licensing of Sunday trading by Jewish traders with conscientious objections to trading on the Jewish Sabbath (1938–1963) see HO 239 ⟨2⟩;
- Rules and activities of Jewish Friendly Societies, Benefit Societies and Loan Societies are reflected in several classes of records of the Registrar of Friendly Societies (FS 1, 3, 9, 15: see 41.4);
- Law suits in Chancery, which dealt with equity cases and mercantile cases, and the High Court of Admiralty dealing with maritime and trading disputes (see 58 and 61);
- Detailed records of some Jewish businesses from the seventeenth to nineteenth centuries may be found as exhibits in Chancery, in C 103–C 114 ⟨2⟩;
- In addition to the usual methods of searching for soldiers, try Adler, *The British Jewry Book of Honour, 1914–1918*. This includes many photographs. There are also many records of anti-Semitism and of the response to it, described in the catalogue in the language of the time: here are some sample entries.

1887–1904	Aliens (Immigration of destitutes). Metropolitan Police reports on immigration into London at the end of the 19th century. Indication of the growing public hostility toward immigrants at this time. Newspaper clippings from articles in the Daily Mail denouncing immigration.	MEPO 2/260
1911–1913	Administration of the Aliens Act 1905: various aspects of Jewish immigration, including representations on proceedings by London Immigration Board. Deserters from Russian Army. Effect of immigration on wages. Discussion of different aspects of Jewish/Alien immigration in the early years of the last century.	HO 45/24610
1931–1940	Jew baiting by fascists	HO 144/21377–21382
1936	Attacks on Jewish individuals, shops and property and examples of anonymous notes and crude anti-Semitic propaganda.	MEPO 2/3042
1936–1939	Approaches to the problem of anti-Semitism in the 1930s. Includes suggestions from the Home Secretary, accounts of individual incidents and instructions to the Metropolitan Police. Could the police prosecute individuals for common assault without the victim pressing charges?	MEPO 2/3043
1937	Disturbances in East London: anti-Semitic activities	MEPO 2/3112
1939–1944	Jew baiting: monthly reports to Home Office	MEPO 2/3127

44.6 Colonial Jewish communities

There are numerous references to colonial Jews in the Colonial Office records relating to the American and West Indies colonies. These are most easily found in the *Calendars of State Papers, Colonial* (to 1738) which has been republished as a searchable CD-Rom.

In the eighteenth century, large numbers of Spanish Jews in Jamaica threw off their New Christian identity to become British Jews; Jews in the colonies could get naturalisation about 85 years before they could in Britain. For denization and naturalisation, look at 19. For changes of names see 22.

44.7 Jews: bibliography

M ADLER, ed. *British Jewry Book of Honour 1914–1918* (London, 1922, reprinted Aldershot 1997)

A BEARE, *Jewish Ancestors? A Guide to Jewish Genealogy in Latvia and Estonia* (Jewish Genealogical Society of Great Britain, 2001)

G BEECH, 'Sources for the study of Jewish migration in the Public Record Office, London', in A Newman and S W Massil eds, *Patterns of migration, 1850–1914*, (Jewish Historical Society, 1996), pp. 233–45

D BERGER, *The Jewish Victorian: Genealogical Information from the Jewish Newspapers 1871–1881* (Oxford, 1999)

D CESARANI, ed., *The making of modern Anglo-Jewry* (Oxford, 1990)

L P GARTNER, *The Jewish Immigrant in England 1870–1914* (London, 1973)

S ISSROFF, Tracing Jewish Roots: see **www.movinghere.org.uk/galleries/roots/jewish/jewish.htm**

A JOSEPH, 'What's New in Jewish Genealogy?', *Family History Monthly* 111 (2004)

P LAIDLAW, 'Moving Here Earlier: Jewish Immigration before the 1880s', *Ancestors* 10 (2002)

I MORDY, *My Ancestors were Jewish* (Society of Genealogists, 2nd edn, 1995)

G RIGAL, 'Researching Jewish Burials', *Ancestors* 10 (2002)

D ROTTENBERG, *Finding our Past. A Guidebook to Jewish Genealogy* (Baltimore, 1986)

T SKYTE and R SCHOENBERG, *A Guide to Jewish Genealogy in Germany and Austria* (Jewish Genealogical Society of Great Britain, 2001)

C TUCKER, 'Jewish Marriages and Divorces in England until 1940', *Genealogists' Magazine*, vol. XXIV, pp. 87–93, 139–143.

D J STEEL and E R SAMUEL, *Sources for Roman Catholic and Jewish Family History and Genealogy* (London, 1974)

R WENZERUL, ed., *Jewish Ancestors? A Beginner's Guide to Jewish Genealogy in Great Britain* (Jewish Genealogical Society of Great Britain, 2000)

R WENZERUL, *Genealogical Resources within the Jewish Home and Family* (FFHS, 2002)

Journals

Avotaynu, The International Review of Jewish Genealogy, quarterly journal (**www.avotaynu.com**)

Jewish Year Book (London, annually from 1896)

Shemot (Names), Jewish Genealogy Society of Great Britain (quarterly journal)

Transactions, Jewish Historical Society of England

45 Blacks and Asians

45.1 General advice

Blacks and Asians have been living in Britain for centuries. Although many people living in the United Kingdom will have one or two ancestors, or most of their family, as a member of either of these groups, large-scale migration did not begin until 1948. This chapter aims to give very basic advice on searching for ancestors, before concentrating on what is available in the National Archives. Very few records are specifically devoted to either of these groups: instead, you will find black or Asian people among most of the modern (later than, say, 1700) records in the National Archives. Records are therefore of four kinds:

- recent migration;
- living in the United Kingdom;
- living in the home country of origin;
- living in the Empire.

We do have a specialist guide called *Tracing Your West Indian Ancestry* by Grannum: although this is obviously most helpful for the West Indies, it does contain very useful explanations of standard sources for other colonies: see also the bibliography. For guidance on searching out South Asian ancestry, see the two articles by Husainy and Trumpbour. Have a look too at **www.movinghere.org.uk/galleries/ roots/default.htm** for both Caribbean and South Asian ancestry. This is a site that you should use anyway, as it has many digitised sources from archives across the country. Other sites you may find interesting are **www.nationalarchives.gov.uk/ pathways/blackhistory** (on Asians and blacks in Britain, 1500–1850) and the Caribbean and Black and Asian History site at **www.casbah.ac.uk**. There are many more to investigate.

45.2 Recent migration

Between 1948 and 1962 workers from the colonies and Commonwealth could migrate to Britain without restriction, and were encouraged to do so to help recovery from the Second World War and to fill labour shortages. Until 1962 every Commonwealth citizen was entitled to enter the United Kingdom at will. This right had been freely exercised for many years but it was only in the 10 years from 1952 onwards that substantial numbers of people from the Commonwealth began to think of settling in Britain. Under the British Nationality Act 1948, citizens of British colonies could simply apply to the Home Office for registration of British nationality and were issued with certificates. Very many people did register, and if these registers were indexed online they would be an excellent source. However, they were not and the National Archives (although it holds the registers) still has to rely on an index kept elsewhere. See 19.11 for more details. The certificates issued may still be among family papers, of course.

Passenger lists for people entering or re-entering Britain between 1890 and 1960 are becoming more easily accessible: see 17.2. Several passenger lists from the height of direct migration (1948–1960) from the West Indies and South Asia can be seen on **www.movinghere.org**.

45.3 Living in the United Kingdom

Most people will be in the standard family history sources (as described throughout this book) but they are not identified as black or Asian. Some may be identifiable as such by birthplace or name. As records registering individuals in the census, the armed forces and the Merchant Navy begin to be catalogued in greater detail, this kind of information is becoming available to be searched. For example, Naval seamen from 1873 onwards can now be searched by birthplace (see 28.4.3), as can merchant seamen from 1941 (and in some cases from as early as 1913: see 35.8). Searching in the census can also be done by birthplace: see 3. Much more remains to be done in this area, and as we now have the technology, no doubt more records will be opened up.

Other people will turn up in law suits or criminal trials, as parties or as witnesses. These can vary from great disputes in Chancery or the High Court of Admiralty by wealthy merchants to criminal trials at the Old Bailey and elsewhere. The Old Bailey website gives useful advice on search strategies for finding black and Asian people among the records of the court, recommending the following search terms:

- 'black man', 'black woman', 'blackamoor' and 'blackmoor', 'black boy', 'black girl', 'negro', 'mulatto' and 'swarthy' for the black community in London;
- 'lascar', 'Alcoran' (for oaths sworn on the Koran), 'East Indian', 'Malay' for the South Asian community in London

For more details on relevant cases in the Old Bailey, have a look at **www.oldbaileyonline.org/history/communities/black.html#searchstrate gies** and see 48.8.

45.4 Living in the home country

If you don't have certificates among family papers, you will need to investigate registers of births, marriages and deaths kept in the home country. The Family History Centres run by the Church of Jesus Christ of Latter-day Saints/The Genealogical Society of Utah (LDS) have copies of the various West Indies registers at their London centre. If London is too far to travel, you can find a nearer centre on **www.familysearch.org**. See 4, 5, 7 and 8 for further guidance.

South Asian families may have come either directly from the Indian sub-continent or by a more roundabout route. After the abolition of slavery, the use of indentured labour from South Asia and China expanded across the Empire, in a reversion to the system of indentured labour originally used to settle large tracts of North America (see 18.4). Indentured labourers were taken from India to colonies such as Mauritius, the West Indies, British Guiana, Ceylon (Sri Lanka), East Africa and South Africa. After a period of service, they either returned home or were offered the opportunity to settle. Some generations later, a further migration brought them to Britain. See the Research Guide on Unfree Labour on our website.

The best sources in the National Archives for finding people tend to be those created by the Colonial Office in correspondence with the local governments, the local Government *Gazettes* (see 17.4) and the mass of documentation created by slavery, the abolition of slavery and the introduction of indentured labour. It is possible to trace people through this latter material: see the article 'Tracing African slave ancestors' by Crooks. You will need to use Grannum's book to find out more.

Mentions of individual people may crop up anywhere among official correspondence. These records can illustrate likely experiences and are a prime source for research into the history of social groups, but not ideal sources for tracing particular families back in time. We are currently running a major cataloguing project, *Your Caribbean Heritage*, which is opening up correspondence between the Colonial Office and the local governments in the West Indies. (Similar correspondence for the Indian sub-continent is kept in the India Office records at the British Library.) This project is producing masses of searchable descriptions of documents of real interest (see 17.4). The terms used in the catalogue are those used in the records, such as negro, mulatto, quadroon, octaroon, maroon. Although now considered pejorative, these were the words in use at the time and many had exact meanings in a highly stratified society: different categories had different levels of legal rights.

Colonial Office records can also produce some real gems, like the disputes between slaves in Berbice (now in Guyana), 1819–1832, reported back in almost word-by-word detail and printed by the House of Commons (CO 116/138–142).

Of course, many people were also involved in local administration in their home community. A good rule here is that if this generated some kind of financial implication for government, there may be some kind of record of such employment somewhere in the archives, either here, in the India Office records or locally. Some of these can even be found on a search in our catalogue:

- Nyasaland: Various requests for approval of the payment of pensions and gratutities to employees in the Nyasaland Native Civil Service. Includes records of service of Mr David Akamanga and Mr Solomon Gangata. 1931 Feb 25–1931 Jun 08. CO 525/140/12;
- British Guiana: Retirements of officials: individual forms showing personal details (age, service, salary, emoluments, pension awards, cause of retirement, etc.): J Howard, Sorter, General Post Office; J Subryan, Interpreter and Depot Keeper, Immigration Dept; E N Edwards, 3rd Class Clerk and Clerk of Court; T B Lambert, Postmaster; Albuoystown. 1928 Dec 12–1929 Nov 7. CO 111/677/1.

45.5 Living as part of the Empire

Blacks and South Asians have formed a significant part of the British Empire's military power since the seventeenth century: see **www.national archives.gov.uk/pathways/blackhistory/work_community/fighting.htm** for a good overview. The Indian regiments and Naval forces of the East India Company, taken over in 1857 by the British government, are well known: most of their records are kept with the India Office records at the British Library (see 17.5 and 27.6).

Many records of the famous black and native regiments of the British Army are kept at the National Archives – the West India Regiment, the King's African Rifles, the Gold Coast Regiment, the Central African Regiment, the West African Regiment, the Nigerian Regiments, Sierra Leone Regiments and the Africa Corps, amongst many others. Try a search in the catalogue by name of the regiment and you may find muster rolls, discharges to pension, pension lists, registers of prize money payments or war diaries. You can also find records of 'negro pensioners' in WO 23 for 1837–1879. See 23–27 for advice on Army records.

Both the Royal Navy and the Merchant Navy had very many black and Asian seamen: as service records become more easily searched, these individuals become much easier to find. See 28 and 35 for advice.

Indian casualties of the First and Second World Wars can be searched in the Commonwealth War Graves' Debt of Honour database at **www.cwgc.org**. So far, it does not seem possible to identify West Indian or many African casualties except by name.

45.6 Blacks and Asians: bibliography

General

G GRANNUM, *Tracing Your West Indian Ancestors* (Public Record Office, 2002)

R KERSHAW, 'Becoming a Brit: The Home Office Naturalisation Papers and the Citizenship Project', *Ancestors* 22 (2004)

R KERSHAW and M PEARSALL, *Immigrants and Aliens* (Public Record Office, 2000)

G E LANE, *Tracing Ancestors in Barbados* (Baltimore, 2006)

M E MITCHELL, *Jamaican Ancestry: how to find out more* (1998)

S D PORTER, *Jamaican Records: A Research Manual* (1999)

Black Ancestry

S J BRAIDWOOD, *Black Poor and White Philanthropists: London's Blacks and the Foundation of the Sierra Leone Settlement, 1786–1791* (Liverpool, 1994)

R N BUCKLEY, *Slaves in Red Coats: The British West India Regiments 1795–1815,* (London, 1979)

T BURNARD and J LEAN, 'Hearing Slave Voices: The Fiscal's Reports of Berbice and Demerara-Essequebo', *Archives* 27, no. 106 (2002), 37–50

Calendar of State Papers, Colonial, America and West Indies, 1574–1738 (London, 1860–1969). (Republished as a searchable CD-Rom, Routledge and Public Record Office, 2000)

P CROOKS, 'Tracing African slave ancestors', *Ancestors* 10 (2002)

B DYDE, *The Empty Sleeve: The story of the West Indian Regiments of the British Army,* (Antigua, 1997)

G GERZINA, *Black London: Life Before Emancipation* (New Jersey, 1995)

House of Commons, *Berbice Fiscal's Returns, printed by order of the House of Commons,* 23rd June 1825

N MYERS, 'The Black presence through criminal records, 1780–1830', *Immigrants and Minorities,* 7 (1988), pp. 292–307

South Asia in Ancestry

Calendar of State Papers, Colonial Series, East Indies 1513–1634, W N Sainsbury (ed.), 5 vols (London, 1862–92)

A HUSAINY and J TRUMPBOUR, 'British Sources for South Asian ancestors', *Ancestors* 13 (2003)

A HUSAINY and J TRUMPBOUR, 'Military Sources for South Asian Ancestors', *Ancestors* 14 (2003)

46 Coroners' inquests

46.1 Introduction

Coroners have been responsible for investigating sudden, unnatural or suspicious deaths, and the deaths of people detained in prisons, ever since 1194. Until 1926 all coroners' inquests were held before a jury. The main surviving record of the coroners' hearings is usually the individual inquest or inquisition, giving the verdict, name, date, time, cause and place of death with the signatures of the jurors. Verdicts were in Latin until 1733, after which English was used. Inquests (or inquisitions) are normally held in public and are regularly reported in the press. The survival of coroners' records after 1850 is not good – it is probably easier and more rewarding to search for a newspaper report rather than for the coroner's record.

Incidentally, coroners' inquests (or the modern post-mortem medical examinations) are not the same as an inquisition post mortem: the latter is concerned with establishing the identity of the heir, not the cause of death (see 49).

Most modern coroners' records are held in local record offices rather than at the National Archives; they are generally not searchable online. The easiest way to find out what survives (and where to look for it) is to consult *Coroners' Records in England and Wales* by Gibson and Rogers. This lists the location of records available, by county, and includes a section on sources in the National Archives. Inquests for many counties have been published by local record societies, so ask the advice of your local record office or reference librarian. The bibliography includes only a few of the published inquests, chosen because they have very good introductions that explain the context of the records and the procedures that created (and kept) them.

If original inquests have not survived, it is sometimes possible to piece basic information (such as the name of the deceased and verdict) together from coroners' bills. These record the coroners' claims for expenses; if they survive at all they will be in local record offices, usually amongst the quarter sessions records. Hunnisett's volume on *Wiltshire Coroners' Bills* will give you a good idea of the quality of information they can provide.

46.2 Coroners' records in the National Archives

A search on coroner in the online catalogue brings up over 2,000 hits: most of them are administrative records. However, some relate to people whose inquests had raised particular policy problems, for example:

- Mr P Le Piper, coroner, forwarding suggestions of jury at inquest on Samuel Henry Bayley, who died of cholera in King's Bench prison, for improvements at the prison during the epidemic 1832 July 18. HO 44/25 folios 197–200;
- Coroners and Inquests: Suicide of a soldier from the 15th Hussars, Hounslow: complaints at inquest delay 1858. HO 45/6551;
- Coroners and Inquests: Inquests held in the absence of a body: various cases including that of Amy Johnson, aviator 1940–1948. HO 45/25555.

However, the basic coroners' holdings at the National Archives are of formal returns by coroners. These start with the many coroners' rolls for the late thirteenth to the early fifteenth centuries in JUST 2 ④. Most coroners' inquisitions are filed with the records of the court of King's Bench. This is because from 1487 coroners were required to bring their inquests to the judges at the twice-yearly assizes. Those that did not result in a trial for murder or manslaughter were forwarded to the King's Bench, where they were filed with the indictments according to the law term in which they were handed in. There are no indexes. For the period 1485–1675, the inquests are in KB 9 ⑦; after 1675 they are in KB 11 ⑦ (for the provincial or 'out-counties') and KB 10 ⑦ (for the City of London and Middlesex). However, the King's Bench clerks stopped filing inquests in the indictment files after 1733 and the general practice of handing in inquests appears to have declined from the mid-seventeenth century, and is commonly thought to have stopped on most assize circuits in about 1750. Inquests survive for 1740–1820 from the Western circuit (Cornwall, Devon, Dorset, Hampshire, Somerset and Wiltshire) in KB 13 ⑦. It may be worth checking in any relevant miscellanea series for a particular assize circuit, as some inquests have been found recently for the nineteenth-century Northern circuit in ASSI 47/24–73 ⑦.

A coroner's inquest could act as an indictment, so both they and related depositions are often found amongst assize papers, even if no trial actually took place (see 48). Such inquests do not simply relate to obvious cases of murder but also cover accidental deaths. From the thirteenth to seventeenth centuries, inquests taken during proceedings that resulted in the granting of pardons can be found by hard research among Chancery files in C 260 ⑦. Copies of the proceedings were often included in the pardons themselves, which, if enrolled, are in C 66 ⑤⑦.

The Palatinates of Chester and Lancaster have extensive coroners' records. The Chester records also include some from Flintshire and Denbighshire. Inquests from 1794 to 1830, with a few earlier and later ones, are in CHES 18 ⑦: from 1830 to 1891 they are in ASSI 66 ⑦, with some from

Anglesey, Denbighshire, Flintshire and Merionethshire. Again there are a few dating back earlier (to 1798) so you may need to look in both series. Inquests from the Palatinate of Lancaster, 1626–1832, are in PL 26/285–29 Ⓣ. For coroners' inquests taken within lands of the Duchy of Lancashire that are outside the county of Lancashire, look at DL 46 Ⓣ. This has inquests for certain lands in Middlesex (1817–1884); Surrey (1823–1896); Essex (1821–1822); Halton in Cheshire (1848–1849); Pontefract in Yorkshire (1822–1894); and Norfolk (1804–1824, 1853–1875, 1885–1889). There are also very informative depositions about accidental deaths and homicides within Lancashire in PL 27 Ⓣ, 1663–1869.

Other sources in the National Archives relate to the deaths of prisoners. The inquests of prisoners (usually debtors) held in the King's Bench prison, 1747–1750 and 1771–1839 (KB 14 Ⓣ), can be informative about previous occupations. There is also a register of deaths of prisoners and of inquests upon them for the Millbank Penitentiary, 1848–1863 (PCOM 2/165). Some deaths fell within the jurisdiction of the High Court of Admiralty (usually of those who died on or in the River Thames or of those who had been prisoners in the custody of the court) and records of inquests survive for 1535–1688 in HCA 1/78–84 Ⓣ and for 1816–1832 in HCA 1/86 and 102–109 Ⓣ.

46.3 Coroners' records outside the National Archives

Modern coroners' records do not survive very well. Records of individual inquests (other than treasure trove) created after 1875 may be weeded or destroyed, unless they are of significant public interest. Even if they do survive, inquest records are usually closed for 75 years. They are normally held in the local record office, unless they remain in the custody of the coroner. It is most unlikely that they will be indexed by name. *Coroners' Records in England and Wales* by Gibson and Rogers is the essential guide. You can find out about holdings of local record offices through A2A (see 1.13).

46.4 Murder

Records relating to murder victims are normally found by searching trial and associated records, published literature (see 48.4) and appeals for mercy (see 47.7). For much of the nineteenth and twentieth centuries many provincial police forces asked the Metropolitan Police Force to assist them in the investigation of murder, so files relating to provincial murders and infanticides may survive alongside those of London cases in MEPO 3 ② ⑥. There are police registers of murders and of deaths by violence (including the deaths of women by illegal abortion) in the Metropolitan Police area for 1891–1909, 1912–1917 and 1919–1966. These give the name, address and occupation of the victim, date and place of death, and subsequent charges or convictions (MEPO 20 Ⓣ).

46.5 Coroners' inquests: bibliography

K CHATER, 'By His Own Hand', *Ancestors* 8 (2002)

J S W GIBSON and C ROGERS, *Coroners' Records in England and Wales* (FFHS, 2000)

R F HUNNISETT, *Calendar of Nottinghamshire Coroners' Inquests, 1485–1558*, Thoroton Society, Record Series, vol. XXV

R F HUNNISETT, 'Medieval Coroners' Rolls', *American Journal of Legal History*, vol.III, pp. 95–221 and 324–359

R F HUNNISETT, *Sussex Coroners' Inquests, 1485–1558*, Sussex Record Society, vol. LXXIV

R F HUNNISETT, *Sussex Coroners' Inquests, 1558–1603* (PRO, 1996)

R F HUNNISETT, *Sussex Coroners' Inquests, 1603–1688* (PRO, 1998)

R F HUNNISETT, *Wiltshire Coroners' Bills, 1752–1796*, Wiltshire Record Society, vol. XXXVI

47 Prisoners and convicts

47.1   Prisoners in the census

As the censuses are now searchable, we are currently experiencing a surge of questions about people found to be in prison on one of the census nights. You should be able to find out more, but it may take some time.

- **1841–1871 census entry.** If the prison was Brixton, Broadmoor, Chatham, Dartmoor, Fulham, Portland, Portsmouth or Woking, try HO 8 ⑥ first. Court orders with details of the convict's penal history are in PCOM 5, with indexes in PCOM 6/18–20. They give the name (and any aliases), age, marital status, trade, crime, date and place of committal and conviction, sentence, previous convictions and character, name and residence of next of kin, literacy level and religion, together with a physical description.
- **1841–1891 census entry.** Try the Criminal Registers in HO 26 ⑦ and HO 27 ④, arranged by county. There are fiche indexes to some of the registers (see 47.3 for more details).
- **1871–1901 census entry.** Try the printed after-trial calendars of prisoners in HO 140 ④ (and for the Central Criminal Court in London from 1855 in CRIM 9 ⑦). These list people tried in each county, and give age and occupation, level of literacy, the name and address of the committing magistrate, details of the alleged offence, verdict and sentence.

47.2   Prison as a punishment

Today we are accustomed to regard imprisonment as one of the most likely punishments for criminal behaviour. This was not so before the mid-nineteenth century. Most offences either carried the death penalty (often commuted to transportation or some other lesser sentence) or were punished by a fine and/or whipping. Each county had its own county gaol, which was primarily used to hold prisoners awaiting trial. Many counties also experimented with new prisons where vagrants and later also criminals could be put to work and subjected to disciplines that were intended to reform them. This kind of prison was often called a bridewell or house of correction. As prison policy was not uniform across the country it is difficult to be precise here, but until the early decades of the nineteenth century most prisons, whether designated as houses of correction or not, were simply used to house prisoners on remand. Those prisoners who were dealt with by magistrates acting alone, in pairs or in petty sessions (that is to say, in all cases acting without a jury) could also sentence prisoners to a 'short, sharp shock' period in the local gaol; but this would only be for a few weeks or months. With certain exceptions (see 47.3), their records, if they survive, are usually held in the local county record office.

From the mid-nineteenth century, local and national prisons began to be built to house long-term prisoners as an alternative to execution, transportation or the hulks; they were sentenced to penal servitude or hard labour, in conditions of deliberate harshness. Penal servitude was imposed for sentences for three years or more, and was carried out in national prisons not local ones. The first six months were served in solitary confinement. The prisoner was then transferred to one of the national public-works prisons of Borstal, Dartmoor, Parkhurst or Portland (or Aylesbury for women), where arduous work was undertaken on extending and fortifying the Naval dockyards at Chatham, Portsmouth and Portland, or in the quarries. Those unfit for such labour were sent to Woking. Remission of up to a quarter of the sentence could be earned by good behaviour. Having earned remission, the prisoner would be released conditionally, on a licence or ticket-of-leave, which could be forfeited quite easily (see 47.6).

For an expert guide, see Paley, *Using Criminal Records*. An overview of the wide range of records relating to imprisonment is provided by Hawkings' *Criminal Ancestors*, which provides transcripts and facsimiles, not only of material in the National Archives but also in local record offices.

47.3 Registers of prisoners in prison hulks

We hold prison registers of the prison ships or 'hulks' that were moored near British Naval bases to house prisoners (often awaiting transportation) between 1776 and 1857, as well as some of those that were used in Gibraltar and Bermuda until 1875. (See 28.6.2 for more on convict labour in the royal dockyards and 28.7.2 for medical care of convicts at Bermuda.) Registers of prisoners on the hulks, 1802–1849, are in HO 9 ▣, with more up to 1860 in PCOM 2 ▣, including registers for prisoners at Gibraltar, 1851–1875 in PCOM 2/11–13.

The quarterly returns of convicts in hulks, from 1824 on, in HO 8 ⑥⑤ can be used to trace details of behaviour, state of health, transfers to other gaols and eventual release. There are also quarterly returns relating to the hulks, 1802–1831, in T 38/310–338 ⑥. Registers and indexes for the *Cumberland* 1830–1833 and *Dolphin* hulks 1822–1835, and a description book of convicts in the hulk *Ganymede* 1834, are in ADM 6/418–423. Registers for the *Antelope, Coromandel, Dromedary* and *Weymouth* hulks, 1823–1828, are in HO 7/3. Some registers and returns of prisoners in the hulks are also found in T 1, but the inadequacy of the lists makes searching extremely difficult. It is worthwhile taking into consideration that some prisoners sentenced to transportation spent their whole sentences on the hulks and never left Britain.

47.4 Registers of prisoners in local and national prisons

Except for a brief period during the nineteenth century, prison records were not collected or retained centrally. Many are still kept by the prisons, or by the authorities that took them over. As a matter of policy, it has been decided that in future prison registers should be deposited in local record offices; essentially this means that most prison registers created after 1878 are more likely to be found in a local record office than in the National Archives. Hawkings' *Criminal Ancestors* has a useful (but now slightly dated) list of prison registers held in local record offices. This is also something that can be checked out on A2A (see 1.13).

Nevertheless, the National Archives does have various registers, mainly from the nineteenth century, of some criminal prisons. One of the most important collections is the Criminal Registers in HO 26 ⑦ and HO 27 ④. These are volumes made up from returns of prisoners. The details were copied from the returns into large volumes and the returns were then destroyed. Those in HO 26 are for London and Middlesex and cover the period 1792 to 1849. From 1805 a separate series was compiled for the rest of England and Wales and these make up the HO 27 series. From 1850 the England and Wales series (HO 27 ④) also includes the London and Middlesex returns; these records stop in 1892. There are fiche indexes to some of the registers.

Similar registers for prisons, also including detailed descriptions of the prisoners, 1838–1875, are in HO 23 and HO 24. Those returns in HO 24 contain details of prisoners convicted across the whole of England, Scotland and Wales. In effect the Home Office was 'renting' cells from county prisons; so people convicted in Perth, Northumberland or Cornwall may be found in the registers for 'Reading Prison'. KB 32/23 has a return of convicts in the Millbank Penitentiary in 1826, which gives name, offence, court of conviction, sentence, age, 'bodily state' and behaviour.

The quarterly returns of convicts in national prisons, from the late

1850s–1876, in HO 8 ⑤ can be used to trace details of behaviour, state of health, transfers to other gaols and eventual release.

There are also a few records of births and burials. The Westminster Penitentiary has a register of baptisms, 1816–1871 (PCOM 2/139) and another of burials, 1817–1853 (PCOM 2/140). There is a register of deaths and inquests at the Millbank Penitentiary, 1848–1863 (PCOM 2/165): in this case, most burials were in the Victoria Park cemetery, whose records are discussed in 6.6. For more on burials, search PCOM using 'burial'.

47.5 Registers of habitual criminals, from 1869

Transportation to Australia (but not Gibraltar or Bermuda) was effectively stopped in 1857, although it was not formally ended until 1867. This meant that prisoners who would previously have been transported were instead kept imprisoned and subsequently released back into the community. In an attempt to dispel some of the anxiety this caused, local prisons were asked to compile registers of 'habitual criminals' – that is, prisoners convicted of any of the many crimes specified by the Habitual Criminals Act 1869 or by the Prevention of Crime Act 1871.

Printed forms were supplied with these registers, which required name and alias, age, description, trade, prison from which released, date of liberation, offence, sentence, term of supervision, intended residence, distinguishing marks and any previous convictions. In addition, photographs were pasted onto the forms. These local registers were supposed to be sent to the central Habitual Criminals Registry, where an alphabetical national register of people thought likely to re-offend was compiled. The idea was to distribute the printed national register to police stations, but it did not include the photographs. The first national register of habitual criminals covered December 1869 to March 1876, and included 12,164 people under 22,115 names, out of a total of 179,601 submitted in the local registers (PCOM 2/404).

The National Archives does not have a full set of these national registers, but since they were compiled for local distribution, others may survive elsewhere. The registers in the National Archives are to be found in PCOM 2/404 (1869–1876) and in MEPO 6/1–52 ⑦ (1881–1882, 1889–1940); they are closed for 75 years from the date of creation. The National Archives also has the local prison registers of habitual criminals for Birmingham, 1871–1875 (PCOM 2/296–299, 430–434 ⑦) and Cambridge, 1875–1877 (PCOM 2/300). A photograph album of prisoners in Wandsworth, 1872–1873, has been listed in detail on the catalogue (PCOM 2/291), with images available to buy in Documents Online.

References to other local registers held locally can be found in A2A for parts of Lancashire, Sussex, Norfolk, Wiltshire – Gloucester has them for 1869–1933 with photographs, while those for Birkenhead cover 1886–1937.

There are similarly informative registers of habitual drunkards, 1903–1914, whose photographs were to be circulated to local pubs by local police forces, to prevent them being served alcohol (MEPO 6/77–88). These are discussed in Paley and Fowler, *Family Skeletons*.

47.6 Licences and 'tickets of leave', 1853–1887

The increased use of imprisonment as a punishment naturally led to increased costs for the criminal justice system, both in terms of the maintenance of individual prisoners and in the costs of prison buildings. By 1853 there were considerable anxieties about the expansion in the prison population that would result from the diminishing numbers of convicts being transported to Australia. A system of licences was introduced to prevent this, allowing convicts of good behaviour to be released before the completion of their sentences. The licences (popularly known as 'tickets of leave') could be revoked in cases of misbehaviour or re-offending (see 47.2).

These registers of licences to be at large give name, physical description, age, marital status, educational level, occupation, details of convictions, conduct whilst in prison, name and address of next of kin, religion and health. They are annotated with details of any subsequent revocation of the licence.

Male convicts	Registers in licence no. order	1853–1887	PCOM 3 Ⓕ
	Indexes	1853–1881	PCOM 6
Female convicts	Registers in licence no. order	1853–1887	PCOM 4 Ⓕ
	Indexes	1853–1885	PCOM 6

47.7 Pardons and appeals for mercy

There were well over 300 offences carrying the death penalty by the end of the eighteenth century. However, only a minority of those sentenced to death were actually hanged. By the later nineteenth century the death penalty had been removed from all but the most serious of crimes.

Pardons were freely granted, either unconditionally or (initially in small numbers in the seventeenth century) on condition of transportation. Those sentenced to lesser penalties also applied for pardons. Petitions were based on such things as youth, extreme age, provocation, the existence of dependent relatives who might become a burden to the poor rates and previous good character. For these reasons, applications for mercy sometimes contain a lot of information and can be very useful for family history purposes.

Before 1784, you will need to look at the correspondence of the secretaries of state in the State Papers, Domestic: there is a research guide on using these available on the website. This correspondence continues after

1782 as Home Office General Correspondence (HO 42 ☑). However, it appears that the numbers of petitions for clemency increased so much at the end of the eighteenth century that they were separated out from the main HO 42 series (see following paragraph) and only a small number are thought to be found in that specific series. For the period 1654–1717, pardons on condition of transportation are entered on the Patent Rolls (C 66 ☒), but such enrolments are in Latin and in any case rarely contain the kind of detail that family historians need. For the majority of the eighteenth century (up to 1782) pardons, respites, remissions and some refusals for pardons can be found in the Criminal Entry Book in SP 44 ☑.

Separate series of papers relating to applications for mercy start in 1784. The judges' reports in HO 47 (1784–1830) (partly ②, ⑤, ⑥) are a particularly rich source of information. Some of the early volumes contain 'circuit letters'; lists compiled by judges at the end of the assizes and Old Bailey sessions, giving the names of capital convicts with recommendations for pardon. However, the majority of this material concerns individual cases, often including virtual transcripts of the trial evidence (sometimes annotated with the judge's opinion of the veracity of witnesses and the credulity of the jurors) together with character references (both for and against the convict) and other personal information. Volunteers are currently cataloguing this series: currently the first 22 volumes covering 1783 to 1799 are listed in detail in the catalogue (from 75 in all, ending in 1830). The remaining volumes will be added over the next few years. The List and Index Society are currently publishing this work (two volumes available so far), cross-referenced to the outcomes, which are recorded in the HO 13 Criminal Entry Books. Other letters and statements (mainly circuit letters) from trial judges, 1816–1840, are in HO 6 ☑. They are somewhat formal but do include recommendations for mercy, together with useful supporting information about the convict and his/her crime.

Surviving petitions for mercy are in HO 17 ☒ (1819–1840) and HO 18 ☒ (1839–1854). These are also being catalogued (by the same volunteer editors as HO 47) to be fully searchable. Currently only a few pieces of these series are in the catalogue and it is expected that this project may take several years to complete. If the period you are interested in has not yet been done, you need to know that they are arranged in coded bundles and that the registers in HO 19 ☑ identify them. The registers are arranged by date of receipt of petition and give the name of the convict, date and place of trial, offence, code number of the bundle in which the petition was filed and, in most but not all cases, the outcome of the application. Incidentally, the indexes do not start in 1819 but in 1797: it appears that many of the earlier petitions simply do not survive or were later filed elsewhere (such as, HO 47). There are also petitions in HO 48 ☑, HO 49 ☑ and PRO 30/45 ☑, but the lists are inadequate to find them easily.

Formal records of pardons and reprieves are given by the Home Office warrants in HO 13 ☑ (1782–1849) and HO 15 ☑ (1850–1871). The modern registers of remissions and pardons, 1887–1960 (HO 188 ⑧), is far more informative as details of the cases and reasons for the decision are given; each volume has its own rough index. You may also find it worthwhile to search through the Home Office General Correspondence in HO 42 ⑦ (1782–1820) and Home Office Criminal Papers Old Series, 1849–1871, in HO 12 Ⓕ (approached via the registers in HO 14). Similar papers after 1871 are in HO 45 ② and HO 144 ②.

47.8 Executions

Few of those who were sentenced to death actually hanged: most were reprieved, or had their sentences commuted to transportation. Published pamphlet and newspaper literature is the best source for finding out about the lives of those who were hanged. If you are really determined, you may find additional information about the costs of imprisonment and execution amongst the financial papers of sheriffs in E 370 ⑦ (1714–1832), T 64 ⑦ (1745–1785), T 90 ⑦ (1733–1822) and T 207 ⑦ (1823–1959).

Although most records about condemned persons should be traced as if they were ordinary convicts, there are some additional series of records (mostly selections or samples) relating specifically to the hanged, mainly in HO 163 ⑦ (1899–1921), MEPO 3 ②, PCOM 8 ② and PCOM 9 ②. HO 336 contains the complete records of nine condemned prisoners (1936–1969) in order to illustrate the kind of information that was kept on such individuals. Background information on the way in which the death penalty was implemented can be found in PCOM 8 ⑥, with more discursive contextual discussion in HO 45 ⑥. There is no comprehensive list either of those executed or of the men who executed them. However, HO 324/1 contains a register of prison burials (1834–1969), which could provide the basis of establishing a list of the executed. Some personal details about executioners can be found in HO 144, PCOM 8 and PCOM 9 (all ①).

47.9 Transportation as a punishment

As explained in 47.2, the range of punishments open to the authorities for serious criminal offences before the nineteenth century was very limited: it was quite literally a choice between enforcing the death penalty or releasing criminals back into the community. The expansion of Britain's overseas territories added a further possibility. Now convicted criminals could be sentenced to a period of exile, during which they would be removed from their previous bad associates, be forced to work productively and thereby learn new habits of industry and self-discipline. At the same time, they would benefit the development of the colonial economy.

For the imperial government, transportation was not a question of simply dumping human refuse on the colonies but was genuinely thought to be effective, efficient and humane. Those who were transported were often quite young; it was, after all, the young who were most likely to benefit from a new life in a new world and who were most likely to be fit enough to supply the productive labour that that new world needed. The colonial authorities, not unnaturally, tended to take a more jaundiced view of the benefits of transportation, and bitterly resented it.

After 1615, as a result of an order by the Privy Council, it became increasingly common for a pardon to be offered to convicts who had been sentenced to death on condition of transportation overseas. In 1718 an act of Parliament standardised transportation to America at 14 years for those who had been sentenced to death and introduced a new penalty – transportation for 7 years – as a sentence in its own right for a range of non-capital offences.

Some 40,000 people had been transported to America from England, Wales, Scotland and Ireland when the system came to an abrupt halt in 1776 because of the outbreak of the American Revolution. Prisoners who had been sentenced to transportation had to be held in prison instead. The overcrowding that ensued soon resulted in the creation of floating prisons or 'hulks' (see 47.3), but of course they too soon became overcrowded. A solution took over ten years to find, but in 1787 the 'first fleet' set out for Australia to found a penal colony in New South Wales. Transportation to Van Diemen's Land (Tasmania) began in 1803.

Transportation was at its height in the 1830s and was probably already in decline when, as a result of the Penal Servitude Act of 1853, it was removed from all but the most serious offences. In 1857 it was effectively abolished, although the Home Secretary retained the right to impose transportation in specific cases until 1867. It is estimated that over 160,000 people were transported to Australia and Tasmania between 1787 and 1867; in the 1830s 4,000 people were being transported every year.

Transportation of convicts had its exact counterpart in Ireland (see **www.nationalarchives.ie/genealogy/transp.htm** for more information and for a searchable database of transported convicts).

47.10 Transportation to America and the West Indies

If you are looking for an individual who may have been transported to America or the West Indies, a good starting point is a CD-Rom incorporating the work of decades: Coldham's *British Emigrants in Bondage, 1614–1788*, based on records in the National Archives and in local record offices. Coldham lists 48,000 felons carried from the jails of England, Wales, Scotland and Ireland and gives, where known:

- date and place of trial
- occupation
- month of embarkation and landing
- name of ship
- destination.

The CD includes a history of the British transportation system, an exhaustive account of the records used in this work and a complete list of convict ships that sailed to America between 1671 and 1788.

You can move on from this to other published works since (with the exception of trial records) most of the National Archives' original sources relating to transportation in this period have been published. An earlier version of Coldham's research findings, published as *Bonded Passengers to America* (but also covering transportation to the West Indies), includes a readable history of the system and gives a detailed overview of the published sources available.

Coldham's works will give you enough to start looking for the trial record. If your convict was transported before 1718 or was transported after 1718 for 14 years, then you should look for the trial amongst the records of assize or assize equivalent courts. If your convict was transported after 1718 for a period of 7 years then the trial could have been either at an assize or assize equivalent court, or at quarter sessions (see 48). Perhaps your convict was unsuccessful in an application for mercy (see 47.7). If your convict was involved in a particularly notorious trial then you may find that there are published works available that will save much time and effort. For example, lists of those transported after the Monmouth rebellion are included in Wigfield's *The Monmouth Rebels 1685*.

The National Archives also holds Treasury money books (T 53 ⑦), which include details of payments by the Treasury to contractors engaged to arrange transportation between 1716 and 1772. Until October 1744 names of all those to be transported from the home counties are listed, together with names of ships and their captains. Thereafter, only totals for each county are given. Until 1742 the colony of destination is usually recorded. Similar information is given in a broken run of transportation lists, 1747–1772, in T 1 (search by 'transportation' to get an idea of what can be found).

Colonial Office correspondence with America and the West Indies (CO 5) includes material on all aspects of transportation to the American colonies; up to 1734 it is included in the *Calendar of State Papers Colonial, America and West Indies*. Much of the material relevant to transportation amongst the records of the Treasury and of the Colonial Office has also been published (47.13) and is therefore available at major reference libraries, as well as at the National Archives. For other records relating to the American and West Indian colonies, which may include details of convicts or ex-convicts and of free emigrants, see 18.4.

47.11 Transportation to Australia

For a general overview of the kind of documents that are available and what sort of information they contain, you will find Hawkings' *Bound for Australia*, and *Criminal Ancestors* particularly useful as they provide transcripts and facsimiles of a wide range of records relating to imprisonment and transportation. Readers in Australia should know that microfilm copies of many National Archives documents are available in Australia at the National Library in Canberra and at the Mitchell Library in Sydney. The National Archives has a copy of an index to convicts who arrived in New South Wales and Van Diemen's Land between 1788 and 1842, and to the ships that transported them, provided by the Genealogical Society of Victoria.

Many family historians start by searching for the trial records, but as explained in 48, such records are rarely very informative. Remember that no matter how short the sentence, few people would ever be able to return from Australia and that the voyage was long and dangerous. Applications for mercy were commonplace and it is far better to start there than with the formal court record.

In order to get started you will need to have some idea *either* of the date and place of trial so that you can trace the convict forward *or* of the date and preferably ship on which the convict arrived in Australia so that you can trace him/her back. You can find this information in a number of ways. The Convict Transportation Registers, 1787–1867 (HO 11 F) provide the name of the ship on which the convict sailed as well as the date and place of conviction and the term of the sentence. They are not indexed by name of convict, but if you know the name of the ship and preferably also when it either left England or arrived in Australia it should be relatively easy to find the convict. The names of the convicts on the first fleet, which left England in May 1787, reaching Australia in January 1788, are listed by Fidlon and Ryan in *The First Fleeters*. A list of convicts transported on the second fleet of ships, which left in 1789, is in Ryan's *The Second Fleet Convicts*. Censuses or musters were taken periodically in New South Wales and Tasmania between 1788 and 1859. Convicts and former convicts had to identify themselves as such and to supply information about their dates and ships of arrival (see 47.12).

It was possible for wives to accompany their convict husbands and some applied to do so. Their petitions survive for 1819–1844 (PC 1/67–92 7) and from 1849–1871 (HO 12 F, identified via the registers in HO 14 7). A register of applications for passages to the colonies for convicts' families, 1848–1873, s CO 386/154.

The Privy Council registers (PC 2 7) can give lists of convicts transported for 14 years or less. Contracts with agents to transport the prisoners, with full lists of ships and convicts, 1842–1867, are in the Treasury Solicitor's Department general series papers (TS 18/460–525 and 1308–1361 6). Reports on the medical condition of the convicts while at sea may be found in the Admiralty medical journals, 1817–1856 (ADM 101 6), and in the Admiralty Transport Department surgeon-superintendents' journals, 1858–1867 (MT 32 6).

47.12 Settlement in Australia

Musters or censuses, primarily but not exclusively concerned with the convict population, were taken periodically in New South Wales and Tasmania between 1788 and 1859 (HO 10 Ⓢ). The New South Wales census of 1828 (HO 10/21–27) is the most complete and is available in a published edition by Sainty and Johnson. It contains the names of more than 35,000 people with details of age, religion, family, place of residence, occupation and stock or land held. Whether each settler came free, or as a convict (or was born in the colony) is recorded; and date of arrival and the name of the ship are given. The musters for New South Wales and Norfolk Island, 1800–1802, for New South Wales, Norfolk Island and Van Diemen's Land, 1811, and for New South Wales in 1822, 1823, 1824, 1825 and 1837 have also been published. Copies of all these works are available at the National Archives. Papers relating to convicts in New South Wales and Tasmania (HO 10 Ⓩ) contain material about convicts' pardons and tickets of leave from New South Wales and Tasmania, 1835–1859. Home Office records also include some information about deaths of convicts in New South Wales, 1829–1834 (HO 7/2). There is a clutch of conditional pardons for convicts in Western Australia, 1863–1873, scattered in HO 45: try a search on 'Australia AND pardons'.

Colonial Office records relating to Australia sometimes note individual convicts as well as policy decisions, but they are not easy to search for particular named individuals. There are, however, lists of convicts, together with emigrant settlers, 1801–1821, in New South Wales Original Correspondence (CO 201 Ⓕ). A microfiche index (the Deane index) to settlers, military men and convicts referred to in some pieces can be found in the Microfilm Reading Room at the National Archives. Names can also be traced in New South Wales entry books from 1786 (CO 202 Ⓩ) and registers from 1849 (CO 360 Ⓩ and CO 369 Ⓩ). Records of the superintendent of convicts in New South Wales, 1788–1825, are now held in the State Archives of New South Wales; the National Archives holds microfilm copies (CO 207 Ⓩ). Some of the lists from these records have been printed in Robson, *The Convict Settlers of Australia*.

For other records that may provide relevant information, see 18.5.

47.13 Prisoners and convicts: bibliography

C M ANDREWS, *Guide to the materials for American history to 1793 in the Public Record Office of Great Britain* (Washington, 1912–1914)

C BATESON, *The Convict Ships, 1787–1868* (Glasgow, 2nd edn 1969)

C J BAXTER, *General muster and lands and stock muster of NSW, 1822* (Sydney, 1988)

C J BAXTER, *General Muster of New South Wales, 1823, 1824, 1825* (Sydney, 1995)

C J BAXTER, *General Musters of NSW, Norfolk Island and Van Diemen's Land, 1811* (Sydney, 1987)

C J BAXTER, *Muster and lists of NSW and Norfolk Island, 1800–1802* (Sydney, 1988)

J M BEATTIE, *Crime and courts in England 1660–1800* (Oxford, 1986)

G Bell, 'Convicts, Colonists And Colliers' [To Australia], *Ancestors*, 30 (2005)

A Brooke and D Brandon, *Bound for Botany Bay: The Story of British Convict Transportation to Australia* (The National Archives, 2005)

A Brooke and D Brandon, 'Little Depraved Felons' [child convicts transported], *Ancestors* 38 (2005))

A Brooke and D Brandon, 'Surgeons at Sea' [Naval surgeons on convict ships], *Ancestors* 40 (2005)

N G Butlin, C W Cromwell and K L Suthern, *General Return of convicts in NSW 1837* (Sydney, 1987)

M Cale, *Law and society, an introduction to sources for criminal and legal history from 1800* (PRO, 1996)

Calendar of Home Office Papers (3 vols, London, 1873–1881)

Calendar of State Papers Colonial, America and West Indies, 1574–1739 (HMSO, 1860–1994; CD-Rom edition, Routledge, 2000)

Calendar of State Papers, Domestic (London, 1856–1972)

Calendar of Treasury Books, 1660–1718 (London, 1904–1962)

Calendar of Treasury Books and Papers, 1729–1745 (London, 1898–1903)

Calendar of Treasury Papers, 1557–1728 (London, 1868–1889)

P Carter, 'Home Office 47: Judges' Reports on Criminals, 1783–1830', *Archives*, 110 (2004)

P Carter, *Pardons and punishments: Judges' Reports on Criminals, 1783 to 1830: HO (Home Office) 47* (List & Index Society, 2004 ongoing)

P W Coldham, *Bonded Passengers to America, 1615–1775* (Baltimore, 1983)

P W Coldham, *British Emigrants in Bondage, 1614–1788* (CD-Rom, 2005)

M Edwards, 'The curious case of Lieutenant Lutwidge', *Ancestors* 25 (2004)

A R Ekirch, *Bound for America: The Transportation of British Convicts to the Colonies, 1718–1775* (Oxford, 1990)

P G Fidlon and R J Ryan eds, *The First Fleeters* (Sydney, 1981)

Friends of the East Sussex Record Office, *East Sussex Sentences of Transportation at Quarter Sessions, 1790–1854* (Lewes, 1988)

D T Hawkings, *Bound for Australia* (Chichester, 1987)

D T Hawkings, *Criminal Ancestors, a guide to historical criminal records in England and Wales* (Sutton, revised edn, 1996)

C Heather, 'Sentenced To Hang' *Ancestors* 17 (2003)

C F E Hollis Hallett, *Forty Years of Convict Labour: Bermuda 1823–1864* (Bermuda, 1999)

R Hughes, *The Fatal Shore: A History of Transportation of Convicts to Australia, 1781–1868* (London, 1987)

W B Johnson, *The English Prison Hulks* (revised edn, Phillimore, 1970)

Journals of the Board of Trade and Plantations, 1704–1782 (London, 1920–1938)

S Keates, 'British Prison Hulks', *Family History Monthly* 81 (2003)

Letters and papers ... of Henry VIII (London, 1864–1932)

S McConville, *English Local Prisons, 1860–1900: next only to death* (London, 1995)

S McConville, *History of English Prison Administration 1750–1877* (London, 1981)

R Paley, *Using Criminal Records* (PRO, 2001)

R Paley and S Fowler, *Family Skeletons: Exploring the lives of our disreputable ancestors* (The National Archives, 2005)

S Rees, *The floating brothel: the extraordinary true story of the Lady Juliana and its cargo of female convicts bound for Botany Bay* (London, 2001)

L L Robson, *The Convict Settlers of Australia* (Melbourne, 1981)

R J RYAN, *The Second Fleet Convicts* (Sydney, 1982)

M R SAINTY and K A JOHNSON eds, *New South Wales: Census ... November 1828* (Sydney, 1980)

S and B WEBB, *English Prisons under Local Government* (reprinted, London, 1963)

R WHITMORE, *Victorian and Edwardian Crime and Punishment* (London, 1978)

W M WIGFIELD, *The Monmouth Rebels 1685* (Somerset Record Society, 1985)

I WYATT ed., *Transportees from Gloucester to Australia, 1783–1842* (Bristol and Gloucester Archaeological Society, 1988)

48 Criminal trials

48.1   Easy sources to search

Trial records in general are not easy to use (although this may depend on the period you are researching) and will not necessarily give you good family history information. They do not, for example, normally include transcripts of evidence given in court. For family history purposes, tracing convicts (especially transported ones) is usually easier and more rewarding (see 47).

The first problem to overcome is the lack of name indexes. Unless you know when and where your ancestor was tried it can be extremely difficult to track down the trial record. There is no central index of persons tried: some searchable data and indexes do exist, but they are far from comprehensive. There are a few exceptions:

- Trials at the Old Bailey between 1674 and 1834 are easily found at **www. oldbaileyonline.org**. There are plans to extend the coverage of this excellent site to 1913 by September 2008;
- Trials at the Court of Great Sessions in Wales from 1730–1830 can be found at **www.llgc.org.uk/sesiwn_fawr/index_s.htm**;
- Trials in the microfiche publication *British Trials 1660–1900* are indexed by defendant, victim and location;
- Trials in the sixteenth and seventeenth centuries at the assizes for the Home Circuit (Essex, Hertfordshire, Kent, Surrey and Sussex) are indexed in the *Calendar of Assize Records*;
- The names of people who made sworn statements on the North Eastern Circuit between 1613–1800 are searchable in the catalogue in ASSI 45;

- The names of those who were tried in Kent in 1602 are indexed in *Kent at Law 1602*;
- *Summary Convictions in Wiltshire, 1698–1903*: a CD produced by the Wiltshire Family History Society, contains 26,500 convictions;
- *Unrolling the Past: Denbighshire Quarter Sessions Rolls, 1706–1800*: a CD produced by Denbighshire Archives Service, 2003;
- *Swing Unmasked* book and CD cover over 3,300 offences from the time of the Captain Swing Riots (1830–1832), produced by the Family and Community Historical Research Society.

Outside these sources, you may be in for a piece of extended research.

48.2 Courts used for criminal trials

Even if you know roughly when and where the trial took place, you still need to know what kind of court tried the offence.

Justices of the Peace, Quarter Sessions, Assizes

Until the sixteenth century, many manorial courts exercised jurisdiction in cases of petty theft, affray, drunkenness and other offences (see 49.2), but from the sixteenth century onwards jurisdiction over minor crimes increasingly passed to Justices of the Peace (also known as magistrates). Justices of the Peace were (then as now) effectively volunteer amateur judges, who were commissioned by the Crown because of their importance in the local community rather than for their legal expertise. Justices of the Peace were empowered to try some offences without a jury: this was called summary jurisdiction. They could do so either singly or in twos or more. Summary courts with more than one Justice were usually called petty sessions. The scope of summary jurisdiction has been steadily widened since the late seventeenth century: far more crimes in England and Wales are tried summarily than by full jury trial. Surviving records of summary trials are held in local record offices, but the survival is generally poor until the mid-nineteenth century. The Justices also convened, usually four times a year, meetings that became known as quarter sessions. Here, until the late nineteenth century, they transacted administrative business of the kind that would now fall to elected local councils and were also empowered to hear certain criminal cases that were to be determined by a jury. With certain limited exceptions (see 48.7), quarter sessions and other records created by Justices of the Peace are usually held in local record offices rather than at the National Archives: see Gibson, *Quarter Sessions Records for Family Historians*.

Criminal cases could also be tried before professional judges acting as justices of gaol delivery: pairs of judges literally rode through groups or circuits of counties in order to hold their courts, which became known as the assizes. They took their authority from commissions of gaol delivery, of the peace and of oyer and terminer. These enabled them to try or 'deliver' anyone imprisoned in the county gaol or on bail from it, and also to 'hear and determine' certain other cases, such as treason, riot, rebellion, coining, murder, burglary, etc. Most parts of England and Wales, therefore, had multiple courts able to try criminal cases. Additionally, the King's Bench (which was a central royal court sitting at Westminster) had an overriding jurisdiction over them all. Records of assize courts and of the King's Bench are held in the National Archives (see 48.6 and 48.9).

In some areas of the country the judicial system worked slightly differently. If the case in which you are interested was tried in Bristol, Wales or one of the Palatinates of Chester, Durham or Lancaster, or in the City of London or the ancient county of Middlesex, read 48.6 and 48.7 below.

LOCAL COURT = LESSER OFFENCE?

It is a fallacy to believe that minor offences were tried in minor courts and that serious offences were tried in the higher courts. Even today there are a number of offences that can be tried with a jury in a county court (the modern equivalent of assizes and quarter sessions) or without a jury in a magistrates court. In the past there was an even greater overlap between the various courts and the kind of cases that they could hear; some offences, such as assault, could be tried at any of the four levels of the court hierarchy. The division of cases between assize courts and sessions was a rough and ready one and depended on convenience and cost as well as on the gravity of the crime. It is possible to generalise only about those crimes for which the penalty was death or transportation.

From at least the sixteenth century, it would have been unusual for capital crimes to be tried anywhere other than assizes (or a court with equivalent power). Anyone who was transported before 1718 or who was transported for 14 years after 1718 was probably tried at assizes (or equivalent). Anyone who was sentenced to transportation for less than 14 years after 1718 could have been tried either at assizes or at quarter sessions. In trying to match the crime to a court, you need to remember that the law kept changing and could influence the kind of trial that could be held. Sheep stealing, for example, was a 'serious' offence in the eighteenth century, normally tried at assizes. But by the middle of the nineteenth century, records of trials for sheep stealing can often be found in quarter sessions or even summary jurisdiction. The reason is simple: the death penalty for sheep stealing was abolished in 1832, and so as far as the law was concerned it suddenly ceased to be a 'serious' offence.

Scotland has a very different legal system, whose surviving records are in the National Archives of Scotland and local record offices in Scotland.

48.3 Using trial records

Another problem is the trial records. The nature and quality of the assizes records varies considerably from period to period and from circuit to circuit (group of counties). Trial records consist of a variety of documents: indictments, witness statements, gaol calendars, recognisances (bonds, usually for bail, but sometimes to testify or prosecute) and minute books. With certain limited exceptions, however, they do not contain transcripts of evidence and will not normally give details of the age of the accused or of his/her family relationships.

The indictments set out the nature of the charge against the accused. As with all formal legal records, until 1733 (with a brief interruption between 1650 and 1660) they are in heavily abbreviated Latin and are written in distinctive legal scripts. Even after 1733, when indictments were written in English and in an ordinary hand, the language used is so convoluted and archaic that it can be difficult to understand exactly what the defendant was being charged with. This does improve over time: by the late eighteenth century you should find them reasonably easy to understand.

Even more disappointing for the family historian is the fact that although the indictments appear to tell you the occupation and parish of residence of the accused, the information given is fictitious. Men are almost always described as labourers, even if they were skilled artisans. The parish of residence is invariably the place at which the crime was committed. If you are prepared to make a thorough search of the indictment and deposition files then you may be able to find more accurate information from some of the associated documents. By doing just this, Knafla has been able to establish correct occupation and place of residence for 87 per cent of the defendants he studied for *Kent at Law 1602*. But remember that a search of this kind will be both time consuming and speculative. It will also require a sound knowledge of trial procedures and records, as well as palaeographic skills, and a lot of background reading: the works listed in the bibliography (48.12), especially by Baker, Beattie and Cockburn, will get you off to a good start.

Pre-trial witness statements may survive either with the indictments or in a separate series (usually described in the National Archives as depositions, but often described in local record offices simply as sessions papers). These are in English and in the ordinary hand of the day, but if you are not familiar with this handwriting you may find them difficult to read. From about 1830, the deposition files have been heavily weeded, so that only depositions in capital cases, usually murder and riot, tend to survive. From the mid-twentieth century, depositions survive for a greater variety of cases. The deposition files (especially more modern ones) may also contain items used as trial exhibits, such as photographs, maps, appeal papers and in one case even a policeman's pocket book. Some of the exhibits are distressing.

Minute books (usually described by the National Archives as Crown books or gaol books) may also survive. These usually list the defendants at each session with a brief note of the charges against them and are often annotated with verdicts and sentences. Similar information is contained in sheriffs' assize vouchers (see 48.5).

Unofficial transcripts of evidence survive for some early nineteenth-century cases in which convicts petitioned for mercy (see 47.7). Official transcripts of selected criminal trials of special interest, 1846–1931, are held amongst the records of the Director of Public Prosecutions in DPP 4 ⊡. The records of the Director of Public Prosecutions also include case papers relating to prosecutions (1889–1992) in DPP 1 ⊡ and DPP 2 ⊡, and registers of cases (1884–1956) in DPP 3 ⊞. Many of these records are closed for 75 years.

48.4 Using other sources

Although the formal trial records might be disappointing, it is worth remembering that even quite ordinary trials attracted much journalistic coverage, which sometimes included transcripts of all or part of the evidence, as well as comments on family or occupational background. If you really want to know what happened at the trial, it is probably better to start with published reports of trials rather than with actual trial records.

Newspaper coverage became common from about 1750. *The Times*, which has been produced since 1786, is available online at most major reference libraries, as well as at the National Archives. Transcripts, confessions, dying statements of those who were hanged and other 'true crime' accounts have been published in pamphlet, magazine and book form from the seventeenth century to the present day. In the early period such publications were sometimes produced as one-off attempts to break into what was obviously a lucrative market, but local printers sometimes also tried to establish a market of their own by producing a series of pamphlets about local trials. The most famous are the *Old Bailey Proceedings*, which have been published since at least the 1690s and are now searchable online at **www.oldbaileyonline.org** (see below 48.8). Similar accounts were produced for other parts of the country too: the earliest known copy of the *Surrey Assize Proceedings* dates from 1678 and the series is known to have continued until at least 1780. Surviving pamphlets of this kind can be traced using the British Library's *English Short Title Catalogue* (previously known as the *Eighteenth Century Short Title Catalogue*). A number of these pamphlets have been re-published on microfiche by Chadwyck-Healey as *British Trials 1660–1900*, together with indexes of defendants, victims and locations; a copy is available at the National Archives. To find out more about how to trace printed works on crime, ask for advice at your nearest central reference library.

48.5 Criminal trial registers and other lists of prisoners to be tried, 1758–1892

Most records of criminals and criminal trials are not easy to use as they are not usually arranged by name. If you have some information, however sketchy, about the date and place of trial then you should try using sheriffs' assize vouchers, the Criminal Registers or the Calendars of Prisoners. These sources will only help you find those who were tried by jury but will not help for trials held in ordinary magistrates' courts without a jury.

Sheriffs' assize vouchers, 1758–1832, give some information about prisoners to be tried at assizes (they do not include those tried at quarter sessions) including their sentences, the length of time they spent in prison and the costs of maintaining them. They are held in E 370/35–51.

The Criminal Registers are returns from the counties, bound up in alphabetical order of county. They show all persons charged with indictable offences, giving the date and result of the trial, sentence in the case of conviction and dates of execution for those convicted on capital charges. The registers are in two series: HO 26 ⑦, which covers Middlesex only, 1791–1849; and HO 27 ⑦, which covers all England and Wales, 1805–1892 (including Middlesex from 1850). For 1807–1811 only, the Middlesex registers in HO 26 relate only to those tried at the Old Bailey; prisoners tried at the Middlesex and Westminster sessions are listed in HO 27.

Printed Calendars of Prisoners, 1868–1971, are held in HO 140 ④ and for London, 1855–1949, in CRIM 9 ⑦. Some are closed for 75 or 100 years. The Calendars list prisoners to be tried at courts of assize and quarter sessions, and for each one give age and occupation, level of literacy, the name and address of the committing magistrate, details of the alleged offence, verdict and sentence. Like the Criminal Registers, they are arranged by county. Printed calendars of this kind were compiled from at least the early nineteenth century, and earlier calendars can sometimes be found in PCOM 2 ⑦ or scattered amongst assizes series. Copies are also sometimes to be found in local record offices. For the Old Bailey (Central Criminal Court) there are returns of prisoners to be tried, 1815–1849, in HO 16 ⑦ and printed lists of defendants, 1782–1853, with the results of their trials, in HO 77 ⑦.

48.6 Quarter sessions and assizes

Before the assizes were created the judges were sent to try cases in the counties at irregular intervals on what became known as general eyres. The surviving records of these cases, both civil and criminal, are described in Crook's *Records of the general eyre*; Crook also lists those that have been published. The records are in JUST 1–JUST 4 ⑦: their use requires a high level of skill. The few quarter sessions records for the fourteenth and fifteenth centuries that survive are mostly in JUST 1; they are listed in Putnam's *Proceedings before the Justices of the Peace in the Fourteenth and Fifteenth Centuries* and many have been published by local record societies.

From the sixteenth century onwards, quarter sessions survive in increasing quantities and are deposited in local record offices: a search on A2A will turn up many references (1.13). Gibson's *Quarter Sessions Records* is probably still the easiest way in, however, as it gives details and locations very conveniently. Ratclif's *Warwick County Records* and Emmison's *County records* give a very full indication of the nature of the records and the sort of information they contain. Again, many have been published by local record societies.

Assizes records are normally held in the National Archives. Those for the fourteenth and fifteenth centuries are mostly in JUST 3 [7], with some others in JUST 1 [7], JUST 4 [7] and KB 9 [7]. After 1559, they are normally in the many ASSI series.

Assizes and Quarter Sessions courts were abolished in 1971.

ENGLISH ASSIZES, 1559–1971 (ALL [7])

County	Crown & Gaol Books		Indictments		Depositions		Other
Bedfordshire	1863–1876	ASSI 33	1658–1698	ASSI 16	1832–76	ASSI 36	ASSI 34,
	1734–1863	ASSI 32	1693–1850	ASSI 94	1876–1971	ASSI 13	ASSI 38,
	1876–1945	ASSI 11	1851–1971	ASSI 95			ASSI 39,
							ASSI 15
Berkshire	1657–1971	ASSI 2	1650–1971	ASSI 5	1719–1971	ASSI 6	ASSI 4,
	1847–1951	ASSI 3					ASSI 9,
							ASSI 10,
							ASSI 93
Buckingham-shire	1863–76	ASSI 32	1642–99	ASSI 16	1832–76	ASSI 36	ASSI 34,
	1734–1863	ASSI 33	1695–1850	ASSI 94	1876–1971	ASSI 13	ASSI 38,
	1876–1876	ASSI 11	1851–1971	ASSI 95			ASSI 39,
							ASSI 15
Cambridgeshire	1902–43	ASSI 31	1642–99	ASSI 16	1834–1971	ASSI 36	ASSI 34,
	1863–1971	ASSI 32	1692–1850	ASSI 94			ASSI 38,
	1734–1863	ASSI 33	1851–1971	ASSI 95			ASSI 39
Cheshire	1532–1831	CHES 21	1341–1830	CHES 24	1831–1944	ASSI 65	ASSI 59,
	1341–1659	CHES 24	1831–1945	ASSI 64	1945–1971	ASSI 84	ASSI 63,
	1831–1938	ASSI 61	1945–1971	ASSI 83			ASSI 66,
	1835–83	ASSI 62					ASSI 67
	1945–51	ASSI 79					
Cornwall	1730–1971	ASSI 21	1801–1971	ASSI 25	1861–1971	ASSI 26	ASSI 24,
	1970–1824	ASSI 23	1971		1951–3	ASSI 82	ASSI 30
Cumberland	1714–1873	ASSI 41	1607–1876	ASSI 44	1613–1876	ASSI 45	ASSI 43,
	1665–1810	ASSI 42	1877–1971	ASSI 51	1877–1971	ASSI 52	ASSI 46,
							ASSI 47,
							ASSI 93
Derbyshire	1818–1945	ASSI 11	1868–1971	ASSI 12	1862–1971	ASSI 13	ASSI 15
			1662–7, 87	ASSI 80			
Devon	1746–1971	ASSI 21	1801–1971	ASSI 25	1861–1971	ASSI 26	ASSI 24,
	1670–1824	ASSI 23			1951–3	ASSI 82	ASSI 30
Dorset	1746–1971	ASSI 21	1801–1971	ASSI 25	1861–1971	ASSI 26	ASSI 24,
	1670–1824	ASSI 23			1951–3	ASSI 82	ASSI 30
Durham	1770–1876	DURH 15	1582–1877	DURH 17	1843–1876	DURH 18	DURH 19,
	1753–1858	DURH 16	1876–1971	ASSI 44	1877–1971	ASSI 45	ASSI 46,
	1858–1944	ASSI 41					ASSI 47,
							ASSI 93

County	Crown & Gaol Books		Indictments		Depositions		Other
Essex	1734–1943	ASSI 31	1559–1688	ASSI 35	1825–1971	ASSI 36	ASSI 34,
	1826–1971	ASSI 32	1689–1850	ASSI 94			ASSI 38,
			1851–1971	ASSI 95			ASSI 39
Gloucestershire	1657–1971	ASSI 2	1662–1971	ASSI 5	1719–1971	ASSI 6	ASSI 4,
	1847–1951	ASSI 3					ASSI 9,
							ASSI 10,
							ASSI 93
Hampshire	1746–1971	ASSI 21	1801–1971	ASSI 25	1861–1971	ASSI 26	ASSI 24,
	1670–1824	ASSI 23			1951–3	ASSI 82	ASSI 30
Herefordshire	1657–1971	ASSI 2	1627–1971	ASSI 5	1719–1971	ASSI 6	ASSI 4,
	1847–1951	ASSI 3					ASSI 9,
							ASSI 10,
							ASSI 93
Hertfordshire	1734–1943	ASSI 31	1573–1688	ASSI 35	1851–1971	ASSI 36	ASSI 34,
	1826–1971	ASSI 32	1689–1850	ASSI 94			ASSI 38,
			1851–1971	ASSI 95			ASSI 39
Huntingdon-shire	1902–1943	ASSI 31	1643–98	ASSI 16	1851–1971	ASSI 36	ASSI 34,
	1863–1971	ASSI 32	1693–1850	ASSI 94			ASSI 38,
	1734–1863	ASSI 33	1851–1971	ASSI 95			ASSI 39
Kent	1734–1943	ASSI 31	1559–1688	ASSI 35	1851–1971	ASSI 36	ASSI 34,
	1826–1971	ASSI 32	1689–1850	ASSI 94			ASSI 38,
			1851–1971	ASSI 95			ASSI 39
Lancashire	1524–1843	PL 25	1660–1867	PL 26	1663–1867	PL 27	PL 28
	1686–1877	PL 28	1877–1971	ASSI 51	1877–1971	ASSI 52	ASSI 46,
							ASSI 53,
							ASSI 93
Leicestershire	1818–64	ASSI 11	1653–1656	ASSI 80	1862	ASSI 13	ASSI 15,
	1864–75	ASSI 32	1864–75	ASSI 35	1863–75	ASSI 36	ASSI 34,
	1876–1945	ASSI 11	1876–1971	ASSI 12	1876–1971	ASSI 13	ASSI 38,
							ASSI 39
Lincolnshire	1818–1945	ASSI 11	1868–1971	ASSI 12	1862–1971	ASSI 13	ASSI 15
			1652–79	ASSI 80			
London & Middlesex	1834–1949	CRIM 6	1834–1957	CRIM 4	1839–1971	CRIM 1	CRIM 7,
			1833–1971	CRIM 5	1923–1971	CRIM 2	CRIM 8,
							CRIM 9,
							CRIM 10,
							CRIM 11,
							CRIM 12,
							CRIM 13
Monmouth-shire	1657–1971	ASSI 2	1666–1971	ASSI 5	1719–1971	ASSI 6	ASSI 4,
	1847–1951	ASSI 3					ASSI 9,
							ASSI 10,
							ASSI 93
Norfolk	1902–43	ASSI 31	1606–99	ASSI 16	1817–1971	ASSI 36	ASSI 34,
	1863–1971	ASSI 32	1692–1850	ASSI 94			ASSI 38,
	1734–1863	ASSI 33	1851–1971	ASSI 95			ASSI 39
Northampton-shire	1818–64	ASSI 11	1659–60	ASSI 80	1862	ASSI 13	ASSI 15,
	1864–76	ASSI 32	1864–75	ASSI 95	1864–75	ASSI 36	ASSI 34,
	1876–1945	ASSI 11	1876–1971	ASSI 12	1876–1971	ASSI 13	ASSI 38,
							ASSI 39
Northumber-land	1714–1944	ASSI 41	1607–1971	ASSI 44	1613–1971	ASSI 45	ASSI 43,
	1665–1810	ASSI 42					ASSI 46,
							ASSI 47,
							ASSI 93
Nottingham-shire	1818–1945	ASSI 11	1868–1971	ASSI 12	1862–1971	ASSI 13	ASSI 15
			1663–4, 82	ASSI 80			

County	Crown & Gaol Books		Indictments		Depositions		Other
Oxfordshire	1657–1971	ASSI 2	1661–1971	ASSI 5	1719–1971	ASSI 6	ASSI 4,
	1847–1951	ASSI 3	1688	PRO 30/80			ASSI 9,
							ASSI 10,
							ASSI 93
Rutland	1818–64	ASSI 11	1667, 85	ASSI 80	1862	ASSI 13	ASSI 15,
	1864–76	ASSI 32	1864–75	ASSI 95	1864–73	ASSI 36	ASSI 34,
	1876–1945	ASSI 11	1876–1971	ASSI 12	1876–1971	ASSI 13	ASSI 38,
							ASSI 39
Shropshire	1657–1971	ASSI 2	1654–1971	ASSI 5	1719–1971	ASSI 6	ASSI 4,
	1847–1951	ASSI 3					ASSI 9,
							ASSI 10,
							ASSI 93
Somerset	1730–1971	ASSI 21	1801–1971	ASSI 25	1861–1971	ASSI 26	ASSI 24,
	1670–1824	ASSI 23			1951–3	ASSI 82	ASSI 30
Staffordshire	1657–1971	ASSI 2	1662–1971	ASSI 5	1719–1971	ASSI 6	ASSI 4,
	1847–1951	ASSI 3	1662	ASSI 80			ASSI 9,
							ASSI 10,
							ASSI 93
Suffolk	1902–1943	ASSI 31	1653–98	ASSI 16	1832–1971	ASSI 36	ASSI 34,
	1863–1971	ASSI 32	1689–1850	ASSI 94			ASSI 38,
	1734–1863	ASSI 33	1851–1971	ASSI 95			ASSI 39
Surrey	1734–1943	ASSI 31	1559–1688	ASSI 35	1820–1971	ASSI 36	ASSI 34,
	1826–1971	ASSI 32	1689–1850	ASSI 94			ASSI 38,
			1851–1971	ASSI 95			ASSI 39
Sussex	1734–1943	ASSI 31	1559–1688	ASSI 35	1812–1971	ASSI 36	ASSI 34,
	1826–1971	ASSI 32	1689–1850	ASSI 94			ASSI 38,
			1851–1971	ASSI 95			ASSI 39
Warwickshire	1818–1945	ASSI 11	1868–1971	ASSI 12	1862–1971	ASSI 13	ASSI 15
			1652, 88	ASSI 80			
Westmorland	1714–1873	ASSI 41	1607–1876	ASSI 44	1613–1876	ASSI 45	ASSI 43,
	1718–1810	ASSI 42	1877–1971	ASSI 51	1877–1971	ASSI 52	ASSI 46,
							ASSI 47,
							ASSI 53,
							ASSI 93
Wiltshire	1746–1971	ASSI 21	1729,	ASSI 25	1861–1971	ASSI 26	ASSI 24,
	1670–1824	ASSI 23	1801–1971		1951–3	ASSI 82	ASSI 30
Worcestershire	1657–1971	ASSI 2	1662–1971	ASSI 5	1719–1971	ASSI 6	ASSI 4,
	1847–1951	ASSI 3					ASSI 9,
							ASSI 10,
							ASSI 93
Yorkshire	1718–1863	ASSI 41	1607–1863	ASSI 44	1613–1863	ASSI 45	ASSI 15,
	1658–1811	ASSI 42	1864–76	ASSI 12	1868–76	ASSI 13	ASSI 43,
	1864–76	ASSI 11	1877–1971	ASSI 51	1877–1971	ASSI 52	ASSI 46,
							ASSI 47,
							ASSI 53,
							ASSI 93

Please note that the covering dates in the table give only a general indication of survival: there may well be unexplained gaps within an otherwise continuous run of records.

48.7 Bristol, the Palatinates of Chester, Durham and Lancaster, and Wales

In Bristol, the right to hear criminal cases was one of the ancient chartered privileges of the Corporation of Bristol. This right was abolished in 1832, after which date assize courts were held for Bristol as for any other county. Surviving trial records before 1832 are held in the Bristol Record Office (address in 62); those after 1832 are in the National Archives amongst the ASSI series.

Records of the Palatinate of Chester, primarily comprising Cheshire and Flint, are held in the National Archives under CHES. Those of the Palatinate of Durham, covering County Durham and certain areas beyond, are in DURH, and the Palatinate of Lancaster, covering Lancashire, in PL. Ely assizes records for the seventeenth and eighteenth centuries are at Cambridge University Library (address in 62).

In Wales, the equivalent jurisdiction to the assizes was exercised from 1542 to 1830 by the Great Sessions of Wales, whose records are in the National Library of Wales. Records of criminal trials at Great Sessions between 1730 and 1830 are searchable in their Crime and Punishment database at **www.llgc.org.uk/php_ffeiliau/sf_s.php**. Petty crimes were heard at the Courts of Quarter Sessions, whose records are held by the Welsh county record offices: see **www.archivesnetworkwales.info/**.

From 1830 to 1971 the Welsh counties were included among the assizes circuits, so the records are in the ASSI series at the National Archives, as below.

WELSH ASSIZES, 1830–1971

County	Crown & Gaol Books		Indictments		Depositions		Other
Anglesey	1831–1938	ASSI 61	1831–1945	ASSI 64	1831–1944	ASSI 65	ASSI 59,
	1835–83	ASSI 62	1945–1971	ASSI 83	1945–1971	ASSI 84	ASSI 63,
	1945–51	ASSI 79					ASSI 66,
							ASSI 67
Breconshire	1841–2	ASSI 74	1834–1945	ASSI 71	1837–1971	ASSI 72	ASSI 73,
	1844–1946	ASSI 76	1945–1971	ASSI 83	1945–1971	ASSI 84	ASSI 77
	1945–51	ASSI 79					
Caernarvon-shire	1831–1938	ASSI 61	1831–1945	ASSI 64	1831–1944	ASSI 65	ASSI 59,
	1835–83	ASSI 62	1945–1971	ASSI 83	1945–1971	ASSI 84	ASSI 63,
	1945–51	ASSI 79					ASSI 66,
							ASSI 67
Cardiganshire	1841–2	ASSI 74	1834–1945	ASSI 71	1837–1971	ASSI 72	ASSI 73,
	1844–1946	ASSI 76	1945–1971	ASSI 83	1945–1971	ASSI 84	ASSI 77
	1945–51	ASSI 79					
Carmarthen-shire	1841–2	ASSI 74	1834–1945	ASSI 71	1837–1971	ASSI 72	ASSI 73,
	1844–1946	ASSI 76	1945–1971	ASSI 83	1945–1971	ASSI 84	ASSI 77
	1945–51	ASSI 79					
Denbighshire	1831–1938	ASSI 61	1831–1945	ASSI 64	1831–1944	ASSI 65	ASSI 59,
	1835–83	ASSI 62	1945–1971	ASSI 83	1945–1971	ASSI 84	ASSI 63,
	1945–51	ASSI 79					ASSI 66,
							ASSI 67
Flint	1831–1938	ASSI 61	1330–1541	CHES 24	1831–1944	ASSI 65	ASSI 59,
	1835–83	ASSI 62	1831–1945	ASSI 64	1945–1971	ASSI 84	ASSI 63,
	1945–51	ASSI 79	1945–1971	ASSI 83			ASSI 66,
							ASSI 67
Glamorgan-shire	1841–2	ASSI 74	1834–1945	ASSI 71	1837–1971	ASSI 72	ASSI 73,
	1844–1946	ASSI 76	1945–1971	ASSI 83	1945–1971	ASSI 84	ASSI 77
	1945–51	ASSI 79					

County	Crown & Gaol Books		Indictments		Depositions		Other
Merioneth-shire	1831–1938 1835–83 1945–51	ASSI 61 ASSI 62 ASSI 79	1831–1945 1945–1971	ASSI 64 ASSI 83	1831–1944 1945–1971	ASSI 65 ASSI 84	ASSI 59, ASSI 63, ASSI 66, ASSI 67
Montgomery-shire	1831–1938 1835–83 1945–51	ASSI 61 ASSI 62 ASSI 79	1831–1945 1945–1971	ASSI 64 ASSI 83	1831–1944 1945–1971	ASSI 65 ASSI 84	ASSI 59, ASSI 63, ASSI 66, ASSI 67
Pembroke-shire	1841–2 1844–1946 1945–51	ASSI 74 ASSI 76 ASSI 79	1834–1945 1945–1971	ASSI 71 ASSI 83	1837–1971 1945–1971	ASSI 72 ASSI 84	ASSI 73, ASSI 77
Radnor	1841–2 1844–1946 1945–51	ASSI 74 ASSI 76 ASSI 79	1834–1945 1945–1971	ASSI 71 ASSI 83	1837–1971 1945–1971	ASSI 72 ASSI 84	ASSI 73, ASSI 77

48.8 London: Old Bailey until 1834 and the Central Criminal Court from 1834

London here means the City of London and the county of Middlesex – not any part of current London south of the Thames. As part of its privileges, the City of London had rights over its neighbouring county of Middlesex. These included control of the county gaol (Newgate), together with the right to deliver the gaol – that is, to try criminals. This meant that for both London and Middlesex, sessions of gaol delivery were held at the Old Bailey in the City. (The Middlesex sessions of the peace were held before the Middlesex Justices of the Peace at their sessions house in Clerkenwell.)

The website **www.oldbaileyonline.org/** has transformed searching for London criminals between 1674 and 1834 (to be extended to 1913 by late 2008). The site gives the full text of the published *Old Bailey Proceedings*. These are virtually verbatim reports of the proceedings in court, giving the name of the accused, the charges, the evidence of witnesses, the verdict (often with the prisoner's age if found guilty) and the sentence. Further work has been done to find the actual records of the case or any supplementary material in the relevant archives, so you may find that you can follow an existing trial. Each case will either be a London or a Middlesex one. This is important as the records of London and Middlesex gaol deliveries were kept separately:

- City of London: Corporation of London Record Office;
- Middlesex: London Metropolitan Archives.

There are very many references on the website from individual cases to related records in the National Archives (still called the Public Record Office in Old Bailey Online): these can therefore be followed up easily.

Remember that those parts of London that had spread south of the Thames were largely in the borough of Southwark. Southwark was normally held to be part of the county of Surrey. If your 'London' crime was committed **south of the river before 1834** you need to look at the records of assize courts for Surrey: you will not find anything in **www.oldbaileyonline.org/**.

The courtrooms of the Old Bailey were also used, from about 1660 to 1834, for the trials of individuals accused of offences within the jurisdiction of the High Court of Admiralty. Trial records in these cases if they survive are to be found amongst the various High Court of Admiralty series in the National Archives (see 48.11)

In 1834 the Old Bailey sessions were abolished and replaced with a court that is officially known as the Central Criminal Court (but which in practice is still called the Old Bailey). The geographical jurisdiction of this new court reflected the continuing spread of London and therefore included parts of Essex, Kent and Surrey as well as the City of London and Middlesex. The court's legal jurisdiction was made equivalent to an assize court for both the City of London and for Middlesex. Between 1834 and 1844, it was also given the jurisdiction over crimes on the high seas that had previously belonged to the High Court of Admiralty (48.11). Under the Central Criminal Court Act 1856, the court was empowered to hear cases from other counties to ensure a fair trial where local prejudice existed or where it could offer an earlier trial and so avoid the delay in waiting for the next assizes.

The actual records of the Old Bailey or Central Criminal Court after 1834 are held in the National Archives. Unfortunately, as a result of the Denning Report, only a two-per-cent sample of depositions in ordinary criminal cases survives, although depositions in cases involving murder, sedition, treason, riot and conspiracy to affect political change, as well as other trials of historic interest, are preserved permanently.

Depositions	1835–1992	CRIM 1	②
Calendars of Depositions	1923–1966	CRIM 2	⑧
Indictments	1834–1971	CRIM 4	⑦
Calendars of Indictments	1833–1971	CRIM 5	⑦
Court Books	1834–1949	CRIM 6	⑦
After Trial Calendars of Prisoners	1855–1949	CRIM 9	⑦
Minutes of Evidence	1834–1912	CRIM 10	⑦

Some additional information for 1782 to 1853 can be found in the Newgate Prison Calendar in HO 77⑦. Conviction details, 1815 to 1849, can be found in HO 16 ⑦.

The power of the court to hear cases outside its ordinary jurisdiction was further extended by the Jurisdiction in Homicides Act 1862.

From 1848 there was a limited right of appeal from decisions of the Central Criminal Court to the new Court of Crown Cases Reserved. Records are in CRIM 11 and CRIM 12 ②.

48.9 King's Bench

The Court of King's Bench was the highest court of common law in England and Wales until it was absorbed into the High Court in 1875. This section considers only its criminal jurisdiction; for a discussion of the records relating to civil litigation, see 57. The Court of King's Bench evolved from the Curia Regis and had become an established institution by the thirteenth century. The court was not itinerant, but since it was attached to the person of the King it necessarily moved with the seat of government. By 1422 the court had settled at Westminster, although the wording of its records still maintained the fiction that it was always held in the presence of the king himself.

The King's Bench gradually developed three separate jurisdictions: original jurisdiction over all criminal matters, supervisory powers over lesser courts and a local jurisdiction over the county in which it sat (which in practice from 1422 onwards was Middlesex). Like all courts in England and Wales, its formal records were written in heavily abbreviated Latin and in distinctive legal scripts until 1733 (except for a brief period during the interregnum). Its procedures were elaborate and created complex, inter-connected series of records for which there is no single or obvious point of entry. The indexes and finding aids are inadequate. In short these are not records that should be attempted by any but the most determined of searchers. As with assize and quarter sessions records, records of King's Bench trials do not contain transcripts of evidence and it may be better to start by looking for a newspaper or other published account of the trial that interests you (see 48.4).

Despite the received wisdom of traditional legal historians that use of this court must have been restricted to the rich and influential, the reality is that the court was accessible to almost all ranks of society. Its wide jurisdiction also meant that cases initiated or referred to the King's Bench (few of which were actually tried) covered a wide range of subject-matter, from minor assaults, disorderly houses and obstructed highways to riot, attempted rape and high treason. The records of the King's Bench are a particularly fruitful source of information about Londoners, but cases also came to the court from all over the country. Occasionally, they even came from the colonies as well.

Records of the King's Bench survive from the thirteenth century until its abolition in 1875. Formal and formulaic narratives of both civil and criminal proceedings are given in the plea rolls: KB 26 ⑦ (1194–1272) and then in KB 27 ⑦ until 1702. After 1702, entries for criminal business are found on the Crown Rolls (KB 28 ⑦). Indictment files, arranged by term, are in KB 9 ⑦ until 1675. Between 1675 and 1845 there are two series of indictments: KB 10 ⑦ for London and Middlesex and KB 11 ⑦ for the provincial or out-counties. From 1845 to 1875 there is once again a single series of indictments (KB 12 ⑦). Indictments in special cases are in KB 8 ② (48.10). For a description of the kind of information that can be gained from indictments see 48.3. Minute books, known as Crown Side rule books, survive from 1589 in KB 21 ⑦. Occasional witness statements survive from the mid-seventeenth century, but the survival is particularly good from the eighteenth century onwards (KB 1 ⑦ and KB 2 ⑦).

From 1329, the controlment rolls in KB 29 ⑦ provide references to the entries of criminal business in KB 27 and KB 28. Some contemporary indexes to indictments exist in IND 1. They are arranged alphabetically by the first letter of the surname of the accused, and then chronologically by term and supply the number of the indictment on the relevant indictment file. There are indexes to London and Middlesex defendants, 1673–1843; to provincial defendants, 1638–1704 and 1765–1843; and to London and Middlesex defendants and some defendants in northern counties, 1682–1699. There is a modern card index to entries on the plea rolls (KB 28) 1844–1859. From 1738, there is also a contemporary listing in KB 39 of the statements in KB 1. The great docket books and modern pye books in IND 1 can also be used as finding aids. Both give information about the way that cases were processed through the courts, but as they are arranged chronologically they are of limited use unless you already have some information about the date of the trial.

48.10 Sedition and high treason

Records of certain treason trials and other special cases were held in the so-called *Baga de Secretis* (KB 8 ②). Unlike the other KB series, KB 8 is well listed so it is comparatively easy to find cases. Some other records of, or relating to, treason trials, including lists of prisoners and convicts, are in KB 33 ②, PC 1②, TS 11② and TS 20 ②: see the research guide *The Jacobite Risings of 1715 and 1745*. Many of the most celebrated cases in King's Bench are reported in detail in the published *State Trials*. Trials for seditious libel should be traced through the King's Bench records in the normal way (see 48.9).

48.11 High Court of Admiralty

The criminal jurisdiction of the High Court of Admiralty was established by act of Parliament in 1535; it lasted until 1834. Commissions of oyer and terminer and of gaol delivery were issued to the Admiral or his deputy authorising them to try cases of piracy and other crimes committed on the high seas according to the procedures of common law. Its criminal jurisdiction also included the English havens and the Thames below London Bridge (then the limit of the tidal Thames). Until about 1660 the court usually met at the Guildhall or in Southwark; after 1660 it began also to use the Old Bailey and from 1700 the Admiralty sessions were always held there. Published reports of cases are sometimes included in the *Old Bailey Proceedings* (48.8). As explained above (see 48.3), all formal legal records are written in heavily abbreviated Latin and in distinctive legal scripts until 1733, the information given in indictments is often fictitious and trial records do not normally include transcripts of evidence.

The main series of criminal records is held in HCA 1 Ⓔ. It covers the period 1537–1834, with a gap between 1539 and 1574. The files contain a variety of different kinds of document, such as lists of prisoners, bails and bonds, jury panels and indictments and depositions. They also contain material about cases tried by Vice Admiralty Courts in the maritime counties of England (excluding the Cinque Ports) and Wales, as well as overseas. An index of persons and ships is available at the National Archives; both list and index are published by the List and Index Society (volumes 45 and 46).

Criminal examinations for 1607–1609, 1612–1614 and 1661–1674 are in HCA 13/98, 99 and 142. Warrants relating to execution of judgement 1802–1856 are in HCA 55 Ⓩ. Records relating to appeals from colonial admiralty courts are in DEL and PCAP.

The jurisdiction of the High Court of Admiralty passed to the new Central Criminal Court in 1834. In 1844 the judges of assize were allowed to try offences in any county. For the period 1834–1844, therefore, you should look for records in the CRIM series (48.8) and after 1844 in the relevant ASSI series (48.6).

The High Court of Admiralty also had jurisdiction over instance and prize cases: for a fuller description, see 61.

48.12 Criminal trials: bibliography

K R ANDREWS, *Elizabethan Privateering* (1969)

J H BAKER, 'Criminal courts and procedure at common law 1550–1800', in *Crime in England 1550–1800*, ed. J S Cockburn (London, 1977)

E BERCKMAN, *Victims of piracy: the admiralty court 1575–1678* (1979)

British Trials 1660–1900 (Chadwyck-Healy, 1990)

M CALE, *Law and society, an introduction to sources for criminal and legal history from 1800* (PRO, Readers' Guide 14, 1996)

J S COCKBURN ed., *Calendar of Assize Records, Home Circuit Indictments* (London, 1975–1995; Woodbridge, 1997)

D CROOK, *Records of the general eyre* (London, 1982)

H DEADMAN and E SCUDDER, *An introductory guide to the Corporation of London Record Office* (London, 1994)

Denbighshire Archives Service, *Unrolling the Past: Denbighshire Quarter Sessions Rolls, 1706–1800* (CD, 2003)

F G EMMISON and I GRAY, *County records (quarter sessions, petty sessions, clerk of the peace and lieutenancy)*. (Helps for students of history 62, 2nd edn, Historical Association, 1987)

Family and Community Historical Research Society, *Swing Unmasked* (Book and CD, 2003)

J S W GIBSON, *Quarter Sessions Records for Family Historians: a Select List* (FFHS, 1995)

D T Hawkings, *Criminal ancestors, a guide to historical and criminal records in England and Wales* (Sutton, 1992)

T B Howell and T J Howell eds, *A complete collection of state trials ...* (London, 1816–1826)

L A Knafla, *Kent at Law 1602, The county jurisdiction: assizes and sessions of peace* (London, 1994 continuing)

List and Index Society, *High Court of Admiralty, Oyer and Terminer Records (HCA 1), 1535–1834* (1969, vols 45 and 46)

J McDonell ed., *Reports of State Trials, New Series* (London, 1858–1898, reprinted Abingdon, 1982)

B H Putnam ed., *Proceedings before the Justices of the Peace in the Fourteenth and Fifteenth Centuries* (1938)

S C Ratclif and others eds, *Warwick County Records* (Warwick, 1935–1964)

G O Sayles, *Select cases in the court of King's Bench under Edward I* (Selden Society, 1936–71), 7 vols

Wiltshire Family History Society, *Summary Convictions in Wiltshire, 1698–1903* (CD-Rom)

49 Manors, Crown lands and wardship

49.1 Manorial records thirteenth to twentieth centuries: an overview

Many records of land holding and transfer relate to property held within a manor. It may not be easy to tell whether or not your ancestor was a manorial tenant. It's easy if you find a copy of a court roll among family papers. Without such a clue, you need first to find out which manor or manors covered your person's township or parish, and then see if any manorial records survive. If someone was a tenant of a particular manor, any surviving records may provide an invaluable source of information about him or her, and possibly about some generations of the family. If court rolls survive, you may find information from before the start of the parish registers. They may also provide continuity where parish registers contain gaps, especially during the Commonwealth period.

Manorial documents of all kinds are scattered between the National Archives and in many other archives. Although for some manors records exist covering many years, this is not the case for the majority of manors and for some no records survive at all. The best way to find out what records exist for a particular manor is to use the Manorial Documents Register. This register, covering England and Wales, mostly consists of a card index held at the National Archives. However, updated information for Wales, the Isle of Wight, Hampshire, Norfolk, Surrey, Middlesex and the three Ridings of Yorkshire is available online at **www.nationalarchives. gov.uk/mdr**. Other counties will follow. In the meantime, you can contact the Manorial Documents Register at the National Archives for information.

The manor is usually defined as a type of estate, in existence before the time of the Norman Conquest, lasting into the twentieth century and in a very few cases to the present day. Its most important feature was the right of the lord of the manor to hold manorial courts within it. Apart from court rolls, manorial administration also produced rentals and surveys (see 49.4) and accounts (see 49.5).

49.2 Manorial courts and court rolls

Manor courts were responsible for the regulation of local affairs, including land holding, as defined in the customs of the manor. These local customs can be among our most ancient laws: they were safeguarded by local knowledge. (Evidence on the customs of a particular manor may be found in depositions now in E 134 ⑤: see 59.4.) The two main courts were sometimes held together. Activity and decisions were recorded in court rolls.

The most frequent court, the **court baron**, was held every two to three weeks. It was mainly concerned with all matters to do with the lands and tenures of customary and villein tenants. These could be the regulation of agriculture in the manor, transfers of property and the settlement of disputes (not involving bloodshed) between tenants. It also chose the lord's officials, such as the reeve and the beadle.

The **court leet** was held every six months or so. Within the manor, all men over the age of twelve were grouped together in bands, called tithing groups, which were responsible for their good behaviour. At the court leet the view of frankpledge was held. This required the tithing groups to report on any crimes, misdemeanours, nuisances and obstructions, which were then punished by the court (although the more serious crimes began to be taken over by justices of the peace from the sixteenth century onwards). The court leet was also responsible for the assizes of bread and ale (to maintain standard weight and quality), as well as the election of manor officials such as the constable, ale-taster and the head of each tithing group.

Court rolls, which may date from the thirteenth to the twentieth centuries, are the central records of the manor court. Although the records are also often highly abbreviated, they make regular use of certain phrases, which once grasped can be easily recognised. During the Commonwealth period (1649–1660) and after 1733, court rolls are written in English: otherwise they are in Latin. For assistance with reading court rolls and other documents, see 49.8 – and particularly the works by Bass, Haydon and Harrop, and Stuart.

As the name suggests, court rolls may be found in roll form, possibly containing records of courts held in one manor over a period of years, or of one court held for several manors. Court rolls might also be found on single sheets of parchment, or sometimes in the form of a series of volumes or court books.

The National Archives has some major series of court rolls from manors that at one time or another had been in Crown hands: most of these can be searched by name of manor.

1441–1950	Court Rolls and other Manorial Documents from Crown Manors	CRES 5	⑥, ④
c.1272–1954	Duchy of Lancaster: Court Rolls	DL 30	⑥, ④
1286–1837	Court Rolls and Other Manorial Documents from Crown Manors	LR 3	⑥, ④

c.1350–1798	Estreats [extracts] of Court Rolls (from Crown Manors)	LR 11	[7]
c.1200–c1900	Special Collections: Court Rolls	SC 2	[6], [4]
1473–1930	Admiralty: Royal Greenwich Hospital: Court Rolls (manors in Cumberland, Northumberland and Kent)	ADM 74	[6]
1386–1926	Manor of Paglesham [Essex] Manorial Documents	MAF 5	[7]

We also have other series court rolls that have come in for safe keeping or as a result of law suits.

1324–1808	Lordship of Ruthin (Denbighshire): Court and Constables' Records	WALE 15	[7]
1294–1808	Chancery: Manor Court Rolls Extracted from Chancery Masters' Exhibits	C 116	[6], [4]

Sometimes the distinction is not clear. Often court rolls are not in a separate series: the best way to find these is to search on the name of the manor and 'court roll' over the whole catalogue.

49.3 Manorial tenants

Deaths of tenants since the last court were reported in the court baron, from which you can get a rough date of death for a tenant (male or female). The subsequent admissions of heirs may also be of interest, as the relationship between the former tenant and his heir should be made plain.

Various patterns of inheritance were used on manors. According to the custom of the manor, the heir might be the eldest son (primogeniture) or the youngest son (Borough English) or in certain areas of the country, such as Kent and parts of Wales, the property might be divided between all the sons or all the daughters if there were no sons (gavelkind). If the heir was not the son or daughter of a former tenant, but a more distant relation, this might also be explained.

Tenants might hold land in a manor by one or more of several types of tenure:

- freehold
- customary hold (in villeinage, copyhold, at will) if this existed in the manor
- leasehold.

Many people held different plots of land by different tenures. Remember, copyhold land could not be left by will until 1815: instead, any transfer had to be dealt with in the manor court. You may find it worth checking the relevant manor court roll around the time of probate to see if land not mentioned in a will had been surrendered and re-granted within the family.

Freehold tenants' property was not regulated by the manor courts and therefore transfers were not recorded there. However, freeholders paid rents, were obliged to attend the court baron, where they might appear as jurors, and made payments on entry into property ('reliefs') and on the death of tenants ('heriots', the 'best beast', or else cash), all of which may be recorded in the court rolls.

Customary tenants' property was entirely regulated by the manor courts and transfers were performed and recorded there – customary tenure being either of inheritance or for life or lives. The commonest form of customary tenure was **copyhold**, so-called because tenants held their land 'by copy of court roll' and according to the custom of the manor. Copyhold land was transferred in the ceremony of surrender and admission, usually carried out on behalf of the lord by the steward of the manor in court. In the nineteenth and twentieth centuries, the steward was very often a solicitor and the ceremony might take place in his office, out of court. First, the land was surrendered to the lord of the manor from whom it was held, then it was re-granted and the new tenants admitted. These conveyances of copyhold property were entered on the court rolls and the tenant generally given a copy of the relevant entry as a record. Copyholders were also obliged to attend the lord's court and paid rents. In the early Middle Ages, they were obliged to perform labour services for the lord, but on most manors by the sixteenth century these were converted into money payments. They might also be liable to make cash payments on entry into property ('fines') and heriots on the death of tenants. Holding by copyhold was not confined to the common people. For example, the magnificent Ham House was originally held by copyhold of the Crown manor of Petersham: the cavalier Earl of Dysart transferred the tenure to his wife in the manor court to prevent the house being confiscated by Parliament.

In the sixteenth century, **leasehold** became more popular. Copyhold tenure was sometimes converted into leasehold. Tenants held leases that either ran for a term of years or for lives, usually that of the tenant and two others. Rents were payable for leasehold property, often with payments in kind and some obligations, as well as heriots and payments on renewal or granting of a lease. Records of such payments may be found in the court rolls and in some cases, in separate registers of leases. However, lists of tenants by type of tenure, their holdings and rents may often be found in the different types of manorial survey (see 49.4).

Copyhold tenure could be converted to leasehold, as noted above, or to freehold ('enfranchised'). The process of **copyhold enfranchisement** was only addressed by legislation from the mid-nineteenth century onwards. Copyhold tenure was finally abolished by the Law of Property Acts, 1922 and 1924, which virtually brought the life of the manor to a close. The National Archives holds nineteenth- and twentieth-century files of copyhold enfranchisements in MAF 9 ②, ④, ⑤ and MAF 20 ⑤. Manorial incidents, the lord's residual financial interest in this newly enfranchised land, including entry fines, reliefs and heriots, were also abolished under the Acts; twentieth-century files relating to compensation for manorial incidents are found in MAF 13 ②, ④, ⑤ and MAF 27 ①, ⑤.

Further material on these subjects will be found in MAF 48 ⑤, MAF 76 ⑦ and MAF 233 ⑦.

49.4 Manorial rentals and surveys

The second major group of manorial records consists of the various types of manorial survey. These contain details of property, tenants, their tenure and rents and, in the early period, services. Among the earliest types of survey are:

- the custumal, a list of tenants with the customs by which they held their property;
- the extent, a list of every item on the manor with its valuation;
- the terrier, a plot-by-plot description of lands;
- the rental, a list of tenants and their rents owed to the lord.

By the sixteenth century, however, some surveys began to consist of three elements:

- a written description of the boundaries of the manor;
- a list of the customs;
- a rental or rent roll.

These were made at a special court baron called the court of survey, before commissioners of survey appointed by the lord and a jury of survey, who would answer a detailed list of questions concerning all aspects of the manor. Tenants were expected to attend the court with their record of title, so that the rental could be compiled. The rental will generally list tenants by type of tenure – freehold, leasehold and customary hold, including copyhold – and may give brief details of the property held by each tenant. This includes acreage, amount of rent payable, services owed, if any, sometimes including names of former tenants or statement of how present tenants came to occupy the property – for example, by inheritance, which may lead to relationships being stated. With leasehold property, the duration of the lease may be given, together with the date of entry.

Although this kind of survey became common, other types, such as rentals and rent rolls, continued to be made. During the sixteenth century, the profession of surveyor began to develop and increasingly a surveyor may have been employed to make the survey and, in some cases, a map may also have been produced, accurately measured and drawn to scale, although manorial maps are very rare before 1600.

Surveys were often created as part of the routine of estate management and may have been made on a regular basis; however, they were often made before or after a change in ownership of the manor, or if the manor was the subject of litigation. Surveys may cover an individual manor, or an estate made up of manors; therefore, they may exist as a single sheet of parchment or in a large volume. By the eighteenth century, documents such as rentals may normally be set out in regular columns under clear headings, kept in a series of annual volumes. The early surveys are in Latin, but from the sixteenth century, surveys are often found in English.

Surveys of all kinds are found among manorial records in the National Archives. The first things to check are the published *List of Rentals and Surveys* and the *List of Rentals and Surveys: Addenda*. These list and index all relevant documents in DL 29, DL 42, DL 43, DL 44, E 36, E 142, E 164, E 315, E 317, LR 2, SC 11, SC 12, SP 10–SP 18 and SP 46 F. Surveys taken as a result of litigation or for other reasons will also be found in the Special Commissions in E 178 F – look in the *List of Special Commissions and Returns in the Exchequer*. Other surveys may be found by searching in the catalogue in general by the name of the manor.

49.5 Manorial accounts: ministers' and receivers' accounts

Manorial accounts are not easy to use and the information they contain is not very helpful for family historians. If you want to investigate them, in the first place look at published editions, such as those for Cuxham, Oxfordshire edited by Harvey (see 49.8).

Accounts in the National Archives include those of Crown lands, or lands held temporarily by the Crown, and are known as 'ministers' accounts' or 'receivers' accounts', depending on the type of official who created them. For the most part, local officials appear to have delivered their accounts to a receiver-general, who in turn submitted his final account to the Exchequer; as a result, the contents will comprise summaries of payments, rather than detailed sections on crops and livestock. Few original accounts for Crown lands survive after the sixteenth century. Most surviving accounts held in the National Archives are in SC 6 4, 5 and DL 29 4, 5. These are also listed in the publications:

- *List of Original Ministers' Accounts, Part I – Henry III to Richard III*;
- *List of Original Ministers' Accounts: Appendix, Corrigenda, and Index to Part I*;
- *List of Original Ministers' Accounts, Part II – Henry VII to Henry VIII*;
- *List of Ministers' Accounts Edward VI – 18th century and analogous documents.*

Material of interest may also be found in the *List of the Lands of Dissolved Religious Houses*.

49.6 Tenants of Crown lands

Many properties have at some time been in the hands of the Crown. For 1786–1830, there is the *Crown Lands Return* of 1831, available in the Map Room. It may be that other similar returns to Parliament exist among the Parliamentary Papers, which can be seen on microfiche in the Library. For Wales, for example, there is the *Crown Lands (Wales and Monmouthshire)*

Return of 1911 (London, 1912). If it is unclear whether certain lands were part of the Crown estates, there is a useful list of Crown manors as at 1827 in CRES 2/1613, and the Annual Reports of the various bodies administering the Crown lands are in CRES 60 ⑦ for 1797–1942. From 1914 to 1961, there is a card index (on open access) to the buyers and lessees of Crown lands; the actual deeds (in LRRO 16) may be closed for up to 100 years. For 1832–1913, there are indexes LRRO 64 ⑦ to buyers, lessees and places mentioned in deeds now in LRRO 13 Ⓕ, LRRO 16 Ⓕ and other series; again the indexes can be seen but documents of more recent date than 100 years ago are also closed.

If there is any evidence to suggest that a piece of property was in the Crown's hands or that a person was a Crown tenant, it is worth exploring the various codes that contain the bulk of material relating to Crown lands – CRES, LR, LRRO and E, particularly series in the E 300s ⑦. There is also FEC, the Forfeited Estates Commission ④, ⑤, ②. The court rolls, rentals and surveys, ministers' and receivers' accounts are particularly fruitful sources for identifying Crown lands and tenants (see 49.2, 49.4 and 49.5).

The Parliamentary Surveys of Crown Lands in E 317 ⑤, recorded in English, can be used to establish both the occupation of lands in the mid-seventeenth century and an indication of the size, extent and layout of the buildings themselves. These surveys were taken under two acts of 1649 and 1650, which authorised the sale of honours, manors and lands formerly belonging to King Charles I, Queen Henrietta Maria and Prince Charles. The trustees appointed to sell the lands employed local surveyors to conduct surveys of the Crown lands. The registrar's books of particulars (based on the surveys) and contracts for sale are in CRES 39/67–74. Individual particulars and contracts for sales of Crown lands are in E 320 ②, ④. Many of these sales were reversed following the Restoration of Charles II in 1660.

49.7 Inquisitions post mortem, homage and wardship to 1660

Before the abolition of feudal tenure in 1660, the death of any holder of land who was thought to have held that land directly from the Crown (called a tenant in chief by knight service) would prompt an inquiry to be held by the escheator of the county involved. The escheator was one of the most important royal officials in the localities and it was his responsibility to maintain the Crown's rights as feudal overlord. When land was deemed to have no owner, for whatever reason, the property reverted to the king as ultimate feudal lord.

Inquisitions post mortem were conducted according to well-established procedures. A local jury would be summoned by the sheriff and had to swear to the identity and extent of the land held by the tenant at the time of his death, by what rents or services they were held and the name and age of the next heir. If there was no heir, the land escheated (reverted) to the

Crown; if the next heir was under age, the Crown claimed rights of wardship and marriage over the lands and the heir until he or she came of age. If the heir was adult, livery of seisin of the lands was granted on performance of homage to the king, and on payment of a reasonable fine or relief. If the heir's age was in doubt, there might have been a separate inquiry to produce proof of age; this inquiry was known as an inquisition *de aetatis probanda*. These proofs often record memories of other notable events to fix the heir's year of birth. Widows also had rights of dower in the lands, which may have continued long after the deaths of their husbands, and there are inquisitions *de assignatio dotis* into this as well. These inquisitions are included with the inquisitions post mortem. The jury's findings were returned to Chancery as an indenture, along with any associated documentation, such as the Chancery writ. A duplicate indenture was kept by the escheator. The documents produced by inquisitions post mortem are a very valuable source for both family and local history; however, it must be remembered that not all the information given is reliable.

The inquisitions give details of what lands were held (a separate inquisition was held for each county involved) and by what tenure and from whom, as well as the date of death and the name and age of the heir. They are in Latin and follow a standard pattern. Each inquisition starts with the county, the name of the escheator (the official holding the inquest) and a list of the jurors. The name of the deceased and the date of their death are given next. Then follows a brief description of each landholding, its value (often underestimated) and the tenure by which it is held. This section may include extracts (in English) from a will or an enfeoffment to use (putting the lands into the hands of trustees, in order to avoid the king's claims to livery and wardship, etc., and also to allow lands to be left to people other than the heir at law). At the end, the next heir is identified, and an age given. If the heir was of age (over 21, or over 14 for an heiress) the actual age given may be an estimate. The next heir is usually one male, or one female or a number of females; lands were split between daughters (who were treated as having an equal claim if there was no male heir) but not between sons.

The main series consists of those returned into Chancery (c 132–c 142): unfortunately they are often illegible. Transcripts of some were sent to the Exchequer (e 149 7, e 150 2, 4, e 152 7) and to the Court of Wards from the reign of Henry VIII (ward 7 2, 4) and are usually in better condition. There are published editions of inquisitions post mortem covering 1236–1432 and 1485–1509 (see 49.8).

1236–1272	Henry III	C 132, E 149	S
1272–1307	Edward I	C 133, E 149	S
1307–1327	Edward II	C 134, E 149	S
1327–1377	Edward III	C 135, E 149	S

1377–1399	Richard II	C 136, E 149	[S]
1399–1413	Henry IV	C 137, E 149	[S]
1413–1422	Henry V	C 138, E 149	[S] C 138 [2], [4]
1422–1461	Henry VI	C 139, E 149	[S] (to 1432) C 139 [2], [4]
1461–1483	Edward IV	C 140, E 149	C 140 [2], [4]
1483–1485	Richard III	C 141, E 149	C 141 [2], [4]
1485–1509	Henry VII	C 142, E 150	[S]
1509–1660	Henry VIII–Charles I	C 142, E 150, WARD 7	All [2], [4]

Inquisitions from the palatinate of Durham are in DURH 3 [F]; for the palatinate of Chester in CHES 3 [F]; and for the duchy of Lancaster in DL 7 [F].

The right to wardship was often sold by the Crown, by no means always to the next of kin; grants of wardship may be found in the Patent Rolls (C 66 [F]). The Close Rolls (C 54 [F]) contain writs of livery of seisin, while the Fine Rolls (C 60 [F]) include grants of wardship and marriage and writs of livery of seisin: see 50.3.

If the heir was underage and did hold land in chief from the Crown, then it is worth investigating the records of the Court of Wards and Liveries, which operated between 1540 and 1660. The records of most potential value are the legal proceedings (see 60.5), and so the records are full, informative, and in English. For more information, consult Bell, *An Introduction to the History and Records of the Court of Wards and Liveries*. For other legal proceedings about the validity or accuracy of inquisitions post mortem, see the records of the plea side of Chancery (57.2).

49.8 Manors, Crown lands and wardship: bibliography

General works

B ENGLISH, 'Inheritance and Succession in Landed Families 1660–1925', *Genealogists' Magazine*, vol. XXIV, pp. 433–438

E GOODER, *Latin for Local History* (2nd edn, London, 1978)

A W B SIMPSON, *A History of the Land Law* (Oxford, 1986)

D STUART, *Latin for Local and Family Historians: A Beginner's Guide* (London, 1995)

Manorial records

R BASS, *Manorial Records: 16th–19th centuries*, University of York, Borthwick Institute of Historical Research, Borthwick Wallet 8 (York, 1998)

J BECKETT, 'Estate Surveys as a Source for Names', *Genealogists' Magazine*, vol. XXIV (1993), pp. 335–341

J H BETTEY, 'Manorial Customs and Widows' Estates', *Archives*, vol. XX (1992), pp. 208–216

M ELLIS, *Using Manorial Records* (revised edn, PRO, 1997)

J GURNEY, 'The manorial documents register', *Ancestors* 23 (2004)

P D A HARVEY, *Manorial Records* (revised edn, Loughborough, 1999)

P D A Harvey, ed., *Manorial Records of Cuxham, Oxfordshire c. 1200–1359* (London, 1976)

E Haydon and J Harrop, eds, *Widworthy Manorial Court Rolls 1453–1617* (Honiton, 1997)

P B Park, *My Ancestors were Manorial Tenants: How can I find out more about them?* (2nd edn, Society of Genealogists, 1994)

D Stuart, *Manorial Records* (Chichester, 1992)

A Travers, 'Manorial Documents', *Genealogists' Magazine*, vol. XXI (1983), pp. 1–10

H Watt, *Welsh Manors and their records* (National Library of Wales, 2000)

Inquisitions post mortem and wardships

H E Bell, *An Introduction to the History and Records of the Court of Wards and Liveries* (Cambridge, 1953)

Calendar of Inquisitions Miscellaneous, Henry III to Henry VII (London, 1916–1968)

Calendar of Inquisitions Post Mortem, Henry III to Henry VI, and Henry VII (London, 1898–2004)

Calendarium Inquisitionum Post Mortem (Record Commission, 1806–1828)

R F Hunnisett, 'The Reliability of Inquisitions as Historical Evidence', *The Study of Medieval Records*, eds D A Bullough and R L Storey (Oxford, 1971)

J Hurstfield, *The Queen's Wards* (London, 1958)

R E Latham, 'Hints on Interpreting the Public Records: III, Inquisitions Post Mortem', *Amateur Historian*, vol. I (1952–1954), pp. 77–81

List of Inquisitions Post Mortem, Henry V–Richard III; Inquisitions ad quod damnum and miscellaneous inquisitions, Henry VII–Charles I (C138–C142) (List and Index Society, vols 268–269, 1998)

M McGuinness, 'Inquisitions Post Mortem', *Amateur Historian*, vol. VI (1963–1965), pp. 235–242

Crown lands

C D Chandaman, *The English Public Revenue, 1660–1688* (Oxford, 1975)

R Hoyle, *The Estates of the English Crown, 1558–1640* (Cambridge, 1992)

W C Richardson, *History of the Court of Augmentations, 1536–1544* (Baton Rouge, 1961)

B P Wolffe, *The Crown Lands, 1460–1536* (London, 1970)

B P Wolffe, *The Royal Demesne in English History* (London, 1971)

50 Land transfer

50.1 Registration of deeds

Because there was no national system of registration before the nineteenth century, records of the ownership and transfer of particular lands in England and Wales are difficult to locate. The national Land Registry was established in 1862, but registration was voluntary and little used. Compulsory registration on sale was gradually introduced from 1899. Most land/property has now been registered and you can find out the current owner at **www.landregisteronline.gov.uk/** or by writing (address in 62). An increasing number of registered deeds can be seen online, for a fee.

Local registries of deeds were established in the Bedford Level in the fens, in the three Ridings of Yorkshire and in Middlesex early in the eighteenth century. The registry in Middlesex closed in 1940, but those in Yorkshire continued to operate until the 1970s. The Bedford Level register can be seen at the Cambridgeshire Record Office and the Middlesex register at the London Metropolitan Archives; the registers for the North, East and West Ridings of Yorkshire are in the county record offices at Northallerton, Beverley and Wakefield respectively (addresses and websites in 62 under Yorkshire).

If you want to know about nineteenth- and early twentieth-century properties, start with the property surveys in 51.

50.2 Deeds in the National Archives

The National Archives holds hundreds of thousands of deeds and property-related records, but not in any registered form. These deeds are here

- because the particular property was at some point in the possession of the Crown or government;
- or because the property was the subject of litigation and documents were presented as evidence to the courts and never reclaimed;
- or because documents were enrolled in the records of a court to demonstrate transfer or proof of ownership.

As a result they are widely scattered among the records. There is no single index, and in many cases their original context has been lost. The overwhelming majority of private deeds came into the Crown's possession either when it acquired property through purchase, forfeiture or other forms of escheat, or when the deeds were produced as evidence in law suits and were not collected afterwards. Most deeds are conveyances and other evidences of title, although various other record types, including wills, bonds and receipts, might also be found.

A typical deed will contain the name of the vendor, the purchaser, details of the property concerned, the sum paid for the property and the date on which the transaction was conducted. Latin is the language of most medieval and Early Modern deeds, with the remainder written in either English or French. Modern deeds are written in English. In some instances, one or more seals may survive, still attached to the original deed.

The large collections of individual deeds emanating from private or monastic sources are primarily in the codes C, DL, DURH, E, LR, PL, WALE and WARD (most ②, Ⓥ and ⑤, Ⓥ). Some series of deeds, C 149, DURH 21, E 44, E 330, E 355, LR 16 and WALE 31, have not been listed and access to them is currently restricted.

It remained common practice until the nineteenth century to enrol private deeds in the central courts as a way of recording ownership; certain types of deed continued to be enrolled up to 1925. The greatest number of deeds was enrolled in the Chancery (C 54); others were enrolled in the Exchequer (E 13, E 159, E 315 and E 368), the Court of Common Pleas (CP 40 before Easter 1583 and 1834–1875 and CP 43, 1583–1834) and the Court of King's Bench (KB 26, KB 27 before 1702 and KB 122, 1702–1875). There are manuscript and typescript indexes and calendars to the deeds in C 54, CP 40, CP 43, E 13, E 315, KB 26 and KB 27. Deeds enrolled in E 368 can be traced by referring to IND volumes, which must be ordered as original documents.

In the City of London and in many other cities and boroughs, transfers of property were often entered on the rolls of the Court of Husting or other courts, and these records should be sought in the appropriate local record office. Also, in most counties, the type of deed known as the 'bargain and sale' was enrolled in the records of Quarter Sessions from 1536 to the early seventeenth century, and these records will also be found locally, if not in Chancery.

In addition, deeds were sometimes used as evidence in law suits and their texts can be found on the plea rolls, the pleadings or as separate series of documents amongst the records of the relevant court. Deeds used as evidence in Chancery suits exist in large number in C 103–C 115, C 171 and J 90 (all ②, ⑤). Deeds used in suits in the Court of Wards and Liveries are in WARD 2, but the list, such as it is, is very difficult to use.

50.3 Chancery enrolments

The records of Chancery contain many useful references to grants of land from the Crown and conveyances. Evidence of early grants from the Crown can be traced on the Charter Rolls (c 53 Ⓢ). The principal source of grants of land, however, is found on the Patent Rolls (c 66 Ⓢ, Ⓕ). There are also contemporary manuscript indexes in c 274 Ⓩ, which survive from 1485 (1 Henry VII) to 1946 (10 George VI). They are arranged in letter order of grantees' names; some have indexes.

The Patent Rolls and Close Rolls were also used to enrol private conveyances. The Close Rolls (c 54 Ⓢ, Ⓕ) became a popular means of recording private deeds, and from 1536 the type of deed known as a 'bargain and sale' was required to be enrolled there or in local records. The Patent Rolls record licences to alienate. These were used by individuals holding property by tenure in chief. This could only lawfully be sold with the Crown's permission. Copies of the licences were enrolled on the Patent Rolls (c 66 Ⓢ, Ⓕ). Using the indexes to the calendars is an easy and sometimes rewarding way of searching for early conveyances. After the printed calendars cease, it is easier to leaf through the Entry Books of Licences and Pardons for Alienation, 1571–1650 (A 4 Ⓩ) as it is to use the contemporary finding aids to the Patent Rolls.

50.4 Fines and recoveries

Other ways to transfer the ownership of land involved the common law and the King's courts: the most usual, fines and common recoveries, were methods of conveying property by means of fictitious legal actions. Conveyancing by fines (also known as final concords) became increasingly common during the late twelfth century. By 1195, the procedure was well established and fines continued to be used until their abolition in 1833. Until the fourteenth century, fines were made in the Court of Common Pleas, the Court of King's Bench and the general eyre, a periodic visitation of the English counties by royal justices. From the fourteenth century onwards, all feet of fines made in the central common law courts were made in the Court of Common Pleas.

A foot of fine was the bottom copy of a series of three or more copies of a final agreement, or concord, written on a single piece of parchment. A copy was given to each of the parties to the agreement to retain as their own record, while the foot was retained by the court. The contents of the documents tend to follow a set formula. The intended purchaser, as plaintiff, claimed the property from the vendor, as defendant (or deforciant); the property was then transferred by a legally sanctioned agreement. The largest series of Feet of Fines are in CP 25/1 Ⓕ and CP 25/2 Ⓕ. Fines can be located by using the manuscript indexes of fines and recoveries in IND 1/1–6605 and IND 1/17183–17216 arranged by date. Furthermore, certain manuscript indexes to fines from the reign of Henry

VIII onwards (for CP 25/2) are available on microfilm. Many fines have also been published, mainly by local record societies: it is best to look first in *Texts and Calendars*, by Mullins, to see if any fines for the relevant shire have been printed. For medieval feet of fines, see the article by Kissock, which includes a catalogue of those published.

The recovery was a method of transferring property developed in the fifteenth century, which also lasted until its abolition in 1833. It was used to enable entailed estates to be broken up so that they could be disposed of at will rather than descending within a specific family line. Having already agreed terms beforehand, the individual who wished to acquire the entailed lands would bring a fictitious action against the person wishing to dispose of the land, known as the tenant-in-tail. The tenant-in-tail named a third party to warrant the title to him. This individual became known as the common vouchee. He would appear to defend the tenant's title but would subsequently default (i.e., not turn up in court). This was a contempt of court, which allowed the justices to make a judgement against the tenant, thus breaking the entail and enabling the smooth transfer of the property in question. The recovery is a distinctive document, taking the form of a type of copy known as an 'exemplification', written on a large sheet of parchment, worded as a royal writ and sealed with the Great Seal.

The majority of common recoveries are in CP 40 Ⓕ and CP 43 Ⓕ. Recoveries can be traced by referring to the manuscript indexes of fines and recoveries in IND 1/1–6605 and IND 1/17183–17216.

50.5 Chester, Durham and Lancaster

The palatinates of Chester, Durham and Lancaster had their own administrations, which paralleled those of the central government, and records created by these administrations will be found in National Archives series CHES, DURH and PL respectively. Fines and recoveries can be found in CHES 2 Ⓕ, CHES 29 Ⓕ, CHES 30 Ⓣ, CHES 31 Ⓣ, CHES 32 Ⓣ, DURH 12 Ⓣ, DURH 13 Ⓣ, PL 15 Ⓣ and PL 17 Ⓣ. Deeds can be found in CHES 2 Ⓕ, CHES 29 Ⓕ, DURH 13 Ⓣ, DURH 21 (unlisted), PL 2 Ⓕ, PL 14 Ⓣ, PL 15 Ⓣ and PL 29 Ⓘ, Ⓢ. For a description of the nature and format of these types of documents, please refer to the relevant subject headings in this chapter.

50.6 Land transfer: bibliography
Deeds and feet of fines

N W ALCOCK, 'In word and deed', *Ancestors* 35 (2005)

N W ALCOCK, *Old Title Deeds* (Chichester, 2001)

J CORNWALL, *How to Read Old Title Deeds XVI–XIX Centuries* (2nd edn, Federation of Family History Societies, 1997)

A A DIBBEN, *Title Deeds* (Historical Association, 1968)

J KISSOCK, 'Medieval feet of fines: a study of their uses, with a catalogue of published sources', *Journal of the Society of Archivists*, vol. XXIV (1994), pp. 66–82

F SHEPPARD and V BELCHER, 'The Deed Registries of Yorkshire and Middlesex', *Journal of the Society of Archivists,* vol. VI (1978–1981), pp. 274–286

K T WARD, 'Pre-Registration Title Deeds: The Legal Issues of Ownership, Custody and Abandonment', *Journal of the Society of Archivists,* vol. XVI (1995), pp. 27–39

Chancery enrolments

Calendar of Charter Rolls (London, 1903–1927)

Calendar of Close Rolls (London, 1892–1963)

Calendar of Patent Rolls Elizabeth I, 1582–1590 (List and Index Society 2000–2004)

Calendar of Patent Rolls, Henry III to Henry VII, and *Edward VI to 1582* (London, 1891–1986)

Letters and Papers of Henry VIII (London, 1864–1932). (This includes a calendar of the Patent Rolls for Henry VIII.)

Patent Rolls ... Henry III (London, 1901–1903)

Rotuli Chartarum (Record Commission, 1837)

Rotuli Litterarum Patentium (Record Commission, 1835)

51 Surveys of land and house ownership and tenancy

51.1 Introduction
51.2 Tithe survey records, *c.* 1830–*c.* 1930
51.3 Enclosure maps and awards, sixteenth to twentieth centuries
51.4 Valuation Office Surveys, 1910–1913
51.5 Surveys of land and house ownership and tenancy: bibliography

51.1 Introduction

For very many parishes of England and Wales there is either a tithe map and apportionment or an enclosure award and map that can provide valuable information about land ownership. The tithe maps and apportionments were created in the mid-nineteenth century, while the enclosure awards and maps usually come from the eighteenth and nineteenth centuries. They give you the opportunity to find out where in a particular parish your ancestors were living, who their neighbours were, what land they owned or occupied, what industries were important locally and a mass of further information.

Less well known but equally important was a survey carried out by the Valuation Office under the Finance (1909–1910) Act, 1910, which has left behind series of maps and field books that between them provide a detailed record of housing and other property, useful for both family and local historians.

In addition, there was an investigation in 1873 of owners of one acre or more of land in England, Wales and Scotland, which was published by Parliament: we have the published version in our Library, but no related records (see 51.5).

We have published two specialist guides in this area: Beech and Mitchell on *Maps for Family and Local History* and Barratt on *Tracing the History of Your House*.

51.2 Tithe survey records *c.* 1830–*c.* 1930

Tithes were originally a tax of one tenth of all produce paid to the local clergyman by his parishioners. After the Reformation many entitlements to receive tithes came into the hands of laymen. That is to say, the right to collect tithes came to be 'owned' by non-clerics and could be bought and sold on the open market. Disputes about tithes were a major part of the business of the equity side of the Exchequer (see 59).

By the nineteenth century there was much popular disenchantment with the system of tithes, and many parishes had local agreements regarding the payment of money in lieu of produce. In 1836, the Tithe Commutation Act set a national framework for all tithes to be fixed as a money payment, which was linked to the changing price of wheat, barley and oats. The maps and apportionments created by Tithe Commissioners set out the names of owners and occupiers for the 75 per cent of parishes and chapelries that were still titheable in the 1830s. These records also provide the name and description of the premises and land (for example, 'Farm House and Out Buildings'), as well as providing details of the extent of land and the state of cultivation. Copies of tithe maps and apportionments are held in some county record offices, as well as in the National Archives (IR 29, IR 30 ⑤, ④).

An easy way to find out the existence of and document reference for maps and apportionments for a particular parish is to look at Kain and Oliver's *The Tithe Maps of England and Wales*. This is available in the Map Room: it is arranged by county, and each parish entry starts with a number. A brief description of the map is also given. To get the apportionment, add IR 29 to this number: for the map, add IR 30. Maps for English counties in the alphabetical sequence Bedfordshire–Middlesex are seen on microfiche. The apportionments in IR 29 are seen on microfilm for all counties.

For some areas no tithe maps and apportionments were made. This is because satisfactory arrangements for money payments had already been agreed or an award of land in lieu of tithes had been made during an enclosure. There were also some districts where no apportionment was made, even though tithes for the area were commuted under the Tithe Commutation Act. This was because either the amount involved was negligible, or because the land owners were themselves the tithe owners and the agreement or award of a gross tithe rentcharge was followed by the redemption or merger of the tithe rentcharges. By this procedure the owners of the land/tithe avoided the need (and expense) of producing a map and apportionment. In these cases the result of the proceedings would still need to be recorded as a formal agreement or instrument of merger (in TITH 3 Ⓕ). There should also be a tithe file (IR 18 ⑤, ④). Although disappointing for genealogists, these may give valuable information to the regional or local historian.

For detailed advice on using tithe maps and apportionments, see Beech and Mitchell's *Maps For Family History*. It is a good idea to look at this before trying to understand an apportionment, because the arrangement of the information is not easy to grasp on film. There is a numerical key at the beginning of each apportionment in which you look up the plot number found on the tithe map (hundreds across the top, tens and units down the side: at their intersection you will find the page number of the apportionment).

51.3 Enclosure maps and awards, sixteenth to twentieth centuries

The term enclosure, as applied to land, usually refers to either the fencing in of commons for private and exclusive landownership or the consolidation of plots of land formerly distributed over the shared open fields into compact blocks, linked together and surrounded by hedges or fences and gates. Useful starting-points before embarking on research (for enclosures from *c.* 1730) among the surviving records are Tate's *A Domesday of English Enclosure Acts and Awards* and Chapman's *A Guide to Parliamentary Enclosure in Wales*. See also Kain, *The enclosure maps of England and Wales: 1595–1918*.

Enclosures of common lands, pastures and manorial wastes were made from an early period, sometimes arbitrarily and sometimes by agreement. Some of the earliest enclosures have left no records, although some will be contained within manorial and estate records, which are usually deposited with the local county record office.

From at least the middle of the sixteenth century it was common to effect enclosures by decree in the equity courts (especially Chancery and Exchequer). There is no full list of enclosures by this means and they are difficult to find with no preliminary information. From the middle of the eighteenth century (there are a small number earlier than this) it became common to effect enclosure by act of Parliament. These are far easier to trace and to use. The act would name the larger owners of property who had promoted the act. As a result of the enclosure, an award and (in many cases) a map would be drawn up. The award would list the people who were allotted land at enclosure, along with the amounts of land involved. These records can usually be found in the county record offices although others have been listed from several classes in the list referred to earlier. The original acts are held at the House of Lords Record Office.

The General Inclosure Acts of 1801 and 1836 did not specify where the awards were to be kept. Some were enrolled at Westminster and these are now at the National Archives in c 54 Ⓕ or e 13 Ⓕ. Where these have been identified they have also been inserted in the list referred to earlier. Others will be found in the county record offices. In 1845 the Enclosure Commission was set up under the Enclosure Act of the same year. The Commission (and its successor departments, the Land Commissioners, the Board of Agriculture and the Ministry of Agriculture and Fisheries) retained copies of the awards. These awards (which include maps) are now in MAF 1 Ⓢ, Ⓐ.

Enclosure material varies in the amount of information given. References to individuals are restricted to those who were allotted land: enclosure awards do not list everyone within a particular parish. Where enclosure maps were created (usually from the late eighteenth century onwards) they often cover only that part of the parish or manor affected.

51.4 Valuation Office surveys, 1910–1913

The survey carried out by the Valuation Office under the Finance (1909–1910) Act, 1910 saw a comprehensive mapping and valuation of the country. Much of the initial work was done starting from existing Ordnance Survey Maps.

Under the Finance Act of 1910, a tax was attached to the profit of house sales if part of the profit was judged to have occurred because of the provision of amenities at the public expense. For example, if a park was opened nearby, trees planted in the road and the road paved, the house price might increase because the site had become more attractive, although the householder had given neither effort nor financial contribution to the improvements. In order to establish a fixed point from which to measure subsequent increases in value, a huge (and expensive) valuation exercise took place between 1910 and 1913 – the largest since 1086 and Domesday Book. The valuers wrote detailed descriptions and valuations of each house, and details of owners and tenants (but not occupiers), in the Field Books (IR 58 F). To find the right entry in a field book, you have to use the maps (IR 121/1–IR 135/9 F) to discover the property number. You may need to ask for help, as actually finding the right map and the right field book can be quite complicated.

A second set of books, known as Domesday Books, was also made: these included the actual occupiers as well as owners and tenants and are particularly useful as most people lived in rented accommodation. Most of these Domesday Books are to be found in county record offices, which may also have duplicates of the Record Maps. The National Archives has only the Domesday Books for the City of London and for Paddington (IR 91 F).

It should be noted that although the valuation was supposed to include all land, even if exempt from payment, there are gaps in the records. Maps covering Portsmouth and Southampton, and an area around Chichester, were all lost during the Second World War. In addition to this many records for around Chelmsford in Essex and for the whole of Coventry appear to be lost. For large properties and estates, the field books may simply have the phrase 'description filed'. This indicates that the information was entered on a separate document in specially created files. These files are not thought to have survived.

As an exercise in raising money, the whole operation proved to be an expensive failure: it was called off in 1920.

51.5 Surveys of land and house ownership and tenancy: bibliography

A Parliamentary Return of Inclosure Awards (House of Commons Sessional Papers, 1904 (50) LXXVIII, 545)

G BEECH, 'Maps for Genealogy and Local History', *Genealogists' Magazine*, vol. XXII, pp. 197–202

N Barratt, *Tracing the History of Your House: A Guide to Sources*, 2nd edition (The National Archives, 2006)

G Beech, 'The 20th Century Domesday Book' [Valuation Office survey], *Ancestors*, 30 (2005), 34–41

G Beech and R Mitchell, *Maps for Family and Local History: The Records of the Tithe, Valuation Office, and National Farm Surveys of England and Wales, 1836–1943*, 2nd edition (The National Archives, 2004)

J Chapman, *A Guide to Parliamentary Enclosure in Wales* (Cardiff, 1992)

J Chapman, 'The interpretation of enclosure maps and awards' in *Maps and history in south-west England*, K Barker and R Kain eds (Exeter, 1991), pp. 73–88

J H Harvey, *Sources for the History of Houses* (British Records Association, 1968)

D Hey, 'Parliamentary Enclosures', *Ancestors* 19 (2004)

R J P Kain, *The enclosure maps of England and Wales: 1595–1918* (2004)

R J P Kain and R R Oliver, *The Tithe Maps of England and Wales* (Cambridge, 1995)

R Mitchell, 'Surveying the Scene: the mid-nineteenth century Tithe Commission Records', *Ancestors* 19 (2004)

Return [to Parliament] of owners of land, 1873 (HMSO, 1874 [Scotland] and 1875 [England and Wales])

B Short and M Reed, 'An Edwardian Land Survey: The Finance (1909–10) Act records', *Journal of the Society of Archivists*, vol. VIII (1986), pp. 95–103

W E Tate, *A Domesday of English Enclosure Acts and Awards* (Reading, 1978)

52 Taxation

52.1 Introduction

Tax records have always been a fruitful source for historians; many before 1680 have been published by local record societies. This is one obvious case when it is better to go first to an up-to-date bibliography (try a search on county and tax in **www.rhs.ac.uk/bibl/bibwel.asp**) to see what is in print, rather than order up original documents.

Most tax records until the late seventeenth century are in the Subsidy Rolls (E 179 ⑤ in the E 179 database at **www.nationalarchives.gov.uk/e179/**). This contains the surviving records of a number of different types of tax that were levied before 1700, the best known of which is the hearth tax (see 52.6). It includes documents relating to scutage (a feudal payment in lieu of knight service), poll taxes, taxes on land, taxes on goods, taxes on aliens, forced loans, sheep tax in 1549, etc. No tax return can be used as a total census of the population – there were always exemptions and evasions. For full details on the taxes, see Jurkowski, Smith and Crook, *Lay Taxes in England and Wales, 1188–1688*. This invaluable book has been produced as part of the large-scale E 179 project run by the University of Cambridge and the National Archives. This has re-examined the lay tax records and entered details of tax and place covered (*not* personal names) into the E 179 database: they are also going in the catalogue.

Many inquisitions and assessments relating to feudal payments based on land, drawing on E 179 and other series, are printed in *Feudal Aids*, which is indexed by place-name and personal name and is on open access. The original records are mainly in Latin, some are damaged and the handwriting can be difficult to read, but lists of names should become legible with practice.

52.2 Lay subsidies, 1290–1332

The earliest type of tax for which the most comprehensive returns survive is the fractional lay subsidies of 1290–1332, a tax on the moveable, personal wealth of individuals, rather than on the land that they owned, which had been levied sporadically throughout the thirteenth century. The tax was granted by Parliament in acts that specified what proportion of an individual's wealth was taxable after agreed exemptions had been made. Exemptions often included equipment necessary to pursue one's occupation, ranging from a knight's armour to a merchant's capital. Apart from in 1301, the grant normally exempted the poorest; for example, in 1297 those assessed at less than a shilling did not have to pay anything. The heading of the lay subsidy roll will normally state what fraction of assessable property has been granted in tax, ranging from a sixth to a twentieth during this period. If two fractions are given, the higher one normally applies to more 'urban' areas. After 1334, assessment of individuals was replaced by fixed quotas levied on individual townships, based on a fifteenth on most taxpayers and a tenth on those living in boroughs or ancient Crown demesne. Glasscock's *The Lay Subsidy of 1334* lists the places assessed, giving modern Ordnance Survey grid references. Although the 'fifteenth' continued to be levied intermittently until the seventeenth century, it was fossilised at these 1334 rates, although local or national disasters, such as the Black Death, might lead to reductions being granted to particular places. They are more fully described in Beresford's *Lay Subsidies and Poll Taxes*.

52.3 Poll taxes, 1377–c. 1670

In 1377, the first poll tax was granted by Parliament, at a flat rate of 4d a head (one shilling for clergy who had a benefice). All men and women were liable – only those under 14 (possibly one third of the population) and those who begged for a living were exempt. It was also granted in 1379 (on those over 16) and 1380 (on those over 15) but at different rates according to status, thus giving details of occupations, although evasion was widespread. See the E 179 database and Fenwick's *Poll Taxes of 1377, 1379 and 1381*. The failure of this unpopular tax led to its abandonment until the seventeenth century when it was intermittently revived in 1641 and on a number of occasions after 1660, although few nominal returns survive of these later poll taxes.

52.4 Subsidies and other taxes after 1522

After 1522, a fresh attempt was made to assess individual wealth, based on income from freehold land, the capital value of moveable goods and income from wages. Not all categories of wealth were taxed in every subsidy and rates varied. Of the four collections of the subsidy granted in 1523, the first two (1524 and 1525) levied one shilling in the pound on land, with the same on goods over £20 in value (6d in the pound on goods under £20) and 4d in the pound on wages (only on those earning £1 or more). The third and fourth collections only taxed those with more than £50 in land (1526) or goods (1527). Aliens (foreigners) had to pay double rates. Wages were not taxed separately after 1525 and the threshold for payment on goods varied (£5 after 1553 and reduced to £3 in 1563). The most informative returns are those relating to the grants of 1523 and 1543; later assessments generally represented only a minority of the population. These subsidies are fully described and illustrated in Hoyle's *Tudor Taxation Records*, which also covers the 'Military Survey' of 1522 and other sources for forced loans required from wealthier individuals, such as the privy seal letters to contributors of 1588–1589 in E 34/16–40. Hoyle argues that values given in assessments are rough estimates rather than precise valuations – 'they describe reputed wealth rather than real wealth'. Under-assessment was endemic. For more on the use of the 1523 lay subsidy returns for economic and local history, see Sheail, *The Regional Distribution of Wealth in England as indicated in the 1524/5 Lay Subsidy Returns*.

Certificates of residence appear in E 115 ②, ④ (mainly from 1558–1625) and were intended to prevent double charging of individuals who resided in more than one county. Each taxpayer was to be assessed at his normal place of residence on all his lands and goods throughout the country.

52.5 Seventeenth century: new taxes

In 1642, a new parliamentary tax, the assessment levied on counties, was imposed and was levied sporadically until c. 1680. County commissioners were to assess and enforce payment, and records of payments by individuals may survive locally. Returns of sums raised are in E 179. In fact, the mid-seventeenth century was a time of great experimentation in tax raising. Details of many taxes not previously described, such as have been discovered by the E 179 Project, are presented in Jurkowski, Smith and Crook, *Lay Taxes in England and Wales, 1188–1688*. See also Gibson and Dell, *The Protestation Returns 1641–42 and other contemporary listings: collection in aid of distressed Protestants in Ireland, subsidies, poll tax, assessments or grants, vow and covenant, solemn league and covenant*.

The list of contributors to the 'Free and Voluntary Present' to Charles II in 1662 provides names and occupations or status of the wealthier members of society. About half the number who paid the hearth tax subscribed to the 'Present'. Returns for Surrey have been published.

The parish lists of contributors to the fund for the relief of Protestant refugees for Ireland in 1642 provide a number of names, but survival is patchy (SP 28/191–195, E 179). The Surrey lists are very good and a typescript list and index is available.

52.6 The hearth tax, 1662–1688

The surviving hearth tax returns and assessments of 1662–1674 relate to the levy of two shillings per year on every hearth: as such, they are one of the obvious sources for family, local and social history. The hearth tax actually continued until 1688, but the later records were not returned into the Exchequer, and most do not survive.

The most complete hearth tax records are those for 25 March 1664. Information supplied includes names of householders, sometimes their status, and the number of hearths for which they are chargeable. The number of hearths is a clue to wealth and status. Over seven hearths usually indicates gentry and above; between four and seven hearths, wealthy craftsmen and tradesmen, merchants and yeomen. Between two and three hearths suggests craftsmen, tradesmen and yeomen; the labouring poor, husbandmen and poor craftsmen usually only had one hearth. There are many gaps in the series of records, partly because of the loss of documentation, and there was also widespread evasion of this most unpopular tax. Hearth tax returns for particular areas have been published by many local record societies, and some records are to be found in county record offices, among the quarter session records.

The hearth tax consisted of a half-yearly payment of one shilling for each hearth in the occupation of each person whose house was worth more than 20 shillings a year, and who was a local ratepayer of church and poor rates.

This actually left out quite large numbers of people, and paupers were not liable at all. Exempt from the tax were charitable institutions with an annual income of less than £100; industrial hearths such as kilns and furnaces (but not smithies and bakeries); people who paid neither church nor poor rate (paupers); and people inhabiting a house worth less than 20 shillings a year who did not have any other property over that value, nor an income of over £100 a year. To prove that you were in the last category, you needed a certificate of exemption from the parish clergyman, churchwardens and overseers of the poor, signed by two JPs. After 1663, the hearth tax returns include lists of those chargeable and not chargeable (exempt), although these may be entered in a block, not necessarily at the end of the parish entry of payers.

From 1670, printed exemption forms were used; many are now in E 179/324–351 arranged by county only. They can give more detail on why someone was exempt, and for the returns which do not include the 'not chargeables' you may need to look at them for information about poorer inhabitants or those engaged in industry. Some of these pieces are unlisted and access to them may be restricted. Those for Norfolk have been published in Seaman and others, *Norfolk Hearth Tax exemption certificates, 1670–1674: Norwich, Great Yarmouth, King's Lynn and Thetford*.

The British Records Society and the Roehampton Institute London are running an on-going project to provide a printed edition of at least one hearth tax return for each county (and ideally one from the 1660s and one from the 1670s). So far, volumes for Kent and Cambridge and on Norfolk exemption certificates have been published (with local records societies). The introductions to these volumes are worth reading, even if you are looking at another county, as they will help in teasing out the implications of any assessment.

52.7 Land and other taxes, from 1689

From 1689 to 1830, there are records of land and assessed taxes in local record offices (which list names) and in the National Archives (which do not, in general). The accounting records of the taxes are in the National Archives, in E 181–E 184 ⑦. They do not list all taxpayers, although defaulters or people whose assessments changed may be listed.

Three groups of taxes were administered centrally by the Board of Taxes, and locally by county commissioners. First was land tax, voted annually from 1692 to 1798, and then made a perpetual charge. Second, assessed taxes, based on the possession or occupation of certain kinds of property, beginning with the window tax in 1696. By 1803, assessed taxes included taxes on inhabited houses, male servants, carriages, horses for riding and drawing carriages, horses for husbandry, dogs, horse dealers, hair powder and armorial bearings. The third was income tax, which began in 1799.

Land tax assessments may be found in county record offices: they give owners and occupiers of land. The National Archives has what is effectively a national snapshot taken in 1798–1799, in IR 23 ⑦. It lists all owners of property subject to land tax in England and Wales in 1798–1799, when the land tax became a fixed annual charge and many people purchased exemption. The arrangement is by land tax parish and there is no index of names. The records of these transactions are also useful and may include maps and plans (IR 22 ④, Parish Books of Redemptions; 1799–1953 and IR 24 ④, Registers of Redemption Certificates; 1799–1963, both partly indexed by IR 22/206–7). The arrangement is again by parish. See the book by Gibson and Mills for lists of records in the National Archives and elsewhere, arranged by county. There is a useful introduction to using local and central land tax records by Pearl, 'Land tax: yesterday's electoral register'. For a scholarly study, see Ginter, *A Measure of Wealth*.

If you are a keen explorer of records and have a lot of time, the particulars of Account in E 182 ④ may be the series to investigate. This series comprises supporting documentation to the tax accounts in E 181. The particulars run from 1689 to 1830 and relate to land tax, assessed taxes and income tax. It has an uninformative list giving no descriptions other than county and covering dates, but the introductory note is good. The records do not in general include lists of names, but can produce the occasional nugget of information. It does not include regular full lists of taxpayers, but it does have information on those whose circumstances and therefore taxes change – including those who died, or who got another horse, etc. Many payments authorised by central government were made at a local level from the tax revenues and not recorded elsewhere (e.g., rewards to informers leading to the arrest of army deserters, bounties paid to parishes for getting people to enlist in the army). It sometimes has lists of militia volunteers. This is certainly a series ripe for a large-scale listing project. At the moment it is not really a suitable series to recommend to novice researchers.

52.8 Death duties, 1796–1903

These records are in IR 26 (currently indexed by IR 27) and can be seen on microfilm at both the Family Records Centre and the National Archives. However, the main means of access to part of these is via the website at **www.nationalarchives.gov.uk/documentsonline/** where those registers for probates and administrations granted by county courts between 1796 and 1811 are searchable by full name.

From 1796 legacy, estate and succession duty (death duties) were payable on many estates over a certain value, which itself changed over time. More people were included as the scope of estate duty was extended throughout the nineteenth century. Before 1805, the registers cover about a quarter of all estates. By 1857, there should be an entry for all estates except those worth less than £20. However, unless the assets were valued at £1,500 or more, the taxes were often not collected, and so the register entry was not filled in with all the details. Britons resident abroad, but with estates in England and Wales, were exempt from the tax. Tax was payable on bequests to people outside a closely defined family circle (whittled down from offspring, spouse, parents and grandparents in 1796 to spouse and parents in 1805, and to spouse only in 1815). Many of the registers for the 1890s were destroyed by fire. There is no such information available after 1903, as the Inland Revenue switched from using registers to individual files, which were destroyed after 30 years.

The register entries use a lot of abbreviations: a research guide is available on the website. You may also find what look like references to correspondence: if they date from 1812–1836, try to follow them up in IR 6 [7], where you will get a different view of the matter – that of the executor or administrator, perhaps struggling to prove a generous will by distributing a too-small estate while being harassed by the Inland Revenue.

For the procedure involved, see *Ham's Inland Revenue Yearbook*, which gives contemporary instructions. The National Archives Library has copies of this annual work (under slightly varying titles) from 1875 to 1930.

Death duty registers give different information than the wills and much better information than administrations (see 9 and 10 for these). In particular they will show what actually happened to a person's estate after death (rather than what they hoped would happen) and what it was actually worth, excluding debts and expenses. They can also give the date of death and information about the people who received bequests (beneficiaries), or who were the next of kin, such as exact relationship to the deceased. Because the registers could be annotated for up to 50 years after the first entry, they can give a wealth of additional information. This can include dates of death of spouse; dates of death or marriage of beneficiaries; births of posthumous children; change of address; references to lawsuits in Chancery delaying the settling of the estate; etc.

52.9 Taxation: bibliography

Search on **www.rhs.ac.uk/bibl/bibwel.asp** *for publications for counties, etc.*

D ANNAL, 'The secret lives of the death duty registers', *Ancestors* 20 (2004)

M W BERESFORD, 'Lay Subsidies', *Amateur Historian*, vol. III pp. 325–328 and vol. IV pp. 101–109

M W BERESFORD, *Lay Subsidies and Poll Taxes* (Phillimore, 1963)

M W BERESFORD, 'Poll Taxes of 1377, 1379 and 1381', *Amateur Historian*, vol. III pp. 271–278

British Records Society and others
* *Cambridgeshire Hearth Tax Returns, Michaelmas 1664*, N Evans, S Rose (2000)
* *Kent Hearth Tax: Assessment Lady Day 1664*, D Harrington, S Pearson and S Rose (2000)

C R CHENEY, *Handbook of Dates for Students of English History* (London, 1991)

S COLWELL, 'Pay As You Go' [Death duty], *Ancestors* 25 (2004)

S CUNNINGHAM, 'Tax trails', *Ancestors* 7 (2002), pp. 22–26

B ENGLISH, 'Probate valuations and the death duty registers', *Bulletin of the Institute of Historical Research*, 57 (1984), pp. 80–91

C C FENWICK, ed., *The Poll Taxes of 1377, 1379 and 1381 Part I Bedfordshire–Leicestershire, Part II Lincolnshire–Westmorland* (British Academy, 1998 and 2001)

Feudal Aids (London, 1899–1920)

J S W GIBSON, *Hearth Tax Returns, other later Stuart Tax Lists, and the Association Oath Rolls* (FFHS, 1996)

J S W GIBSON and A DELL, *The Protestatation Returns 1641–42 and other contemporary listings: collection in aid of distressed Protestants in Ireland, subsidies, poll tax, assessments or grants, vow and covenant, solemn league and covenant* (FFHS, 1995)

J S W GIBSON, M MEDLYCOTT and D MILLS, *Land and Window Tax Assessments, 1690–1950* (FFHS, 1997)

D E GINTER, *A Measure of Wealth: English Land Tax in Historical Analysis* (Montreal, 1992)

R E GLASSCOCK, ed., *The Lay Subsidy of 1334* (British Academy Records of Social and Economic History, new series, II, 1975)

D R GREEN and A OWENS, 'Metropolitan estates of the middle class, 1800–50: probates and death duties revisited', *Historical Research*, 70 (1997), pp. 294–311

D T HAWKINGS, 'Listing the Landowners' [land tax], *Ancestors* 28 (2004)

D HEY, 'Family Names and the Hearth Tax', *Ancestors* 7 (2002)

R W HOYLE, *Tudor Taxation Records* (PRO, 1994)

M JURKOWSKI, C L SMITH and D CROOK, *Lay Taxes in England and Wales 1188–1688* (PRO, 1998)

S LEWIS, *Topographical Dictionary of England* (London, 4th edn, 1840)

S Lewis, *Topographical Dictionary of Wales* (London, 1840)

L M Marshall, 'The Levying of the Hearth Tax; 1662–1668', *English Historical Review*, vol. LI, pp. 628–646

C A F Meekings, *Introduction to the Surrey Hearth Tax, 1664* (Surrey Record Society, vol. XVII)

E L C Mullins, *Texts and Calendars* (Royal Historical Society, 2 vols, 1958, 1983: continued on the HMC website)

S Pearl, 'Land tax: yesterday's electoral register', *Family Tree Magazine*, June 1991

K Schurer and T Arkell, *Surveying the people: the interpretation and use of document sources for the study of population in the later 17th century* (Oxford, 1992)

P Seaman, 'Going up in Smoke' [hearth tax], *Ancestors* 34 (2005)

P Seaman, J Pound and R Smith, *Norfolk Hearth Tax exemption certificates, 1670–1674: Norwich, Great Yarmouth, King's Lynn and Thetford* (Norfolk Record Society, 65, 2001)

J Sheail, *The Regional Distribution of Wealth in England as indicated in the 1524/5 Lay Subsidy Returns* (List and Index Society, *Special Series*, vols 28 and 29, 1998)

C Webb, *Calendar of the Surrey Portion of the Free and Voluntary Present to Charles II* (West Surrey Family History Society, 1982)

C Webb and East Surrey Family History Society, *Surrey Contributors to the Relief of Protestant Refugees from Ireland, 1642*

F A Youngs Jr., *Guide to the Local Administrative Units of England*, 2 vols (Royal Historical Society, 1980, 1991)

53 Tontines and annuity records

53.1 Tontines

The *tontine* is named after Lorenzo Tonti, a Neapolitan banker who started such a scheme in France in 1653. Each subscriber paid a sum into the fund, and in return received dividends from the capital invested. As each person died his share was divided among all the others until only one was left, who reaped all the benefits. The capital reverted to the state when the last subscriber died.

53.2 State tontines and annuities

In the late seventeenth and eighteenth centuries, the British government organised several money-raising schemes by selling tontines and annuities. These schemes and the records produced are described by Colwell in *Family Roots*.

There were three English State Tontines, in 1693, 1766 and 1789, and three Irish State Tontines, in 1773, 1775 and 1777. In return for an original investment, participants were guaranteed a yearly income for the life of a living nominee chosen by the investor. People usually nominated their youngest relative. As the nominees died off, the central fund was distributed between fewer and fewer people and the annuity therefore became more valuable as the years passed. There were in all about 15,000 participants.

Surviving records often involve proof of identity, or proof of continued existence. The records continue long after the original date of issue: for example, the last surviving nominee of the 1766 Tontine died in 1859. Most of the records are in NDO 1–NDO 2 ⑧ for the English Tontines, and NDO 3 ⑧ for the Irish. The registers have integral indexes, so are easy to use. They may give details concerning the marriages, deaths and wills of contributors and nominees. Contributors were usually substantial people. Many were spinsters.

Annuities were similar to tontines, in that an original investment paid out an annuity for term of life. However, the annuity did not grow as other annuitants died off. Annuities were offered throughout the eighteenth century. Again, the records obviously extend way beyond the date of issue. NDO 1–NDO 2 ⑦ are once more the main series, but Colwell's *Dictionary of Genealogical Sources in the Public Record Office* includes many other detailed references to tontine and annuity records.

53.3 Private tontines

Examples of private tontines are known to date back to the seventeenth century. Private tontines needed to establish some form of collateral to guarantee payments, so the organisers bought financial securities with the initial contributions of the participants. Many of these private (and sometimes small scale) tontines can be traced in A2A, and also among records of Friendly Societies in FS 15 ⑥.

A much larger-scale one was the British Tontine, set up from 1792. Its records were called into Chancery as evidence in a lawsuit brought by the participants. Several volumes listing subscribers are in C 114/166–168.

53.4 Tontines and annuity records: bibliography

S COLWELL, *Dictionary of Genealogical Sources in the Public Record Office* (London, 1992)

S COLWELL, *Family Roots: Discovering the Past in the Public Record Office* (London, 1991)

F LEESON, *A Guide to the Records of the British State Tontines and Life Annuities of the 17th and 18th Centuries* (Shalfleet Manor, 1968)

54 Business records

54.1 Companies' registration, from 1844
54.2 A company's own records
54.3 Business records: bibliography

54.1 Companies' registration, from 1844

Until 1844, companies could only be incorporated by Royal Charter or special act of Parliament. From 1844 onwards, various Companies Acts enabled companies to be formed cheaply and easily. Some information about directors and shareholders of registered companies can be found in the companies' registration records,

For records relating to live companies, and to those that have ceased to function within the last 20–30 years, you should contact the Companies Registration Office (**www.companieshouse.gov.uk**, address in 62). For a small fee they will produce a microfiche copy, which contains all the required documents relating to any one company.

At the National Archives are registration records for dissolved companies from 1844 until about 30 years ago. For companies registered under the 1846 and 1856 Acts, and dissolved before 1860, search by name of the company in BT 41 ⑥. For registered companies dissolved after 1860, use the same method in BT 31 ⑥. Records have been kept for only a sample of companies dissolved after 1860 – a large sample at first, dwindling to 5 per cent for modern records. If you do locate a file for your company, you will find that the file itself has been weeded, so that it only contains certain documents. These include memoranda and articles of association, and lists of shareholders, directors and managers, for the first, last and some intermediate years of the company's operation. They give name, address, occupation, sometimes date of death and very rarely change of name. Between 1918 and 1948 they also give nationality if not British.

Notices of receiverships, liquidations and bankruptcies appear in the *London Gazette* (available at the National Archives as ZJ 1 ⑦).

54.2 A company's own records

The National Archives has the records of canal and railway companies nationalised in 1947 (in RAIL: see 36); other transport undertakings and chartered and commercial companies that have passed into public ownership or whose records have come into public custody; and numerous records of various companies and other commercial undertakings among the exhibits used in litigation in C 103–C 114 and J 90 (see 58.11) and bankruptcy (see 55).

For companies in general, try a search in A2A or in the National Register of Archives. You are also strongly recommended to look at the research guide *Sources for Business History* on the website **www.nationalarchives. gov.uk/researchguidesindex/asp.**

54.3 Business records: bibliography

J ARMSTRONG, *Business Documents: their origins, sources and uses in historical research* (London, 1987)

H A L COCKERELL and E GREEN, *The British Insurance Business, 1547–1970* (London, 1976)

K JENNS, 'Women who meant business', *Ancestors* 41 (2006)

D J JEREMY, *Dictionary of Business Biography: Biographical Dictionary of Business Leaders active in Britain in the Period 1860–1980* (London, 1984–1986)

E D PROBERT, *Company and Business Records for Family Historians* (Federation of Family History Societies, 1994)

A RITCHIE, 'Business History and the National Register of Archives', *Business History* 80 (2000)

C T WATTS and M J WATTS, 'Company Records as a source for the Family Historian', *Genealogists' Magazine*, vol. XXI, pp. 44–54

55 Insolvent debtors and bankrupts

55.1 Insolvency and bankruptcy

The court and prison records held in the National Archives and locally include very many references to legal proceedings against 'insolvent debtors'. These were people who had debts but were unable to pay them: they remained subject to common law proceedings and indefinite imprisonment, if their creditors so wished. The insolvent debtor was a pitiful figure.

However, debtors who were traders and owed large sums were usually exempt from the laws relating to debtors and from imprisonment as debtors. They were subject instead to bankruptcy proceedings. The legal status of being a bankrupt was confined to traders owing more than £100 (reduced to £50 in 1842). The legal definition of 'trader' came to embrace all those who made a living by buying and selling, and by the late eighteenth century included all those who bought materials, worked on them and then re-sold them: in other words, most skilled craftsmen. Farmers were specifically excluded but, nonetheless, do appear in the records. Those who wished to qualify as bankrupts, and thus avoid the awful fate of an insolvent debtor, sometimes gave a false or misleadingly general description of their occupations: *dealer and chapman* was very common.

Bankruptcy was a process whereby a court official declared qualifying debtors bankrupt, took over their property, and distributed it to their creditors in proportion to what they were owed: bankrupts could then usually be discharged from their debts and escape imprisonment. Their annual numbers increased from a few hundreds to many thousands between the eighteenth and twentieth centuries. Partnerships of individuals could also declare themselves bankrupt, but companies were not covered until after 1844.

From 1861, insolvent debtors were at last allowed to apply for bankruptcy.

55.2 Published sources for debtors and bankrupts

Official notices relating to many bankrupts (from 1684) and insolvent debtors (from 1712) in England and Wales were placed in the *London Gazette* (ZJ 1). Scottish notices were placed in the *Edinburgh Gazette*, although a few are found in the *London Gazette*. Details were also published in *Perry's Bankruptcy and Insolvent Weekly Gazette* (later *Perry's Gazette*) from 1827. From 1862 official notices relating to county court proceedings were placed in local newspapers, held by the appropriate local record office or by the British Library Newspaper Library (address in 62). Records relating to Scottish bankruptcies ('sequestrations') are held in the National Archives of Scotland (address in 62).

These publications rarely give more than the names, addresses and occupations and sometimes those of their creditors, with formal details of conviction and imprisonment, where appropriate.

55.3 Insolvent debtors before 1862

For an overview of debtors' process, read the article by Innes.

Insolvent debtors were held in local prisons, and often spent the rest of their lives there: imprisonment for debt did not stop until 1869. Records are kept in local record offices. The National Archives holds records for the prisons of the central courts, and of the Palace Court. The Palace Court, 1630–1849, was used for the recovery of small debts in the Westminster area (PALA 1–PALA 9: all ⑦). Records of the Fleet, King's Bench, Marshalsea and Queen's prisons for debtors, 1685–1862, are in PRIS 1–PRIS 11 (all ⑦).

PCOM 2/309 is a register of Lincoln Gaol, 1810–1822, which lists the names of many people imprisoned for debt: other PCOM records may be worth exploration. Try also the returns of imprisoned debtors made to the Court of Bankruptcy, 1862–1869, from the Queen's Prison and London's Whitecross Street and Horsemonger Lane prisons (B 2/15–32).

The periodic passing of Acts for the Relief of Insolvent Debtors allowed for their release if they applied to a Justice of Peace and submitted a schedule of assets. Records relating to this process may be with quarter sessions records held by local county record offices: exceptionally, some for the Palatinate of Chester, 1760–1830, are here in CHES 10 ⑦.

In 1813, the Court for the Relief of Insolvent Debtors was established. After 1847, this court also dealt with London bankruptcies under £300. Petitions for the discharge of prisoners for debt in England and Wales, 1813–1862, were registered by this Court (B 6/45–71 Ⓕ: indexes in B 8). Petitions by debtors (who were not traders or who were traders owing small amounts) for protection orders against the laws relating to debtors were registered by the Court of Bankruptcy, 1842–1847. After this, they were registered by the Court for the Relief of Insolvent Debtors, 1847–1861 (B 6/88–89, 94–96 ⑦), and also by local courts of bankruptcy jurisdiction. The Court of Bankruptcy recorded proposals for repayments by insolvent debtors, 1848–1862 (B 6/97–98 ⑦).

55.4 What you can expect to find in bankruptcy records

In most bankruptcy cases, the records held by the National Archives are confined to brief, formal entries in various register series that will establish the fact of bankruptcy but will not provide much background detail. Additional information can sometimes be found in the court records of legal actions against them: see 56.

Bankruptcy records usually give only the name, address and occupation of the debtors and of their creditors, and a formal summary of court proceedings. Detailed case files only survive for a very small sample (B 3 ③, B 9 ①, BT 221 ③, BT 226 ②) or where the proceedings were subjected to legal review (B 1, B 7), but they may provide interesting information about the bankrupts' family and business links, trading activities and economic circumstances.

From 1842 separate records of bankruptcy proceedings outside the London area were kept by district bankruptcy courts (1842–1869) and by county courts with bankruptcy jurisdiction (from 1861). You will need to look in local record offices for these (you could start with a search on A2A).

Registers of petitions in bankruptcy in England and Wales from 1912 to date are held in the Thomas More Building, Royal Courts of Justice, where searches may be made on payment of a fee.

Throughout, legal issues relating to bankruptcy were heard separately in local and central courts, and especially in Chancery (see 58). Bankrupts guilty of fraud, dishonesty or misconduct remained liable to imprisonment and may be found in the gaol records referred to in 55.3.

55.5 Bankruptcy before 1869

Commissioners of bankrupts could be appointed to allow a bankrupt legally to discharge his debts to his creditors by an equitable and independent distribution of his assets, and then begin trading again with his outstanding debts wiped out. The creditors petitioned the Lord Chancellor for a commission of bankruptcy (a fiat after 1832 when the Court of Bankruptcy was established).

For the period after 1759, search B 3 first. This contains a sample (about 5 per cent only) of bankruptcy case files, listed by name (*D.C.* stands for *Dealer and Chapman*). Most files date from after 1780 and before 1842. A further sample of case files after 1832 is in B 9 – after 1869, most relate to the London area. Case files may contain balance sheets submitted by the bankrupt. These are usually very general statements, rather than itemised accounts, and assignees' accounts. If your bankrupt is not listed in B 3 or B 9, you will have to search various register and enrolment series that will normally only lead to brief formal entries. These will confirm the fact of bankruptcy, if it took place, but will not provide much detail. Some case files of proceedings under the Joint Stock Company Acts, 1856–1857, for 1858–1862, are in B 10.

Registers of commissions of bankruptcy and fiats issued are in B 4 ⑦ for 1710–1849. Entries vary in detail over this period and may give the address and trade of the bankrupt (not between 1770 and 1797) and the names of either the petitioning creditors or those of the bankrupt's agent or solicitor. Enrolments of bankruptcy commissions (after 1758) and fiats may be in B 5 ⑦.

The Commissioners published notices in the *London Gazette* (seen here in ZJ 1 ⑦) to inform creditors about their proceedings. Such notices are found from 1684 and are indexed from 1790: before 1832, they include many bankruptcies not included in the surviving B series. Bankruptcy notices also appear in *The Times* (searchable and viewable online at the National Archives and many local libraries). The records of these commissions, in the B series, only survive from 1710 and are incomplete until after 1832 (1821 for London). Earlier commissions of bankruptcy can be found enrolled on the Patent Rolls (C 66–C 67 Ⓔ); conveyances of bankrupts' estates are enrolled on the Close Rolls (C 54 Ⓔ); and relevant petitions are sometimes found in the State Papers (SP Ⓔ).

After 1849, creditors petitioned for an Adjudication in Bankruptcy, the registers of which (to 1869) are in B 6 ⑦. The Commissioners took statements from the bankrupt and his creditors about his debts and the creditors then elected trustees or assignees to value his assets and distribute them as dividends. To prevent fraud Official Assignees were also appointed after 1831 (appointments made 1832–1855 are in B 5 ⑦) and thereafter assignees had to pay cash from the sale of a bankrupt's estates into the Bank of England – AO 18 ⑦ contains records of their accounts for the period 1832 to 1851. Miscellaneous accounts, dating after 1844, are in BT 40 ⑦.

When sufficient creditors (the proportion varied from 3/4 to 4/5, by number and value) were satisfied, they signed a request for a Certificate of Conformity (a statement that the bankrupt had satisfied all the legal requirements). The Commissioners could then issue the certificate, which effectively discharged the bankrupt, although dividends might continue to be paid after that date. From 1849 to 1861, there were three classes of certificate:

I – where the bankrupt was blameless;

II – where some blame could be attributed;

III – where it was entirely the bankrupt's fault.

Indexed Registers of Certificates of Conformity for 1733–1817 and deposited Certificates for 1815–1856 are in B 6 ⑦. These give the name and address of the bankrupt and the date of the certificate. Enrolled copies of some certificates of conformity, 1710–1846, some assignments of assets to trustees, 1825–1834, and some appointments of trustees, 1832–1855, are in B 5 ⑦. After 1861, Orders of Discharge were issued instead. Records relating to issues the Commissioners were unable to resolve or appeals in bankruptcy cases are in B 1 ⑦ and B 7 ⑦. Actions against individual bankrupts or their assignees may sometimes be found in the records of other courts – Chancery, Exchequer, King's Bench and Common Pleas – many cases coming before the Palace Court (PALA), which dealt with small debt cases in the Westminster area (see 55.3).

55.6 District bankruptcy courts, after 1842

District bankruptcy courts were set up after 1842 to deal with cases outside London, sometimes defined as a 20-mile radius from the centre, and after 1869 (in part from 1847, for sums under £20) their jurisdiction passed to the county courts. After 1842, records relating to bankruptcy cases outside London may be held by county record offices and, after 1869, should normally be held there with the records of county courts, although sometimes 'country' cases were heard in London.

From 1849 until 1869, when the London Court of Bankruptcy was established, the two series of London District and Country District General Docket Books in B 6 ⑦ show the class of certificate awarded. After 1861 they give instead the date of discharge, name, address and trade of the bankrupt and sometimes the names of petitioning creditors. For London Court cases, 1861–1870, deeds of composition with creditors or of assignment to trustees are summarised in a series of registers in B 6 ⑦, Ⓕ (indexes in B 8). Registers of Petitions for protection from bankruptcy process in county court cases, from 1854, are in LCO 28 ⑦.

55.7 Bankruptcy, 1869–1884

After 1869, routine imprisonment for debt ceased, other than in cases of fraud or deliberate refusal to pay, and the Court for the Relief of Insolvent Debtors was wound up. Creditors who were owed more than £50 could petition for bankruptcy proceedings. Cases in London were dealt with by the London Court of Bankruptcy and records are in the National Archives. London was defined as the City and the areas covered by the metropolitan county courts of Bloomsbury, Bow, Brompton, Clerkenwell, Lambeth, Marylebone, Southwark, Shoreditch, Westminster and Whitechapel. Cases outside London were normally heard by the county courts after 1861 (they had some jurisdiction since 1847) although they could be transferred to the London Court by special resolution of the creditors. The appropriate local record office normally holds county court records. Registers of Petitions for protection from bankruptcy process in county court cases, from 1854, are in

LCO 28 ☑. There is a Register of London bankruptcies for 1873–74 in BT 40/27 and one for County Court bankruptcies for 1879 in BT 40/46.

After 1883, the London Court of Bankruptcy was incorporated into the Supreme Court as the High Court of Justice in Bankruptcy. It subsequently became responsible for the additional metropolitan county court areas of Barnet, Brentford, Edmonton, Wandsworth, West London and Willesden. Bankruptcy petitions were only to be presented to the High Court if the debtor had resided or carried on business within the London Bankruptcy District for six months, if he was not resident in England or if the petitioning creditor could not identify where he lived. A High Court judge could, however, transfer any bankruptcy case to or from a county court. After 1883, official receivers supervised by the Bankruptcy Department of the Board of Trade took over responsibility for the administration of the bankrupt's estate, once a court had determined the fact of bankruptcy and made a receiving order. Its records therefore cover cases dealt with by both the High Court and the county courts.

The Registers of Petitions for Bankruptcy for 1870–1883, in B 6/184–197 ☑, are arranged alphabetically by initial letter of the bankrupt's surname. They cover both London and Country cases but only give a very brief entry with the case number, bankrupt's name, occupation and address. There are also registers of bankrupts, in both the London Bankruptcy Court and the county courts, for 1870–1886 in BT 40 ☑. These give dates of orders of discharge. More detail, for cases heard by the London Court of Bankruptcy, is given in the Registers of Creditors' Petitions (B 6/178–183 ☑), the best place to begin a search for cases heard in London 1870–1883. They are arranged chronologically and in alphabetical order of the first letter of the bankrupt's surname. They give his name, address and occupation and that of the petitioning creditor(s); details of what formal act of bankruptcy was committed; the date (and place if outside London) of adjudication as a bankrupt; the date of advertisement in the *London Gazette*; the names of any trustees appointed; the amount of any dividend paid, as shillings in the pound; and the date when proceedings closed. Indexes to Declarations of Inability to pay (London Court cases only after 1854), which were one means of committing a formal act of bankruptcy, give the date of filing and basic details of the name, address and occupation of the debtor and name of his solicitor, 1825–1925, and are also in B 6.

Official Assignees' accounts, before 1884, are in BT 40 ☑.

55.8 Bankruptcy, from 1884

After 1884, the Board of Trade supervised the work of the official receivers, who had the status of court officials. After a receiving order had been made by the court, the receivers held meetings of creditors, investigated the circumstances of the bankruptcy and acted as interim administrators of the bankrupt's assets, pending, or in default of, the appointment of a trustee chosen by the creditors. If the bankrupt's assets were likely to be less than £300, the official receiver normally acted as trustee. When the trustee had realised as much of the bankrupt's assets as possible to pay his debts, he could apply for a release, discharging his responsibility.

For the period 1884–1923, Board of Trade registers in BT 293 ⑦, which are indexed alphabetically by name, should contain entries for all persons served with a petition for bankruptcy, whether the case was heard in London or locally – although it should be noted that not all petitions resulted in formal bankruptcy. Each entry should give the name, address and occupation of the debtor; the date of filing of the petition for bankruptcy; the dates of orders in case, including final discharge; the names of any trustees and the rate of dividend paid to the creditors. The incomplete set of Estate Ledgers in BT 294 ⑦, arranged alphabetically by name, may show how the assets were distributed.

From 1888, registration of Deeds of Arrangement, made privately between debtors and creditors outside normal bankruptcy proceedings, became compulsory and the registers are in BT 39 ⑦, with some case files in BT 221 ③. These case files, dating from 1879, may also deal with audits and official releases. Case files of the Official Receiver relating to High Court cases from 1891 are in BT 226 ②, sampled after 1914. Most cases are personal bankrupts, ranging from comedians to stockbrokers.

From 1924, you need to contact the Insolvency Service (**www.insolvency. gov.uk** or see 62). They hold docket books with internal indexes that continue the kind of information previously found in BT 293 up to 1923. These docket books include the date of the announcement in the *London Gazette*, which can be seen at the National Archives in ZJ 1.

55.9 Petitions to the High Court, from 1884

Registers of petitions to the High Court, by or against debtors, chronologically arranged by initial letter of surname from 1884, record the names, addresses and occupations of the debtors and petitioning creditors; the name and address of the solicitor; and the alleged act of bankruptcy committed: they are in B 11 ⑦. The actual petition will only have survived if there is a case file in B 9 ① on which it has been filed. Registers of receiving orders from 1887 (orders from 1883 are noted in the B 11 Registers) are in B 12 ⑦. They give the dates of formal court orders, including the receiving order, the order of discharge with a note of any conditions attaching to it and the date of the trustees' release. Names of trustees may also be given, although not if the official receiver was acting as trustee. For London and High Court bankruptcies after 1869, there is a very small sample (less than 5 per cent) of bankruptcy case files, arranged roughly chronologically by date of filing of petition, in B 9 ①. These files may be one or more substantial volumes – those for A W Carpenter, trading as the Charing Cross Bank, run to 152 volumes.

55.10 Bankruptcy appeals

Before 1875, minutes of appeal cases are in B 7 ☷, with entry books of orders in B 1 ☷. Thereafter, appeals were directed to the Supreme Court's Court of Appeal (J 15, J 56, J 60 and J 69–70 ☱). From 1883, appeals in county court cases went to a divisional court of the High Court (J 60, J 74 and J 95). An incomplete series of registers of petitions for protection from process in county court cases, covering the period 1854–1964, is in LCO 28 ☷.

55.11 Insolvent debtors and bankrupts: bibliography

W BAILEY, *List of Bankrupts, Dividends and Certificates, 1772–1793* (London, 1794)

H BARTY-KING, *The Worst Poverty: A History of Debt and Debtors* (Alan Sutton, 1991)

Edinburgh Gazette (Edinburgh, 1699 continuing)

J EDWARDS, 'Forever in their Debt: using bankruptcy and insolvent debtor records', *Family History Monthly* 111 (2004)

M FINN, *The Character of Credit: Personal Debt in English Culture, 1740–1914* (Cambridge, 2003)

J INNES, The King's Bench Prison in the later eighteenth century', in J Brewer and J Styles, eds, *An Ungovernable People* (London, 1980)

London Gazette (London, 1665 continuing) in ZJ 1

S MARRINER, 'English Bankruptcy Records and Statistics before 1850', *Economic History Review*, 2nd series, vol. XXXIII, pp. 351–366

Perry's Bankrupt and Insolvent Weekly Gazette (London, 1827–1881)

Perry's Gazette (London, 1882 continuing)

56 Civil litigation: an introduction to the legal system

56.1   Civil litigation

Civil litigation (legal disputes between two parties) makes up a very large – and under-used – part of the National Archives' holdings. The records cover disputes about land, property rights, debts, inheritance, trusts, frauds, etc., and they can provide unparalleled levels of information about people in the past. However, they can also be difficult to find and to understand – especially if you are coming to them without any knowledge of the legal systems in use at the time. This chapter gives you a very brief overview of a very complicated subject, before the records of the individual courts are described in 57–61.

56.2   Common law and equity

The development of law in medieval England was quite different to that of the rest of Europe. (Scotland has a very different legal system, whose surviving records are in the National Archives of Scotland and local record offices in Scotland.) In England, the common law provided a powerful centralised system of justice, which was based on principles derived from the common customs of the country but was essentially unwritten.

The remedies offered by the common law did not always meet litigants' needs. It was difficult, for example, to enforce trusts and wills at common law. In cases of breach of contract the common law remedy would ensure the payment of damages, but it could not compel enforcement of the terms of the contract (a remedy that lawyers describe as specific performance). This law was used by the ancient royal courts of Common Pleas and King's Bench, in the civil actions heard at the assizes and in the Exchequer of Pleas and the common law side of Chancery.

Courts of equity, which developed alongside common law courts, were able to provide a different kind of remedy as they were empowered to give judgements according to conscience and justice, rather than according to law. Courts of equity such as Chancery and the Equity Side of the Exchequer could (and did) order specific performance (but they could not award damages for non-compliance). Royal prerogative courts such as Star Chamber and Requests also existed, using equity-type procedure for a mixture of civil and criminal cases to short-circuit the normal routes: these were abolished in 1641 as an unacceptable use of royal power.

The two systems of justice co-existed until the nineteenth century when the Common Law Procedure Acts allowed equitable pleas to be considered in common law actions.

In addition to these royal courts, there were similar common law and equity courts in the palatinates of Chester, Durham and Lancaster, and in Wales: the records of Welsh courts are now in the National Library of Wales. The duchy of Lancaster (not the same as the palatinate) had its own courts, available to tenants of duchy lands throughout the kingdom.

56.3 Civil law, ecclesiastical law and customary law

Three other systems of law also operated in England. Civil law (a branch of Roman law) was used in the High Court of Admiralty and in the High Court of Delegates; ecclesiastical law (another branch of Roman law) was used in the church courts; and customary law, used in the many local courts, based on the jurisdiction of the lord rather than the king.

56.4 The Supreme Court of Judicature

All these legal systems (except for the ecclesiastical and local courts) were brought together in a series of mid-nineteenth-century reforms, which resulted, in 1875, in a single Supreme Court of Judicature, with separate Divisions of Chancery, Common Pleas, Exchequer, King's Bench, and Probate, Divorce and Admiralty.

56.5 Civil litigation: the records

Records of civil litigation differ according to the kind of law and procedure used by the court in which they were heard. Cases heard in the common law courts were usually known as 'actions' and those in equity courts as 'suits.' They are usually given a short title such as Smith v Jones (Smith versus Jones), sometimes Smith con Jones (Smith contra Jones), which obscures the fact that there may be several plaintiffs disguised under Smith, and several defendants under Jones.

Unfortunately, surviving common law records relating to civil litigation (although extensive) are extremely difficult to use. They are very formal and are largely composed of standard legal formulae. It requires considerable expertise to understand the meaning that lies behind the formulae and the records rarely contain useful detail.

In contrast, the records of the equity courts are full and informative and provide a wonderful source for social, family and local history. However, the complexity of the filing procedures of the equity courts and the inadequacy of the available lists and indexes mean that it can be difficult to search for a particular case. This is a problem that will eventually disappear, as more of the equity finding aids become searchable online.

56.6 Civil litigation: an introduction to the legal system: bibliography

J H BAKER, *An Introduction to English Legal History* (London, 2002)

W R CORNISH and G DE N CLARK, *Law and Society in England 1750–1950* (London, 1989)

A H MANCHESTER, *A modern legal history of England and Wales, 1750–1950* (London, 1980)

57 Civil litigation: the central common law courts

57.1 The central common law courts before 1875

Since the creation of the Supreme Court in 1875, we have become accustomed to the idea that legal business is organised on functional lines: that is, one division of the court deals with matters relating to trusts and real estate, another with personal actions and so on. Before 1875, the division of business was not by type of case but by type of litigant. Thus Exchequer dealt with litigation between those who were Crown debtors, Common Pleas dealt with actions between subjects of the Crown and King's Bench dealt with actions between Crown and subjects. Civil litigation in the King's Bench was heard on the 'Plea Side' (for information about its criminal jurisdiction, known as 'Crown Side', see 48.9).

Common law actions based on similar subject-matter could therefore be heard in any of these courts, so that even if you know that someone was involved in a civil case and what the subject-matter was, it will still be difficult to predict the court in which the action took place. Predicting which court a litigant might choose is further complicated by the fact that over the centuries a series of legal fictions were developed that enabled each of the courts to extend its clientele and effectively therefore to poach business from one another.

These central common law courts were based in Westminster, but it was possible, and indeed usual, for trials to be held locally under a writ known as *nisi prius*. In effect this meant that the cases were heard at the next visit of the circuit judges to hold assize courts, and some records of trials held at *nisi prius* are therefore found amongst the records of the clerks of assize in the ASSI series.

57.2 The records before 1875

Although much research has been undertaken on the medieval records, the more modern ones have been under-used and are still imperfectly understood. The procedures – and hence the records – of the common law courts were extraordinarily complicated, and the task of understanding how they fit together is not helped by the fact that they were heavily, systematically and unsympathetically weeded in the early twentieth century.

You also need to be aware that, with the exception of a short period during the interregnum of 1649 to 1660, all formal legal records were written in abbreviated Latin and in distinctive legal scripts until 1733. Even after that date the use of archaic legal phraseology and of legal fictions mean that it can be difficult to interpret the records accurately. There are as yet no published guides to using these records; the lists are inadequate and there are no modern indexes (although there are a number of contemporary finding aids). Researching common law records is not for the faint-hearted and you will have to be exceptionally determined even to attempt it. However, as the article by Watts and Watts shows, determination can occasionally pay handsome dividends.

Since we know that even in the present day most legal actions are compromised or dropped well before any formal legal hearing, the wisest course of action, in theory, would be to attempt to trace cases from the earliest initiation of procedure to the last conceivable entry. However, in the current state of knowledge, such an approach is not practical. It is far better, and very much easier, to concentrate on a few major series of records, such as plea rolls, posteas and judgement books/rolls. Most of these records were not created until the closing stages of cases that were either tried or came very near to being tried, and they will not therefore pick up the many cases that faltered soon after the initial steps of process.

Plea rolls are the formal record of the court's business. They are made up of individual parchment rotuli (a Latin term which literally means 'little rolls') on which are set out, in formulaic language, the nature of the action and an account of the process and final judgement (if any). Those of the King's Bench are in KB 26 (1194–1272), then in KB 27 Ⓕ until 1702, and are continued, for plea side only, in KB 122 Ⓕ. (These rolls also include the texts of deeds enrolled in the court.) Reference to plea side enrolments, 1656–1839, is by means of a contemporary series of dockets now held in IND 1 Ⓩ, which give, term by term, alphabetical lists of defendants' names together with the appropriate rotulus numbers in the plea rolls. The practice of filing rotuli on the plea rolls declined after 1760, so much so that by 1841, 90 per cent of rotuli went unfiled. For this period, therefore, it is essential to use the Entry Books of Judgements, 1699–1875, in KB 168 and J 89, which are arranged chronologically and give the date, county, names of plaintiffs, defendants and attorneys and brief details of the sum in dispute. There are indexes in the same series.

The plea rolls of Common Pleas, 1273–1874, are in CP 40 Ⓕ. Between 1583 and 1838 they include personal and mixed actions only, as pleas of land were enrolled separately on the recovery rolls (CP 43 Ⓕ). Although there are no indexes, there are a number of contemporary finding aids that can be used to help a search. These include the prothonotaries' docket rolls in CP 60 ⑦, 1509–1859 (formerly in IND 1). The docket rolls were probably compiled for the collection of fees, but they do give direct references to the rotuli and so can be useful as a means of reference. From the middle of the sixteenth century the termly entries give the county, the names of the attorney, plaintiff and defendant and the kind of entry made. Until 1770 there are three separate series of docket rolls: one for each of the three prothonotaries. In order to check all the entries for a particular term, you have to use all three rolls. There are gaps in each of the three series. No docket rolls survive for the period 1770–1790. From 1791 onwards there is a single series, which ends in 1859. Thereafter similar information, 1859–1874, is contained in the Entry Books of Judgements in CP 64 ⑦. There are also docket books, 1660–1839, in IND 1, which give the rotulus numbers of cases reaching judgement, and various calendars of entries, also in IND 1 ⑦.

The plea rolls of the Exchequer of Pleas, 1325–1875, are in E 13 Ⓕ. The most useful means of reference to them are the docket books of judgements, 1603–1839, which are in IND 1/4522–4567. These are arranged first by legal term, then alphabetically by name of the defendant against whom judgement was given. They usually give the name of the plaintiff, the type of suit (and sum in dispute in cases of debt), the amount of damages awarded and the resolution of the case. Two series of (selective) calendars of the records down to 1820 have been compiled. The first, arranged by date, is in IND 1/7344–7363; the other, arranged alphabetically by persons and places, is in E 48 and is available on open access in the National Archives. Repertory rolls, in E 14 ⑦, can also be used as a means of reference, but the series is very broken and covers only the periods 1412–1499, 1559–1669 and 1822–1830. Entry books of judgements, 1830–1875, are in IND 1/4243–4425. These give the dates of interlocutory and final judgements, but do not give any direct references to the plea rolls.

Chancery also had a common law jurisdiction, called the plea side of Chancery. Its basic jurisdiction covered relations between Crown and subject on such matters as royal grants, royal rights over its subjects' lands as discovered through inquisitions post mortem and inquisitions of lunacy, feudal incidents due to the Crown and division of lands between joint heiresses. It also had an increasing role in debt jurisdiction, on actions for recognisances for debt entered in Chancery. Pleadings for Edward I–James I are well listed in C 43 and C 44 (both ①Ⓥ); pleadings for Elizabeth I to Victoria are in C 206 ⑦. There are remembrance rolls in C 221 and C 222, and writs in C 245 (all ⑦).

57.3 The Supreme Court of Judicature, from 1875

In 1875, the existing superior civil courts were amalgamated into a new Supreme Court, consisting of a High Court of Justice and a Court of Appeal, which was able to apply either common law or the rules of equity as needed. The High Court consisted of five divisions: King's (or Queen's) Bench, Common Pleas, Exchequer, Chancery, and Probate, Divorce and Admiralty. In 1881, the Common Pleas, Exchequer and Queen's Bench Divisions were amalgamated. Records are split under the codes J, C and HCA.

Theoretically all jurisdiction belongs to all divisions alike, but in practice the exercise of jurisdiction in particular matters is assigned to particular divisions. The Queen's Bench Division deals with actions founded on contract or tort (causing harm or injury to a person without legal justification) and in commercial cases. The Chancery Division deals with actions relating to land, trusts, mortgages, partnerships and bankruptcy. In 1971 the Probate, Divorce and Admiralty Division was renamed the Family Division; its Admiralty business was transferred to the Queen's Bench Division and contentious probate actions were transferred to the Chancery Division.

The records of the High Court are filed by type rather than by case, so it can be extremely difficult and time-consuming to trace and assemble all the surviving material for any particular action. You also need to be aware that it is rarely possible to gain detailed information about the cases after 1945. A sample of judgement books is in J 89 ⑦. The entry books of decrees and orders (J 15 Ⓕ) can be useful in tracing cases heard in the Chancery Division; there are contemporary annual indexes (A and B books) to these orders under the name of the first plaintiff (in several sequences in IND 1: see the paper list of J 15 to find the reference for each year's set of indexes). If you are tracing a case heard in the Queen's Bench Division you should start with the cause books in J 87 Ⓕ (indexed in J 88 ⑦) and J 168 ⑦. There are a few exhibits from Queen's/King's Bench Division, the Court of King's Bench and the Exchequer in J 90: most are from Chancery so for this series, see 58.

The Appeal Court, which was also created as part of the Supreme Court in 1875, heard civil appeals only until 1966. Its surviving records are in J 83 and J 84 with judgements (1907–1926) in J 70 ⑦. Such records are rarely informative, since the cases were argued verbally, usually on points of law rather than on new evidence.

57.4 Civil litigation: the central common law courts: bibliography

J H BAKER, *An Introduction to English Legal History* (London, 2002)

M CALE, *Law and Society: An Introduction to Sources for Criminal and Legal History from 1800* (PRO, 1996)

W R CORNISH and G DE N CLARK, *Law and Society in England 1750–1950* (London, 1989)

A H MANCHESTER, *A modern legal history of England and Wales, 1750–1950* (London, 1980)

58 Civil litigation: Chancery proceedings

58.1 An introduction and overview of current cataloguing

Increasingly, anyone searching by surname on the National Archives website will find that they are getting unexpected hits with references starting with a c or a j including somewhere in the description a phrase such as *Smith v Jones*. You may even find that you have similar hits with a TS reference. These are references to law suits heard by the court of Chancery (later the Chancery Division). If you have got such a hit, you may be about to start on an exploration of some of the most interesting records held by the National Archives.

Many people may find they have picked up an intriguing reference from the catalogue that is actually to a later stage in a suit – to a receiver's account in c 30, for example, or to a set of family papers used as evidence in c 104 or to a record of the government's interest in a particular case in TS. This chapter actually takes you through the records of the various stages in a Chancery suit from the beginning: if you have landed in the middle of a suit, look through it to get an idea of what else might exist.

If you can do it for yourself, you will be in for many trips to the National Archives. If you can't and want to employ a researcher, ask for a précis of any information rather than a full transcript. These documents can be very large (especially after 1714) and are written in verbose style with phrasing often repeated – the clerks in Chancery were among the richest in government as a result!

Over the centuries, the Lord Chancellor or his deputies heard hundreds of thousands of disputes over inheritance and wills, lands, trusts, debts, marriage settlements, apprenticeships and other parts of the fabric of daily life. People turned to his court of Chancery because it was an equity court, promising a merciful justice not bound by the strict rules of the common law courts. The procedure was quite different, and involved the gathering of written pleadings and evidence to be examined by officers of the court. These still exist in such quantity – in millions of documents – that today the equity records of the court of Chancery are one of the treasures of the National Archives and a major resource for social and economic history. Many family historians have accessed them from the Bernau Index, but it would be fair to say that they have not had the popularity they deserve. This chapter may appear dry – but the records themselves can be the nearest we get to a window into people's lives and worries for the fourteenth to the late nineteenth centuries.

Most Chancery records are in English: many appear (misleadingly) to be written speech. The initial pleadings are the best known, but behind them is a huge hinterland of investigation (and administration of properties in dispute) by the court. Chancery suits, and the subjects of dispute, have not been easy to research because of the difficulties of the Chancery filing system, and the lack of good catalogues and indexes. I am currently working on a major project to improve access to Chancery records – and I hope to be doing so for the next fifteen years before passing on the baton to another.

The advent of the online catalogue has started to transform searching for the initial stages of a Chancery suit. Already, simple name searches on the catalogue bring up many references to suits in 'c', and many more people are exploring records they had never considered before. In particular, the catalogue has opened up the fifteenth- and early sixteenth-century suits in c 1, which are well catalogued – although with such weird contemporary spellings that using wild cards in searching is a necessity.

After 1558, the various series of initial pleadings are not catalogued in so much detail, but their finding aids are slowly being added to the catalogue: we are currently working on c 2, c 10 and c 13. However, several series of pleadings between about 1558 and 1714, and 1860 onwards, as yet have no searchable list online. The years 1860–1875 in c 16 are likely to be the next to be added, but even this will take some time.

Later stages of the suits are even less visible from the lists, and still require use of contemporary 'indexes' or 'alphabets' available at the National Archives only. Subject or place searching is almost impossible where the cataloguing is only by the titles of suits. If you want an overview of what material it is possible to find, look at Horwitz, *Samples of Chancery Pleadings and Suits: 1627, 1685, 1735 and 1785.*

Part of c 6 was entered into a separate database, funded by the Pilgrim Trust, the Transport History Trust and the Friends of the National Archives and the National Archives. The database is now available and searchable at **www.nationalarchives.gov.uk/equity/default.asp**, but the decision has been made to add any further improvements to the catalogue itself, rather than to a separate database.

The records of any one equity suit heard in Chancery were not kept together. Instead of being filed by the suit, they were filed by the type of document. This makes it difficult to trace all the documents in a suit, and at each point you will have to search for relevant records. To track a case in Chancery, you must currently have some idea of the title of the suit. If you have got into exploring Chancery records by finding an interesting reference on the catalogue, or by a reference from, say, *The Times* or a death duty index, this is not a major problem. You may even have found references to suits in Chancery from family papers or from locally held archives, as the court generated so much paperwork: A2A has over 4,000 references to copies of Chancery material held locally. If you just know of a suit in Chancery by family tradition with no idea of the title, you may have a harder time looking.

58.2 Titles of suits: some new discoveries

Titles of suits were assigned by the clerks of Chancery when they removed the proceedings from the active office to the record rooms – when they were archived, usually about two years after the case began. As parts of proceedings often ended up away from their original file (they were borrowed by other clerks to be copied to send to other parties in the suit), so the clerks wrote down in their archive lists what they saw on the document they were sending to their archives, rather than what the original name of the suit was (which they would have had to look for elsewhere). These archive lists are the foundation of all current Chancery catalogue entries from 1714 to 1842, and for some series as far back as 1625.

As a result of these practices, suit titles were very slippery before 1842. A suit with one plaintiff and one defendant would indeed be reliably catalogued as *Smith v Jones*, even if the various documents in it had been scattered. But a suit with two or more defendants could have as many titles as there were defendants, if they had responded separately and their documents had been misfiled. Thus Fitzwilliam Darcy v Elizabeth Bennet and Charlotte Lucas could be listed as both *Darcy v Bennet* or *Darcy v Lucas* – while remaining the same case. A suit with five defendants could end up being catalogued as five separate suits. Add to this the complication that the name of the plaintiff could also change if the first named plaintiff died or changed her name on marriage.

This problem of misfiling and misnaming was solved in 1842 by the introduction of a simple system of assigning to each suit as it was started a unique number based on the year, the first letter of the first plaintiff's surname and a unique number. Our example above would then have been known as 1842 D35: the thirty-fifth suit to have been started by a D plaintiff in 1842. This easy code was written on documents relating to the case, even those added to it years later, which meant they could be quickly reunited with the file if they were ever removed from it. The same system was used in cross-referencing decrees and so on.

This system solved so many problems that we are starting to apply it retrospectively in the catalogue to cases dating from before 1842. It will take a very long time to do, but in the end it will transform Chancery searching. If you have found one reference with a code such as 1869 A47, try a search in c and j using '1869 A47' as the search term: you may get related material. The divide between c and j is very irregular: you should try both.

Suits are sometimes named *In re Dashwood* or *In the matter of Wickham*: these tend to be where the court is acting on behalf of someone incapable of acting for themselves – a minor or a lunatic, perhaps. From the 1850s onwards, suits sometimes have a double title: *In the matter of Hallam; Carr v Crook*, for example. These will be cases settling points about a will – in this case the will of Hallam.

58.3 The five main record categories

The records fall into five main categories.

- Pleadings: statements made by the parties to a case. These bills, answers, replications and rejoinders are collectively known as **Chancery Proceedings**.
- Evidence: depositions (sworn examinations of persons chosen by the parties), affidavits (voluntary statements on oath) and exhibits brought into court.
- Decrees and orders: in the course of a suit.
- Chancery Masters' reports and accounts: on evidence and subjects remitted for investigation or administration.
- Final decrees – and appeals against them.

Spoken activity before the court is *not* recorded.

58.4 The pleadings: the beginning of a suit

Anyone wishing to start a suit in Chancery would get a lawyer to draw up a bill of complaint to submit to the Lord Chancellor. This would set out the offences of the defendant. It needed to claim that because of his or her lack of resources and power, or some other factor, the common law courts could not deliver justice. An equitable solution was therefore asked of the Lord Chancellor. The name of the Lord Chancellor can sometimes be the best clue to the date of the bill in the early centuries of the court's existence.

Bills (apart from the earliest ones) are in English, and give the plaintiff's name, occupation, rank and place of abode: the lawyer's name usually appears written by itself in a top corner. The defendant was required to make a similar written answer to all the points raised. The plaintiff could submit a replication, which might in turn produce a rejoinder from the defendant, and so on until the allegations of the bill had been whittled or 'pleaded' down to a set of agreed points at issue. These were then used for the next stage, the gathering of evidence (see below, 58.5).

You will not always find bills and answers filed together under the same reference: carry on looking, but remember that if the dispute was settled out of court you will find no further record. If the documents in the suit are described as 'bill only' or 'single bill' you can assume that this particular suit stopped there, or was settled out of court (for which we have no evidence). If you are looking among the series c 1–c 10, you may find that a bill is filed separately from its answers on occasion, so you can't as yet assume that the case did not proceed.

All the catalogues, etc., mentioned below can be seen at the National Archives, except for the Bernau Index. The Bernau Index is available on microfilm at the Family History Centres and at the Society of Genealogists (see 2.1). It is a good source, with a few minor drawbacks: it can be difficult to read, it gives obsolete references and it makes no attempt to standardise variant spellings of the same surname. It rarely gives any additional information (such as address) that would allow individuals with common surnames to be identified without recourse to the original documents.

If you use the Bernau Index, *please* copy the Bernau reference in full, as you will otherwise be lacking vital clues when it comes to translating the obsolete references given into modern National Archives references. If you have references to translate, ask at the Map Room desk for Sharp's *How to use the Bernau Index* or use Lawton's articles in *Family Tree Magazine*; you may still need to ask for advice.

Some series have published catalogues, which can be accessed through public and other libraries as well as at the National Archives: see the bibliography for details

PLEADINGS c. 1386–1558

c. 1386–c. 1558	Early Chancery Proceedings	C 1	2V, 5V, 4, 6
1401–1660	Answers, etc. (stray answers, replications, rejoinders, etc., with some bills)	C 4	2V

c 4 is not all searchable as yet: it is being catalogued from the original documents, and this should be finished within the next three years.

1558–1625	Chancery Proceedings: Series I: Elizabeth I and James I • Detailed list in process of entry onto the catalogue: check at C 2 level for progress • Detailed paper lists, including name and place indexes • Some published catalogues: see 58.15 • Some but not all are included in the Bernau Index	C 2	Becoming [2][V], [5][V], [4], [6] but very little in as yet
1625–1649	Chancery Proceedings: Series I: Charles I • No detailed list • Indexes to first plaintiff and first defendant at the National Archives • Published list of suit titles; online searchable version at www.originsnetwork.com/ (paid service): also viewable free at the National Archives	C 2	[W]
1558–1660	Chancery Proceedings: Series II. [V] • Fuller details available at the National Archives from published lists: see 58.15	C 3	1st plaintiff, 1 defendant [1][V] and [4]
1401–1660	Answers etc.	C 4	[2][V]
1570–1714	Six Clerks Series: Mitford • Manuscript lists at the National Archives	C 8	No descriptions in catalogue
1613–1714	Six Clerks Series: Bridges • published catalogues at the National Archives: see 58.15	C 5	1st plaintiff, 1 defendant [1][V] and [4]
1620–1714	Six Clerks Series: Hamilton • Manuscript lists at the National Archives	C 7	No descriptions in catalogue
1625–1714	Six Clerks Series: Collins • Fully searchable in the equity database • Browsable in papers lists at the National Archives • Manuscript lists at the National Archives	C 6 1–419 420–611	 70 per cent is fully searchable in Equity Database 30 per cent [F]
1640–1714	Six Clerks Series: Whittington 50 per cent poorly entered into the catalogue by surname only with many misreadings This series is slowly having full details entered from the detailed manuscript lists at the National Archives Miscellaneous pleadings from other series are listed at the end of the C 10 volumes	C 10	Part [1][V] Part [2][V], [5][V], [4], [6] Part [F]
1649–1714	Six Clerks Series: Reynardson • Some published catalogues: see Bibliography	C 9	1st plaintiff and 1 defendant [1][V]

An online index to the catalogue references for over 26,000 disputed wills litigated in Chancery (the Inheritance Disputes Index 1574–1714) is searchable online for a fee at **www.originsnetwork.com** (also searchable for free at the National Archives, thanks to British Origins and the compiler P W Coldham).

1715–1758	Various Six Clerks, Series I • The Bernau Notebooks are arranged by reference and give (for all parties) surname, forename, occupation and date: available at the National Archives • The Bernau Index at the Society of Genealogists indexes these notebooks	C 11	1st plaintiff and 1 defendant ⊡
1758–1800	Various Six Clerks, Series II	C 12	1st plaintiff and 1st defendant ⊡
1800–1842	Various Six Clerks, Series III Becoming searchable for 1st plaintiff and all defendants ☐2 [3 days notice to produce these] See research guide on www.nationalarchives.gov.uk for more details	C 13	1st plaintiff and 1 defendant ⊡

PLEADINGS AFTER 1842

1842–1852	Modern Series: Pleadings [3 days notice to produce these]	C 14	1st plaintiff and 1 defendant ⊡
1844–1864	Miscellaneous Pleadings	C 18	1st plaintiff and 1st defendant ☐2
1853–1860	Modern Series: Pleadings	C 15	1st plaintiff and 1 defendant ⊡
1861–1875	Modern Series: Pleadings	C 16	Ⓕ
1876 onwards	Chancery Division: Pleadings, Common Law Orders etc. Index for 1876–1890 only in IND 1/2218–2226	J 54	Ⓕ

If you have found a reference in C 14, C 15, C 16 or J 54 before 1880, you are very strongly advised to look at the relevant Cause Book in C 32 ☐7 before even ordering the pleadings (see 58.13 for more details). The cause books are arranged by the coding (e.g., 1842 H 45) and will give you, most importantly, the full names of all the plaintiffs and all the defendants. This is vital as these series are otherwise only listed as Smith v Smith. They also record the progress of each suit.

A shortcut into some at least of the suits after 1861 is to search C 30 ⊡. This series contains the accounts of receivers appointed by the court (see 58.10).

58.5 Depositions and affidavits

When the pleadings were finished, and the issues in dispute defined, the court commissioned neutral men of substance to examine an agreed list of people (deponents) and report back in writing (in English, with commissions and some small amount of material in Latin before 1733). Both sides drew up separate lists of numbered questions, called interrogatories, to be put to the deponents under oath. The answers, called depositions, provide information about the case and often about the parties involved in the dispute that was not included in the pleadings. They also give the deponent's name, place of abode, age and occupation at the head of his or her deposition. Affidavits were voluntary statements made upon oath during the progress of a suit.

Indexes at the National Archives are to the title of the suit, not to the person giving the deposition or affidavit. For indexes to these people (deponents), try the Bernau Index (see 58.4) at the Society of Genealogists. The only trouble with this is that the Bernau Index will give you a reference to a whole box full of depositions from many different suits – with no clue as to which suit to read to find the name in the index. One point to note is that you cannot order a copy of depositions in the usual way from a Bernau reference as our copying service will not read through a hundred plus documents to find the relevant one for you. If you cannot come yourself, you will need to use an independent researcher.

The depositions fall into two groups: town depositions taken in London and country depositions taken elsewhere, usually before local worthies commissioned by Chancery to do so.

Town depositions

1534–1853	Mostly listed by term: use IND 1/16759 and IND 1/9115–9121 Deponents indexed in Bernau Index	C 24 Ⓕ
1854–1880 March	Filed with the pleadings in these series: see previous table	C 15, C 16, J 54
1880 April– 1925	See Country depositions in next table	J 17

Country depositions

1558–1649	Deponents indexed in Bernau Index	C 21	1st plaintiff and 1 defendant Ⓣ
1649–1714	Deponents indexed in Bernau Index for C 22/1–75, and for all cases where the plaintiff's name began with A: about 8 per cent of total	C 22	1st plaintiff and 1 defendant Ⓣ
1714–1842	Filed in the same series as the pleadings Add 'AND dep*' to your search to find them No information on deponents	C 11, C 12, C 13	1st plaintiff and 1 defendant Ⓣ
1842–1880 March	Filed with the pleadings. No information on deponents	C 14	1st plaintiff and 1 defendant Ⓣ
1880 April– 1925	Town and Country depositions No information on deponents Use IND 1/16748–16752	J 17	Ⓕ

If you cannot find the interrogatories, you could try the annual bundles of Detached Interrogatories, 1598–1852, in C 25 Ⓣ. In addition, there are the Sealed, or Unpublished, Depositions taken for use in contingencies which never arose. These are in C 23, but they are not listed. You would have to be really dedicated to look through either of these series as there is nothing to help you.

1611–1800	Indexes in IND 1/14545–14567 Entry marked with a cross: the original affidavit is in C 31 No cross: try the copies in C 41, for 1615–1747 only	C 31, C 41	F
1801–1875	Indexes in IND 1/14575–14684 The name listed after the plaintiff and defendant is that of the solicitor, initiating the affidavit	C 31	F
1876 onwards	There are indexes in IND 1: ask at the Map Room desk in the National Archives	J 4	F

Further (i.e., different) affidavits are known to be in the Chancery Master's Documents in c 117–c 125 F; see 58.9.

58.6 Decrees and orders in the course of a suit

Any orders made during the course of a case, and the final judgement, are recorded in the Entry Books of Decrees and Orders. These also give the date for the recording of the depositions and affidavits, the hearing and the final decree. Decrees and order before 1733 may be in Latin.

1544–1875	Accessed by contemporary annual indexes No indexes for 1544–1546	C 33	4
1876–1954	Accessed by contemporary annual indexes	J 15	4
1955–1966	Destroyed	–	

The Entry Books are in two sequences known as 'A' and 'B'. Until Trinity term 1629, both 'A' and 'B' books list suits (by plaintiff v defendant) from A to Z. From 1629, entries for plaintiffs A–K are in the 'A' books, and entries for plaintiffs L–Z are in the 'B' books. In 1932 the 'A' and 'B' books were amalgamated.

The annual indexes (which are nearly all on the open shelves) reflect the A and B arrangement. Although annual, they start their year from the Michaelmas term. This means the dates on the spines are out by one year for the other three law terms. For example, the index listed as 1849 covers Michaelmas 1849 and Hilary, Easter and Trinity terms 1850. From 1860 each index covers a calendar year, not a 'legal' year. The reference found in the index has to be matched up to the c 33 or J 15 series list: make sure the IND volume number matches as well to ensure that you have the right year.

Sometimes, of course, the case did not proceed after the bill and answer had been filed and thus no orders will be found.

acco^{tt} accountant	*exor* executor	*mre* matter
affd^{t} affidavit	*fur^{r}* further	*Ora^{r}* Orator (plaintiff)
Appo^{t} appointment	*hrinbef^{e}* hereinbefore	Ors others
Bequed bequeathed	*hrs* heirs	*ppr* paper
Co^{l} Counsel	*incon* or *inion* injunction	*rev^{r}* revivor
Co^{t} Court	*indre* indenture	*suppl* supplement
Conson consideration	L C Lord Chancellor	*testor* testator
declon declaration	M R Master of the Rolls	*tree(s)* trustee(s)
Excepons Exceptions	Mr Master	*w^{o}* widow

58.7 Involvement of the 'Treasury Solicitor'

The records of the Treasury Solicitor are full of material relating to (mostly nineteenth-century) cases being heard in Chancery – and their descriptions in the catalogue have the huge merit of giving the subject of the dispute. Try a search by surname in plain TS: you may be surprised. Some appear because the Attorney General was involved, either in bringing the suit, often at the relation of a third party, or defending the Crown's interest. These tend to be cases involving charities or a wider interest, as in the following examples.

- 1832–1842 Attorney General (at the relation of John Gage) and others v. David Columbine, Henry Martinson and others and the Solicitor General. Proceedings to determine use of the French Church at Norwich. Court: Chancery TS 11/176
- 1808 Thomas POWELL v Attorney-General. Suit concerning validity of a bequest under will of James Pendleton dated 10 July 1802 to widows and children of seamen belonging to town of Liverpool: Chancery, bill filed 21 Nov 1808 TS 11/1066

However, from the descriptions of other cases, there does not appear to be any obvious public interest.

58.8 Masters' reports and certificates

In many Chancery suits, the judge referred matters for investigation or action to one or more of the Chancery Masters in Ordinary. The Masters' investigated the evidence (including depositions, affidavits and exhibits), administered the estates that were in Chancery care during the (often very lengthy) course of a suit and reported to the court.

The Master's report back to the court often formed the basis for the court's final decrees. The Masters also sometimes acted as arbitrators and the reports are therefore full of arbitrations and awards of various sorts. Until 1842, the reports include dealings with the infant and lunatic wards of court. The draft reports were submitted to both parties, who were allowed to review the reports and to submit their response in the way of 'exceptions'. Longer reports can include detailed material taken from the pleadings and other papers being examined by the Master, and can provide a very useful summary or overview of a case. The Masters also returned short certificates into court, for example, authorising the delivery of money. Masters were also responsible for assessing costs. From 1842 taxing masters did this instead. In 1852 the Masters' other functions were transferred to the judges. The judges then started referring many matters to their chief clerks (who soon took on the title of Master). The clerks' and taxing masters' reports were filed in the same series as the earlier Masters' reports. To find specific reports and certificates, you will need to use the contemporary 'indexes' in IND 1.

1544–1605	C 38 Ⓕ	Reports: main series	No indexes
1606–1759	C 38 Ⓕ	Reports: main series	IND 1/1878–2028
1760–1800	C 38 Ⓕ	Reports: main series	IND 1/10700/1–41
1801–1875	C 38 Ⓕ	Reports: main series	IND 1/14919–14993
1756–1859	C 39 ⑦	Oversize documents	No indexes
1756–1859	C 40 Ⓕ	Exceptions to the reports: appeals by either party	1836–1840 only: IND 1/30785–1/30786
1875–1962	J 57 Ⓕ	Reports: main series	IND 1: many sequences

58.9 Masters' documents

These may contain the affidavits, examinations of witnesses, estate accounts, wills and other documents on which the Masters founded their reports, together with the drafts of reports. As such, they can form an absolute treasure chest of information – but they are not always easy to find.

You will need to know the name of the Master dealing with the suit. The various c series are named for the last Master to occupy the office on its abolition in 1852. Look at the succession lists of Masters filed with c 103 paper list, at the National Archives only, to see where the papers of your Master will be. There are contemporary indexes to these records: these indexes are not always reliable.

Master Blunt	C 124 ①	
Master Brougham	C 117 Ⓕ	IND 1/6625
Master Farrar	C 122 Ⓕ	IND 1/6624
Master Horne	C 118 Ⓕ	IND 1/6620 to IND 1/6621
Master Humphrey	C 123 Ⓕ	IND 1/6618
Master Kindersley	C 126 Ⓕ	IND 1/6622
Master Lynch (no separate collection)	C 123; C 124 ①	IND 1/6618, IND 1/6616
Master Richards	C 121 Ⓕ	IND 1/6626 to IND 1/6627
Master Rose	C 119 Ⓕ	IND 1/6619
Master Senior	C 125 Ⓕ	IND 1/6623
Master Tinney	C 120 Ⓕ	IND 1/6617

Master Romer's Miscellaneous Books	1850–1911	J 23	[7]
Master Romer's Papers	1860–1890	J 24	[7]
Master Satow's Miscellaneous Books	1855–1899	J 26	[7]
Master Satow's Papers	1850–1900	J 27	[7]
Master Fox's Miscellaneous Books	1828–1895	J 29	[7]
Master Fox's Papers	1870–1910	J 30	[7]
Master Watkin Williams' Miscellaneous Books	1850–1909	J 32	[7]
Master Watkin Williams' Papers	1850–1900	J 33	[7]
Master Hulbert's Miscellaneous Books	1850–1903	J 35	[7]
Master White's Miscellaneous Books	1850–1903	J 36	[7]
Master Ridsdale's Miscellaneous Books	1855–1907	J 37	[7]
Master Ridsdale's Papers	1850–1938	J 38	[7]
Master Keen's Papers	1850–1910	J 40	[7]
Master Jobson's Miscellaneous Books	1850–1900	J 42	[7]
Master Jobson's Papers	1850–1910	J 43	[7]
Master Chandler's Miscellaneous Books	1847–1877	J 45	[7]
Master Chandler's Papers	1850–1890	J 46	[7]
Master Mosse's Papers	1852–1917	J 63	[7]

As yet there is no succession list for these later masters to show where records of a particular master will be found. The papers have been quite heavily weeded.

PEDIGREES

Pedigrees were often created in the course of a Chancery dispute to help the Master. There are four dedicated series:

	Dates created	Dates covered		
Master Hawkins' Pedigrees	1849–1925	from 1770	J 64	[2], [1]
Master Hulbert's Pedigrees	1849–1926	from 1583	J 66	[2], [1]
Master Newman's Pedigrees	1893–1931	from 1742	J 67	[2], [1]
Pedigrees (Various Masters)	1852–1977	from 1850	J 68	[2], [1]

These tend to be listed by the 'principal person' – the pivotal person in the legal proof of entitlement to whatever was being claimed – and the name of the law suit.

A few pedigrees can be found by searching in J 90 and in c 104–c 115 (see below 58.11). There are likely to be more waiting to be discovered in the Masters' Documents.

58.10 Accounts of disputed estates

The Masters had to receive annual accounts of the estates they administered while the ownership was in dispute in Chancery, or while the owner was a ward of the court, from trustees to whom the care of the estate had been remitted. The accounts are a very under-used source, but need to be listed better to be accessible for local or business history.

The accounts for c. 1750–c. 1850 are in C 101 ☐ (suit title): unfortunately no dates are given. Some cataloguing work is being done on this series, but it will take a long time for much impression to be made on a very large series. For later accounts try C 30 ☐ (suit title), covering 1859–1901 (but no dates are given in the catalogue). These are the accounts of receivers appointed by the court for the protection or collection of property, in actions concerning the administration of estates of deceased persons or in the dissolution of partnerships.

Other records of estates administered by Chancery are still held by the Supreme Court of Justice: we expect to receive some of these in the near future.

58.11 Masters' exhibits

Exhibits are private papers brought into court as part of litigation: most were reclaimed at the end of a suit, but some were not. The minority that remained unclaimed now form the National Archives' lucky dip – a major collection of sources for social, economic and business history, as well as family papers.

The Chancery Masters' exhibits range in date from the twelfth to the nineteenth centuries; although the cases they come from are mostly of the eighteenth and nineteenth centuries. They were handed on from each of the twelve Masters to his successor, and the collections are named after the last Master to hold them before the abolition of the office.

The subject range is that of life itself – you can find papers relating to dentists; privateers; lunatics; the Great Fire of London; alum works; loyalist troops in America; West Indian plantations; the diamond trade; the newspaper trade; monastic records; and estate papers galore. The series also include major collections relating to the Royal African Company, the Million Bank and the religious houses of Llanthony by Gloucester, Reading, Repton and Sudbury.

The lists are all searchable online, but their quality is patchy. Some descriptions are good, others ludicrously brief. You are likely to get one or more boxes of papers, sometimes in their original order and with the schedule (a list drawn up on their deposit with the Master) still attached.

In theory, if the exhibits exist you should be able to match them up with the relevant case. This is not easy, as many of the pleadings are unindexed. The Master's documents, reports, accounts, etc. (C 117–C 129) are also in theory a source to move on to. If you can work out which Master was involved, use the various lists of Masters attached to the C 103 paper list to find out who was the last holder of that Mastership, and whose name was therefore given to the surviving records inherited from his predecessors.

See the introductory notes filed with the paper lists of C 103–C 114 for advice on this.

	Last date			
1295	1808	Court Rolls (extracted from the other C series)	C 116	④, ⑤
1481	1829	Master Lynch	C 105	①, ②, ④, ⑤, ⑥
1235	1837	Master Kindersley	C 113	①, ②, ④, ⑤, ⑥
1566	1841	Unknown Masters	C 114	①, ②, ④, ⑤, ⑥
1085	1842	Duchess of Norfolk Deeds	C 115	①, ②, ④, ⑤, ⑥
1220	1847	Master Farrar	C 108	①, ②, ④, ⑤, ⑥
1350	1850	Six Clerks' Office	C 171	①, ②, ④, ⑤, ⑥
1250	1851	Master Senior	C 107	①, ②, ④, ⑤, ⑥
1200	1853	Master Richards	C 106	①, ②, ④, ⑤, ⑥
1306	1853	Master Horne	C 110	①, ②, ④, ⑤, ⑥
1200	1856	Master Tinney	C 104	①, ②, ④, ⑤, ⑥
1180	1857	Master Humphrey	C 109	①, ②, ④, ⑤, ⑥
1200	1857	Master Brougham	C 111	①, ②, ④, ⑤, ⑥
1270	1857	Master Rose	C 112	①, ②, ④, ⑤, ⑥
1200	1859	Master Blunt	C 103	①, ②, ④, ⑤, ⑥
1250	1930	Chancery Masters' Exhibits	J 90	①, ②, ④, ⑤, ⑥

58.12 Final decrees, arbitrations and appeals

Decrees (and orders) could be enrolled in the Decree Rolls at an extra cost. Any appeal against such enrolled decrees or order would have to be made to the House of Lords: try the House of Lords Record Office. As a result, very few decrees were enrolled, as it made a case more difficult to reopen. After 1875, the only decrees enrolled related to railway schemes and orders of other courts.

1534–1903	C 78 Decree Rolls	Ⓕ	IND 1/16950–16961B
1534–1903	C 79 Supplementary Series	Ⓕ	IND 1/16960B

There is a place-name index for enrolled decrees, Henry VIII to George III, in IND 1/16960A. Work undertaken to calendar the rolls in C 78 is described in M W Beresford, 'The decree rolls of Chancery as a source for economic history 1547–c. 1700'. Parts of this series have been calendared and indexed as a result of projects undertaken by Professor Beresford (1974–1976) and Professor R W Hoyle (1992). As a result, there is a detailed list and index of C 78/1–130, while for C 78/131–750 there is a detailed list with no index. After this, every fifth roll was listed, covering C 78/755–1250. These rolls appear to cover about 1534 to 1700, but the enrolling system was not by date, so it is difficult to be sure if they include all decrees of that period. The List and Index Society have published these calendars. As yet, they have not been put on the catalogue. There are also a number of contemporary indexes, arranged in alphabetical order by the first letter of the name of the parties in the dispute.

If final decrees were not enrolled, they will be found in the Decree and Order Books (see 58.6). *Not* enrolling had advantages in some cases, as appeals were made back to the Lord Chancellor, and cases could be reopened more easily.

Appeals against unenrolled decrees (and orders) are among the Petitions. These also include 'ordinary' petitions, for example for winding up associations or for the appointment of new trustees to administer an estate.

1774–1875	C 36 Ordinary and Appeal Petitions	F	IND 1/15029–15047
1876–1925	J 53 Chancery Division Petitions	F	IND 1/15048–15051 and 15282

Many suits were ended by arbitrations, mediations, compositions and awards of various sorts, made by commissioners appointed by Chancery. Quite frequently they were the Chancery Masters.

1544–1844	C 38 Reports on arbitrations by Masters	See 58.8
1544–1694	C 33 Awards enrolled	See 2.3
1694–1844	C 42 Awards not enrolled	No indexes

58.13 Cause Books, 1842–1880: an integrated record

For 1842–April 1880 only, Cause Books survive in C 32 ⑦, F. If you have found a reference to pleadings in C 14, C 15, C 16 or C 17, you are strongly advised to look at the relevant C 32 volume before even ordering the pleadings. They are arranged by the coding (e.g., 1842 H45) and will give you most importantly the full names of all the plaintiffs and all the defendants. They also bring together for convenience all references to decrees and orders, reports and certificates made during the course of a case, together with the names of any solicitors and the dates of all their appearances. Indexes for 1860 to 1880 are in IND 1/16727–16747.

Cause Books from April 1880 onwards were destroyed on the recommendation of the Denning Committee on Legal Records, leaving no primary means of access to the records after 1880. Specimens only are preserved in J 89 ⑦ for April–December 1880, 1890, 1900, 1910, 1920, 1930 and 1940.

58.14 Dormant funds in court

There are various kinds of Funds in Court, often loosely called 'Estates in Chancery' or 'Money in Chancery'. The law courts (particularly Chancery) have traditionally accepted responsibility for money and property belonging to people who cannot be found, or who have a disability which prevents them looking after it themselves. Any property was sold and turned into money, and the money was administered on their behalf. After a fixed period of inaction (set by the statute under which they are lodged) accounts become Dormant Funds and no longer attract interest.

These funds may be claimed back from the court upon sufficient proof. On occasion, claimants have received large sums of money they were unaware of, and great public interest is shown in the idea of 'funds in court'. However, such cases are very rare: money is not waiting for everyone. Even where funds do exist, they are usually less than £150 in value. The main types of funds in court include:

- awards of the Family Court;
- compensation from the Civil Injuries Compensation Board;
- compensation under Compulsory Purchase Acts, in cases where either the ownership of the property is unknown or the owner refuses to accept it;
- legacies, where missing heirs cannot be found;
- money lodged for dissenting shareholders;
- mortgage foreclosures, when the mortgagor cannot be traced: the net proceeds of sale.

Be very wary of statements made (in the media and on the internet) by people claiming to be 'Unclaimed Money Agents' able to recover 'money in Chancery' on payment of fees or a percentage, or to act on behalf of the 'Court of Chancery'. The Supreme Court of Judicature has no such agents. They strongly recommended that you take independent advice before making a payment to any agency in respect of money alleged to be in Court.

To find out if there are any dormant funds in a particular case, you can write to the Court Funds Division (address in 62) and ask them to search their index for you. You will have to give

- the title of the Court proceedings (Smith v Jones and the suit number if you have it – e.g., 1867 S346);
- the name of the Court;
- the name(s) of the person(s) who lodged the money into Court;
- for whose benefit the money was lodged;
- relevant dates;
- the assumed link between you and any of the above, i.e. evidence of beneficial interest.

Do not send any original documents such as certificates of birth, marriage or death: copies are acceptable. You can also go to this address yourself to consult the index on a computer kept at the North Entrance of 22 Kingsway.

58.15 Civil litigation: Chancery proceedings: bibliography

M W BERESFORD, 'The decree rolls of Chancery as a source for economic history 1547–c. 1700', *Economic History Review*, 2nd series, 32 (1979), pp. 1–10

Calendar of Chancery Decree Rolls (C 78/1–14) List and Index Society Vol. 160, 1979

Calendar of Chancery Decree Rolls (C 78/15–45) List and Index Society Vol. 198, 1983

Calendar of Chancery Decree Rolls (C 78/46–85) List and Index Society Vol. 253, 1994

Calendar of Chancery Decree Rolls (C 78/86–130) List and Index Society Vol. 254, 1994

P W COLDHAM, 'Genealogical Resources in Chancery Records', in *Genealogists' Magazine*, vol XIX, pp 345–347 and vol XX, pp 257–260

D GERHOLD, *Courts of Equity ... A Guide to Chancery and other Legal Records* (Pinhorn, 1994)

D GERHOLD, 'Searching for Justice: Chancery records on the Internet', *Ancestors* 13, 2003

A HANSON, A Litigant in the Family [C4 cataloguing and discoveries], *Ancestors* 13, 2003

H HORWITZ, *Chancery Equity Records and Proceedings 1600–1800* (PRO, 1998)

H HORWITZ, *Samples of Chancery Pleadings and Suits: 1627, 1685, 1735 and 1785* (List and Index Society, vol 257, 1995)

W J JONES, *The Elizabethan Court of Chancery* (Oxford, 1967)

S T MOORE, *Family Feuds: an Introduction to Chancery Proceedings* (Federation of Family History Societies, 2003)

G V SANDERS, *Orders of the Court of Chancery* (1845)

H SHARP, *How to Use the Bernau Index* (Society of Genealogists, 1996)

Published finding aids

The level of detail given in these published catalogues is not always included in the online catalogue.

C 2	• 1558–1603, Calendar of Proceedings in Chancery in the Reign of Queen Elizabeth I ed. J Caley and J Bayler (London, Record Commission, 1827–1832)
	• 1603–1624, Index of Chancery Proceedings, James I, A–K only, PRO Lists and Indexes, vol. XLVII (1922) Index of Chancery Proceedings, 1603–1625, A–L only, ed. R Topham, The Genealogist, n.s. vols IV, VI–IX (1887, 1889–1892)
	• 1625–1649, Calendar of Chancery Proceedings, Bills and Answers filed in the reign of Charles I, vols 1–3, ed. W P W Phillimore, vol. 4, ed. E A Fry (British Record Society Index Library, 1903–1904). [This is much the same information as is searchable at www.originsnetwork.com (paid service): also viewable free at the National Archives – best to use that in preference to this book]
C 3	Index of Chancery Proceedings, PRO Lists and Indexes • 1558–1579, vol. VII (1896) • 1579–1621, vol. XXIV (1908) • 1621–1660, vol. XXX (1909)
C 5	Index of Chancery Proceedings, Bridges' Division, 1613–1714, PRO Lists and Indexes • A–C, vol. XXXIX (1913) • D–H, vol. XLII (1914) • I–Q, vol. XLIV (1915) • R–Z, vol. XLV (1917)
C 9	Index of Chancery Proceedings, Reynardson's Division, 1649–1714, ed. E A Fry (British Record Society, Index Library, 1903–1904)

Many local record societies have published catalogues of Chancery Proceedings for their own county. A quick way to check what exists is to go to **www.rhs.ac.uk/bibl/bibwel.asp** and search this excellent bibliography using the county and Chancery as search terms.

59 Civil litigation: Exchequer equity proceedings

59.1 Introduction to Exchequer equity records

Many people will access the Exchequer equity records in the first place by discovering an interesting and surprisingly full description with a reference starting E 134 in the course of searching the website or catalogue. This can advance family history several steps in one go – for example:

- Stephen Pitcher and his wife Mary. v. Mary Cox, widow: Legacy given by the will of Sarah Painter, of Beaminster, widow. Touching the whereabouts of Bernard Newman, heretofore of Beaminster (Dorset), apothecary or physician (son of Bernard Newman, late of Netherbury (Dorset), and grandson of said testatrix), who is said to have gone to Jamaica in the West Indies, and to have succeeded there as a physician. [The names of John Newman, of Netherbury, husbandman, Wm. Newman and Thos. Newman, brothers of said Bernard, Sarah Newman (mother of said Bernard and sister of the defendant Mary Cox), Samuel Cox, of Beaminster, merchant, Onesiphorus Symes, and Tobias Symes are mentioned.]: Somerset; Dorset.

Ref: E 134/29Geo2/Hil2

What is this court? What are these records, recently described by Milhous and Hume as an astonishingly rich potential source? In the mid-sixteenth century, the Exchequer developed an equity jurisdiction, which ran alongside the ancient common law Exchequer of Pleas. Its business included disputes over titles of land, manorial rights, tithes, mineral rights, ex-monastic land, debts, wills, etc. – anything where the plaintiff could allege (usually fictitiously) that the Crown had some kind of revenue interest in getting the matter sorted out. In effect, any suit that could be brought in Chancery could equally well be brought in the Exchequer. For decades the court provided a quicker forum than Chancery. As more people started using the Exchequer court, so its advantages disappeared and the court became over-burdened. In 1841, the Exchequer lost its equity side, and its outstanding business was transferred to the court of Chancery.

There is a specialist guide to these records, Horwitz's *Exchequer Equity Records and Proceedings 1649–1841*, which may be useful once you have started using them. This chapter should help get you started.

If you begin to investigate Exchequer equity proceedings by following up an interesting E 134 reference, you will find on that you are in fact in the middle of a law suit. This is because the depositions in E 134 are the only Exchequer equity records to be listed in any detail, giving plaintiffs, defendants and subjects in dispute. Most descriptions up to early 1773 have been incorporated into the catalogue: most of those from Easter 1773 to 1841 are currently awaiting entry.

Using E 134 for an initial search can be an easy way to start exploring the records, but remember that E 134 only includes depositions taken in the country, and the catalogue does not include the names of the deponents. If depositions were taken in London only, or if the case did not involve depositions, you will have to try tracing the case from other series of records. These have not been listed at anything like the same level of detail, and need to be accessed by contemporary 'indexes' available only at the National Archives. There is no union index of names. Few of the contemporary indexes are in strict alphabetical order.

59.2 Working through a case

Documents relating to cases heard in the Exchequer fall into many different categories – pleadings, evidence and court decisions and opinions, each filed separately. Almost all are in English. In general, Exchequer cases are easier to follow through than Chancery ones, as the Exchequer clerks developed a rational filing system early, and stuck to it.

If you suspect from other information that an equity dispute was heard in the Exchequer, try a keyword search (using variant spellings) in E 134 (②, ⑤, ⑥ for 1558–1773) or look in the manuscript calendar of E 134 (Ⓕ for 1773–1841). If searching, watch out for abbreviations of forenames (see 1.6) and variant spellings of surnames. If nothing turns up but you know the case was heard in the Exchequer, then look at the pleadings (see below) and proceed logically through the case. The most important documents are the pleadings, the depositions and the decree, if any.

For named people. If nothing turns up from a keyword search in E 134, then a speculative search can be difficult. The Bill Books, which are the original filing registers for the pleadings, are subdivided by county and are not alphabetically arranged, although the full names of the plaintiffs and defendants are given. Many defendants are recorded in the appearance books (E 107 ⑦): these are arranged by date, but are not indexed. However, the Bernau Index (see 58.4) indexes deponents and defendants in Exchequer Depositions (E 134) but may not be complete. A list of deponents, 1559–1695, is available at the National Archives and at the Society of Genealogists, but is not indexed.

For places/subjects. Try a keyword search restricted to E 134 for 1558–1773. You may also wish to look through the paper versions at the National Archives, which are arranged in three sequences, by county and also by date up to 1772 and then in manuscript calendars by date until 1841. Read through the Bill Books for the county at the National Archives to find any pleadings that did not produce depositions in E 134. The Board of Celtic Studies has published details of cases relating to Wales before 1625.

Some commissions in the series of Special Commissions (E 178 ②, ⑤), which are arranged by county in a chronological sequence, also relate to equity disputes. To find the title of the suit (if any) you will have to read the commission itself (in Latin until 1733) or look for an endorsement or other annotation on the return. The exhibits (E 140 ①, ⑤) and exhibits in Clerks' Papers (E 219 ⑥) may also be worth checking.

59.3 Pleadings

Pleadings were statements made by the parties to a suit: these bills, answers, replications and rejoinders are collectively known, for short, as bills and answers.

A bill of complaint submitted by the plaintiff initiated a suit by setting out the case against the defendant. It conventionally included a statement that the parties were 'Debtors and accountants to his/her Majesty'. This was to imply that if the wrong was not righted the revenues of the Crown would be affected, either directly or indirectly, because the plaintiff would then be less able to pay his own debts or dues to the Crown. There is a possibility that fairly lowly tenants of Crown manors were likely to use this court, but in many cases the status as a Crown debtor was fictional.

The bills and answers usually give much circumstantial detail. In addition to the plaintiffs' and defendants' names, the pleadings give their occupation, rank and address. When brought by the Attorney General the bill was known as an 'Information'.

The defendant replied to the bill with his answer; the plaintiff might respond with a replication, and the defendant with a rejoinder, and so on. A purely legal objection given by way of reply was called a demurrer. Because both bills and answers are *ex parte*, each party setting out his case at length and in the most favourable light, they may include a wealth of background detail: but may not necessarily be true or accurate representations of the facts.

Bills, answers, etc., in each suit were strung together in a single file, and given a reference number, which is entered on the top left-hand corner of the bill. The bills and answers are in two series:

c. 1485–	Early	Most of these are NOT Exchequer documents but	E 111	②,
c. 1558	Bills and	strays from the records of other courts, such as		⑤
	Answers	the Court of Requests.		

c. 1558–	Bills and	These are arranged by reign, subdivided by county	E 112	Ⓕ
1841	Answers	Not searchable online.		
		To find individual pleadings, you		
		• order up the Bill Books described below		
		• get a suit number and county		
		• key this up in the E 112 list to find the modern		
		number of the portfolio		
		• use the suit number to find the right papers in		
		the portfolio		

BILL BOOKS (ELIZABETH I–VICTORIA)

These are the original, and still the best, means of access to the bills in E 112. They still serve as the main 'index'. The Exchequer clerks entered the bills under different sections for each county. They are indexed by plaintiff, and give the full names of the parties. Before 1700, and sometimes after, they give the subject. Entries up to 1733 are usually in Latin – but as you are looking for names this is not usually a problem. Some of the very early ones are faded, and need to be seen under ultra-violet light.

Bedford, Buckingham, Cambridge, Cheshire, Cornwall, Cumberland, Devon, Essex, Hampshire, Hereford, Hertford, Huntingdon, Kent, Lancashire, Lincoln, Middlesex and all Welsh counties

Elizabeth I	1558–1603	IND 1/16820
James I	1603–1625	IND 1/16822
Charles I	1625–1649	IND 1/16824
Commonwealth	1649–1660	IND 1/16826
Charles II	1660–1674	IND 1/16828
	1669–1685	IND 1/16830
James II	1685–1688	IND 1/16832
William and Mary	1688–1694	IND 1/16834
William III	1694–1702	IND 1/16836
Anne	1702–1714	IND 1/16836
George I	1714–1727	IND 1/16838
George II	1727–1760	IND 1/16840
George III	1760–1801	IND 1/16842
	1776–1820	IND 1/16844
	1779–1820	IND 1/16846
George IV	1820–1830	IND 1/16848
William IV	1830–1837	IND 1/16850
Victoria	1837–1841	IND 1/16852

☐ p. 566

Berkshire, Derby, Dorset, Durham, Leicester, Monmouth, Norfolk, Northampton, Northumberland, Nottingham, Oxford, Rutland, Shropshire, Somerset, Stafford, Suffolk, Surrey, Sussex, Warwick, Westmorland, Wiltshire, Worcester, York

Elizabeth I	1558–1603	IND 1/16821
James I	1603–1625	IND 1/16823
Charles I	1625–1649	IND 1/16825
Commonwealth	1649–1660	IND 1/16827
Charles II	1660–1674	IND 1/16829
	1669–1685	IND 1/16831
James II	1685–1688	IND 1/16833
William and Mary	1688–1694	IND 1/16835
William III	1694–1702	IND 1/16837
Anne	1702–1714	IND 1/16837
George I	1714–1727	IND 1/16839
George II	1727–1760	IND 1/16841
George III	1760–1801	IND 1/16843
	1776–1820	IND 1/16845
	1779–1820	IND 1/16847
George IV	1820–1830	IND 1/16849
William IV	1830–1837	IND 1/16851
Victoria	1837–1841	IND 1/16853

There are two manuscript indexes available at the National Archives. One indexes plaintiffs and defendants for James I–Victoria: Miscellaneous Bundles, referring to the bundles of miscellaneous material grouped at the end of each reign in E 112. The other is a calendar of Elizabethan cases in E 112 for the counties Bedford–Kent. This gives a brief description of the subject of the suit: it is arranged by name of plaintiff, with defendants' names cross-referred.

Replications and rejoinders, the responses to the bill and answer, are often found with the bills and answers in E 112 before about 1700. However, there are others in E 193 ⑦. Before 1700 the replications and rejoinders in E 193 appear to be strays from E 112. Those dated before 1660 add details on the alleged facts of the case. After that date, they are formulaic and add nothing material to our knowledge of the case. They are listed by date.

The appearance in court of the defendant, whether in person or, as was usual, by his attorney, was noted in the appearance books (E 107 ⑦). Before 1815 the books record the names of defendants both in cases on the Memoranda Rolls (E 159 Ⓕ) 'Per Rec'; and in equity disputes 'Per Bill Anglican' or, where the Attorney-General was the plaintiff, 'Per Informac'. The early books sometimes enter subsequent proceedings under the first entry. Since the defendant's name is given first, the order of the parties should be reversed to obtain the title of the suit, if this is not already known.

59.4 Evidence: depositions, surveys, affidavits and exhibits

Evidence took the form of affidavits (statements on oath); depositions (examinations of witnesses on lists of questions filed in advance by the parties); surveys (enquiries conducted by commissioners acting on instructions from the Exchequer); and exhibits.

DEPOSITIONS

When the pleadings were finished, and no more counter-replies remained to be filed, the court commissioned certain persons to examine witnesses. Both sides drew up a list of simple questions, called interrogatories, to be put to the witnesses. Each question was given a number, and was subject to vetting by the court. The answers to these questions, called depositions, provide information about the case and often about the parties involved in the dispute, which may not be included in the pleadings. The answers can be fully understood only by reference to the numbered questions of the interrogatories; and separate sets of depositions were taken to answer each party's interrogatories. The deponent's name, address, age and occupation are set out at the head of his deposition.

The depositions fall into two groups: those taken before the barons of the Exchequer at Westminster and those taken in the country by commissioners appointed by the court. In a few cases, especially those in which the Crown had an interest, the court appointed commissioners to conduct an inquiry into the facts of the case, such as, for example, the boundaries of a manor. The parties might themselves request such a survey after filing an affidavit (E 103 ⑦). The records are arranged in the following series:

1558–1841	Depositions before the Barons [in London]	Searchable online for plaintiff or defendant: no dates These are listed in three groups • alphabetically by plaintiff, excluding Crown cases • Crown cases listed alphabetically by defendant • cases in which the plaintiff is not known, plus miscellanea	E 133	①
		For 1558–1603, there is a manuscript calendar, giving date, parties and subject		Ⓕ
1558–1841	Depositions taken by Commission [in the country]	1558–1773	E 134	②, ⑤
		1773–1841	E 134	Ⓕ
1774–1841	Affidavits	In a minority of cases involving mis-understanding or malpractice, deponents could swear an affidavit in the Exchequer, sometimes giving additional details about themselves as well as about the case	E 103	⑦

The Bernau Index at the Society of Genealogists includes many deponents and defendants, although the coverage may not be complete. Deponents are also listed in a county arrangement, 1559–1695, in a typescript list, copies of which are in the National Archives and at the Society of Genealogists. The National Archives' copy is not indexed, but the Bernau Index (see 58.4) includes references to this list.

COMMISSIONS AND SURVEYS

Commissions of enquiry, c. 1558–1841, in both equity and revenue causes are in E 178 ②, ⑤. The return of executed commissions (and depositions) into the Exchequer is recorded in E 221 ⑦.

There are also Commission Books, which record the issue of commissions, writs etc., in both revenue and equity proceedings. They therefore include commissions to take the answers of defendants, or the depositions of witnesses, although the majority of entries relate to revenue proceedings on the Memoranda Rolls (E 159 Ⓔ) rather than equity disputes.

1578–84	E 165/43
1624–30	E 165/44
1725–45	E 165/45. Gives the names of the commissioners, identifying those appointed at the suggestion of the plaintiff and of the defendant
1725–1842	E 204

AFFIDAVITS

These are sworn statements made before the court or, in the country, before commissioners of oaths. Most are procedural, and many relate to the service of process, especially of the subpoena intended to secure the appearance in court of the defendant. They are usually in common form, but some add considerable circumstantial detail; others enlarge on the status of individual deponents, on the evidence or the circumstances of the case. Affidavits in equity causes and in revenue cases enrolled on the Memoranda Rolls (E 159) are filed in the same bundles. There are three series:

1558–1774	Bille: contain much other procedural matter Date list, no index	E 207	⑦
1774–1841	Date list only: the later indexes relate solely to revenue proceedings	E 103	⑦
1695–1822	Date list only, no index	E 218	⑦

EXHIBITS

Documents produced in court as supporting evidence, but not subsequently reclaimed by the parties. With the transfer of outstanding business to the Chancery in 1841 one of the Exchequer clerks became a Chancery Master. Exhibits in Exchequer cases can therefore found in the following series:

E 140	1319–1842	Exhibits. Some exhibits are described in more detail in ①, ⑤, Ⓕ OBS 1/752: this list has to be keyed with the modern list
E 219	17th–19th century	Exchequer Office, Clerks' Papers. Includes exhibits. ①, Ⓕ Card index of plaintiffs where known

C 106	13th–19th century	Chancery Masters' Exhibits, Master Richards. Most are ②, ⑤ exhibits in Chancery actions, but the series includes Exchequer cases also (although the list does not identify them as such)
C 121	c. 1600– c. 1900	Chancery Masters' Documents, Master Richards. Ⓕ Most relate to Chancery actions, but the series also includes Exchequer cases

59.5 Court decisions and other formal records

Court decisions are recorded in several overlapping series of decree and order books, and in reports by the officers of the court.

DECREES AND ORDERS

At each stage of a dispute, an order of the court was required to move on to the next stage. Orders therefore appointed days for hearing, authorised the issue of commissions and the like and, on occasion, made interim settlements. Most orders ran 'of course' and were little more than formalities; a few add substantially to our knowledge of the case. The first notice of an order was a brief entry in the Minute Books (E 161 ⑦); orders were then written out in full (Original Orders, E 128, E 131 ⑦) and registered (E 123–125, E 127 ⑦). The final judgement was called a decree. Many cases were either withdrawn or settled out of court before they reached this stage, so that the court would reach no conclusion.

The first notice of a decree was an entry in the Exchequer Chamber Minute Books (E 162 ⑦). These, with the clerks' papers (E 219 ①, Ⓕ), are the only records which give any indication as to what actually happened in court, as distinct from the decisions of the court. Like the orders, decrees were first written out in full (E 128, E 130 ⑦) and then registered (E 123–124, E 126 ⑦). Some drafts and copies of both decrees and orders are in the Clerks' papers (E 219). A full description of the interrelationship of the several series is given in the introduction to the E 123 paper list. The series overlap, and entries relating to any one case may be found in more than one series.

You could also try Martin, *Index to Repertories, Books of Orders, and Decrees, and other Records in the Court of Exchequer*, which is a place-name index for the earlier records. The references have to be keyed to modern lists.

REPORTS AND CERTIFICATES

At any stage in the dispute the written pleadings, interrogatories etc. might be referred for comment to the officers of the court. Many surviving reports represent a fairly late stage in the proceedings, dealing with funds in court or the taxation of costs. A few contain very detailed accounts of the disposition of estates. Reports and Certificates (1648–1841) are in E 194 ⑦.

The Court could order that disputed monies should be paid into court, to be held in trust pending settlement of the dispute in question. Where the quarrel was over the estate of a deceased person, the court sometimes ordered the sale or realisation of the profits of that estate. Monies paid into court were frequently invested in consolidated stock: that is, in the Bank of England. Initially administered by the King's Remembrancer or his deputy those funds were, from 1820, administered by the Accountant General of the Court. Account Books of Funds in Court (1675–1841) are in E 217 ⑦. E 217/1–6, which are indexed, are detailed accounts under the titles of the suits. Other volumes in the series are chronologically arranged, and the entries brief. They contain many entries unrelated to equity proceedings: see the introduction to the list.

Many of the Equity Petitions (1627–1841) in E 185 ⑦ were made after the filing of the decree, and relate either to the taxation of costs or the payment of funds into or out of court. Petitions earlier than 1800 are mostly for admission to sue as a poor person.

59.6 Civil litigation: Exchequer equity proceedings: bibliography

W H BRYSON, *The Equity Side of the Exchequer* (Cambridge, 1975)

D B FOWLER, *The Practice of the Court of the Exchequer* (2 vols, London, 1795). A manual produced by a working officer of the court, and much the best guide, at least to eighteenth century procedure.

H HORWITZ, *Exchequer Equity Records and Proceedings 1649–1841* (PRO, 2001)

E G JONES, *Exchequer Proceedings (Equity) Concerning Wales. Henry VIII–Elizabeth* (Cardiff, University of Wales, Board of Celtic Studies, *History and Law* series, 1939)

T I JEFFREYS JONES, *Exchequer Proceedings Concerning Wales in Tempore James I* (Cardiff, University of Wales, Board of Celtic Studies, *History and Law* series, 1955)

G LAWTON, 'Using Bernau's Index', *Family Tree Magazine*, vol VIII, 1991–2 (3 parts)

A MARTIN, *Index to Various Repertories, Books of Orders, and Decrees and other Records preserved in the Court of Exchequer* (London, 1819). Selective index to places mentioned in decrees and orders, memoranda rolls etc.

J MILHOUS and R D HUME, 'Eighteenth Century Equity Lawsuits in the Court of Exchequer as a Source for Historical Research', *Historical Research* vol. 70, no 172, pp. 231–246, 1997

H SHARP, *How to use the Bernau index* (Society of Genealogists, 1996)

T TROWLES, 'Eighteenth century Exchequer records as a genealogical source' in *Genealogists' Magazine* vol. 25, pp. 93–8

60 Civil litigation: Courts of Star Chamber, Requests, Augmentations, Wards and palatine equity

60.1   Bill procedure courts, but different law systems

All these courts can provide wonderful information about the circumstances and relationships of people's lives. They all used the English bill procedure that was very similar to that used by the equity sides of Chancery and Exchequer: for a description, see 58. However, although the palatine courts were equity courts, the other courts were not. The Court of Augmentations was set up to deal with solving problems relating to landholding and other rights caused by the dissolution of the monasteries and chantries in the 1530s and 1540s and the transfer of their land to the Crown and out to new owners. The Court of Wards handled disputes arising from the Crown's control of wardships arising from feudal tenures: most again relate to land.

60.2   The Court of Star Chamber, 1485–1641

Star Chamber (named after the room in the Palace of Westminster in which it met) was effectively the King's Council sitting as a tribunal to enforce law and order in both civil and criminal matters. There are many cases alleging the fixing of juries, or the corruption of local officials, for example. Many of these cases were bought by the Attorney General. Cases bought by the King's Almoner relate to suicides (whose goods were supposed to go to the almoner to be used for charity). Most business of the court, however, was handling private disputes about property rights described as if they were about offences against public order.

James I and Charles I used the court to suppress opposition to royal policies, and it became increasingly unpopular in Parliament (though not with litigants). Star Chamber was abolished in 1641, and most of the 'current' records from Charles I's reign have disappeared.

Star Chamber used written procedures in English. The case papers or proceedings are well listed (except for STAC 5), but not all the information for James I has been transferred onto the catalogue. However, most cases can be searched for on the catalogue by surname, even if subject or place searches are not always available.

Assigned to	Actual date range		
Henry VII	1485–1509	STAC 1	[2][V], [5], [6]
Henry VIII	c. 1450–1625	STAC 2	[2][V], [5], [6]
Edward VI	Hen VII–Eliz I	STAC 3	[2][V], [5], [6]
Mary	Hen VII–Eliz I	STAC 4	[2][V], [5], [6]
Elizabeth I	1558–1601	STAC 5	[1][V]
		STAC 7	[2][V], [5], [6]
James I	1601–1625	STAC 8	[1][V]: for more detail use [F]
Charles I	1625–1641	STAC 9	[2][V], [5], [6]

There is a published version of the list of STAC 1–STAC 4 (Henry VII– Mary), with a separate index, which is useful for picking up variant spellings of names and places. For STAC 8 (James I), there are two supplementary finding aids: a full listing giving details of the suits and the Barnes Index to this list. Barnes produced three volumes of indexes relating to parties, places, offence and counties in considerable detail, using a numeric code system which is explained in each volume. Copies are available at the National Archives. These indexes are quite difficult to get used to, but very helpful for local history, or for the history of offences, as well as for people searching for particular parties. You will need to read the introductory material, explaining the codes used, and you have to identify which index and which column to look in.

The records of Star Chamber do not survive in entirety. There are large numbers of proceedings, but no decree or order books survive. You can find out a great deal of detail about a case, but have little chance of discovering its final outcome. Barnes has argued that every Star Chamber case in which at least one defendant was convicted resulted in a fine, and that notes of these fines were recorded on the Exchequer Memoranda Rolls in E 159 [F]. Another old computer print-out at the National Archives lists these for 1596–1641. The series E 101 and E 137 also contain some accounts of fines: search these or Star Chamber and then browse to identify likely documents.

A detailed list of cases relating to Wales is in Edwards, *A Catalogue of Star Chamber Proceedings Relating to Wales*. It is also worth exploring the publications of local record societies, which cover many cases: see for example the volumes for Somerset, Sussex, Yorkshire and the North in the bibliography. For more information, try Guy's handbook to Star Chamber, and Barnes' article.

60.3 The Court of Requests, 1483–1642

The Court of Requests was an offshoot of the king's council, intended to provide easy access by poor men and women to royal justice and equity. It was established in 1483, when the Chancery official responsible for sorting petitions from the poor became clerk of the council of requests. A cheap and simple procedure attracted many suitors (not all of them poor, but particularly including women). The Court used procedures like those of the equity courts, so the main series of records are in English. The records of the court cease in 1642. Although the court was never formally abolished, much of its caseload eventually passed to local small claims courts. Types of case heard included title to property, annuities, matters of villeinage, watercourses, highways, wilful escape, forgery, perjury, forfeitures to the king by recognisance and dower, jointure and marriage contracts.

Requests proceedings in REQ 2 are only just being entered onto the catalogue, currently at the rate of about five bundles a year. Otherwise you will need to use these supplementary finding aids at the National Archives (or at the Society of Genealogists in the case of the Bernau Index):

Monarch	Date range	Bundles in REQ 2	Finding aids
Henry VII–Henry VIII	1485–1547	1–13	Beginning to be ☑☑, ☑ and ☑ Listed in *List and Index, XXI, Proceedings in the Court of Requests* (gives parties, subject and place): 1–40 also listed with a little more detail, and some dates, in the lists marked 'Hunt's series' Indexed in *List and Index Supplementary, VII, vol. 1* Included in the Bernau Index
Edward VI	1547–1553	14–19	As above
Mary I	1553–1558	20–25	As above
Elizabeth I	1558–1603	26–136	As above
		137–156	Listed in the manuscript 'Atkin's Calendar', and indexed in *List and Index Supplementary, VII, vol. 1*
		157–294	Listed in a further unnamed manuscript list, and indexed by person, subject and location in: bundles 157–203 in *List and Index Supplementary, VII, vol. 2*; bundles 204–294 in *List and Index Supplementary, VII, vol. 3*
		369–386	None

Monarch	Date range	Bundles in REQ 2	Finding aids
James I	1603–1625	295–311	Listed in a further unnamed manuscript list, and indexed by person, subject and location in *List and Index Supplementary, VII, vol. 4.*
		387–424	Bundles 387–409 are listed in a further unnamed manuscript list, indexed by person, subject and location in *List and Index Supplementary, VII, vol. 4.*
		425–485	None
Charles I	1625–1649	486–806	None
	various dates	807–829	None

Unlike the Star Chamber, the judicial and administrative records (in English and Latin) of the Court of Requests have survived fairly well: most are in REQ 1 ⑦, but there may be some unsuspected material in REQ 2/369–386. REQ 1 includes:

		REQ 1/	
Order and decree books	Hen VII–Chas I	1–38, 209	orders, decrees, final judgements and, before 1520, appearances
Order books	Eliz I–Chas I	39–103	draft orders, decrees and memoranda
Appearance books	Hen VIII–Chas I	104–117	records of appearance by defendants, usually by attorney
Contemporary indexes to affidavits	1637–1641	118, 150	incomplete
Affidavit books	1591–1641	119–149	signed affidavits (by servers) that process, especially writs of summons, had been served
Note books	1594–1642	151–170	outline records of the progress of suits
Process books	1567–1642	171–197	recording the issue of writs of privy seal, attachments for arrest, appointment of commissions, injunctions, and orders for appearances
Witness books	Eliz I–Chas I	198–206	
Register of replications	1632–1636	207	
Commission book	1603–1619	208	recording return dates of depositions by commission

For a general overview, see Leadam, *Select Cases in the Court of Requests.*

60.4 The Court of Augmentations, 1536–1554

The Court of Augmentations was founded in 1536 to deal with the transfer of land to the Crown when the monasteries were dissolved. Most historians consider it to be an administrative court, and it was certainly involved in a huge amount of administration. However, it was also a court of law, using English bill procedure, to settle disputes relating to the land and other rights claimed by monastic tenants, pensioners, founding families, local communities, debtors and creditors, charities and so on.

Records of the legal proceedings are scattered among several series.

	Date	Series	Finding aid	Indexes
Pleadings (and some depositions)	1536–1554	E 321 E 315/19–23, 165 and 516–522	MS list filed as [refers to E 321 vol. 1], [refers to E 321 vol. 2], [refers to E 315 vol. 1] Gives plaintiff, defendant, subject and county	Place index to all three lists, filed as [refers to E 315 vol. 2]
Depositions	1536–1554	E 315/108–134	MS list filed as [refers to E 315 vol. 1] Gives plaintiff, defendant, subject and county	
Decrees and orders	1536–1553	E 315/91–105	MS list filed as [refers to E 315 vol. 5] [refers to E 315 vol. 7]	Indexes at [refers to E 315 vol. 6] [refers to E 315 vol. 8]

The court of Augmentations was absorbed into the Exchequer in 1554. There are many later suits relating to the lands of the monasteries and charities in the Exchequer equity proceedings (see 59).

60.5 The Court of Wards, 1540–1646

As well as running the money-raising side of collecting feudal dues on the death of major holders of Crown lands, the Court of Wards handled the subsequent disputes about widows' remarriage, sales of wardships of minors, idiots and lunatics and fines for leases of wards' lands. (See 49 for more on the Court of Wards.)

Pleadings	1547–1646	WARD 13	7
Supplementary Pleadings	1540–1646	WARD 15	7
Decrees, Orders, Affidavits, etc.	1540–1646	WARD 1	7
Deeds and Evidences	c. 1200–Charles I	WARD 2	F
Depositions	1540–1646	WARD 3	7
Miscellaneous Books	1540–1826	WARD 9	7
Miscellaneous Documents	Henry II–c. 1650	WARD 10	7
Miscellaneous Records in Bundles	1540–1646	WARD 11	7

Unfortunately, many of the court's records are unfit to be produced: after the court was abolished its records were thrown into in a fish yard near Westminster Hall. They survive, and await attention. The deeds in WARD 2 are a very large collection – and almost inaccessible because of the extraordinary difficulty of their (incomplete) finding aid.

60.6 The Palatinate of Chester: Exchequer equity court

The local equity jurisdiction of the Chester equity court, known as the Exchequer, lasted from the fifteenth century to 1830. If properly listed it would be a wonderful resource for Cheshire family history. There are detailed finding aids for 1509–1558 and for 1760–1820 at the National Archives.

Pleadings in cases mostly relating to land	c. 1509–1830	CHES 15	F
Pleadings in cases mostly relating to debts and personal property	1559–1762	CHES 16	7
Depositions	1558–1603	CHES 12	7
Affidavits, exhibits and other miscellaneous papers	c. 1200–1673; 1501–1830	CHES 11; CHES 9	2 V
Decrees and orders	1559–1790	CHES 13	7
Entry books of decrees and orders	1562–1830	CHES 14	7

A printed calendar to CHES 15/1, covering pleadings from the reigns of Henry VIII, Edward VI and Philip and Mary, is contained in the *Deputy Keeper's Twenty-fifth Report* (1864), pp. 23–31. The suit files are listed from 1 to 196 in alphabetical order by first plaintiffs' names. The names of the first defendants are then listed with a note of the types of documents surviving in each file, e.g., Bill, Answer, Depositions, etc., followed by a brief indication of the subject of the dispute as well as the date where known. There is also an alphabetical index to all the parties and places named in the pleadings. The numbers in the calendar correspond to the numbered labels on the individual suit files in CHES 15/1.

A manuscript index exists for the pleadings and associated documents in CHES 15/156–178, covering 1760–1820. This is IND 1/17578. The pleadings across the reign have been arranged in alphabetical order by the name of the first plaintiff and numbered from 1 to 4941. The index lists these suits in alpha-numerical order, giving the name of the first defendant to each suit, the types of surviving documents and the date by calendar year and regnal year.

60.7 The Palatinate of Durham: Chancery equity court

The local equity jurisdiction of the Chancery of Durham similarly used equity procedure. These records would repay investigation by local historians.

Pleadings	1576–1840	DURH 2	F IND 1/8849
Interrogatories and depositions	1557–1804	DURH 7	2
Affidavits, exhibits and other miscellaneous papers	1657–1812	DURH 1	7
Decrees and orders	1633–1958	DURH 4	7
Decrees and orders: drafts	1613–1778	DURH 5	7
	1749–1829	DURH 6	7

60.8 The Palatinate of Lancaster: Chancery equity court

Investigation of the local equity jurisdiction of the Chancery of the County Palatine of Lancaster is being started by a group of family and local historians of Lancashire, working with Sean Cunningham of the National Archives. They have been astounded at the wealth of material they are uncovering. Sample work indicates a very valuable collection linked to the Liverpool maritime trade (including slavery), the development of Lancashire cloth industries, land use, social history and mining. The project as envisaged will cover PL 6, PL 7 and PL 10: look out for catalogue improvements that will make these series fully searchable by name, place and subject. Descriptions up to 1734 should be available fairly soon, as these are being created from existing indexes.

Pleadings: bills	1485–1853	PL 6	F 7
Pleadings: answers	1474–1858	PL 7	F 7
Pleadings: replications	1601–1856	PL 8	7
Depositions	1581–1854	PL 10	F 7
Affidavits, exhibits and other miscellaneous papers	1610–1678; 1793–1836; 1795–1860	PL 9; PL 12	7
Reports and certificates	1813–1849	PL 30	7
Decrees and orders: entry books	1524–1848	PL 11	7

There are few cases from the fifteenth and sixteenth centuries: records survive in number from about 1606 onwards. For background information, see Cunningham, 'Untold Riches'.

60.9 The Duchy of Lancaster: Duchy Chamber equity court

The equity court of the Duchy of Lancaster, known as the Duchy Chamber, started in the fourteenth century and still exists in theory. The Duchy of Lancaster is not the same as the county of Lancaster or Lancashire: the Duchy holds lands in many other parts of the country, and its tenants were able to use its court centred on the Savoy in London. Pleadings in DL 1 and DL 3 from 1485–1603 are calendared in three indexed volumes known as *Ducatus Lancastriae*. Unpublished indexes are also available for the pleadings from the reign of James I to 1832 in IND 1/16918–16922 and ZBOX 1/59. For the decrees in DL 5, try IND 1/16923–16935 and 17616.

Pleadings	1485–1835	DL 1	F
	1558–1818	DL 3	F
	1502–1853	DL 49	1
Draft injunctions	1614–1794	DL 8	7
Depositions	1485–1818	DL 3	F
		DL 4	F
Depositions (sealed)	1695–1739	DL 48	1
Affidavits, exhibits and other miscellaneous papers	1502–1853; 1560–1857	DL 49; DL 9	1 7
Decrees and orders: entry books	1472–1872	DL 5	F
Decrees and orders: drafts	1509–1810	DL 6	F

60.10 Civil litigation: Courts of Star Chamber, Requests, Augmentations, Wards and palatine equity: bibliography

Abstracts of Star Chamber proceedings relating to the county of Sussex: Henry VII to Philip and Mary (Sussex Record Society, 1913)

J H BAKER, *An Introduction to English Legal History* (London, 3rd edn, 1990)

T G BARNES, 'The archives and archival problems of the Elizabethan and early Stuart Star Chamber', *Journal of the Society of Archivists*, II (1963)

C G BAYNE and W H DUNHAM, *Select cases in the council of Henry VII* (Selden Society, 1958)

G BRADFORD, *[Somerset] Proceedings in the Court of the Star Chamber in the reigns of Henry VII and Henry VIII* (Somerset Record Society; v. 27, 1911)

S CUNNINGHAM, 'Untold Riches: how the North-West was run' [Palatinate of Lancaster], *Ancestors* 21, 2004

Ducatus Lancastriae (Record Commission, 1823–1834)

I EDWARDS, *A Catalogue of Star Chamber Proceedings Relating to Wales* (Cardiff, University of Wales, Board of Celtic Studies, *History and Law* series, 1929)

K EMSLEY and C M FRASER, *The courts of the County Palatine of Durham* (Durham County Local History Society, 1984)

J A GUY, *The court of Star Chamber and its records to the reign of Elizabeth I* (HMSO, 1984)

R W HOYLE, *A handlist of Star Chamber pleadings before 1558 for Northern England* (List and Index Society vol. 299, 2003)

G LAWTON, 'Using Bernau's Index', *Family Tree Magazine*, vol. VIII, 1991–2 (3 parts)

I S LEADAM, *Select cases in the Court of Requests* (Selden Society, 1898)

I S LEADAM, *Select cases … in Star Chamber* (Selden Society, 1903)

E A LEWIS and J CONWAY DAVIES, *Records of the Court of Augmentations relating to Wales and Monmouthshire* (Cardiff, University of Wales, Board of Celtic Studies, *History and Law* series, 1954)

List of proceedings in the Court of Star Chamber preserved in the Public Record Office (Public Record Office, Lists and Indexes vol. XIII, 1901 and Lists and Indexes Supplementary vol. IV, 1966)

H SHARP, *How to use the Bernau index* (Society of Genealogists, 1996)

R SOMERVILLE, 'The palatinate courts in Lancaster', *Law and law makers in British History, papers presented to the Edinburgh Legal History Conference 1979* (Royal Historical Society Studies in History Series, XXII)

R STEWART-BROWN, *Lancashire and Cheshire cases in the Court of Star Chamber* (Lancashire and Cheshire Record Society, 1916)

Yorkshire Star Chamber proceedings (Yorkshire Record Society, 4 vols, 1909–1927)

61 Civil litigation: Admiralty, Delegates and Privy Council appeals

61.1 High Court of Admiralty

This court was a civil law court, generally applying Roman or 'civil' international law. Civil disputes (concerning commercial disputes, wages, salvage and damage to ships or cargoes) were normally heard in the High Court of Admiralty (which also had a common law criminal jurisdiction: see 48.11). The civil business of the High Court of Admiralty was conducted from about 1660 in a separate Instance Court. The records of the Instance jurisdiction are extensive, but like other legal records they can be difficult to use. Although part of the Supreme Court since 1875, later records of the High Court of Admiralty are still found in HCA, not J.

The records most likely to interest family and social historians are:

- the examinations and answers in HCA 13 ⑤ (1531–1768): in English and contain detailed accounts of evidence tendered by witnesses including the witness's name, address, occupation and age; there is an index of examinations in IND 1/10322;
- the instance papers in HCA 15–HCA 18 (1586–1874) ⑦, ⑤, which contain a variety of papers including affidavits, allegations, answers, decrees, petitions and exhibits.

If you are interested in a particular ship, try the 1772–1946 indexes to ships' names in HCA 56.

61.2 High Court of Delegates

The High Court of Delegates was established during the reign of Henry VIII to hear appeals from the ecclesiastical courts, which, before the break with Rome, would have been made to the Pope: as such it used canon law. It also had appellate jurisdiction from the instance court of the High Court of Admiralty, the Court of Chivalry and the courts of the chancellors of Oxford and Cambridge Universities. Every appeal necessitated the appointment of a special commission under the great seal directed to judges delegate appointed by the lord chancellor. Proceedings are in DEL 1 ① and DEL 2 ①. The Court was abolished in 1833.

61.3 The Judicial Committee of the Privy Council

The Privy Council devolved its judicial authority to a committee in 1833. It took over the old High Court of Delegates jurisdiction in matrimonial, ecclesiastical and maritime appeals until 1858 (1879 for maritime cases). Proceedings are in PCAP 1 ②, ⑤.

The National Archives does not hold records of the Judicial Committee's criminal or modern civil appeal jurisdiction as the court of appeal for colonial or ex-colonial jurisdictions. These are still kept by the Judicial Committee, and an appointment is needed to see them (address in 62). If you are following a Privy Council appeal, it would be worth checking for related material in the correspondence from the relevant colony (see 17.4).

However, the records of the Treasury Solicitor do contain related records about appeals brought before both the Privy Council and the Judicial Committee: for example, a search in TS using Council as a search term brought up:

- c. 1756 Old John UNCAS and greater part of tribe of Moheagan Indians, by Samuel MASON, their guardian v Governor and Company and His Majesty's English colony of Connecticut in New England, America and George RICHARDS and several other persons, intruders on lands in question: Privy Council TS 11/1006;
- 1820–1821 Gerald Shaw and others v. A–G of St. Vincent on behalf of Jenny and children. Appeal from Chancery of St. Vincent establishing devise and bequest to a negro woman, and declaration of freedom for her and her children. Court: Privy Council TS 11/130;
- 1831 Appeal of Marie Saladin (a slave) to HM in Council against a judgment of the Court of Appeal in Mauritius TS 25/17;
- 1834–1836 Janokee Doss v. The King at the prosecution of Bindabun Doss. Appeal from Supreme Court of Bengal sentencing appellant and four others for conspiring to procure imprisonment of Bindabun Doss. Court: Privy Council TS 11/130.

I never cease to be amazed at what can be found at the National Archives. I hope you too find something amazing.

61.4 Civil litigation: Admiralty, Delegates and Privy Council appeals bibliography

J H BAKER, An Introduction to English Legal History (London, 3rd edn, 1990)

G I O DUNCAN, The High Court of Delegates (Cambridge, 1971)

P A HOWELL, The Judicial Committee of the Privy Council, 1833–1876, its origins, structure, and development (Cambridge, 1979)

R G MARSDEN, *Select pleas in the Court of Admiralty* (Selden Society, 1897)

M J PRICHARD and D E C YALE, *Hale and Fleetwood on Admiralty Jurisdiction* (Selden Society, 1992)

E S ROSCOE, *Reports of prize cases determined in the High Court of Admiralty: before the Lords Commissioners of Appeals in Prize Causes and before the Judicial Committee of the Privy Council from 1745 to 1859* (London, 1905)

62 Useful addresses

ALDERNEY, CLERK OF THE COURT, Queen Elizabeth II St, Alderney GY9 3AA, Channel Islands • 01481 822817

ARMY *see* Ministry of Defence

ARMY MEDICAL SERVICES MUSEUM, Keogh Barracks, Ash Vale, Aldershot GU12 5RQ • 01252 340212 • www.army.mod.uk/medical/ams_museum

BEDFORDSHIRE AND LUTON ARCHIVES, County Hall, Cauldwell Street, Bedford MK42 9AP • 01234 228833/22 • archive@bedscc.gov.uk • www.bedfordshire.gov.uk/archive

BERKSHIRE RECORD OFFICE, 9 Coley Avenue, Reading, RG1 6AF • 0118 901 5132 • ARCH@Reading.gov.uk • www.berkshirerecordoffice.org.uk

BOARD OF DEPUTIES OF BRITISH JEWS, 6 Bloomsbury Square, London, WC1A 2LP • 020 7543 5400 • info@bod.org.uk • www.bod.org.uk

BODLEIAN LIBRARY, Broad Street, Oxford OX1 3BG • 01865 277158 • www.bodley.ox.ac.uk

BORTHWICK INSTITUTE FOR ARCHIVES, University of York, Heslington, York YO10 5DD • 01904 321166 • www.york.ac.uk/borthwick

BRISTOL RECORD OFFICE, 'B' Bond Warehouse, Smeaton Road, Bristol BS1 6XN • 0117 922 4224 • bro@bristol-city.gov.uk • www.bristol-city.gov.uk/recordoffice

BRITISH ASSOCIATION FOR CEMETERIES IN SOUTH ASIA (Secretary), 76½ Chartfield Ave., London SW15 6HQ • www.bacsa.org.uk

BRITISH EMPIRE AND COMMONWEALTH MUSEUM, Clock Tower Yard, Temple Meads, Bristol BS1 6QH • 0117 9254980 • collections2@empiremuseum.co.uk • www.empiremuseum.co.uk

BRITISH IN INDIA MUSEUM, 1 Newtown St, Colne, Lancashire BB8 0JJ • 01282 613129

BRITISH LIBRARY, 96 Euston Rd, London NW1 2DB • 0870 444 1500 • www.bl.uk/

BRITISH LIBRARY, Newspaper Library, Colindale Ave., London NW9 5HE • 020 7412 7353 • www.bl.uk/collections/newspapers.html

BRITISH LIBRARY, Oriental and India Office Collections, British Library, 96 Euston Rd, London NW1 2DP • 020 7412 7873 • www.bl.uk/collections/orientalandindian.html

BRITISH POSTAL MUSEUM AND ARCHIVE, Freeling House, Phoenix Place, London WC1X 0DL • 020 7239 2570 • info@postalheritage.org.uk • www.postalheritage.org.uk

BRITISH RED CROSS MUSEUM AND ARCHIVES, 44 Moorfields, London EC2Y 9AL • 020 7877 7058 • enquiry@redcross.org.uk • www.redcross.org.uk

CAMBRIDGE UNIVERSITY LIBRARY, Department of Manuscripts and University Archives, West Road, Cambridge CB3 9DR • 01223 333000 • mss@lib.cam.ac.uk • www.lib.cam.ac.uk/MSS

CAMBRIDGESHIRE COUNTY RECORD OFFICE, Shire Hall, Cambridge CB3 0AP • 01223 717281 • county.records.cambridge@cambridgeshire.gov.uk • www.cambridgeshire.gov.uk/archives

CANTERBURY CATHEDRAL ARCHIVES, The Precincts, Canterbury CT1 2EH • 01227 865330 • archives@canterbury-cathedral.org • www.canterbury-cathedral.org/archives.html

CATHOLIC CENTRAL LIBRARY, St Michael's Abbey, Farnborough Road, Farnborough, Hants GU14 7NQ • 0207 732 8379 • librarian@catholic-library.org.uk • www.catholic-library.org.uk/

CENTRE FOR BUCKINGHAMSHIRE STUDIES, County Hall, Walton Street, Aylesbury HP20 1UU • 01296 382587 • archives@buckscc.gov.uk • www.buckscc.gov.uk/archives

CENTRE FOR KENTISH STUDIES, County Hall, Maidstone ME14 1XQ
• 01622 694363 • archives@kent.gov.uk
• www.kent.gov.uk/e&l/artslib/archives/home.html

CHAMBERS B, 39 Chatterton, Letchworth Garden City, England SG6 2JY
• bjchambers@genfair.com • www.genfair.com/shop/pages/bjc

CHANNEL ISLANDS FAMILY HISTORY SOCIETY, PO Box 507, St Helier, Jersey
JE4 5TN, Channel Islands • www.channelislandshistory.com

CHESHIRE AND CHESTER ARCHIVES, Duke Street, Chester CH1 1RL
• 01244 602574 • recordoffice@cheshire.gov.uk
• www.cheshire.gov.uk/recoff/home.htm

CHILD MIGRANTS TRUST, 28a Musters Road, West Bridgford, Nottingham
NG2 7PL • 0115 982 2811

CHURCH OF ENGLAND RECORD CENTRE, 15 Galleywell Road, London SE16 3PB
• 020 7898 1030 • archivist@c-of-e.org.uk
• www.lambethpalacelibrary.org/holdings/CERC.html

CHURCH OF JESUS CHRIST OF LATTER DAY SAINTS, Genealogical Society of Utah,
50 East North Temple, Salt Lake City, Utah 84150, USA

CHURCH OF JESUS CHRIST OF LATTER DAY SAINTS, Genealogical Society of Utah,
British Isles Family History Service Centre, 185 Penns Lane, Sutton Coldfield,
West Midlands B76 8JU • 08700 102 051

CHURCH OF JESUS CHRIST OF LATTER DAY SAINTS, Hyde Park Family History
Centre, Hyde Park Chapel, 64–68 Exhibition Rd, London SW7 2PA
• 020 7589 8561

CITY OF LONDON POLICE RECORDS OFFICE, 26 Old Jewry, London EC2R 8OJ.
Correspondence Address 37 Wood Street, London EC2P 2NQ

CITY OF WESTMINSTER ARCHIVES CENTRE, 10 St Ann's Street, London SW1P 2DE
• 020 7641 5180 • archives@westminster.gov.uk
• www.westminster.gov.uk/archives/index.cfm

COLLEGE OF ARMS, Queen Victoria Street, London EC4V 4BT • 020 7248 2762
• www.college-of-arms.gov.uk

COMMONWEALTH WAR GRAVES COMMISSION, Information Office, 2 Marlow Rd,
Maidenhead, Berks SL6 7DX • 01628 634221 • www.cwgc.org

COMPANIES REGISTRATION OFFICE (Isle of Man), Finch Rd, Douglas, Isle of Man

COMPANIES REGISTRATION OFFICE (Northern Ireland), IDB House,
64 Chichester St, Belfast BT1 4JX • www.companieshouse.gov.uk

COMPANIES REGISTRATION OFFICE (Scotland), 102 George St, Edinburgh EH2 3DJ
• www.companieshouse.gov.uk

COMPANIES REGISTRATION OFFICE, Crown Way, Maindy, Cardiff CF4 3UZ
• 0870 3333 636 • www.companieshouse.gov.uk

COMPANIES REGISTRATION OFFICE, London Information Centre, 21 Bloomsbury
Street, London WC1B 3XD • 0870 3333 636 • www.companieshouse.gov.uk

CORNWALL RECORD OFFICE, Old County Hall, Truro, Cornwall
TR1 3AY • 01872 323127 • CRO@cornwall.gov.uk
• www.cornwall.gov.uk/cro/default.htm

CORPORATION OF LONDON RECORD OFFICE, 40 Northampton Rd, London
EC1R 0HB • 020 7332 1251
• www.cityoflondon.gov.uk/Corporation/leisure_heritage/

COURT FUNDS DIVISION, 22 Kingsway, London WC2B 6LE • 020 7947 7648

CUMBRIA RECORD OFFICE, The Castle, Carlisle CA3 8UR • 01228 607285
• carlisle.record.office@cumbriacc.gov.uk • www.cumbria.gov.uk/archives

DERBYSHIRE RECORD OFFICE, New Street, Matlock, Derbyshire DE4 3AG
• 01629 580000 • record.office@derbyshire.gov.uk
• www.derbyshire.gov.uk/recordoffice/

DEVON RECORD OFFICE, Great Moor House, Bittern Road, Sowton, Exeter
EX2 7NL • 01392 384253 • devrec@devon.gov.uk
• www.devon.gov.uk/record_office.htm

DORSET HISTORY CENTRE, Bridport Road, Dorchester, Dorset DT1 1RP
• 01305 250550 • archives@dorsetcc.gov.uk • www.dorsetcc.gov.uk/archives

DR WILLIAMS'S LIBRARY, 14 Gordon Square, London, WC1H 0AR • 020 7387 3727
• enquiries@DWLib.co.uk • www.dwlib.co.uk/dwlib

DURHAM UNIVERSITY LIBRARY, Archives and Special Collections, Palace Green,

Durham DH1 3RN • 0191 334 2972 • PG.Library@durham.ac.uk
• www.dur.ac.uk/library/asc

EAST RIDING OF YORKSHIRE ARCHIVES SERVICE, The Chapel, Lord Roberts
Road, Beverley, Yorkshire • 01482 392790 • archives.service@eastriding.gov.uk
• www.eastriding.gov.uk/libraries/archives/archives.html

EAST SUSSEX RECORD OFFICE, The Maltings, Castle Precincts, Lewes, Sussex
BN7 1YT • 01273 482349 • archives@eastsussex.gov.uk
• www.eastsussex.gov.uk/useourarchives

ESSEX RECORD OFFICE, Wharf Road, Chelmsford, Essex CM2 6YT • 01245 244644
• ero.enquiry@essexcc.gov.uk • www.essexcc.gov.uk/ero

EXON, the Queen's Bodyguard of the Yeomen of the Guard, St James's Palace,
London SW1A 1JR

FAMILY RECORDS CENTRE, 1 Myddelton St, London EC1R 1UW • 020 8392 5300

FEDERATION OF FAMILY HISTORY SOCIETIES, Administrator, PO Box 2425,
Coventry CV5 6YX • admin@ffhs.org.uk • www.ffhs.org.uk

FLEET AIR ARM MUSEUM, Records & Research Centre, Box D6, RNAS Yeovilton,
near Ilchester, Somerset, BA22 8HT • 01935 840565 • www.fleetairarm.com

FOREIGN AND COMMONWEALTH OFFICE, Records and Historical Service Unit,
Hanslope Park, Hanslope, Milton Keynes MK19 7BH (medal entitlement for
Palestine Police)

FRIENDS HOUSE LIBRARY, Euston Rd, London NW1 2BJ • 020 7663 1135

FRIENDS OF THE NATIONAL ARCHIVES, The National Archives, Kew, Richmond,
Surrey TW9 4DU • 020 8876 3444 ext. 2226

GENEALOGICAL SOCIETY OF SOUTH AFRICA, Suite 143, Postnet X2600, Houghton,
2041 South Africa • www.rootsweb.com/~zafgssa/

GENEALOGICAL SOCIETY OF UTAH see Church of Jesus Christ of Latter
Day Saints

GENERAL REGISTER OFFICE (NORTHERN IRELAND), Oxford House,
49–55 Chichester St, Belfast BT1 4HL • 028 9025 2000 • www.groni.gov.uk

GENERAL REGISTER OFFICE (SCOTLAND), New Register House, Edinburgh
EH1 3YT • 0131 334 0380 • www.scotlandspeople.gov.uk

GENERAL REGISTER OFFICE OF ENGLAND AND WALES
• Adoptions Section, Trafalgar Rd, Southport PR8 2HH • 0151 471 4830
• Certificate enquiries, PO Box 2, Southport, Merseyside PR8 2JD
• 0845 603 7788, (+44 (0)1704 569 824 from overseas)
• Overseas Section, The General Register Office, Smedley Hydro,
Trafalgar Road, Birkdale, Southport, Merseyside PR8 2HH • 0151 471 4801
• www.gro.gov.uk

GENERAL REGISTER OFFICE OF IRELAND, 8–11 Lombard St, Dublin 2, Republic of
Ireland • 003531 6354000 • www.groireland.ie

GLOUCESTERSHIRE RECORD OFFICE, Clarence Row off Alvin Street, Gloucester
GL1 3DW • 01452 425295 • records@gloucestershire.gov.uk
• www.gloucestershire.gov.uk/archives

GRAY'S INN LIBRARY, 5 South Square, Gray's Inn, London WC1R 5EU
• www.graysinn.org.uk

GUERNSEY, THE GREFFE (HM Greffier), Royal Court House, St Peter Port,
Guernsey, Channel Islands • 01481 725277

GUILD OF ONE NAME STUDIES, Box G, c/o 14 Charterhouse Buildings,
Goswell Rd, London EC1M 7BA • www.one-name.org

GUILDHALL LIBRARY, Aldermanbury, London EC2P 2EJ • 020 7332 1868,
Manuscripts: 020 7332 1863 • www.cityoflondon.gov.uk

HAMPSHIRE RECORD OFFICE, Sussex Street, Winchester, Hampshire SO23 8TH
• 01962 846154 • enquiries.archives@hants.gov.uk
• www.hants.gov.uk/record-office/index.html

HARTLEY LIBRARY, Special Collections, University of Southampton, Highfield,
Southampton SO17 1BJ • 023 8059 2721 • archives@soton.ac.uk
• www.archives.lib.soton.ac.uk/

HEREFORDSHIRE RECORD OFFICE, Harold Street, Hereford HR1 2QX
• 01432 260750 • archives@herefordshire.gov.uk
• www.herefordshire.gov.uk/archives

HERTFORDSHIRE ARCHIVES AND LOCAL STUDIES, County Hall, Hertford

SG13 8EJ • 01438 737333 • hertsdirect@hertscc.gov.uk
• www.hertsdirect.org/hals
HMS *Belfast*, Symons Wharf, Vine Lane, Tooley St, London SE1 2JH
• http://hmsbelfast.iwm.org.uk/
HMS *Victory*, HM Naval Base, Portsmouth, Hampshire PO1 3PZ
• www.hms-victory.com
HOME OFFICE, Departmental Records Officer, 4th Floor, Seacole Building, Home
Office, 2 Marsham Street, London SW1P 4DF
HOUSE OF LORDS RECORD OFFICE, House of Lords, London SW1A 0PW
• 020 7219 3074 • www.parliament.uk
HOUSEHOLD CAVALRY MUSEUM, Combermere Barracks, Windsor, Berkshire
SL4 3DN (Closed until 2007: no research possible until then)
• www.householdcavalry.gvon.com/museum.htm
HUGUENOT LIBRARY, University College London, Gower St, London WC1E 6BT
• 020 7697 7094 • www.ucl.ac.uk/Library/huguenot.shtml
HUNTINGDON RECORD OFFICE (Cambridgeshire County Record Office,
Huntingdon), Grammar School Walk, Huntingdon PE29 3LF • 01480 375842
• county.records.hunts@cambridgeshire.gov.uk
• www.cambridgeshire.gov.uk/archives
HYDE PARK FAMILY HISTORY CENTRE, Hyde Park Chapel, 64–68 Exhibition Rd,
London SW7 2PA • 020 7589 8561
IMMIGRATION AND NATIONALITY DEPARTMENT, Nationality Office, B4 Division,
India Buildings, Water Street, Liverpool L2 0QN • 0845 010 5200
• www.ind.homeoffice.gov.uk
IMPERIAL WAR MUSEUM, Duxford, Cambridgeshire CB2 4QR • www.iwm.org.uk
IMPERIAL WAR MUSEUM, Department of Documents, Lambeth Rd, London
SE1 6HZ • 020 7416 5221 • www.iwm.org.uk
INDIA OFFICE *see* British Library, Oriental and India Office Collections
INNER TEMPLE LIBRARY, Inner Temple, London EC4Y 7DA
• www.innertemplelibrary.org.uk
INTERNATIONAL COUNCIL OF THE RED CROSS, Archives Division, 19, Avenue de
la Paix, CH–1202 Geneva • www.icrc.org
ISLE OF MAN GENERAL REGISTRY, Deemsters Walk, Buck's Rd, Douglas, Isle of
Man IM1 3AR • 01624 687039 (Births, Marriages and Deaths) or 01624 685250
(Probate) • www.gov.im/registries/
JERSEY ARCHIVE, Jersey Heritage Trust, Clarence Road, St Helier Jersey JE2 4JY,
Channel Islands • 01534 833333 • archives@jerseyheritagetrust.org
• www.jerseyheritagetrust.org
JERSEY, JUDICIAL GREFFE, Morier House, Halkett Place, St Helier, Jersey JE1 1DD,
Channel Islands • 01534 502300 • jgreffe@super.net.uk • www.jersey.gov.uk/
JEWISH GENEALOGICAL SOCIETY OF GREAT BRITAIN, PO Box 13288, London
N3 3WD • www.jgsgb.org.uk/
JEWISH MUSEUM, 80 East End Rd, London N3 2SY; and Raymond Burton House,
129–131, Albert St, London NW1 7NB • 020 7284 1997
• www.jewishmuseum.org.uk/
JEWISH REFUGEES COMMITTEE, Jubilee House, Merrion Avenue, Stanmore,
Middlesex HA7 4RL • 020 8385 3070 • enquiries@ajr.org.uk • www.ajr.org.uk
JUDICIAL COMMITTEE OF THE PRIVY COUNCIL, Privy Council Office, Downing
Street, London SW1A 2AJ • 020 7276 0483
• judicial.committee@pco.x.gsi.gov.uk • www.privy-council.org.uk
LAMBETH PALACE LIBRARY, London SE1 7JU • 020 7898 1400
• www.lambethpalacelibrary.org
LANCASHIRE RECORD OFFICE, Bow Lane, Preston PR1 2RE • 01772 533039
• record.office@ed.lancscc.gov.uk • www.archives.lancashire.gov.uk
LAND REGISTRY, Lincoln's Inn Fields, London WC2A 3PH • 020 7917 8888
• www.landreg.gov.uk
LAW SOCIETY ARCHIVES, Ipsley Court, Berrington Close, Redditch,
Worcestershire, B98 0TD • 020 7242 1222
LEICESTERSHIRE, LEICESTER AND RUTLAND RECORD OFFICE, Long Street,
Wigston Magna, Leicester LE18 2AH • 0116 257 1080
• recordoffice@leics.gov.uk • www.leics.gov.uk

LICHFIELD RECORD OFFICE, Lichfield Library, The Friary, Lichfield, Staffordshire WS13 6QG • 01543 510720 • lichfield.record.office@staffordshire.gov.uk • www.staffordshire.gov.uk/archives/

LINCOLN'S INN LIBRARY, Lincoln's Inn, London WC2A 3TN • www.lincolnsinn.org.uk

LINCOLNSHIRE ARCHIVES, St Rumbold Street, Lincoln LN2 5AB • 01522 525158 • lincolnshire_archive@lincolnshire.gov.uk • www.lincolnshire.gov.uk

LIVERPOOL UNIVERSITY, Sydney Jones Library, Chatham Street, Liverpool L7 7AY • 0151 794 2696 • http://sca.lib.liv.ac.uk/collections

LONDON METROPOLITAN ARCHIVES, 40 Northampton Rd, London EC1R 0HB • 020 7332 3820 • www.cityoflondon.gov.uk/archives/lma/

MANX MUSEUM AND NATIONAL HERITAGE LIBRARY, Douglas, Isle of Man, IM1 3LY • 01624 648000, enquiries@mnh.gov.im • www.gov.im/mnh/

MARITIME HISTORY ARCHIVE, Memorial University of Newfoundland, St John's Newfoundland, Canada A1C 5S7 • 001 709 737 8428 • www.mun.ca/mha

MERSEYSIDE MARITIME MUSEUM NMGM, Albert Dock, Liverpool L3 4AQ • 0151 478 4418 • www.liverpoolmuseums.org.uk/maritime/

METROPOLITAN POLICE ARCHIVES, New Scotland Yard, Victoria St, London SW1 0BG • www.met.police.uk

METROPOLITAN POLICE MUSEUM, c/o Room 1334, New Scotland Yard, Victoria St, London SW1 0BG

MIDDLE TEMPLE LIBRARY, Middle Temple Lane, London EC4Y 98T • www.middletemple.org.uk

MINISTRY OF DEFENCE: ARMY
For officers discharged since 1922, and for soldiers and NCOs discharged since 1921 but before 1996: Army Personnel Centre, Historic Disclosures, Mailpoint 400, Kentigern House, 65 Brown Street, Glasgow, G2 8EX • 0845 600 9663 • disc4.civsec@apc.army.mod.uk
For serving soldiers or officers and those discharged since 1996: Army Personnel Centre, Disclosures 1, Mailpoint 520, Kentigern House, 65 Brown Street, Glasgow, G2 8EX • 0845 600 9663 • disc1.civsec@apc.army.mod.uk
For soldiers and NCOs in the Footguard Regiments (Grenadier, Coldstream, Scots, Welsh and Irish Guards): Regimental Headquarters, The (name) Guards, Wellington Barracks, Birdcage Walk, London SW1E 6HQ
For soldiers and NCOs in the Household Cavalry Regiments (Life Guards, Royal Horse Guard, Royal Dragoons, Horse Grenadier Guards, Blues & Royals) enlisting between 1799–1919): Household Cavalry Museum, Combermere Barracks, Windsor, Berkshire SL4 3DN (closed until 2007)

MINISTRY OF DEFENCE: MEDALS
Army, Navy, Marine and Air Force Medal Office, RAF Innsworth, Gloucester GL3 1HW • 0800 085 3600

MINISTRY OF DEFENCE: MILITARY GRAVES OUTSIDE THE WORLD WARS: PS4(CAS)(A), Bourne Avenue, Hayes, Middlesex, UB3 1RF

MINISTRY OF DEFENCE: POLISH SERVICE
Ministry of Defence, APC Polish Enquiries, Building 28B, RAF Northolt, West End Road, Ruislip, Middlesex HA4 6NG • 0208 833 8603 • apcsec@btconnect.com

MINISTRY OF DEFENCE: ROYAL AIR FORCE
Air Historical Branch, Building 266, Royal Air Force, Bentley Priory, Stanmore, Middlesex HA7 3HH
PMA Sec IM1B, Room 5, Building 248A, RAF Personnel Management Agency, RAF Innsworth, Gloucester GL3 1EZ

MINISTRY OF DEFENCE: ROYAL MARINES
For Commissioned Officers and Non-Commissioned Ranks enlisted during or after 1923: DPS(N) 2, Bldg 1/152, Victory View, PP36, HMNB, Portsmouth PO1 3PX • 02392 727531

MINISTRY OF DEFENCE: ROYAL NAVY
*For non-commissioned ranks who enlisted after 1923 or commissioned officers who entered service after 1916 **and have died:*** Navy Search, TNT Archive Service,

Tetron Point, William Nadin Way, Swadlincote, Derbyshire DE11 0BB
• 01283 227 913 • navysearchpgrc@tnt.co.uk
*For non-commissioned ranks who enlisted after 1923 or commissioned officers who
entered service after 1916 **and are still alive:*** Data Protection Cell (Navy), Victory
View, Building 1/152, HM Naval Base Portsmouth, Portsmouth PO1 3PX
• 02392 727381
MITCHELL LIBRARY, State Library of New South Wales, Macquarie St, Sydney
NSW 2000, Australia • www.sl.nsw.gov.au/
MODERN RECORDS CENTRE, University of Warwick, Library, Coventry CV4 7AL
• 024 7652 4219 • www2.warwick.ac.uk/services/library/mrc/
MUSEUM OF IMMIGRATION, 19 Princelet Street, London E1 6QH
• 020 7247 5352 • information@19princeletstreet.org.uk
• www.19princeletstreet.org.uk
NATIONAL ARCHIVES AND RECORDS ADMINISTRATION [OF THE US], 700
Pennsylvania Avenue, NW, Washington, D.C. 20408, USA
• 00 1 1800 234 8861 • www.nara.gov
NATIONAL ARCHIVES OF SCOTLAND, HM General Register House, Edinburgh EH1
3YY • 0131 535 1314 • www.nas.gov.uk
NATIONAL ARCHIVES OF AUSTRALIA, PO Box 7425, Canberra Mail Centre, ACT
Australia 2610 • 00 61 2 6212 3600 • www.naa.gov.au
NATIONAL ARCHIVES OF CANADA, 395 Wellington St, Ottawa, Ontario K1A 0N3,
Canada • 00 1 613 995 5138 • www.archives.ca
NATIONAL ARCHIVES OF IRELAND, Bishop St, Dublin 8, Ireland • 003531 4072300
• www.nationalarchives.ie
NATIONAL ARMY MUSEUM, Department of Records, Royal Hospital Rd, London
SW3 4HT • 020 7730 0717 • www.national-army-museum.ac.uk
NATIONAL LIBRARY OF AUSTRALIA, Parkes Place, Canberra, ACT 2600, Australia
• 00 61 2 6262 1111 • www.nla.gov.au
NATIONAL LIBRARY OF IRELAND, Kildare St, Dublin 2, Republic of Ireland
• 003531 6618811 • www.nli.ie
NATIONAL LIBRARY OF SCOTLAND, George IV Bridge, Edinburgh EH1 1EW
• 0131 226 4531 • www.nls.uk
NATIONAL LIBRARY OF WALES, Aberystwyth, Dyfed SY23 3BU • 01970 632800
• www.llgc.org.uk
NATIONAL MARITIME MUSEUM, Maritime Information Centre,
Romney Rd, London SE10 9NF • 020 8858 4422
• www.nmm.ac.uk
NATIONAL RAILWAY MUSEUM, Leeman Rd, York YO26 4XJ • 01904 621261
• www.nrm.org.uk
NATIONAL REGISTER OF ARCHIVES (SCOTLAND), West Register House, Charlotte
Square, Edinburgh EH2 4DF • 0131 535 1314
NAVAL DOCKYARDS SOCIETY, c/o 44 Lindley Avenue, Southsea, Hampshire PO4
9NV • www.hants.gov.uk/navaldockyard
NORFOLK RECORD OFFICE, The Archive Centre, Martineau Lane, Norwich,
Norfolk NR1 2DQ • 01603 222599 • norfrec@norfolk.gov.uk
• http://archives.norfolk.gov.uk
NORTH YORKSHIRE COUNTY RECORD OFFICE, Malpas Road, Northallerton,
North Yorkshire DL7 8TB • 01609 777585 • archives@northyorks.gov.uk
• www.northyorks.gov.uk/libraries/archives/default.shtm
NORTHAMPTONSHIRE RECORD OFFICE, Wootton Hall Park, Northampton
NN4 8BQ • 01604 762129 archivist@northamptonshire.gov.uk
• www.northamptonshire.gov.uk/Community/record/about_us.htm
NOTTINGHAMSHIRE ARCHIVES, County House, Castle Meadow Road,
Nottingham NG2 1AG • 0115 958 1634 archives@nottscc.gov.uk
• www.nottinghamshire.gov.uk/archives
OXFORDSHIRE RECORD OFFICE, St Luke's Church, Temple Road, Cowley, Oxford
OX4 2HT • 01865 398200 • archives@oxfordshire.gov.uk
• www.oxfordshire.gov.uk
PIETERMARITZBURG ARCHIVE REPOSITORY, Private Bag X9012, Pietermaritzburg
3200 South Africa • +27 (0)33 – 342 4712 • pmbarch01@hotmail.com
PRESBYTERIAN HISTORY SOCIETY, Church House, Fisherwick Place, Belfast

BT1 6DW • www.presbyterianireland.org/phsi
PRIAULX LIBRARY, St Peter Port, Guernsey, Channel Islands • 01481 721998
PRINCIPAL REGISTRY OF THE FAMILY DIVISION, Decree Absolute Section, First
  Avenue House, 42–49 High Holborn, London WC1V 6NP
  • 020 7947 6000 (Royal Courts of Justice switchboard)
PRIVY COUNCIL OFFICE, 2 Carlton Gardens, London SW1Y 5AA • 020 7210 1033
  • pcosecretariat@pco.x.gsi.gov.uk • www.privy-council.org.uk
PROBATE SEARCHROOM, Principal Registry of the Family Division, First Avenue
  House, 42–49 High Holborn, London WC1V 6NP • 020 7947 6000 (Royal
  Courts of Justice switchboard)
PUBLIC RECORD OFFICE OF NORTHERN IRELAND, 66 Balmoral Ave., Belfast
  BT9 6NY • 028 9025 1318 • http://proni.nics.gov.uk
RAILWAY ANCESTORS FAMILY HISTORY SOCIETY
  • www.railwayancestors.fsnet.co.uk
REGISTRY OF DEEDS, King's Inn, Henrietta St, Dublin 1, Republic of Ireland
  • 003531 6707500 • www.landregistry.ie
REGISTRY OF DEEDS, YORKSHIRE: see East Riding, North Yorkshire and West
  Yorkshire
REGISTRY OF SHIPPING AND SEAMEN (MARITIME AND COASTGUARD AGENCY),
  MCA Cardiff, Anchor Court, Ocean Way, Cardiff, CF24 5JW • 02920 448800
  • registryofshippingandseamen@mcga.gov.uk
ROYAL AIR FORCE MUSEUM, Department of Aviation Records (Archives),
  Hendon Aerodrome, London NW9 5LL • 020 8205 2266
  • www.rafmuseum.com
ROYAL AIR FORCE see Ministry of Defence
ROYAL ARCHIVES, Windsor Castle, Windsor, Berkshire, SL4 1NJ • 01753 868286
  • www.royal.gov.uk/output/Page2556.asp
ROYAL CHELSEA HOSPITAL, London SW3 4SR • 020 7881 5204
  • info@chelsea-pensioners.org.uk • www.chelsea-pensioners.co.uk
ROYAL COLLEGE OF NURSING ARCHIVES, 42 South Oswald Road, Edinburgh,
  EH9 2HH • 0131 662 6122 • archives@rcn.org.uk
  • www.rcn.org.uk/resources/historyofnursing/
ROYAL COURTS OF JUSTICE, Room 81, Strand, London WC2A 2LL (For recent
  enrolled changes of name) • 020 7947 6528
ROYAL MARINES MUSEUM, Eastney, Southsea, Hampshire PO4 9PX
  • 023 9281 9385 • www.royalmarinesmuseum.co.uk
ROYAL NAVAL MUSEUM, HM Naval Base, Portsmouth, Hampshire PO1 3NH
  • 023 9272 7577 • www.royalnavalmuseum.org
ROYAL MARINES see Ministry of Defence
ROYAL NAVY see Ministry of Defence
SARK, REGISTRAR, La Vallette, Sark, Channel Islands
SHAKESPEARE BIRTHPLACE TRUST, The Shakespeare Centre, Henley Street,
  Stratford-upon-Avon, Warwickshire CV37 6QW • 01789 201816
  • records@shakespeare.org.uk • www.shakespeare.org.uk/records.htm
SOCIÉTÉ GUERNESIASE, Family History Section, PO Box 314, Candie, St Peter Port,
  Guernsey GY1 3TG • www.societe.org.gg
SOCIÉTÉ JERSIAISE, Lord Coutanche Library, 7 Pier Rd, St Helier, Jersey JE2 4XW,
  Channel Islands • 01534 730538 • www.societe-jersiaise.org
SOCIETY OF GENEALOGISTS, 14 Charterhouse Buildings, Goswell Rd, London
  EC1M 7BA • 020 7251 8799 • www.sog.org.uk
SOMERSET ARCHIVES, Obridge Road, Taunton, Somerset TA2 7PU • 01823 337600
  • Archives@somerset.gov.uk • www.somerset.gov.uk/archives
SOUTHAMPTON ARCHIVES OFFICE, South Block, Civic Centre, Southampton
  SO14 7LY • 023 8083 2251 • city.archives@southampton.gov.uk
  • www.southampton.gov.uk/education/libraries/arch.htm
SPANISH AND PORTUGUESE JEWS' CONGREGATION, Honorary Archivist,
  2 Ashworth Rd, London W9 1JY • 020 7289 2573
ST ANTONY'S COLLEGE, Middle East Centre Archive, Oxford, OX2 6JF (Palestine
  Police service cards) • 01865 284706 • www.sant.ox.ac.uk/mec/meca.shtml
SUFFOLK RECORD OFFICE, Gatacre Road, Ipswich, Suffolk IP1 2LQ • 01473 584541
  • ipswich.ro@libher.suffolkcc.gov.uk • www.suffolkcc.gov.uk/sro/

Superintendent Registrar of Births, Marriages and Deaths Jersey, The
  States Building, St Helier, Jersey, Channel Islands
Thomas Coram Foundation, 40 Brunswick Square, London WC1N 1AZ
  • 020 7841 3600 • enquiries@foundlingmuseum.org.uk
  • www.foundlingmuseum.org.uk
Trinity House Corporation, Trinity House, Tower Hill, London, EC3N 4DH
Ulster Historical Foundation, Balmoral Buildings, 12 College Square East,
  Belfast, BT1 6DD Northern Ireland • 028 90 332288 • enquiry@uhf.org.uk
  • www.ancestryireland.co.uk
Wapping Police Museum, 98 Wapping High Street, London E1
Warwickshire Record Office, Priory Park, Cape Road, Warwick CV34 4JS
  • 01926 738959 • recordoffice@warwickshire.gov.uk
  • www.warwickshire.gov.uk/countyrecordoffice
Wellcome Library for the History and Understanding of Medicine,
  210 Euston Road, London NW1 2BE • 020 7611 8486
  • http://library.wellcome.ac.uk
Wellington Barracks see Ministry of Defence: Army
West Riding Registry of Deeds, West Yorkshire Archives Service, Wakefield
  Headquarters, Newstead Rd, Wakefield WF1 2DE • 01924 305980
West Sussex Record Office, Sherburne House, 3 Orchard Street, Chichester,
  West Sussex PO19 1RN • 01243 753600 • records.office@westsussex.gov.uk
  • www.westsussex.gov.uk/ccm/navigation/libraries-and-archives
West Yorkshire Archive Service, Leeds, 2 Chapeltown Road, Sheepscar,
  Leeds LS7 3AP • 0113 214 5814 leeds@wyjs.org.uk • www.archives.wyjs.org.uk/
West Yorkshire Archives Service, Wakefield Headquarters, Registry of
  Deeds, Newstead Rd, Wakefield WF1 2DE • 01924 305980
Wiltshire and Swindon Record Office, Bythesea Road, Trowbridge,
  Wiltshire BA14 8BS • 01225 713709 • wsro@wiltshire.gov.uk
  • www.wiltshire.gov.uk/heritage/html/wsro.html
Worcestershire Record Office, County Hall, Spetchley Road, Worcester WR5
  2NP • 01905 766351 • RecordOffice@worcestershire.gov.uk
  • www.worcestershire.gov.uk/records/
York Probate Sub-Registry, First Floor, Castle Chambers, Clifford Street, York,
  YO1 9RG • 01904 666777

Series index

Index

Bold entries indicate major references

police forces *cont.*
  South Africa 33.8
  Wales 33.6
poll books 21.1
poll taxes 52.3
Poor Laws **41**
  new Poor Law of 1834 41.2
  old Poor Law of 1601 41.1
  Poor Law unions 41.2
  union staff 41.3
port books 18.4
Post Office 34.3
POWs *see* prisoners of war
Prerogative Court of Canterbury (PCC) 9.4,
    9.5, 10.1
  litigation before 1858 10.11
  original and other wills 10.4
  proving a will in 10.5
  users of 10.2
  wills online and search tips 10.3
Prerogative Court of York 9.5
preventive services **32**
  before Coastguard 32.1–2
  Coastguard *see* Coastguard
  service records 32.2, 32.4
Preventive Water Guards 32.1
  see also Coastguard; preventive services
Principal Registry of the Family Division
    6.5
prison hulks 47.3, 47.9
prisoners and convicts **47**
  in the census 18.5, 47.1
  executions 47.8
  habitual criminals register 47.5
  insolvent debtors 55.3
  licences (tickets of leave) 47.6
  lists of prisoners to be tried 48.5
  Naval dockyards 28.6.2
  pardons and appeals for mercy 47.7
  in prison hulks 47.3
  prison as a punishment 47.2
  registers of prisoners in prisons 47.4
  transportation 47.9–12
prisoners of war (POWs) **31**
  pre 1793 31.2
  1793–1914 31.3
  1914–1919 31.4
  1939–1945
    British/Commonwealth in enemy hands
      31.5
    in British hands 31.7
    merchant seamen 31.6
  1950–1953 (Korea) 31.8
  see also internees
private acts of Parliament 22.5
private tontines 53.3
Privy Council 11.3
  Judicial Committee of 6.3, 61.3
  Privy Council Proceedings and *Acts* 11.3
PRO Guide 1.9
Probate, Court of 9.3, 10.13
probate **9, 10**
  see also administrations; wills
probate clauses 10.5
proctors 10.11, 38.7
professional researchers 2.6

Protestant Dissenters' Registry of births 5.6
Protestant nonconformists 43.5
  burial grounds 6.6
  registers 5.4, 5.5–8
proving wills 9.5, 10.5
Public Record Office (PRO) 1.2

Quaker registers 5.8
quarter sessions, criminal trials 48.2, 48.6
Queen Alexandra's Imperial Military Nursing
    Service (QAIMNS) 27.3
Queen Alexandra's Royal Naval Nursing
    Service (QARNNS) 28.7.3
Queen's Nursing Institute 40.5

Railway Benevolent Institution 36.3
railways **36**
  companies 36.1, 36.5
  other sources of information 36.3
  railway police 36.4
  staff records 36.2
    at the National Archives 36.5
receivers' accounts 49.5
recoveries 50.4
Recusant Rolls 43.4, 43.5
refugees 19.4, 19.6, 44.4
register offices 4.3
registration certificates (R certificates) 19.11
regnal years 2.9
Relief of Insolvent Debtors, Court for the 55.3,
    55.7
religious registration of births, marriages and
    deaths **5**
  Anglican registers in the National Archives
    5.11
  Army chaplains' registers 24.1.1
  British Lying-In Hospital 5.12
  Catholic registers 5.9
  Channel Islands 16.1, 16.2
  Fleet marriage registers 5.13
  Ireland 14.1
  Isle of Man 15.1
  marriages before 1837 and online indexes 5.2
  National Burial Index 5.3
  Nonconformist registers 5.5
  non-parochial registers 5.4
  overseas 8.2
  parish registers and online indexes 5.1
  Protestant Dissenters' Registry of births 5.6
  Quaker registers 5.8
  registers of foreign churches in England
    5.10
  Scotland 13.1
  Wesleyan Methodist Metropolitan Registry
    of births 5.7
rentals, manorial 49.4
repatriation 17.3
reprieves, prisoners 47.7
Requests, Court of 11.3, 60.3
Revenue Cruisers 32.1
  see also Coastguard; preventive services
Riding Officers 32.1
  see also Coastguard; preventive services
RNAS *see* Royal Naval Air Service
RNR *see* Royal Naval Reserve
RNVR *see* Royal Naval Volunteer Reserve

Finding your detailed document references

If you have found a record series in this book that you want to explore, check its 'square note' in the table below and follow the advice given.

1	Searchable online by surname
2	Searchable online by forename AND surname (James AND Maltby)
3	Searchable online by initial AND surname (J AND Maltby)
4	Searchable online by county
5	Searchable online by place
6	Searchable online by subject or by name of regiment, unit or ship
7	Brief description in catalogue (sometimes just a date range, or ranges of names or numbers): no searchable data on individuals. May need to browse the catalogue (or search by V and date), or use the paper catalogue and then read the most likely record. For how to browse the catalogue, see 1.7
8	Brief description in catalogue: no searchable data on individuals. The document itself contains an index
P	Best searched in paper catalogue at the National Archives: detailed descriptions are not in online catalogue
S	Best searched in published work: detailed descriptions are not in online catalogue
F	Best searched in or with a supplementary finding aid at the National Archives: detailed descriptions are not in online catalogue
V	Use variant spellings or wildcards
W	Searchable on another website (often free at the National Archives)

- You can find out more about this system at 1.8 (pp. 12–13).
- You can access our online catalogue at **www.nationalarchives. gov.uk/catalogue**.
- You can see paper catalogues and indexes at the National Archives.